No Higher Law

No Higher Law

American Foreign Policy and the
Western Hemisphere since 1776

BRIAN LOVEMAN

The University of North Carolina Press   Chapel Hill

All rights reserved. Designed by Courtney Leigh Baker and set in Minion Pro by
Achorn International, Inc. Manufactured in the United States of America. The paper in this
book meets the guidelines for permanence and durability of the Committee on Production
Guidelines for Book Longevity of the Council on Library Resources. The University of North
Carolina Press has been a member of the Green Press Initiative since 2003.

Library of Congress Cataloging-in-Publication Data
Loveman, Brian.
No higher law : American foreign policy and the Western Hemisphere since 1776 /
Brian Loveman.
    p. cm.
Includes bibliographical references and index.
ISBN 978-0-8078-3371-1 (cloth : alk. paper)
1. United States—Foreign relations. I. Title.
E183.7.L79 2010
327.73—dc22   2009045321

14 13 12 11 10   5 4 3 2 1

Contents

Illustrations, Maps, and Tables

TABLES

No Higher Law

We can not fail, under the favor of a gracious Providence, to attain the high destiny which seems to await us.

—JAMES MONROE, Inaugural Address, 1817

The same force that had once guided Pilgrim sails to Plymouth Rock had impressed our ships at Manila and our army at Santiago. Upon us rested the duty of extending Christian civilization, of crushing despotism, of uplifting humanity and making the rights of man prevail. Providence has put it upon us.

—SENATOR ORVILLE PLATT (R.-Conn.), 1898

A gray ship flying the American flag in every corner of the world is a statement about who we are, what we are interested in, and how we assure and deter in the far reaches of the earth.

—ADMIRAL GARY ROUGHEAD, Chief of Naval Operations, 2007

Introduction

Writing history is almost always an effort to make the past speak to the present. I have written *No Higher Law* in that spirit. My research has been guided by concerns about the United States and the world in the first decades of the twenty-first century, even as I write about the Alien and Sedition Acts of 1798, the campaign against pirates of the Caribbean in the 1820s, America's first treaty protectorate regime in Colombia in 1846, and Senate debates on treaties from 1794 to the end of World War II. Asking the past to speak to the present is not the same as seeing and describing the past strictly through modern perspectives, ideas, or morality. Rather, such a historical inquiry reconsiders the past both to better understand it on its own terms and to reframe our understanding of the present.

As I wrote this book, the United States was engaged in a Global War on Terror.[1] Unilateral, preemptive, and even preventive military intervention was official American policy. President George W. Bush proclaimed this policy with less stealth than Thomas Jefferson and James Madison, but with hardly more imperiousness than James Polk, more swagger than Theodore Roosevelt, or more cynicism than Richard Nixon. President Bush's predecessor, Bill Clinton, had declared: "When our national security interests are threatened, we will, *as America always has*, use diplomacy when we can, but force if we must. We will act with others when we can, but alone when we must."[2] And George W. Bush's successor, Barack Obama, had told the Chicago Council of Global Affairs on April 23, 2007: "No president should ever hesitate to use force — unilaterally if necessary — to protect ourselves and our vital interests when we are attacked or imminently threatened."

U.S. presidents since the Republic's first decades had announced their willingness to use force unilaterally to protect U.S. citizens and the country's security interests, a disposition consistent with conventional notions of the right of sovereign nation-states to act in self-defense to preserve their independent existence and vital interests.[3] Likewise, American policymakers resorted to preemptive use of military force and justified policies toward Spain, England, and France in the Western Hemisphere as anticipatory self-defense from the 1790s.

In more modern times, preemptive war in self-defense is recognized in customary international law and under the United Nations Charter.[4] Preventive war is much more controversial but, on balance, plausibly justified in the name of self-defense (if intelligence on enemy intentions and capabilities indicates that the risks of inaction are too great to tolerate).[5] U.S. support for "regime change," that is, overt or clandestine operations to overthrow the governments of sovereign nations, may be more controversial but is also without historical novelty. Indeed, American-sponsored regime change preceded annexation of West Florida in 1810, Texas in 1845, California in 1850, and Hawaii in 1898.[6]

To make sense of policies that took U.S. armed forces to Afghanistan in 2001 and Iraq in 2003 and engaged them around the world in hundreds of more or less clandestine operations before and after September 11, 2001, we need to look to the evolution of America's foreign policy from the beginnings of the Republic. We need to ask how American policies were shaped in response to changes in the international system and how they were influenced by domestic politics and by underlying American religious and cultural premises.[7] *No Higher Law* is such a historical inquiry. It seeks to uncover the sources of present American foreign policy by taking a long view of ideological, institutional, and political development within a dynamic international system.

No Higher Law reveals a continuity in certain beliefs, institutions, policies, and practices in the American experience as part of the country's evolving grand strategy. These continuities persisted despite ongoing changes in the international system and dramatic augmentation in American economic power and military capabilities since the late nineteenth century.[8] *No Higher Law* demonstrates not only that American foreign policy was rarely inspired by benevolence — not a surprise, since consistent saintly behavior is too much to expect of any nation-state in a dangerous international system — but that to achieve its foreign policy objectives the United States engaged in aggressive diplomacy, often deployed military force into foreign territory, and orchestrated regime change to overthrow the governments of sovereign nations judged inimical to U.S. interests.[9]

In these respects the United States behaved much like other powers in the international system, within constraints imposed by geography, technology, economic resources, and military capabilities. However, unlike the great powers of Europe, which relied on shifting alliances and balance-of-power politics as instruments of foreign policy, from the birth of the Republic American policymakers adopted unilateralism as their guiding principle in international affairs. Unilateralism, understood as *autonomy, aversion to permanent alliances*, and *armed neutrality*, remained a basic principle of American foreign policy until after World War II. American unilateralism derived largely from the interplay among the international system, the construction of American national identity and nationalism, and the dynamics of domestic politics.

From the outset, U.S. presidents and policymakers, like leaders of other nations, sought to shape global politics in what they took to be their country's interest and to respond to their perceptions of emerging threats and opportunities in the international system. How they defined foreign policy objectives and how they elaborated and implemented foreign policy depended on international circumstances, the current economic, technological, and military capabilities of the United States, and conjunctures in domestic politics. Foreign policy was always the product of contestation within a progressively more pluralistic political system, though certain underlying premises, beliefs, doctrines, and practices gradually emerged as the core elements of American diplomacy and policies abroad.[10] Of these, unilateralism was the most widely shared until World War II.

Understanding U.S. foreign policy requires the same sort of analytical frame as does comprehending the foreign policy of other nation-states.[11] How best to do that is disputed by the various "schools" of international relations theorists, including disagreements regarding the relative emphasis on geography, natural resources, "power politics," political culture, definition of national interests and security, international norms and regimes, symbolic power, and the interplay of geopolitics and domestic politics. The history I have written draws eclectically and selectively on these literatures without worshiping exclusively at any of the branch churches. For me, the question, "Why did the United States adopt particular policies and implement them the way it did (whether the Monroe Doctrine of 1823 or the Truman Doctrine of 1947)," almost always is answered with "for a variety of reasons" — from concerns about security, economic interests, and partisan politics, to underlying religious and secular values and the evolution of American political culture.[12]

Whatever the immediate circumstances that evoked particular policy decisions, however, there developed a uniquely American political culture and institutional framework that tied formulation of foreign policy to domestic politics in ways that often generated policies at odds with the formative myths of America. Despite the original sins of the American Constitution, most notably its reaffirmation of slavery, and the corruption of political life that quickly became endemic, Americans came to believe, or said they believed, in their political and moral exceptionalism. America claimed to be a beacon of hope to the oppressed and an example to the world of democracy. It claimed for itself an unheard-of benevolence in its foreign policies. And it claimed a special Providence (the belief that America was a nation called by God to a worldly mission): to promote liberty and freedom, first in the Western Hemisphere, then throughout the world.[13]

These mantras of American politics endured. Embellished periodically with public declarations of new foreign policy principles, doctrines, and corollaries to the doctrines, they became a shared liturgy in the rituals of American political life.[14] President Calvin Coolidge synthesized this liturgy in his inaugural address of 1925: "America seeks no earthly empire built on blood and force. No ambition, no temptation, lures her to thought of foreign dominions. The legions which she sends forth are armed, not with the sword, but with the cross. The higher state to which she seeks the allegiance of all mankind is not of human, but of divine origin."

Yet America's domestic politics and foreign policies often belied these claims of political and moral exceptionalism. Deciphering how and why this happened requires reconsideration of the special place of the peoples and nations of the Western Hemisphere in the construction of American national identity and the country's evolving grand strategy. The story begins with the rupture of the colonial regime in the late eighteenth century, when postindependence leaders aimed to form and maintain a federal Union and to create a sense of national identity while surrounded by Native American peoples and the colonial possessions of the strongest European powers. Enmeshed inevitably in European balance-of-power politics, commercial competition, and wars, America's first governments designed the country's foreign policies to insert the fragile new nation opportunistically into the international system.

A quest for Union and national security, dreams of territorial expansion, and the lure of global commerce melded to shape the policies of America's first governments. These governments adopted as first principle the idea that the United States should "command its own fortune," based foremost on a developing belief in the country's special Providence and its exceptionalism.[15] Americans constructed a national myth that gradually transformed their global ambitions into a righteous crusade, ostensibly for liberty, democracy, and *civilization* writ large in Anglo-Saxon idiom. There would be no law for the United States in its foreign relations higher than decisions made by its own government — no matter international norms or the sovereign interests and rights of other nations. Partly, Americans adopted unilateralism as the basic rule of their foreign policy because they believed it best served their interests, in their circumstances, given their place and ambitions in the international system. Partly, Americans adopted unilateralism because they believed that they "were a chosen people delivered from bondage to Promised Land, and you can't get more exceptional than that."[16]

Unilateralism is not, and was not, isolationism. Chapters 1 through 6 of this book revisit the first century of American national development and challenge the enduring myth of American foreign policy isolationism. They also reconsider the role of Latin America in international politics and in U.S. and European foreign policy. *No Higher Law* focuses on U.S. policy toward Latin America and inter-American relations because American foreign policy made Latin America a crucial element in the country's relations with the rest of the world. Despite often-expressed disdain for the region and its peoples, America sought to construct and consolidate a bastion in the Western Hemisphere from which to execute an expanding global project. The nascent United States promulgated a doctrine declaring the Western Hemisphere a "separate sphere" from Europe — a sphere in which monarchy, absolutism, alliance politics, and eternal warfare would not prevail. Instead, the United States would create in the Western Hemisphere a bastion for republican institutions, a formally secular government constructed on a profoundly religious foundation. In this scheme, Spanish America and Brazil would become a laboratory for foreign policies that were later "exported," with some tailoring, to the rest of the world as the United States became a global power.

Spanish America and Brazil were much more important in defining emergent American national identity and the American role in the international system than is commonly understood. Latin America's importance for American policymakers resulted because American territorial aspirations, commercial ambitions, and security concerns necessarily, and immediately, confronted the challenges posed by contiguous and nearby European colonies that eventually became Spanish-American republics. Latin America's importance also stemmed from construction of an American nationalism and political culture that emphasized the unique and exceptional nature of the American republican experiment by invidious deprecation of Spanish and Latin American culture, religion, institutions, and peoples.[17] Latin America also warranted close attention from American policymakers because European nations contested U.S. hegemony in the Western Hemisphere, as part of their own grand strategies, much longer than most master narratives of international relations suggest. Indeed, contestation of American hegemony in the Western Hemisphere by European (and now, Asian) powers continues in the twenty-first century.

Taking the long view of the role of Latin America in the international system, and of U.S.-European competition in the Western Hemisphere, uncovers the steady accretion of foreign policy–making experience and ideas regarding

Latin America that resulted in the complex bundle of interests, doctrines, ideologies, prejudices, and practices that later shaped U.S. actions elsewhere in the world. Transformed into an economic and military power, the United States would adapt the political, economic, and military interventionism applied in the Western Hemisphere to its policies in the Pacific, Asia, the Middle East, and Africa. Just as many Latin Americans came to distrust and fear the United States even before the war with Mexico (1846–48) and to resent the United States fiercely after the 1898 war against Spain, other peoples who did not share America's exaltation of (and desire to export) Christianity and capitalism around the world came to detest U.S. interventionism, racism, and sense of cultural superiority as they confronted American power and its religious, economic, and military agents.

From the beginning, American foreign policies and practices often contradicted the political principles and idealism proclaimed by the country's leaders. At home and abroad, American governments acted in ways that tarnished the country's claim to moral and political exceptionalism. Ethnic cleansing against Native American peoples, an economy based on slavery, contempt for people of color, and institutionalized racism belied the noble phrases of the Declaration of Independence. Shibboleths regarding democracy and civilizing missions imperfectly veiled American intentions to establish political and economic hegemony, first in the Western Hemisphere and then, more recently if less successfully, around the globe.[18]

Yet there were always groups of Americans, sometimes conflicted among themselves, who opposed these dominant tendencies towards unilateralism, interventionism, racism, colonialism, and the accompanying erosion of civil liberties at home. At each critical juncture — from the Quasi-War of 1798–1800 against France, to the Mexican War and the expansionist policies of the administration of James Buchanan (1857–61), to the Spanish-American War in 1898 — voices in Congress and in the press and among cultural and political elites and a minority of religious leaders called on America to live up to its proclaimed ideals at home and abroad. The history of these opposition movements and eclectic political coalitions, their successes and failures, also forms an essential part of the long view of the American mission and U.S. relations with its neighbors in the Western Hemisphere.

In the last half of this book, the story begun in the late eighteenth century is brought forward from 1898, when the United States became an imperial power, into the first decade of the twenty-first century. On September 20, 2001, President George W. Bush declared that the country was engaged in a global war on terror in response to the attacks by al Qaeda operatives flying sequestered commercial aircraft with their civilian passengers aboard into the

World Trade Center Twin Towers in New York and the Pentagon in Washington, D.C. The attacks resulted in several thousand deaths and a nation shocked by its vulnerability and angered by the assault on its territory and people. President George W. Bush told America: "Our war on terror begins with al Qaeda, but it does not end there. It will not end until every terrorist group of global reach has been found, stopped and defeated. Americans are asking, why do they hate us? They hate what we see right here in this chamber — a democratically elected government. . . . They hate our freedoms — our freedom of religion, our freedom of speech, our freedom to vote and assemble and disagree with each other."[19]

Did al Qaeda attack the United States because it hated our freedoms? Was President Bush right in 2006 when he told the country, resurrecting the historical American belief in its manifest destiny and special Providence (and the recent memory of "victory" in the Cold War), that, "like the Cold War, America is once again answering history's call with confidence — and like the Cold War, freedom will prevail"?[20]

Like American leaders since the 1776 Declaration of Independence, President Bush claimed that America was answering history's (and Providence's) call. But what has history called upon America to do? How has America responded to history's call? What have Americans done in the world and at home since 1776? How is America's response to history's call seen around the world? Making sense of the long story leading to the terrorist attacks of September 11, 2001, and to the political, economic, moral, and military morass of the United States in 2010 requires rethinking the dilemmas of American domestic politics, the country's strategic vision, and its foreign policies since shortly after the Treaty of Paris ended the American war for independence in 1783.[21] It also requires a more critical history of the interplay of domestic politics, changes in the international system, the U.S. role in that system, and the special place of the Western Hemisphere in U.S. grand strategy from the early nineteenth century to the first decade of the twenty-first century. In *No Higher Law*, I seek to provide this more critical history as a way of asking the past to speak to the challenges of American foreign policy in the first decades of the twenty-first century.

Chapter One

The Isolationist Myth

We are met together at a most interesting period. The situation of the principal powers of Europe are singular and portentous. Connected with some by treaties and with all by commerce, no important event there can be indifferent to us. — JOHN ADAMS, First Message to Congress, 1797

Making sense of U.S. foreign policy in the twenty-first century requires rethinking America's historical role in the community of nations. It also requires understanding the connection between partisan and sectional politics and the foreign policy challenges confronted by the new nation in the first half century after independence.

The American colonies' war for independence from Britain was part of a major conflict among European powers that stretched from India and the Mediterranean into the West Indies and North America. French and Spanish arms, supplies, money, naval assets, and troops deployed against the British made possible American independence.[1] In the decades after its independence, America's leaders devised policies for inserting the country into an international system dominated by the European powers. Although never entirely consensual, the emerging policies were rooted in concerns for the new nation's security, ambitious commercial and territorial aspirations, and an assertive nationalism. In its first half century, American foreign policy was expansionist, self-congratulatory, far reaching, aggressive, and sometimes idealistic — but never isolationist.

There is abundant scholarship debunking the myth of U.S. foreign policy isolationism after independence.[2] Yet there persists among many Americans the idea that until 1898 U.S. foreign policy conformed to an isolationist vision bequeathed by George Washington's Farewell Address in 1796 or Thomas Jefferson's admonition against "entangling alliances" in 1801.[3] But Washington and Jefferson were not isolationists. They did not promote American disengagement and separation from international politics, international diplomacy, or international commerce or even from meddling in European politics and influencing the balance of power in European affairs. Neither did their successors in America's first half century. As Alexander H. Everett, America's minister to Spain, wrote in 1827: "A complete separation of our political interests from those of all other countries could only be effected by a complete abstinence from all intercourse with them; a plan which it would be extremely difficult to realise, which would be highly impolitic if practicable, and has never been avowed nor defended by anyone."[4]

Given the historical record, the persistence of the idea that America had an isolationist tradition before 1898 is remarkable. It is not merely a curiosity or a semantic dispute over how best to characterize the United States' foreign policy. Professional historians, political scientists, policy analysts, and popular writers insist on the reality of America's isolationist past despite significant revisionist scholarship since at least the 1950s. Thus, historian Dexter Perkins, who spent much of his life writing about American policy toward Latin America, told readers in 1962 that during the first period of American foreign policy, before 1898, the country evolved "an isolationist viewpoint regarding Europe."[5] In 1966, political scientist Leroy Rieselbach wrote in a study on Congress and foreign policy that "isolationism has been a force in American politics since the founding of the nation."[6] Historian Howard Jones's widely used textbook on American foreign relations notes in passing that "the war with Spain [in 1898] also furthered the decline of American isolationism." In 2006, the author of a major study of American foreign policy and strategy declared that "when, toward the end of the nineteenth century, a united Germany proved to be too powerful to be restrained by its European neighbors without American help, America's first strategy of isolationism became obsolete."[7] And a well-known policy analyst reminded readers in 2007: "Isolationism, recall, was America's response to the wrangling world and remained so throughout much of the nation's history. . . . The isolationist instinct lives in America."[8]

The persistence of the idea that America had a tradition of isolationism reflects crucial aspects of American national identity. Americans have been taught to think, and like to think, that the country did not meddle in the affairs of other nations, that in its dealings with other peoples the United States has been magnanimous, that, unlike other great powers, the United States has usually followed the moral high ground and resorted to force only in self-defense. Americans like to believe that the wars they have fought were provoked by other nations and that the United States has promoted freedom and liberty around the world, fighting against tyranny from the early nineteenth century to the first decade of the twenty-first.

Such premises mistake American unilateralism for isolationism. To defend the new nation and its supposed Providential destiny, the country's leaders adopted a unilateralist foreign policy.[9] Unilateralism is not an epithet; it refers to a principle that guided American policymakers, consisting of *armed neutrality* in European wars, *autonomy*, and *refusal to join in alliances*. Unlike the leaders of Europe, American statesmen, after allying with France and Spain in their global war against Britain to win their own independence, rejected formal alliances as an instrument of foreign policy, preferring instead unilateral action to achieve the country's objectives.[10] This made the United States a singular exception to the general practices of foreign policy of European nations in the eighteenth and nineteenth centuries. Nevertheless, the United States deployed naval forces around the globe, sent diplomats and a growing merchant marine to every continent, and "operated, in foreign politics, according to the assumptions of power politics that dominated contemporary European statecraft."[11] As an American political scientist writing in 1940 put it, "Americans may do well to consider that the true objective of their historic caution was not isolation, a friendliness which may subject their destiny to their enemies, but an ideal interpreted to the nation by [George] Washington as 'the command of its own fortunes.'"[12]

Americans inherited much of British political culture and legal institutions. They had also participated actively in Britain's global commerce and empire. By fighting a war for independence and creating a federal republic, however, they challenged the hegemony and legitimacy of European monarchy and colonialism. The origins, political ideology, and very existence of the United States of America represented a threat to the colonial interests of major European powers, particularly in the Western Hemisphere.

George Washington, America's first president, well understood that the United States operated *in*, not isolated from, a dangerous international system. Washington warned Congress: "The United States ought not to indulge a persuasion that, contrary to the order of human events, they will forever keep at a distance those painful appeals to arms with which the history of every other nation abounds. . . . If we desire to avoid insult, we must be able to repel it; if we desire to secure peace, one of the most powerful instruments of our rising prosperity, it must be known that we are at all times ready for war."[13] Washington asked Congress in 1793 for a larger budget for munitions, armaments, and military stores specifically because "the connection of the United States with Europe has become extremely interesting." Two years later, Washington returned to the need for military preparedness, partly to protect the country's shifting and vulnerable frontiers against European nations and their Native American allies.[14]

George Washington was a realist. He presided over a militarily weak new nation in an international system dominated by European powers with which the United States had important commercial relations but also trade disputes and territorial conflicts. War between France and England threatened to involve the United States and divided its political elite between Anglophiles (Federalists) and Francophiles (Jeffersonian Republicans). Under these circumstances, Washington intended to avoid disunion and to achieve American foreign policy objectives through *armed neutrality*.[15] In his Farewell Address, he defined his policy of neutrality as a temporary tactic not an enduring principle: "With me, a predominant motive has been to endeavor to gain time to our country to settle and mature its yet recent institutions, and to progress without interruption to that degree of strength and consistency which is necessary to give it, humanly speaking, the command of its own fortunes."[16]

Three months later, in his last annual message to Congress, Washington lamented the depredations of France on American commerce in the West Indies; he urged on Congress a program of naval construction and a policy of military deterrence to defend the country's shipping, not only in the West Indies but in the Mediterranean: "The most sincere neutrality is not a sufficient guard against the depredations of nations at war. To secure respect to a neutral flag requires a naval force organized and ready to vindicate it from insult or aggression. This may even prevent the necessity of going to war by discouraging belligerent powers from committing such violations of the rights of the neutral party as may, first or last, leave no other option."[17] Washington believed in deterrence through military strength. He asked Congress to create a credible navy to defend the nation's shores and deter attacks on its merchant ships around the world.

If American leaders wished for the country to command its own fortunes, then it followed that their foreign policies and decisions on military preparedness would depend partly on changing perceptions of threats to national security and also on economic opportunity and possibilities for territorial expansion. Among themselves, however, Americans disagreed on how to define and achieve the country's foreign policy objectives. They disagreed also on the desirability of territorial expansion. And, among the expansionists, there existed no consensus on which territorial annexations had priority. America's leaders also contested alignment, alliances, and ideological affinity with the conflicting European powers. The two political parties that competed for control of the Union from the early 1790s, the Federalists and the

Democratic-Republicans (or Jeffersonians), emerged in part from these differences on foreign policy. Likewise, Americans had not yet firmly established the workings of their new constitutional system. Conflicts over foreign policy would contribute to defining the nature of congressional-executive relations. Gradually, contentious partisan politics and congressional debates, in which the contending parties and factions sought to "out-patriot" their competitors, contributed to the consolidation of unilateralism as a first principle of American grand strategy.

Washington's successors aspired to expand American commerce around the globe and to wrest control of much of the North American continent, including Canada and the Floridas, from European powers and Native Americans. There could be no isolation from trade negotiations, nor from the need to counter European political, economic, and military initiatives in the Western Hemisphere.[18] Even before independence, the North American colonials participated actively in international trade; Thomas Jefferson had written in *A Summary View of the Rights of British America* (1774) that the colonists had a "natural right" to trade freely with all parts of the world.[19] British North American colonial traders defied European mercantile restrictions in the Caribbean, Asia, and Africa, carrying American cargoes along with the commodities and manufactures of other nations to all points of the compass. In this enterprise, they enjoyed the protection of the British navy until they struck out on their own in 1776. After independence, the new nation would have to defend its own commerce, in competition with the British and other European powers.

The Founders' generation thus gave priority to international trade. America's first treaty — an independence war alliance with France in 1778 — adopted free trade and reciprocity as the cornerstone of the country's commercial policies. Tariff policy and customs revenues occupied George Washington in the first moments of his administration. He signed legislation imposing duties on imported goods on July 4, 1789. Customs revenues became the most important source of federal government revenue until World War I.[20]

In the Washington and John Adams administrations, the annual value of American exports almost quadrupled, from 22 million dollars in 1790 to 81 million in 1800, and then fluctuated, with some declines, during the Napoleonic wars (1803–15), which involved major European powers and commercial warfare in the West Indies.[21] For the period 1790 to 1814, approximately one-third of American exports went to European colonies in the Caribbean and South America.[22] Perhaps more important, the American merchant marine and receipts from shipping services made possible, along with European loans and investment, the relatively high level of imports experienced by a predominantly agricultural nation, thus making the protection of neutral shipping a key to the American economy and balance of payments.[23]

Defense of neutral rights and commerce would become a primary concern of American foreign policy. This commitment took the country into war against France, the Barbary powers (Morocco, Algeria, Tunis, and Tripoli), and Britain in the first decades after independence.[24] The new nation could not isolate itself, or the Western Hemisphere, from international conditions that defined its commercial opportunities, constrained its territorial expansion, and, sometimes, directly threatened the very survival of the Union.[25] In this context, America adopted unilateralism as the first principle of its foreign policy.

Beginnings

When the United States gained its independence it was encircled by vast territories of the major European powers. In the first half century of independence, American presidents and the Congress repeatedly addressed threats from France, England, Spain, and Russia (on the Pacific Coast) as well as recurrent warfare with Native American peoples.[26] America's commercial ambitions and security concerns required diplomatic missions and small naval and military expeditions to the Pacific rim, the Caribbean, Asia, and the South Atlantic. In the case of North Africa, America went to war against the Barbary powers rather than continue to pay tribute to avoid assaults on American shipping in the Mediterranean. Americans characterized their victory against the Barbary powers as a blow "for liberty and Christianity" against "Islamic Despotism."[27]

In the country's first decades, several basic preoccupations framed its foreign policy: (1) preventing fragmentation of the Union *as a result of foreign meddling*;[28] (2) territorial consolidation and expansion; (3) growth and protection of American commerce, *globally*, through opening new markets, reciprocal trade agreements, and naval reprisal against attacks on merchant shipping *anywhere in the world*; (4) impeding further European colonization in the Western Hemisphere and then eliminating or neutralizing European rivals;[29] and (5) exclusion of European "systems" and their political "legitimacy" (at first, monarchy, but later other "systems" and political doctrines) from the New World. All of these concerns stemmed from the perceived designs of European nations in the Western Hemisphere and (after 1822) from initiatives by Latin American governments to favor European interests over those of the United States. The policies took into account nonstate actors such as financiers, investors, merchants, missionaries, fishermen, whalers, smugglers, privateers, pirates, and slave traders.[30]

What American legislators defined as domestic politics — tariff legislation, public lands policy (which spurred the quest for more territory and hence conflicts with Native Americans and European rivals), the slavery question, and even subsidies for canals, railroads, and merchant marine — had unavoidable foreign policy implications.[31] Votes by congressmen on foreign policy issues sometimes turned on patronage and public works contracts for family members or constituents. Partisan politics or even bribes decided Senate votes on treaties.[32] Policies affecting other nations might be determined by federal government revenue requirements, electoral considerations, and the momentary coalition put together to bring legislation through Congress rather than by coherent grand strategy.[33] Thus, foreign policy and domestic politics were inextricably intertwined from the conception of the American Republic — a phenomenon that modern political scientists have called "intermestic politics."

Beyond the domestic determinants of foreign policy, the evolving definition, through practice, of presidential authority in foreign affairs also inspired America's global and regional initiatives. American presidents stretched constitutional authority to its limit and beyond. They launched covert operations, subverted foreign governments, and promoted regime change as a transition to annexation into the Union of former European territories or to a reconfiguration of the hemispheric balance of power through decolonization in Spanish America. They sent agents to bribe foreign officials and financed and cultivated insurrections in foreign territory from their "contingency fund" (introduced at the suggestion of Alexander Hamilton).[34] They also authorized "exploratory expeditions" into foreign territory, ostensibly for scientific purposes but with clearly strategic objectives. This included Thomas Jefferson's authorization of the Lewis and Clark expedition in 1804 and the 1806 Zebulon Pike mission into the territory (mostly Spanish) drained by the Arkansas and Red Rivers. It also included "scientific" expeditions from Mexico to South America.[35] In all this, American leaders took unilateral decisions (sometimes influenced by electoral considerations) — but they could not isolate themselves from European or Native American resistance or reprisals.

As the United States engaged the European powers, Congress recognized the sometime need for secrecy in conducting foreign affairs. The initial legislation providing contingent funds for secret operations instructed President Washington to account for expenditures "in all instances, wherein the expenditure thereof may, *in his judgment*, be made public." For expenditures "that he [the President] may think it advisable *not to specify*," the president could provide an annual statement to Congress.[36] Congress initially budgeted $40,000 for George Washington's secret fund; four years later this amount had increased to 1 million dollars, approximately 12 percent of the national budget.[37] American political leaders thus created, in Washington's first term, the beginnings of secret government.

Fundamental philosophical and pragmatic differences divided the American political elite on the role of the president and Congress in foreign policy, on the balance between state and federal authority, and on a variety of foreign policy issues. Almost all legislators agreed that expansion of U.S. commerce and containment of European influence in the Western Hemisphere was crucial. Most agreed that success in this realm depended on increasing military, especially naval, forces. Disagreement existed, however, on the particulars of relations with Great Britain, France, and Spain, including policies in the Floridas and toward Spanish-French claims in what came to be called the Louisiana Territory. Differences also existed regarding policies toward European colonies in the Caribbean and Canada. Likewise, legislators were not of a common mind regarding policies that should be adopted regarding annexation of new territories into the Union or the extension of slavery into any newly acquired territory or, once annexed, how such territory should be divided for the purpose of creating new states, with their respective representation in the House of Representatives and the Senate.[38] Foreign policy, particularly annexation of new territory acquired by purchase, infiltration, or war, had critical implications for the balance of sectional and partisan politics. On the resolution of these issues turned the nature, even the survival, of the Union.

Foreign policy thus involved intense conflicts among partisan, sectional, and economic interests. It also brought conflictive engagement with the major European powers over territory — Canada, Oregon, Texas, Florida, and even Cuba — coveted by some American leaders. The complexities of American intermestic politics encouraged dynamic and pragmatic unilateralism as a basic strategy of American foreign relations to defend the new nation against foreign threats, to limit European influence in domestic politics, to pursue territorial ambitions in the Western Hemisphere, and to exploit commercial opportunities around the globe.

Grand Strategy and the Western Hemisphere

In America's first half century, policies intended to create a secure home bastion in the Western Hemisphere became the linchpin for the country's insertion into the global system. National security and economic growth required territorial expansion to control the Mississippi basin, south to New Orleans and Florida, with its outlets to the Caribbean and the Atlantic. American security also required a policy of strategic denial toward European powers. These two premises underlay the foreign policies of the Federalists in the late 1790s when Alexander Hamilton presented his summary of the global situation and explained U.S. interest in (1) preserving the balance of power in Europe; and (2) promoting U.S. territorial expansion at the expense of Spain: "Besides eventual security against invasions, we ought certainly to look to the possession of the Floridas and Louisiana, and we ought to squint at South America."[39] Hamilton observed that France's aim was the destruction of Great Britain, "which had repeatedly held the balance of power [in Europe] in opposition to the grasping ambition of France." If the French were successful, "the foundation will be laid for stripping [Spain] of South America and her mines; and perhaps for dismembering the United States. The magnitude of this mischief is not easily calculated."[40] Hamilton, thus, informed his advice on foreign policy with strategic analysis of the European balance of power and its implications for U.S. security. He knew that isolationism was an impossibility. The trick was how to play the European powers against one another to achieve American aims. Hamilton focused directly on policies that might influence *the balance of power in Europe* to American advantage.

Hamilton's political adversary, Thomas Jefferson, shared his concern with the policies of France, Spain, and England in the Western Hemisphere. Jefferson saw danger in British policy toward the United States, but after 1800 he also came to detest Napoleon as a tyrant and as a menace to American interests. His writings and correspondence illustrate, long before he became president, how perceptively he linked the prospects for the United States to European wars and politics. Jefferson wrote in 1790 that he expected that the United States would "fatten on the follies of the old [nations] by winning new territory and concessions from their wars."[41] His prescience on this score was remarkable; during his presidency the country would acquire the Louisiana Territory from Napoleon's France, thereby doubling the size of the nation, precisely because Napoleon had fought a losing battle against a slave revolt in Saint Domingue (Haiti) and required funds to fight a global war against England and its European allies.

Retracing the story of American diplomacy, war making, territorial expansion, and formulation of foreign policy doctrine and practice from the 1790s to the early 1820s belies the phoenix-like myth of isolationism. It also reveals the gradual formulation of a grand strategy premised on construction of a secure bastion in the Western Hemisphere. Key episodes in this story were the Quasi-War with France (1798–1800, fought mainly in the Caribbean and West Indies), the Louisiana Purchase (1803), annexation of West Florida (1810–11), failed efforts at regime change and annexation of East Florida (1811–19), the War of 1812, the Seminole War (1817–18), the Adams-Onís Treaty (1819), and final acquisition of East Florida (1819–21). Taken together, these key moments in America's first three decades under the federal Constitution defined the practical meaning of foreign policy unilateralism for the new nation and also established the framework for partisan and congressional politics in the formulation of foreign policy.

Quasi-War: 1798–1800

Before securing independence, the American colonies had entered into the defensive Treaty of Alliance with France in 1778. The treaty required that the United States come to the aid of France to defend its West Indies colonies against an attack by Great Britain and that "neither of the two parties shall conclude either truce or peace with Great Britain, without the formal consent of the other first obtained; and they mutually engage not to lay down their arms until the independence of the United States shall have been formally, or tacitly, assured by the treaty or treaties, that shall terminate the war."[42] A revolution that began in 1789 eventually ousted the French monarch, Louis XVI. A month after the French Convention ordered the king's execution by guillotine (January 21, 1793), George Washington held his first cabinet meeting as president of the United States (February 25). In the interim, on February 1, 1793, France went to war with Great Britain, the Netherlands, and Spain.

Federalist leader Alexander Hamilton advised President Washington to issue a proclamation of American neutrality. Thomas Jefferson also preferred neutrality but favored recognition of the French republic and argued that only Congress could commit the country to neutrality in accord with its war-making powers. Debates over foreign policy and the proper roles of Congress and the president in foreign affairs thus became partisan political issues.

Washington favored Jefferson's views on upholding the treaty with France and Hamilton's views on presidential authority. In April, he proclaimed that the United States would pursue a "conduct friendly and impartial toward the belligerent powers."[43] To avoid a constitutional debate over authority to declare "neutrality," Washington's neutrality proclamation avoided the word "neutrality." (Congress would pass a "Neutrality Act" in June 1794). Since France had declared war on Great Britain, the United States avoided any obligation to provide military aid to the French.[44] *Neutrality* in European conflicts became the guiding rule for American policymakers, but the meaning of "neutrality" at each juncture and how to protect American interests and shipping amid

European wars provoked considerable partisan disagreement and practical obstacles as the belligerents targeted American shipping and embargoed American commerce, especially in the Caribbean and the West Indies.

France viewed America's 1794 Jay Treaty with England as a breach of its 1778 Treaty of Alliance, which ostensibly required the United States to defend France's West Indian colonies.[45] In 1796, France began seizing American ships that were trading with its British enemy. In the so-called XYZ affair, a delegation sent by President John Adams to negotiate peace with France was told that the United States would have to pay a large bribe, help finance the French war effort against the British, and apologize for anti-French declarations by the president. Adams told Congress: "Such attempts ought to be repelled with a decision which shall convince France and the world that we are not a degraded people, humiliated under a colonial spirit of fear and sense of inferiority, fitted to be the miserable instruments of foreign influence, and regardless of national honor, character, and interest."[46]

Revelation of the XYZ affair ramped up anti-French sentiments. Adams instructed the armed vessels of the United States "to seize, take and bring into any Port of the United States, to be proceeded against according to the Laws of Nations, any armed Vessel sailing under Authority, or Pretense of Authority, from the Republic of France, which shall have committed, or which shall be found hovering on the Coasts of the United States for the purpose of committing, Depredations on the Vessels belonging to Citizens thereof; and also to retake any Ship or Vessel of any Citizen or Citizens of the United States, which may have been captured by any such armed Vessel." In July 1798 Congress rescinded all treaties with France and authorized the navy and privateers to attack and seize French shipping in the West Indies until the French refrained from their "lawless depredations and outrages."[47] Secretary of the Navy Benjamin Stoddert ordered *offensive* operations in the Caribbean, where most of the French cruisers were based.[48] In the next two years, Congress passed a raft of laws authorizing further measures against France.[49]

President Adams wavered between declaring war against France and secret peace negotiations. Initially, the majority of Adams's cabinet favored a declaration of war against France, forming an alliance with Great Britain, and invading Spanish Louisiana and Florida. Yet Adams could not rely on moderate Federalists and the Jeffersonians to approve a declaration of war.[50] Moreover, his administration's policies, and Hamilton's prowar rhetoric, generated a vitriolic political opposition to the Federalist party by the Democratic-Republicans, led by Vice President Thomas Jefferson. The policies also divided the Federalists among factions looking toward the 1800 presidential elections.[51] Congressional debates on the war centered on the president's constitutional authority, the size of military forces required, logistics, war taxes, cost overruns, profiteering, and corruption — issues that would re-emerge in future American wars.[52] Congress conceded contingent authority to the president, in this case to increase the size of the army and call up the state militia, to order seizure of French shipping, and to expand (really, to re-create) the navy.[53]

As Congress debated the undeclared war against France, the ideological and political issues surrounding the Quasi-War shaped the outlines of the first American political party system. The Federalists and the Jeffersonians (and factions within the two camps) exchanged vicious personal attacks in partisan newspapers.[54] The Supreme Court also made its first determination regarding the president's war powers and the effects of undeclared war. In a case involving an award for salvage for the recapture of an American vessel taken by the French, Justice Bushrod Washington (George Washington's nephew) wrote: "Every contention by force, between two nations, in external matters, under the authority of their respective governments, is not only war but public war," although no official declaration of war existed.[55] Only Congress could *declare* war, but the Supreme Court ruled that the United States could *make* war, constitutionally, without such a declaration.[56]

To stifle dissent against the Quasi-War, the Federalist-controlled Congress passed the Alien and Sedition Acts (June–July 1798) — the first "internal security" legislation of the new republic. The Alien and Sedition Acts authorized the president to deport aliens (for example, recent Irish Catholic immigrants) "dangerous to the peace and safety of the United States"; allowed the wartime arrest, imprisonment, and deportation of any alien subject to an enemy power; and established that any treasonable activity, including the publication of "false, scandalous and malicious writing," was a high misdemeanor, punishable by fine and imprisonment.[57] In practice, this meant repression of the political opposition, including editors of Democratic-Republican newspapers.[58]

Manufactured fear of foreign ideologies precipitated the country's first bout of legislative repression against internal dissent.[59] Sedition Act trials and the Senate's use of its contempt powers to suppress opponents of the war also sparked anger against the Federalists and contributed to their defeat in the election of 1800, despite the settlement of the conflict with France in the Treaty of Mortefontaine.[60] In the fall of 1800, with the Federalist Party divided among various presidential candidates and between those who preferred peace and those, led by Hamilton, who desired full-scale war with France, John Adams lost his bid for reelection to Thomas Jefferson.[61] In his inaugural address in 1801, Jefferson told the country that among the principles of government he deemed essential were "peace, commerce, and honest friendship with all nations, entangling alliances with none."[62] Jefferson, like Washington, preferred unilateralism to alliance politics. Although his admonition against "entangling alliances" is frequently confused with a policy of isolationism, Jefferson envisioned an America fully engaged in commerce and cooperative relations with "all nations" to the extent that international circumstances permitted.

In retrospect, the largely forgotten Quasi-War significantly influenced the initial development of congressional-executive relations and the role of Congress in war making with *resolutions* and *appropriations* rather than *declarations* of war. Naval war with France in the Caribbean, an area that would become a central focus of American strategic doctrine, thus presaged the link between American global security policy and hegemony in the Western Hemisphere. It also irreversibly connected partisan politics, foreign policy, and the fate of civil liberties in America in times of crisis. The Quasi-War made clear that America's internal security, partisan politics, economy, and commercial ambitions could not be isolated from events in Europe and access to European colonies in the Western Hemisphere.

Louisiana

Even as the United States made peace with France, Spain retroceded the Louisiana Territory (with boundaries unspecified) to France in the (temporarily) secret Treaty of San Ildefonso (1800). President Jefferson was keenly aware of the international and partisan implications of the Spanish retrocession, with the possibility of French troops landing at New Orleans and demands from the Federalists for an alliance with England to renew war on France.

In February 1800, Napoleon Bonaparte established himself as First Consul of France's ruling triumvirate — a transition to dictatorship. (In 1802 Napoleon was "elected" Consulate for life, and he became Emperor of France in 1804.) Napoleon dreamed of a restored North American and Caribbean empire to reverse France's defeat in the Seven Years War (1756–63). His ambitions represented a serious threat to the United States and to the British. President Jefferson wrote in 1802 to French economist and diplomatic intermediary Pierre Samuel du Pont de Nemours: "This little event, of France's possessing herself of Louisiana, is the embryo of a tornado which will burst on the countries on both sides of the Atlantic and involve in its effects their highest destinies."[63]

Jefferson preferred negotiations to a "tornado burst." His Federalist opponents fulminated over Spanish treachery and French trickery and sought to push the country back into war. Exacerbating this situation, in 1802 the Spanish intendant at New Orleans suspended the right of Americans to deposit cargoes for transshipment without paying duties. This decision created a significant burden for American commerce at the Mississippi and the Gulf outlet for American exports. Alexander Hamilton called this decision a justifiable cause for war.[64]

Congress debated a resolution by Senator James Ross (Federalist-Pa.) authorizing the president to take immediate possession of New Orleans and environs, "as he may deem fit and convenient for the purposes of [obtaining the right of deposit] and to adopt such other measures for obtaining that complete security as to him in his wisdom shall seem meet."[65] Ross claimed that the Spanish had violated provisions of the Treaty of Amity with the United States of 1794, spoliated its commerce on the high seas, and blocked access and navigation on the Mississippi River, to which the United States had an "undoubted right of nature." Federalists saw a chance to "out-patriot" Jefferson, appealing to westerners and southerners who relied on New Orleans for transshipment of their agricultural products. In the Senate, Gouverneur Morris (Federalist-N.Y.) questioned Spain's right to transfer Louisiana back to France: "Had Spain a right to make this cession without our consent? Gentlemen have taken the position for granted that she had. But I deny the position. No nation has a right to give to another a dangerous neighbor without her consent . . . as between nations, who can redress themselves only by war, such transfer is in itself an aggression. He who renders me insecure; he who hazards my peace, and exposes me to imminent danger, commits an act of hostility against me, and gives me the rights consequent on that act."[66] Morris's position anticipated more modern justifications for preemptive self-defense.

For now, war would not be necessary to enforce the new American security principle. Defeat of Napoleon's troops by Haitian revolutionaries (and yellow fever) in 1803, France's turn toward its adversaries in Europe, and Napoleon's need for cash made the Louisiana Territory expendable. President Jefferson instructed his representative in France, James Monroe, to take advantage of the international situation to acquire New Orleans: "You cannot too much hasten it, as the moment in France is critical. St. Domingo delays their taking possession of Louisiana, and they are in the last distress for money for current purposes."[67] Jefferson's instructions reflected an astute and realist analysis of America's immediate opportunities to buttress its security, expand its territory, and push the French entirely out of North America. Despite the legend of Jefferson's attachment to limited government, Congress had not been consulted. He acted on his own, arguably beyond his constitutional authority.

Only two months after Morris's bombastic speech, France signed the Louisiana Purchase Treaty, on April 30, 1803. On signing the treaty, American

Minister to France Robert Livingston proclaimed: "Today, the United States take their place among the powers of the first rank."[68] The treaty doubled the size of the United States, adding approximately 828,000 square miles, which encompassed parts of fifteen of today's states and two Canadian provinces. It left Spain, rather than France or England, as the Americans' southern and southwestern neighbor. More important, the idea that imminent danger, including threats to American commerce, justified preemptive war, set the stage for grander American claims and military operations. So, too, did the disposition of some legislators to authorize broad presidential discretion to achieve the nation's foreign policy objectives and to ratify retroactively "facts-on-the-ground" resulting from presidential initiatives undertaken without congressional approval.

The treaty authorizing the Louisiana Purchase was not approved without opposition in the Senate (24–7) from Federalists who feared that southern and western influence in Congress would increase disproportionately and that slavery would spread into the western territories. A plot led by Senator Timothy Pickering (Federalist-Mass.) to form a "Northern Confederacy" failed, but the aftermath, in 1804, included a duel between Aaron Burr (Jefferson's vice president) and Alexander Hamilton, who suffered mortal wounds.

The overlap of foreign policy and partisan politics could be deadly serious. It could also make a huge difference in electoral politics. Jefferson garnered 72 percent of the popular vote in the 1804 presidential election, and the Democratic-Republicans took 80 percent of the seats in the House of Representatives. The Federalist Party was on its way to extinction.

West Florida

For seven years after acquiring the Louisiana territory, the United States negotiated unsuccessfully with Spain for the adjacent West Florida territory.[69] In 1810, President Madison sent covert agents and then troops into the territory, ostensibly to protect American lives and property. The United States informed Spanish diplomats that it was taking possession of the land between the Perdido and Mississippi Rivers. Meanwhile, an independent West Florida Republic had been established. It would endure for approximately three months.

A former American diplomat, Fulwar Skipwith, who had helped James Monroe to negotiate the Louisiana Purchase, became West Florida's first and only president/governor. Diplomatic cover for the West Florida operation was a claim that this territory had been included in the Louisiana Purchase. On October 27, 1810, President James Madison (1809–17) annexed the West Florida territory by proclamation. But if the territory had been included

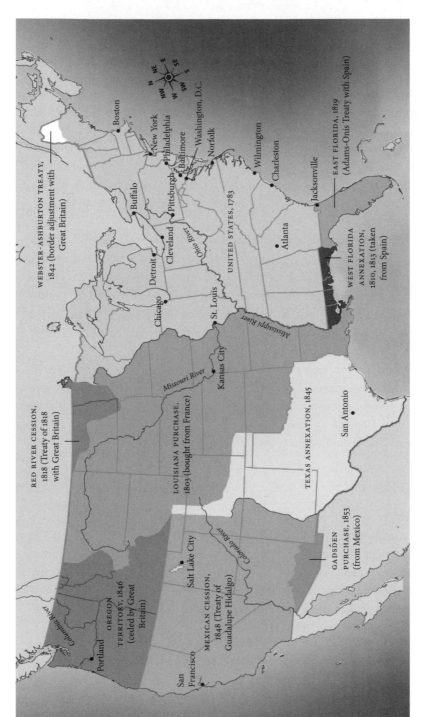

Map 1.1. The territorial growth of the United States

in the Louisiana Purchase, what need was there for Madison's annexation proclamation?

No constitutional authority existed for Madison's proclamation. He explained this operation to Congress in early December, appealing to international law, "necessity," and the immediate economic and security threats posed by the uncertain situation of the Spanish colonies in the Western Hemisphere. (Napoleon had usurped the Spanish throne in 1808, ensconcing his brother Joseph as ruler of Spain.) Madison's West Florida initiative combined pragmatism, opportunism, and "soft power" (appeals to international norms, even if the particular terms of the Louisiana Purchase had been contested by the Bourbon Monarchy before Napoleon's invasion of Spain in 1808).[70] Madison justified his West Florida operation to Congress in December 1810:

> Among the events growing out of the state of the Spanish monarchy, our attention was imperiously attracted to the change developing itself in that portion of West Florida which, though of right appertaining to the United States, had remained in the possession of Spain, awaiting the result of negotiations for its actual delivery to them. The Spanish authority was subverted, and a situation produced exposing the country to ulterior events which might essentially affect the rights and welfare of the Union. In such a conjuncture I did not delay the interposition required for the occupancy of the territory west of the river Perdido, to which the title of the United States extends, and to which the laws provided for the territory of Orleans are applicable. . . . The legality and necessity of the course pursued, assure me of the favorable light in which it will present itself to the legislature, and of the promptitude with which they will supply whatever provisions may be due to the essential rights and equitable interests of the people thus brought into the bosom of the American family.[71]

Madison presented Congress with a fait accompli: West Florida was now declared to be part of the Union. As had Adams and Jefferson before him, Madison wished to ensure that the annexation "was [plausibly] compatible with the law of nations and would eventually be accepted as such by settlers on the Gulf Coast and by governments in London, Madrid and Paris."[72] Madison understood the intricate links between American domestic politics and the country's position *in* the international system.

In Congress, Madison, his allies, and opposition congressmen debated the constitutionality of the annexation proclamation and sources of the U.S. territorial claim on West Florida (going back to seventeenth-century colonial settlements and eighteenth- and nineteenth-century treaties among the European powers). Madison's opponents and supporters appealed alike to "universal law," supposed treaty rights, and the threat of a Spanish and French military response. Reviewing these debates immerses the reader in a surprisingly modern-sounding discussion of constitutional and political issues as they pertain to immediate foreign policy challenges.[73]

In the debates over the West Florida annexation, the beginnings of executive-legislative complicity in American aggressive unilateralism in relations with foreign powers were forged. Congress accepted the conclusions of Henry Clay (Democratic-Republican–Ky.), which supported the president's constitutional, international law, and pragmatic rationale for seizing West Florida and for moving toward the same policy regarding East Florida and even Cuba.[74] Clay told Congress: "I have no hesitation in saying, that if a parent country will not or cannot maintain its authority in a colony adjacent to us, and there exists in it a state of misrule and disorder, menacing our peace, and if moreover such colony, by passing into the hands of any other power, would become dangerous to the integrity of the Union, and manifestly tend to the subversion of our laws; we have a right, *upon eternal principles of self-preservation, to lay hold of it.*[75] *This principle alone, independent of any title, would warrant our occupation of West Florida. But it is not necessary to resort to it, our title being in my judgment incontestably good.*"[76]

Like Gouverneur Morris, Clay appealed to the "principles of self-preservation" to justify covert operations and preemptive deployment of military force. In March 1811, Congress officially approved a joint resolution that made up the legislation on Spanish Florida and also the joint resolution that established the No Transfer Principle (see below), a *secret* policy undergirding American grand strategy in the Western Hemisphere.[77] Secret government, covert operations, and regime change had been established as national policy within the American constitutional system.[78] According to historian J. C. A. Stagg, Madison had acted preemptively, fearing that consolidation of Napoleon's reign in Spain would provoke the collapse of the Spanish-American empire, thereby putting Cuba and the Floridas at risk of British possession.[79] The president had resorted to anticipatory self-defense in the West Florida gambit to defend American commerce and the security of the Union against potential threats from England or other European competitors in the hemisphere. In the same month that Congress learned (and approved) of Madison's West Florida operation, it also considered the prospect of war with England, the advantages of invading and taking Canada, and the implications of admitting the Orleans Territory into the Union.[80]

East Florida and the No Transfer Resolution

Madison did not intend to end his territorial grab with West Florida. In secret sessions during the first months of 1811, Congress debated legislation recommended by the president authorizing him "to take possession of any part or parts of the said territory [East Florida], in pursuance of arrangements which may be desired by the Spanish authorities; and for making provision for the government of the same during such possession." Madison had alerted Congress to "the seasonableness of a declaration that the United States could not see, without serious inquietude, any part of a neighboring territory, in which they have, in different respects, so deep and so just a concern, pass from the hands of Spain into those of any other foreign Power."[81] He asked for secret authority regarding East Florida, having already enunciated a more general security principle for U.S. foreign policy — what came to be called the No Transfer Principle.[82]

Congress accommodated the president with legislation and a joint No Transfer Resolution in January 1811. Although aimed for the moment at Spain and England, the principle enunciated in the No Transfer Resolution was more generic: the United States might define any transfer of territory in the Western Hemisphere from one European power to another as a threat or potential threat to its security and national interests. This principle would become a bedrock of U.S. regional security doctrine and a foundation for the better-known Monroe Doctrine proclaimed in 1823. American policymakers would repeatedly return to this principle as an anchor of security policy from 1812 through World War II. In modified versions, the No Transfer Principle would eventually be applied to the Sandwich Islands (Hawaii) and other Pacific islands and then to other parts of the world, much to the distress of Great Britain and other European powers.[83]

By its actions regarding the Floridas, Congress approved Madison's covert operation in West Florida and authorized the upcoming invasion of East Florida. Congress's enactment was supposedly a secret law (not published officially for seven years), though, in practice, the legislators had lifted the lid in 1812.[84] Between January and March, Congress continued to discuss the Florida situation.[85] In the course of the debates, the executive branch selectively provided to legislators intercepted correspondence from Spanish and British officials, purportedly confirming the grave risk to American security.

In West Florida, the cover of law for U.S. seizure was at least somewhat plausible, if not unambiguous.[86] In East Florida, American claims were negligible to nonexistent. Nevertheless, Madison sought legal justification in unpaid claims against Spain for spoliation of American commerce going back to the independence wars and the more recent suspension of the concession to deposit merchandise for re-export via New Orleans. Eventually, he also resorted to the legal fiction of a local rebellion and separation from Spain — a precedent for what would later occur in Texas (1836–45), California (1846), Hawaii (1893–94), and Panama (1902).[87]

With Spain occupied by French troops and England supporting guerrilla warfare against the French occupation, the British sought to represent Spanish concerns about Florida to the American government. Diplomatic correspondence between July and November 1811 reveals the realpolitik that would lead to the failed effort to seize East Florida. The American secretary of state wrote to his British counterpart: "Situated as East Florida is, cut off from the other possessions of Spain, and surrounded in a great measure by the territory of the United States, and having also an important bearing on their commerce, no other Power could think of taking possession of it, with other than hostile views to them. Nor could any other Power take possession of it without endangering their prosperity and best interests."[88] Many months before the secretary of state had this message delivered to the English diplomat, President Madison had sent an American agent, the ex-governor of Georgia, General George Mathews, to Spanish East Florida. Controversy still exists over Madison's intent and Mathews's instructions. Mathews promoted a failed rebellion in East Florida.[89] According to Madison, his actions exceeded the authority conveyed by his instructions, or at least that was the claim by the spring of 1812, just before Congress declared war on Great Britain, Ireland, and their dependencies, on June 18, 1812.

Mathews received written instructions in early 1811, only months after Madison had annexed West Florida. Under several contingencies, acting as a secret operative, he was to take possession of East Florida. Seemingly, the instructions left him ample discretion in carrying out this commission. Further, they specified: "If, in the execution of any part of these instructions, you should need the aid of a military force, the same will be afforded you upon your application to the commanding officer of the troops of the United States on that station, or to the commanding officer of the nearest post, in virtue of orders which have been issued from the War Department."[90]

Mathews essentially had authorization to subvert Spanish authorities, promote what now would be called regime change, and facilitate the eventual annexation of East Florida to the United States. As historian Stephen Knott writes, James Madison "believed covert operations were an essential part of America's foreign policy arsenal."[91] When Mathews's covert operation failed, the U.S. president and the secretary of state determined that he had exceeded his authority and, as came to be expected in later times with outed covert operatives, Mathews took the rap as a rogue warrior.[92] According to Stagg, the complexity and Machiavellian realism of covert operations in the Spanish Floridas (and also in British Canada) by American agents "made a mockery of the idealism that justified its foreign policy, while in East Florida itself the American-backed revolutionaries inflicted widespread devastation on the local populations."[93] Devastation notwithstanding, the East Florida gambit failed. Thomas Jefferson, James Madison, and their allies would have to wait until 1819 to force Spain to part officially with this piece of its dissolving empire.

Meanwhile, Congress debated the advisability and justice of war with England, the political and military situation in Europe, the position to take regarding Spain's loosening hold on its colonies in the Western Hemisphere (a first declaration of independence occurred in Venezuela in 1811), and the relative emphasis to place on naval and land forces as the country prepared for war. In their debates of 1811 and early 1812, the legislators considered the Napoleonic wars in Europe, their spread into the Caribbean, the desirability of invading, occupying, and eventually incorporating Canada into the Union, and the U.S. military and commercial role in the global system. The executive branch sent emissaries and covert agents to Europe and Spanish America and sought to encourage rebellion in Mexico and South America.[94] Whatever shorthand label is pasted on these policies, it cannot be isolationism. Americans sought, as Washington had urged, to "command their own fortune."

The War of 1812

War against the British in 1812 resulted from failure to settle a panoply of conflicts dating from the late 1790s and from the immediate intricacies of the Napoleonic wars. According to President James Madison's war message to Congress, the main provocations for the war were the ongoing harassment and seizure of American shipping, impressment of sailors for the British navy, and encouragement by British garrisons and traders of "the warfare just renewed by the savages on one of our extensive frontiers."[95] For the British, however, the war was another front in the battle against Napoleon, in which American commercial policy and territorial ambitions had figured since the 1798–1800 Quasi-War against France. As the war progressed, it briefly threatened the survival of the United States. New England states refused to call up their militia to fight the war. Radical Federalists even proposed a separate peace between New England and Britain.

President Jefferson had implemented embargoes on American shipping from 1807 to 1809 in efforts to end British and French seizures of American ships. Jefferson defended the principle of neutrality (a similar principle would underlie Woodrow Wilson's policies from 1914 to 1917, before American entry into World War I). American ships carried provisions of all sorts for the European belligerents. Both sides sought to prevent their adversaries from receiving supplies that assisted the war effort. England's blockade of the continent was intended to cut France off from the Western Hemisphere (as England would attempt to do to Germany from 1914 to 1917). France reciprocated by interdicting shipping bound from the United States and the West Indies to England. Ultimately, the American principle (really the Dutch principle) of "free ships make free goods" would be the victim of the necessities of war. Between 1804 and 1810 Americans could have chosen on various occasions to make war against either the French or the British over their attacks on the country's neutral shipping.

Jefferson's embargo policy provoked violence, corruption, and severe economic hardship in the United States while failing to deter either England or France from seizing American ships. Jefferson sought to keep America out of war, but this was not due to a dedication to isolationism.[96] He had made war on the Barbary powers, had proposed a small naval construction program, and, in the run-up to the Louisiana Purchase, had allowed American deliveries of arms and supplies to the Haitian insurrectionists in their war against Napoleon. Jefferson also supported resources for port fortifications and coastal gunboats. He created a military school at West Point. As he made efforts to create an army staffed by Republican rather than Federalist officers, he tripled the size of the military establishment by 1808.[97]

Jefferson's failed embargo strategy engaged the Union in complex intermestic politics. He applied the trade embargoes, which carried the country toward the War of 1812, as the tactic of a weak nation drawn into the cross fire of the Napoleonic wars. Reluctantly, he approved a relaxation of the embargoes just prior to leaving office, but not before he had deployed the regular army throughout much of New England and along the Canadian border to enforce his foreign policies on a reluctant northeast and Federalist opposition.

When Congress finally passed Macon's Bill Number 2 on May 1810 to lift the embargo, Napoleon seized on the opportunity to agree to halt attacks on American shipping, subject to the English doing the same. The English did not follow suit, leaving the Americans with an undeclared maritime war with Britain. Eventually, for this and other sundry reasons, the United States would go to war with Great Britain, though not without substantial opposition in the House of Representatives (79–49) and the Senate (19–13). Opponents would derisively label the conflict "Mr. Madison's War." It was a "war of choice," which need not have been fought and which would settle almost none of the issues over which Madison and Clay took the United States to war against Great Britain.

Neither the United States nor England was fully committed to the War of 1812. Diplomatic negotiations continued throughout the war, which was fought at sea, on Lake Erie and Lake Champlain, and on land. The British defeated two American efforts to occupy Canada, but in 1813 the Americans sacked and burned York (Toronto). In turn, in August 1814, the British occupied Washington, D.C., and burned public buildings, including the White House. The most-remembered battle of the war took place at New Orleans, where Andrew Jackson's army defeated an invading British force on January 8, 1815 — two weeks after the peace treaty ending the war had been signed but six weeks before the news reached New Orleans.

Opposition to the War of 1812 in New England generated widespread civil disobedience and talk of secession, especially among the Federalists. New England merchants sold supplies to the British army. The antiwar movement culminated with the so-called Hartford Convention in December 1814. The delegates demanded significant reforms of the U.S. Constitution: representation in the House should be based on the free population alone; there would be no reelection of presidents; no embargo should extend more than sixty days; prohibition of commerce, admission of new states, declarations of hostilities or war should require a two-thirds vote of both houses, except in defense against an invasion of the United States; and no naturalized citizen could henceforth be a member of Congress.[98] By the time the Hartford Convention made public its report, the Treaty of Ghent (1814) had ended the war. But, as George Washington had feared, the mix of partisan and sectional politics with foreign policy had briefly threatened the survival of the Union.

In the aftermath of the War of 1812, the Federalist Party virtually dissolved when voters punished its candidates in the 1816 elections. Despite the subsequent reframing of the war as a "second war of independence" and Andrew Jackson's victory at New Orleans, the United States failed to annex Canada, to stop Indian resistance to the push westward, and to take Florida from England's Spanish ally, and, more broadly, it failed, for the moment, to further expand or consolidate the United States' Western Hemisphere bastion or to dislodge the European presence in North America.[99]

Spanish America

Just prior to the 1812 war with the United Kingdom, Congress had reached out to Spain's colonies, inviting them to gain their independence, but without risking direct confrontation with Spain and its British ally:

Be it,

Resolved, by the Senate and House of Representatives of the United States of America in Congress assembled, That they behold, with friendly interest, the establishment of independent sovereignties by the Spanish provinces in America, consequent upon the actual state of the monarchy to which they belonged; that, as neighbors and inhabitants of the same hemisphere, the United States feel great solicitude for their welfare; and that, when those provinces shall have attained the condition of nations, by the just exercise of their rights, the Senate and House of Representatives will unite with the Executive in establishing with them, as sovereign and independent States, such amicable relations and commercial intercourse as may require their Legislative authority.[100]

This backhanded encouragement for independence movements throughout Spanish America only made sense in the context of the global moment: the United States faced war with England, and Madison plotted the invasion of East Florida.[101] Congress would pass the No Transfer Resolution in January 1811, aimed at deterring possible British intervention in Cuba or Florida. Felix Grundy (R.-Tenn.) told his colleagues:

We now stand on the bank; one movement more, the Rubicon is passed, we are in Italy; and we must march to Rome. . . . The rapid growth of our commercial importance, has not only awakened the jealousy of the commercial interests of Great Britain, but her statesmen, no doubt, anticipate with great concern, the maritime greatness of this Republic. . . . Sir, I prefer war to submission. . . . This war, if carried on successfully, will have its advantages. We shall drive the British from our Continent — and they will no longer have an opportunity of intriguing with our Indian neighbors, and setting on the ruthless savages to tomahawk our women and children. . . . I feel anxious therefore not only to add the Floridas to the South, but the Canadas to the North of this empire.[102]

Grundy not only imagined an American empire; he also assessed the impact of war on relations with France and other European powers. His appeal to domestic economic interests and patriotism and to the defense of women and children against "savages" sounds as modern as effective rallying-round-the-flag coalition-building. His global framework sharpens the significance of the 1811 resolution declaring that the United States would "behold, with friendly interest, the establishment of independent sovereignties by the Spanish provinces in America." Isolationism was not Grundy's plate of choice.

For Spain, American support for independence of its colonies in 1812 represented a significant threat. If the United States did not enforce its neutrality legislation, rebels could buy provisions and arms, attack Spanish shipping, and mount expeditions into Mexico, the Caribbean, and northern South America. For England, the United States' pretensions signified a challenge to its commerce and threats to its Caribbean colonies and Canada. Much of what became U.S.-Latin American relations for the next half century would be partly the spin-off of Anglo-American rivalry in the hemisphere.[103]

Viewed by the British in 1814, the fates of Texas, Oregon, Canada, and the Spanish northern territories, including California, the West Indies, and the Central American isthmus, were hardly sealed with the stamp of the Eagle.[104] Spain had reconquered some of its Western Hemisphere possessions with counterrevolutionary military campaigns; Mexico and Peru, the centers of the colonial empire, and Cuba, its most important military base in the Caribbean, had remained under Spanish control. What in retrospect seems "inevitable" — Latin American independence, American acquisition of Texas and the Oregon Territory, and incorporation of California into the Union — was not deemed so by policymakers in 1815. The British, French, Portuguese, Dutch, and Russians had not yet given up on the Western Hemisphere. To create a secure bastion in the hemisphere, American foreign policy would, of necessity, contest the ambitions of the major European powers for the foreseeable future. In the meantime, the Spanish-American wars of independence engaged the United States in messy diplomacy with Spain and other European powers, as well as clandestine military and commercial operations into the early 1820s.

The Seminole War: Ungoverned Spaces and Self-Defense

Even after the Treaty of Ghent ending the war with Great Britain, U.S. agents continued to foment rebellion in Florida. In 1818, justified as a defensive response to pirate activities, smuggling, and general disorder, American forces invaded and occupied Amelia Island. The island served as a base for Spanish-American revolutionaries sending arms and supplies to the insurgents seeking independence from Spain. Numerous American (and still more British) privateers, seamen, military officers, and merchants participated directly, for profit, in the wars against Spain, although the U.S. and British governments repeatedly declared their neutrality.[105]

Secretary of State John Quincy Adams sought to sell the 1818 invasion of East Florida to Congress based on its own No Transfer Resolution of 1811 — a big stretch, inasmuch as Spain, which admittedly did not and could not control the pirates, smugglers, runaway slaves, and rebels on the island, had not proposed to transfer the territory to a foreign power. Adams then argued that the right of self-defense under international law justified the incursion. In modern terms, Florida and Amelia Island were "ungoverned spaces" or "sanctuaries" used by pirates, privateers, slavers, revolutionaries, runaway slaves, and "savages," all of which posed security threats to the United States.[106]

As negotiations continued, the American government ordered General Andrew Jackson to retaliate against a band of Seminole Indians and free blacks who had attacked an American ship and killed approximately thirty American citizens. Jackson was authorized to engage in hot pursuit into Spanish territory, but he was cautioned not to attack Spanish posts, except under designated circumstances. He also had instructions to prevent Spanish Florida from becoming a haven for runaway slaves.[107] By May, Jackson's forces had taken Pensacola, proclaimed martial law, and summarily executed several Indian prisoners and two British subjects, one an ex–military officer.

Jackson appointed one of his officers as military governor of Pensacola and immediately applied American revenue laws and customs. He proclaimed that "the Seminole Indians inhabiting the territories of Spain have for more than two years past, visited our Frontier settlements with all the horrors of savage massacre — helpless women have been butchered and the cradle stained with the blood of innocence." Under these conditions, "the immutable laws of self-defense, therefore, compelled the American government to take possession of such parts of the Floridas in which the Spanish authority could not be maintained."[108]

Jackson appealed to a "no sanctuary for 'savages'" doctrine, not only to invade Spanish territory but to occupy it and install military government, and he urged his government to annex the territory. Whether or not Jackson exceeded his authority was debated at the time and remains contested to the present.[109] Some in Washington proposed a court martial for him; others honored him as a hero.[110] Secretary of State Adams justified Jackson's incursions in terms easily transportable to the twenty-first century, despite its racist premises:

> By the ordinary laws and usages of nations, the rights of pursuing an
> enemy, who seeks refuge from actual conflict within a neutral territory
> is incontestable. . . . The territory of Florida was not even neutral. It
> was itself, as far as Indian savages possess territorial right, the territory

TABLE 1.1. America at War: 1798–1819

	Adversaries	Years
Quasi-War	France	1798–1800
Barbary Coast War	Tripoli, Barbary powers	1801–5
Embargo Act "war"	France, Great Britain	1807–10
Incursions into Florida	Spain	1807–19
Shawnee War	Native Americans	1811
War of 1812	Great Britain, "Canadians"	1812–14
Creek War	Native Americans	1813–14
Seminole War	Native Americans, Free Blacks, Great Britain/Spain	1814–19

of Indians, with whom the United States were at war. It was their place of abode; and Spain was bound by treaty to restrain them by force from committing hostilities against the United States — an engagement which the commanding officer of Spain in Florida had acknowledged himself unable to fulfill. The possession which [Jackson] took of the fort of St. Mark, and subsequently of Pensacola, [was] . . . necessary upon the immutable principles of self-defense.[111]

Jackson had defied judicial writs and set himself up as military governor of New Orleans. But Adams defended his actions in the name of self-defense. Moreover, Monroe subsequently (in 1821) appointed Jackson as military governor of Florida, pending its organization as the Florida Territory. Jackson's correspondence to the Spanish governor regarding "taking delivery" of the former Spanish colony makes evident that Monroe was not displeased with his service to the nation.[112]

For the moment (1818), however, to avoid war and allow negotiations over territorial transfer to proceed, President Monroe decided to restore to Spain the forts that Jackson's forces occupied. Jackson maintained that his instructions authorized his actions and that he had informed Monroe that he intended to conquer Florida in early January 1818. During congressional hearings on the Florida incursion, Jackson sent a private letter to Monroe explaining that St. Augustine, Florida, and Cuba were essential to American security and could be taken "whenever thought necessary."

The Adams-Onís Treaty

After vigorous, and sometimes vituperative, hearings in the House of Representatives and the Senate regarding Jackson's behavior and questions regarding Monroe's constitutional authority to send him to Florida in the first place, a Senate committee report concluded that Jackson had exceeded his authority and "seems to have been [*sic*] to involve the nation in a war without her consent." The full Senate never considered the report. John Quincy Adams credited Jackson's campaign with being "among the most immediate and prominent causes that produced a treaty" (the Adams-Onís Treaty of 1819), which conveyed Florida to the United States, established the Sabine River as the boundary between the United States and the viceroyalty of New Spain (Mexico), and gave to the United States the territory claimed by Spain in the Columbia River basin.[113]

Some congressional opponents of the 1819 treaty lamented that Texas had not also been acquired. Monroe had threatened the Spanish with full-scale military occupation of East Florida and beyond (meaning Texas) if they continued to delay ratification of the proposed treaty. Unfortunately for Spain, it could not count on British intervention to resist the American advance. Writing in 1817, the British foreign secretary had observed that "there can be no question that we have an obvious motive for desiring that the Spaniards should continue to be our neighbours in East Florida rather than that our West Indian possessions should be so closely approached by the territory of the United States, but this is a consideration which we are not prepared to bring forward in the discussion at the present moment in bar to a settlement between Spain and North America."[114]

American aggression against Spain carried out under cover of international law and the justification of "necessity" and "self-defense" carried the day. The No Transfer Principle had become a foundation of U.S. regional security policy and a pretext for interventionism, regime change, and territorial annexation. U.S. diplomats negotiated with Spanish diplomats to acquire Florida and eliminate Spanish claims south of the Oregon Territory.[115] European politics, alliances, wars, and the balance of power system left Spain unable to do better. In the Adams-Onís Treaty of 1819, eventually ratified in 1820 by Spain and 1821 by the United States, Spain retained Texas and what would become the American southwest, including California.

American unilateralism carried the day. International law would not restrain American policy in its engagement of European powers, its quest for security and commercial expansion, and its efforts to create a protectorate over the "separate sphere" it sought to create in the Western Hemisphere. Two years later, President James Monroe would announce, unilaterally, new rules for international politics in the hemisphere. In 1823, Monroe proclaimed — in what came to be known as the Monroe Doctrine — that "the American continents . . . are henceforth not to be considered as subjects for future colonization by any European powers; [the United States] should consider any attempt on their part to extend their system [monarchy] to any portion of this hemisphere as dangerous to our peace and safety." By unilateral determination the American president presumed to impose new rules on the system of international politics and to assume supervision over the Western Hemisphere.

Chapter Two

The Monroe Doctrine and Manifest Destiny

We cannot obscure ourselves, if we would; a part we must take, honorable or dishonorable, in all that is done in the civilized world. — CONGRESSMAN DANIEL WEBSTER, 1823

From the 1780s into the 1820s, Americans constructed an emergent nationalism based partly on their cultural, religious, and political traditions, partly through engagement and war with Native peoples and the European powers, and partly through the creation of new national myths. America's exceptionalism, its example to all the world, its rightful role as protector of the Western Hemisphere, and its Providential destiny became the stuff of national identity and popular culture, which informed U.S. policy.[1] Such notions also became stock rhetoric in the halls of Congress as Americans came to see themselves and their unique political experiment in contradistinction to the tyranny of European monarchies and in contraposition to negative images of Catholic Spain and Spanish America. Spain, its culture, institutions, and religion was "what the United States should not become" — a decadent empire, the antithesis of the American beacon of freedom and liberty. And, as intellectual historian Iván Jaksić discovered, "Latin America did not fare any better. All the negative characteristics ascribed to Spain were simply transferred across the Atlantic [by American writers], where the element of race added ever darker overtones."[2]

Like foreign policy more generally, American policy toward the Western Hemisphere was shaped by domestic politics as well as international circumstances. In the years following the War of 1812, the interplay between foreign policy and domestic politics vectored America toward ascendancy in the Western Hemisphere. President Madison's (1809–17) incursions into the Floridas and his invasion of Canada during the War of 1812, followed by President James Monroe's renewed aggression against East Florida (1817–19), set the United States against Spain and England. Calls from American legislators to support Spain's rebellious colonies, beginning in 1811, provoked Spanish, French, and even Russian anger. As wars raged across the Spanish American empire (1810–26), American merchants, mercenaries, and emissaries undermined Spanish rule. In 1822, the United States became the first nation to recognize the independence of several Spanish American republics — a unilateral and revolutionary initiative challenging the European monarchies and the rules of "legitimacy" in the existing international system.[3]

In December 1823, President James Monroe announced foreign policy principles regarding the Western Hemisphere, which would come to be called the Monroe Doctrine. Americans slowly converted this doctrine into a foundation of the country's foreign policy. Yet, at the time Monroe delivered his message to Congress, his intent was not to create doctrine but only to address immediate domestic political concerns and the foreign policy challenges posed by Britain and the Holy Alliance that supported Spain's King Ferdinand VII and monarchism in Europe. Given the virtually sacred status achieved later by the Monroe Doctrine in American politics, it is worth asking what confluence of domestic and international circumstances led to this defining moment in inter-American relations and in American foreign policy more generally.

The Monroe Doctrine

James Monroe had been reelected unopposed in 1820. He received all but one of the votes in the electoral college. Monroe's first term (1817–21) is often referred to as the "era of good feelings." Despite the good feelings, an economic downturn in 1819, sectional disputes over protective tariffs, and the battle over the future of slavery complicated Monroe's presidency. Indeed, the vituperative debates in January and February of 1820 on slavery and statehood for Missouri and Maine belie the appellation "good feelings." With the perspective of hindsight, congressional speeches of the period scream "civil war!" to the modern reader.[4] More than one southern legislator warned that banning slavery in Missouri carried the risk of "dissolution of this Government." Some compared northern opposition to slavery to the radicalism and terror of Robespierre in the French Revolution.[5]

Himself a slaveholder and member of the American Colonization Society, which advocated the eventual relocation of blacks to Africa (resulting in the creation of Liberia and the name of its capital, Monrovia), Monroe successfully averted a political crisis with the Missouri Compromise in 1820. The crisis had resulted from the application for statehood by the Missouri Territory, part of the Louisiana Purchase, which Monroe had helped to negotiate in 1803. The Missouri Compromise divided the Louisiana Territory into a free north and a slave south, with the exception of Missouri (a line was drawn at 36°30' north latitude, north of Arkansas). Missouri entered the Union as a slave state — the first state entirely west of the Mississippi River. Maine entered as a free state.[6] The Compromise made the City on the Hill a nation literally half free and half slave, both in number (twelve free states and twelve slave states) and, most important, in the Senate.[7] The law also provided that slaves "escaping into any . . . state or territory of the United States . . . may be lawfully reclaimed and conveyed to the person claiming his or her labor or service."[8]

The urgency of the slavery question formed part of the domestic political background for the Monroe Doctrine message to Congress. It also directly affected negotiations with European powers regarding suppression of the slave trade, piracy, and recognition of the independence of Spanish America. With the uncertain fate of Spain's Caribbean colonies in 1822, American slave owners worried about the fate of Cuba and Cuban slavery. The island represented not only a strategic position in the Caribbean, but also either a potential slave state should it be acquired or a potential "bad example" for the South, should Cuba, like some other former Spanish colonies, obtain its independence and decree abolition or even gradual emancipation.[9] Debates in Congress repeatedly featured speculation on British intrigue to control Cuba and foment slave insurrections in America. A resolution by the House of Representatives requesting that Monroe negotiate a treaty with European powers for suppression of the slave trade and its treatment as piracy under international law further linked domestic politics and policy toward Spanish America.[10] Adding to these concerns, in 1819 Congress had enacted "An Act to Protect the Commerce of the United States and Punish the Crime of Piracy." Renewed in 1820 and then again without a time limit in January 1823 (eleven months before the Monroe Doctrine message to Congress), this legislation targeted pirates and privateers operating out of Cuba and Puerto Rico. President Monroe and Congress had created and deployed the West Indian Squadron to the Caribbean in 1822, running the risk of direct confrontation with Spanish authorities who resisted U.S. naval operations in their colonial territories — especially Cuba (see chapter 4).

Campaigning for the 1824 presidential election to succeed Monroe had begun the same year that the United States deployed its West Indian Squadron to the Caribbean, raising critical issues in the context of which the Monroe Doctrine would be formulated. The candidates differed significantly on tariff policy, the role of the federal government in internal development, slavery, suppression of the slave trade, relations with Spanish America, and policy

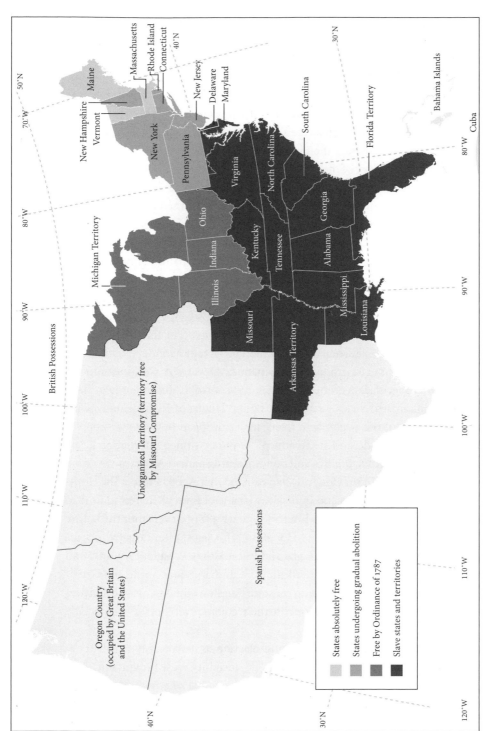

Map 2.1. The United States and adjoining territories in 1821. The Missouri Compromise prohibited slavery in the Louisiana Territory, north of the Arkansas Territory at latitude 36°30', with, however, no restriction on slavery in Missouri.

toward the European powers.[11] Candidate Andrew Jackson had served as governor of Florida, managing implementation of the Adams-Onís Treaty. As a war hero and "Indian fighter," he was identified with an aggressive anti-British, anti-Spanish, anti-Indian, and expansionist foreign policy that made him popular in the West. As senator from Tennessee and a slave owner and slave trader, Jackson had significant support in the South. Jackson began his campaign in 1822, as had John Quincy Adams (secretary of state and the eventual author of the Monroe Doctrine), Henry Clay (Speaker of the House, 1811–21, expansionist, and advocate of Spanish American independence), and William Crawford (secretary of the treasury, ex-minister to France, and slave owner). Clay and Adams differed on the risk of recognizing Spanish American independence; Adams had repeatedly expressed his disdain for the Latin Americans.[12] Between Clay and Jackson, personal animosity went deep. Clay wrote in 1825: "I cannot believe that killing 2,500 Englishmen at New Orleans qualifies for the various, difficult, and complicated duties of the Chief Magistracy."[13] Crawford opposed the anti–slave trade treaty, tying it to old fears of British search and seizure of American ships. In turn, Adams defended the treaty, telling the Senate that it was part of "sundry other negotiations" ongoing with the British, "intimately connected with the welfare, and even the peace of our Union." These other negotiations included "the whole system of South American concerns, connected with general recognition of South American independence, [that] may again, from hour to hour, as it has already been, [be] an object of concerted operations of the highest interest to both nations, *and to the peace of the world*."[14] Thus the panoply of intermestic issues confronting the Monroe administration, from tariff debates and suppression of piracy and the slave trade to the "peace of the world," provided a very complex background for the December 2, 1823, message that contained what became the Monroe Doctrine.

As it turned out, the November 1824 election gave no candidate a majority in the electoral college, reflecting the sharp personal, factional, and sectional divisions in the country. For the first time, a presidential election would be decided in the House of Representatives.[15] Of course, Monroe could not know what would be the outcome in late 1823, as he prepared his message to Congress — only that his own party was factionalized and that policy toward Europe and the Western Hemisphere was controversial.[16]

Beyond partisan and presidential politics, Monroe's message responded to changes in European politics and the course of the independence movements in the Western Hemisphere.[17] In 1823, 100,000 French troops reinstalled Ferdinand VII as absolute ruler of Spain, who then contemplated an expeditionary force to reimpose colonial rule in the Western Hemisphere. Speculation existed that France and Russia might assist Spain's efforts at reconquest.[18] At the same time, Britain opposed Spanish reconquest of the colonies but was not yet ready to officially recognize Spanish American independence, for reasons related to European balance-of-power politics. Additionally, British commercial interests had come to dominate much of Spanish America's trade and finance. Hence Britain proclaimed its neutrality in the independence wars, although English and Irish mercenaries and navy officers fought against the Spanish from southern South America into the northern Andes. By 1822, only the United States had recognized the independence of any of the Spanish American republics.

British foreign secretary George Canning proposed to the Monroe administration a joint declaration on the undesirability of Spanish reconquest and French influence in the Western Hemisphere. Consistent with the unilateralist motif established early in U.S. foreign relations and taking into account the personalities and issues that dominated the upcoming presidential elections, Monroe and John Quincy Adams — the eventual victor in the presidential race — decided on an exclusively American proclamation.[19]

In April 1823, Secretary of State John Quincy Adams instructed the new minister plenipotentiary to Spain, Hugh Nelson: "You will not conceal from the Spanish government the repugnance of the United States to the transfer of the island of Cuba by Spain to any other power . . . [and] that the condition of Cuba cannot be changed without affecting in an eminent degree the welfare of the Union, and consequently the good understanding between us and Spain."[20] Adams added that if such an effort to transfer Cuba to another power occurred, the inhabitants of Cuba would be justified in asserting their independence — as most of Spanish America had already done — and that "the United States will be fully justified in supporting them to carry it into effect."[21] He reiterated his concerns over the possible French invasion of Cuba or transfer of Cuba to Great Britain to the new head of the U.S. Mission to Spain on April 28, 1823, calling Cuba "an object of transcendent importance to the political and commercial interests of our Union."[22] In short, six months before the Monroe Doctrine message, the United States (and its future president) reasserted the No Transfer Resolution and intimated support for regime change (decolonization) in Cuba if Spain ceded the island to England or another European power.

Monroe's personal connection to slavery also indirectly influenced the aggressiveness of the 1823 message. In 1800, then-Virginia governor James Monroe harshly suppressed a slave insurrection. Some slaves were hanged; others, at the suggestion of Thomas Jefferson, were pardoned, delivered to slave traders, or "reprieved for transportation" to Spanish Louisiana. The presumed leader of the insurrection, Gabriel Prosser, was hanged in the middle of the first round of voting in the fall state elections, which would bring Thomas Jefferson to the presidency.[23] Such events made fearmongering that connected slave rebellions to British policy in the Caribbean an effective electoral tactic. The Federalists were associated with pro-British orientations. The Democratic-Republicans in Virginia, like Governor Monroe, were not tainted with Anglophile sentiments, but they did have to demonstrate that they were not allies of the French or its revolution, nor a threat to law and order — nor to the "peculiar institution" of slavery that underlay the prosperity and political system of the American republic.[24]

The year before the Monroe Doctrine message, Charleston, South Carolina, where blacks outnumbered whites by three to one, was confronted by what has been labeled the largest slave conspiracy in American history. Denmark Vesey, a West Indian ex-slave and leader of the African Methodist Episcopal Church, which preached abolition, allegedly conspired to liberate slaves in a Bastille Day (July 14) uprising, kill their masters, and sail to Haiti — at the invitation of Haitian president Jean-Pierre Boyer. The Haiti connection again raised the specter of the "contagion" effect of free blacks — and the danger of any changes in the status of Cuba. An informant gave up the supposed plot; Charleston's mayor called up the city militia and convened a special court to try the captured insurgents.[25] The court, in secret hearings, convicted and ordered the execution of Vesey and, eventually, more than thirty other supposed conspirators. Some forty more were sold outside the United States; some were re-enslaved in Cuba.[26]

Meanwhile, both Mexico and Colombia conjured up plans for invading Cuba to rid the hemisphere of Spanish colonialism. Such Spanish American schemes worried southern legislators and the Monroe cabinet that insurgency in Cuba might provoke "race war" and then slave rebellion in the American South. Periodic slave rebellions in Cuba, elsewhere in the Caribbean, and in British Guyana (Demerara) in the previous decade added to these southern fears.[27] Thus, the Monroe message of 1823 was framed by a complex intermestic situation: (1) the upcoming presidential election; (2) debates in the press and Congress about the antipiracy campaign and the treaty with Britain to suppress the slave trade; (3) concern over potential European intervention to support Spain's reconquest of its colonies; (4) American policy toward Spanish America; (5) the abolitionist threat to the Slave Power; and (6) fear of slave insurrections in the United States.[28]

Domestic "tranquility" depended on the Faustian bargain made in the 1820 Missouri Compromise.[29] With the Compromise debates still fresh, annexation of Spain's Caribbean colonies (with the slaves of Cuba and Puerto Rico) to the United States would provoke renewed threats of "disunion." And should Spain depart, leaving a weak Colombian or Mexican tutelage over Cuba, Britain or France might be tempted to intervene.[30] Adams and Monroe could thus assure the British that the United States (for the moment) "aim[ed] not at the possession of them [Cuba and Puerto Rico] ourselves" — though the United States would not tolerate the islands' transfer to another European power.[31] Spain's continued possession of Cuba meant that the United States would not confront a Haitian-like independence movement, abolition of slavery in Cuba and Puerto Rico, another British outpost in the Caribbean, or a bitter sectional conflict in Congress over annexation of the Pearl of the Antilles.

By 1823, Monroe's life and career embodied the themes of American politics of the time. He had suppressed slave insurrections. After completing his term as governor, he went to France to help negotiate the Louisiana Purchase. He then served as secretary of war during the War of 1812 and then as secretary of state. Monroe also exhibited a certain American pragmatism, or ideological "flexibility." He distrusted the federal government — until his party took power. Initially antitariff and pro–states' rights, as president he would support the 1824 protective tariff and use presidential authority as if he were a disciple of Hamilton. Monroe even served as president of the Second National Bank — the first bank having been anathema to the Democratic-Republicans and the second a target of Andrew Jackson's venom. As the last of the "Virginia Dynasty" (from Washington to Monroe), Monroe epitomized the schizophrenia of the reformers who abominated the slave *trade* but tolerated slavery, even making their livelihood from the sweat and misery of slaves on their own plantations. During the 1820 Missouri Compromise debates, Monroe had written to Jefferson: "I have never known a question so menacing to the tranquility and even the continuance of our Union as the present one. All other subjects have given way to it." For Monroe, the slavery question threatened the survival of the Union — and both domestic and foreign policy had to take that primordial reality of American politics into consideration — though slavery was not a topic in the *Federalist Papers*, coauthored by Madison, Hamilton, and John Jay (all slave owners).[32]

In this highly charged political context, Monroe delivered his 1823 message to Congress. Unlike the secret congressional No Transfer Resolution of 1811, the Monroe message was a public, unilateral policy declaration by the American president. Although its wording had been controversial within the cabinet, Monroe purported to impose new rules on European powers for their activities in the Western Hemisphere and to alert them to American pretensions in the region. Monroe's message was bold, even outrageous. He declared that "the American continents . . . are henceforth not to be considered as sub-

TABLE 2.1. Monroe and the Western Hemisphere

Rush-Bagot Agreement	1817	Demilitarizes the boundary with Canada
Andrew Jackson attacks Seminoles/ Spanish Florida	1817–18	Jackson defeats Seminoles and escaped slaves; destroys Spanish forts, British plantations; seizes Spanish territory; proclaims provisional military government at Pensacola; operation divides Republican Party among anti-Jackson faction and pro-Jackson faction, headed by Adams
Anglo-American Convention	1818	Provides for joint Anglo-American occupation of the Oregon Territory; United States requests return of slaves ("property") in British territory or on British ships when the Treaty of Ghent (1814) was signed
Adams-Onís Treaty	1819	Acquisition of East Florida from Spain and demarcation of the U.S. boundary with Spanish territory across the Rocky Mountains to the Pacific Ocean
Missouri Compromise	1820	Establishes north/south boundary for expansion of slavery in territory of the Louisiana Purchase at latitude 36°30'; maintains balance of slave and free states in the Senate
Diplomatic Recognition	1822	United States recognizes independence of five Spanish American republics: Gran Colombia (Ecuador, Colombia, Venezuela after 1830); Mexico, Chile, Peru, La Plata (Buenos Ayres)
Creation of the West Indian Squadron	1822	War on pirates in the Caribbean; conflict with Spanish authorities in Cuba and Puerto Rico
Monroe Doctrine	1823	Announced in December message to Congress
Russo-American treaty	1824	Limits Russian expansion south on the Pacific Coast
Anglo-American treaty	1824	Suppression of slave trade through naval interdiction by American and British ships (not ratified by Britain)
Gran Colombia	1824	First American trade and navigation treaty with a Spanish American republic; incorporates principle of "free ships make free goods"

jects for future colonization by any European powers; that [the United States] should consider any attempt on their part to extend their system [monarchy] to any portion of this hemisphere as dangerous to our peace and safety."[33]

Monroe's message complemented his aggressive transcontinental policies since 1817. On taking office he boasted of America's great advances since independence, the bravery of its soldiers and sailors, and its victories in war. Monroe told his fellow citizens that "the heart of every citizen must expand with joy when he reflects how near our Government has approached to perfection; that in respect to it we have no essential improvement to make. . . . If we persevere in the career in which we have advanced so far and in the path already traced, we can not fail, under the favor of a gracious Providence, to attain the high destiny which seems to await us."[34]

Delighted with America's works, Monroe had pushed forward in his first term with territorial aggrandizement and military intervention in foreign territory. He also encouraged Indian peoples "to retire west and north of our States and Territories on lands to be procured for them by the United States, in exchange for those on which they now reside," anticipating Andrew Jackson's Indian Removal policies of the 1830s.[35] Each of Monroe's initiatives had contentious implications for domestic politics, whether over public lands policy, the proposed tariff legislation, or the slavery question or for partisan and presidential politics.[36] By recognizing Spanish American independence in 1822, he asserted U.S. leadership in the Western Hemisphere and appealed to the Clay faction of his party; by refusing to support Cuban independence and warning against British meddling, he balanced sectional interests and partisan factions. When it came time to sign a commercial treaty with Gran Colombia in 1824, he sought, during the presidential election campaign, to walk a thin line that divided supporters of protective tariffs (favored by Henry Clay and John Quincy Adams and opposed by Vice President John Calhoun) and those seeking markets in the West Indies and Spanish America.[37]

Expanding the Monroe Doctrine?

In the same message in which Monroe announced this new "doctrine," he also proclaimed America's "most ardent wishes" for the success of the Greek rebellion, which sought independence from the Ottoman Empire, raising some concern in Congress that he, and some of his idealistic allies, intended to meddle in that distant conflict.[38] Congressman Daniel Webster (National Republican Party–Mass.) entered a motion that Congress authorize the president to appoint an agent or commissioner to Greece, "whenever the President shall deem it expedient," noting that the United States "had diverse interests in the Mediterranean, which might be seriously affected, more or less, by the course of events in that quarter."[39] Webster linked the Greek struggle for freedom with that of the Spanish Americans and the "rumored combination of foreign Sovereigns to interfere in the concerns of South America."[40] He invoked the cause of freedom against tyranny as an American mission: "Ours is now the great Republic of the earth; its free institutions are matured by the experiment of half a century; . . . As a free Government, as the freest Government, its growth and strength compel it, willingly or unwillingly, to stand forth to the contemplation of the world."[41]

Monroe, Webster, Adams, and others associated the Holy Alliance's attack on the cause of freedom in Spain and across Europe with the Greek revolution and the possibility that the European monarchies might "extend their plans across the Atlantic and that their attention would next be directed to the Republics of South America."[42]

Notwithstanding the urge of some Americans to crusade for freedom outside the Western Hemisphere, part of Monroe's message proclaimed that the United States would not interfere in the affairs of Europe. In this spirit, many legislators resisted an expansive and overly zealous interpretation of Monroe's message as global policy. They preferred it to be understood as a response to immediate security concerns and economic interests in the Western Hemisphere. Congressman Samuel Breck (Federalist-Pa.) asked his colleagues to consider the trade that might be lost in Asia Minor, Smyrna, and Egypt by offending the Turkish government. Congressman Joel Poinsett (D.-S.C.), who had served as special agent to South America in the early stages of the Spanish American independence movements and then as minister to Mexico, also urged caution in applying Monroe's new policies beyond the Western Hemisphere: "We ought to be slow to adopt any measure which might involve us in a war, except where those great interests are concerned."[43] He also warned his colleagues not to confuse the Greek revolution with that of Spanish America. Rather, the comparison ought to be to U.S. policy toward Italy if it sought independence from Austria, or Poland from Russia, or Ireland from England. In short, in matters of European politics and balance of power, the United States should not intervene, idealistically, in the name of self-determination.

Poinsett continued with a surprisingly modern analysis of the European alliance system, its implications for the Middle East and North Africa, and the dangers for the United States of provoking war with Turkey allied with the Barbary powers and European monarchies.[44] He put on the record a letter from John Quincy Adams sent to an agent of the Greeks, in which Adams reaffirmed the American position of neutrality with regard to belligerents and de facto recognition if government control were established, as in the case of the new Spanish American republics. Adams had essentially exported Jefferson's recognition policy adopted for Spanish America to Greece, Poland, and Ireland — an early instance of U.S. policy toward Latin America serving as a testing ground for later application to far reaches of the planet.[45] Poinsett concluded that if the United States were forced to resist the "fearful combination of Sovereigns against the liberties of mankind," that "it is here [in the Western Hemisphere] that we ought to meet it. . . . If there is danger to be apprehended from the avowed principles of the Holy Alliance, it is in America that we must resist them."[46] The debate that followed took in the implications of the Greek and Spanish American events for the global balance of power and the alliance system in Europe and potential dangers to the American republic.[47] Congress debated how best to defend American security and further the country's commercial interests within the complicated and menacing international system. The debates made clear that policy toward the Western Hemisphere formed a crucial element in American global strategy.

Monroe's 1823 speech elicited a range of response among American legislators and partisan newspapers, and it sent different messages to the various European powers. To the Russian czar, who had issued an edict (*ukase*) in 1821 that seemed to claim territory to the 51st parallel, Monroe declared: "The American continents, by the free and independent condition which they have assumed and maintain, are henceforth not to be considered as subjects for future colonization by any European powers." To the Spanish and French, Monroe proclaimed that "we could not view any interposition for the purpose of oppressing them [the Spanish Americans], or controlling in any other manner their destiny, by any European power in any other light than as the manifestation of an unfriendly disposition toward the United States." For European monarchists more generally, the president warned: "It is impossible that the allied powers should extend their political system to any portion of either continent without endangering our peace and happiness; nor can anyone believe that our southern brethren, if left to themselves, would adopt it of their own accord."

The American president had "forbidden" not only further European colonization but also the future export of monarchical dynasties and institutions to the Western Hemisphere (a foreshadowing of the post–World War II global project of ideological and institutional containment — of communism instead of monarchism). Monroe also promised the Europeans that "our policy in regard to Europe, which was adopted at an early stage of the wars which have so long agitated that quarter of the globe, nevertheless remains the same, which is, not to interfere in the internal concerns of any of its powers."[48] Promising not to interfere in the *internal* affairs of the European monarchies, Monroe lied when he proclaimed: "With the existing colonies or dependencies of any European power we have not interfered and shall not interfere." Despite its official neutrality in the Spanish American independence wars, agents of the American government and freebooters had been stirring the pot of rebellion from Mexico to Chile since at least 1811.[49]

With his sweeping set of claims, admonitions, and prevarications, Monroe's name became associated with an idea that evolved, along with increasing American power, to become the doctrinal foundation of U.S. policy toward European powers in the Western Hemisphere. Like Monroe and Adams, American legislators across the political spectrum saw their country immersed in international politics. The realists among them — the majority — wished to avoid the costs of departing from official neutrality regarding European conflicts in Europe. A small minority, like Clay and Webster, urged that the "Great Republic of the Earth" carry the torch of freedom around the world, anticipating the rhetoric of America's liberal internationalist crusaders in the twentieth century.[50]

Although the United States had no fleet capable of enforcing exclusion of European influence in the hemisphere and no army capable of defending any Spanish American republic against European intervention, Monroe did not believe it would be necessary. The predominance of British commerce and naval power, along with French reluctance to engage in reconquest of Spanish colonies, made illusory most of the threats to which Monroe addressed his message. In contrast, the dangers which Monroe enumerated struck the chords of fear and ambition for diverse domestic political constituencies, particularly in the context of the 1824 presidential election.[51]

For years, the European powers and the Spanish Americans would take little practical notice of Monroe's claim to an American protectorate over the hemisphere. If Americans gradually came to believe that the Monroe Doctrine established principles or even rights in international law, Europeans thought less of it. As the British and the Americans contested commercial privileges and political influence during the next half century, British diplomatic correspondence repeatedly revealed the low opinion held for America's unilateralism and the challenges it raised for international law and to European possessions in the region — but also the extent to which the Monroe Doctrine became patriotic pulp for domestic politics in the United States. In private correspondence to Lord Clarendon in 1853 regarding American regional policy and tolerance for filibustering operations in Cuba, England's chief diplomat in Washington, D.C., wrote:

By eternal repetition this so-called doctrine is gradually becoming, in the minds of the Democracy here, one of those habitual maxims which are no longer reasoned upon but felt, and any imagined "violation of the Monroe Doctrine" is now vehemently taken up as a just reason for peremptory demand for satisfaction from any Foreign Power who may have committed it.

Now altho' I know that a great deal of this language is held for home political purposes, each party out-bidding the other in its offer of "Americanism," still it cannot be denied that a very dangerous effect is produced upon the Masses by such doctrines, and it becomes a very grave question what position Foreign Powers ought to adopt in regard to them. It seems to me quite clear that if carried out to their full effect, we should be forced to resist them somewhere, and the question remains as to the point at which it would be advisable to make a stand.[52]

By the 1840s, an expanded Monroe Doctrine had become a foundation of American foreign policy but also a bipartisan pillar of jingoism in American politics. As a unilateral doctrine aimed at European powers, its meaning, the circumstances when it would be applied, and its reach were strictly matters for U.S. policymakers to decide as they sought for America to command its own fortune and the fortune of the Western Hemisphere.

The First American Protectorate and the Central American Isthmus

Dreams, schemes, and failed projects that aimed at constructing a canal across the Central American isthmus dated from Spanish conquest. From the 1780s into the 1830s, European and American visionaries and entrepreneurs periodically resurrected the canal dream.[53] American policymakers looked toward Panama, Tehuantepec (Mexico), and Nicaragua with increased interest. With a trans-isthmian route in mind, American presidents and Congress encouraged exploratory expeditions to Central America. Notably, a Senate resolution in 1835 requested that President Andrew Jackson "consider the expediency of entering negotiations" with Central American governments and New Grenada (Colombia), with regard to its northern province (Panama) to secure "forever . . . the free and equal right of navigating such a canal [across the Central American isthmus] to all such nations, on the payment of such reasonable tolls as may be established, to compensate the capitalists who may engage in such an undertaking and complete the work."[54]

American policymakers considered the necessity of such a canal for both commercial and security purposes. Entrepreneurs, often encouraged by government officials and legislators, obtained concessions for canal and railroad projects across Central America from as early as the 1820s. After Congress's resolution in 1835, President Jackson sent Charles A. Biddle to investigate the possibility of a concession from Nicaragua, Guatemala, or Colombia. Biddle did not visit Nicaragua, but he did succeed in negotiating a private concession, in which he held two-thirds of the stock, for construction of a macadamized road (stone and hard surface), railway, and steamship project across the Isthmus of Panama.[55] According to historian E. Taylor Parks, "[Biddle's] early death probably saved him from the most violent of Jacksonian reprimands [for his private profiteering from his government assignment]." Meanwhile, Robert McAfee, the American representative in Bogotá from 1833 to 1837, had been instructed "to disclaim all connection with the project on the part of . . . [his] government."[56]

Jackson reported to Congress in January 1837 that his "agent returned to the United States in September last; and although the information collected by him is not as full as could have been desired, yet it is sufficient to show that the probability of an early execution of any of the projects which have been set on foot for the construction of the communication alluded to, is not so great as to render it expedient to open a negotiation at present with any foreign Government upon the subject."[57] Worries remained, however, that a European-controlled project would compromise American security and economic interests.

In 1845–46, as the United States annexed Texas, invaded Mexico, and wrested Oregon Territory from the British, the country entered into a treaty with Colombia in the effort to control a trans-isthmian route. In the Bidlack-Mallarino Treaty (December 12, 1846), the United States pledged, in exchange for transit rights by "any road or canal that might be made by the government of New Granada, or by the authority of the same," to guarantee the neutrality of the zone and "the rights of sovereignty and property, which New Granada has and possesses over the said territory."[58] Whether such a proviso represented an "entangling alliance," thus contravening a basic principle of American foreign policy, was debated vigorously within the administration and in the Senate, which eventually ratified the treaty, in 1848.[59] A year later, U.S. policymakers gave the treaty a more cautious but also more unilateralist spin: "The obligations which we have incurred [to guarantee the neutrality of the isthmus and Colombian sovereignty] gives us the right to offer, unasked, such advise [sic] to the New Granadian Government in regard to its relations with other powers, as might tend to avert from that Republic a rupture with any nation which might covet the Isthmus of Panama."[60] According to this interpretation, the treaty with New Granada had not only created an obligation to intervene to protect Panama from foreign aggression but the right to do so at American discretion and convenience — whether or not Colombia requested American assistance.

For American policymakers, beyond improving commercial relations with Colombia the 1846 treaty represented part of great power competition for control of transit across Central America between the oceans. The treaty blurred, but also bridged, the boundary between the limited commitments implied by the 1811 No Transfer Resolution and the Monroe Doctrine and outright interventionism. The United States had created its first protectorate. The 1846 treaty directly connected American foreign policy and global ambitions to the country's rising tide of nationalism and belief in its manifest destiny. In the next decades, both with and without Colombian authorization, American forces would often intervene in Panama "to prevent the obstruction of traffic by the contending national and revolutionary armies."[61]

As Bidlack negotiated the treaty with Colombia, America went to war with Mexico — a war that provoked bitter partisan opposition from abolitionists and Whigs against the Polk administration's dedication to manifest destiny and to expansion of the slave system.[62] During the war, Congress debated repeatedly the implications of annexation of all or parts of Mexico for the expansion of slavery and whether to apply the Missouri Compromise line (latitude 36°30' straight to the Pacific) to any territory acquired. When Polk requested funds in 1846 to facilitate negotiation with Mexico of territorial "compensation," parliamentary delaying maneuvers by the opposition led to an amendment presented by Congressman David Wilmot (D.-Pa.), proposing that slavery be prohibited in any territory acquired. Lewis Cass (D.-Mich.) argued instead that "popular sovereignty" should determine whether new territories and states be free or slave.[63] In the end, neither the Wilmot Proviso nor any other restriction on expansion of slavery would be included in the Treaty of Guadalupe Hidalgo (1848), which ended the Mexican War.

Meanwhile, the British challenge in Central America persisted. England seized San Juan (1848) and Tigre Island in the Gulf of Fonseca (1849) and effectively occupied the Mosquito Coast (Nicaragua) and Belize (British Honduras). The Monroe Doctrine — even Polk's elastic interpretation of it — had not kept European powers out of the hemisphere nor prevented them from controlling most of the region's commerce and financial transactions. In the short term, however, the United States and Britain negotiated the Clayton-

Bulwer Treaty (1850), which would keep the two Anglo rivals from each other's throats:

> The governments of the United States and Great Britain hereby declare, that neither the one nor the other will ever obtain or maintain for itself any exclusive control over the said ship canal; agreeing that neither will ever erect or maintain any fortifications commanding the same or in the vicinity thereof, or occupy, or fortify, or colonize, or assume or exercise any dominion over Nicaragua, Costa Rica, the Mosquito coast, or any part of Central America; nor will either make use of any protection which either affords or may afford, or any alliance which either has or may have, to or with any State or people, for the purpose of erecting or maintaining any such fortifications, or of occupying, fortifying, or colonizing Nicaragua, Costa Rica, the Mosquito coast, or any part of Central America, or of assuming or exercising dominion over the same.[64]

This treaty, affecting potential transit routes across Central America, did not include any Central American states as signatories. The United States and Great Britain determined the immediate terms and conditions for getting between the Atlantic and Pacific oceans and appropriated to themselves the task of "granting such protection as the United States and Great Britain engage to afford." For the moment, given British imperial reach and American pretensions of manifest destiny, such arrangements made pragmatic sense, though it rubbed many Americans wrong that the British would be given equal footing regarding a future Central American canal.

After 1850, the United States repeatedly intervened in Panama and Central America to protect its commercial interests, guarantee "law and order," and restore "stability." Executing such a policy engaged the United States in negotiations and occasional threats of war with major European powers and provoked the anger of Latin Americans.[65] As historian Thomas O'Brien put it: "During the late 1850s a firestorm of anger swept Latin America in response to the U.S. annexation of Texas, the invasion of Mexico, and the plague of filibusters that had been visited upon Central America and the Caribbean."[66]

Policy toward Central America and the Caribbean provoked repeated debate in Congress, which contributed to incremental definition, in practice, of the meaning of the American Constitution in the area of foreign affairs, including the character of congressional-executive relations, the scope of presidential authority as commander in chief, and the role of secrecy and clandestine operations.[67] As American politicians and judges struggled over the interconnected domestic and foreign policy challenges presented by expansionism, national security, and global commerce, the presidency gradually aggrandized its power. In part this resulted because some of the Framers, both Federalists and Jeffersonians, had accepted secrecy and covert operations as an implicit element of the Constitution. Hamilton, Jefferson, and Madison had provided the example for Monroe and, to the chagrin of many of their political allies, for the aggressive foreign policy initiatives of Andrew Jackson and the presidents who followed from 1837 to 1861.[68]

The Idea of Manifest Destiny

For Americans, the idea of manifest destiny took over where defense against European intrusions and the myth of the City on the Hill left off in justifying and explaining territorial expansion and intrusions into other nations' internal affairs. In part, Americans inherited the idea of manifest destiny from Anglo-Teutonic notions of racial superiority, from the British imperial "civilizing mission," and from the Puritan call to "be as a City upon a Hill, [and that] the eyes of all people are upon us."[69] Many Americans believed they were part of a new political experiment, a nation guided by divine Providence, which would bring a particular version of Christianity and Freedom to the rest of the world, or at least provide an example for others to follow. Thomas Paine had captured this spirit in his 1776 pamphlet *Common Sense*: "We have it in our power to begin the world over again. A situation, similar to the present, hath not happened since the days of Noah until now. The birthday of a new world is at hand." Other Americans had a less messianic, more territorial interpretation of the new Republic's destiny. Thus John Quincy Adams prophesied in 1811 that "the whole continent of North America appears to be destined by Divine Providence to be peopled by one nation."[70] (Ironically, in this same year, Russian settlers founded Fort Ross just up the coast from Bodega Bay, north of San Francisco.)

On the other hand, there existed no one-time definition of the territorial limits of this manifest destiny. Americans differed on the political, geographical, and racial limits for inclusion in the Union. At each juncture, proposed expansion into new territory occasioned congressional debates: the Louisiana Purchase, the Floridas, Texas, the Southwest, the Oregon Territory, California, Alaska, Cuba, the Dominican Republic. And then extra-hemispheric territories such as Samoa, Hawaii, and the Philippines were all the subject of extensive political contention.[71]

For some few Americans, their mission included "saving" the rest of humankind from tyranny and bestowing the blessing of American institutions and Christianity upon them. For most, however, Providence and American manifest destiny meant domination by a superior race over inferior peoples, who could be taught, but only with great difficulty, the rudiments of civilization. It also meant recurrent warfare with Native American peoples, pushing them off their land, concentrating them in reservations, and removing them as an obstacle to America's westward expansion.

By the late 1830s, the idea of manifest destiny signified a racist nationalism that preferred to incorporate into the Union "unsettled" and "empty" lands — such as those taken from Native American peoples and, soon thereafter, Mexico. Manifest destiny was also a missal of exclusion — from 1790 when the Founders determined that only "free white persons" could become American citizens. The outcome of debates on annexing all of Mexico, Cuba, Panama, or the Yucatán peninsula turned on the undesirability of accepting inferior peoples as citizens.[72] Racism cut at least three ways. It inspired and justified American territorial expansion, but it also limited its reach due precisely to the indisposition of many Americans to incorporate into the Union "inferior peoples" as equals and citizens. It also underlay the slave/free divide in American domestic politics.[73] Congressional debates from 1804 to the 1870s on annexation of Caribbean and Mexican territories turned on the potential effects of such annexation on sectional representation and the balance between slave and free states in Congress, especially in the Senate.[74] The appeal to manifest destiny, therefore, had complex implications for American domestic politics and foreign policy.

By the 1830s, the idea of exceptionalism and Providential destiny directly inspired American nationalism and also the emulation of European treatment of "inferior" peoples. Congress and the president authorized reprisals by naval units against communities and groups that mistreated American merchants and overseas residents. Andrew Jackson, for example, sent the frigate *Potomac* against the Sumatran village of Quallah Battoo in 1831 because an American trader vessel, the *Friendship*, had been attacked and pillaged by a "Malay pepper boat." The *Friendship*'s crew suffered casualties and lost its cargo of pepper, opium, and other commodities. The *Potomac*'s crew was to seek reparations, but its commander, Captain John Downes (who had fought in 1804 in Tripoli, had commanded the Mediterranean Squadron, and was now commanding the Pacific Squadron), reported that it had not been possible to do so — that the local leaders (*rajahs*) recognized no international law and that his attacking party of some 250 men neither gave quarter nor took prisoners. The American foray killed some 150 villagers and burned four native villages.[75] Downes wrote that he had informed a messenger bearing a white flag that "if forbearance should not be exercised hereafter from committing piracies and murders upon Americans citizens, other ships-of-war would be dispatched to inflict upon them further punishment."[76]

Explaining the expedition to Congress, President Jackson claimed that the villagers "were a band of lawless pirates" and that the operation would "inflict such a chastisement as would deter them and others from like aggressions." Arguing that there was no "regular government" to deal with, Jackson essentially had given instructions permitting Captain John Downes to treat the Sumatrans, in their own villages, as outlaws beyond the protection of international law.[77] As a follow-up measure, the secretary of the navy reported that "to guard against their perfidy, orders were given that the *Potomac* should be followed by a detachment from the [United States] Brazilian squadron, part of which detachment has since sailed, and has instructions to touch not only at Sumatra, but such places in India, China, and on the eastern coast of Africa as may be conducive to the security and prosperity of our important commercial interests in those regions."[78] In his history of U.S. foreign relations, George C. Herring concluded: "His [Jackson's] gunboat diplomacy put the United States very much in the mainstream of Western imperialism rather than outside of it, as Americans have boasted, belying the nation's claims of its exceptionalism."[79]

In the years that followed, presidents Andrew Jackson, Martin van Buren, and John Tyler all extended broad discretion to naval officers to carry out their patrols around the world, some leading to the use of force (Falkland Islands, 1833; Fiji, 1840; Samoa, 1841; China, 1843; Ivory Coast, 1843), bordering on undeclared war, to protect American interests and defend its commerce.[80] In some cases, Congress challenged presidential authority, especially where it might provoke war. By and large, however, American presidents continuously, if fitfully, enlarged America's global military, diplomatic, and commercial reach.

By 1843, a report of the secretary of the navy made clear that the Home Squadron "was designed when occasion required, to course over the world of waters — to pass beyond the Pillars of Hercules, which bounded the view of the ancient mariner, and to carry the protection of our fleets to the most distant quarters of the globe."[81] Congressman Edward J. Morris (Whig-Pa.) added that the country had small squadrons in the Mediterranean, off the coast of Brazil and Africa, in the Pacific, and elsewhere — and that the navy needed more resources to protect American commerce and citizens around the world.[82] In March 1844, Senator James Semple (D.-Ill.) urged that, in order to counteract British commercial and naval activity in the Caribbean, perhaps the president might "produce an order to send our vessels of war more frequently into those places [the circuit of the West Indies and Gulf of Mexico, once a month, touching at the principal ports in the islands of Cuba, Santo Domingo, and Puerto Rico] where . . . our commerce had been heretofore much neglected."[83] In the next weeks, the Senate discussed by what means to acquire the Oregon Territory from the British and how best, if at all, to annex the republic of Texas, over Mexico's objection, into the Union.

Credited with devising the term "manifest destiny," journalist and Democrat Party partisan John L. O'Sullivan wrote in 1839 that "so far as regards the entire development of the natural rights of man, in moral, political, and national life, we may confidently assume that our country is destined to be the great nation of futurity." He added: "This will be our future history, to establish on earth the moral dignity and salvation of man — the immutable truth and beneficence of God. For this blessed mission to the nations of the world . . . has America been chosen; and her high example shall smite unto death the tyranny of kings, hierarchs, and oligarchs, and carry the glad tidings of peace and good will where myriads now endure an existence scarcely more enviable than that of beasts of the field."[84] While O'Sullivan's version of manifest destiny proclaimed America's global moral and political mission, his territorial focus highlighted North America. He proclaimed in 1845 "the right of our manifest destiny to over spread and to possess the whole of the continent which Providence has given us. . . . It is a right such as that of the tree to the space of air and the earth suitable for the full expansion of its principle and destiny of growth."

The 1840s marked a high point for the influence of manifest destiny in American policy, justifying war with Mexico (1845–48), occupation of the conquered territories from the Rio Grande into California and north to Colorado, and the acquisition of the Oregon Territory from England in 1846 after threatening war with the provocative slogan "54°40′ or fight" — a reference to the southern boundary of Russian Alaska.[85] The more comprehensive idea of manifest destiny also inspired lustful advances toward Cuba, efforts at commercial penetration of Japan and China, and annexationist sentiments regarding Hawaii (in competition with British and French interests).[86] From the 1850s, U.S. naval units exercised a sort of oversight of Hawaii and routinely patrolled off the coasts of Hispaniola (Santo Domingo and Haiti) and in the rest of the Caribbean.[87] The British minister to the United States warned Lord Clarendon in 1853 that "the time has come for the English and French Government to take some steps in the matter [regarding the Sandwich Islands (Hawaii)] if they think it important that those Islands should not fall into the hands of the United States." He had earlier (1852) complained that "with regards to these Islands, you will recollect that the United States has held to us exactly the same language as with regards to Cuba, viz. That they will *not allow us* to become possessed of them, declining to make any renunciation of them on their own part."[88] By British reckoning, before the middle of the nineteenth century the United States had already extended the reach of the No Transfer Principle and the Monroe Doctrine far beyond Mexico, California, and the Oregon Territory to distant islands of the Pacific Ocean.

At mid-century, American self-righteous, self-laudatory nationalism and belief in the country's manifest destiny had become a mainstay of popular culture and the expected message of electioneering. The Democrats campaigned in the 1852 presidential election with the slogan "We Polked you in 1844; we shall Pierce you in 1852!" The Whig opposition countered with "a hero of many a well-fought bottle" — a reference to Franklin Pierce's Mexican War experience and his reputation as a hard drinker. Pierce's opponent, Winfield Scott, had fought in the War of 1812, the Blackhawk War (1832), and the Second Seminole War (1835–42). He had also been a general in the Mexican War, indeed had been Pierce's commanding officer, and he headed the forces that occupied Mexico City at war's end. Despite their differences on slavery (Scott's antislavery stance made him unpalatable to the South), both presidential candidates in the 1852 election were army generals who represented an aggressive American foreign policy and expansionism. The idea of manifest destiny and the practice of frontier militarism against Native Americans, Europeans, and Mexicans, ingrained in the popular spirit, had "chosen" America's leaders at mid-century.[89]

Like President James Polk, Pierce was a proslavery expansionist. He brought with him to the presidency, as secretary of war, Jefferson Davis, later the president of the Confederacy during the Civil War. His administration negotiated the Gadsden Purchase from Mexico in 1853, filling out the continental United States and acquiring a railroad route in southern Arizona and New Mexico. Pierce unsuccessfully pushed for annexation of Cuba, recognized the William Walker filibuster government in Nicaragua (and brief relegalization of slavery in that country), issued (and then retracted) the Ostend Manifesto on Cuba (1854), and supported the Kansas-Nebraska Act of 1854.[90] This legislation overturned the Missouri Compromise of 1820 in the name of "popular sovereignty" to support expansion of slavery, leading to bloodshed in Kansas and pushing the country ever closer to civil war. It also incited opponents to found the Republican Party.[91] In the Kansas violence, Pierce supported the rogue proslavery legislature and used federal troops against the "freesoilers" (opponents of slavery).

In the quest to realize their ambiguously defined manifest destiny, Americans collided in political battles over slavery, territorial expansion, interpreta-

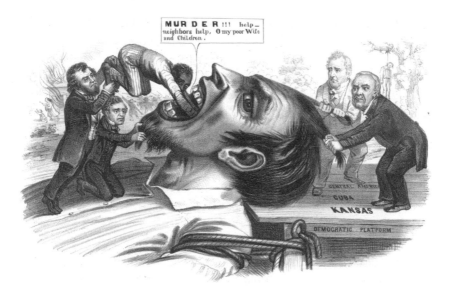

Forcing Slavery Down the Throat of a Freesoiler (1856), lithograph by J. L. Magee. A giant Free Soiler is being held down by Democratic presidential candidate James Buchanan and Senator Lewis Cass standing on the Democratic platform marked "Kansas," "Cuba," and "Central America." President Franklin Pierce holds down the giant's beard as Senator Stephen Douglas shoves a black man down his throat. Douglas's nickname was "little giant" (he was 5′4″ and weighed less than 100 pounds). The balloon caption coming out of the Free Soiler's mouth says: "MURDER!!! Help neighbors help, O my poor wife and children." (Alfred Withal Stern Collection of Lincolniana, Rare Book and Special Collection Division, Library of Congress)

tions of American federalism, and emergent empire. During the presidency of James Buchanan, from 1857 to 1861, reverberations from foreign policy adventurism and interventionism, especially in the Western Hemisphere, would further erode the ever-more-fragile bonds of Union, ultimately inscribing civil war into the story of the nation's manifest destiny.

Appendix: Instances of Use of United States Armed Forces Abroad, 1798–1844[92]

1798–1800 — *Undeclared Naval War with France.*

1801–5 — *Tripoli.* The First Barbary War included the USS *George Washington* and USS *Philadelphia* affairs and the Eaton expedition, during which a few marines landed with Agent William Eaton to raise a force against Tripoli in an effort to free the crew of the *Philadelphia*. Tripoli declared war, but the United States did not.

1806 — *Mexico (Spanish territory)*. Captain Zebulon M. Pike, with a platoon of troops, invaded Spanish territory at the headwaters of the Rio Grande on orders from General James Wilkinson.

1806–10 — *Gulf of Mexico*. American gunboats operated from New Orleans against Spanish and French privateers.

1810 — *West Florida (Spanish territory)*. Governor Claiborne of Louisiana, on orders of the president, occupied territory in dispute east of the Mississippi as far as the Pearl River.

1812 — *Amelia Island and other parts of east Florida, then under Spain.* Temporary possession was authorized by President Madison and by Congress to prevent occupation by any other power.

1812–15 — *War of 1812.*

1813 — *West Florida (Spanish territory)*. On authority given by Congress, General Wilkinson seized Mobile Bay in April with 600 soldiers.

1813–14 — *Marguesas Islands (French Polynesia)*. U.S. forces built a fort on the island of Nukahiva to protect three prize ships that had been captured from the British.

1814 — *Spanish Florida*. General Andrew Jackson took Pensacola and drove out the British.

1814–25 — *Caribbean*. Engagements between pirates and American ships or squadrons took place repeatedly, especially ashore and offshore around Cuba, Puerto Rico, Santo Domingo, and Yucatán. 3,000 pirate attacks on merchantmen were reported between 1815 and 1823. In 1822, Commodore James Biddle employed a squadron of two frigates, four sloops of war, two brigs, four schooners, and two gunboats in the West Indies.

1815 — *Algiers*. The second Barbary War was declared by the opponents but not by the United States. Congress authorized an expedition. A large fleet under Stephen Decatur attacked Algiers and obtained indemnities.

1815 — *Tripoli*. After securing an agreement from Algiers, Decatur demonstrated with his squadron at Tunis and Tripoli, where he secured indemnities for offenses during the War of 1812.

1816 — *Spanish Florida*. U.S. forces destroyed Nicholls Fort, also called Negro Fort, which harbored raiders making forays into U.S. territory.

1816–18 — *Spanish Florida — First Seminole War*. The Seminole Indians were attacked by troops under Generals Jackson and Gaines and pursued into northern Florida. Spanish posts were attacked and occupied, and British citizens were executed.

1817 — *Amelia Island (Spanish territory off Florida)*. Under orders of President Monroe, U.S. forces landed and expelled a group of smugglers, adventurers, and freebooters.

1818 — *Oregon.* The USS *Ontario* landed at the Columbia River and in August took possession of Oregon territory. Britain had conceded sovereignty, but Russia and Spain asserted claims to the area.

1820–23 — *Africa.* Naval units raided the slave traffic pursuant to the 1819 act of Congress.

1822 — *Cuba.* U.S. naval forces suppressing piracy landed on the northwest coast of Cuba and burned a pirate station.

1823 — *Cuba.* Brief landings in pursuit of pirates occurred on April 8 near Escondido; on April 16 near Cayo Blanco; on July 11 at Siquapa Bay; on July 21 at Cape Cruz; and on October 23 at Camrioca.

1824 — *Cuba.* In October, the USS *Porpoise* landed bluejackets near Matanzas in pursuit of pirates.

1824 — *Puerto Rico (Spanish territory).* Commodore David Porter with a landing party attacked the town of Fajardo, which had sheltered pirates and insulted American naval officers. He landed with 200 men in November and forced an apology. Commodore Porter was later court-martialed for overstepping his powers.

1825 — *Cuba.* In March, cooperating American and British forces landed at Sagua La Grande to capture pirates.

1827 — *Greece.* In October and November, landing parties hunted pirates on the islands of Argenteire, Miconi, and Androse.

1831–32 — *Falkland Islands.* Captain Duncan of the USS *Lexington* investigated the capture of three American sealing vessels and sought to protect American interests.

1832 — *Sumatra.* On February 6 to 9, a naval force landed and stormed a fort to punish natives of the town of Quallah Battoo for plundering the American ship *Friendship*.

1833 — *Argentina.* From October 31 to November 15, a force was sent ashore at Buenos Aires to protect the interests of the United States and other countries during an insurrection.

1835–36 — *Peru.* From December 10, 1835, to January 24, 1836, and August 31 to December 7, 1836, marines protected American interests in Callao and Lima during an attempted revolution.

1836 — *Mexico.* General Gaines occupied Nacogdoches (Texas), disputed territory, from July to December during the Texan war for independence, under orders to cross the "imaginary boundary line" if an Indian outbreak threatened.

1838–39 — *Sumatra.* From December 24, 1838, to January 4, 1839, a naval force landed to punish natives of the towns of Quallah Battoo and Muckie (Mukki) for depredations on American shipping.

1840 — *Fiji Islands.* In July, naval forces landed to punish natives for attacking American exploring and surveying parties.

1841 — *Drummond Island, Kingsmill Group.* A naval party landed to avenge the murder of a seaman by the natives.

1841 — *Samoa.* On February 24, a naval party landed and burned towns after the murder of an American seaman on Upolu Island.

1842 — *Mexico.* Commodore T. A. C. Jones, in command of a squadron long cruising off California, occupied Monterey, California, on October 19, believing war had come. He discovered peace, withdrew, and saluted. A similar incident occurred a week later at San Diego.

1843 — *China.* Sailors and marines from the USS *St. Louis* landed after a clash between Americans and Chinese at the trading post in Canton.

1843 — *Africa.* From November 29 to December 16, four U.S. vessels demonstrated and landed various parties (one consisting of 200 marines and sailors) to discourage piracy and the slave trade along the Ivory Coast and to punish attacks by the natives on American seamen and shipping.

1844 — *Mexico.* President Tyler deployed U.S. forces to protect Texas against Mexico, pending Senate approval of a treaty of annexation (which was later rejected). He defended his action against a Senate resolution of inquiry.

Chapter Three

Providential Nursery?

What has miserable, inefficient Mexico — with her superstition, her burlesque upon freedom, her actual tyranny by the few over the many — what has she to do with the great mission of peopling the new world with a noble race? Be it ours, to achieve that mission!
— Walt Whitman, Editorial, *Brooklyn Daily Eagle*, 1846

Between 1800 and 1867 the United States more than tripled in size. But American territorial aggrandizement did not happen Providentially.[1] American diplomats successfully negotiated treaties with European powers transferring territory to the United States. American policymakers also made war on European nations, Native Americans, and Mexico. They gradually subverted foreign claims over vast territories across North America. War, annexation proclamations, covert operations, filibusters, skillful diplomatic negotiations, land purchases, westward migration, immigration, and technological innovation all combined to transform a fragile, militarily weak federal republic into an increasingly potent nation-state.

European wars spilled over into the Western Hemisphere, engaging the United States alternately against British, French, and Spanish forces from the Floridas to Canada. War proffered both danger and opportunity. Each conflict spawned internal dissent along partisan and sectional lines, which threatened the country with disunion but also provided the chance to expand the nation's territorial domain and increase its weight in the international system. The European wars, and especially the Napoleonic wars, also revolutionized the Western Hemisphere by undermining the Spanish colonial empire.

After Napoleon invaded Spain in 1808, independence movements erupted in parts of Spanish America (1810–14). The Spanish American insurgencies challenged American policymakers and merchants to balance the country's territorial ambitions (especially in the Floridas) and its economic interests between Spanish claims and the affection for the United States of the insurgents from Mexico to southern South America. American government agents went to Buenos Aires, Chile, and Venezuela (1811–12), then throughout South America. Although the United States reaffirmed its policy of neutrality in 1818, mercenaries, merchants, and political missionaries with copies of the American Declaration of Independence weighed in on the side of the insurgents.[2] American ports were opened to Spanish American rebels — Monroe made this official policy in messages to Congress in 1817 and 1818. With final ratification of the Adams-Onís Treaty in 1821, Monroe finally sent a message to Congress on March 8, 1822, urging recognition of the Spanish American republics and requesting appropriations for "such missions to the independent nations on the American continent as the President of the United States may deem proper."

Less than two months before Mexican independence, Secretary of State John Quincy Adams delivered a Fourth of July speech in 1821 which would become a classic referent in the mythology of American foreign policy. He told the House of Representatives that America has "in the lapse of nearly half a century, without a single exception, respected the independence of other nations while asserting and maintaining her own. She has abstained from interference in the concerns of others, even when conflict has been for principles to which she clings, as to the last vital drop that visits the heart. . . . she goes not abroad, in search of monsters to destroy. She is the well-wisher to the freedom and independence of all."[3]

By the time John Quincy Adams delivered this speech, American foreign policy had departed markedly from the claims of his myth-in-the-making moment. Although perhaps good advice, especially the trope on avoiding quests for monsters to destroy, Adams's assertion that "she [the United States] has abstained from interference in the concerns of others" rang hollow to Native peoples, European powers, North African potentates, and even the Spanish Americans. Efforts to open markets, acquire territory, civilize and Christianize "savage" and "inferior" peoples, and influence foreign governments contradicted almost all of Adams's claims. As conservative historian Max Boot put it: "The U.S. has been involved in other countries' internal affairs since at least 1805, when, during the Tripolitan War, William Eaton tried to topple the Pasha of Tripoli and replace him with his pro-American brother."[4]

Two years after Adams's July 4th foreign policy address, President James Monroe, with Adams's assistance, concocted the Monroe Doctrine under circumstances detailed in chapter 2. Monroe announced American intentions to oversee the New World and warned Europe to discard any thought of renewed colonization or political influence in the Western Hemisphere. Monroe shared his generation's vision of an American dominion stretching between the seas, "under the favor of a gracious Providence, to attain the high destiny which seems to await us."[5]

From Monroe to Polk

American political development and foreign relations in the first half of the nineteenth century depended greatly on the use of military force or the threat of force. Native peoples resisted as the army and settlers appropriated their lands and destroyed their way of life. The Spanish sought to defend the Floridas from U.S. advances and small-scale filibusters. In the course of losing their Western Hemisphere colonies, they could no longer resist U.S. pressures and ceded Florida in the 1819 Adams-Onís Treaty. Monroe's successors, John Quincy Adams (1825–29) and Andrew Jackson (1829–37), added no European-held or Mexican territory to the United States, but both supported acquisition of Texas from Mexico.[6] Then, in 1836, Mexico lost Texas in a U.S.-supported rebellion. Texas became an independent republic, achieving recognition by several continental European powers, England, and the United States despite Mexican opposition.[7] Before leaving office in 1837, Andrew Jackson threatened Mexico with use of force if it refused to resolve certain outstanding claims of U.S. citizens. The language in Jackson's message was menacing; it called upon Congress to authorize the president to use the navy to "take reprisals" against Mexico if it should fail to satisfy American demands.[8] Jackson then urged Congress to recognize the independence of the Republic of Texas with appointment of a chargé d'affaires.[9]

Eight years later, in late February 1845, ignoring Mexican admonitions that annexation of Texas would be considered the equivalent of a declaration of war, Congress voted in a joint resolution to do just that. The question of Texas annexation had been an important issue in the presidential campaign of 1844. Factionalism within the Democratic Party and partisanship between Democrats and Whigs in the Senate had cost President John Tyler his party's nomination and led to the election of Democrat James K. Polk.[10] Lame-duck president Tyler could not obtain the necessary two-thirds vote in the senate for approval of a treaty between Texas and the United States for Texas's annexation.[11] The votes of twenty-five Whigs against the treaty made annexation by joint resolution Tyler's only viable option.[12]

Congress's joint resolution was aimed partly at countering British and French policies intended to persuade Mexico to recognize Texas's independence *so long as it did not accede to annexation by the United States.*[13] In January 1845 British foreign secretary Lord Aberdeen had written: "Her Majesty's

Government are of opinion that the continuance of Texas as Independent Power, under its own Laws and institutions, must conduce to a more permanent balance of interests in the North American continent, and that its interposition between the United States and Mexico offers the best chance of a preservation of friendly relations between those two Governments."[14] France also favored an independent Texas, as made clear by Foreign Minister François Guizot in June 1845: "There are in America [the Western Hemisphere] three powers, the United States, England, and the states of Spanish origin. . . . What is the interest of France? It is that the independent states remain independent, that the balance of forces between the great masses which divide America continue, that no one of them become exclusively preponderant."[15] Contemporary diplomatic correspondence thus makes clear that, notwithstanding the Monroe Doctrine, for the European powers the Western Hemisphere remained part of the global chessboard.

When President James K. Polk and his allies deliberately misinterpreted a Spanish American treaty regarding boundaries between the United States and northern Mexico, citing the unilateral boundary resolution of the Texas rebels in 1836, war ensued. Mexican troops attacked American forces within the disputed territory. President Polk, in his own words, had "anticipated" the conflict, if not actually provoked it:

> Anticipating the possibility of a crisis like that which has arrived, instructions were given in August last, "as a precautionary measure" against invasion or threatened invasion, authorizing General Taylor, if the emergency required it, to accept volunteers, not from Texas only, but from the States of Louisiana, Alabama, Mississippi, Tennessee, and Kentucky, and corresponding letters were addressed to the respective governors of those States. . . . In further vindication of our rights and defense of our territory, I invoke the prompt action of Congress to recognize the existence of the war, and to place at the disposition of the Executive the means of prosecuting the war with vigor, and thus hastening the restoration of peace.[16]

Polk pushed the country into war. According to political scientist Scott Silverstone, Congress was focused on the Oregon Territory debate, giving Polk wide leeway for his aggressive policies toward Mexico.[17] According to Polk, the United States could foment secession, independence, and subsequent annexation of "independent" republics into the Union. The Europeans, in contrast, had nothing to say about it, could not transfer colonies among themselves in the hemisphere, and could not acquire territory from former Spanish dependencies — even if the new republics willingly ceded such territory to them. In Polk's version, the Monroe Doctrine purported to limit not only European intrusions into the hemisphere but also the sovereignty of Latin American nation-states (or even the Texas Republic) in their dealings with the Europeans:

> We must ever maintain the principle that the people of this continent alone have the right to decide their own destiny. Should any portion of them, constituting an independent state, propose to unite themselves with our Confederacy, this will be a question for them and us to determine without any foreign interposition. We can never consent that European powers shall interfere to prevent such a union because it might disturb the "balance of power" which they may desire to maintain upon this continent. . . . In the existing circumstances of the world the present is deemed a proper occasion to reiterate and reaffirm the principle avowed by Mr. Monroe and to state my cordial concurrence in its wisdom and sound policy.[18]

By this interpretation, the Spanish American republics' right to "command *their* own destiny" did not include sale, transfer, or cession of territory to European nations, but it did include the right to be annexed to the United States.

Polk further extended the Monroe Doctrine toward the end of the Mexican War when an Indian insurrection in Yucatán brought a request from that territory's elite for assistance or even annexation to the United States, Britain, or Spain. Polk asked Congress for authorization for temporary military occupation of Yucatán to prevent English or other European intervention and to protect the white population from "Indian savages" in revolt. A bill to support Polk's request was introduced in Congress, but, after impassioned debates over three weeks, it was withdrawn — since the revolt had ended.[19] Polk hesitated to deploy troops to Yucatán without congressional approval, but his rationale for sending troops — military occupation to protect the white population or to *preempt* intervention by European powers — was not contested.

The debates over intervention in Yucatán revealed the complex relationships in American politics among annexationist sentiments, competing interpretations of the Monroe Doctrine, manifestations of Anglo-American rivalry in the Western Hemisphere, and the racialist foundations of American foreign policy.[20] Polk's supporters urged quick approval of the president's request to protect "people of white blood" from attacks by "the merciless savages."[21] Senator Lewis Cass (D.-Mich.), past secretary of war under Andrew Jackson and future secretary of state under James Buchanan, added that "some civilized nation should interpose, else the white population of Yucatán would be swept out of existence."[22] Cass, as secretary of war, had implemented Jackson's Indian Removal program and supported "popular sovereignty" on the slavery issue (that is, the expansion of slavery if territorial residents desired it) and would be the Democrats' presidential candidate in 1848. He favored what would later be called "humanitarian intervention" in Yucatán to protect the white elite from the virtually enslaved Indian peoples.

To the protection of white people against the Indians, Senator Edward Hannegan (D.-Ind.), who would serve as U.S. minister to Prussia (1849–50), added the danger of British ambitions: "England cherishes the design, at this moment, to secure the most practicable route for an artificial means of communication between the two oceans; and to effect that object she is gradually and rapidly absorbing the entire Isthmus. Unless we act she will accomplish her purpose. The possession of Yucatán by England would soon be followed by the possession of Cuba."[23] Hannegan argued that the Congress should "say to the people of Yucatán we will preserve you from destruction — we will prevent the seizure of your territory by any foreign Power."[24]

Democratic senator James Westcott, one of Florida's first two senators after admission to the Union in 1845, mixed racism, fear of slave revolts, and the British threat. He contended that "Britain meant to emancipate the slaves in Cuba in order to strike at the South and the Yucatán with ex-slaves from Jamaica, as part of a scheme for surrounding Florida with a Cordon of Negro freedmen." Moreover, he claimed that "she [Britain] wants Yucatán as an important naval position, from which she can, in time of war, harass and annoy our commerce in the Gulf of Mexico, and that which goes through the Caribbean Sea further south."[25] Westcott urged that Congress mandate intervention in Yucatán, not merely authorize the executive to do so.

Senator Jefferson Davis (D.-Miss.) told his colleagues that since war with Mexico already existed, the president did not require further congressional authorization for sending troops to Yucatán, a part of Mexico. As to the British question: "We have seen Great Britain year after year extending her naval stations, until, by a line of circumvallation, she almost surrounds the Gulf of Mexico. . . . Yucatán and Cuba are the salient points commanding the Gulf of Mexico, *which I hold to be a basin of water belonging to the United States. The cape of Yucatán and the island of Cuba must be ours.*"[26]

In this now hardly remembered debate over possible military intervention in Yucatán, Congress gave painstaking attention to manifest destiny, territorial expansion, regional security, Anglo-American competition for influence and commerce in the Western Hemisphere, and American grand strategy. It also considered American "domestic tranquility" — meaning the possibility of slave insurrections provoked by the British. White people had to be protected against all sorts of "savages" — including Indians in Yucatán and black insurrectionists in the United States, like those involved in the Nat Turner rebellion in Virginia in 1831, which killed over fifty whites, sowed panic throughout the South, and brought repression from Virginia to Florida against blacks imagined to be conspiring.[27]

Polk's nationalist resurrection and amplification of the Monroe Doctrine secured for its elastic interpretation a permanent place in American foreign policy mythology. The Monroe Doctrine, as interpreted by American leaders in 1848, now clearly included the possibility of preemptive military deployments and humanitarian intervention, whether to protect the Central American isthmus and Tehuantepec from British domination, to guarantee the right of Western Hemisphere nations — like Texas (and perhaps Yucatán or Nicaragua) — to be annexed to the Union, or to preserve the norms of white supremacy.[28]

In defense of the war on Mexico, Polk also resorted to a rhetorical device that had been used since 1800 and would be used by future presidents over and over again to justify American intervention: self-defense. Polk explained that "though the United States were the aggrieved nation, Mexico commenced the war, and we were compelled in self-defense to repel the invader and to vindicate the national honor and interests by prosecuting it with vigor until we could obtain a just and honorable peace."[29]

The voices of restraint in the American wars of 1798, 1812, and 1846 found it difficult to overcome the momentum of the "facts on the ground" created through already-executed covert action, troop or naval deployments, and misinformation (or disinformation) provided by the executive branch to Congress and the popular media.[30] Yet such opposition to wars of choice and imperial ventures, with the concomitant attack on civil liberties at home, also became part of the American political tradition.[31] Illustratively, Senator Thomas Corwin (Whig-Ohio), who would become Abraham Lincoln's ambassador to Mexico, called on his senatorial colleagues in 1847 to limit presidential war making and to defend constitutional government against presidential "despotism":

> Tell me, ye who contend that, being in war, duty demands of Congress for its prosecution all the money and every able-bodied man in America to carry it on if need be, who also contend that it is the right of the President, without the control of Congress, to march your embodied hosts to Monterey, to Yucatán, to Mexico, to Panama, to China, and that under penalty of death to the officer who disobeys him — tell me, I demand it of you — tell me, tell the American people, tell the

nations of Christendom, what is the difference between your democracy and the most odious, most hateful despotism, that a merciful God has ever allowed a nation to be afflicted with since government on earth began? You may call this free government, but it is such freedom, and no other, as of old was established at Babylon. . . . Sir, it is not so; such is not your Constitution; it is something else, something other and better than this.[32]

Corwin's clarion call against imperialism and presidential war making fell mostly on deaf ears. Americans celebrated their victorious war and the Treaty of Guadalupe (1848), which deprived Mexico of over 40 percent of its territory. A war ostensibly fought over annexation of Texas and disputed borders allowed acquisition of California and New Mexico (the future U.S. states of Arizona, California, Nevada, New Mexico, and Utah, as well as portions of the states of Colorado, Kansas, Oklahoma, and Wyoming).[33] With American annexation of Mexican territory, the admonition in 1828 of the Mexican secretary of foreign relations, Lucas Alamán, had been realized:

They commence by introducing themselves into the territory which they covet, upon pretence of commercial negotiations, or of the establishment of colonies, with or without the assent of the Government to which it belongs. . . . These pioneers excite, by degrees, movements which disturb the political state of the country . . . and then follow discontents and dissatisfactions, calculated to fatigue the patience of the legitimate owner, and to diminish the usefulness of the administration and of the exercise of authority. . . . Sometimes more direct means are resorted to; and taking advantage of the enfeebled state, or domestic difficulties, of the possessor of the soil, they proceed, upon the most extraordinary pretexts, to make themselves masters of the country, as was the case in the Floridas; leaving the question to be decided afterwards as to the legality of the possession, which force alone could take from them.[34]

In 1853, the Gadsden Purchase added a little less than 30,000 square miles more of Mexican territory to the United States, south of the Gila River and west of the Rio Grande. The United States paid 10 million dollars for the territory and also secured the rights, which were never used, to build a canal across the isthmus of Tehuantepec.[35] In 1857, President Buchanan would propose a draft treaty whereby the United States would purchase Baja California, nearly all of Sonora, and part of Chihuahua for 12 million dollars. He instructed the American minister to Mexico, John Forsyth, to stress "the slight value of these provinces to Mexico and the fact they were largely occupied by savage tribes of Indians."[36] Ongoing internal strife in Mexico provided Forsyth opportunities to influence Mexican officials with promises of loans to finance repression of regime opponents. Civil war ensued in Mexico, with Forsyth, on his own, "suspending" relations with the de facto government and favoring the liberal insurgent, Benito Juárez. Buchanan ordered his new minister to Mexico, Robert McLane, to recognize a government headed by Juárez (to whose forces Americans had provided supplies and arms). Buchanan then asked Congress for authority to establish a temporary protectorate over parts of northern Mexico — a request that Congress, on the brink of the Union's disintegration, ignored. Nevertheless, the 1846–48 war, followed by further U.S. nibbling at Mexican territory and meddling in Mexican civil wars into the 1860s, epitomized the linkage between partisan and sectional politics, the mantra of manifest destiny, and U.S. foreign policy at mid-century.[37]

The Oregon Territory

Victory in the war with Mexico expanded U.S. territory south and west. Prior resolution of long-standing differences with Britain over the Maine-Canadian border and the Oregon Territory facilitated military success in the Mexican campaign. After the War of 1812, the Treaty of Ghent had created a joint commission to settle the boundary between the United States and Canada. In 1818, the two countries signed a Treaty of Joint Occupation of Oregon; this treaty was renewed in 1827. Spain, Great Britain, Russia, and the United States claimed parts of the Oregon Territory, which encompassed present-day Oregon, Washington, and most of British Columbia. In 1819, under terms of the Adams-Onís Treaty, Spain ceded its claims in Oregon to the United States. Shortly thereafter, the United States contested a Russian move to grant some of its citizens a fishing, whaling, and commercial monopoly from the Bering Straits to the 51st parallel. Promulgation of the Monroe Doctrine in 1823 put the Russians on notice that the United States would resist any further European penetration into North America.

From 1827 until the early 1840s, Britain and the United States reached no definitive solution to the U.S.-Canada boundary question.[38] Rebellions in Canada in 1837 involved some U.S. citizens, and cross-border raids continued in 1838. Requests for extradition of slaves (as criminals, perhaps for stealing food, clothing, or a horse to escape) and the activities of U.S. slave catchers in pursuit of fugitive slaves added friction to U.S.-British (Canadian) relations.[39] To settle these difficulties, the British sent a special mission to Washington in 1842 headed by Foreign Secretary Lord Ashburton. On August 9, 1842, the Webster-Ashburton Treaty provided partial solutions to outstanding disputes: the United States promised halfheartedly to police the slave trade with its navy in Africa; the two states accepted a division of disputed territory, giving 7,015 square miles to the United States and 5,012 to Great Britain (Canada). The agreed-upon boundary line went through the Great Lakes to the Lake of the Woods. The issue of the definitive Oregon border was left to be settled at a later date. Canada's role as destination for the Underground Railroad for fugitive slaves was not resolved.

Migration of U.S. settlers into Oregon country continued, creating pressure for a more definitive resolution of the boundaries. At the same time that the Polk administration prepared for war with Mexico, jingoists demanded that the British cut loose all the territory to the 54°40′ parallel — popularizing the slogan "fifty-four forty or fight." Debates in Congress reflected the rising tide of nationalism. In June 1844, Senator Thomas Hart Benton waxed passionately on the global implications of acquiring the Oregon territory: "We want thirty thousand rifles in the valley of Oregon; they will make all quiet there, in the event of a war with Great Britain for the dominion of that country. The war, if it comes, will not be topical; it will not be confined to Oregon; but will embrace the possession of the two powers throughout the Globe."[40]

Even Senator Benton did not join the "fifty-four forties," as they came to be called — in reference to the 1824 treaty that defined the southern boundary of the Russian settlement (Alaska).[41] Focused on Mexico, and seemingly content with the 49th parallel for an Oregon settlement, with some adjustments for Vancouver Island, President Polk eventually took the moderate position in the Oregon dispute. In his December 1845 message, he informed Congress that negotiations were under way on the matter. And, as America invaded Mexico and emigrants continued pouring into Oregon, the British accepted most of the American demands. After extensive debates and reviews of the various claims going back to the eighteenth century, the U.S. Senate ratified the treaty with Great Britain settling the "Oregon question" (which encompassed modern-day Oregon, Washington, Idaho, and western Montana) by a vote of 41–14, in June 1846.[42] All the nay votes came from Democrats, who held out for a northern boundary beyond the 49th parallel.

Beyond the North American Continent:
The Caribbean and Cuba

New territory created tension over the extension of slavery and threatened to upset the balance of sectional and economic interests in Congress. Nonetheless, by mid-century, expansionist and nationalist sentiments dominated the country. President Millard Fillmore (1850–53), taking office after President Zachary Taylor's (1849–50) death, signed the so-called Compromise of 1850, which compensated Texas for land west of the Rio Grande, established the New Mexico Territory, terminated the slave trade (but not slavery) in the District of Columbia, admitted California as a free state, and approved the Fugitive Slave Act (September 18, 1850).[43] This legislation authorized federal commissioners to pursue fugitive slaves anywhere in the country, return them to their owners, and receive compensation. No statute of limitations applied. Thus, while the South espoused the principle of states' rights, its leaders sought to require the federal government to protect slave owner property rights throughout the country — an ironic feature of the Fugitive Slave Act glossed over by the Slave Power in 1850, given their previous efforts to limit federal authority regarding establishment of a national bank, road and canal building, and even tariffs.[44]

The 1850 compromise brought temporary "peace" among the conflicting interests but angered abolitionists and inspired legislative resistance in some northern states. The compromise left unsettled the slave/free status of future states while reinforcing the institution of slavery itself. It also further complicated the possibility and significance of a future annexation of Cuba. As Fillmore noted in his December 1852 message to Congress: "Were this Island comparatively destitute of inhabitants, or occupied by a kindred race, I should regard it, if voluntarily ceded by Spain, as a most desirable acquisition. But, under existing circumstances, I should look upon its incorporation into our Union as a very hazardous measure. It would bring into the Confederacy a population of different national stock, speaking a different language, and not likely to harmonize with other members."[45] Fillmore's message captured the sense of the "scientific" racism that permeated American academia and popular opinion, as well as defenders of slavery.[46] It also reflected the ideas of many northern abolitionists, who were both racists and anti-imperialists. Thus northern Free Soiler journalist (chief Washington correspondent for the *New York Tribune*) James Shepherd Pike wrote in 1853 that the United States did not want a territory "filled with black, mixed, degraded, and ignorant or inferior races."[47] (Abraham Lincoln appointed Pike as the U.S. minister to the Netherlands, where he served from 1861 to 1866.)

Fillmore's successor, Franklin Pierce (1853–57), was a northern Democrat who favored southern causes — even repeal of the 1820 Missouri Compromise. He served as a brigadier general in the Mexican War and supported further territorial expansion (he would declare his support for the Confederacy during the Civil War). Pierce saw Cuba, Central America, and Kansas as part of the same field of opportunity for extension of the slave system and America's Providential destiny, southern version. His inaugural address in 1853 reaffirmed the No Transfer Principle of 1811 and the 1823 Monroe Doctrine as foundations of American foreign policy. He further proclaimed that armed force might be used to protect American citizens around the world: "The rights which belong to us as a nation are not alone to be regarded, but those which pertain to every citizen in his individual capacity, at home and abroad, must be sacredly maintained. . . . He must realize that upon every sea and on every soil where our enterprise may rightfully seek the protection of our flag American citizenship is an inviolable panoply for the security of American rights."[48]

President Pierce's vision of global protection for American citizens in their commercial ventures, though not backed by a powerful navy, virtually paralleled the imperial claims of England's Lord Palmerston (and the practice by other European powers of protecting nationals overseas). Palmerston, who supported Texas's independence as a "buffer state" in North America to advance England's strategic vision and perhaps even preferred the dismembering of the Union to dilute American influence in global politics, explained to Parliament his use of the fleet to protect British citizens in 1850 by reference to the Roman Empire: "As the Roman, in days of old, held himself free from indignity, when he could say *Civis Romanus sum*; so also a British subject, in whatever land he may be, shall feel confident that the watchful eye and the strong arm of England, will protect him against injustice and wrong."[49] Americans like President Pierce had picked up the Roman and British mantle. Beyond protection for Americans overseas, Pierce believed in America's manifest destiny and that expansion was critical not only for the United States but for "the peace of the world." He had declared in his inaugural address of 1853 that "the policy of my Administration will not be controlled by any timid forebodings of evil from expansion. Indeed, it is not to be disguised that our attitude as a nation and our position on the globe render the acquisition of certain possessions not within our jurisdiction eminently important for our protection, if not in the future essential for the preservation of the rights of commerce and the peace of the world."[50]

In the second year of Pierce's presidency, American diplomats in Belgium, including future president James Buchanan, badgered Spain to sell Cuba to the United States in the ill-fated Ostend Manifesto of 1854. Commerce tied Cuba to American markets. In the 1850s, the United States accounted for perhaps one-third of the island's foreign trade (mostly sugar), and Cuba ranked third or fourth among sources of American imports. Although Pierce's secretary of state, William L. Marcy, repudiated the Ostend Manifesto, it accurately interpreted the expansionist and southern aspirations regarding Cuba, as well as the broad interpretation of American national security and commercial interests: "It must be clear to every reflecting mind that, from the peculiarity of its geographical position, and the considerations attendant on it, Cuba is as necessary to the North American republic as any of its present members, and that it belongs naturally to that great family of States of which the Union is the providential nursery."[51]

Periodic rumors in the American press denounced an alleged British-Spanish plot to "Africanize" Cuba, abolish slavery, and establish a British protectorate — an act that might have inspired American slaves to rebellion. England disputed these stories, especially as it found itself engaged in the Crimean War against Imperial Russia (1853–56). England feared that the United States would take advantage of British preoccupation with Russia to annex Cuba and make further inroads in Central America.[52] In sum, British and American policies in the Caribbean were tied, as always, to broader geostrategic considerations and also to domestic politics in Britain and America.

U.S. policymakers dreaded repetition of the Haitian model in the Caribbean — a free black republic that emerged from a slave rebellion. The Ostend Manifesto expressed these fears plainly: "We should . . . be recreant to our duty, be unworthy of our gallant forefathers, and commit base treason against our posterity, should we permit Cuba to be Africanized and become a second St. Domingo [Haiti], with all its attendant horrors to the white race, and suffer the flames to extend to our own neighboring shores, seriously to endanger or actually to consume the fair fabric of our Union." The language of the Ostend Manifesto integrated several, sometimes contradictory, concerns that underlay American policy in the Western Hemisphere since the early nineteenth century: desire for territorial expansion; fears of slave insurrections; quest for hemispheric security; American grand strategy; and how to interpret, in practice, the spirit of manifest destiny that would cultivate the "Providential nursery." Significantly, the Ostend Manifesto referred to continued Spanish possession of Cuba as a possible threat to *internal peace* of the United States and even to survival of the Union — a departure from earlier acquiescence on Spanish rule so long as Spain did not transfer the colony to another European power:

> The Union can never enjoy repose, nor possess reliable security, as
> long as Cuba is not embraced within its boundaries. . . . After we shall
> have offered Spain a price for Cuba far beyond its present value, and

this shall have been refused, it will then be time to consider the question, does Cuba, in the possession of Spain, seriously endanger our internal peace and the existence of our cherished Union? . . . Should this question be answered in the affirmative, then, by every law, human and divine, we shall be justified in wresting it from Spain if we possess the power, and this upon the very same principle that would justify an individual in tearing down the burning house of his neighbor if there were no other means of preventing the flames from destroying his own home.[53]

In January 1859, Senator John Slidell (D.-La.) observed, not entirely accurately, that "the ultimate acquisition of Cuba may be considered a fixed purpose of the United States — a purpose resulting from political and geographical necessities which have been recognized by all parties and all Administrations."[54] Despite repudiation of the Ostend Manifesto, the 1860 presidential platforms of Southern Democrat John C. Breckinridge and Northern Democrat Stephen Douglas both urged annexation of Cuba. Douglas, as chairman of the Senate Committee on Territories, had proposed what became the Kansas-Nebraska Act. As late as Christmas 1860, he sought to avoid civil war by suggesting to prominent Democrat Alexander Stephens (who became vice president of the Confederacy) that Mexico be annexed as a slave state. Breckinridge, who served as Buchanan's vice president and had demanded congressional protection for southern slavery through adoption of a national slave code, was elected senator from Kentucky in 1860. He was expelled from the Senate in December 1861 for his support of the Confederacy, though Kentucky stayed in the Union. Breckinridge served as a general in the Confederacy's army, then as Confederate secretary of war until war's end.

Opposition notwithstanding, Buchanan had reiterated his policy of acquiring Cuba in his last message to Congress.[55] Abraham Lincoln's election and the onset of civil war in the United States put the Cuban issue temporarily to rest. Upon southern defeat in 1865, Breckinridge, who would have liked to see Cuba as a slave state, would flee to Cuba and then to exile in Canada.

Civil War and Reconstruction

Four years of civil war threatened the Union's survival and engaged both the government in Washington and the Confederacy in complex and sometimes byzantine diplomacy with Europe's major powers and the Spanish American republics.[56] Worried that diplomatic recognition of the Confederacy might permanently sanction disunion, the federal government worked tirelessly to prevent that outcome. For their part, southern diplomats sought arms, commerce, and recognition from European powers and Mexico. Civil War in America allowed a French-supported emperor, Maximilian I of the House of Habsburg, to establish a Mexican monarchy (1864–67). The French intervention, along with the Spanish reoccupation of Santo Domingo (1861–65) and Spanish bombardment of Peruvian and Chilean ports in the so-called Guano War (1865–66), directly violated Monroe's doctrine proclaiming the Western Hemisphere off-limits to European powers. At war's end, the U.S. government sent 50,000 troops to the Mexican border as a reminder to the French that time was running out on its empire in Mexico. A U.S. naval blockade, along with arms and supplies for Benito Juárez's armies, facilitated Mexican victory over Maximilian's forces and the eventual French withdrawal in 1867.

Meanwhile, aspirations for territorial expansion northward to Canada and even beyond the continent persisted.[57] Secretary of State William Seward set his eyes on a number of new territories, including Alaska, Hawaii, the Danish West Indies, and Santo Domingo. Seward visited Santo Domingo in 1866, intent on securing a Caribbean naval base. Presidents Andrew Johnson and Ulysses S. Grant both proposed annexation of Santo Domingo to the United States Senate. However, in the midst of post–Civil War Reconstruction, racial concerns shaped, and in a curious way curtailed, expansionist impulses. It was bad enough that freed blacks demanded equal rights and contested white supremacy in the defeated Confederate states; adding more "inferior" peoples to the Union lacked the appeal for Southern and Northern Democrats that imperialism and expansion of slavery had had before 1860.

Opposing the annexation of Santo Domingo, Senator Carl Schurz (R.-Mo.) claimed that the Dominicans were "indolent and ignorant." In the House of Representatives, Congressman Fernando Wood (D.-N.Y.) told his colleagues that the people of Santo Domingo were "of a most degraded character, being mostly composed of a race whose blood is two-thirds native African and one-third Spanish creole."[58] In June 1870, the Santo Domingo Annexation Treaty failed on a tie vote (two-thirds being necessary for approval). In his last message to Congress, President Grant lamented the failure to annex Santo Domingo. Meanwhile, Seward's efforts to convince Congress to approve annexation of the Danish West Indies and (Swedish) St. Bartholomew (which, in direct contravention of the No Transfer Principle, Sweden sold to France in 1878) also failed.

In contrast to setbacks for the expansionists in the Western Hemisphere, American commercial and military operations in the Pacific had "opened" Japan in 1854, reaffirmed a military and missionary presence in China in 1858, and obtained a navy base at Pago Pago Bay, Samoa, in 1878. Historian George C.

Herring writes that in "opening" Japan, Commodore Matthew Perry threatened that "if Japan did not treat with him it might suffer the fate of Mexico."[59] Thus, not only policy doctrines would be exported from the Western Hemisphere but also the use (and threat of use) of military might to achieve objectives where diplomacy failed. Shortly thereafter would come the "opening" of Korea in 1882 and definitive control over Pearl Harbor, Hawaii, in 1887.

Limited annexationist sentiment also resurfaced after the Civil War regarding Cuba, now in the midst of its own insurrection against Spain (1868–78). American mercenaries, adventurers, and traders supported the Cuban rebels. Some of the American press also sympathized with the insurgents, but diplomatic efforts to obtain reparations from England for damage done by the Confederate raider *Alabama*, built in English yards during the Civil War, complicated official assistance for Cuban "secessionists." Such support would put the United States in the position that the British had been in, in relation to the Confederacy, only several years earlier. Thus Caribbean (and Cuban) policy remained enmeshed in competing American, British, and European grand strategies and diplomatic conflicts.

Political instability in Spain during the Cuban insurrection confounded debates on the Cuba issue in the U.S. Congress and complicated policies toward the rebels' accomplices operating out of American bases. The American government was divided over recognition of the Cuban rebels as belligerents, which would have legalized loans and some supply operations favoring the rebels. President Grant was tempted; his secretary of state, Hamilton Fish, opposed annexation. He harked back to the No Transfer Resolution, telling the German minister privately that "the United States would 'resist at all hazard' any Spanish effort to sell the island to another European power."[60] Reaffirmation of the No Transfer Principle and the Monroe Doctrine was no novelty by the 1870s. But neither of these policy pronouncements offered succor to the Cuban *insurrectos*. So long as Spain controlled Cuba, rather than a more powerful European power, the United States could accept continued vestiges of European colonialism in the hemisphere.

In the short term, contingencies unplanned by policymakers framed diplomatic and military decisions. In October 1873, Spain captured a side-wheel steamship (the *Virginius*, a blockade runner captained by a Confederate navy veteran) leased to Cuban insurgents. The ship illegally flew the American flag. It had made previous runs to Cuba and was carrying war supplies to the Cuban rebels. The Spanish commander eventually ordered the execution of the *Virginius*'s captain and some fifty other prisoners.

Protests followed from the United States and England (the Spanish had seized the vessel in Jamaican waters). Negotiated reparations avoided war between Spain and the United States, despite a yellow press that shrilly called for revenge. Such demands abated when litigation in American courts demonstrated that the *Virginius* had been engaged in illegal activities that compromised American neutrality. The *Virginius* incident thus proved a poor cause célèbre, hardly justifying diplomatic remonstrance against Spain, let alone war. In any case, annexationist sentiment veiled by denunciation of Spanish atrocities against the Cubans faced the same dilemma as Grant's failed treaty for Santo Domingo: public opinion resisted incorporating more people of color into the Union. On Cuba, the *Nation* opined in 1873: "when we talk of annexing Cuba, as some of our orators do most glibly, we mean the admission to a share in this government of a motley million and a half of Spaniards, Cubans, and negroes, to whom our religion, manners, political traditions and habits, and modes of thought are, to tell the honest truth, about as familiar as they are to the King of Dahomey."[61] Racial politics could not be separated from the country's foreign relations, and race desirability conditioned what seeds would willingly be planted in the Providential nursery. In any case, Reconstruction and recovery after the Civil War required a respite from more grandiose foreign adventures and further territorial annexation, except for Alaska in 1867.[62]

Domestic politics also played an important role in temporarily curtailing the expansionist urge. By the mid-1870s, much of official Washington wished to be done with Reconstruction policies that entailed concern for the rights of African Americans. In the highly contested 1876 presidential election, the outcome ultimately turned on votes from Florida, Louisiana, and South Carolina. In exchange for agreeing to election of their candidate, Rutherford B. Hayes, the Republicans negotiated renewed Democrat control of state politics in the South. Reconstruction came to an end as federal troops left the South to local leaders. In the next two decades, blacks lost voting rights as the old Confederacy established a Jim Crow regime of segregation, humiliation, and repression, which endured with variations until the 1960s.[63] In these circumstances, annexation of Cuba, Santo Domingo, or other tropical territory with people of color lost most of its allure for American politicians and presidents.

And the Indian Nations

Avoiding direct involvement in the European wars of the 1870s, America celebrated its 1876 centennial in Philadelphia with its first World's Fair: the International Exhibition of Arts, Manufactures, and Products of the Soil and Mine.[64] Thirty nations participated in the event, which was opened by President Ulysses S. Grant and Dom Pedro II, the emperor of Brazil. In keeping with the pervasive ideology of "scientific" racism, which was then reaching a high point in American intellectual circles, racial classifications dictated the way the World's Fair was to be organized. Buildings from foreign nations were grouped by race: Anglo-Saxons, Teutons, Latins, and so on.[65] As the celebration took place, Chiefs Sitting Bull, Crazy Horse, and Gall led Sioux Indian resistance against General George Custer's 7th Cavalry, annihilating his force in the Montana Territory at the Little Big Horn on June 25, 1876.

The tragic experience of Native American peoples after contact with European invaders and their descendants is a well-known story. It is rarely viewed, however, as part of American and European grand strategy.[66] In North America, the British, French, and Spanish recruited Indian allies in their wars against one another. In the War of 1812, the British allied with Shawnee leader Tecumseh, who spent much of his life rallying Indian alliances against European and then American encroachment on Native American lands. Tecumseh died at the Battle of the Thames in Upper Canada in 1813, where American general and future president William Henry Harrison made part of his reputation as an "Indian fighter." Tecumseh remains a hero of North American Indian peoples and also of Canada — for his defense of Canadian autonomy from the United States. His story, like that of many Indian peoples, intertwined with European colonialism and then U.S. nation-building and state creation. The Europeans and the Americans used treaties with the Native peoples to achieve temporary alliances and to define boundaries between Indian territory and the claims of the non-Indian powers. In North America, the British repeatedly signed agreements with Indian nations but never effectively curtailed westward European expansion.

After independence, the U.S. government systematically pushed Indian peoples westward. Through military expeditions and chicanery, the Sauk, Fox, and Cherokee nations lost territory to the United States in present-day Illinois, the Mississippi Territory, Georgia, and Tennessee. Some bands of Shawnee ceded land in Indiana in 1809 — and the process continued into the mid-1820s, when representatives of northwestern tribes signed the initial Treaties of Prairie du Chien, Wisconsin, in which they sold millions of acres of land in return, supposedly, for reservations in the West. As candidly summarized by the U.S. Department of State, Bureau of Public Affairs Office, Historian website, in June 2008, "The U.S. Government used treaties as one means to displace Indians from their tribal lands, a mechanism that was strengthened with the Removal Act of 1830. In cases where this failed, the government sometimes violated both treaties and Supreme Court rulings to facilitate the spread of European Americans westward across the continent."

American *foreign policy* toward the Indian peoples after the Indian Removal Act of 1830 had been to "remove them" from land east of the Mississippi in exchange for land to its west — and then to keep removing them further as white settlement required Indian land.[67] In one of the more notorious operations, Chief Black Hawk led a group of Sauk (Sak) and Fox Indians against American troops in Illinois and Wisconsin in 1831–32, seeking to overturn a fraudulent treaty of 1804. After Black Hawk's defeat, the American soldiers massacred Indian women, children, and elderly (Bad Axe Massacre, 1832). A monument erected in 1955 near Victory, Wisconsin, reads: "The Battle of Bad Axe fought near here August 1–2, 1832 ended the Black Hawk War. Driven into the river by their pursuers, the Indians — warriors, old people, women and children — were shot down or drowned as they attempted to escape."

Andrew Jackson referred to the Indian Removal policy in seven of his eight messages to Congress. His fifth message (December 3, 1833) — after detailing relations with Europe and the Spanish American republics — offers a most explicit insight into Indian Removal: "That those tribes can not exist surrounded by our settlements and in continual contact with our citizens is certain. They have neither the intelligence, the industry, the moral habits, nor the desire of improvement which are essential to any favorable change in their condition. Established in the midst of another and a superior race, and without appreciating the causes of their inferiority or seeking to control them, they must necessarily yield to the force of circumstances and ere long disappear."[68] This policy (which passed in the House of Representatives after months of bitter debate and a 102–97 vote) would be characterized in modern parlance as "ethnic cleansing," if not genocide. Critics of this anachronistic use of the term might point out that it decontextualizes the policy and uses human rights language before modern human rights law came into existence. Yet some congressional opponents of the policy appealed to humanity at the time — including Daniel Webster and Davy Crockett (D.-Tenn.), whose opposition to Indian Removal legislation cost him reelection. Crockett explained his opposition in *A Narrative of the Life of David Crockett, of the State of Tennessee, Written by Himself* (1834): "I told them [Congress] I believed it was a wicked, unjust measure, and that I should go against it, let the cost to myself be what it might; that I was willing to go with General Jackson in everything that I believed was honest and right; but further than this I wouldn't go for him, or any other man in the whole creation. I voted against this Indian bill, and my conscience yet tells me that I gave a good honest vote, and that I believe will not make me ashamed in the day of judgment." In whatever context it occurred, Indian Removal meant virtual cultural and physical genocide against many Native peoples, just as slavery, however "decontextualized," meant vicious dehumanization of people — as many opponents of the "peculiar institution" proclaimed at the time.

Jackson's Indian Removal policy also exacerbated conflicts among the Indian peoples as the American military forced various groups further west into the Oklahoma Territory. By the end of his presidency, Jackson had signed into law almost seventy removal treaties, resulting in the forced migration of perhaps 50,000 Indians to "Indian Territory," — defined as U.S. territory west of the Mississippi River (excluding the states of Missouri and Iowa as well as the Territory of Arkansas). In practice, the government intended to confine the expelled Indian peoples to what later became eastern Oklahoma.[69]

The Cherokee resisted the 1830 legislation in court, claiming that they were a sovereign nation and that any such policy as the Removal Act would require a treaty between them and the U.S. government. The U.S. Supreme Court agreed with the Cherokee, in *Worcester v. Georgia* (1832).[70] By this interpretation, Indian Removal would require a treaty with two-thirds vote in the Senate, as with any sovereign nation. Chief Justice John Marshall ruled that the Cherokee Nation was sovereign, making the removal laws invalid. (President Jackson reputedly responded: "John Marshall has made his decision. Now let him enforce it.") Whether the remarks attributed to Jackson are apocryphal or close to accurate, Marshall's decision did not stop implementation of the Indian Removal policy.

In 1835, with the Cherokees divided, the U.S. government negotiated the Treaty of New Echota (approved in the Senate by a one-vote margin in 1836), providing Jackson with the legal basis for enforcing Indian Removal. President Jackson told the Cherokees: "I am sincerely desirous to promote your welfare. Listen to me, therefore, while I tell you that you cannot remain where you now are. Circumstances that cannot be controlled, and which are beyond the reach of human laws, render it impossible that you can flourish in the midst of a civilized community."[71]

The most notorious Indian Removal operation, called retrospectively the "Trail of Tears," involved Jackson's successor. In 1838, President Martin Van Buren ordered his army to remove the Cherokee from their ancestral lands in Georgia to the West. General Winfield Scott, of soon-to-be conquest of Mexico fame, informed the Cherokee: "The President of the United States has sent me, with a powerful army, to cause you, in obedience to the Treaty of 1835, to join that part of your people who are already established in prosperity, on the other side of the Mississippi. . . . The full moon of May is already on the wane, and before another shall have passed away, every Cherokee man, woman and child . . . must be in motion to join their brethren in the far West."[72] On the U.S. National Park Service website in 2008, the Trail of Tears was listed as one of the country's National Historic Trails. A lesson plan for teachers regarding the Trail comments: "No one knows exactly how many died during the journey. Missionary doctor Elizur Butler, who accompanied one of the detachments, estimated that nearly one fifth of the Cherokee population died. The trip was especially hard on infants, children, and the elderly. An unknown number of slaves also died on the Trail of Tears. The U.S. government failed to pay the five million dollars promised to the Cherokees in the Treaty of New Echota."[73]

In the following decades, numerous broken treaties and military campaigns pushed the Indian peoples ever westward, destroyed their way of life, decimated their populations, and forced them onto reservations.[74] This was part of the American geopolitical vision; it shared the ideological, religious, and racialist premises of manifest destiny that underlay territorial expansion south and west into the Floridas and Mexico and to the Pacific Coast. The same army officers who led campaigns against the French, Spanish, and British fought against the Indian peoples. The Indian wars, in turn, trained and blooded the officers who fought against Mexico and then led both sides in the American Civil War. Several American presidents — Andrew Jackson, William Henry Harrison, Zachary Taylor — owed their fame, if not their presidencies, to their days as "Indian fighters."

By 1876, the Indian fighters had largely taken the homelands of the Native American peoples. Some of the Indian fighters from the 1870s would later find their way to Cuba and the Philippines after 1898, adopting brutal counterinsurgency tactics and treating America's new subjects as they had dealt with the Indians in North America. In 1899, Theodore Roosevelt explicitly compared policy toward the Indian peoples to America's new Philippine "wards." He explained: "For the barbarian will yield only to force. [Indian-White warfare] had to continue until we expanded over the country. . . . The same will be true of the Philippines . . . so that one more fair spot of the world's surface shall have been snatched from the forces of darkness."[75]

With few exceptions, Native American nations had been purged from the American South and Midwest, east of the Mississippi River, by the mid-1840s. Wars against the Indian peoples continued until almost the end of the nineteenth century, when resistance to a broken treaty by the Lakota Sioux culminated in the massacre at Wounded Knee, South Dakota, in 1890. Army forces of the 7th Cavalry, General Custer's old unit, slaughtered Indian men, women, and children. Summarizing the post–Civil War army operations against the

Indian people, the U.S. Army's *American Military History* recounts: "The Battle of Wounded Knee was the last Indian engagement to fall in the category of warfare; later incidents were more in the realm of civil disturbance. The nineteenth century was drawing to a close and the frontier was rapidly disappearing. . . . In the quarter century of the Indian wars the Army met the Indian in over a thousand actions, large and small, all across the American West . . . while at the same time it helped shape Indian policy, contributed to the red man's acculturation, and was centrally involved in numerous other activities *that were part and parcel of westward expansion and of the nation's attainment of its "manifest destiny."*[76]

America's Providential nursery had gradually weeded out the Native peoples, who represented an obstacle to its manifest destiny. With the exception of Canada, the Americans also gradually eliminated European rivals. Nevertheless, England, other European powers, and Latin Americans themselves continued to contest American hegemony in the New World. In much of the hemisphere, American commercial, cultural, and military influence remained weaker than that of British, French, and even German competitors. The desired Western Hemisphere bastion was not yet entirely secure, though "Providence," with the assistance of aggressive American policies and wars against its neighbors, had transformed the thirteen colonies on the eastern seaboard into a continental republic.

Appendix 1: Key Treaties, 1795–1850

1794 — *Jay Treaty (Treaty of London)*. Attempts to settle post-Revolution disputes with Great Britain.

1795 — *Pinckney Treaty (Treaty of San Lorenzo)*. Defines boundaries with Spain; provides access to Mississippi and right of deposit at New Orleans.

1795 — *Treaty with Algeria*. Regularizes trade relations on same basis as with British, Dutch, and Swedes; agreement not to attack American shipping.

1796 — *Treaty with Tripoli*. Tribute payments to Tripoli to protect Americans from seizure and ransom.

1797 — *Treaty with Tunis*. Increases tribute payments to Tripoli.

1800 — *Convention of 1800 (Treaty of Môrtefontaine)*. Ends the Quasi-War between France and the United States.

1803 — *Louisiana Purchase from France*.

1805 — *Treaty with Tripoli*. Secures release of Americans being held and proclaims peace and amity.

1814 — *Treaty of Ghent*. Ends the War of 1812 between the United States and Great Britain.

1817 — *Rush-Bagot Treaty*. United States and Great Britain agree to demilitarize the Great Lakes.

1818 — *Convention of 1818*. Resolves boundary issues between United States and Great Britain; provides for joint occupation and settlement of Oregon.

1819 — *Adams-Onís Treaty*. Purchase of Florida from Spain.

1824 — *Russo-American Treaty*. Resolves Russian claims on land off the Northwest Pacific Coast of North America (north of Oregon country).

1842 — *Webster-Ashburton Treaty*. Settles boundary disputes between the United States and Britain (Canada).

1846 — *Bidlack-Mallarino Treaty* New Granada (Colombia). Establishes first American protectorate.

1846 — *Oregon Treaty*. Ends the Oregon boundary dispute with Britain.

1847 — *Treaty of Cahuenga*. Ends the Mexican War in California.

1848 — *Treaty of Guadalupe Hidalgo*. Ends the Mexican War and cedes territory to United States.

1850 — *Clayton-Bulwer Treaty*. United States and Britain agree to share control over any eventual canal across Central America.

*Appendix 2: Instances of Use of U.S.
Armed Forces Abroad, 1846–1876*[77]

1846–48 — *Mexican War*.

1849 — *Smyrna*. In July, a naval force gained release of an American seized by Austrian officials.

1851 — *Turkey*. After a massacre of foreigners (including Americans) at Jaffa in January, a demonstration by the Mediterranean Squadron was ordered along the Turkish (Levant) coast.

1851 — *Johanns Island (east of Africa)*. In August, forces from the U.S. sloop of war *Dale* exacted redress for the unlawful imprisonment of the captain of an American whaling brig.

1852–53 — *Argentina*. From February 3 to 12, 1852, and September 17, 1852, to April 1853, marines were landed and maintained in Buenos Aires to protect American interests during a revolution.

1853 — *Nicaragua*. From March 11 to 13, U.S. forces landed to protect American lives and interests during political disturbances.

1853–54 — *Japan*. Commodore Perry and his expedition made a display of force leading to the "opening of Japan."

1853–54 — *Ryukyu and Bonin Islands*. Commodore Perry, on three visits before going to Japan and while waiting for a reply from Japan, made a naval demonstration, landing marines twice, and secured a coaling concession from the ruler of Naha on Okinawa. He also demonstrated in the Bonin Islands with the purpose of securing facilities for commerce.

1854 — *China*. On April 4 and June 15–17, American and English ships landed forces to protect American interests in and near Shanghai during Chinese civil strife.

1854 — *Nicaragua*. From July 9 to 15, naval forces bombarded and burned San Juan del Norte (Greytown) to avenge an insult to the American minister to Nicaragua.

1855 — *China*. From May 19 to 21, U.S. forces protected American interests in Shanghai and, from August 3 to 5, fought pirates near Hong Kong.

1855 — *Fiji Islands*. From September 12 to November 4, an American naval force landed to seek reparations for depredations on American residents and seamen.

1855 — *Uruguay*. From November 25 to 29, U.S. and European naval forces landed to protect American interests during an attempted revolution in Montevideo.

1856 — *Panama, Republic of New Granada*. From September 19 to 22, U.S. forces landed to protect American interests during an insurrection.

1856 — *China*. From October 22 to December 6, U.S. forces landed to protect American interests at Canton during hostilities between the British and the Chinese and to avenge an assault upon an unarmed boat displaying the U.S. flag.

1857 — *Nicaragua*. In May, Commander C. H. Davis of the U.S. Navy, with some marines, received the surrender of William Walker, who had been attempting to get control of the country, and protected his men from the retaliation of native allies who had been fighting Walker. In November and December of the same year, U.S. vessels *Saratoga*, *Wabash*, and *Fulton* opposed another attempt of William Walker on Nicaragua. Commodore Hiram Paulding's act of landing marines and compelling the removal of Walker to the United States was tacitly disavowed by Secretary of State Lewis Cass, and Paulding was forced into retirement.

1858 — *Uruguay*. From January 2 to 27, forces from two U.S. warships landed to protect American property during a revolution in Montevideo.

1858 — *Fiji Islands*. From October 6 to 16, a marine expedition chastised natives for the murder of two American citizens at Waya.

1858–59 — *Turkey*. The secretary of state requested a display of naval force along the Levant after a massacre of Americans at Jaffa and mistreatment elsewhere "to remind the authorities (of Turkey) of the power of the United States."

1859 — *Paraguay*. Congress authorized a naval squadron to seek redress for an attack on a naval vessel in the Paraná River that had taken place in 1855. Apologies were made after a large display of force.

1859 — *Mexico*. Two hundred U.S. soldiers crossed the Rio Grande in pursuit of the Mexican bandit Cortina.

1859 — *China*. From July 31 to August 2, a naval force landed to protect American interests in Shanghai.

1860 — *Angola, Portuguese West Africa*. On March 1, American residents at Kissembo called upon American and British ships to protect lives and property during problems with natives.

1860 — *Colombia, Bay of Panama*. From September 27 to October 8, naval forces landed to protect American interests during a revolution.

1863 — *Japan*. On July 16, the USS *Wyoming* retaliated against a firing on the American vessel *Pembroke* at Shimonoseki.

1864 — *Japan*. From July 14 to August 3, naval forces protected the U.S. minister to Japan when he visited Yedo to negotiate concerning some American claims against Japan and to make his negotiations easier by impressing the Japanese with American power.

1864 — *Japan*. From September 4 to 14, naval forces of the United States, Great Britain, France, and the Netherlands compelled Japan and the Prince of Nagato in particular to permit the Straits of Shimonoseki to be used by foreign shipping in accordance with treaties already signed.

1865 — *Panama*. On March 9 and 10, U.S. forces protected the lives and property of American residents during a revolution.

1866 — *Mexico*. In November, to protect American residents, General Sedgwick and 100 men obtained the surrender of Matamoras. After three days, he was ordered by the U.S. government to withdraw. His act was repudiated by the president.

1866 — *China*. From June 20 to July 7, U.S. forces punished an assault on the American consul at Newchwang.

1867 — *Nicaragua*. Marines occupied Managua and Leon.

1867 — *Formosa*. On June 13, a naval force landed and burned a number of huts to punish the murder of the crew of a wrecked American vessel.

1868 — *Japan (Osaka, Hiolo, Nagasaki, Yokohama, and Negata)*. On February 4 to 8, April 4 to May 12, and June 12 and 13, U.S. forces were landed to protect American interests during the civil war in Japan over the abolition of the Shogunate and the restoration of the Mikado.

1868 — *Uruguay*. On February 7 and 8 and 19 to 26, U.S. forces protected foreign residents and the customhouse during an insurrection at Montevideo.

1868 — *Colombia.* In April, U.S. forces protected passengers and treasure in transit at Aspinwall during the absence of local police or troops on the occasion of the death of the president of Colombia.

1870 — *Mexico.* On June 17 and 18, U.S. forces destroyed the pirate ship *Forward*, which had been run aground about forty miles up the Rio Tecapan.

1870 — *Hawaiian Islands.* On September 21, U.S. forces placed the American flag at half mast upon the death of Queen Kalama, when the American consul at Honolulu would not assume responsibility for so doing.

1871 — *Korea.* On June 10 to 12, a U.S. naval force attacked and captured five forts to punish natives for depredations on Americans, particularly for murdering the crew of the *General Sherman* and burning the schooner and for later firing on other American small boats taking soundings up the Salee River.

1873 — *Colombia (Bay of Panama).* On May 7 to 22 and September 23 to October 9, U.S. forces protected American interests during hostilities over possession of the government of the State of Panama.

1873–96 — *Mexico.* U.S. troops crossed the Mexican border repeatedly in pursuit of cattle and other thieves. There were some reciprocal pursuits by Mexican troops into border territory. Mexico protested frequently. Notable cases were at Remolina in May 1873 and at Las Cuevas in 1875. Washington orders often supported these excursions. Agreements between Mexico and the United States, the first in 1882, finally legitimized such raids. They continued intermittently, with minor disputes, until 1896.

1874 — *Hawaiian Islands.* From February 12 to 20, detachments from American vessels were landed to preserve order and protect American lives and interests during the coronation of a new king.

1876 — *Mexico.* On May 18, an American force was landed to temporarily police the town of Matamoros while it was without other government.

Chapter Four

The Good Neighbor

When we wanted this country we came and took it. If we want Central America, the cheapest, easiest and quickest way to get it is to go and take it, and if France and England interfere, read the Monroe doctrine to them. — SENATOR ALBERT GALLATIN BROWN (D.-Miss.), September 11, 1858

Looking backward from 1860, many Latin American leaders and intellectuals had come to distrust and fear the United States. Beyond the anger, it was difficult for Latin Americans — as well as for historians to the present — to make sense of how U.S. partisan and sectional politics influenced American policy in the hemisphere. Such an understanding requires reconsideration of the relationship between American political and economic development and the country's international relations.

Until the Civil War, America had lived off slavery. Slaves produced most of America's important cash crops such as cotton, tobacco, rice, indigo, and sugarcane. With Eli Whitney's invention of the cotton gin in 1793, southern agriculture became gradually less diversified; cotton was king and the perpetuation of slavery was assured.[1] The American South grew 60 percent of the world's cotton and provided some 70 percent of the cotton in the British textile industry in 1840. Thus, slavery paid for a substantial share of the capital, iron, and manufactured goods that fueled American economic growth.[2] Duties on those imports financed the federal government, whose main source of revenue was land sales and customs duties.[3] In 1850, almost 2 million slaves worked on cotton plantations, and cotton accounted for more than half of the value of exports — ten times more than its nearest competitor, the wheat and wheat flour of the North.[4] By 1860, slaves represented almost 15 percent of the American population, and this figure reached over 45 percent in states such as Georgia and Alabama. In South Carolina, slaves outnumbered free persons.[5]

Embedded in global commercial and financial networks, the cotton plantations linked America to all continents, to manufacturing workers in England and Europe, to labor markets in Africa and Asia, and to the world's financial centers. British capital financed southern banks, which extended credit to planters to open up new lands for cotton cultivation.[6] New England shipping and finance supported and was supported by the slave economy. In 1860, U.S. cotton manufacturing still generated more income than the iron industry; it too relied indirectly on slavery.[7] As settlers moved west, western farmers sold corn, wheat, and livestock products to the southern plantations. Slaves served as collateral for loans, were themselves commodities, and, through taxes on their sale and value, funded local and state governments. In short, slavery was a bedrock of American economic and political development.[8]

Slavery, and conflict over its perpetuation and expansion, also figured centrally in American politics. Compromise on the "slavery question" had been crucial in the transition from the Articles of Confederation to the federal regime established in the 1787 constitution. The so-called three-fifths principle (article 1, section 2, of the Constitution) allowed southern states to count slaves for purposes of political representation, guaranteeing disproportionate southern influence in Congress and presidential elections. The Constitution also required states to return fugitive slaves to their owners, thereby restricting the authority of states, should they so decide, to provide refuge to escaped slaves.[9] A major threat to the survival of the Union posed by the debate on admission of Missouri and Maine as states was resolved by the Missouri Compromise of 1820. The Compromise avoided disunion by admitting Missouri as a slave state and Maine as a free state, making the country "half slave and half free" (in the Senate). The slavery question continued to plague domestic politics and foreign relations until 1861. A growing abolitionist movement threatened the political and economic foundations of the nation, especially of the South. Southern Democrats and American presidents in the 1850s repeatedly called for further territorial expansion and extension of slavery into new territory. These conflicting forces linked partisan and sectional politics to the "slave question" and to foreign policies regarding Mexico, the Caribbean, and Central America.[10]

Sectionalism and Tariff Politics

Along with slavery, tariff and commercial policy overlapped domestic politics and foreign policy. Alexander Hamilton's *Report on Manufactures* (1791) recommended protectionism as a way to encourage American industry and generate employment. The report generated immediate controversy. Protec tionism disadvantaged important southern and, later, western interests. On the other hand, tariff revenues provided the main source of income for the federal government.[11] Striking a balance between revenue collection and protectionism became a constant political battle.

Although some southern support existed for moderate protective tariffs, in 1828 the so-called Tariff of Abominations provoked a constitutional crisis — foreshadowing the Civil War. In response to the Tariff of 1828 (and its revision in 1832), South Carolina's legislature passed the Nullification Act.[12] The state legislature claimed that Congress had gone too far, and South Carolina "nullified" the federal tariff. Congress responded with a "force bill" authorizing President Jackson to use the federal military to impose the tariff. Jackson sent a naval flotilla to Charleston, North America's main port of entry for slaves before abolition of the slave trade in 1808 and the scene of the Vesey slave insurrection conspiracy only a decade earlier (see chapter 2). Jackson recognized the fundamental threat presented by South Carolina's challenge to federal authority: "I consider, then, the power to annul a law of the United States, assumed by one State, incompatible with the existence of the Union, contradicted expressly by the letter of the Constitution, unauthorized by its spirit, inconsistent with every principle on which It was founded, and destructive of the great object for which it was formed."[13]

Disunion and even war seemed possible before Congress approved a compromise tariff in 1833. Importantly, it was not the "slavery question" per se that had generated the constitutional crisis, but tariff policy, a "domestic" issue that, by its nature, could not be neatly separated from foreign policy nor from fundamental disagreements about the nature of American federalism. Thus, two of America's most important domestic political issues, slavery and tariff legislation, significantly affected its foreign policies and relations with Latin America and the rest of the world.

In principle, the United States had agreed in 1808 to collaborate in stifling the slave trade. In practice, American commitment to this effort left much to be desired.[14] Most Spanish American republics eventually outlawed slavery, but others, along with Brazil and Spain's colonies in Cuba and Puerto Rico, retained slave systems into the late nineteenth century. Both the clandestine slave trade and the threat to the American South of slave rebellion and abolition affected American trade and security policy in the Western Hemisphere, especially relations with Spain regarding its Caribbean possessions. Britain abolished slavery in its Western Hemisphere colonies in 1834; the French and Danes did so in 1848. As the abolition movement in the United States intensified and territorial expansion from 1803 to 1850 brought contestation over the slave-versus-free status of new territories and states, Congress repeatedly debated the implications of British, Spanish, and Spanish American policies toward slavery and slave rebellions in the Western Hemisphere.

In regard to trade policy, although proposals for a broader "American System" trade regime surfaced from time to time, the U.S. government generally favored bilateral treaties of amity and commerce with the Latin American nations.[15] Most of the Spanish American republics adopted even higher tariffs than the United States, making penetration of Latin American markets for American exports relatively difficult. In any case, Great Britain, Spain, and the other European nations controlled *legal* access to the markets of their colonies in the West Indies, making trade policy with Cuba, Puerto Rico, Jamaica, and the other plantation societies of the Caribbean matters for U.S.-European relations.

Slavery, tariff, and commercial policy were further complicated after 1810 by American territorial ambitions in the Floridas and the wars of independence being fought against Spain from Mexico to Chile. Notwithstanding grandiose American ambitions, the War of 1812 made evident the military weakness of the United States. The burning by British forces of Washington, D.C., in 1814, in retaliation for American destruction of the parliament buildings and looting at York (Toronto), Upper Canada, in 1813, was followed by the raising of the Union Jack over the city. Although the war ended in a draw, American designs on Canada and East Florida had been thwarted (see chapter 1).

Meanwhile, with Napoleon's defeat in Europe, King Ferdinand VII returned to Spain, denounced the liberal constitution of 1812, and reestablished absolute monarchy. Spanish forces reimposed imperial authority in Mexico, much of northern South America, and Chile. For American policymakers, the independence wars in the Western Hemisphere presented threats to national security and commerce as well as complicated diplomatic challenges with Spain, Great Britain, and France. As previously detailed, this tangled web of intermestic politics — the battle to acquire East Florida from Spain, the Missouri Compromise, the fears of slave rebellion, the conflicts over tariff policy and commercial treaties, the debates on recognition of the emerging Spanish American republics, the anxiety over the Holy Alliance's possible intervention in the Western Hemisphere, and worries over British designs on Cuba — generated the Monroe Doctrine. It also brought the United States to its first war on terror in the Western Hemisphere.

The First War on Terror: Pirates of the Caribbean

The independence wars in Spanish America presented numerous challenges to American policymakers. Among the immediate threats were pirates, smugglers, slavers, gunrunners, and privateers — a world of organized and disorganized crime and rebellion.[16] Rebels in Mexico, Colombia, and Venezuela issued commissions to intercept Spanish vessels and other "enemy shipping." Spanish efforts to blockade trade with the insurgents upped the risk for American and British merchants and mercenaries in service to the rebel navies and armies.

In response to the ongoing conflicts and pirate operations, James Monroe signed into law the previously mentioned antipiracy legislation of 1819 and deployed the West Indian Squadron in 1822 under the command of Captain James Biddle. Congress debated the size and composition of naval forces necessary to carry out the antipiracy policy and the discretion to be given to the naval officers tasked with this mission. Debates centered on the roles of Congress and the president in deciding on the means and tactics to employ in the fight against piracy versus the authorization and funding — which were more clearly legislative responsibilities. Legislators discussed the constitutional limits of legislative and executive authority regarding foreign policy and raised questions on Congress's role in micromanaging military operations.

The piracy debate also raised crucial questions of international law. If pirates were found at sea and then they retreated to Spanish territory — Cuba, Puerto Rico, or smaller islands — was there a right of "hot pursuit"? What if Spanish authorities forbade such pursuit? What if Spanish troops or vessels confronted American forces? How much discretion should the president confer on ship captains? Should Congress legislate in detail instructions for ship captains or should that be left exclusively to the president as commander in chief? Did the country run the risk that a naval officer, without clear instructions and faced with protecting his own force or in his zeal to capture pirates, might push the country into war with Spain or other European powers?

None of these issues proved merely hypothetical. Repeated incidents with privateers, pirates, Spanish authorities, and American naval units gave urgency to the tactics used to suppress piracy. Several weeks after proclamation of the Monroe Doctrine, in December 1823, the secretary of the navy asked Congress for authorization to pursue the pirates "wherever they may fly. . . . The rights to follow should be extended to the settled as well as unsettled parts of the islands." If this failed to suppress the pirates, the next step would be to blockade the area.[17] President Monroe supported this request.[18]

Senator James Barbour (Anti-Democrat–Va.) introduced legislation authorizing the president to instruct naval commanders to pursue pirates "on the Island of Cuba, or any other part of the Islands of Spain, in the West Indies, to land, whenever it may be necessary to secure the capture of the said pirates, and there to subdue, vanquish, and capture them, to deliver them up to the authority of the Island where captured, or to bring them to the United States for trial and adjudication; as the said instructions of the President of the United States may prescribe."[19] Such authorization would confer on naval officers authority to (1) decide who was a pirate; (2) remove the person from Spanish territory or other islands in the West Indies by force; and (3) bring the person to the United States for trial. Barbour affirmed that pirates combined two heinous crimes, the slave trade and piracy, the "Sodom and Gomorah" of international law, and are "the enemies of the human race" — *hostes humani generis*. He claimed that the whole island of Cuba "is infected with moral leprosy — from head to foot."[20] Of course, carrying out the policy urged by Barbour (a states' rights advocate, who had presided over the Senate's debates on the Missouri Compromise in 1820) might conflict with Monroe's desire to avoid direct confrontation with Spain.[21]

Congress debated the proposed legislation for several months.[22] Some legislators objected to the broad discretion that would be granted to the president and navy officers. Others argued that "there did not exist any necessity for granting [the pursuit] provision since the President has it already by the law of nations." For those who objected that Spanish rights might be violated, Barbour added that pirates are "the common enemies of the human race, towards whom there can be no neutrals; therefore, it is perfectly lawful to pursue them into any territory in which they may have taken refuge, and any nation who should assert that their rights had been violated by such a pursuit, would make themselves parties in their crimes, and become obnoxious to all civilized Governments, for the refuge afforded to the enemies of mankind."[23]

After extensive debate, the Senate approved an amended version of the antipiracy bill with language inspired by Daniel Webster's admonition that Congress should decide what resources to give the president, but not restrict the use of those resources in carrying out his defense of the country. Opponents had successfully removed authorization to establish a blockade, after asking what would happen should British or French ships headed to Spanish ports be stopped by U.S. warships. Congress had reservations about turning the country's destiny — war or peace — entirely over to the president or to the bravado of an American naval squadron commander. In short, in making policy for the war against pirates, Congress took into account the international political and military realities of the moment as well as fundamental constitutional issues that would recur to the first decade of the twenty-first century.

With the end of the Spanish American independence movements in the mid-1820s, and with the sometimes-collaboration of the British navy and Spanish authorities in the West Indies, piracy in the Caribbean was largely suppressed.[24] President John Quincy Adams reported in his last message to

Congress that "the repression of piracy in the West Indian and in the Grecian seas has been effectually maintained, with scarcely any exception."[25] Adams's conjunction of "West Indian" and "Grecian" required not even a deep breath; he had a vision of grand strategy and American destiny not limited by oceans or continents — as the debates in 1823 on the Monroe Doctrine, which Adams had largely conceived, made evident.

Legislative sessions regarding the war on piracy anticipated what would be an ongoing debate on the role of Congress and the president in defining and implementing foreign policy and making war. In this first war on "enemies of humanity," Congress confirmed the right of hot pursuit, accepted invasion of foreign soil to capture and render (back to the United States or to the British) international criminals for punishment, and began to define, for itself, the broad, but still limited, authority of the president to deploy military force to protect American citizens, commerce, and security.[26]

When President John Quincy Adams first reported to Congress on suppression of piracy in his 1825 message, he had requested maintenance of a force sufficient to police the Caribbean and also informed Congress that piracy in the Mediterranean and off the Pacific coast of Chile and Peru remained a problem. In retrospect, his rationale for what would be called in the late twentieth century forward presence and forward deterrence sounds eerily contemporary: "It were, indeed, a vain and dangerous illusion to believe that in the present or probable condition of human society a commerce so extensive and so rich as ours could exist and be pursued in safety without the continual support of a military marine — the only arm by which the power of this Confederacy can be estimated or felt by foreign nations."[27] No clearer expression of foreign policy realism could be imagined; military power alone, ultimately, could protect American economic interests. Naval forces, forward deployed, would become a key to America's rising star in the international system.

Spain, Spanish America, and U.S. Regional Policy

Spain refused to give up the battle against decolonization into the 1830s despite U.S., then British and French, recognition of the new republics. After 1823, both Colombia and Brazil asked for interpretations of the Monroe Doctrine and the possibility of defensive alliances against European efforts at reconquest. Colombia's representative in Washington, D.C., wrote: "The Government of Colombia is desirous to know in what manner the Government of the United States intends to resist on its part any interference of the Holy Alliance for the purpose of subjugating the new Republic or interfering in the political forms; if it will enter into a treaty of Alliance with the Republic of Colombia to save America in general from the calamities of a despotic system; and finally if the Government of Washington understands by foreign interference the employment of Spanish forces against America at a time when Spain is occupied by a French Army, and its Government under the influence of France and her Allies."[28] More than a month later, the Colombians received a disappointing response: "The United States could not undertake resistance to them by force of arms, without a previous understanding with those European Powers whose Interests and whose principles would secure from them an active and efficient cooperation in the cause." The Brazilian request for a defensive and offensive alliance, to come into force upon European intervention, or renewal of hostilities by Portugal against its newly independent ex-colony, received much the same answer from Secretary of State Henry Clay. The United States "reserved the right to act as convenient, in each instance, and without any obligation to do so."[29]

Congress thus established a precedent for American reticence toward hemispheric collective security and alliances that would persist (with the exception of the 1846 treaty with Colombia) until the Rio Treaty of 1947 (see chapter 10). In 1825–26, the Senate Foreign Relations Committee reported against the mission to the Panama Congress organized by Simón Bolívar with the following resolution: "Resolved, that it is not expedient, at this time, for the United States to send any Ministers to the Congress of American Nations assembled in Panama."[30] Part of the American reluctance came from the projects by Colombia and Mexico to liberate Cuba, Puerto Rico, and perhaps even the Canary and Philippine Islands. Moreover, since some of the Spanish Americans sought to abolish slavery in the region, Senator John Holmes (D.-Maine) feared that "the blacks will take fire, and the scenes of St. Domingo [Haiti] will be re-enacted at home."[31]

Other legislators warned against entangling the United States in the wars of the Spanish Americans among themselves and against Spain. Senator Robert Hayne (D-S.C.), an ardent states' rights and slavery advocate, called the Panama Congress a project by Bolívar to form a "Confederacy of belligerent States" based on existing defensive treaties among Chile, Colombia, Mexico, and other states with belligerent purposes toward Spain.[32] He insisted that the United States' permanent policy of neutrality would be violated by participation in the Panama Congress.[33] Despite objections, the bill appropriating funds for the Panama Congress mission received approval by a vote of 23–19 — but only after taking so long to enact that the U.S. delegates would not have time to get to the Panama Congress.[34]

As the United States molded its foreign policies from the bastion it sought to create in the Western Hemisphere, Latin Americans found their interests and aspirations sacrificed to Anglo-American rivalries, to balance of power politics in Europe, and to the vicissitudes of U.S. domestic politics. In turn, Latin American governments and diplomats sought to play the Americans and Europeans off against one another, for whatever benefit might be obtained. Correspondence from American and European diplomats repeatedly revealed exasperation with the desires of Latin Americans to resist imposition of "solutions" preferred by "superior peoples." What seemed a constant, however, was the contempt and cynicism demonstrated by American and European governments alike toward Spanish America and Brazil. Recurring threats of military intervention to enforce American and European claims and pressures for special privileges fill the diplomatic dispatches. For the United States, policy regarding its closest neighbors—Cuba, the Caribbean islands, Central America, Colombia (Panama), and Mexico—took priority in the years before the 1880s.

Cuba

In the first decades after American independence, Cuba figured prominently in U.S. strategic and commercial thinking. It became the "most consistent object of application of the No-Transfer Principle in American diplomacy."[35] It also became the subject of various schemes for occupation, annexation, and creation of naval stations. Debates over policy toward Cuba frequently occupied U.S. policymakers from 1808 when France, which had invaded Spain, offered to support a forcible occupation of the island in exchange for a military alliance against Great Britain. James Madison's slippery reply well illustrated the global implications of U.S. regional policy: "Should circumstances demand from the United States a precautionary occupation against the hostile designs of Great Britain, it will be recollected with satisfaction that the measure has received his Majesty's [Napoleon's] approbation."[36] Clearly, Madison referred to the possibility of what might be called, in the twenty-first century, anticipatory self-defense or preemptive attack, should "circumstances demand" such a measure.

With Napoleon's invasion of Spain, President Thomas Jefferson's cabinet agreed on "sentiments which should be 'unauthoritatively expressed' to influential persons in Cuba and Mexico": "If you remain under the dominion of the kingdom and family of Spain, we are contented; but we should be extremely unwilling to see you pass under the dominion or ascendency of France or

England. In the latter case should you choose to declare independence, we cannot now commit ourselves by saying we would make common cause with you but must reserve ourselves to act to the then existing circumstances, but in our proceedings we shall be influenced by friendship to you, by a firm belief that our interests are intimately connected, and by the strongest repugnance to see you under subordination to either France or England, either politically or commercially."[37]

Recurrent rumors circulated that Spain would transfer the island to Great Britain, and American diplomats received repeated instructions to monitor any such developments. Even before President Madison orchestrated the seizure of West Florida in 1810, he had written to Minister Plenipotentiary William Pinkney: "The position of Cuba gives the United States so deep an interest . . . that we could not be a satisfied spectator at its falling under any European government, which might make a fulcrum of that position against the commerce and security of the United States."[38]

The value of trade with Spain and Cuba — where no serious independence movement developed — exceeded that of all of the commerce with Buenos Aires, Chile, New Granada, and Mexico. Until after 1818, only at Buenos Aires could the Spanish American insurgents maintain their independence against Spanish forces. Previous administrations had recognized the rights of belligerents of the Spanish Americans, most notably with a neutrality proclamation in September 1815, permitting their ships into American ports and the rights afforded to belligerent naval forces under existing international law. Still, Secretary of State John Quincy Adams stuck to Jeffersonian principles: only when the rebels essentially controlled the territory over which they claimed independent sovereignty would the United States afford diplomatic recognition. He also opposed authorization for large arms purchases sought by a Colombian agent in the United States to further the war against Spain and carry the offensive to Cuba.

Cuban independence and then annexation on the West Florida model was a temptation but also a risk for both the South (should independence be accompanied by insurgency and abolition) and for antislavery interests (should Cuba be annexed and slavery retained). Adding Cuba as a slave state after 1820 would upset the Missouri Compromise (and the balance of power in the Senate). Inability to control the consequences for American domestic politics of a change in the status quo impeded consensus on Cuban policy. Jefferson and John Quincy Adams both expressed their views on the importance of Cuba to President Monroe in 1823. Jefferson wrote that "Cuba alone seems to present to hold up a speck [specter] of war to us. Its possession by Great Britain would indeed be a great calamity to us."[39] Adams, in Congress, went much further: "It is scarcely possible to resist the conviction that the annexation of Cuba to our federal republic will be indispensable to the continuance and integrity of the Union itself."[40]

Adams and Henry Clay worked to persuade Russia, Great Britain, and France to convince Spain to end hostilities with its colonies and requested that Colombia and Mexico suspend expeditions against Cuba.[41] Adams wrote to the American minister in Spain that "in the *maritime* Wars of Europe we have indeed a direct and important interest of our own; as they are waged upon an element which is the common property of all [the oceans], *and as our participation in the possession of that property is perhaps greater than that of any other nation.* To all maritime wars Great Britain can scarcely fail of becoming a party; and from that moment arises a collision between her and the United States, peculiar to the situation, interests and rights of the two countries."[42]

With the end of the Spanish American independence wars in the mid-1820s, American presidents and secretaries of state repeatedly warned European powers against interference in Cuba or its acquisition. Great Britain, which would take the lead in combating the international slave trade after 1833, sent missions to Cuba to report on conditions of the trade—which Spain had promised to curtail. The American representative at Madrid received instructions regarding Cuba that again made a clear commitment to Spain's possession of the island: "You are authorized to assure the Spanish government, that in case of any attempt, from whatever quarter, to wrest from her this portion of her territory, she may securely depend upon the military and naval resources of the United States to aid her in preserving or recovering it."[43]

Consistent with the No Transfer Policy and also with the original Monroe Doctrine (no *further* colonization), the United States would tolerate continued Spanish control of Cuba. However, it now appeared that the U.S. government threatened (promised?) a military response against "any attempt, from whatever quarter" to transfer the island from Spain to another power. This was not the oblique language of the No Transfer Resolution, nor even the ambiguous warnings of the Monroe Doctrine. To keep Cuba out of English or French possession it seemed that the United States would engage in preemptive war.[44]

With the rising tide of American nationalism in the late 1840s, annexationist aspirations toward Cuba increased. Offers to purchase Cuba from Spain came from the Polk administration (1845–49). Spain rejected them.[45] Southerners dreamed of expanding the realm of American slavery to the Caribbean, Central America, and even Mexico, a dream that would foster various filibustering expeditions as the idea of manifest destiny, in the words of historian Robert May, translated into "sectional destiny."[46] Failed expeditions by Venezuelan-born Cuban exile Narciso López from 1849 to 1851 were followed by numerous filibuster plots headed by John Quitman, military governor of Mexico City after its surrender in 1847 and Mississippi governor (1850–51).[47] Quitman had supported López; both hoped to make Cuba a slave state after winning independence from Spain.[48] Quitman explained that "our destiny is intertwined with that of Cuba. If slave institutions perish there they will perish here."[49]

In response to the filibuster expeditions, the British and French notified Washington that their fleets would "repel by force any attempts of invasion from any quarter." The United States replied that such action could "not but be regarded by the United States with grave disapproval, as involving on the part of European sovereigns combined action of protectorship over American [Western Hemisphere] waters."[50] Again, in 1852, Secretary of State Daniel Webster reminded Great Britain and France that "it has always been declared to Spain that the government of the United States could not be expected to acquiesce in the cession of Cuba to an European power." The British proposed a tripartite convention wherein France, Britain, and the United States all "disclaim now and forever hereafter all intention to obtain possession of the Island of Cuba." Webster, though agreeing with the sentiments expressed by the British, reminded them that "the policy of the United States has uniformly been to avoid alliances or agreements with other States, and to keep itself free of national obligations except such as affect, directly, the interests of the United States themselves."[51] Webster's convenient reiteration of American unilateralism also avoided mention of the strong annexationist sentiments among some Americans.

Taking office in 1853, Franklin Pierce took a still more aggressive stance toward the Cuban question. Provoked in part by Spanish seizure in March 1854 of the American ship *Black Warrior* for failure to produce a required cargo manifest, Secretary of State (and Polk's secretary of war during the Mexican War) William L. Marcy arranged a secret meeting of U.S. diplomats at Ostend, Belgium, to consider American policy toward Cuba. At Ostend, and then at Aix-la-Chapelle, the U.S. minister to Britain and future president James Buchanan, minister to France (Polk's secretary of navy during the Mexican War and ardent states' rights and slavery advocate) John Y. Mason, and minister to Spain Pierre Soulé (a prominent supporter of slavery and proponent of American manifest destiny) produced the bellicose and embarrassing Ostend Manifesto.[52] Soulé's version of manifest destiny extended to the "absorption of the entire continent and its island appendages," a view diametrically opposed to the position Webster had expressed to the British and French at the end of 1852.[53]

Dated October 18, 1854, at Aix-la-Chapelle, the same year that Congress approved the Kansas-Nebraska Act repealing the Missouri Compromise, the Ostend Manifesto again justified what might be called, in modern terms, preemptive attack and military occupation to avoid future security risks — if Spain refused to *sell* Cuba to the United States. Thus the Ostend document went well beyond the No Transfer Policy in identifying security risks to the United States. Such risks included "Africanization" of Cuba (abolition of slavery and immigration of free blacks), which might threaten the U.S. economy and its political "tranquility." Buchanan, Mason, and Soulé wrote in their Manifesto: "We should . . . be recreant to our duty, be unworthy of our gallant forefathers, and commit base treason against our posterity, should we permit Cuba to be Africanized and become a second St. Domingo, with all its attendant horrors to the white race, and suffer the flames to extend to our own neighboring shores, seriously to endanger or actually to consume the fair fabric of our Union."

The Ostend Manifesto complicated U.S. relations with Spain, which refused to sell Cuba and was offended by threats of invasion. Marcy's State Department repudiated the Manifesto, but James Buchanan would win the presidency less than two years later, and the southern dream of expanding the Slave Power to Cuba and then throughout the Caribbean and Central America — even to Brazil — persisted. As an editorial in the *Richmond Enquirer* expressed this southern version of manifest destiny, "If we hold Cuba . . . in the next fifty years we will hold the destiny of the richest and most increased commerce that ever dazzled the cupidity of man. And with that commerce we can control the power of the world."[54] Meanwhile, the Pierce administration continued its flirtation with filibusters headed for Cuba, even sending the Home Squadron off the Cuban coast in 1855, ostensibly to protect American shipping.

The 1856 presidential campaign pitted proslavery, annexationist James Buchanan against a Republican platform that called the Ostend Manifesto the "plea of the highwayman." The Republican presidential candidate, General John C. Frémont, called for prohibition of slavery in the territories. In contrast, Buchanan urged Congress not to interfere with popular sovereignty on the slavery question in the territories or new states and called for American ascendancy in the Gulf of Mexico.[55] Upon victory, Buchanan strongly supported the *Dred Scott* decision by the Supreme Court upholding the property rights in slavery of southerners who took their slaves to northern territories where slavery was banned.[56] He also sought congressional authorization to purchase Cuba, reiterating this request again in 1859.

After the American Civil War, a Cuban independence movement (1868–78) again challenged Spanish control of the island. Early leaders of the Cuban rebel movement called for American annexation and then recruited Confederate Civil War general Thomas Jordan to head their army (1869–70). Spain held on tightly to its colony, defeating the insurgents in a vicious ten-year counterinsurgency campaign. Although Cuba would remain a Spanish colony, becoming progressively more open to American commerce for another twenty years, American policy on Cuba from 1811 until the late nineteenth century was emblematic of the complex interplay between U.S. hemispheric policies, its relations with European powers, and American partisan, sectional, and presidential politics. Above all else, the United States insisted that it would determine, *unilaterally*, the limit of European initiatives toward Cuba.

Colombia: The First Treaty Protectorate Regime

Internal strife and international intrigue marked Colombia's first years of independence as the Republic of New Granada, then the Republic of Colombia, and then Gran Colombia. In 1830, the country fragmented into three nations: Colombia, Venezuela, and Ecuador. From the time of recognition and appointment of its first agents in Gran Colombia, American diplomats meddled intrusively and incompetently in the nation's internal affairs. Among the worst of these meddlers was William Henry Harrison, renowned Indian fighter and senator from Ohio (1824–28) — and later president of the United States in 1841. Simón Bolívar's supporters claimed, correctly, that Harrison had involved himself in insurrectionary conspiracies against the Liberator. With Harrison's departure, Bolívar's death (1830), and dissolution of Gran Colombia, U.S. relations with Colombia for the next decade increasingly focused on commerce and the possibility of an isthmian railroad and canal — always in the context of British-American rivalry in the region.

In 1842, the American minister in Bogotá claimed that the British had been approached with a plan to make the province [of Panama] an independent state "and placed under the protection of England, France and the United States, with Treaty stipulations, calculated to avoid all jealousies."[57] Toward the end of his mission, American chargé William Blackford continued to report about the "insidious efforts of the British Government to wrest from the Republic of New Granada the Territory in question."[58]

Benjamin Bidlack replaced Blackford in early December 1845, just before President Polk formally approved annexation of Texas. Bidlack wished to negotiate a treaty with Colombia assuring the establishment of American rights in trans-isthmian routes for roads, rails, or a canal and warding off European private concessionaires and government initiatives in any isthmian designs. He also sought more favorable treatment for American merchants, who faced discrimination in relation to British commerce under the existing Colombian tariff regulations. In November 1846, Bidlack wrote to the secretary of state and future president James Buchanan: "Sir: I am anxiously awaiting authority and instructions to make a Treaty with this government abolishing the differential duties which are now charged against us. . . . I think it proper allso [sic] to observe from various causes which I will not now stop to mention [that] I consider it important that a Treaty should *imediately* [sic] be made with New Granada securing to the Government of the United States *the right of way across the Isthmus of Panama*. I think I have prepared the way for such a treaty."[59]

It was not only Bidlack's efforts that prepared the way. British and French military interventions in the Rio de la Plata region (1837–38, 1843–51) caused concern throughout South America. Fears in the Andes regarding the expedition by Juan José Flores (ex-president of Ecuador and lieutenant of Bolívar in the independence wars), which was ostensibly being prepared in England with the intent to invade Ecuador and establish a monarchy, and aggressive British commercial intrusions conspired to convince the Colombians that a treaty with the United States might be desirable.

Despite the hoopla, England prevented the Flores expedition from sailing for the Western Hemisphere. Nevertheless, the U.S. minister to Ecuador, Van Brugh Livingston, was instructed to say that "the intervention or dictation, direct or indirect, of European Governments in the affairs of the Independent States of the American Hemisphere will never be viewed with indifference by the government of the United States. On the contrary, all the *moral* means, at least, within their power, shall upon every occasion be employed to discourage and arrest such interference."[60] Such instructions followed within the lines of the Monroe Doctrine's original formulation: no further colonization and no transfer of the European system (monarchy) to the Western Hemisphere. But the United States had usually limited such warnings to territory north of Colombia and had done nothing of consequence to contest British or French military intervention in South America.

By the mid-1840s, however, American territorial pretensions, geostrategic concerns, and military capabilities had greatly expanded, giving the Monroe

Doctrine a much enlarged significance. Polk told the country that annexation of Texas and war with Mexico were consistent with the Monroe Doctrine, as were taking the Oregon Territory from the British and even creation of a protectorate regime in Colombia — an entangling alliance that might lead to war with England or France. It seemed that the Monroe Doctrine was as elastic in foreign policy as the "necessary and proper clause" of the U.S. Constitution had been for domestic politics since it was first invoked by Alexander Hamilton to justify creation of the First Bank of the United States, chartered for twenty years in 1791.[61]

Colombian minister of foreign affairs Manuel María Mallarino wrote in a secret and confidential report in December 1846:

> The conduct observed by Great Britain in various parts of the South American Continent — especially in the Argentine Republic (where that power pretends the right of extraterritoriality for her flag in the lengthy course of the mighty rivers of that country) — upon the Orinoco, in Eastern Venezuela — and in the Mosquito Shore on the Isthmus [threatens that] . . . the Empire of the American seas, in its strictly useful or mercantile sense, would fall into the hands of the only nation that the United States can consider as a badly disposed rival. . . . This dominion or ascendancy would be equally ruinous for the commerce of the United States and for the nationality of the Spanish American Republics.[62]

In December 1846, Bidlack sent a draft treaty to Buchanan for the abolition of all differential duties and also for free passage over the Isthmus of Panama for the United States. He advised Buchanan of private negotiations with President Tomás Mosquera in which the Colombian president considered Bidlack as having full powers to negotiate. Thus Bidlack negotiated a commercial treaty, a guarantee of freedom of religious practice for Americans in Colombia, and "the right of transit & free passage over the Isthmus," in exchange for a guarantee of the "integrity and neutrality of the Territory" (that is, the isthmus). He did so without clear instructions and with the recognition that in the U.S. Senate there would likely be objections to what amounted to a defensive alliance with Colombia, a sea change precedent in American foreign policy, which since the time of Jefferson had been governed by the doctrine of no entangling alliances.[63] Bidlack explained: "I wish neither to *exceede* or *neglect* my duty. . . . I considered it dangerous 'to let the golden moment pass.'" He then added in a postscript, by way of assurance, that "the *guarantee* of possession and neutrality, in the Isthmus . . . does not include the Mosquito Shore [the British protectorate of the Mosquito kingdom]."[64]

President Polk submitted the treaty to the Senate in a message of February 10, 1847, five months after General Zachary Taylor's troops captured Monterrey, Mexico. Opponents of the treaty looked askance at a commitment that would "entangle" the United States and further enhance the authority of a wartime president to commit American armed forces abroad — in this case to guarantee the sovereignty of Colombia over Panama against European rivals. Among other reasons for submitting the treaty to the Senate, Polk argued that it was virtually indispensable to the construction of a railroad or a canal across the isthmus. The war against Mexico and potential incorporation of the southwest and California territories into the nation made the isthmus even more important.

The Colombian Senate ratified the treaty in May 1847. Colombia then sent a special emissary to lobby the U.S. Senate to approve the treaty; he warned the senators regarding British aggressions and plots on the Mosquito Coast. Colombians, for their own reasons, judged American guarantees of sovereignty over Panama a lesser risk than further British and French intrusions in the isthmus. The U.S. Senate gave its advice and consent on June 8, 1848 (29 yeas, 7 nays), despite concern regarding the obligation of the United States to guarantee Colombia's sovereignty over the isthmus.[65] It had waited to ratify the treaty until after the Mexican territorial cession (Treaty of Guadalupe Hidalgo, ratified in March 1848). By ratification of the Bidlack-Mallarino Treaty, Congress created America's first official protectorate.

Uncomfortable with the extent to which the 1846 treaty might impair America's traditional unilateralism, the next secretary of state, John Middleton Clayton (1849–50), attempted to reinterpret its reach: "Hence the obligations which we have incurred give us a right to offer, unasked, such advice to the New Granadian Government in regard to its relations with other powers, as might tend to avert from that Republic a rupture with any nation which might covet the Isthmus of Panama."[66] Rather than a defensive alliance, Clayton wished to return to a narrower interpretation that conveyed to the United States rights to meddle and, if necessary, to intervene, but without the reciprocal obligations to consult with Colombia prior to "guaranteeing" its sovereignty. Clayton wished to convert what seemed to be a guarantee to Colombia into Colombia's formal approval of U.S. unilateral intervention *as judged necessary by the United States.*

In 1850, the Colombian government granted a contract to an American firm for construction of a rail line connecting the Pacific and Atlantic Coasts. Two years later, for the first time, the United States sent troops across the isthmus without consulting the Colombian authorities, claiming that the 1846 treaty implied a right to do so, despite Colombian protests to the contrary. In

1855, William Aspinwall's Panama Railroad Company — according to the *Panama Star and Herald*, the "ultimate triumph of Yankee enterprise" — began operation across the isthmus. By then, thousands of adventurers had transited the isthmus on their way to the California gold rush, which began in 1849. In 1853, with the line less than half completed, it carried more than 32,000 passengers.[67]

The Panama Railroad Company had its own "police" force to enforce law and order in Panama. The commander of this force, Randolph Runnels, earned the nickname *El Verdugo* ("the hangman"), for his penchant for vigilante justice and mass hangings of evildoers. The local *Star and Herald* managed to equate these executions with the Monroe Doctrine and America's civilizing mission: "We rise to say that if the work of Mr. Runnels is allowed to continue, and bear its deadly fruit — if we may assay a bit of grim humor — we may soon see the dawn of a new era when the rights of God-fearing, law-abiding, *civilized* citizens will be fully protected according to the principles laid down by the late President Monroe."[68]

Notwithstanding the mass executions and frontier justice it imposed, the Panama Railroad was a success story both for American government policy and for American entrepreneurship. It extended and confirmed the country's manifest destiny. In February 1855, the *New York Mirror* told its readers: "The stupendous enterprise of uniting the two oceans which embrace the greater portion of the globe, we are proud to say, was conceived and executed by our own citizens in the frowning face of obstacles that none but Americans could have overcome. The swamps, the mists, and miasmata of the Isthmus drove all the engineers of Europe home in despair who contemplated the gigantic undertaking and the herculean work was left to the hands and hearts of men in whose vocabulary 'there is no such word as fail.'" The *Aspinwall Courier* added: "To the United States belongs the honor of this work. From its inception to its consummation, it is purely American — American genius conceived the plan; American science pronounced it practicable; American capital has furnished the sinews; and American energy has prosecuted the gigantic enterprise to its completion in spite of the most formidable difficulties."[69] The article neglected to mention the thousands of blacks (West Indians), Native Indians, Chinese, Irish, and Germans who had actually built the line across "hell strip," many losing their lives to tropical disease and construction accidents.

American disdain for Colombians and the rowdiness of some travelers somewhat marred the "honor of this work" of American genius. On April 15, 1856, an altercation between passengers on an American steamer and a fruit vendor in Colón (called Aspinwall by the Americans) escalated into the "water melon war." American hotels and businesses were pillaged and the railway station was attacked. At least fifteen Americans died in the attacks. An official report by Amos B. Corwine in July 1856 concluded that "the dispute relative to the slice of watermelon was seized upon as a pretext by the colored population to assault the Americans and plunder their property . . . but the assault on the railroad station was deliberately planned by the Police and mob." Corwine concluded that "the Government of New Granada is unable to enforce order and afford adequate protection to the transit. . . . I recommend the immediate occupation of the Isthmus, from Ocean to Ocean, by the United States, unless New Granada can satisfy us as to her ability and inclination to afford proper protection and make speedy and ample atonement."[70] To Senator (and former Secretary of War) Jefferson Davis, Corwine wrote the next year that Panama "must sooner or later fall into the hands of the United States. . . . The fruit [was already] ripe — we need only come and take it."[71]

Under legal cover of the 1846 treaty, American forces commanded by Commodore William Mervine occupied the railway station in Panama City in September 1856. As U.S. presidential elections approached in 1856, the Democratic platform called for "timely and efficient control" over the isthmus. During the next months, American diplomats sought reparations for damages from the "water melon war" and guarantees of future security — blaming Panamanian officials for the riots and the failure to punish the guilty. They also demanded that New Granada transfer its rights over the railway to the U.S. government; cede to the United States the islands in Panama Bay for use as naval installations; and make Colón and Panama free ports with "semi-independent" municipal governments. The Granadian government rejected these demands but did eventually agree to make reparations. The U.S. Senate accepted the arrangement in 1860 by approving the Cass-Herrán Treaty.[72]

American naval forces under Commander W. D. Porter would again occupy Panama City for ten days in September and October 1860 in response to an incident in which "six white inhabitants of Panama City were killed and three others wounded" during a local insurrection. Meanwhile, Aspinwall's Pacific Mail Company and the Panama Railroad reaped increasing profits from passengers, freight, and the contract for transporting U.S. mail from Panama to the West Coast of the United States from 1855 to 1859. The U.S. Army also used the railroad to move troops across the isthmus and on to California.

During the U.S. Civil War, Colombia attempted to limit transit of military forces across the Panama isthmus. Secretary of State William Seward contended that "the obligation to protect [in the Treaty] obviously implied the right of unimpeded troop movements, otherwise protection would be impossible." He added that if American rights were not recognized Congress might be asked to authorize the adoption of "other measures to maintain and secure them."[73]

After the Civil War and until the presidency of Theodore Roosevelt, canal schemes framed by the 1846 treaty dominated U.S.-Colombian relations. During his tenure as the U.S. minister to Bogotá (1869–72), General Stephen A. Hurlbut (commander of the Union Army of the Gulf at the end of the Civil War) used resources from the secret service fund to suborn Colombian policymakers and to fill Colombian newspapers with articles favorable to U.S. interests. In the mid-1870s, President Rutherford Hayes stated unequivocally: "It is the right and duty of the United States to assert and maintain such supervision and authority over any interoceanic canal across the Isthmus . . . as will protect our national interests."[74] American presidents continued to order military interventions in Panama to maintain order, to protect American lives and property, and to discourage Colombian taxes on American transit, shipping, and commercial enterprises.[75]

Finally, in 1903, to protect the "neutrality" of the future canal route, the United States impeded troops sent by the Bogotá government to put down the last Panama rebellion — effectively ending Colombian sovereignty over the isthmus, in direct contravention to the 1846 treaty. Not until 1914 would a canal open, permitting naval vessels and commercial ships to transit between the Pacific and the Atlantic. For more than seventy years after its nominal independence, Panama would be an American protectorate, as specified in the Republic's American-approved constitution and the Hay-Bunau-Varilla Treaty (1903). Thus the first U.S. treaty protectorate regime resulted eventually in U.S. control and occupation of Panama for most of the twentieth century.

The Caribbean, Central America, and the Isthmian Canal Routes

With the acquisition of Texas, California, and the Oregon Territory and with expanding American Pacific and Asian trade, transit between the Atlantic and the Pacific took on ever more importance. American filibustering expeditions, some with designs on annexation and addition of slave states to the Union, framed regional policy and complicated Anglo-American rivalries in the Caribbean and Central America.[76] Secession and independence of the Dominican Republic from Haiti in 1844 provided another target of opportunity for the Europeans and the United States in the quest for commerce and naval stations. Great Britain, France, the Netherlands, Denmark, and Sweden all retained possessions in the Caribbean. Britain had important settlements and bases in Jamaica and Barbados and outposts in Belize, Campeche, and the Mosquito (Nicaragua/Honduras) Coast.

In the Caribbean, British efforts to enforce the ban on slave trading sometimes brought the detention and seizure of American-owned ships. British antislavery politics aggravated sectional tensions in the United States, which were based in the fear that England would acquire Cuba and Puerto Rico and then declare slavery's abolition. Beyond the specter of British-inspired slave insurrections and the collapse of the southern economy, the most important long-term issue involved potential transit routes across the Central American isthmus wherever they might be established.[77] From the 1820s, schemes for canals, toll roads, steamship connections, and rail lines alternately enthused and disappointed investors, entrepreneurs, engineers, naval officers, and diplomats. The American and British governments sent agents to negotiate deals, diplomats to bribe Central American politicians, and naval forces to protect citizens and involve themselves in local politics.[78]

In the most flamboyant case, American filibusterer William Walker, seeking to create a U.S. slave state in Nicaragua with the collaboration of the American minister to Nicaragua, made himself president of that country (1855), reestablished slavery, and promised to bind the country to the southern states "as if she were one of themselves." President Pierce recognized the Walker government on May 20, 1856.[79] But Walker's schemes crossed too many interests, including those of steamboat entrepreneur Cornelius Vanderbilt, and his filibustering career (four invasions of the isthmus — 1855, 1857, 1858, 1860) ended with execution by a firing squad, after being turned over by the British to local (Honduran) forces.

Colombian poet José María Torres Caicedo, living in Paris, responded to the Walker episode and American filibustering in Cuba and Central America with *Las dos Americas* (The Two Americas), a bitter denunciation of the betrayal by the United States of its own revolutionary past and its aggression against the poet's *América Latina*:

> The Latin American race
> is confronted by the Saxon Race
> Mortal enemy who now threatens
> To destroy its liberty and its banner.[80]

The Walker intervention, along with other filibuster expeditions and repeated American and European interventions in the region, are seen by one school of Latin American scholars as the origin of popularization of the term *América Latina* (Latin America) and for a growing sense of Pan-Latinism (*Latinidad*) in reaction to Anglo-American presumptions of political hegemony and cultural superiority.[81] President Pierce's recognition of the Walker government made the filibuster much more than the story of a "loose cannon." Central American and Mexican nationalism would have anti-Americanism as a basic ingredient in the future.

The nations of Central America and the Caribbean experienced ongoing European and American interventions. In the words of historian David Long, "Perhaps never in U.S. History have naval officers, operating almost on their own, carried on a more aggressive foreign policy than those in Central America during the 1850s."[82] Resistance to such interventions had limited success. The British, Americans, Germans, and to some extent the French, agreed fundamentally on one thing: the Central Americans and other Latin Americans, including the Brazilians, were an untrustworthy, violent, and generally despicable lot who really did not matter much except as they affected great power interests.

Although the Americans sought to convince the British to divest themselves of their settlements and colonies along the Mosquito Coast, in Belize, and on the Bay Islands in Honduras, the British maintained their presence in the Western Hemisphere. They did agree, as Lord Lyons wrote to Palmerston, that it was difficult to make "the Central American Petty Republics to behave reasonably. I cannot help thinking that the local objections raised by those small governments should be put aside at once — at all events that they should weigh now but as the dust in the balance as compared with the consideration of Relations between England and the United States."[83]

Beginning with the 1846 treaty with Colombia and the Treaty of Guadalupe Hidalgo (1848), the United States secured southerly and northerly routes over the isthmus of Tehuantepec and across Central America. The United States stretched its military, commercial, and diplomatic presence well into the heart of the Caribbean. On the eve of the American Civil War, Nicaraguan and Costa Rican reticence to sign an "acceptable" agreement with the United States (the Cass-Yrisarri Treaty) prompted President James Buchanan to remark: "Both Costa Rica and Nicaragua should be made to understand that the American people and government have yielded enough to the weakness of those republics. . . . They will now take care to do justice to themselves."[84]

Secretary of State (1857–60) Lewis Cass, for his part, had already expressed the idea that "it was our duty to require that this important passage [the Central American isthmus] not be interrupted by the civil wars and revolutionary outbreaks which have so frequently occurred in that region."[85] President Buchanan acknowledged in his 1858 message to Congress that the United States had no authority to enter Nicaragua, even to prevent the destruction of transit, but that in a sudden emergency, "he would direct any armed force in the vicinity to march to their relief." He then asked Congress for authority "to employ the land and naval forces of the United States in preventing the transit from being obstructed and in protecting when necessary the lives and property of American citizens travelling theron."[86] Buchanan wished to make Nicaragua a protectorate without a treaty. He lamented in his February 18, 1859, message to Congress that the British and French executive powers had such authority without resort to legislative approval and that the American executive ought to have the same discretion for protecting Americans abroad and defending American interests.

Buchanan seemed determined to oversee any contracts that Nicaragua let with British, French, or other investors and to protect American citizens where "no impartial tribunal can be said to exist, or when the courts have been arbitrarily controlled by the Government, or when a foreign government becomes a party to contracts and not only fails to fulfill them, but capriciously annuls them."[87] In the interim, James B. Clay (D.-Ky.) delivered a lengthy speech in Congress linking the "three questions, which have of late, more than any other connected with foreign affairs, occupied the public attention; they are intimately connected in principle, and full of importance to the destiny of the nation: 1. England, Central America, and the Clayton-Bulwer Treaty. 2. The slave trade and our engagements to Great Britain for its suppression. 3. The acquisition, in any manner, of the Island of Cuba."[88] No doubt existed for Clay that the slavery question, U.S. sectional politics, isthmian politics, Cuba, and Anglo-American relations formed part of a complex intertwined policy dilemma critical to the "destiny of the nation."

Without taking Central Americans into account, the United States and England negotiated a treaty to resolve one part of the Central American contest between the two powers. The U.S. Senate debated alternate versions of a treaty to amend the Clayton-Bulwer agreement of 1850, and the British parried in response to what they considered undesirable American proposals.[89] The British negotiator for Central America, Sir William Gore Ouseley, had instructions to acknowledge Nicaragua's sovereignty over the Mosquito Coast and Honduran sovereignty over the Bay Islands and to negotiate a border settlement with Guatemala for British Honduras (Belize). British and American negotiators, without Central American participation, eventually worked out sticking points regarding bilateral British treaties with the Central American states.

Buchanan had criticized the Clayton-Bulwer Treaty at the time of its signing, claiming that it "altogether reverses the Monroe Doctrine, and establishes it against ourselves rather than European governments."[90] His presidency gave him a chance to undo the mistake. In his final message to Congress, he reported that the "discordant constructions of the Clayton-Bulwer treaty between the two governments, which at different periods of the discussion bore a threatening aspect, have resulted in a final settlement entirely satisfactory to this government."[91]

Characteristically, throughout the negotiations England and the United States viewed the Central Americans dismissively. Only gradually would the British accede to American hegemony in Central America and parts of the Caribbean. The Clayton-Bulwer agreement remained formally in effect until its mutual abrogation by the Hay-Pauncefote Treaty of 1901, which left the matter of an isthmian canal entirely in the hands of the United States — unless some "petty republic" could mount effective resistance.

Buchanan: The Good Neighbor

Debates over further extension of the Colombian treaty protectorate regime to other Latin American nations shaped legislative-executive relations in the realm of hemispheric policy. President Buchanan's communications to Congress regarding Mexico, Central America, and even Paraguay in the late 1850s directly raised constitutional and security issues of great concern. Having served as Polk's secretary of state and sharing the Southern Democrats expansionist dreams, Buchanan faced the constraints imposed by the Republican Party faction opposed to slavery and, if less so, to imperialism — sentiments that framed pre–Civil War partisan conflict. Indeed, for some of the congressional opposition, slavery and imperialism entwined so inextricably that Buchanan's push to expand presidential discretion in foreign policy could not be separated from domestic political issues that threatened the survival of the Union.

Significantly, Buchanan, in his expansionist and interventionist initiatives, still deeply involved Congress in making foreign policy. On more than one occasion, Congress refused authority for presidential use of force where "local authorities do not possess the physical power, even if they possess the will, to protect our citizens." Emblematic was Senator William Seward's rejection of the "preposterous idea, of the President of the United States making hypothetical wars, conditional wars, without any designation of the nation against which war is to be declared; or the time, or place, or manner, or circumstance of the duration of it, the beginnings or the end; and without limiting the number of nations with which war may be waged."[92] Buchanan lamented but did not frontally challenge congressional constraint on executive authority. Nevertheless, his arguments for expanding executive branch discretion to protect American citizens abroad, the country's commercial interests, and national security presaged developments later in the century.

A synthetic rereading of President Buchanan's messages and requests to Congress regarding Latin America reveals a persistent effort to enlist Congress in a regional policy of establishing military protectorates to advance American hegemony and impede further influence in the hemisphere from European powers. Buchanan justified such a regional strategy on realist grounds, but also as "a good neighbor" extending a "helping hand" to neighbors afflicted by incessant internal strife, as reflected in his observations on Mexico:

> [Mexico] is entirely destitute of the power to maintain peace upon her borders or to prevent the incursions of banditti into our territory. In her fate and in her fortune, in her power to establish and maintain a settled government, we have a far deeper interest, socially, commercially, and politically, than any other nation. She is now a wreck upon the ocean, drifting about as she is impelled by different factions. *As a good neighbor*, shall we not extend to her a helping hand to save her? If we do not, it would not be surprising should some other nation undertake the task, and thus force us to interfere at last, under circumstances of increased difficulty, for the maintenance of our established policy.[93]

This first use by an American president of the term "good neighbor" to characterize relations with a Latin American nation justified a request that Congress authorize American military intervention into Mexico to restore order and to protect American property. It also reflected Buchanan's repeated expressions of contempt for Mexicans when he served as Polk's secretary of state and promoted annexation of Texas: "Only thus can we fulfill our high destinies, and run the race of greatness for which we are ordained. . . . The Anglo-Saxon blood could never be subdued by anything that claimed Mexican origin."[94] Mexicans could perhaps be forgiven for not thanking Buchanan, the Good Neighbor, for his "helping hand."

In October 1859, England's minister to Washington, Lord Lyons, had written a private letter to London, reporting that disturbances in Mexico might prompt U.S. intervention: "It seems probable that the President [Buchanan] may apply to Congress for leave to occupy the frontier Provinces; or even that he may take occasion . . . to send Troops, upon his own responsibility, to maintain order in those Provinces. . . . I see no means which we possess of interfering with effect, even if our interest lay that way; and there is nothing which has so bad an effect upon our relations with this Country as making remonstrances which we do not enforce and showing what the Papers civilly call 'impotent discontent and ill-will.'"[95] Apparently the British minister hoped that the Mexican question would not spill over into the negotiations that were ongoing over interpretations of the Clayton-Bulwer Treaty and British bilateral negotiations with Central American nations.

 Buchanan's representative to Mexico negotiated a "Convention" that conferred on the United States a general police power over Mexico, which would allow the United States to treat any attack on Mexico or threats to its domestic tranquility as an attack on itself.[96] The U.S. Senate rejected this proposed treaty by a vote of 27–18 on May 21, 1860.[97] A separate treaty (McLane-Ocampo), in exchange for 4 million dollars, provided permanent transit rights for U.S. military forces across Mexico and the Tehuantepec isthmus and a right to intervene, in case of grave danger, without the consent of Mexico. The Senate also failed to ratify this agreement despite Buchanan's insistence on its importance for U.S. security.[98] In Europe, these treaties were seen as the prelude to American annexation of Mexico.[99]

Buchanan's annual message to Congress in 1859 further illustrated his disposition to establish additional treaty protectorate regimes — this time in Central America. It also raised again the question of loosening congressional reins on executive discretion in deploying American armed forces.

> I deem it to be my duty once more earnestly to recommend to Congress the passage of a law authorizing the President to employ the naval force at his command for the purpose of protecting the lives and property of American citizens passing in transit across the Panama, Nicaragua, and Tehuantepec routes against sudden and lawless outbreaks and depredations. . . . In the progress of a great nation many exigencies must arise imperatively requiring that Congress should authorize the President to act promptly on certain conditions which may or may not afterwards arise.[100]

Seven months earlier, Buchanan had commended the U.S. minister to Nicaragua, General Mirabeau B. Lamar, for his efforts to negotiate a treaty assuring American transit rights across that country. Lamar's successor, Alexander Dimitry, received instructions in August 1859 from Secretary of State Lewis Cass "to impress on the Nicaraguan Government the folly of vain endeavors to convert her local position into the means of preventing the union of two great oceans which are separated by a narrow territory over which she happens to possess jurisdiction."[101] Happened to possess jurisdiction — unless the United States or Great Britain decided otherwise?

The Water Witch: Buchanan on Paraguay
(and the South Atlantic)

At times, Buchanan stretched the Caribbean and Mexican gambits further south. In February 1855, the USS *Water Witch*, a wooden-hulled, sidewheel gunboat, ostensibly engaged in a scientific expedition to determine the navigability of the Paraná River, took fire from a Paraguayan fort, resulting in one dead and three wounded. Paraguay had prohibited foreign warships from navigating the river. Almost four years of inept diplomacy produced no apology or reparations satisfactory to the United States.

In 1858, President Buchanan claimed that the *Water Witch* was not a warship (despite its hostile operations in Paraguayan waters, in defense of American businessmen).[102] He demanded Paraguayan reparations, though the United States had presented no formal claims. To back up these demands, Buchanan asked Congress for authority to deploy naval forces to encourage Paraguay to provide satisfaction.

Debates in Congress included some reservations on giving the president such broad authority. Jacob Collamer, an antislavery Republican from Vermont, seeking to amend the resolution extending such authority to Buchanan, argued that the president had traditionally been regarded as competent to employ force against "savage" people to obtain redress of grievances (for example in Fiji and Greytown), but with Paraguay the United States had diplomatic intercourse. Notwithstanding the senator's objection to gunboat diplomacy and a parallel debate on giving the executive such "unlimited power," both houses of Congress authorized the naval expedition against Paraguay.[103]

Nineteen U.S. warships arrived at Montevideo, Uruguay, and headed upriver toward Rosario, from which two, including the *Water Witch*, continued to Asunción. Within three weeks, Paraguayan president Antonio López extended an apology to the United States, indemnified the family of the slain *Water Witch* crewman and granted the United States a new commercial treaty.[104] Buchanan reported to Congress in 1859: "It affords me much satisfaction to inform you that all our difficulties with the Republic of Paraguay have been satisfactorily adjusted. It happily did not become necessary to employ the force for this purpose which Congress had placed at my command under the joint resolution of 2d June, 1858." For Buchanan, *deploying* the fleet to Paraguay did not constitute *employing* it. Buchanan added that "the appearance of so large a force, fitted out in such a prompt manner, in the far-distant waters of the La Plata, and the admirable conduct of the officers and men employed in it, have had a happy effect in favor of our country throughout all that remote portion of the world."[105]

That the United States would send nineteen ships to menace Paraguay to resolve an unfortunate (four-year-old) incident resulting in one death and three injuries to the crew of a ship engaged in questionable activities in Paraguayan waters sent a clear message: the United States was willing to use military force in all the Western Hemisphere, even for matters that barely affected anything but the country's "honor." The only "happy effect" of the *Water Witch* incident was that, unlike the French and the British (1838–50), the United States had not blockaded the Paraná River nor invaded Argentina, Paraguay, or Uruguay.

Buchanan on Protectorate Regimes and Regional Security

In 1860, the last year of his presidency, Buchanan submitted a treaty with Honduras to the Senate for its advice and consent; the Senate already had under consideration treaty agreements regarding Nicaragua. In calling for ratification, the president provided the legislators a mini-history of recent "progress," starting with the 1846 Bidlack-Mallarino Treaty protectorate regime for Colombia. He reminded the Senate of Britain's regional ambitions and of the *global* implications of U.S. policies toward Central America, including their relevance to commerce and regional stability and to "preventing revolutions."[106] Buchanan's brief to Congress for extending the protectorate regime model from Colombia into Central America vividly illustrates the relationship between U.S. domestic politics and hemispheric policies as the foundation for its grand strategy before the Civil War.[107]

Domestic tranquility depended increasingly on balancing the conflicting versions of manifest destiny and competing interpretations of American federalism with maintenance of the slave regime — and preventing slave rebellions. The No Transfer Policy and the Monroe Doctrine, updated by Polk and his successors, were foreign policy counterparts to the Missouri Compromise and subsequent domestic "compromises" whereby the political elites sought to achieve this illusive balance. Once the Louisiana Purchase, the Floridas, Texas, the Oregon Territory, and the territory wrested from Mexico were incorporated into the Republic, sustaining the Union required increasing political and economic influence in the Western Hemisphere. To achieve its objectives, the United States would negotiate treaties with European colonial powers and with Latin American governments. But America also asserted its "natural" right of self-defense, understood as unilateral deployment of military force, whether to impede further European colonization, to augment its own territory, to protect its overseas citizens, or to defend its "national honor." The quirks of American domestic politics and the country's underlying political culture of exceptionalism "naturally" produced a foreign policy of aggressive unilateralism in the Western Hemisphere.

To the end of the U.S. Civil War, American regional ambitions confronted the reality of continued British and French economic dominance in most of the Western Hemisphere, especially south of Colombia. During the Civil War, Spain briefly recolonized the Dominican Republic and France established a European monarchy in Mexico (1864–67). Moreover, Europeans still controlled Latin American trade and financial markets. Successful foreign policy after the Civil War would depend first on putting the Union back together. It would also depend on developing commercial and financial networks, along with naval doctrine and fleets to permit the United States to consolidate its hold on the Western Hemisphere and to project its growing economic and military power around the world.

To these tasks, presidents Andrew Johnson (1865–69) and Ulysses S. Grant (1869–77) and their successors dedicated themselves after 1865.[108] In the last thirty-five years of the nineteenth century, Latin Americans would rarely have an opportunity to experience or imagine the United States as the Good Neighbor.

Chapter Five

The New Manifest Destiny

The race that gained control of North America must become the dominant
race of the world and its political ideas must prevail in the struggle for life.
— JOHN FISKE, *American Political Ideas*, 1880

The Civil War bloodied the United States and threatened it with dissolution.
It had not, however, cured the country of an inveterate belief in its special
Providence and manifest destiny. Notwithstanding the postwar tribulations
of Reconstruction, racial strife, cyclic economic crises, and labor conflict, the
country's leaders recast and expanded America's regional and global mission
while maintaining unilateralism as its basic foreign policy principle.[1]

On Abraham Lincoln's assassination in April 1865, Vice President Andrew
Johnson (1865–69) assumed the presidency. Johnson had never been a Republican but rather a "Unionist," and he was the only southerner not to leave the
Senate at the outset of the Civil War. In his first annual message to Congress,
he reaffirmed his faith in America's Providential origin and destiny: " 'To form
a more perfect Union,' by an ordinance of the people of the United States,
is the declared purpose of the Constitution. The hand of Divine Providence
was never more plainly visible in the affairs of men than in the framing and
adopting of that instrument. It is, beyond comparison, the greatest event in
American history; and indeed, is it not, of all the events in modern times, the
most pregnant with consequences for every people of the earth?"

Johnson's message dwelt primarily on the task of reconstruction at home,
but he also included glowing reports on American commercial relations as
well as technological and scientific cooperation with the emperors of China,
Russia, and Brazil. He ended his message with a remarkable celebration of
American exceptionalism, especially coming only seven months after General
Robert E. Lee's surrender at Appomattox Courthouse on April 9, 1865, and

Abraham Lincoln's assassination on Good Friday, April 14: "Where, in past history, does a parallel exist to the public happiness which is within the reach of the people of the United States? Where, in any part of the globe, can institutions be found so suited to the habitats, or so entitled to their love as their own free Constitution?"[2]

Blood had been shed over the meaning of American federalism and the abolition of slavery. Johnson emphasized that the Union would be perpetual; but abolition of slavery did not mean full citizenship for freedmen or other people of color. Like many moderate and conservative Republicans, Johnson opposed extending civil rights and the vote to African Americans. (He also opposed granting citizenship to Chinese, Indians, gypsies, mulattos, and "people of African blood" — and found the idea of marriage between blacks and whites "revolting.")[3] He wrote to Missouri governor Thomas C. Fletcher: "This is a country for white men, and by God, as long as I am President, it shall be a government for white men."[4] Johnson's racist conception of America would prevail in domestic politics and permeate foreign policy for most of the next century.[5]

Although Johnson was preoccupied with postwar political challenges, he had been bequeathed immediate difficulties in the Western Hemisphere. During the Civil War, at the request of white and mulatto leadership in Santo Domingo, Spain had recolonized the Dominican Republic. Calculating that the United States would not seek to enforce the Monroe Doctrine in March 1861, Spain made the Dominican Republic's president, Pedro Santana, captain general of the recolonized territory. The Haitian government, fearing the return of slavery to Hispaniola, as existed in Spanish Cuba and Puerto Rico, supported an insurgency in the Dominican Republic. The War of Restoration (1863–65), led by Haitian-born general Ulises Heureaux and General Gregorio Luperón, forced Spain to de-annex its former colony, just one month before General Lee surrendered to General Ulysses S. Grant. The second independence for the Dominican Republic offered both business and military opportunities for the United States. These opportunities would also create political and diplomatic dilemmas for Johnson — and more so for his successor, President Grant, as Secretary of State William Seward eyed the possibility of annexing the Dominican Republic and establishing naval stations in Haiti.

Lincoln also bequeathed Johnson a French-supported European empire in Mexico, headed by Habsburg Archduke Maximilian of Austria. Constrained by Franco-Anglo maneuvering that threatened the Union war effort, Lincoln had objected to the French intrusion in the hemisphere but could not do much more until Union forces overcame the secessionists. To avoid war with the North, France's Louis Napoleon withheld recognition of the Confederacy, as did England, which profited greatly from the American conflict and the wartime decline of the U.S. merchant marine.[6] By late 1863, however, Louis Napoleon told a confidant: "I realize that I have gotten myself into a tight corner . . . [and] the affair has to be liquidated." In June 1865, Maximilian wrote: "It must be said, openly, that our military situation is very bad. The American Civil War has ended and threat of war with the United States looms."[7]

During peace negotiations in February 1865 at the failed Hampton Roads Conference, presidential adviser Francis Blair had suggested to Lincoln that an armistice be forged between the Union and the Confederacy, allowing the two sides to turn their attention to removing the French-supported regime in Mexico. By this arrangement, enforcement of the Monroe Doctrine would ease the Confederate states back into the Union. Despite his adherence to the Monroe Doctrine, Lincoln did not approve of a joint attack on the French, or any sign of recognition of the Confederacy as a separate nation. He insisted that restoration of the Union was the sine qua non for peace.[8]

In 1866, rumors circulated that by a treaty of "military supplementary convention" Austria would send reinforcements to Maximilian in Mexico. President Johnson, via Secretary of State Seward, made it known to the government of Austria that "the despatch of military expeditions by Austria . . . would be regarded with serious concern by the United States."[9] Seward warned that Austria and all other European powers should know that the United States "cannot consent" to European intervention and establishment of European imperial military despotism in the Western Hemisphere. In December 1866, President Johnson announced that "a friendly arrangement was made between the Emperor of France and the President of the United States for the withdrawal from Mexico of the French expeditionary military forces."[10]

To encourage this French decision, the U.S. government deployed to the border an "army of observation" of 50,000 troops commanded by Union war hero General Philip Sheridan.[11] In addition to threatening the French with invasion, the Americans provisioned the Mexican resistance with munitions and other supplies, while financing the insurgents by purchase of Mexican war bonds (with heavy discounts). The French Mexican empire dissolved in June 1867 with Maximilian's execution after capture and "trial" by Juárez's forces. After Juárez returned to the Mexican presidency in July 1867, unsatisfied claims by bondholders, a wave of American investment schemes, and ambitions by some to annex parts of northern Mexico soured relations between the two countries.[12]

Beyond hemispheric issues, Lincoln had left Johnson with a diplomatic conflict with England over British supplies of armaments and ships to the southern insurgents. In particular, the so-called *Alabama* claims were a sensitive issue. A warship built in England, the *Alabama* was delivered to the Confederacy and caused havoc during the war. Radical Republican senator Charles Sumner of Massachusetts initially proposed reparations of 2 billion dollars or cession of Canada to the United States. President Johnson wished to negotiate an amicable settlement on the *Alabama* claims, but his conflict with the Senate on Reconstruction policy impeded Senate ratification of a treaty with the British.

Meanwhile, attacks by the Irish Republican Brotherhood — the Fenians — into Canada from the United States beginning in 1866 further complicated relations with England. The Fenians, many of them Irish and Irish American Civil War veterans calling themselves the Irish Republican Army, attacked British forts and customs posts with pretensions of pressuring British withdrawal from Ireland or even U.S. annexation of Canada.[13] Johnson denied any American involvement but did ask the British to extend clemency to the captured Irish Americans.[14] Some historians have asserted that Johnson met with the Fenian leadership, gave tacit approval for the raids, and then applied American neutrality laws against them as a bargaining chip in negotiations on the *Alabama* claims.[15] Whatever the veracity of this claim, America would not add Canada to its Providential nursery. The Fenian raids had unintended consequences: they encouraged Parliament's approval of the British North America Act, creating the Canada Confederation in 1867, thereby removing any chance for annexation by the United States.[16]

Thus Canada was not available for incorporation into the Union, but Secretary of State Seward had other grand designs for American expansion. He favored annexation of Hawaii and negotiated a treaty with Denmark for purchase of St. Thomas and St. John. The U.S. Navy took Midway Island in the Pacific in 1867, the same year that Seward completed the Alaska purchase from Russia.[17] To Seward's dismay, the House of Representatives adopted a resolution in November 1867 declaring that "in the present financial condition of the country any further purchases of territory are inexpedient, and this House will hold itself under no obligations to vote money to pay for such purchase unless there is greater present necessity for the same than now exists."[18] The Senate failed to approve the treaty with Denmark. With the exception of the Alaska purchase in 1867, Americans and their Congress seemed in no mood for further territorial aggrandizement.[19]

During these years, Congress maintained military occupation of the former Confederate states, partly to protect African Americans and partly to assure Republican control over state and local politics in the South. Over Johnson's objections, Congress enfranchised African American voters and, according to Johnson, subjected the South to "Negro domination," despite that "negroes have shown less capacity for government than any other race of people."[20] Johnson protested that "of all the dangers which our nation has yet encountered none are equal to those which must result from the success of the effort now making to Africanize half of our country."[21] According to the president, secession and the Civil War were less dangerous than "Africanizing" the South.

Disagreements with the Radical Republicans, who gained control of Congress in 1866, over the character of Reconstruction in the South, led eventually to Johnson's impeachment in the House in 1868 — though the impeachment trial itself centered on Johnson's violation of the Tenure of Office Act and the effort to fire his secretary of war, Edwin Stanton.[22] Johnson avoided conviction in the Senate by one vote on May 16, 1868, largely because his successor would have been Benjamin Wade, president of the Senate pro tem and a Radical Republican feared by other factions in the party. As one of his last acts as president, Johnson granted an unconditional amnesty, on Christmas Day 1868, to all Confederates, including high-ranking officers and civilians in the Confederate government.

In his last annual message to Congress, Johnson lamented that "the attempt to place the white population under the domination of persons of color in the South has impaired, if not destroyed, the kindly relations that had previously existed between them." Looking to international relations, Johnson reported that commercial and diplomatic relations around the world had been generally cordial; he dedicated almost three pages of a seventeen-page document to Latin America, including plans for an expedition to survey a canal route in Panama. In the spirit of the new manifest destiny championed by Seward, Johnson complained that "too little has been done by us . . . to attach the communities by which we are surrounded [Santo Domingo, the West Indies] to our own country." Anticipating the debates on American annexation policy into the 1890s, Johnson observed: "Comprehensive national policy would seem to sanction the acquisition and incorporation into our federal Union of the several adjacent continental and insular communities as speedily as it can be done, peacefully and lawfully, and without any violation of national justice, faith or honor. Foreign possession or control of these communities has hitherto hindered the growth and impaired the influence of the United States."[23]

Johnson seemed to refer to parts of Mexico and Cuba — to which James A. Scrymser's International Ocean Telegraph Company had extended a telegraph cable from Florida in 1866.[24] He urged the Senate to approve the annexation treaty negotiated for St. Kitts and St. Thomas and to consider annexation of Santo Domingo. He recommended that Hawaii should be treated like the West Indies. And, in a call to extend the blessings of American institutions and principles to the rest of the world, Johnson told Congress in the same 1868 message that "the conviction is rapidly gaining ground in the American mind that, with the increased facilities for intercommunication between all portions of the earth, the principles of free government, as embraced in our Constitution, if faithfully maintained and carried out, would prove of sufficient strength and breadth to comprehend within their sphere and influence the civilized nations of the world."

The Grant Presidency

Andrew Johnson could not persuade the Democratic Party to nominate him for reelection. Instead, the Democrats chose Horatio Seymour, former governor of New York, who had supported the Kansas-Nebraska Act in 1854 and antiwar draft riots during the war. Seymour had been critical of Lincoln's emancipation proclamation and supported Johnson's views on Reconstruction policies in the South. Republican campaign propaganda portrayed Seymour as a traitor (Macbeth!) with blood on his hands. In turn, the Democratic platform railed against the tyranny (of black voters and federal troops) imposed by the Radical Republicans and promised a "white man's government." The Democrats called for increased disposal of the public lands and, lastly, expressed their gratitude to President Johnson for "resisting the aggressions of Congress against the constitutional rights of the states and the people."[25]

The Republicans chose Civil War hero Ulysses S. Grant as their candidate. The Republican Party platform deplored the death of Abraham Lincoln and expressed its regret "for the accession of Andrew Johnson to the presidency, who has acted treacherously to the people who elected him and the cause he was pledged to support."[26] In a hotly contested election (the popular vote gave Grant 52.7 percent and Seymour 47.3 percent), Grant's victory came in the first election after the 1867 Military Reconstruction Act that enfranchised African American males in ten former Confederate states (but not in the North). About 450,000 blacks voted in ex-Confederate states in the 1868 presidential election; Grant's margin over Seymour was approximately 300,000 votes.

On taking office, Grant immediately addressed issues of Reconstruction, the public debt, taxes, and tariffs. Looking to the Western Hemisphere, he reaffirmed the No Transfer Principle and asked the Senate to approve annexation of Santo Domingo. He also raised the specter of European occupation of Samaná Bay if the United States refused to act ("I have information, which I believe reliable, that a European power stands ready now to offer two millions of dollars for the possession of Samaná Bay alone. If refused by us, with what grace can we prevent a foreign power from attempting to secure the prize?").

Lady *******. *Time* midnight. *Scene*, New York City Hall: "Out, damned spot! Out, I say! . . . Here's the smell of the blood still: all the perfumes of Democracy will not sweeten this little hand. Oh! oh! oh!" Cartoon by Thomas Nast, published in *Harper's Weekly*, September 5, 1868. Horatio Seymour, the Democratic presidential nominee, as Shakespeare's Lady Macbeth cannot wash the blood of his crime—support of the Civil War draft rioters—off his hands. In 1863, Seymour, then governor of New York, addressed the New York City draft rioters as "My friends" and voiced his opposition to the draft. Thomas Nast continually reminded his audience of Seymour's purported complicity in that violent and, in the cartoonist's view, disloyal event. It was also standard for Nast to draw Seymour's curly hair to resemble Satan's horns. (Provided courtesy HarpWeek, LLC)

Opponents in Congress questioned Grant's claims. To convince the Senate on the Dominican annexation, Grant made an appeal to national security and to almost every political constituency imaginable from canal promoters and farmers in search of markets to global abolitionists. He also resorted to the Monroe Doctrine ploy:

> The acquisition of San Domingo is an adherence to the Monroe doctrine; it is a measure of national protection; it is asserting our just claim to a controlling influence over the great commercial traffic soon to flow from east to west by the way of Isthmus of Darien; it is to build up our merchant marine; it is to furnish new markets for the products of our farms, shops, and manufactories; it is to make slavery insupportable in Cuba and Porto Rico at once, and ultimately in Brazil; it is to settle the unhappy condition of Cuba and end an exterminating conflict; it is to provide honest means of paying our honest debts without overtaxing the people; it is to furnish our citizens with the necessaries of life at cheaper rates than ever before; and it is, in fine, a rapid stride toward that greatness which the intelligence, industry, and enterprise of the citizens of the United States entitle this country to assume among nations.[27]

Secretary of State Hamilton Fish went further, melding the No Transfer Policy and the Monroe Doctrine into a most revealing reaffirmation of the American sense of superiority and the hope for a time when European influence in *its* neighborhood would be erased:

> It will not be presumptuous . . . to say . . . that, the United States by the priority of their independence, by the stability of their institutions, by the regard of their people for the forms of law, by their resources as a government, by their naval power, by their commercial enterprise, by the attractions they offer to European immigration, by the prodigious internal development of their resources and wealth, and by the intellectual life of their population, occupy of necessity a prominent position on this continent which they neither can nor should abdicate, which entitles them to a leading voice, and which imposes on them duties of right and honor regarding American questions, whether those questions affect emancipated colonies or colonies still subject to European dominion.[28]

Fish confronted a panoply of pressing issues: tensions with Spain regarding insurrection in Cuba and American filibusters supporting the rebels; ongoing negotiations with England on the *Alabama* claims; discussions with England,

France, Prussia, and other European powers regarding possible "good offices" and other matters related to the Franco-Prussian War (1870–71); negotiations with Spain, again, in the *Virginius* matter (see chapter 3); and then diplomacy with European powers for enforcing claims against China after riots in Tientsin (June 21, 1870). Although Fish reaffirmed American neutrality in European wars and balance of power conflicts, his policies demonstrated the extent to which American concerns for the Western Hemisphere were enmeshed in webs of global foreign policy to which America brought a conviction of its new manifest destiny.[29]

Grant and Fish saw the Santo Domingo annexation scheme as part of grand strategy. The country needed coaling stations; it needed to defend the Central American isthmian transit routes, for the moment railroads and roads but possibly an interoceanic canal. Yet, once the Santo Domingo annexation treaty had been rejected by the Senate in 1870, Latin America figured little as a topic in domestic political discussion, with the exceptions of Cuba, Mexico, and the Central American isthmus. Congress even reduced budgets for American diplomatic representation in other parts of Latin America.[30]

Grant refused to recognize belligerent status for the Cuban rebels (he had no love for secessionists). Secretary of State Fish saw American support for Cuban insurgents and British support for the Confederacy as analogous; he urged Grant to remain neutral and, unlike Pierce and Buchanan, to restrain filibusters in order to avoid charges of hypocrisy as he sought to resolve the *Alabama* claims with Great Britain. (Unknown at the time, the Cuban rebels had given bonds to the U.S. secretary of war that would have enriched him — but only if the rebels achieved Cuban independence.) To the end of his presidency, Grant wrestled with policy toward Spain and Cuba. He maintained U.S. neutrality despite the divisions within his cabinet and pressure from jingoists in the news media, such as James Gordon Bennett Jr. in the *New York Herald*, Charles Dana in the *New York Sun*, and the wealthy Cuban exile community in New York City, for intervention on behalf of the rebels. In the end, Grant simply reaffirmed that the Monroe Doctrine precluded the transfer of Cuba or other Western Hemisphere territory to a European power. America could still live with a Spanish colony in Cuba and its slave economy.

Domestic politics in the 1870s continued intertwined with regional and global policy. In the early postwar years, a boom in railroad construction, accelerated westward migration, and impressive economic growth accompanied unregulated financial speculation. The bubble burst in 1873, bringing on an economic crisis that endured through the remainder of the Grant administration. With the Panic of 1873, the opposition Democrats gained control of Congress and attacked Grant for massive corruption in the Interior, War, and Navy Departments. Bribes, profiteering on government contracts, tax evasion, and graft undermined the Grant presidency. Grant pardoned key administration personalities and cronies, adding to the evolving tradition of impunity for political wrongdoing and incestuous government-corporate collusion as an integral feature of American politics. But the economic crisis again focused attention on the need for new markets for American products, for an isthmian canal, and for naval stations for a larger navy to protect the country's commerce. More aggressive foreign policy in support of American business, especially in Latin America, was viewed as a salve for America's economic crisis.

Beyond the hemisphere, Grant's foreign policy shared with his predecessors the commitment to protect American "honor" and its citizens abroad. He had promised "to deal with nations as equitable law requires individuals to deal with each other, and I would protect the law-abiding citizen, whether of native or foreign birth, wherever his rights are jeopardized or the flag of our country floats."[31] To make good on this promise, Grant deployed American naval forces in the Pacific, Asia, Mexico, Central America, and south to Uruguay. Notwithstanding the bitterness and violence of Reconstruction, along with the numerous corruption scandals that marred his presidency, Grant's diplomatic initiatives achieved some successes: resolution of the *Alabama* claim against England; agreement on the boundary line between the United States and British possessions from the northwest angle of the Lake of the Woods to the Rocky Mountains; and a commercial reciprocity treaty with Hawaii, prohibiting lease of Hawaiian ports to other powers and making Hawaii a virtual protectorate.[32]

Despite these successes, Grant's last message to Congress in 1876 lamented again the Senate's refusal to annex Santo Domingo. He claimed that Santo Domingo might serve to reduce American imports from Cuba, that great opportunities existed for U.S. capitalists, and that the island would allow for emigration from the United States of "the emancipated race of the South."[33] None of this convinced the Senate or the American public that adding more people of color to the Union was desirable.

Hemispheric Policy after Reconstruction

Grant's term ended with the withdrawal of federal troops from Florida as part of the Compromise of 1877, which brought Republican Rutherford B. Hayes to the presidency, despite having received fewer popular votes than his opponent, Democrat Samuel Tilden. Tilden, a New York Democrat, opposed the Republican Reconstruction policies in the South, and rumors circulated that if he were elected slavery would be restored. Political violence and intimidation were rampant throughout the South before and during the election. When Tilden won a clear popular vote victory, which was challenged by Republicans in several key states (Louisiana, Florida, and South Carolina), some pro-Democrat newspapers headlined "Tilden or War."[34] After formation of an independent electoral commission to decide the disputed returns and several months of negotiations in and out of Congress, Hayes secured the electoral votes necessary to occupy the White House. He then removed the remaining federal troops from Louisiana and South Carolina.[35]

To retain the presidency and its vast network of patronage, the Republican Party abandoned African Americans to the southern "Redeemer Democrats." Hayes appointed William M. Evarts, who had been President Johnson's counsel during the impeachment proceedings, as secretary of state. He filled his cabinet with railroad directors and corporate lawyers. They would make the "right" connections between domestic and foreign policy. A vicious normalcy gradually returned to the South, with disenfranchisement of the freed slaves and people of color, as well as the beginning of what would become in the 1890s the segregationist Jim Crow regime, which would endure into the 1960s.[36] And while the federal army would no longer protect African Americans in the South, it would finish the conquest of Indian peoples in the West and it would be repeatedly deployed to repress striking workers, beginning with the Great Railroad Strike of 1877.[37]

The depression of the 1870s commenced with the failure of the Jay Cooke and Company banking firm. The Cooke firm had engaged in egregious financial speculation and had overextended itself in railway loans. The railroads were the largest business in the country and were directly connected to local and state political machines. They had been the beneficiaries of generous federal subsidies and land grants and were up to their gills in political corruption. With the massive economic depression and unemployment between 1873 and 1877, the railroads became targets of public animosity.

In the months after Hayes came to the White House, railroads announced wage cuts. On July 16, 1877, rail workers struck the Baltimore and Ohio Railroad. The strike quickly spread, virtually suspending rail traffic east of the Mississippi River. It turned into a violent social movement from West Virginia and Maryland to Indiana and west to Illinois and Missouri. When railroad magnates, militias, and local authorities could not control the violence, President Hayes deployed federal army troops to "suppress domestic violence and insurrection," to protect federal property, and to aid federal marshals as a *posse comitatus*. One of the "robber baron" railroad investors, Thomas Scott of the Pennsylvania Railroad, who had helped to broker Hayes's election, reportedly called for the strikers to be given "a rifle diet for a few days and see how they like that kind of bread." According to military historians Clayton D. Laurie and Richard H. Cole, army intervention in the Great Strike of 1877 "established an Army internal defense mission and a firm precedent for future domestic use of regular federal military forces in labor disputes and civil disorders."[38] Boom and bust cycles would follow for the next two decades. With each episode, politicians would tell the country that America's new manifest destiny depended on expanded markets abroad to ward off unemployment and labor violence at home.

A century of social and economic development and the recent civil war had greatly transformed the United States. Western expansion, enhanced connections by canal, better roads, railroads, and telegraph (and in 1876 the first telephone call), surging farm output, industrialization, and urbanization made employment and new markets key domestic political issues that directly connected to foreign policy. European powers had initiated in earnest the era of "new imperialism" in Asia and Africa, with dramatic modernization and expansion of German, French, Dutch, and British naval capabilities.[39] Innovations in transportation, communication, and weapons technology brought America "closer" to other parts of the globe. Proximity meant opportunity but also potential danger. And in much of the Western Hemisphere, no matter the Monroe Doctrine, England dominated commerce and finance. European cultural and economic influence exceeded that of the United States in most of the hemisphere.

As the era of Reconstruction came to an end in 1877, American foreign policy returned, in some ways, to the beginning. It focused on expanding commerce around the world, assuring the rights of neutrals (with flexible enforcement of U.S. neutrality law), pushing the doctrine of "free ships, free goods," protecting American citizens wherever they might be, and worrying about the possible transfer to European rivals of Cuba, Puerto Rico, or territory in Central America.[40] A year after Hayes assumed office, the Spanish in Cuba finally suppressed the insurrection, which had lasted for ten years. For the moment, the Redeemer Democrats did not need to fear the "bad example" of radical black politics in another free Caribbean republic.

Domestic politics and the economic crisis made efforts to increase American influence in Latin America a key issue for policymakers. In his first message to Congress, President Rutherford B. Hayes told legislators: "The long commercial depression in the United States has directed attention to the subject of the possible increase of our foreign trade and the methods for its development, not only with Europe, but with other countries, and especially with the States and sovereignties of the Western Hemisphere. . . . The importance of enlarging our foreign trade, and especially by direct and speedy inter-change with countries on this continent, can not be overestimated."[41] In each of the next three years, Hayes returned to the focus on expansion of foreign trade but otherwise only briefly mentioned relations with Spanish America and Brazil, with the exception of violence on the U.S.-Mexican border and concern for European ventures to build a canal across Panama. Despite the apparently low salience of Latin American policy, Hayes's last message again stressed U.S. obligations (and rights!) under the 1846 treaty with Colombia as part of American custodianship over a "gateway and thoroughfare" for the navies and merchant ships of the world: "It is the right and duty of the United States to assert and maintain such supervision and authority over *any* inter-oceanic canal across the isthmus that connects North and South America as will protect our national interest."[42]

Hayes kept his promise not to seek reelection in 1880. The Republican can-didate, James A. Garfield, defeated the Democrat nominee, Civil War hero Winfield Scott Hancock, by the tiny margin of 2,000 votes but captured 214 of 339 votes in the electoral college. (In 1878, the Democrats had regained con-trol over both houses of Congress, making them hopeful in the presidential contest.) Issues played a minor role in the campaign. The parties were even internally divided on the tariff issue, though Republicans were perceived to be supporters of protectionism and Democrats of a more liberal trade policy. Ultimately, mudslinging and personal attacks dominated the electioneering, which featured a satiric Republican pamphlet called "A Record of the States-manship and Political Achievements of General Winfield Scott Hancock" containing only blank pages.

On assuming the presidency, Garfield named James Blaine as his secre-tary of state. Blaine intended to promote American commerce in the Western Hemisphere and to encourage peaceful relations and stability that would en-courage American exports. To that end, he sought, unsuccessfully, to mediate the ongoing boundary dispute between Mexico and Guatemala over Chiapas; he also involved American diplomats, with little skill and plenty of hubris, in trying to negotiate an end to the War of the Pacific, in which Chile, largely due to its naval supremacy, defeated Bolivia and Peru and incorporated their mineral-rich southern territories as its northern provinces. Blaine attempted to mediate the conflict, but the American "diplomats" he sent to the region, both former Civil War generals, took the sides of the countries to which they had been accredited, bungled negotiations beyond repair, and left Peru, Chile, and Bolivia resentful of American meddling.[43]

Blaine's aspirations to convene a general conference of American states in Washington — a Pan American Conference — also came to naught when his successor, Frederick Frelinghuysen, withdrew invitations to the event at the direction of President Chester Arthur, who had succeeded to the presidency on Garfield's assassination on July 2, 1881. (Garfield lingered until September 19).[44] Meanwhile, Frelinghuysen provided secret correspondence on the diplomatic efforts in the War of the Pacific to Congress. This correspondence was leaked to the press and published in Chile before the American diplomats were apprised, causing further embarrassment.

British newspapers and the partisan U.S. press magnified Blaine's failings. The *New York Herald* accused him of seeking to provoke war with Great Britain and reopen the wounds of the Clayton-Bulwer Treaty debates and of having "bullied Chile under the pretense of friendly mediation, whether in the interests of speculations or not: 'in either case the issue was necessarily war, and war in a bad cause, unnecessary and to us disgraceful.'"[45] However, critics may not have fully appreciated the larger aims of Blaine's efforts. As in the past, American policy in the Western Hemisphere during and after the War of the Pacific was part of a bigger story — competition with British, French, and German interests for control of natural resources, commercial opportunities, and coaling stations at the beginning of what would become a naval armaments race pitting the Americans against the world's foremost naval powers.[46]

American fixation on British and European "intrusions" in the hemisphere mucked up diplomacy with the Spanish American governments. Blaine's initiatives toward Latin America had been a disaster, whether or not the charges of corruption and warmongering and even the desire to annex Peru, or at least lease a coaling station at Chimbote, were entirely true. Yet, like his successors, Blaine's policies toward Latin America linked U.S. internal security, labor peace, and "tranquility" to increased commercial opportunities in the hemisphere. As Blaine put it himself in 1886 (after his third unsuccessful run for president in 1884): "What we want, then, are the markets of these neighbors of ours that lie to the south of us. We want the $400,000,000 annually which to-day go to England, France, Germany and other countries. With these markets secured new life would be given to our manufactories, the product of the Western farmer would be in demand, the reasons for and inducements to strikers, all their attendant evils, would cease."[47]

Blaine saw Latin American markets as part of the answer to the increasing social and political strife in the United States. European Marxists, even before Lenin published *Imperialism: The Highest Stage of Capitalism*, would easily understand the reasoning: American economic aspirations in the hemisphere were a response to the internal contradictions and political tensions of capitalism in the United States just as in Europe. By expanding the territorial and political reach of manifest destiny to include much of the Western Hemisphere and the Pacific, the United States had entered, in its own manner, the wave of the "new imperialism" that characterized European policy from the 1870s onward. American initiatives to modify tariff regimes and to abrogate the Clayton-Bulwer Treaty with Britain were a response to regional dimensions of a global agenda. The "social question," that is the battle of organized labor and rural social movements against capitalists, banks, and industrialists had come to America. In response, American policymakers sought new markets for the country's products and, gradually, new opportunities for its investors. A key feature in this vision was the eventual construction of a canal across the Central American isthmus.

President Chester A. Arthur returned to the issue of the interoceanic canal at length in his first message to Congress. Arthur expressed his concern with any dilution of the American protectorate over Panama or British reaffirmation of their rights in the Clayton-Bulwer Treaty of 1850. Indeed, he looked for the British to accept modification of the treaty in order to bring it into compliance with the Monroe Doctrine and America's interpretation of the 1846 treaty with Colombia.[48] Arthur's bluster on control of the isthmus did not conform with American military capabilities. Despite its economic and commercial growth, the United States remained a relatively weak military power into the 1880s. As France and Germany built modern professional armies and England continued to dominate the seas, the U.S. Army had demobilized after the Civil War, and the U.S. Navy went from over 700 to a bit more than 50 ships — according to the U.S. Navy Historical Center, "a collection of antiquated, obsolescent men-of-war, notable for their quaintness rather than their prowess as warships."[49] Moreover, European military missions penetrated much of Latin America, bringing not only professional and technical expertise but also contracts for European arms industries from the 1870s into the early twentieth century.[50] England dominated the shipping and financial systems in Spanish America and Brazil, and it sold modern warships to South American navies. European manufactures competed favorably with those from the United States throughout most of the region. All this riled American policymakers. During the next two decades, overcoming American vulnerability and expanding its commercial reach in the Western Hemisphere would become an issue in domestic politics and a central focus in the development of the country's strategic doctrine. It would also be the rationale for modernization and expansion of the U.S. Navy.

After Reconstruction, margins of less than 1 percent (along with some backroom skullduggery) typically defined electoral outcomes in presidential elections. Foreign policy debates, including the tariff issue and quests for foreign markets, could play a subtle, even defining, role in campaigns. To rally voters, candidates also created war scares, largely based on supposed threats to U.S. security and economic interests in Latin America. These tactics consolidated a bipartisan consensus on the need for enhanced military budgets. In 1882, President Arthur pushed legislation through Congress authorizing construction of a new steel navy, a benchmark in the emergence of America as a global military power (see chapter 6). Arthur also sought markets for American products and intended to guarantee American control over isthmian transit routes.[51] His policies "fit" the mesh of domestic economic concerns and ascendant imperial ambitions — the new manifest destiny of late nineteenth-century America. Of course, rote appeals to the "spread of civilization" and the "blessings of liberty" continued to spice congressional speeches and presidential messages as the country competed with the Europeans for markets, access to raw materials, strategic ports, coaling stations, and military control over the Central American isthmus and the Caribbean basin.

In failing health, Arthur lost the Republican nomination in 1884 to James Blaine. Blaine then lost the election to the first Democratic president after the Civil War, Grover Cleveland. Blaine's reputation for corruption, aggressive foreign policies, protective tariffs, and intimate relations with big business lost him the election — but only barely.

The Tariff, Trade, and Labor Conflict

In Grover Cleveland's inaugural address, he reaffirmed the U.S. policy of unilateralism (which he called a policy of "independence") in foreign affairs. He claimed that the policy of independence was favored "by our position and defended by our known love of justice and by our power." Cleveland put himself squarely in the tradition of the Founders; he would follow a policy "of neutrality, rejecting any share in foreign broils and ambitions upon other continents and repelling their intrusion here. . . . The policy of Monroe and of Washington and Jefferson — 'Peace, commerce, and honest friendship with all nations; entangling alliance with none.' "[52]

In his first term, Cleveland would slow somewhat the imperial thrust of U.S. policy. Nine days after taking office, he withdrew from Senate consideration treaties with the Dominican Republic, Spain, and Nicaragua, the latter seeking to create a semiprotectorate in order to construct a trans-isthmian canal.[53] He announced early and iterated often his opposition to further protectorate regimes and to acquisition of new territory, even insisting on neutrality (rather than U.S. control) of any canal constructed across the isthmus.[54] He also sought to impede white encroachment on Indian lands, overturning his predecessor's policies, which had opened Indian reservations to white settlement by their illegal reincorporation into the public domain.[55] In all these respects Cleveland was an exception among the late nineteenth-century presidents.

Cleveland opposed further territorial expansion (and would oppose annexation of Hawaii in his second term in 1893). But he would not halt the incipient naval modernization program. As was becoming the rule, military contracts favored partisans of the incumbents: the underlying web of relationships that tied American politics to big donors and political machines — and tied foreign policy to the competition among domestic economic interests — had become established.[56] Corruption, a growing addiction to an incipient military-industrial complex, and antilabor policies were bipartisan fundaments of American politics.

Within this emerging frame for U.S. politics, the tariff issue became emblematic. No reliable studies existed on the effects of whatever tariffs were adopted, leaving policymakers and congressmen with ideological commitments and rhetorical flourishes but without good information on which to base their decisions. Moreover, the beneficiaries of protectionist measures might themselves experience higher prices for imported raw materials and intermediate goods as a result of relatively high tariffs. Of course, with 40 to 50 percent protective barriers, American iron, coal, steel, sugar refineries, and other favored industries (and their labor forces) had consumers trapped.

Many Latin American countries exported goods that competed with, rather than complemented, U.S. exports: beef, hides, lard, wool, wheat, cotton, copper, iron ore. In the decade 1880–89, agriculture still accounted for over 75 percent of all American exports, as it had in 1800. As is true today (2010), American agriculture sought protection behind tariffs to the disadvantage of Latin America.[57] Grover Cleveland attacked protective tariffs: "When we consider that the theory of our institutions guarantees to every citizen the full enjoyment of all the fruits of his industry and enterprise . . . it is plain that the exaction of more than [minimal taxes] is indefensible extortion and a culpable betrayal of American fairness and justice." He also quickly implemented legislation passed in the previous administration that provided for reciprocal elimination of tonnage duties on imports from Central America and the West Indies.[58]

The tariff issue figured prominently in the 1888 presidential election. Cleveland lost the election in the electoral college, although he defeated Benjamin Harrison, the Republican candidate, in the popular vote by some 93,000 votes (49 percent–48 percent). The electoral divide was almost entirely North-South, and whether the tariff debates decided the outcome remains arguable. During the election, Republican congressman and future president William McKinley became the spokesperson for the protectionist side. He proclaimed that "free foreign trade gives our money, our manufactures, and our markets to other nations to the injury of our labor, our tradespeople, and our farmers. Protection keeps money, markets, and manufactures at home for the benefit of our own people."

In 1890, McKinley, as chairman of the House Ways and Means Committee, would shepherd a complicated tariff bill through the Congress. In addition to its protectionist dimension — the highest tariffs in American history — it added, for the first time, discretionary authority for the president to apply punitive charges against nations that refused to extend favorable access to their markets for American products. This provision, which would be eliminated in 1894 but would later again be made part of the executive's discretionary foreign trade arsenal, served immediately to influence American relations with producers of sugar, molasses, coffee, tea, and hides, such as Brazil, Cuba and Puerto Rico (Spain), Jamaica, and the countries of Central America. It even allowed the president to negotiate for elimination of German bans (ostensibly for health concerns) on U.S. pork in exchange for not imposing punitive duties on the German sugar beet producers.

Historian Walter LaFeber concluded that with this protectionist measure some Americans sought to break the colonial ties between Canada and Great Britain and that the Canadians would beg to be annexed. LaFeber also suggests that the tariff precipitated the 1893 Hawaiian revolt (white planters wanted access to the U.S. market through annexation) and provoked disorder in Cuba: "When the 1894 tariff ended reciprocity and removed Cuban sugar's favored access to U.S. markets, the island spun into revolution."[59] LaFeber correctly underscores that U.S. tariff policy, with all its domestic complexities, had serious foreign policy dimensions and often even more serious, if unintended, economic and political consequences for foreign nations and colonies seeking access to U.S. markets.

Democrats campaigned energetically against the McKinley tariff of 1890 and scored sweeping electoral gains. They restored Cleveland to the White House in 1893. Cleveland again proposed a much lower tariff. But the Democratic electoral successes brought to Congress Democrats from industrial districts, who were willing to raise rates to benefit favored constituents and campaign donors. The tariff issue cut across party lines. After byzantine backroom bargains had been struck, the Wilson-Gorman Tariff Act of 1894 lowered overall rates from 50 percent to 42 percent but contained so many concessions to protectionism that Cleveland, symbolically, refused to sign it. It became law without his signature because he lacked support in his own party to sustain a veto.[60]

Tariffs, industrial policy, labor conflict, and military budgets melded foreign affairs to domestic politics. Republicans and Democrats alike collaborated with their industrial, financial, and railroad corporate supporters in repressing labor disputes. In the most emblematic strikes of the era, President Cleveland sent the army against striking railway workers in the 1894 Pullman Strike, just as Hayes had done in 1877 in the Great Strike, Cleveland had done in his first term at Haymarket in 1886 (the origins of Labor Day), and Harrison had done at Carnegie's Homestead Mill in 1892. Democrats and Republicans alike deployed the army against organized labor.[61]

Cleveland's second term coincided with the Panic of 1893, the most severe economic depression suffered by the country to that time, once again making unemployment — and therefore a search for new markets overseas and therefore the tariff issue — hot political topics. The march of "Coxey's Army" on Washington, D.C., and the arrest of its leader, populist businessman Jacob Coxey, revealed the desperation of the working classes in the early 1890s. Coxey called himself the commander of the Commonweal of Christ. Police arrested him for walking on the Capitol's grass (May 1, 1894). President Cleveland refused to meet with Coxey, and though Coxey's speech would not be made at the White House, it was read into the *Congressional Record*. Coxey's program, considered radical at the time, called for government public works programs, particularly roads, to provide jobs to the unemployed.[62] In the weeks between the panic over the Coxey march and the Pullman Strike, which began in May 1894, the *New York Tribune* discovered "an anarchist plot to blow up the capitol."[63]

America needed markets but also protectionism to provide jobs and curtail internal strife. Militarism and its associated "military-industrial complex," in the terminology of President Dwight D. Eisenhower over a half century later, might be part of the solution. The cost would be engagement, interventionism in Latin America, and global competition with the European powers, if not for colonies (with some few exceptions in the Pacific), then for markets, investment opportunities, and control of transportation and communication networks and raw materials. All this would require a massive naval construction program.

In 1896, in the midst of the economic crisis, McKinley campaigned heavily on the tariff issue. Protectionism, he claimed, was necessary to combat the severe depression and to protect American jobs and industry from foreign competition. After an impressive victory at the polls, Republicans ramrodded through Congress the Dingley Tariff of 1897. Rates returned to the 50 percent level. In all this, Latin America was generally an afterthought, if thought about at all, though there were exceptions, especially Spain's Cuban and Puerto Rican colonies (sugar), Central America (the eventual interoceanic canal across the isthmus), and Brazil (coffee, rubber).

What present-day libertarian and leftist critics of the U.S. political system have called "corporate liberalism" was jelling. Corporate liberalism entailed an alliance of big business and the federal government to formulate neo-mercantilist regulation of the economy, including selective protectionism through tariff policy, restriction of competition, and cartelization of the domestic market. Simultaneously, some of the same corporate leaders (in and out of government service) pushed overseas economic expansion.[64]

Perhaps the most revealing snapshot of the political class that dominated foreign policy, especially toward Latin America, in the era of the new manifest destiny is a list of the participants in the First International Conference of American States in 1889. When President Benjamin Harrison brought back James Blaine as secretary of state in 1889, Blaine revived his project for a conference of Latin American diplomats in Washington to push for arbitration of international conflicts, commercial agreements, the possibility of a customs union, an inter-American railroad network, an isthmian canal, and sundry other topics.[65] Despite opposition by outgoing president Cleveland, a joint congressional resolution had called for invitations to be issued to Latin American representatives.

According to the guidelines for the conference, each country could send as many delegates as it desired, but each delegation would have but one vote on any resolutions presented. The Latin Americans states sent one to three delegates each, mostly diplomats. In contrast, the American delegation of ten, among whom only one spoke Spanish passably, consisted almost entirely of industrial magnates and politicians.

The U.S. organizers had assumed that the Latin Americans would speak English, like their diplomats in Washington, but only six of the seventeen Latin American delegates spoke English, and they generally preferred Spanish in the formal sessions as a matter of national and cultural pride. The conference organizers scrambled to find translators and interpreters, some of whom understood how to soften bombast as they translated, while others provided literal renditions of heated debates "without sugar or honey."[66]

From the opening session, it was clear that most of the Latin American delegations, and especially the Argentine and Chilean representatives, resisted Blaine's agenda, a clear effort to control the hemisphere's economies and commerce by Washington, along with a thoroughly unacceptable imposition of a

TABLE 5.1. American Delegates to the First International Conference
of American States, 1889

Andrew Carnegie	Carnegie Steel, largest producer of steel, pig iron, and rails in the world and supplier of armor plate for the New Navy
Cornelius N. Bliss	Textile magnate; chair of New York Republican state committee (1887–88); founder of American Protective Tariff League; treasurer of the Republican National Committee (1892); secretary of the interior under McKinley (1897–99)
Thomas Jefferson Coolidge	Boston financier and banker; directorships of Merchants National Bank of Boston and the New England Trust Company; management of various railroads; U.S. minister to France, 1892
Clement Studebaker	World's largest manufacturer of carriages and wagons; since the late 1850s, the family company had sold wagons to the U.S. Army; after 1897 gradually entered automobile manufacturing
Charles R. Flint	Ship owner, exporter, arms merchant, speculator, only member of the delegation with long-standing interest in Latin America; major exporter to Brazil; business associate of Brazilian minister Salvador de Mendoça (Brazilian delegate to the conference); Chilean consul at New York City, a post he filled from 1876 to 1879, at which time he became consul general to the United States for Nicaragua and Costa Rica
Henry Gassaway Davis	Former U.S. senator (D.-W.Va., 1871–83); lumber, coal, and railroad magnate; by 1892, Davis Coal & Coke was among the largest in the world; also represented the United States at the 1901 Pan American Conference; unsuccessful vice-presidential candidate in 1904
John F. Hanson	Bibb Manufacturing Company, a Georgia textile manufacturer; by 1900, the company owned the largest cotton mill in the country; newspaper owner; a founder of Georgia Tech University
Morris M. Estee	California fruit grower and lawyer; secretary of the state Republican Central Committee (1871–75); state assemblyman representing Sacramento; established vineyards in Napa, California; delegate to the 1888 Republican National Convention; in 1890, appointed to the U.S. District Court in Hawaii; interested in Nicaraguan canal project
John B. Henderson	Former U.S. senator from Missouri; coauthor of Thirteenth Amendment; Washington lawyer; presided over Republican National Convention (1884)
William H. Trescot	Diplomat; counsel for the United States before the Halifax Fishery Commission (1877); commissioner for the revision of the treaty with China (1880); minister to Chile (1881–82); in 1882, with General U.S. Grant, negotiated a commercial treaty with Mexico

quasi-mandatory arbitration scheme to settle regional and bilateral conflicts. Blaine's ideas were contrary to Latin American notions of sovereignty and, in any case, most likely would have been unacceptable to the U.S. Senate had acceptance been achieved.

While the conference was meeting, the Republican-controlled U.S. Congress worked on a new protectionist tariff clearly disadvantageous for most of the Latin American republics. In the end, the first Conference of American States achieved little and reconfirmed many Latin American prejudices regarding American lack of diplomatic skills and respect for their southern neighbors. Latin Americans were also reminded of the idiosyncratic and corrupt operation of the U.S. Congress, the conflicting interests of American businessmen among themselves, and the fragility of American promises. The experience made desperately clear that U.S.–Latin American policy derived from a bizarre mixture of U.S. partisan politics and the U.S. global agenda. That meant, for the countries of the Caribbean basin and Central America especially, that their sovereignty would be hostage to America's ascendant nationalism and its renewed fear of European or Asian threats, which made any eventual canal through the isthmus, in the words of America's most prominent geostrategist, "a strategic centre of vital importance."[67] For the rest of Latin America in 1889–90, the United States presented both an inspiring model of economic and technological progress and a threat to sovereignty and national dignity as the American behemoth sought to control more firmly *its* hemisphere.

Foreign Threats and Imperial Ambitions

After 1877, each presidential administration provided Congress and the country with its version of present and imminent dangers and its interpretation of the No Transfer Principle and the Monroe Doctrine and of how Latin America figured in its regional and global security agenda. Whether the supposed menace came from Great Britain, France, Spain, Germany, or even Chile, policymakers and the partisan media crafted for American public opinion a world of insults, disrespect, and danger emanating from some adversary. Always, it seemed, the United States confronted an enemy — even when domestic critics understood and proclaimed that political corruption, patronage, and an increasingly close relationship between government and business subverted American claims of righteousness.

The Republic ran on "pork," sinecures, scams, and double talk.[68] Perhaps most important, the same cabinet members, legislators, industrialists, railroad bosses, and financial speculators who created trusts and monopolies, which concentrated economic power, controlled tariff policy, and repressed organized labor, also made foreign policy. Small, overlapping groups of influential people controlled both spheres of policymaking. In this sense, "linkage politics" and logrolling took on a very personal meaning in the backrooms of Congress and the salons of the affluent and in private meetings with the president, whether at the White House or on other convenient premises.

The post-Reconstruction administrations, with the exception of Cleveland's first term, renewed and extended the imagined territorial reach of the No Transfer Principle, the Monroe Doctrine, and the country's manifest destiny. Three decades earlier (1842), President John Tyler (in the "Tyler Doctrine") had adapted language from the No Transfer Policy and the Monroe Doctrine to tell Congress that European acquisition of the Hawaiian islands would be inimical to the interests of the United States.[69] Now, twenty-five years after the California gold rush, annexation of Hawaii became a recurrent topic of discussion in Congress. American planters and missionaries had come to control Hawaii's land and business. They hoped for annexation or at least favorable treatment of sugar exports to the U.S. market.[70] Congressman Fernando Wood (D.-N.Y., former Tammany politician and New York mayor), shepherding a reciprocity treaty with Hawaii through the House Ways and Means Committee, took testimony in 1876 from Admiral David D. Porter. Porter told the committee that the British had long had their eyes on Hawaii as "a principal outpost *on our coast* where they could launch forth their ships upon us with perfect impunity."[71] Congressman Wood observed:

> The Pacific Ocean is an American Ocean, destined to hold a far higher place in the future history of the world than the Atlantic. . . . [It is] the future great highway between ourselves and the hundreds of millions of Asiatics who look to us for commerce, civilization, and Christianity. . . . [The Hawaiian islands lie] midway between us and them as the necessary post provided by the Great Ruler of the universe as points of observation, rest, supply, military strategy, and command, to enable each other to unite in protecting both hemispheres from European assault, aggression and avarice.[72]

Of course, transit routes over the Central American isthmus, a maritime canal, and a greatly expanded and modernized navy would be essential to fulfill the "Great Ruler's" plan for the United States.

In the summer of 1879, Ferdinand de Lesseps, the French engineer who had completed the Suez Canal ten years earlier, contracted with the Colombian government to build a canal across Panama. Hamilton Fish's successor as secretary of state, William A. Evarts, concluded that "no contract or negotiations could ever be entered into between private projectors and the Government of Colombia except in contemplation of the position of the United States under the treaty [of 1846]."[73] The United States thus reaffirmed that its protectorate over Colombia must be taken seriously and that Colombia should seek American approval for even a private concession to build a canal across Panama.

As in the past, policy toward Colombia (Panama) was part of a larger grand strategy. With the end of Reconstruction, the United States intended to increase its global presence. In 1878–79, President Hayes had deployed the USS *Ticonderoga* to Africa (Liberia, Congo, Zanzibar) and into the Persian Gulf, then to Aden, which the British were making the "Gibraltar of the East," and then to Muscat, another British protectorate, to Basra (then Turkish), and on to India. Commodore Robert W. Shufeldt sent back to Secretary of State Evarts and Navy Secretary Richard W. Thompson his impressions of the territory visited and its commercial possibilities for the United States, reporting almost everywhere the presence of the British gunboat navy — "the real exponent of British Naval Power on all distant seas."[74] Simultaneous naval operations in China, an expedition up the Amazon by the USS *Enterprise*, deployments off the Pacific coast of South America (during the 1879–84 War of the Pacific, which pitted Chile against Bolivia and Peru), all pointed to a grandiose commercial and strategic vision backed up, so far, with only a small, technically inferior and aging navy.

Events across the world and in the hemisphere highlighted American vulnerability. In July 1882, British naval units bombarded Alexandria, Egypt, destroying coastal fortifications without suffering significant damage from the outmoded Egyptian shore artillery — the sort of artillery that defended the American coast. Descriptions of the British ships and guns provoked deep concern among some U.S. policymakers.[75] With British bases and coaling stations in the Caribbean and Central America, the United States could not defend itself on the seas against the British navy, nor could it enforce the No Transfer Principle or the Monroe Doctrine in a military confrontation. Moreover, according to congressional testimony, when Chile bombarded Peru's port at Callao in 1880 during the War of the Pacific, "her gunboats were armed with breech-firing guns while the shore batteries consisted of smoothbore guns, which proved ineffective. The United States lay behind smoothbore batteries, but every potential foe was equipped with long-range modern guns! Not one American gun could penetrate the armor of the Chilean ironclads. . . . The American Navy [was] an instrument too weak to oppose . . . a minor American state."[76] According to one historian of the U.S. Navy, "There was not a single day of debate on navy bills in the decade of the eighties in which the

Chilean affair was not summoned to support the case for naval expansion."[77] Senator Eugene Hale (R.-Maine) told Congress in 1884: "I confess with a sense of shame . . . there is nothing whatever to prevent Chile or any South American power which has in its possession . . . a second or third-rate ironclad from steaming along the Pacific coast and laying our towns under contribution, and burning and destroying . . . the metropolis of the Pacific coast."[78]

In these debates, legislators and the executive branch used *fear* of the most unlikely foreign threats, as well as some more likely contingencies, to promote expanded military budgets and modernization. Whether Chile, France, Spain, Germany, or — many times over — Great Britain, discursive construction of plausible enemies and journalistic dissemination of these fears persuaded legislators and their constituents that America must become a naval power on a grand scale. Thus Randall Lee Gibson (D.-La.), in the spirit of the "new manifest destiny," told his colleagues in 1888 that the day was "not far distant when the dominion of the United States will be extended to every part of the American continent — British America, Mexico, Cuba, Central America, and the islands on our coast."[79]

Not only concern for control of a future canal and the Caribbean Sea, but defense of the Pacific Coast, Hawaii, and Samoa and commerce to China against German, French, British, and Japanese navies linked Latin American policy to further-reaching issues of foreign policy. In 1878, a treaty with Samoa mimicked the 1846 treaty protectorate regime with Colombia. In exchange for allowing a coaling station at Pago Pago, the U.S. government agreed to "intercede" with third parties in case of disputes.[80] A similar but more complex agreement was signed with the Hawaiian Kingdom in 1884 as a supplement to the 1875 Reciprocity Treaty, conceding to the United States "the exclusive right to enter the harbor of the Pearl River in the Island of Oahu, and to establish and maintain there a coaling and repair station for the use of vessels of the United States, and to that end the United States may improve the entrance to said harbor and do all other things needful to the purpose aforesaid." The U.S. Navy obtained a coaling station at Pearl Harbor and permission to use it as a naval base. Hawaii's sugar planters received duty-free entry into U.S. markets for their sugar. According to historian Kenneth Hagan, "Hawaii attracted the new navalists because the islands seemed ideal as a western sentinel for the proposed Central American canal, which the Harrison administration hoped to build through Nicaragua."[81]

Treaty obligations enhanced executive discretion in foreign affairs and military deployments. In deciding to negotiate treaties, in the instructions given to diplomats, in the meddling in the affairs of other nations entailed by such initiatives, the executive branch could create "conditions on the ground," which required congressional response. Often, by the time Congress received a presidential request for the authorization to take action, consuls, navy officers, businessmen, executive agents, and missionaries had so complicated the American position that legislators faced ugly faits accomplis. Legislators increasingly confronted such moments after the mid-1870s.

As an illustration, President Hayes asked Congress for approval to obtain coaling stations in Central America. When Congress failed to act, the president announced that, under existing authority (the 1846 treaty), the secretary of the navy would establish coal depots on the east side of the isthmus at Chiriqui Lagoon, and also on the Pacific, at the Bay of Golfito.[82] Congressman John Goode (D.-Va.), former member of the Confederate congress, offered an amendment to an appropriation bill in February 1881 to establish naval *stations* (not just coal depots) at the isthmus of Panama for "steamships of war." The amendment passed. Once the naval stations were created, the president could act under his constitutional powers as commander in chief to protect American lives and property, which required no congressional authorization, and to defend American interests by deployment of ships from the navy stations necessary to comply with American obligations and defend rights derived from the 1846 treaty.[83]

Presidents Arthur, Cleveland, and Harrison became bolder in exercising their elastic foreign affairs authority. Harrison even threatened Chile with war, put the navy on a war footing, and sent a war message to Congress over a matter that seemed to involve little more than Chilean police brutality against a crew of carousing U.S. sailors. As historian Henry B. Cox wrote: "Harrison's impatience for war apparently outstripped his eagerness for congressional action. . . . Harrison arguably went further than some of his contemporaries by planning events in a way that preempted Congress's authority to declare peace or war."[84] In this incident, the so-called *Baltimore* affair (the USS *Baltimore* was the ship whose crew was involved in the fracas), Chile eventually caved in entirely, having just emerged in 1891 from a brief but tragic civil war and facing a U.S. Navy much stronger than it had been a decade earlier.[85]

During Chile's civil war, Secretary of State Blaine had initially favored the side of President José Manuel Balmaceda. In 1889, he had named Patrick Egan as U.S. minister to Chile. Egan, a naturalized American citizen, had fled Ireland in 1882 when faced with arrest for his anti-British activities in the Irish independence movement. Egan despised the British, who dominated Chile's nitrate industry.[86] American diplomats and the navy had strict orders to stay neutral in the civil war. But neutrality did not mean Americans particularly respected Chileans on either side of the conflict. The U.S. consul in the port of Talcahuano wrote to Blaine, requesting the protection of an American naval vessel: "We have no guarantee of any kind and I should feel as safe amongst the Hottentots, as here."[87]

The rebels, who claimed to be constitutionalists opposed to Balmaceda's presidential "dictatorship," had purchased arms in the United States. The U.S. Navy seized the *Itata*, a ship carrying arms toward Chile's northern nitrate port of Iquique, which was controlled by Balmaceda's adversaries. This gave the appearance of American support for the Balmaceda government. An American court sided with the owners of the *Itata*, ruling that the seizure had been illegal.[88]

President Harrison treated this issue, and the spin-offs for U.S.-Chilean relations of the recently concluded Chilean civil war, at length in his December 9, 1891, message to Congress. He lamented the decision against the seizure of the *Itata* in the Southern District Court of the United States and threatened that if Chile did not provide proper reparations and demonstrate remorse for the *Baltimore* affair, "I will by a special message bring this matter again to the attention of Congress for such action as may be necessary."[89]

The anti-Balmaceda forces won the civil war, supported by British diplomacy and naval units and also by French prohibition of delivery of warships to the Balmaceda government. The Americans had chosen the wrong side. Egan granted asylum in the American embassy to several leaders of the Balmaceda administration and refused to surrender them to the new Chilean government. Thus the *Baltimore* affair was more than an incident involving drunken sailors in Valparaíso; it encapsulated the poor relations between the United States and the victors in the Chilean civil war. According to the secretary of the British legation in Washington, D.C., Cecil Spring Rice, "The President [Benjamin Harrison] and the Secretary of the Navy [Tracy] wish for war; one to get re-elected, and the other to see his new ships fight and get votes for more."[90] This would not be the last time that an American president invented a foreign "crisis" for electoral purposes or that quests for military appropriations drove public discourse and foreign policy decisions.[91] It was, perhaps, the first time since the *Water Witch* affair that the United States came close to war against a Western Hemisphere nation over an incident of so little moment, though some of those fanning the flames of war demanded that Harrison protect the "dignity and honor of this country, even to the extent of war."[92]

Growing presidential discretion in foreign affairs made presidential personality and temperament ever more crucial in shaping foreign policy. Even when the Senate rejected treaties or annexation of territory, authority to "protect American lives and property" and to "maintain the honor and dignity of the country abroad" meant a great deal more with a larger and more powerful

"A Very Mischievous Boy." Cartoon by Herbert Merrill Wilder, published in *Harper's Weekly*, November 14, 1891. The U.S. minister to Chile, Patrick Egan, is depicted inciting "The Chilian [*sic*] War Scare." (Provided courtesy HarpWeek, LLC)

navy deployed throughout the Western Hemisphere and around the globe (see chapter 6). Deciding *which* Americans to protect and which interests meshed with the overall pursuit of expanded commerce and investment overseas could depend on which private citizens had access to cabinet officials, party leaders, and the president himself. Invisible networks of politicians and railroad, commercial, banking, and industrial magnates spun further the web among the American federal government, domestic political patronage, and an incipient navy-industrial complex, which would promote militarization of foreign policy.[93] As historian Steven Topik wrote, "The U.S. Navy was becoming more than just a servant of foreign policy and overseas expansion; it was becoming a vested interest in the emerging industrial society."[94]

In the next decades, a "New Navy" would become an ever-more-important element in American foreign policy in search of the country's "manifest destiny, understood in its broadest sense."[95] Increasing economic and military intervention in Latin America would be part of the recipe concocted by naval strategists, nationalists, imperialists, industrialists, and other patriots. As the country entered the 1890s, both political parties reaffirmed the policy of American unilateralism and called for constructing a canal across the Central American isthmus, expanding commerce within the Western Hemisphere and beyond, and increasing naval expenditures to maintain "a navy strong enough for all purposes of national defense, and to properly maintain the honor and dignity of the country abroad."[96] Once created, the New Navy would allow presidents and policymakers to cast aside the relative caution of the early post-Civil War era and to transform the "new manifest destiny" into an era of American imperialism.

Chapter Six

The New Navy

Our interest and our dignity require that our rights should depend upon the will of no other state, but upon our own power to enforce them. — CAPTAIN ALFRED THAYER MAHAN, 1898

In the year of the First International Conference of American States, President Harrison appointed Benjamin F. Tracy as secretary of the navy. Tracy, influenced by Alfred Thayer Mahan, who was working at the newly created (1884) Naval War College, recommended construction of two fleets of battleships, twelve ships for the Atlantic, eight for the Pacific, all of them equal to the best in the world in regard to armor, armaments, structural strength, and speed. He also proposed adding sixty fast cruisers for commercial raiding and coastal defense.[1]

In 1890, Mahan published *The Influence of Sea Power on History, 1660–1783*. This book became an intellectual foundation for a massive naval modernization program and for American imperial expansion. According to Mahan, economic prosperity and national security could not be separated. The key to both was a powerful navy deployed to every region of the planet. Since military and economic power were interdependent, some sort of imperialism, however euphemized, could not be avoided if American destiny "in the broadest sense" was to be fulfilled. Mahan argued that "when a question arises of control over distant regions . . . whether they be crumbling empires, anarchical republics, colonies, isolated military posts, or [small] islands, it must ultimately be decided by naval power." Mahan saw potential threats to America almost everywhere and warned that action must be taken to deter or destroy them. European and Asian rivals would not be constrained by international law — only by American military power. Most notably, Mahan sought to instill *fear* of potential enemies and their capabilities, or even their potential capabilities, into public and congressional debates on naval budgets and doctrine.[2]

Mahan's analysis made control of Central America and the Caribbean the starting point for American grand strategy. He understood the *political* usefulness of updating the No Transfer Policy and the Monroe Doctrine. Mahan told the country: "The precise value of the Monroe doctrine is very loosely understood by most Americans, but the effect of the familiar phrase has been to develop a national sensitiveness, which is a more frequent cause of war than material interests; and over disputes caused by such feelings there will preside none of the calming influence due to the moral authority of international law, with its recognized principles, for the points in dispute will be of policy, of interest, not of conceded right."[3] Mahan believed that, ultimately, the United States would have to defend the Western Hemisphere not only from European competitors but also from "a wave of barbaric invasion" that would come from Asia.

Beginning with the passage of the Naval Act of 1890, Congress bought into most of Mahan's basic premises. To achieve the "manifest destiny of the Republic *in the broadest sense*" required a world-class navy to protect and project American economic and political influence and to gain undisputed hegemony over the Caribbean and Central America. Accepting Mahan's strategic vision on the Western Hemisphere, the Democratic Party platform of 1892 proclaimed that, "for purposes of national defense and the promotion of commerce between the States, we recognize the early construction of the Nicaragua Canal and its protection against foreign control as of great importance to the United States."[4]

Debates over the type and size of navy to deploy and the nature of contingent threats continued during the decade, with Mahan contributing frequently to popular discussion and policy decisions in Congress.[5] He insisted that American prosperity and security required control over the Western Hemisphere and that such control started with naval domination of the Caribbean basin. Both Navy Secretary Tracy and Secretary of State Blaine worked to obtain Caribbean naval bases and coaling stations for the United States. They also sought to promote canal projects across the Central American isthmus. Initial efforts focused on a canal treaty with Nicaragua, on a naval base at Môle St. Nicholas in Haiti, and, once again, on Samaná Bay in Santo Domingo.

Each of these initiatives turned into ugly political ventures for President Harrison, involving the United States in Central American and Caribbean civil wars, charges of corruption, and some nasty diplomatic interchanges with England. Historian David Healy's account of these initiatives in his biography of Blaine is material for opera buffa or, alternately, a modern *tele-*

novela spoof, but at the time they reinforced Latin American perceptions of heavy-handed American interventionism.[6] Virtually everywhere they looked, Latin Americans saw U.S. warships off their coasts, in their ports, seeking to influence commercial treaties, menacing their political autonomy, meddling in their bilateral relations with other Latin American nations, and, not infrequently, participating directly, if "unofficially," in deciding the outcome of contests for political power.[7]

In April 1891, the *Baltimore* affair in the port of Valparaíso, involving the second protected cruiser in America's New Navy (commissioned in 1890), threatened war between the United States and Chile. Two years later, Secretary of State Walter Gresham put himself into the boundary dispute between Colombia and Costa Rica (1893–94), provoking resentment from both sides. The American minister to Colombia noted that "there is a good deal of prejudice among a large class of people in Colombia against the United States." He recommended keeping a gunboat close to the Panamanian isthmus "in case of revolution."[8] Then, in 1893–94, the United States deployed a significant portion of its navy to Brazil, ostensibly to protect its merchant ships in Rio de Janeiro but more plausibly to influence the outcome of a civil war and to demonstrate America's new naval power and global reach.

Brazil, 1893–1894

On September 6, 1893, the leaders of Brazil's navy declared themselves "at war" with the incumbent government. The Brazilian navy imposed a blockade in Rio de Janeiro and refused to allow foreign merchants to off-load cargoes.[9] The U.S. government initially proclaimed its neutrality in the conflict, but Secretary of State Gresham labeled the rebels "pirates" and sent warships of the New Navy to break the blockade.

Motivating the U.S. naval operations were fears of secessionist movements in southern Brazil, perhaps encouraged by pan-Germanists' aspirations for closer ties to a growing German immigrant population in Brazil. Also at play were direct requests from American industrialists, bankers, and Standard Oil to protect their interests against British and German competitors and, in principle, the more traditional American concern with protecting neutral shipping.[10] Harrison's successor, Grover Cleveland, reported to Congress on the Brazilian mission and numerous other naval deployments to protect American interests: "There have been revolutions calling for vessels to protect American interests in Nicaragua, Guatemala, Costa Rica, Honduras, Argentina, and Brazil, while the condition of affairs in Honolulu has required the constant presence of one or more ships."[11]

To Guanabara Bay, the United States deployed the most powerful fleet it had ever sent abroad.[12] Historian Steven Topik recounts in detail the operations of the American fleet and also of a parallel mercenary fleet ("Flint's Fleet") organized in the name of the Brazilian government by Charles Flint. Flint, an industrial and shipping magnate with business ties to the Brazilian minister in Washington, had been an American delegate at the first Inter-American Conference in 1889.[13] According to Topik, Admiral Andrew Benham's powerful squadron had been placed in Rio not only to protect American commerce from the insurgents but to impose the will of the United States on the other Great Powers.[14] Benham initiated his own "diplomacy" with the rebel forces, the Brazilian president, and European naval commanders to end the revolt — and may have negotiated the election of Brazil's first civilian president, though the evidence is circumstantial.[15] Topik concluded that "Benham's actions were an important first step in asserting American supremacy over the British in Latin America. . . . After the Admiral's success, he was sent directly to Nicaragua to challenge the British claim to the Misquito Coast."[16]

The Brazilian episode illustrated the collaborative relationship of American financiers, industrialists, mercenaries ("private contractors," in modern parlance), and the New Navy in making and implementing foreign policy. It also demonstrated the connection between intervention in Latin American politics and the broader U.S. global project. As Navy Secretary Hilary Herbert (a Confederate officer in the Civil War and vocal white supremacist) put it, "We must make and keep our Navy in such a condition of efficiency as to give weight and power to whatever policy it may be thought wise on the part of our government to assume."[17] He added, three years later, that the United States required a navy that could "afford unquestionable protection to our citizens in foreign lands, render efficient aid to our diplomacy, and maintain under all circumstances our national honor."[18]

Maintaining national honor under "all circumstances" would require a forward presence on a scale beyond anything imagined before the 1880s. Herbert placed the Brazilian episode in the broader context of the protective and humanitarian role pursued by the U.S. Navy in the world's trouble spots. He explained that it would "have far-reaching and wholesome influence in quite a number of countries where revolutions are so frequent as to almost constantly imperil the rights of American citizens."[19]

The American fleet was still no match for the navies of Great Britain, France, or Germany in an extended conflict, but it did give the American president leverage in formulating and implementing a global strategy. It also provided temptation. As the fleet grew and deployed around the world, what would be the limit of America's manifest destiny "in the broadest sense"? Correlatively, with augmented worldwide naval deployments, the military capabilities and political conflicts of the remotest nations became potential threats to what both Republicans and Democrats called American interests, national dignity, and honor. Would the temptation for U.S. presidents, commercial interests, missionaries, and mercenaries to achieve America's destiny make the New Navy a never-ending pretext for increased military expenditures to meet the inevitable threats occasioned by American intrusion on foreign shores?

Following the Brazilian operation, Assistant Secretary of the Navy William G. McAdoo anticipated "constant upheavals" in the Far East and Latin America. He called for the creation of a large two-ocean battle fleet (instead of the small independent regional squadrons). Naval historian Kenneth Hagan notes that this call by McAdoo, a Democrat, confirmed that Mahan's vision now had extensive bipartisan support.[20]

The Mosquito Coast, 1895

British recognition and protection of the Misquito Kingdom had long been an issue in Anglo–Central American and Anglo-American relations.[21] Britain first created the "Miskito Kingdom" in the late seventeenth century; the British government had notified the Central American republics in 1847 that the "de la mosquitia" coast extended from the Cape of Honduras to the southern bank of the San Juan River, and that the Misquito Kingdom should be recognized as a sovereign nation under the protection of Great Britain. Great Britain sought resolution of ongoing conflict over the area through a treaty with Nicaragua in 1860, which acknowledged Nicaraguan sovereignty. However, in the 1870s, the British efforts to protect the Indian peoples (and maintain a commercial foothold and small port on the isthmus) renewed the diplomatic controversy. Nicaragua agreed to arbitration by the emperor of Austria in 1879, by which the Indian peoples theoretically gained a certain autonomy from the Nicaraguan government. In practice, the British maintained an informal protectorate in the region.

So things stood until 1893–94, when Nicaraguan president José Santos Zelaya attempted to extend control more fully over the Misquito territory, to the displeasure of British and American settlers, lumbermen, and merchants. Nicaraguan claims and (English-speaking) Indian desires for autonomy were the subplot. Since the 1850s, the Misquito Kingdom had been largely a cover for indirect British rule; the local government, called the Bluefields Council, in 1893–94 had only three "Indians" among its sixteen members. British, U.S., and other merchants carried out their business free from regulation or taxation by authorities in Managua. They spoke English and appealed to English law. The American government accused the British of maintaining their presence with the pretext of defending the Indians because the territory commanded control of any eastern end of a potential Nicaraguan canal route.

Some fifty U.S. citizens and the U.S. consul requested that the United States send a warship to protect their lives and property against the Zelaya government. An American ship sent for that purpose sank en route. A British naval unit arrived first, landed marines, and reached an agreement to govern Bluefields with local authorities. Eventually the USS *Marblehead* reached Bluefields and embarked troops, and its commander took control of the very complicated situation involving American investors, British subjects (the majority of them Jamaicans), Nicaraguan political factions, and a diplomatic mess dating from even before 1847. According to the U.S. Navy Historical Center, "On 7 July, in response to dispatches from the American consul, she [the *Marblehead*] put ashore a landing party of marines and bluejackets to keep order and protect American interests. Reinforced by a second party 31 July, this force remained ashore until 7 August. Five days later, *Marblehead* departed Bluefields to continue cruising the Caribbean, showing the flag in Latin American waters until 26 November."[22]

The New Navy had become the arbiter of Nicaraguan politics and relations between England and Nicaragua. In the end, the U.S. minister in London, Thomas Bayard, wrote to Secretary of State Gresham: "His lordship [British Foreign Secretary Lord Kimberly] repeated to me . . . that he had no other wish than to act in accord and with the approval of the United States in matters concerning political control in Central America."[23] Nicaragua gained sovereignty over its Atlantic coast as the United States sought to ease England out of the isthmus and overturn the Clayton-Bulwer Treaty of 1850. As historian Thomas Leonard recounts: "The British withdrew quietly, to the satisfaction of Managua and Washington."[24] The *Marblehead*, a cruiser commissioned in 1894, had been enough to "resolve" over half a century of confused Anglo-American isthmian diplomacy. More important, with this mission, the *Marblehead* reaffirmed the broader *political* significance of the recent victory of the American fleet in Brazil and presaged the ultimate ascent of the New Navy as a principal instrument of an American global grand strategy.

Like the Brazilian operation, the intervention in Nicaragua sent a larger message to Great Britain and the European powers. It demonstrated also that Mahan's strategic vision had taken hold among civilians and navalists alike. An isthmian canal would be the key to a coming struggle for global dominance that "would enable the Atlantic coast to compete with Europe, on equal terms, as to distance, for the markets of eastern Asia" but would also weaken the strategic security of the Pacific coast — making naval expansion ever more a necessity — as would defense of the [still-to-be-constructed] canal itself. Nicaragua mattered as a potential site for a canal across the isthmus, an integral part of Mahan's regional security doctrine, and was crucial in the broader grand strategy.[25] And every "success," like that of the *Marblehead*, demonstrated the necessity of further naval expansion to implement American foreign policy.

The Venezuelan Boundary Dispute and the Olney Corollary

Twisting the British lion's tail for electoral gain and to marshal public opinion in the United States had enjoyed, by 1895, over a century of good use. As Cleveland looked forward to securing his party's nomination for reelection in 1896, faced with congressional hearings on labor conflict and financial crisis, the British bogeyman would now serve to divert attention, temporarily, from domestic woes. It also provided further public support for the New Navy.

British presence in what came to be British Guiana dated from a cession from Spain in an 1814 treaty. Treaty language made boundaries between Venezuela and the British colony vague. Since the early 1840s, Venezuela and Great Britain had failed in various diplomatic efforts to fix an agreeable boundary. In the mid-1880s, the dispute led to temporary suspension of diplomatic relations between the two nations.

In 1893, the British-Venezuelan dispute had again heated up. President Cleveland made it a topic in his message to Congress on December 3, 1894: "The Boundary of British Guiana still remains in dispute between Great Britain and Venezuela. Believing that its early settlement on some just basis alike honorable to both parties in the line of our established policy to remove from this hemisphere all causes of difference with powers beyond the sea, I shall renew the efforts heretofore made to bring about a restoration of diplomatic relations between the disputants and to induce a reference to arbitration." Congress passed a joint resolution on February 22, 1895, calling on Great Britain and Venezuela to subject the dispute to arbitration.

Venezuela had hired William Lindsay Scruggs as a public relations man in the United States. In 1894 he published *British Aggressions in Venezuela, the Monroe Doctrine on Trial* and obtained some success in getting ink in American newspapers across the country. He also caught the ear of congressmen with an anti-British bent. Scruggs had served as U.S. minister to Colombia in 1872 and spent almost twenty years in the diplomatic service, including from 1889 to 1893 as minister to Venezuela. In this last post, he bribed the Venezuelan president to help solve a claim against the government by an American citizen, acting simultaneously as a lawyer and in his official capacity. Secretary of State John Foster removed him: "Such conduct on your part, involving the bribery of the President of the country to which you are accredited, is unworthy of a diplomatic representative of the United States."[26]

Upon his separation from diplomatic service, the Venezuelan government hired Scruggs as a lobbyist. He knew the ropes, had owned a newspaper in his younger days, and could find and get the ear of the legislators. Scruggs found ways to incorporate into his messages Mahan's preaching on the strategic importance of the Caribbean and all the outstanding issues between Great Britain and the United States.

By the time Senate committee members, the cabinet, the president, and the American public had digested Scruggs's message, one thing was clear: the British were up to their old imperial tricks. Now they wanted to control the mouth of the Orinoco River, a major artery leading to the heart of South America. By the title given to Scruggs's book, readers learned that not only Venezuela was at risk, but the Monroe Doctrine was on trial. In April 1895, Great Britain helped Venezuela's case. British ships blockaded the port of Corinto, Nicaragua, and occupied the customs house to force the Zelaya government to pay an indemnity for affronts to the British vice consul and other subjects after the Nicaraguans expelled the Miskito King and his cabinet, who fled to Jamaica.[27] The U.S. secretary of the navy ordered gunboats to Greytown and San Juan del Sur "to protect American lives and property, *following the policy always pursued in such contingencies*," while claiming that the deployments were "not on any business connected with the situation at Corinto."[28]

Neither Cleveland nor Gresham wished to provoke war with England. The U.S. government recognized the right of the British to take reprisals for indignities suffered at the hands of the Central Americans. Deploying the navy was a reminder to the Central Americans and the British of "the policy [now] always followed" in matters affecting American lives and property and also affecting American interests in any future canal across Nicaragua or Panama. So, too, in the Venezuelan case, the American president and secretary of state did not care much about the substance of Venezuela's boundary dispute with the British, notwithstanding Cleveland's more romanticized version of events delivered in lectures at Princeton in 1904 and republished, posthumously, in 1913.[29] What was at stake was consolidation of American hegemony in the hemisphere. Naval presence became the most obvious marker in this strategic design.

In May 1895, Secretary of State Gresham died, to be replaced by the attorney general, Richard Olney. Olney had criticized President Grant for "usurpation" of states' rights during the initial period of Reconstruction. He opposed equal rights and the vote for African Americans. Olney had close ties to the

Morgan banking house; he detested labor organizations, "which threaten the stability of our institutions and the entire organization of society as now constituted." As attorney general during the May 1894 Pullman Strike, Olney had ordered detention and arrest of strikers "by such numbers of deputies or such possee as may be necessary."[30] To defend the corporations and trusts, but not black voters or civil rights, the federal government would use the army and "government by injunction" (against the unions).[31] Olney was the near-perfect face for the new manifest destiny; he epitomized the corrupt, racist, corporate cliques that had come to dominate U.S. politics, control both political parties, and define the country's foreign policies. That he gave his name to a corollary of the Monroe Doctrine that claimed its legitimacy in international law, or at least in the law of "necessity," was an ironic final touch of the Gilded Age.[32]

By June 1895, Cleveland and Olney had agreed on a message to be sent to the British, insisting that the Monroe Doctrine required them to agree to some form of arbitration or to a commission to settle the boundary dispute. On July 25, 1895, Olney sent a message to be delivered in London by the U.S. ambassador. The message, what Cleveland later referred to as Olney's "twenty-inch guns" — a metaphorical reference to the powerful guns of the New Navy — included historical meanderings on the boundary itself, the failed negotiations, and the evolution of the Monroe Doctrine.[33] In the latter regard, Olney claimed that British unwillingness to submit the controversy to arbitration violated the Monroe Doctrine, in effect, because it constituted an expansion of European territorial dominion within the Western Hemisphere. Many of his facts were wrong, and his claims were rubbish. Yet Olney's message is still remembered for its imperious announcement of American hemispheric hegemony as the nineteenth century came to a close: "Today, the United States is practically sovereign on this continent, and its fiat is law upon the subjects to which it confines its interposition."

Olney virtually claimed that the Monroe Doctrine had become international law and threatened that it would be enforced with American naval power. President Cleveland maintained that "the Monroe Doctrine finds it recognition in those principles of international law which are based upon the theory that every nation shall have its rights protected, and its just claims enforced."[34] But if the Monroe Doctrine were merely the "right of self-defense," what did it have to do with a boundary dispute between Venezuela and England over a colony in northern South America?[35]

The British responded with diplomatic formality but also with a certain incredulity. On the Monroe Doctrine itself, Lord Salisbury remarked that "no statesman, however eminent, and no nation, however powerful, are competent to insert into the code of international law a novel principle which was never recognized before, and which has not been since accepted by the governments of any other country."[36] On boundary disputes in the Western Hemisphere, the British responded that "Her Majesty's Government . . . [is] not prepared to admit that the interests of the United States are necessarily concerned in every frontier dispute which may arise between any two States who possess dominion in the Western Hemisphere; and still less can they accept the doctrine that the United States are entitled to claim that the process of arbitration shall be applied to any demand for the surrender of territory which one of those States may make."[37]

In a special message to Congress on December 17, 1895, Cleveland implicitly threatened the British with war if they did not accept arbitration: "While it is a grievous thing to contemplate the two great English-speaking peoples of the world as being otherwise than friendly competitors in the onward march of civilization and strenuous and worthy rivals in all the arts of peace, there is no calamity which a great nation can invite which equals that which follows a supine submission to wrong and injustice and the consequent loss of national self-respect and honor, beneath which are shielded and defended a people's safety and greatness." Cleveland received support from Republican senator Henry Cabot Lodge, who connected the Venezuelan border controversy to broader regional and global concerns: "Let England's motives or feeling be what they may; we are concerned for the interests of the United States. If Great Britain is to be permitted to occupy the ports of Nicaragua and still worse take the territory of Venezuela, [then] France and Germany will do it also. . . . The American people are resolved that the Nicaraguan canal shall be built and absolutely controlled by the United States. The supremacy of the Monroe Doctrine must be established and at once — peaceably if we can, forcibly if we must."[38] Theodore Roosevelt did Lodge one better: "Let the fight come if it must. I don't care if our seacoasts are bombarded or not; we could take Canada."[39]

In the end, the British agreed to arbitration; they received by the settlement almost 90 percent of the territory they had claimed. The British and the Americans allowed the Venezuelans to name only one of five arbiters. When the agreement was reached, "it was published in the Venezuelan press as a 'memorandum,' together with a letter from Cleveland, recommending to the President of Venezuela that the treaty be signed in the form agreed upon by the United States and Great Britain."[40]

For Cleveland and Olney, as for the British, the issue was not Venezuela, its sovereignty, its internal politics, or its future development. The American ambassador in London reminded President Cleveland of the "wholly unreliable character of the Venezuelan rulers and people." For the American government, the fundamental issue was simply British acknowledgment of American hegemony in the Western Hemisphere and to make clear that the United States would intervene, unilaterally, anywhere in the hemisphere, at any time it chose, if it decided its interests might be affected.

With or without a treaty, all of the hemisphere would be a protectorate at American discretion. As one British diplomat put it, thinking of Venezuela but also of Hawaii, "Monroeism cannot tolerate a foreign flag in the Pacific, 2000 miles from the nearest American port; and therefore, so that the bones of Monroe may rest in peace, the American coast-line is to be pushed 2000 miles west. . . . The Monroe Doctrine can be stretched so as to cover everything; and when the Monroe Doctrine is preached, it is a jehad to which all the faithful must give heed."[41] That American policy in the Western Hemisphere and beyond in the late nineteenth century might be viewed as "jehad" from London did not give pause to the American government or public opinion. Nor would the term be remembered more than a century later when jihad was declared against America by other adversaries.

In his final message to Congress, President Cleveland reported that "the Venezuelan boundary question has ceased to be a matter of difference between Great Britain and the United States, their respective Governments having agreed upon the substantial provisions of a treaty between Great Britain and Venezuela submitting the whole controversy to arbitration." But the Anglo-Venezuelan controversy had been a minor issue among the country's more global ambitions. The outgoing president told Congress that American businessmen and missionaries were entitled to protection wherever they went in the world and that the country now had a real navy for such purposes, including deployments in the Mediterranean: "Our Government at home and our minister at Constantinople have left nothing undone to protect our missionaries in Ottoman territory. . . . Several naval vessels are stationed in the Mediterranean as a measure of caution and to furnish all possible relief and refuge in case of emergency. . . . I do not believe that the present somber prospect in Turkey will be long permitted to offend the sight of Christendom." Cleveland did not remember that Monroe's message of 1823 was accompanied by concerns for Christians in Greece at risk of Turkish oppression. Historical memory is sometimes conveniently blurry. As in the first decade of the twenty-first century, in the 1890s the New Navy sought to cover the oceans to protect commerce and U.S. citizens, to deter, if possible, "the rage of mad bigotry and cruel fanaticism" emanating from non-Christian lands that "so mars the humane and enlightened civilization."[42]

Latin America, Grand Strategy and the War with Spain

Reflecting the fundamental role of Latin America in U.S. global policies, both major political parties referred explicitly to the region in their presidential platforms for 1888, connecting it to the need for commercial expansion and naval modernization. In 1892, the Democrats again reminded the country of the need for friendly relations "with our neighbors on the American continent, whose destiny is closely linked with our own. . . . We favor the maintenance of a navy strong enough for all purposes of national defense, and to properly maintain the honor and dignity of the country abroad."[43] The Republican platform did the Democrats one better: "We reaffirm our approval of the Monroe doctrine and believe in the achievement of the manifest destiny of the Republic in its broadest sense." Summing it up on foreign relations, the Republicans were candid: "We favor extension of our foreign commerce, the restoration of our mercantile marine by home-built ships, and the creation of a navy for the protection of our National interests and the honor of the flag."[44] It was not yet clear, however, what the Republicans meant by "manifest destiny in its broadest sense."

By the time the 1896 election rolled around, an insurrection in Cuba gave both parties a chance to expand on their foreign policy visions. The Democrats extended their "sympathy" to the Cuban insurgents and claimed to favor Cuban independence from Spain: "The Monroe doctrine, as originally declared, and as interpreted by succeeding Presidents, is a permanent part of the foreign policy of the United States, and must at all times be maintained. We extend our sympathy to the people of Cuba in their heroic struggle for liberty and independence."[45] But President Cleveland, who had rejected annexation of Hawaii in 1893, also opposed overt support for the Cuban insurgents. For his deviation from the rising tide of American populism, along with his collaboration with J. P. Morgan to save U.S. gold reserves in 1895, he was harpooned in the press. The country was still suffering from the early 1890s economic crisis that had generated a wave of violent strikes, from Carnegie's Homestead Steel plant and Idaho silver miners in 1892 to the Pullman Railroad Strike in 1894. Cleveland's continuing support for the gold standard (instead of free coinage of silver) amid the economic hard times lost him his own divided party's nomination in 1896.

At their convention in Chicago in 1896, a divided Democratic party repudiated the "Gold Democrats" and Cleveland, choosing William Jennings Bryan to replace him as their presidential candidate. Bryan's memorable "cross of gold speech" at the convention set off a nationwide campaign, supported also by the Populist Party, that railed against bankers, big business, and the gold standard: "Having behind us the producing masses of this nation and the world, supported by the commercial interests, the laboring interests and the toilers everywhere, we will answer their demand for a gold standard by saying to them: You shall not press down upon the brow of labor this crown of thorns, you shall not crucify mankind upon a cross of gold." Bryan was against bankers (especially, but not only, British-Jewish bankers) and American empire. Like the Republicans, however, Bryan favored the Cuban insurgents' cause against Spain. His defeat would initiate a succession of Republican presidents until Woodrow Wilson's electoral victory in 1912. And it would inaugurate an era of American imperialism made possible and symbolized by the New Navy.[46]

The Republican candidate, William McKinley, ran on the slogan "Sound Money, Protection, and Prosperity." Republicans called for a foreign policy that would always be "firm, vigorous, and dignified, and all our interests in the western hemisphere should be carefully watched and guarded." They added that "the Hawaiian islands should be controlled by the United States, and no foreign power should be permitted to interfere with them. The Nicaraguan Canal should be built, owned and operated by the United States. And, by the purchase of the Danish islands we should secure a much needed Naval station in the West Indies."[47] Appropriating Mahan's globalism and navalism as the party program, the Republicans proclaimed: "American citizens and American property, must be absolutely protected at all hazards and at any cost. . . . The peace and security of the Republic and the maintenance of its rightful influence among the nations of the earth demand a naval power commensurate with its position and responsibilities. We, therefore, favor the continued enlargement of the navy, and a complete system of harbor and sea-coast defense."[48]

In a nutshell: exclude the Europeans to the extent possible from the Western Hemisphere; consolidate the Caribbean bastion and approaches to a future canal; connect the Atlantic to the Pacific; reach to Hawaii and then to Asia with commerce and the navy; show the flag and protect American commerce and citizens around the world. Mahan's global project for militarizing foreign policy joined to the agendas of domestic corporate magnates, protectionists, and the growing "navy-industrial complex" had been, with slight variations, absorbed into the platforms of both major parties.

Parallel to the diplomacy with England over the Venezuelan boundary dispute, Cleveland and Olney had turned their attention to the insurrection in Cuba against Spain. In part, American tariff policy had precipitated the violence in Cuba. Responding to the 1893 economic crisis, Congress passed the Wilson-Gorman Tariff (1894). The tariff eliminated preferential access of

Cuban sugar to the U.S. market. Spain retaliated by eliminating duty concessions for U.S. products, raising prices for foodstuffs and consumer goods in Cuba. As world sugar and tobacco prices dropped precipitously, Cuba experienced a brutal economic contraction that exacerbated long-standing animosity against Spain and rekindled separatist sentiments.

Failed rebellions in the name of *Cuba Libre* ("Free Cuba") had broken out recurrently since the end of the Ten Years War (1868–78). In February 1895, the call for a "Free Cuba" again resounded across the island. This time, however, according to historian Louis Pérez, "the separatist enterprise was conceived as both a rebellion against Spanish political structures and a revolution against the Cuban social system."[49] In September of the same year, America's New Navy commissioned the battleship *Maine*.

By 1895, the Cuban "social system" significantly implicated American investors, merchants, and landowners. American investments in Cuba exceeded 50 million dollars, annual trade exceeded 100 million dollars, and the United States imported 90 percent of Cuba's sugar.[50] Secretary of State Olney had personal and professional connections to the Morgan banking house, and Edwin Atkins, a millionaire sugar grower in Cuba and a partner in the Morgan octopus, was also a close friend.[51] Olney worried that the Cuban insurgents were neither white enough nor decent enough to merit independence, though he told President Cleveland that they "were not the scum of the earth" and their cause "was just in itself."[52]

In April 1896, three months before the Democratic convention in Chicago, Olney indirectly threatened Spain with U.S. intervention in Cuba: "It is not proposed now to consider whether existing conditions would justify such intervention at the present time, or how much longer those conditions should be endured before such intervention would be justified. That the United States cannot contemplate with complacency another ten years of Cuban insurrection, with all its injurious and distressing incidents, may certainly be taken for granted."[53] That is, Spain could not be permitted by the United States to fail to suppress the insurrection much longer because it negatively affected American interests and had become a hot potato in Congress — with elections upcoming.

Notwithstanding his own repudiation by the Democratic Party and the Republican victory in the November election, Cleveland's last message to Congress (December 18, 1896) reiterated the No Transfer Principle and hinted at future American intervention, which would bring the Cubans "the blessings of peace" — but not independence: "I have deemed it not amiss to remind the Congress that a time may arrive when a correct policy and care for our interests, as well as regard for the interests of other nations . . . will constrain our government to such action as will subserve the interests thus involved, and at the same time promise to Cuba and its inhabitants an opportunity to enjoy the blessings of peace."

Spain proved unable to suppress the insurrection. Elite Cubans, fearful of the social and political consequences of a revolutionary victory, urged President Cleveland — and then his successor in the coming year — to intervene or even to annex the island. As a last gasp effort to retain control of the island, Spain offered the rebels "autonomy" but not independence. The insurrectionists rejected the offer. As it became apparent that the Cuban revolutionaries would be successful (or at least that Spain could not restore order) and that their program included land reform and attacks on racial inequality, American military and political leaders contemplated what action to take to mitigate the risks of a truly independent Cuba.

In late January 1898, President McKinley sent the *Maine* to Havana harbor on a "courtesy visit," reluctantly approved by the Spanish government. On February 15, an explosion destroyed the *Maine* and killed more than 250 of its crew. In the United States, a shrill press demanded retribution for the *Maine*, although Spain denied responsibility for the ship's sinking. Indeed, the Spanish navy had contributed heroically to saving survivors in the hellacious aftermath of the *Maine*'s destruction. Between February and April, the Spanish position in Cuba deteriorated, and victory for the insurgents and Cuban independence seemed imminent.

Despite Spanish protestations of innocence and diplomatic efforts to avoid war with the United States, the tragic loss to the New Navy provided the U.S. government with the pretext for "forcible intervention . . . *as a neutral* to stop the war." Chants of "Remember the *Maine*, to Hell with Spain" were translated into a joint resolution by Congress calling for "the recognition of the independence of the people of Cuba" and demanding "that the Government of Spain relinquish its authority and Government in the island of Cuba." Congress directed the President of the United States "to use the land and naval forces of the United States to carry these resolutions into effect." McKinley signed the joint resolution on April 20, 1898.

Spain rejected Congress's demands. On April 25, 1898, President McKinley recommended to Congress "the adoption of a joint resolution declaring that a state of war exists between the United States of America and the Kingdom of Spain." On the same day, by joint resolution, Congress declared that war existed with Spain "since the 21st day of April, A.D. 1898."

McKinley disavowed any desire to annex Cuba. Anti-annexationists wanted more assurance. To this end, Senator Henry Teller (R.-Colo.) had attached an amendment to the joint resolution whereby Congress authorized American intervention in Cuba.[54] The Teller amendment declared that the United States "hereby disclaims any disposition of intention to exercise sovereignty, jurisdiction, or control over said island except for pacification thereof, and asserts its determination, when that is accomplished, to leave the government and control of the island to its people." The amendment had opponents in the Senate (45 yeas, 35 nays), but once approved it went through the House of Representatives without significant opposition.

McKinley explained to Congress that American intervention would be in accord "with the precepts laid down by the founders of the republic and religiously observed by succeeding administrations to the present day." He claimed that successive insurrections in Cuba over the last half century had "subjected the United States to great effort and expense in enforcing its neutrality laws, caused enormous losses to American trade and commerce, caused irritation, annoyance, and disturbance among our citizens." Most important, McKinley affirmed that "the present condition of affairs in Cuba is a constant menace to our peace, and entails upon this government an enormous expense." Last he proclaimed that "the destruction of the *Maine,* by whatever exterior cause, is a patent and impressive proof of a state of things in Cuba that is intolerable." Intervention, therefore, was essential, but McKinley told Congress: "*I do not think it would be wise or prudent for this government to recognize at the present time the independence of the so-called Cuban Republic.* Such recognition is not necessary in order to enable the United States to intervene and pacify the island."[55] Thus, while the Teller amendment precluded annexation, the declaration of war did not reaffirm the first joint resolution of Congress calling for Cuban independence.

America officially made war on Spain. It also intended to "pacify" the Cuban liberation movement. But the war to pacify Cuba began in Spain's Philippines colony. Commodore George Dewey took the Asiatic Squadron from its station in Hong Kong to Manila Bay and destroyed the Spanish fleet, which had no armored ships, in a single battle on May 1, 1898. Dewey's flag ship, the protected cruiser *Olympia,* had been commissioned, like the Maine, in 1895. It was accompanied by the protected cruisers *Boston* (as the second cruiser of the New Navy it had participated in the Hawaii regime change in 1893), *Raleigh* (commissioned in 1894), and *Baltimore* (commissioned in 1890 and infamous for the incident in Chile in 1891), two gunboats, and two auxiliary vessels. Thus, the New Navy had its first test in war — against an antiquated Spanish squadron whose largest ship was wooden. According to the U.S. Navy Historical Center: "Beginning in 1894 [that is, four years before the War with Spain] the Naval War College examined the possibility of war with Spain over trouble in Cuba. An attack by the U.S. Asiatic Squadron against the Spanish forces in the Philippines first became a part of the Navy's plans in 1896. The objective of the offensive operation was not to conquer all or part of the Spanish colony, but to tie down or divert enemy ships and give the United States a stronger bargaining position at the peace settlement. Nevertheless, the consequences of Dewey's triumph were much different."[56] Dewey became an instant hero in the United States.

Unknown to most Americans, Philippine insurgents had been fighting the Spanish for independence since the early 1890s. As subsequently occurred in Cuba, American occupation of the Philippines would subvert that nation's independence. Six weeks after Dewey's victory in Manila, U.S. forces invaded Santiago de Cuba. The navy quickly destroyed a poorly maintained, outgunned Spanish squadron. A month later, Spain signed a protocol of peace. The United States suffered less than 400 killed in action in Cuba in what Secretary of State John Hay, who helped negotiate the Treaty of Paris ending the war with Spain, would call a "splendid little war." The New Navy had proved itself against a feeble empire in decline. At war's end, Spain relinquished to the United States "all claim of sovereignty over and title to Cuba."[57] In addition, Spain ceded to the United States Puerto Rico, Guam, and the Philippines. Acquisition of Asian and Pacific colonies further justified expansion of the New Navy.

For Cuban liberation fighters, the bitter fruit harvested after years of terrible sacrifice would be American military occupation (1899–1902) and then the fiction of independence under an American protectorate regime. As a condition for ending the military occupation, the U.S. Congress would require that Cubans accept the terms specified in the Platt amendment of 1901: eight ignominious limitations on Cuban sovereignty and a blank check for repeated American intervention.[58] Conditions III, VII, and VIII of the Platt amendment read:

III. That the government of Cuba consents that the United States may exercise the right to intervene for the preservation of Cuban independence, the maintenance of a government adequate for the protection of life, property, and individual liberty, and for discharging the obligations with respect to Cuba imposed by the treaty of Paris on the United States, now to be assumed and undertaken by the government of Cuba....

VII. That to enable the United States to maintain the independence of Cuba, and to protect the people thereof, as well as for its own defense, the government of Cuba will sell or lease to the United States lands necessary for coaling or naval stations at certain specified points to be agreed upon with the President of the United States.

VIII. That by way of further assurance the government of Cuba will
embody the foregoing provisions in a permanent treaty with the
United States.[59]

In imposing the Platt amendment, the requirements of the New Navy had
high priority. Guantánamo Bay would become an important Caribbean base
for carrying out Mahan's global project. The Platt amendment protectorate
regime would remain in effect until 1934, frustrating the hopes for *Cuba Libre*
despite the country's formal independence from Spain.

Imperial America

As America created its New Navy and an imperial America was being born,
Japan defeated China in the Sino-Japanese war (1894–95), ostensibly fought
over control of Korea and Formosa (Taiwan). Japan's victory raised questions
among the European powers of spheres of commercial, political, and religious
influence in China. The United States wished not to be left out of the division
of spoils. Meanwhile, Turkish repression of its Armenian Christian minority
(1894–96) forced European powers to rethink the 1878 Treaty of Berlin, by
which they had guaranteed to "secure Christian subjects their full liberty of
religious worship and belief." By 1896, many of the missionaries in Turkey
were Americans, thus raising the issue of American joint intervention with
European powers to protect the Armenians against Turkish massacres. Editorial
cartoons depicting the "cruel and heathen Turks" reinforced President
Cleveland's last message to Congress that the U.S. Navy had global missions
to perform in the name of Christian Civilization.

Like it or not, the United States was "entangled" — not in foreign alliances
but in global dreams. Those dreams depended for their fulfillment on the
New Navy and consolidation of hegemony in the Western Hemisphere. That
meant excluding German and other European naval bases and coaling stations
in the Caribbean and protecting potential transit routes across Central
America.

German ambitions and occasional probing (as in Guatemala, Venezuela,
Costa Rica, Mexico, and Brazil) provided an obvious potential enemy. Increased
German investment and immigration and the role of German military
missions in South America made plausible the ongoing military planning
to counter European intrusions into the hemisphere.[60] Fueling and servicing
requirements of the world's most advanced warships (until conversion from
coal to oil was introduced just before World War I) made naval stations in the

"Uncle Sam as a Peacemaker": "I've just settled my quarrels at home, and you fellers will find I'm ready to attend to you, if you don't keep quiet." Cartoon published in the *Overland Monthly*, December 1896. Uncle Sam is pointing his finger at Hawaii (where a native woman kneels), Cuba (where a Spanish soldier confronts a kneeling Cuban and a prone Cuban woman), Armenia (where a Turk threatens a kneeling Armenian), and Venezuela (where Britain confronts a Venezuelan). A Japanese ship is coming from the rear. (Courtesy of the University of California Southern Regional Library Facility)

Caribbean necessary to mount a sustained assault on the U.S. East Coast, one scenario considered repeatedly by the Germans and the U.S. General Board of the Navy (created in 1900). According to legal scholar William Kane, "The inevitable conclusion [of U.S. Army and Navy war planning] was that European lodgement — especially German lodgement — would constitute an intolerable alteration of the strategic position of the United States."[61]

Theodore Roosevelt, then assistant secretary of the navy, had neatly summarized this global vision in a letter to Alfred Thayer Mahan, just before the Spanish-American War:

> THIS LETTER MUST, of course, be considered as entirely confidential, because in my position I am merely carrying out the policy of the secretary and the President. I suppose I need not tell you that as regards Hawaii I take your views absolutely, as indeed I do on foreign policy generally. If I had my way we would annex those islands tomorrow. If that is impossible I would establish a protectorate over them.

I believe we should build the Nicaraguan canal at once, and, in the meantime, that we should build a dozen new battleships, half of them on the Pacific Coast; and these battleships should have large coal capacity and a consequent increased radius of action.

I am fully alive to the danger from Japan, and I know that it is idle to rely on any sentimental goodwill toward us. . . . There are big problems in the West Indies also. Until we definitely turn Spain out of those islands (and if I had my way that would be done tomorrow), we will always be menaced by trouble there. We should acquire the Danish Islands and, by turning Spain out, should serve notice that no strong European power, and especially not Germany, should be allowed to gain a foothold by supplanting some weak European power. I do not fear England — Canada is a hostage for her good behavior but I do fear some of the other powers.[62]

Underlying agreement existed among the imperialists and the navalists on the need to defend the Caribbean and expand the New Navy, but differences of opinion existed on strategy and tactics. Mahan, for example, hesitated on annexation of the Philippines. Once taken, the islands would have to be defended, placing a severe burden on the navy if challenged by Japan or Germany. Some of the navalists favored annexation of Cuba; others preferred a protectorate over a nominally independent republic. On the Central American isthmus, some believed that the 1846 treaty with Colombia could be used, along with cash, to control a Panamanian canal. Others, like Roosevelt, had no patience for the Colombians' insistence on treatment as a sovereign country. In any case, for the moment, they preferred a Nicaraguan canal. But Roosevelt did not favor annexation of Nicaragua, Panama, or the Dominican Republic. He shared doubts about their peoples' suitability as citizens and preferred stable protectorate regimes to their acquisition by the United States.[63]

The Hawaii Connection

Fears of German and Japanese pretensions in the Philippines encouraged American annexation after the 1898 war against Spain, despite President McKinley's initial hesitancy. Regarding Hawaii, the Spanish American War somewhat changed domestic and international calculations. The United States had acquired Pacific and Asian colonies. Recent migration of Japanese to the Hawaiian islands supposedly made annexation urgent, despite racial "problems," if control by the white planters and sugar interests were not later to be lost.[64] Hawaii's value lay not only in its naval base but also, according to the

McKinley administration, as a stepping-stone across the Pacific to markets in Asia, especially China. McKinley's secretary of state, John Hay, first sought an "open door" and equal commercial opportunity for the United States in China (while closing off the Philippines market to competitors with tariff barriers). Hay even attempted to export Mahan's Western Hemisphere coaling station and naval base model to China at Samsah Bay but was thwarted by the Japanese, who reminded the Americans of the need to protect Chinese "territorial integrity."[65]

McKinley's policy on Hawaii differed markedly from President Cleveland's opposition to annexation in 1893 when planters under the leadership of Samuel Dole, in collusion with the American minister and naval forces from the USS *Boston*, overturned the government of Queen Liliuokalani. Cleveland's forceful stance against Hawaiian annexation was a rare confession of wrongdoing and contrition by an American president:

> It appears that Hawaii was taken possession of by the United States forces without the consent or wish of the government of the islands, or of anybody else so far as shown, except the United States Minister.
>
> Therefore the military occupation of Honolulu by the United States on the day mentioned was wholly without justification, either as an occupation by consent or as an occupation necessitated by dangers threatening American life and property.
>
> . . . I believe that a candid and thorough examination of the facts will force the conviction that the provisional government owes its existence to an armed invasion by the United States. Fair-minded people with the evidence before them will hardly claim that the Hawaiian Government was overthrown by the people of the islands or that the provisional government had ever existed with their consent.
>
> . . . On that ground the United States can not properly be put in the position of countenancing a wrong after its commission any more than in that of consenting to it in advance. On that ground it can not allow itself to refuse to redress an injury inflicted through an abuse of power by officers clothed with its authority and wearing its uniform; and on the same ground, if a feeble but friendly state is in danger of being robbed of its independence and its sovereignty by a misuse of the name and power of the United States, the United States can not fail to vindicate its honor and its sense of justice by an earnest effort to make all possible reparation.[66]

Cleveland withdrew the annexation treaty from the Senate's consideration, initially disowning the white planter insurgency supported (covertly) by

"The Boxers." Uncle Sam to the obstreperous Boxer: "I occasionally do a little boxing myself." Cartoon by William A. Rogers, published in *Harpers Weekly*, June 9, 1900. President William McKinley and Secretary of State John Hay formulated the Open Door policy (1899), seeking to secure for the United States its "fair share" of the China trade. McKinley sent American ships and soldiers from the Philippines to protect American lives and property during the 1900 Boxer rebellion—without congressional authorization. (Provided courtesy HarpWeek, LLC)

President Harrison. A year later, however, bowing to political pragmatics, Cleveland recognized the provisional government of the "Republic of Hawaii," with Samuel Dole as its president. Rebellions by insurgents seeking to restore the Hawaiian monarchy had failed.

Unlike Cleveland, President McKinley strongly favored Hawaiian annexation. He sent a new treaty to the Senate in 1897, negotiated with a government dominated by a committee of planter annexationists.[67] This shift in policy demonstrated once again the importance of presidential personality and sense of mission and also the influence of key advisers in formulating American foreign policy. No matter the underlying continuities, the particulars at any moment could depend critically on the occupant of the White House. McKinley's policy toward Hawaii recalled previous presidents' tactics with West Florida and Texas — regime change followed by stalking-horse "republics" as a transition to annexation.

The Hawaii episode also illustrates the complex nature of opposition to expansion and empire. Cane growers in Louisiana fearing competition from the Hawaii plantations, organized labor, anti-imperialists, and racists who believed that native Hawaiians (about 30 percent of the population at the time of annexation) were not suited for U.S. citizenship formed a diverse opposition coalition against annexation. Native Hawaiians also opposed the annexation treaty with petitions presented to the Senate and the secretary of state.

With the declaration of war against Spain in April 1898, the obvious strategic importance of Hawaii for the New Navy tipped the balance. Even so, the strength of the opposition to the annexation treaty in the Senate forced McKinley to resort to a joint resolution of Congress to legitimate the annexation (thereby overcoming the need for two-thirds of the Senate required for treaty approval). The House approved the Newlands Resolution annexing Hawaii on June 15, 1898, by a vote of 209–91; the Senate followed suit on July 6 (three days after destruction of the Spanish squadron at Santiago de Cuba), by a vote of 42–21 (with 6 abstentions). McKinley signed the legislation the next day.[68]

Francis G. Newlands (D.-Nev.) had introduced this resolution in the House of Representatives in early May 1898, when it became clear that McKinley could not obtain the necessary two-thirds vote in the Senate to approve the annexation treaty. In August 1898, the Hawaiian Patriotic League delivered a protest to the U.S. secretary of state against the American actions in Hawaii since 1893. The league challenged the legality of annexation by joint resolution rather than treaty.[69] Such protests went for naught. According to the U.S. Department of State official website (2008), after annexation "racial attitudes and party politics in the United States deferred statehood until a bipartisan compromise linked Hawaii's status to Alaska, and both became states in 1959."[70]

The debates on the Hawaii Organic Act of 1900 make clear that the 2008 State Department summary of the racist objections to annexation and to subsequent Hawaii statehood for the next fifty-nine years were incomplete. Newlands and his allies in the Senate wished also to make Hawaii an outlet for immigrants from the mainland by "providing that the people in Hawaii employing labor shall gradually give preference to our people by requiring that at least 10 percent of their employees shall be citizens, adding to this 10 percent each year until all employees are citizens, allowing them to take the colored people from this country to displace the Asiatics if they so desire." Opponents of this amendment to the legislation argued that "the peculiar conditions and kinds of work in that country may demand the employment of the Asiatics, who by the bill are denied the right of citizenship."[71]

Importantly, both sides on the debate over Asian contract labor in the new Hawaii territory agreed on two fundamentals: restrictive citizenship and voting laws to maintain white rule and the need to increase the white population of the islands to impede eventual control by Hawaiians. As Newlands put it: "I take it, the purpose and aim of our legislation is to increase the immigration of free white persons to those islands."[72] Congressman John Sharp Williams (D.-Miss.), who had opposed annexation for the same reason others had opposed annexation of Santo Domingo in 1870, was not convinced by Newlands's policy of gradual "whitening" of the islands: "Does the gentleman imagine that we of the South take any pride in the fact that we have been compelled to restrict suffrage in order to preserve civilization? . . . I stated in the Hawaiian debate that whenever I was faced with that problem that, if I were the only Democrat in the United States to do so, I would stand for white supremacy in Hawaii just as I had stood for it in Mississippi, and I will. . . . I am prepared to say that the very worst thing that can happen to the Hawaiian Islands to-day or to-morrow would be to have Kanaka rule or colored-race rule in Hawaii."[73]

Grand Strategy and Colonialism

Annexation of ports for global deployment of the New Navy in Hawaii, the Philippines, Guam, Wake Island, and Puerto Rico confronted American empire directly with the racist underpinnings of the country's exceptionalism. (The annexation treaty with the Philippines in 1899 barely obtained the required two-thirds: 57–27, with anti-imperialists and Democrats in opposition.) On the one hand, new territories might expect to become states; on the other, the populations of Spain's former colonies and Hawaii were not deemed racially suitable for American citizenship. But whatever the political, military, racial, and cultural dilemmas, the new territories were essential for implementation of the post-1898 grand strategy. In skeletal form, the "large policy" consisted of the following agenda: (1) expanding U.S. markets in Latin America and Asia, including an "open door" (equal access) to China;[74] (2) a system of naval and coaling stations in the Pacific; (3) controlling Cuba and Puerto Rico after expelling Spain from the hemisphere; (4) construction of an American-controlled canal across Central America to link the eastern seaboard with the Pacific; (5) continued expansion and modernization of the navy, with forward presence in Asia, the Mediterranean, the Pacific, and the South Atlantic; (6) gradual expulsion of European influence in the Caribbean, though recognizing that the British would remain in Jamaica and in other West Indian possessions; (7) war plans to counter potential Japanese threats in the Pacific and German threats in Latin America; and (8) defense of the eastern seaboard against German attack (this in response to German war gaming and Kaiser Wilhelm II's volatility).[75] As usual, for some Americans this grand strategy coincided with a higher calling. Attorney-journalist (and later a voice of the Progressive movement in California) Arthur J. Pillsbury proclaimed in the *Overland Monthly and Out West Magazine* shortly after the peace treaty with Spain: "The Measure of American conquests and colonizations will be the measure of American duty to the higher claims of humanity, duties which will arise out of events not of our shaping, but owing their causation to a Power greater than that of nations and which makes for the redemption of the world. . . . Whatever duty, under the Providence of God, is laid upon the shoulders of the American people will be assumed with thanksgiving and discharged with fidelity."[76]

Latin America, especially Mexico, the Caribbean, and the Central American isthmus, were at the core of the expansionists' grand strategy. During the next thirty years, repeated American interventions and military occupations would occur in the Caribbean basin. The treaty protectorate regime first created in Colombia in 1846 would be modified and "improved" to control several of the Central American republics, Santo Domingo, and Haiti. The Platt amendment protectorate regime covered Cuba and provided the navy with Guantánamo, in addition to bases in Puerto Rico. Panama would be taken from Colombia and transformed into a permanent (until 1977) American protectorate.

This sea change in American foreign policy after 1898 created military occupation regimes in Asia and Latin America and, in some cases, American engagement in counterinsurgency operations on a large scale against Native peoples outside the continental United States. American political cartoons, letters home from soldiers, and even congressional debates referred to the Philippine insurgents as "Indians," "dagos," and "niggers": "We have been in this nigger-fighting business now for twenty-three days, and have been under fire for the greater part of that time. . . . The morning of the 6th a burying detail from our regiment buried forty-nine nigger enlisted men and two nigger officers, and when we stopped chasing them the night before, we could see 'em carrying a great many with them" (Frank M. Erb, of the Pennsylvania Regiment).

Not all Americans took pride in the imperial thrust. An Anti-Imperialist League formed to contest the country's entry into the company of the European imperialists. Created in 1898 to oppose annexation of the Philippines, the league finally disbanded in 1921. Likewise, more than a few American soldiers detested the war they had been sent to fight, just as would occur years later in Haiti, the Dominican Republic, Nicaragua, Vietnam, and Iraq: "I deprecate this war, this slaughter of our own boys and of the Filipinos, because it seems to me that we are doing something that is contrary to our principles in the past. Certainly we are doing something that we should have shrunk from not so very long ago" (Sergeant Elliott, of Company G, Kansas).[77] Yet the country, overall, seemed to enjoy its debut as a world military and naval power.

Shortly after the war with Spain, Britain agreed, in the Hay-Pauncefote Treaty of 1901, to nullify the Clayton-Bulwer Treaty (1850) and extend exclusive rights to the United States to build and control a canal across the Central American isthmus. In exchange, the United States would guarantee passage without discrimination to other nations, on the same basis as adopted for the Suez Canal in the Convention of Constantinople (1888).[78] Still, mastery of the Western Hemisphere was not complete. European powers insisted on the right to protect their citizens, enforce debt collection with military interventions, and maintain their own possessions in the hemisphere.

Venezuela and the New Navy

British and German naval attacks on La Guaira and bombardment of a fort at Puerto Cabello in Venezuela in 1902 to collect debts, followed by a blockade in which Italy joined, provoked the usual response from the United States: so long as the Europeans only sought to collect debts but not take territory, the United States would not intercede.[79] The U.S. government even agreed to international arbitration of the *priority* of claims against Venezuela — once the Europeans properly understood that the United States would not brook territorial pretensions or permanent military presence.

Yet appearances could be deceiving. In early October, the *New York Times* reported that a Caribbean division of the North Atlantic Squadron had been created, with Culebra, on the east coast of Puerto Rico, as headquarters. The flagship would be the *Olympia*, Admiral Dewey's flagship at Manila Bay. In accord with Mahan's geostrategic doctrine regarding the importance of the Caribbean, Culebra island would serve as "the rendezvous for the North Atlantic, South Atlantic, Pacific, and European squadrons when they assemble for command manoeuvres under the command of Admiral Dewey."[80]

President Theodore Roosevelt, not sure whether the 1902 Venezuelan episode represented a new German (and British) test of the Monroe Doctrine and suspicious of German desires for Western Hemisphere bases, had approved naval exercises in the Caribbean under Dewey's temporary command. (Both the German and American navies had conducted war games with Caribbean scenarios, including a German plan for taking Puerto Rico and invading the U.S. East Coast.) Dewey still had not forgiven the Germans for their interference in the Philippines in 1898. From its new naval station in the Western Hemisphere bastion, Roosevelt threatened implicitly that Dewey would have a chance to exact revenge. On December 8, Roosevelt warned the German ambassador in private conversation that he would use force if it appeared that the Germans sought acquisition of territory in Venezuela or elsewhere in the Caribbean.[81] The next day the Germans seized four Venezuelan gunboats, destroying three of them. Venezuela's president requested American intercession, proposing arbitration of the dispute with the European creditors.

For the Christmas holidays, Dewey's battleships went to Trinidad, 500 miles closer to Venezuela than the naval station at Culebra. The rest of the fleet dispersed among ports at St. Kitts, St. Thomas, Antigua, and Curaçao.[82] As the crisis continued, the German ambassador in Washington consulted with Secretary of State Hay regarding U.S. intentions. He learned that the Americans, now having deployed battleships, cruisers, and gunboats within quick range of Venezuela and having the gunboat *Marietta* at La Guaira (the harbor for Caracas), preferred arbitration between the Europeans and the Venezuelans but would use the fleet if necessary.[83] Germany and England requested U.S. arbitration of the dispute with Venezuela.[84]

Despite the request for arbitration, German and British pressure on Venezuela continued, as did the naval blockade. The German cruiser *Panther* bombarded the fort at Maracaibo in mid-January 1903. Nevertheless, the Anglo-German alliance had accepted arbitration rather than *occupation* of Venezuelan ports and direct debt collection or worse. The New Navy had enforced the Monroe Doctrine, as understood by Theodore Roosevelt, against two of the most powerful naval powers in the world.[85] When Germany's new ambassador, Hermann Speck von Sternberg, arrived in Washington, he told the American press, however insincerely: "The [German] Emperor understands the Monroe Doctrine thoroughly. . . . He would no more think of violating it than of colonizing the moon."[86]

The Roosevelt Corollary to the Monroe Doctrine

A similar "debt-collection crisis" afflicted the Dominican Republic in 1904–5. President Roosevelt now felt the need for a more permanent U.S. policy toward such incidents wherein European nations sought to "adjust disputes" with Latin American states but might, thereby, cross the line — wherever it was — on the now reified Monroe Doctrine. Having clarified the meaning of the Doctrine *in practice* in the Venezuelan episode, Roosevelt followed up with what came to be called the Roosevelt Corollary to the Monroe Doctrine. In his December 6, 1904, message to Congress, Roosevelt proclaimed: "Any country whose people conduct themselves well can count upon our hearty friendship. If a nation shows that it knows how to act with reasonable efficiency and decency in social and political matters, if it keeps order and pays its obligations, it need fear no interference from the United States. Chronic wrongdoing, or an impotence which results in a general loosening of the ties of civilized society [however], may in America, as elsewhere, ultimately require intervention by some civilized nation, and in the Western Hemisphere the adherence of the United States to the Monroe Doctrine may force the United States, however reluctantly, in flagrant cases of such wrongdoing or impotence, to the exercise of an international police power."[87]

The United States was a self-anointed international police power. Respect for Latin American nations' sovereignty depended upon U.S. perceptions of whether they were "obey[ing] the primary laws of civilized society." To prevent European intrusions to collect debts from Latin Americans, America would intervene to collect the debts on behalf of the creditors. The New Navy would enforce the Roosevelt Corollary as part of America's global strategy. Roosevelt told the country:

> There is no more patriotic duty before us as a people than to keep the
> Navy adequate to the needs of this country's position. . . . We have
> undertaken to secure for ourselves our just share in the trade of the
> Orient. We have undertaken to protect our citizens from improper
> treatment in foreign lands. We continue steadily to insist on the appli-
> cation of the Monroe Doctrine to the Western Hemisphere. Unless our

attitude in these and all similar matters is to be a mere boastful sham we can not afford to abandon our naval programme.[88]

Luis María Drago, an Argentine jurist and diplomat, had invited the Americans in 1902 to oppose coercive debt collection in the hemisphere (in exchange for support of his own version of the Monroe Doctrine). This "merger" never took hold. Latin American nationalists forgot (and forget) that Drago packaged his doctrine as an appendage to the Monroe Doctrine. American policymakers never seriously considered abandoning the unilateralism of the greatly expanded Monroe proclamation to support Drago, although the principles he espoused would shortly become part of international law.

Notwithstanding the pending discussion of Drago's proposal at the Hague Peace Conference, Roosevelt embarked on a new American policy for the hemisphere — really the Caribbean and Central America — which consisted of: (1) American imposition of customs house receiverships to guarantee European loan payments; (2) American political administration, to the extent necessary, of Latin American countries unable to "obey the primary laws of civilized society"; and (3) U.S. military occupation to "clean up" conditions leading to "chronic wrong doing" or "impotence." Roosevelt initially did this on his own authority in the Dominican Republic, establishing a receivership on his signature and that of the secretary of state. His action represented a novel stretch of presidential authority in foreign affairs.

Writing in 1916, historian Albert Bushnell Hart noted that "to send down what were practically Federal officials to collect, bank, and apply the customs revenue of a nominally independent state went beyond any responsibility up to that time assumed by the President, and made a doubtful precedent."[89] To prevent European intervention, Roosevelt also gave a consortium of New York bankers "a direct and personal interest in the making and continuing of financial control." Hart added that, despite what seemed to be overreach, followed by almost two years of refusal by the Senate to ratify the treaty negotiated by Roosevelt's team, "the system has stood the test of ten years' experience *and is now the accepted policy of the State Department.*"[90]

The Roosevelt Corollary claimed for the United States the right (though not the obligation) to intervene in Latin American nations to counter European intrusions and "for their [the Latin Americans'] own good." According to Roosevelt, such conditions made, ipso facto, the United States "a party in interest."[91] The 1846 Bidlack-Mallarino protectorate regime model had afforded the United States some right to intervene, unilaterally, for purposes stated in a bilateral treaty. In Cuba, the United States had a right to intervene under conditions specified by treaty and the Cuban constitution. The

Roosevelt Corollary went well beyond these juridical foundations for "international police work." Threats to U.S. security and interests, as decided by the U.S. government, made the United States a "party of interest" with the implied authority to enforce the "primary laws of civilized society." American security interests, as defined by the grand strategy of Mahan, Roosevelt, the navalists, and the imperialists, warranted unilateral intervention, military occupation, and transformation of sovereign states into political and economic protectorates. And the justification for this policy was primarily self-defense.

In Roosevelt's December 5, 1905, message to Congress, seeking ratification of the proposed treaty with the Dominican Republic to put in place the first customs house receivership, the president explained the rationale for the Dominican operation at length. He emphasized U.S. security interests, humanitarian concerns, and international law. He also referred to more general principles, to U.S. global interests in a changing world, and to the importance of a flexible interpretation and implementation of the Monroe Doctrine, as it had come to be "accepted" by the European powers: "One of the most effective instruments for peace is the Monroe Doctrine as it has been and is being gradually developed by this Nation and accepted by other nations. . . . It is useful at home, and is meeting with recognition abroad because we have adapted our application of it to meet the growing and changing needs of the hemisphere."[92]

According to Roosevelt, the United States wished to strengthen the "forces of right" and apply the Golden Rule to international politics, to the extent possible, but never eschewing the right of unilateral military intervention in self-defense or to safeguard its own rights and interests. Neither could America allow inferior peoples or unstable governments to put its interests or security at risk by exercising imperfect sovereignty over their own territory — especially not in the Western Hemisphere. Projection of power with the New Navy, in the Western Hemisphere and beyond, had thus come to play a central role in achieving the objectives of American foreign policy. The naval-industrial complex that undergirded the New Navy and America's new manifest destiny anticipated by six decades the even more politically impressive military-industrial complex against which President Eisenhower would warn the country in the 1950s.[93]

Chapter Seven

Protective Imperialism

[God] has made us the master organizers of the world to establish system where chaos reigns. . . . He has marked the American people as His chosen nation to finally lead in the regeneration of the world. This is the divine mission of America.
— SENATOR ALBERT J. BEVERIDGE, Washington, D.C., 1900

President Theodore Roosevelt's recovery of the No Transfer Principle and his expansive interpretation of the Monroe Doctrine inaugurated a decade of American military intervention and colonialism. American policymakers intended not only to consolidate hegemony in the Western Hemisphere and enhance the country's global power; they also sought to remake the political and social systems of their new possessions. As General Leonard Wood, military governor of Cuba (1899–1902) and then commander of the Philippines Division and commander of the Department of the East (1902–3), put it, the United States "became responsible for the welfare of the people, politically, mentally, and morally."[1] The new possessions were populated by colonial subjects, like the Indian Nations within the United States, defined by Chief Justice John Marshall in 1831 as "domestic dependent nations [that] occupy a territory to which we assert a title independent of their will. . . . Their relation to the United States resembles that of a ward to his guardian."[2]

By 1885, the U.S. Supreme Court had transformed the Indians into "local dependent communities" rather than dependent *nations* and had decided that Indians born on reservations were "nationals," owing allegiance to the United States without the privileges of citizenship.[3] For the expansionists and imperialists after 1898, policy toward the Caribbean and Pacific protectorates had much to emulate from the country's subjugation of the Indian peoples. In his acceptance speech for the Republican vice presidential nomination in 1900,

Theodore Roosevelt made clear the connection between Indian policy and colonial policy: "[On Indian reservations,] the army officers and the civilian agents still exercise authority without asking the 'consent of the governed.' We must proceed in the Philippines with the same wise caution."

For colonial administration in the Philippines and the Caribbean, the War Department created in 1898 a Division of Insular Affairs; in 1902 it became the Bureau of Insular Affairs, on the model of the Bureau of Indian Affairs. It retained this status until 1939. As historian Walter L. Williams noted, "The Bureau of Insular Affairs drew upon the background of its leaders in Indian affairs. Both Major John J. Pershing, who set up and headed the bureau in 1899, and General Clarence R. Edwards, who directed it from 1900 to 1912, had military backgrounds in the West with Indians."[4] All four military governors of the Philippines between 1898 and 1902 had seen extensive "Indian service."

Where the United States had not conquered territory in war, the Dominican Republic customs receivership of 1905 provided an alternative model for civil-military protectorate regimes. Initially, Roosevelt's policy in the Dominican Republic created a constitutional mini-crisis. The president implemented the Dominican treaty *provisionally*, while the Senate debated its approval. When the Senate rejected this approach, Roosevelt presented a more limited treaty for approval in 1907, but not before he transferred a team of colonial administrators, headed by Colonel George Colton, to the Dominican Republic from the Philippines. According to historian Richard Collin, "To make the transition less difficult, the entire administrative apparatus from the Philippines was retained so that Colton remained in the Bureau of Insular Affairs and reported directly to the secretary of war."[5] As in the Philippines and Cuba, American military officers in Santo Domingo would exercise joint, and sometimes parallel, authority over daily life.

In the case of Cuba, the initial U.S. occupation lasted for four years. Secretary of War Elihu Root drafted a set of articles in 1901 (later transformed into the Platt amendment) as guidelines for future United States–Cuban relations. Root's views of hemispheric relations were well known. In 1904, he would write: "The inevitable effect of our building the Canal must be to require us to police the surrounding premises. In the nature of things, trade and control, and the obligation to keep order which go with them, must come our way."[6] Cuban nationalists resisted Root's hemispheric vision, but U.S. warships, economic pressure, and refusal to end the occupation until the Platt amendment had been adopted destined Cuba to be an American protectorate until 1934, when President Franklin Delano Roosevelt's Good Neighbor Policy allowed its abrogation.

Cuba and the Platt Amendment

As previously related, the Platt amendment was in part a response to anti-annexationist sentiments in Congress, which had resulted in the Teller amendment in 1898. However, it also embodied fully the No Transfer Principle and requirements for American security, broadly understood. Congress directed the president to leave the government and control of the island of Cuba to its people,

> so soon as a government shall have been established in said island under a constitution which, either as a part thereof or in an ordinance appended thereto, shall define the future relations of the United States with Cuba, substantially as follows: That the government of Cuba shall never enter into any treaty or other compact with any foreign power or powers which will impair or tend to impair the independence of Cuba, nor in any manner authorize or permit any foreign power or powers to obtain by colonization or for military or naval purposes or otherwise, lodgement in or control over any portion of said island.

The Platt amendment gave legal cover for repeated U.S. military interventions and unremitting meddling in Cuban affairs and also protection for the avalanche of U.S. investment and commerce that came to dominate the island's economy. It confirmed the transformation of the Cuban liberation war into the Spanish American War, making Cuba, like Puerto Rico and the Philippines, spoils of victory.[7] It allowed for a permanent presence in Cuba of U.S. naval forces standing guard over the Caribbean and the soon-to-be constructed Panama Canal.

The Panama Canal Treaty and the Panama Constitution

In the year that saw Cuba's reluctant acceptance of the Platt amendment provisions into its constitution, the United States would assist insurgents in Panama to create an "independent" nation, severing from Colombia its northern province. Warships of the New Navy impeded the Colombian military response to the secessionist forces. In his December 7, 1903, message to Congress, President Roosevelt provided a colorful "history" of the Panama episode and the rationale for the quick recognition of the new country's "sovereignty." He explained the rapid (two weeks after Panamanian independence) approval of the Hay-Bunau-Varilla Treaty regarding the canal to be built across Panama. Phillipe Bunau-Varilla, a French citizen, represented Panama in Washington. No Panamanians participated in the treaty negotiations.

Much like Madison's and Monroe's incursions into the Floridas (1810–18), Roosevelt sought color of law for the Panama operation. He pointed to "international obligations" under the Bidlack-Mallarino Treaty, the insulting rejection by the Colombian Senate of the Hay-Herrán Treaty (August 12, 1903), and the many times that Colombia had called on the United States to maintain order and keep transit open across the isthmus since 1850. He even reached back for justification to Secretary of State Lewis Cass's 1858 remarks regarding the duties that accompanied sovereignty — duties to the international community that Colombia obviously had not fulfilled. According to Roosevelt, the United States had acted "for the sake of our own honor, and of the interest and well-being, not merely of our own people, but of the people of the Isthmus of Panama and the people of the civilized countries of the world." He explained that "all that remains is for the American Congress to do its part, and forthwith this Republic will enter upon the execution of a project colossal in its size and of well-nigh incalculable possibilities for the good of this country and the nations of mankind."

The day before this speech, Roosevelt met with Colombia's incoming president, Rafael Reyes. Reyes had favored the American canal project. Roosevelt told him that had he been president of Colombia, instead of conservative nationalist José Marroquín, Panama could have been saved for Colombia "because you would have known how to safeguard its rights and the interests of all and would have avoided the revolution which caused its secession from Colombia."[8] Reyes's efforts at reconciliation aside, most Colombians did not easily forget the "crime of Panama." In 1909, the Colombian senate rejected a treaty with the United States and Panama, in which Colombia would provide its ports to the United States for defense of the canal zone. Amid student protests and political violence, Reyes resigned, to spend most of the rest of his life in self-imposed exile.

In 1911, Roosevelt explained his actions in Panama to a group at the University of California at Berkeley. His impatience with Congress and his ample view of executive authority to "do right" for America in foreign policy came through endearingly to the audience:

> The Panama Canal would not have been started if I had not taken hold
> of it, because if I had followed the traditional or conservative method
> I should have submitted an admirable state paper occupying a couple
> of hundred pages detailing all of the facts to Congress and asking Con-
> gress' consideration of it. In that case there would have been a num-
> ber of excellent speeches made on the subject in Congress; the debate
> would be proceeding at this moment with great spirit and the begin-

"The News Reaches Bogotá." Cartoon by William A. Rogers, published in the *New York Herald*, December 1903. Theodore Roosevelt supports the Panamanian independence movement and signs a treaty for construction of the Panama Canal — sending the news to Bogotá, where the Colombian senate had rejected American terms for a canal.

ning of work on the canal would be fifty years in the future. [Laughter and applause.] Fortunately the crisis came at a period when I could act unhampered. Accordingly I took the Isthmus, started the Canal and then left Congress not to debate the canal, but to debate me.[9]

Roosevelt deliberately sought to enhance presidential authority. As he told readers in his autobiography:

My belief was that it was not only [the President's] right but his duty to do anything that the needs of the Nation demanded unless such action was forbidden by the Constitution or by the laws. Under this interpretation of executive power I did and caused to be done many things not previously done by the President and the heads of departments. I did not usurp power but I did greatly broaden the use of executive power. In other words, I acted for the common well being of all our people whenever and whatever measure was necessary, unless prevented by direct constitutional or legislative prohibition.[10]

Roosevelt's view of the presidency was not immediately accepted; indeed it was resisted into the 1960s, especially by conservatives, Southern Democrats, and many mainline Republicans. Nevertheless, Roosevelt's initiatives in the Caribbean, Central America, and further afield represented an important benchmark in the development of what came to be called the "imperial presidency." It also reflected Roosevelt's belief that peace would come to the world only through "the warlike power of a civilized people" — a quintessential American blend of messianic righteousness, missionary zeal, and unilateralist interventionism.[11] For this to happen, as Roosevelt had written in 1897, the United States must, of necessity, consolidate its Western Hemisphere bastion:

> I wish we had a perfectly consistent foreign policy, and that this policy was that ultimately every European power should be driven out of America, and every foot of American [Western Hemisphere] soil, including the nearest islands in both the Pacific and the Atlantic, should be in the hands of independent American states, and so far as possible in the possession of the United States or under its protection . . . I would treat as cause for war any effort by a European power to get as much as a fresh foothold of any kind on American soil.[12]

As part of the quick-and-dirty recognition of Panama by the United States, the Hay-Bunau-Varilla Treaty provided for an American protectorate over Panama, including sovereign authority over a strip through the center of the new country. Article XXIV even anticipated that should Panama slip back into Colombia's control, the rights of the United States acquired under the treaty should not be affected. A greatly shortened version of the Platt amendment, Article 136 of the Panama constitution, was carte blanche for intervention at American discretion. As in Cuba, some unsuccessful local resistance developed to this constitutional provision, which gelded Panamanian sovereignty at birth.

A country of less than 400,000 residents, sliced in half by the Canal Zone and permanently occupied by U.S. military forces, Panama was a linchpin in the Mahan-inspired U.S. grand strategy at the beginning of the twentieth century. With the protectorate in Cuba, the Puerto Rican colony and naval station, and the customs receivership protectorates, beginning with the Dominican Republic in 1905, Panama figured centrally in America's consolidation of hemispheric hegemony.[13] American military interventions repeatedly reaffirmed this intention in the Caribbean, Central America, and Mexico from 1907 into the 1930s.

Interventionism and Grand Strategy

For some Latin Americans, the United States seemed much more fearsome than any European power that might want to collect debts or extend its influence in the Western Hemisphere. For Colombian author and journalist José María Vargas Vila, the United States had become the principal enemy of the Latin American people. In *Ante los Bárbaros* (Facing the Barbarians), first published in 1900 and then reprinted and "updated" on the anniversary of the Monroe Doctrine in 1923, Vargas Vila was less than subtle: "*El Yanki; He ahí el Enemigo*" (The Yanki, Here We Have the Enemy).[14] Latin American intellectuals from Mexico to South America responded eloquently to America's imperial pretensions. Nicaraguan poet Rubén Darío wrote in his *To Roosevelt* (1904):

> You are the United States,
> you are the future invader
> of the naive America that has Indian blood,
> that still prays to Jesus Christ and still speaks Spanish.
> . . . Catholic America, Spanish America,
> the America in which noble Cuahtemoc said:
> "I'm not in a bed of roses"; that America
> that trembles in hurricanes and lives on love,
> it lives, you men of Saxon eyes and barbarous soul.
> And it dreams. And it loves, and it vibrates, and it is the daughter
> of the Sun.
> Be careful. Viva Spanish America!
> There are a thousand cubs loosed from the Spanish lion.
> Roosevelt, one would have to be, through God himself,
> the terrible Rifleman and strong Hunter,
> to manage to grab us in your iron claws.[15]

Latin American nationalists and Hispanists urged solidarity against U.S. aggression and neocolonial imposition of its "superior culture" and institutions.[16] These themes, dating as we have seen from Simón Bolívar's distrust of American leaders and the warnings to his people by the first Mexican ambassador to the United States, would remain central to Latin American opposition to American policies in the hemisphere into the twenty-first century.

When Theodore Roosevelt left office in 1909, William Howard Taft inherited a grand strategy premised on updated versions of the No Transfer Principle, the Monroe Doctrine and its Olney and Roosevelt Corollaries, and the geopolitics and navalism of Mahan. Threat scenarios and war planning focused on defense of the Caribbean and the Central American isthmus as the United States joined more fully in competition with European powers and the Japanese for global influence, markets, and even colonial possessions. Plausible treaty cover for recurrent interventions in the region buttressed the grand strategy.

By way of illustration, the U.S. military "Hi-Sd Plan" — referring to Haiti–Santo Domingo, that is, the island of Hispaniola — anticipated the opening of the Panama Canal and ongoing German pretensions in the hemisphere. It called for preemptive seizure of Hispaniola by a marine strike force, prepositioned at League Island in Philadelphia, followed by full-scale military occupation.[17] As would occur in the post-1990s period, from 1909 to 1933 the United States applied international law and treaties flexibly when it decided, unilaterally, that its security or other vital interests (very broadly understood) might be at stake. International law expert William Kane wrote: "The Hi-Sd plan is rivaled in its disregard for legal norms of international behavior only by the German Schlieffen Plan, which has been so-much decried for its disregard of Belgian neutrality."[18]

To dramatize America's global presence, Roosevelt had sent his "Great White Fleet" on a fourteen-month cruise, showing the flag on all continents and in all corners of the earth. According to the U.S. Navy Department:

> The four squadrons of warships, were manned by 14,000 sailors and marines under the command of Rear Adm. Robley "Fighting Bob" Evans — a civil war veteran who had earned his nickname as commander of the gunboat *Yorktown* during the *Baltimore* incident in Chilean waters in 1891, and who commanded the *Iowa* during the American attack on Santiago, Cuba in 1898. All were embarking upon a naval deployment the scale of which had never been attempted by any nation before — the first round-the-world cruise by a fleet of steam-powered, steel battleships. The 43,000 mile, 14-month circumnavigation would include 20 port calls on six continents; it is widely considered one of the greatest peacetime achievements of the U.S. Navy.[19]

According to naval historian Dr. A. A. Nofi, the fleet's voyage was also "a message to Japan [which had defeated Russia in 1905] that said that unlike Russia, if America has to cross the ocean to fight you, its navy will be there in force and ready."[20] The voyage of the Great White Fleet also demonstrated the risks of global deployment, from inconvenient "incidents" like that of a drunken brawl by sailors in Brazil to threats against the fleet: "In Rio the first of many wild rumors about threats to the fleet began circulating. The Rio chief of police had been advised, through unknown sources, that anarchists were plotting to blow up the fleet. Nothing came of it, although Washington did cable for details. These rumors would follow the fleet throughout its voyage and eventually gave the folks back home the impression that the Great White Fleet was in constant peril." On the positive side, the cruise also provided opportunities for creating goodwill and humanitarian intervention, as with American naval assistance to victims of the devastating Messina (Italy) earthquake and tsunami in December 1908.[21]

Roosevelt's chosen successor, William Howard Taft, had easily defeated Democrat William Jennings Bryan (in his third run for the presidency) in November 1908. With President Taft (1909–13), who had served as civilian governor of the Philippines after annexation, and his secretary of state, Philander Chase Knox, the promise to "substitute dollars for bullets"[22] gave even more credence to Latin Americans and Europeans who saw crass economic interests underlying U.S. regional policies. In some ways, however, dollar diplomacy anticipated the missionary zeal with which post-1990 American policymakers would push free trade and globalization as foundations of world peace and democracy. Concern for U.S. economic interests in the Caribbean and Central America before World War I were part of American policymakers' global strategic thinking. This included the drive to provide stability for American banking, manufacturing, and commercial ventures that sought regional markets. The success of American business interests formed part of the grand strategy; separating economic and security interests was illusory.[23]

In the spirit of the times, the Department of State published in 1912 a memorandum prepared by its solicitor, J. Reuben Clark Jr., that sought to justify the right to protect citizens in foreign countries by landing armed forces. As an illustration, the memorandum listed forty-seven instances in which force had been used to protect citizens overseas, almost all of them without congressional authorization. Apparently written to justify Taft's desire to intervene in Mexico during the first years of the Revolution (something that would not occur until Woodrow Wilson became president), it would be consulted by future presidents, including John F. Kennedy during the Cuban Missile Crisis of 1962.[24]

Taft's first assistant secretary of state, Fred J. Huntington Wilson, told the world that dollar diplomacy meant the "creation of prosperity," that financial soundness was a factor in political stability, and that prosperity "means contentment and contentment means repose."[25] Wilson reaffirmed the Roosevelt Corollary to the Monroe Doctrine and anticipated later policy and doctrine regarding the necessity to intervene when weak or "unenlightened" governments threatened U.S. interests: "In these days the interests of one nation are so intertwined with those of all others that the financial recklessness or

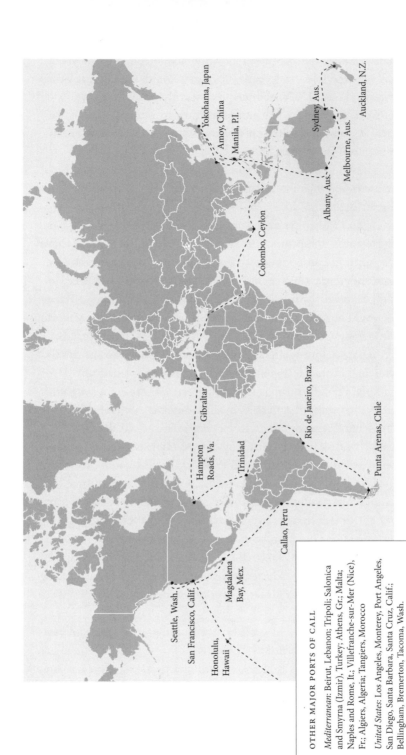

OTHER MAJOR PORTS OF CALL

Mediterranean: Beirut, Lebanon; Tripoli; Salonica
and Smyrna (Izmir), Turkey; Athens, Gr.; Malta;
Naples and Rome, It.; Villefranche-sur-Mer (Nice),
Fr.; Algiers, Algeria; Tangiers, Morocco

United States: Los Angeles, Monterey, Port Angeles,
San Diego, Santa Barbara, Santa Cruz, Calif.;
Bellingham, Bremerton, Tacoma, Wash.

Map 7.1. The voyage of the Great White Fleet, 1907–1909

heresy of one becomes the peril of all. As well leave the slum to manage its own sanitation and thus infect the whole city, as to allow an unenlightened government, unopposed, to create or maintain a financial plague spot to the injury of the general interest."[26]

That U.S. intervention and treaty protectorate regimes provided economic opportunities and promoted financial "soundness" in Latin America did not mean inattention to military requirements. The naval base at Guantánamo was enlarged, and Knox understood that the Monroe Doctrine "does not depend upon technical legal right, but upon policy and power."[27] On Knox's watch, the U.S. government allied with filibusters, bankers, and ambitious businessmen, like the Fletchers of Philadelphia and Sam Zemurray (the "banana man"), who overturned governments in Nicaragua (1909) and Honduras (1911). Dollar diplomacy did not mean *only* dollars — only that naval and military power would be used to leverage and promote American investments as part of the large policy of consolidating the Western Hemisphere bastion while extending investments and bank loans in Asia and even Africa.

Banks and commercial interests profited from U.S. policies. Frequently, however, government policymakers encouraged American private investments considered of strategic importance in efforts to supplant German, British, French, or other European influence in the hemisphere. They also sometimes guaranteed the investments with American firepower, most literally as part of a global policy agenda.[28] According to historian Albert B. Hart, Knox's global application of dollar diplomacy "caused an uproar when it was applied in China, and was very repugnant to the Latin American states."[29]

Although Taft did not share Roosevelt's expansive views of the American presidency, he persisted in Roosevelt's policies of protective imperialism.[30] He reminded Americans of the importance of the Monroe Doctrine in his first message to Congress on March 4, 1909: "We should have an army so organized and so officered as to be capable in time of emergency . . . to resist all probable invasion from abroad *and to furnish a respectable expeditionary force if necessary in the maintenance of our traditional American policy which bears the name of President Monroe.*"[31] Taft accepted and implemented American unilateralist doctrine in its latest version. It had become the *natural* and traditional policy of the country. Americans expected their government to act unilaterally, to protect their investments overseas, and to dominate the Western Hemisphere. The Monroe Doctrine, in whatever manner the incumbent administration chose to interpret it, was virtually a canon of American political religion.

Toward the end of Taft's presidency, a principal spokesperson for the expansionists, Senator Henry Cabot Lodge, stretched the Monroe Doctrine even further, to include U.S. veto of the lease or possession by foreign private firms in the Western Hemisphere of assets that might threaten U.S. security. His resolution responded to the possible acquisition by a Japanese firm of a concession in Magdalena Bay, Mexico, but its reach extended, in principle, to any "place in the American continents so situated that the occupation thereof for naval or military purposes might threaten the communications or the safety of the United States." Preemptive intervention or "interference" thus became a right as well as a duty of the United States where foreign presence in the hemisphere might be "prejudicial to its safety." There seemed no limit to America's "right" to interfere.

Self-defense and global grand strategy à la Mahan required U.S. policing and hegemony in the Western Hemisphere. But Monroe had not mentioned Japan in 1823, nor other powers outside Europe, nor had he referred to private businesses, even of the Europeans. The 1811 No Transfer Policy likewise neglected to suggest American prohibitions on private commercial concessions extended by Latin American governments. In what became known as the Lodge Corollary, Latin Americans saw an unusually contorted effort to restrict their sovereignty. They also saw an assertion of a right to preemptive self-defense and strategic denial that went well beyond anything in international law, though Lodge referred to an incident involving English objections to German presence in a Moroccan port at Agadir as precedent: "This resolution rests on a generally accepted principle of the law of nations, older than the Monroe Doctrine. It rests on the principle that every nation has a right to protect its own safety, and that if it feels that the possession by a foreign power, for military or naval purposes, of any given harbor or place is prejudicial to its safety, it is its duty as well as its right to interfere."[32]

Lodge and his political allies anticipated American interpretations of article 51 of the UN Charter almost a century later. For Americans, the "law of nations" and the right to "self-defense" — as determined by American leadership — would always trump commitments to the principle of sovereign equality of states and nonintervention. Threats or potential threats always existed or could be imagined or fabricated. Having absorbed Mahan's views into popular and political culture, Americans would be required frequently to decide when to exercise their right to interfere in self-defense, as Lodge put it, "where foreign presence might be prejudicial to [their] interests."

The North American Peril and "Benevolent Leadership"

As Taft and Knox applied dollar diplomacy to the region and Senator Lodge proclaimed an expanded version of American security doctrine, Peruvian intellectual and diplomat Francisco García Calderón published *Latin America: Its Rise and Progress*. He began a chapter called "The North American Peril" with affirmations and questions that might concern Americans had they taken seriously what many Latin Americans were thinking:

> To save themselves from Yankee imperialism the American democracies would almost accept a German alliance or the aid of Japanese arms; everywhere the Americans of the North are feared. In the Antilles and in Central America hostility against the Anglo-Saxon invaders assumes the character of a Latin Crusade. Do the United States deserve this hatred? Are they not as their diplomatists preach, the elder brothers, generous and protecting? And is not protection their proper vocation in a continent rent by anarchy? . . . The better to protect the Ibero-Americans, it has proudly raised its Pillars of Hercules against the ambition of the Old World. . . . But who will deliver the Ibero-Americans from the excess of this influence? Quis custodiet custodem? An irresponsible supremacy is perilous.[33]

García Calderón did not stop here. He attacked the "political and financial tutelage of the imperial democracy" and lamented the racist foundations of American policy in Latin America:

> The people of the United States hate the half-breed, and the impure marriages of whites and blacks which take place in Southern homes; no manifestation of Pan-Americanism could suffice to destroy the racial prejudice as it exists north of Mexico. The half-breeds and their descendants govern the Ibero-American democracies, and the Republic of English and German origin entertains the same contempt which they feel for the slaves of Virginia whom Lincoln liberated. In its friendship for them there will always be disdain; in their progress a conquest; in their policy, a desire of hegemony.[34]

García Calderón understood well the racist underpinnings of American domestic politics and political culture. In 1900, Josiah Strong, author of the best-selling book *Our Country, Its Possible Future and Its Present Crisis* (1885), had declared that all people of color, whether within the United States or not, were "many centuries behind the Anglo-Saxon in development and seem as incapable of operating complex machinery as they are of adopting and successfully administering representative government."[35] A two-volume turn-of-the-century "study" of Latin America summed up popular American attitudes: "The belief that a republic is the best form of government for all countries, and that all people are capable of self-government, has been entirely abandoned by men whose opinions are of any weight. In this there is no question involved as to the supremacy of the Anglo-Saxon race or the subordination of the Latin. . . . The only question involved is the imperative necessity for opening up these countries to civilization. All other considerations are beside the issue."[36]

American racism and its connection to missionaries around the world made it easier to ignore international law and sovereignty in the Western Hemisphere and elsewhere. McKinley, Roosevelt, Taft, and Woodrow Wilson shared but slightly different versions of piety and patriotism, more or less sincere in each case but grounded in a belief in America's righteous cause and racial superiority.[37] In one often-told story, McKinley, while praying on his knees, heard God; he knew that the country had to take the Philippines and then Christianize and civilize the Natives. (Apparently, centuries of Catholic influence had not sufficiently "Christianized" Spain's former colony.) When it came Woodrow Wilson's turn, "this president kept his Bible and his watch by his bedside and every day he read the Book."[38] He would teach Latin Americans to "elect good men" and to "discredit and defeat usurpations of power [like that of Victoriano Huerta in Mexico] that menace the peace and put the lives and fortunes of citizens and foreigners alike in constant jeopardy."[39]

Wilson would renounce dollar diplomacy; he called on Latin Americans to enact just government based upon law, not upon arbitrary or irregular force. But Wilson's religious fervor and supposed political idealism did not preclude U.S. interventionism. To the contrary, Wilson and his administration, which historian Samuel Flagg Bemis called "missionaries of democracy," routinely practiced "protective imperialism."[40] With William Jennings Bryan (a phlegmatic populist who accepted the Democratic Party's attachment to the Jim Crow regime) as secretary of state (1913–15), the United States sent troops, on presidential authority and then with congressional support, into Mexico, ostensibly to overturn General Huerta and foreclose the possibility of increased German influence just south of the United States. An incident involving the USS *Dolphin* provided the pretext for seizure of the customs house at Vera Cruz (April 21, 1914). According to navy captain John N. Petrie, writing in 1995 as U.S. Navy professor of National Security Policy and director of research at the National War College:

> The President, as Commander-in-Chief, already had the authority and the obligation to use the armed forces to protect U.S. rights. In asking Congress for their cooperation and approval to use force as necessary, Wilson foreshadowed the war powers debate that ensued decades later. Wilson must have seen this as a task that exceeded his direct respon-

sibilities regarding defense of U.S. rights (especially in the case of our "rights" regarding a salute to the flag). In essence, the President sought Congressional authority to go to war with Huerta under international law without appearing to do so in the eyes of the U.S. Constitution.[41]

Although Wilson appealed to security concerns to gain support for the invasion, historians such as John Mason Hart and Thomas F. O'Brien have demonstrated that he decided on this intervention after being dissuaded from a more ambitious invasion of Mexico, due to its potential cost and lack of public support, in order to protect American investors and to provide military assistance to Huerta's adversaries, much as had occurred with U.S. support for the overthrow of Nicaragua's President José Santos Zelaya in 1909.[42] Uncharacteristically, Wilson agreed to mediation by Argentina, Brazil, and Chile to resolve this first military incursion into Mexico and significant determinant of the outcome of the ongoing revolution. He succeeded, ultimately, in ousting Huerta, and U.S. forces abandoned Vera Cruz on November 23, 1914.

In the next three years, the United States intervened again in Mexico several times, as well as in the Dominican Republic, Haiti, and Nicaragua, looking sometimes to Theodore Roosevelt's customs receivership model for administering the interventions and sometimes to the Platt amendment model of Cuba, with treaty regimes modeled on the 1903 U.S.-Cuban Treaty of Relations. William Jennings Bryan favored acquisition of a naval base in Haiti, and Rear Admiral Colby N. Chester remarked that Haiti was "practically part of the shore line of our republic."[43] In 1916, the United States finally acquired the Danish West Indies by purchase, seeking to keep this potential Caribbean base out of German hands as World War I unfolded — and returning to the No Transfer Principle as well as the Monroe Doctrine to justify this acquisition.

In the same year, the U.S. Senate ratified the Bryan-Chamorro Treaty (signed in 1914 and remaining in effect until 1970), giving the United States a ninety-nine-year option on a naval base at the Gulf of Fonseca on Nicaragua's Pacific coast and guaranteeing American control of any future canal built across Nicaragua. Nicaragua received 3 million dollars, which it used to pay down its debt, administered by American financial interests. Costa Rica, Honduras, and El Salvador objected to the treaty, which violated their claims over territory and, in the case of El Salvador and Honduras, their rights in the Gulf of Fonseca, which they shared with Nicaragua. They took the case to the U.S.-inspired Central American Court of Justice (created at the Washington Peace Conference among the Central American states in 1907). Nicaragua defied the court's decision. The U.S. government supported the Nicaraguan position, undermining the court and maintaining the bilateral treaty in force.

"A New Sentry in the Caribbean." Cartoon published in the *News* (Dayton, Ohio) and reprinted in the *American Review of Reviews*, September 1916. Uncle Sam signs a treaty to acquire Danish possessions in the Caribbean to impede German purchase or use during World War I.

Shortly thereafter, Nicaragua withdrew from the court, which was dissolved in 1918.[44]

After signing the Bryan-Chamorro Treaty, Nicaragua's president, Adolfo Díaz, requested that the agreement be amended to "embody the substance of the Platt Amendment." Not only did the United States seek stable and obsequious elected governments, but some Latin American politicians and would-be presidents — in Cuba, Nicaragua, Honduras, Haiti, and the Dominican Republic — would learn to twist protective imperialism to their own ends. In this case, however, the opposition in the U.S. Senate, led by anti-imperialists such as Senator Borah, but also by Senator Elihu Root (R.-N.Y.), legal counsel to banks and railroads, whose work to establish the Central American Court of Justice would be destroyed by the Wilson-Bryan diplomacy in Nicaragua, rejected amending the treaty with Platt amendment–like provisions. Thus, there was not unanimity among policymakers or the public on the desirability of protective imperialism in the hemisphere or around the world. As in the past, interventionism and imperial reach had their critics in the United States, as did initiatives that violated the tradition of armed neutrality and further expanded presidential autonomy in making foreign policy.

Wilson had barely won the 1916 presidential election against Supreme Court justice Charles Evan Hughes (277–254 in the electoral college, with the difference being California's thirteen electoral votes). Seeking reelection, he promised to keep the country out of war, and his opponent accused him of not protecting American neutrality. Ironically, Wilson would take the country to war a year later, officially as a response to attacks by Germany on American neutral vessels. Like the pirates of the Caribbean in the early Republic, the Germans, who had emerged before World War I as financial, commercial, and military rivals of the British and the United States, had made themselves enemies of all mankind:

> The present German submarine warfare against commerce is a warfare against mankind. . . . It is a war against all nations. American ships have been sunk, American lives taken, in ways which it has stirred us very deeply to learn of, but the ships and people of other neutral and friendly nations have been sunk and overwhelmed in the waters in the same way. There has been no discrimination.
>
> The challenge is to all mankind. . . . There is one choice we cannot make, we are incapable of making: we will not choose the path of submission and suffer the most sacred rights of our Nation and our people to be ignored or violated. The wrongs against which we now

array ourselves are no common wrongs; they cut to the very roots of human life.[45]

A year before Congress declared war on Germany (April 6, 1917), Albert Bushnell Hart published a remarkable tome interpreting the meaning and evolution of the Monroe Doctrine from its beginnings (*The Monroe Doctrine: An Interpretation*). Hart characterized the Monroe Doctrine as a "frame of mind" *that had been extended from the Western Hemisphere to relations with Europe and Asia* and then suggested its adaptation as a "Doctrine of Permanent Interest," involving the global role of the United States' "benevolent leadership." He concluded that "the American people, some with joy and some with regret, consider themselves bound by ties both of interest and honor, to maintain the permanent interest of the United States in American [Western Hemisphere] questions, in the teeth of European or Asiatic interference."[46] The Monroe Doctrine, whatever its current application, had become an article of faith and dogma. It had become an instrument for virtually infinite extension to all matters affecting the Western Hemisphere — and perhaps, in the spirit of America's "benevolent leadership," far beyond the New World sphere.

The Dominican and the Haitian interventions authorized under Wilson led to longer-term military occupations. Although American concerns revolved primarily around German or other European incursions or occupation of Hispaniola, this did not soften the impact of intervention for the affected Caribbean peoples.[47] American military and civilian agents in these two occupation regimes reinforced regional sentiments regarding American disdain for Latin Americans. The brutality of the military campaigns and the manifest racism of the occupation authorities blighted the idealistic pronouncements emanating from Washington. Both of these episodes, as well as the U.S. Marines presence in Nicaragua, contributed to long-term resentment of American policy in Latin America. The Haitian intervention, which perdured until 1934, was particularly horrific, as described by journalist and civil rights activist Herbert J. Seligmann in 1920:

> To Belgium's Congo, to Germany's Belgium, to England's India and Egypt, the United States has added a perfect miniature in Haiti. Five years of violence in that Negro republic of the Caribbean, without sanction of international law or any law other than force, is now succeeded by an era in which the military authorities are attempting to hush up what has been done. The history of the American invasion of Haiti is only additional evidence that the United States is among those Powers in whose international dealings democracy and freedom are mere words, and human lives negligible in face of racial snobbery, po-

litical chicane, and money. . . . The American disease of color prejudice has raged virulently.[48]

American protective imperialism condensed racism at home and abroad with the quest for hegemony in the Western Hemisphere. World War I would consolidate American domination of the hemisphere. Germany's defeat and the provisions of the Versailles Treaty limited its military and commercial influence for the near future. France and England became debtor nations — debtors to the United States. The United States replaced European and British investors in much of Latin America, substituting its products for those of European origin. By supplying its raw materials, food, and fiber to both sides in the war, Latin America profited, though the devastation in Europe also pushed most of Spanish America and Brazil further into the American orbit.[49]

Under these conditions, with no plausible extra-hemispheric threat, President Woodrow Wilson hesitated to further enmesh the country in new military operations in the hemisphere, even when, according to historian Joseph Tulchin, local U.S. diplomats, as in Costa Rica (1918–19), "labored to the utmost to bring about the active intervention of the United States."[50] Instead, Wilson relied on nonrecognition of "bad" governments or, in the case of Mexico, threats to break off diplomatic relations, when jingoists in Congress and even Secretary of State Robert Lansing favored intervention to uphold national honor. In Lansing's views, privately expressed to President Wilson in 1915, "The Monroe Doctrine should not be confused with Pan Americanism. . . . In its advocacy of the Monroe Doctrine, the United States considers its own interests. The integrity of other nations is an incident, not an end."

Protective imperialism and World War I left the United States where Jefferson, Madison, John Quincy Adams, and James Blaine had desired. America faced no immediate extra-hemispheric threats and it enjoyed an expanding intra-hemispheric commerce. What these Founders of the Republic had not foreseen was that this position would make possible, and would have resulted from, becoming the decisive participant in Europe's bloodiest and costliest rearrangement ever of the balance of power. America sent more than 2 million military personnel to Europe and emerged from the war as the world's premier economic and military power. Although the United States refused to officially join an alliance during World War I (fighting the war as an "associated" power), George Washington's policy of armed neutrality and Jefferson's exhortations against entangling alliances had been abandoned in practice.

Not just entangled, but fully engaged — and the arbiter of victory and defeat in the Old World — the U.S. government would, nevertheless, continue to insist on unilateralism and on "commanding its own fortune" from the 1920s until World War II. The United States refused to support even the innocuous multilateralism and annoyance of the Central American Court of Justice (which, in any case, had no jurisdiction over the United States), let alone the potential restraint represented by the League of Nations, created after World War I. Contradictions persisted among policies pursuing regional and global commercial ambitions, reciprocity, "open door" treaties, and protective tariffs. So, too, questions arose over how to defend American business interests and investments, with force if necessary, but still retain some congressional control over overseas troop and naval deployments. Most of all, contradictions would persist among international ambitions, moralistic, evangelical promotion of the "American way of life," and the coercive means required to enforce American policies, whether in the Philippines, China, the Pacific, or the Caribbean.[51]

What next, then, for U.S. relations with Latin America? What new imaginable threats, what new global vision and ambitions of the United States would reshape U.S.–Latin American relations? How would Latin America and Latin Americans figure into the United States' post–World War I plans for the planet and for its own prosperity and security in a world confronting revolutions in China, Mexico, and Russia, along with dissolution of the Ottoman Empire? With U.S. troops in the newly founded Soviet Union, in China, in the Philippines, spread around the Pacific, and in Europe, how would the Western Hemisphere bastion fit into post–World War I grand strategy and be shaped by America's "benevolent leadership"?

Appendix: American Foreign Military Deployments, 1894–1921[52]

1894 — *Brazil.* January. A display of naval force sought to protect American commerce and shipping at Rio de Janeiro during a Brazilian civil war.

1894 — *Nicaragua.* July 6 to August 7. U.S. forces sought to protect American interests at Bluefields following a revolution.

1894–95 — *China.* Marines were stationed at Tientsin and penetrated to Peking for protection purposes during the Sino-Japanese War.

1894–95 — *China.* A naval vessel was beached and used as a fort at Newchwang for protection of American nationals.

1894–96 — *Korea.* July 24, 1894, to April 3, 1896. A guard of marines was sent to protect the American legation and American lives and interests at Seoul during and following the Sino-Japanese War.

1895 — *Colombia.* March 8 to 9. U.S. forces protected American interests during an attack on the town of Bocas del Toro by a bandit chieftain.

1896 — *Nicaragua.* May 2 to 4. U.S. forces protected American interests in Corinto during political unrest.

1898 — *Nicaragua*. February 7 and 8. U.S. forces protected American lives and property at San Juan del Sur.

1898 — *Spanish American War*. On April 25, 1898, the United States declared war on Spain. The war followed a Cuban insurrection against Spanish rule and the sinking of the USS *Maine* in the harbor at Havana.

1898–99 — *China*. November 5, 1898, to March 15, 1899. U.S. forces provided a guard for the legation at Peking and the consulate at Tientsin during a contest between the dowager empress and her son.

1899 — *Nicaragua*. American and British naval forces landed to protect national interests at San Juan del Norte, February 22 to March 5, and at Bluefields a few weeks later in connection with the insurrection of General Juan P. Reyes.

1899 — *Samoa*. February–May 15. American and British naval forces landed to protect national interests and to take part in a bloody struggle over the succession to the throne.

1899–1901 — *Philippine Islands*. U.S. forces protected American interests following the war with Spain and conquered the islands by defeating the Filipinos in their war for independence.

1900 — *China*. May 24 to September 28. American troops participated in operations to protect foreign lives during the Boxer rebellion, particularly at Peking. For many years after this experience, a permanent legation guard was maintained in Peking, which was strengthened when trouble threatened.

1901 — *Colombia (State of Panama)*. November 20 to December 4. U.S. forces protected American property on the isthmus and kept transit lines open during serious revolutionary disturbances.

1902 — *Colombia*. April 16 to 23. U.S. forces protected American lives and property at Bocas del Toro during a civil war.

1902 — *Colombia (State of Panama)*. September 17 to November 18. The United States placed armed guards on all trains crossing the isthmus to keep the railroad line open and stationed ships on both sides of Panama to prevent the landing of Colombian troops.

1903 — *Honduras*. March 23 to 30 or 31. U.S. forces protected the American consulate and the steamship wharf at Puerto Cortez during a period of revolutionary activity.

1903 — *Dominican Republic*. March 30 to April 21. A detachment of marines landed to protect American interests in the city of Santo Domingo during a revolutionary outbreak.

1903 — *Syria*. September 7 to 12. U.S. forces protected the American consulate in Beirut (modern Lebanon) when a local Muslim uprising was feared.

1903–4 — *Abyssinia*. Twenty-five marines were sent to Abyssinia to protect the U.S. consul general while he negotiated a treaty.

1903–14 — *Panama*. U.S. forces sought to protect American interests and lives during and following the revolution for independence from Colombia over construction of the isthmian canal. With brief intermissions, marines were stationed on the isthmus from November 4, 1903, to January 21, 1914, to guard American interests.

1904 — *Dominican Republic*. January 2 to February 11. American and British naval forces established an area in which no fighting would be allowed and protected American interests in Puerto Plata, Sosua, and Santo Domingo City during revolutionary fighting.

1904 — *Tangier, Morocco*. "We want either Perdicaris alive or Raisula dead." A squadron demonstrated to force release of a kidnapped American. Marines landed to protect the consul general.

1904 — *Panama*. November 17 to 24. U.S. forces protected American lives and property at Ancon at the time of a threatened insurrection.

1904–5 — *Korea*. January 5, 1904, to November 11, 1905. A guard of marines was sent to protect the American legation in Seoul during the Russo-Japanese War.

1906–9 — *Cuba*. September 1906 to January 23, 1909. U.S. forces sought to restore order, protect foreigners, and establish a stable government after serious revolutionary activity.

1907 — *Honduras*. March 18 to June 8. To protect American interests during a war between Honduras and Nicaragua, troops were stationed in Trujillo, Ceiba, Puerto Cortez, San Pedro, Laguna, and Choloma.

1910 — *Nicaragua*. May 19 to September 4. U.S. forces protected American interests at Bluefields.

1911 — *Honduras*. January 26. American naval detachments landed to protect American lives and interests during a civil war in Honduras.

1911 — *China*. In October, as the nationalist revolution approached, an ensign and ten men tried to enter Wuchang to rescue missionaries but retreated on being warned away, and a small landing force guarded American private property and the consulate at Hankow. Marines were deployed in November to guard the cable stations at Shanghai; landing forces were sent for protection in Nanking, Chinkiang, Taku, and elsewhere.

1912 — *Honduras*. A small force landed to prevent seizure by the government of an American-owned railroad at Puerto Cortez. The forces were withdrawn after the United States disapproved the action.

1912 — *Panama*. Troops, on request of both political parties, supervised elections outside the Canal Zone.

1912 — *Cuba*. June 5 to August 5. U.S. forces protected American interests on the Province of Oriente and in Havana.

1912 — *China*. August 24 to 26, on Kentucky Island, and August 26 to 30, at Camp Nicholson. U.S. forces protected Americans and American interests during revolutionary activity.

1912 — *Turkey*. November 18 to December 3. U.S. forces guarded the American legation at Constantinople during a Balkan war.

1912–25 — *Nicaragua*. August to November 1912. U.S. forces protected American interests during an attempted revolution. A small force, serving as a legation guard and seeking to promote peace and stability, remained until August 5, 1925.

1912–41 — *China*. The disorders that began with the overthrow of the dynasty during the Kuomintang rebellion in 1912, which were redirected by the invasion of China by Japan, led to demonstrations and landing parties for the protection of U.S. interests in China continuously and at many points from 1912 to 1941. The guard at Peking and along the route to the sea was maintained until 1941. In 1927, the United States had 5,670 troops ashore in China and 44 naval vessels in its waters. In 1933, the United States had 3,027 armed men ashore. The protective action was generally based on treaties with China concluded from 1858 to 1901.

1913 — *Mexico*. September 5 to 7. A few marines landed at Ciaris Estero to aid in evacuating American citizens and others from the Yaqui Valley, made dangerous for foreigners by civil strife.

1914 — *Haiti*. January 29 to February 9, February 20 to 21, October 19. Intermittently, U.S. naval forces protected American nationals in a time of rioting and revolution.

1914 — *Dominican Republic*. June and July. During a revolutionary movement, U.S. naval forces used gunfire to stop the bombardment of Puerto Plata and by threat of force maintained Santo Domingo City as a neutral zone.

1914–17 — *Mexico*. Undeclared Mexican-American hostilities followed the *Dolphin* affair and Villa's raids and included capture of Vera Cruz and later Pershing's expedition into northern Mexico.

1915–34 — *Haiti*. July 28, 1915, to August 15, 1934. U.S. forces maintained order during a period of chronic political instability.

1916 — *China*. American forces landed to quell a riot taking place on American property in Nanking.

1916–24 — *Dominican Republic*. May 1916 to September 1924. American naval forces maintained order during a period of chronic and threatened insurrection.

1917 — *China.* American troops were landed at Chungking to protect American lives during a political crisis.

1917–18 — *World War I.* On April 6, 1917, the United States declared war on Germany and on December 7, 1917, on Austria-Hungary. Entrance of the United States into the war was precipitated by Germany's submarine warfare against neutral shipping.

1917–22 — *Cuba.* U.S. forces protected American interests during insurrection and subsequent unsettled conditions. Most of the U.S. forces left Cuba by August 1919, but two companies remained at Camaguey until February 1922.

1918–19 — *Mexico.* After withdrawal of the Pershing expedition, U.S. troops entered Mexico in pursuit of bandits, at least three times in 1918 and six times in 1919. In August 1918, American and Mexican troops fought at Nogales.

1918–20 — *Panama.* U.S. forces were used for police duty, according to treaty stipulations, at Chiriqui, during election disturbances and subsequent unrest.

1918–20 — *Soviet Russia.* Marines were landed at and near Vladivostok in June and July to protect the American consulate and other points in the fighting between the Bolshevik troops and the Czech army, which had traversed Siberia from the Western Front. A joint proclamation of emergency government and neutrality was issued by the American, Japanese, British, French, and Czech commanders in July. In August 7,000 men landed in Vladivostok and remained until January 1920, as part of an allied occupation force. In September 1918, 5,000 American troops joined the Allied intervention force at Archangel and remained until June 1919. These operations were in response to the Bolshevik revolution in Russia and were partly supported by czarist or Kerensky elements.

1919 — *Dalmatia.* U.S. forces landed at Trau at the request of Italian authorities to keep order between the Italians and the Serbs.

1919 — *Turkey.* Marines from the USS *Arizona* landed to guard the U.S. consulate during the Greek occupation of Constantinople.

1919 — *Honduras.* September 8 to 12. A landing force was sent ashore to maintain order in a neutral zone during an attempted revolution.

1920 — *China.* March 14. A landing force was sent ashore for a few hours to protect lives during a disturbance at Kiukiang.

1920 — *Guatemala.* April 9 to 27. U.S. forces protected the American legation and other American interests, such as the cable station, during a period of fighting between Unionists and the government of Guatemala.

1920–22 — *Russia (Siberia).* February 16, 1920, to November 19, 1922. A U.S. Marine guard was sent to protect the American radio station and property on Russian Island, Bay of Vladivostok.

1921 — *Panama–Costa Rica.* American naval squadrons demonstrated in April on both sides of the isthmus to prevent war between the two countries over a boundary dispute.

Chapter Eight

Return to Normalcy

When Europe turns to the rehabilitation and reconstruction of peace, there will be a struggle for commercial and industrial supremacy such as the world has never witnessed. And if this land of ours desires to maintain its eminence, it must be prepared for that struggle.

— WARREN HARDING, Speech to the National Association of Manufacturers, New York, 1915

Following American foreign policy tradition since the time of George Washington, in August 1914 President Woodrow Wilson declared U.S. neutrality in the conflict that became World War I. Secretary of State William Jennings Bryan called on the belligerents to accept the Declaration of London as the definition of neutral rights.[1] Britain illegally mined the North Sea and extended a blockade of Germany to foodstuffs and other noncontraband (non–war-making) items. In February 1915, Germany announced that British attempts to starve Germans with an illegal blockade required exceptional countermeasures. The waters around the British Isles would be considered a war zone. Enemy merchant ships found in the zone would be destroyed without provision for the safety of passengers or crew. Neutral ships should avoid the zone, lest they be mistaken for British ships and sunk inadvertently.

In response to the German decision, President Wilson issued his "strict accountability" message: "The government of the United States would be constrained to hold the Imperial German Government to a strict accountability for such acts of their naval authorities, and to take any steps it might be necessary to take to safeguard American lives and property, and to secure to American citizens the full enjoyment of their acknowledged rights on the high seas." He added: "It is stated for the information of the Imperial Government that representations have been made to his Britannic Majesty's Government in respect to the unwarranted use of the American flag for the protection of British ships."[2] In March 1915, Britain declared a blockade of all German ports and warned that merchant ships bound to or from such ports would be subject to seizure and confiscation. The British interdicted American shipping, seizing some vessels, and impeded American trade with Germany. Like American presidents from 1793 to 1815, Wilson faced the dilemma of defending neutral rights and American commerce while avoiding the crossfire in a European war that extended worldwide.

Amid an escalating naval and land war, British, French, and German agents sought to influence American public opinion to favor their side. Increasingly, however, Wilson's policies — acceptance of the British blockade of northern Europe, allowing loans to the belligerents, mounting trade with the British and their allies, and dramatic declines in trade with Germany and the Central Powers — put the United States, de facto, on the Allies' side. German submarine warfare sometimes resulted in American casualties, most infamously on the liner *Lusitania* in May 1915, an event that left almost 1,200 dead, among them 128 Americans. Although the ship carried ammunition and other contraband of war, its sinking enraged the American public. For the next year, loss of American lives on ships destroyed by German submarines, charges of German industrial sabotage in the United States, German meddling in Mexico, threats to bring the Japanese into the war against the United States, and effective British propaganda pushed the United States closer to war. In May 1916, President Wilson asked Congress to appropriate funds to create for the United States a "navy second to none."

Germany had warned the United States in April 1916 that "neutrals cannot expect that Germany, forced to fight for her existence, shall, for the sake of neutral interest, restrict the use of an effective weapon if her enemy is permitted to continue to apply at will methods of warfare violating the rules of international law." Faced with the "hunger blockade" and stalemate in the European land war, Germany announced in late January 1917 a renewal of unrestricted submarine warfare. On February 3, 1917, the Wilson government broke off diplomatic relations with Germany; three weeks later Wilson requested authorization from Congress to arm merchant ships. When the Armed Ship Bill failed to overcome a filibuster by Senator Robert La Follette (R.-Wis.), Wilson, on the advice of Secretary of State Robert Lansing (who had tried to suppress information on the war supplies headed to England on the *Lusitania*), decided that he had constitutional authority to order arming merchant ships without congressional approval, and he did so. Wilson's decision marked another step in the expansion of executive authority in the name of defending the nation's security.[3]

From 1915 to 1917, the Germans had attempted to persuade the American government to take a more evenhanded approach to the war. The decision to renew unrestricted submarine warfare in 1917 reflected German frustration with what had essentially become American provisioning of the Allies' war against the Central Powers and the stalemate in the land war — and also the belief by some German naval strategists that submarine warfare would contribute to defeat of the Allies before Wilson could convince Congress to declare war. The Germans had declared in a memorandum handed to the secretary of state on January 31, 1917: "Germany will meet the illegal measures of her enemies by forcibly preventing, after February 1, 1917, in a zone around Great Britain, France, Italy and in the Eastern Mediterranean, all navigation, that of neutrals included, from and to England and from and to France, etc. All ships met within the zone will be sunk."

During February and March of 1917, German submarines sank several American merchant ships. Americans continued to insist, unsuccessfully, as they had during the Napoleonic wars, on respect for neutral shipping. The powder keg only needed a spark to set it off. The idea that Germany intended to create a North American front in the war, should the United States respond forcefully when submarine warfare renewed, eliminated any doubt in American public opinion regarding "Hun treachery." With the Zimmermann note, released to the American press on March 1, 1917, the Kaiser's government lit the ready fuse. The note, intercepted by British intelligence, proposed an alliance with Mexico and recovery of lost territory from the Mexican War of 1846–48 upon German victory:

Berlin, January 19, 1917

We intend to begin unrestricted submarine warfare on the first of February. We shall endeavor in spite of this to keep the United States neutral. In the event of this not succeeding, we make Mexico a proposal of alliance on the following basis: Make war together, make peace together, generous financial support, and an understanding on our part that Mexico is to reconquer the lost territory in Texas, New Mexico, and Arizona. The settlement in detail is left to you.

You will inform the President [of Mexico] of the above most secretly as soon as the outbreak of war with the United States is certain and add the suggestion that he should, on his own initiative, invite Japan to immediate adherence and the same time mediate between Japan and ourselves.

Please call the President's attention to the fact that the unrestricted employment of our submarines now offers the prospect of compelling England to make peace within a few months.

[Signed,] Zimmermann.[4]

The idea of a German alliance with Mexico and restoration of the South-west and Texas to Mexico after German victory not only defied the Monroe Doctrine and threatened U.S. national security but brought the monster of European intrusion into the Western Hemisphere back out of the historical closet. Involving Japan in the conflict would disrupt American commerce in the Pacific and threaten the Philippines, Hawaii, and the American West Coast. President Wilson told Congress: "The present German submarine warfare against commerce is a warfare against mankind. It is a war against all nations." He added that "neutrality is no longer feasible or desirable where the peace of the world is involved and the freedom of its people, and the menace to that peace and freedom lies in the existence of autocratic governments backed by organized force which is controlled wholly by their will, not by the will of their people. . . . The world must be made safe for democracy."[5] The vote for war in the U.S. Congress on April 4, 1917, was overwhelming but not unanimous (82–6 in the Senate and 373–50 in the House of Representatives). The Declaration of War against Austria-Hungary on December 17, 1917, was unanimous in the Senate and opposed only by one person in the House, the first American congresswoman, suffragist and pacifist Jeannette Rankin (Progressive Republican, Mont.). (Rankin returned to Congress in 1940, casting the only vote against U.S. entry into World War II.) Without formal alliance, the United States "associated itself" with Great Britain, France, Italy, and Japan to make war on the Central Powers.

Emergency war measures adopted by President Wilson and Congress further centralized American government, expanded its reach and bureaucratic complexity, and reinforced the evolving relationships among the federal government, industry, and finance.[6] Wilson also authorized an overseas propaganda campaign by the newly created Committee on Public Information. Directly under his control rather than subordinated to the State Department, the new agency established a precedent for presidential autonomy in public diplomacy, infiltrating and suborning foreign media outlets, and enlisting Americans overseas in "informational" and covert disinformation campaigns.[7] The incipient military-industrial complex of the 1880s and post-1898 period mushroomed; the graduated income tax approved in 1916 would finance a growing federal regime.

In January 1918, eleven months before the war's end, Wilson announced his "Fourteen Points" for world peace. The plan focused on Europe and great power politics. It was not so much visionary, except with respect to his design for a League of Nations, as it was a patchwork of boundary settlements, dissolutions of defeated empires, and ideological abstractions.[8] Wilson viewed the League of Nations as a way to keep the United States out of future wars

1 Abolition of secret treaties

2 Freedom of navigation of the seas

3 Equality of trade and removal, so far as possible, of economic barriers

4 Reduction of armaments to the extent compatible with security

5 Adjustment of colonial claims (decolonization, self-determination)

6 Russia to be assured independent development and international withdrawal from occupied Russian territory

7 Restoration of Belgium to antebellum national status

8 France evacuated; Alsace-Lorraine to be returned to France from Germany

9 Italian borders redrawn on lines of nationality

10 Autonomous development for peoples of Austria-Hungary as the Austro-Hungarian Empire is dissolved

11 Romania, Serbia, Montenegro, and other Balkan states to be granted integrity and have their territories evacuated, and Serbia to be given access to the Adriatic Sea

12 Sovereignty for Turkey, but autonomous development for other nationalities within the former empire; free passage through Dardanelles for ships and commerce of all nations

13 Establishment of an independent Poland with access to the sea

14 General association of the nations to enforce the peace (a multilateral international association of nations to enforce the peace)

and to provide hope for Europe and Russia's people. He accepted the need for repression of Bolshevism — what he called "the poison of disorder" — in Europe, the United States, and the Western Hemisphere. He also hoped that the League of Nations would limit the need for a gigantic American military establishment to police the trouble spots of the planet.[9] None of Wilson's Fourteen Points related directly to Latin America, unless Latin Americans saw in the "decolonization" language some hope for U.S. abandonment of its protectorates and military occupation regimes in the Caribbean and Central America. But Wilson's own policies had offered just the opposite between 1914 and 1919: repeated military intervention in Mexico, Nicaragua, Haiti, Cuba, and the Dominican Republic, along with nonrecognition of governments that did not live up to his standards or kowtow to his wishes.

American troops and supplies poured into Europe, turning the tide in the stalemated horrors of trench warfare. Russia, Austria-Hungary, Germany,

France, and England each had lost around 1 million dead. Germany signed an armistice agreement with the Allies on November 11, 1918.[10] President Wilson went to France to stump for the Versailles Treaty, then across the United States until he physically collapsed, thus taking him out of the day-to-day struggle over peace treaty ratification. Disabled by a series of strokes, Wilson would finish his term as an invalid.

In Europe, the victors sought revenge, especially against Germany. They redesigned the map of Europe with the independence of Czechoslovakia, Estonia, Finland, Latvia, Lithuania, Poland, and Yugoslavia. They required that Germany and the Central Powers accept full responsibility for the war, that they disarm, and that they make reparations to the Allies. Indeed, in tentatively accepting Wilson's Fourteen Points as a basis for peace with Germany, the Allies had stipulated that

> clause 2 [of the Fourteen Points], relating to what is usually described as the freedom of the seas, is open to various interpretations, some of which they could not accept. They must, therefore, reserve to themselves complete freedom on this subject when they enter the peace conference. Further, in the conditions of peace laid down in his address to Congress of January 8, 1918, [in which] the President declared that invaded territories must be restored as well as evacuated and freed, the Allies feel that no doubt ought to be allowed to exist as to what this provision implies. By it they understand that compensation will be made by Germany for all damage done to the civilian population of the Allies and their property by the aggression of Germany by land, by sea and from the air.[11]

The Allies carved up spheres of influence, protectorates, and semicolonies in Asia, North Africa, and the Middle East (pretty much in accord with secret treaties concluded among them in 1915, to which the United States was not a party), setting the stage not only for World War II (1939–45) but also (viewed with hindsight) for the tragedy of the Middle East, the Persian Gulf, and Mesopotamia in the last half of the twentieth century.[12]

Communism, Radicalism, Racism, and the First War on Drugs

Toward the end of World War I, the collapse of Russia provided Americans with a new foreign threat: international communism. The United States applied its nonrecognition policy, practiced against Latin American regimes not to its liking, against the new Russian government.[13] America sent troops to Russia in August 1918, along with the Japanese, the French, and the British. President Wilson authorized 50 million dollars in secret payments to the White armies fighting the Bolsheviks, engaged some 5,000 American soldiers in combat, and did not withdraw U.S. forces until June 1919, six months after Germany signed the Armistice. He sent another expedition to Siberia, on exclusively presidential authority, ostensibly to rescue Czech forces besieged by the Communists and to support Czech independence (recognized in October 1919).[14] But military intervention failed to undo the Russian Revolution. U.S. troops withdrew from Siberia in April 1920; the Russian ally had become the Bolshevik enemy.[15] Beginning in the early 1920s, the Soviet regime reached out to nascent communist parties and labor organizations from Mexico to South America. For the next seven decades, the Monroe Doctrine would be applied to contain the influence of international Marxism and the Soviet Union in Latin America instead of that of European monarchies and commercial interests.

The new Russian challenge coincided with labor conflicts and racial violence across the United States in the summer of 1919. Fear of imported Bolshevism and anarchism led to a repressive campaign against "radicals," "reds," and "suspected reds." Pacifists and socialists suffered incarceration, prosecution, and even deportation.[16] Simultaneously, postwar unemployment, a wave of lynching in the South and Midwest, and a resurgence of the Ku Klux Klan (resurrected in 1915, the same year that the epic racist film *Birth of a Nation* swept the nation and drew favorable response from President Woodrow Wilson) drove black immigrants to northern cities in the hope of escaping violence and the oppressive Jim Crow regime. De facto segregation in the North, large increases in African American competition for jobs, housing, and urban space, and homespun racism ignited mob violence in Chicago, Washington, D.C. (where Wilson ordered federal troops to intervene), Omaha (where martial law was imposed), St. Louis, and more than a dozen other cities.[17] African American war veterans, the NAACP, and the Negro press resisted a return to prewar "normalcy" — that is, to institutionalized racial subordination and coercion.[18]

To confront the Red Scare, the Military Intelligence Division (MID) of the army, whose modern birth dated from counterintelligence and counterinsurgency operations in Cuba, Puerto Rico, and the Philippines and whose official rebirth dated from 1917, engaged in extensive domestic surveillance of "radicals." It also monitored what was called "the racial situation."[19] Created by Captain (later Major General) Ralph H. Van Deman, the father of modern American military intelligence, the MID infiltrated organized labor, reform groups, the NAACP, and pacifist organizations. It assisted local authorities, "patriots," and the army in suppressing strikes and "racial disturbances." The

"He Would Turn the Clock Back a Thousand Years." Cartoon by Neal McCall, published in the *Portland Telegram*, reprinted in the *American Review of Reviews*, June 1919. The cartoonist points out the dangers of Bolshevism to the world and the United States after World War I in the midst of the "Red Scare" and with American troops in Russia supporting the counterrevolutionaries.

personalities, practices, and prejudices of U.S. colonial administration came home to repress radicals and "uppity" people of color in the United States.

To suppress "radical-led disorders," the War Department concocted Emergency Plan White.[20] In a 1919 memorandum, Major Elbert Cutler (who had a doctorate from Yale University) expressed his concern for the dangerous fusion of demands for racial equality with socialist and anarchist movements. His African American colleague, Major W. H. Loving, who had served in the Philippine constabulary created by the American occupation force, lamented the growing appeal of the "torch of socialism" to "Negroes" seeking to overcome Jim Crow, the lynching regime, and disenfranchisement.

During World War I, President Wilson had signed the Espionage Act (1917) and the Sedition Act (1918, an amendment to the former), which outlawed the use of "disloyal, profane, scurrilous, or abusive language" about the United States government, flag, or armed forces. The act also allowed the postmaster general to curtail mail delivery to dissenters against government policy during wartime. Reminiscent of the Alien and Sedition Acts implemented by John Adams in 1798, Wilson's internal security legislation brought the beginnings of what would become, after World War II, a permanent U.S. national security apparatus focused on "internal enemies" who drew their inspiration from foreign ideologies.

Senator Robert M. La Follette Sr. (Progressive Republican-Wis.) denounced Wilson's repression of dissent during the war and would continue to oppose the attack on free speech and civil liberties in the postwar years. In October 1917, addressing the Senate, La Follette defended the right of free speech and open opposition to the war. He reminded Wilson of the patriotic opposition to the Mexican War by Henry Clay, Daniel Webster, Abraham Lincoln, and many other great Americans. He also called on Congress to define the country's objectives in the war recently entered into and asserted that

> on this momentous question there can be no evasion, no shirking of duty of the Congress, without subverting our form of government. If our Constitution is to be changed so as to give the President the power to determine the purposes for which this Nation will engage in war, and the conditions on which it will make peace, then let that change be made deliberately by an amendment to the constitution proposed and adopted in a constitutional manner. It would be bad enough if the Constitution clothed the President with any such power, but to exercise such power without constitutional authority can not long be tolerated if even the forms of free government are to remain.[21]

La Follette rejected the idea that the president had powers not stipulated explicitly in the Constitution. The Founders had created no "inherent" powers. He interpreted the commander-in-chief authority strictly in military terms, denying that it gave any political authority to the president, still less any authority to declare war, to make war without congressional authorization, or to define the objectives of any war entered into by the United States. La Follette found himself on the losing side of a constitutional debate and political process that had gradually enhanced executive authority in foreign affairs and for deployment of armed forces abroad in the name of "self-defense" and national security — a process that would intensify in the post–World War I era.

As in the early years of the Republic, fear of foreign enemies, imported revolutionary ideas, revolutionaries, and political dissent led to domestic repression. Parallel to the operations of the MID, Attorney General A. Mitchell Palmer put in place in August 1919 the General Intelligence Division of the Bureau of Investigation. Appointed as its chief, J. Edgar Hoover sought to uncover Bolshevik conspiracies and to repress "Red" agents across the country, especially within the labor movement and among African American organizations seeking an end to the white supremacy regime. Hoover would come to personify American anticommunism for the next half century. The so-called Palmer Raids of 1919 were followed by anticommunist legislation in some thirty states; thousands of arrests resulted. The holy and patriotic mission of fighting communists and communism would become a pervasive element of domestic politics and of policy toward Latin America and Europe.

For Woodrow Wilson, the communists were anathema. He also was no racial liberal. As president of Princeton University, he discouraged black applicants (no African Americans were accepted at Princeton, officially, until 1940). In the Washington bureaucracy, Wilson condoned full segregation. He seemed to mostly accept the southern version of Reconstruction, and, though he denounced Ku Klux Klan terrorism, he could "understand" the Klan as a response to injustices done to the conquered Confederacy. In this context, along with his righteous and aloof personality, must be understood his obdurate commitment to democracy in the abstract and his authoritarian, imperious, and racist policies in practice, overseas and at home.

Woodrow Wilson said that he abhorred lynching but opposed federal antilynching laws because he believed such crimes ought to be managed under the jurisdiction of the individual states. And, notwithstanding his campaign promises to support female suffrage, he opted to remain uncommitted rather than openly to oppose expansion of the vote to women in his first term, apparently still believing that, like antilynching legislation and disenfranchisement of African Americans, expansion of the suffrage to women should be left to the states. In short, Woodrow Wilson had a limited notion of democracy. Making the world "safe for democracy" did not include equality for all Americans and it did not include self-determination for peoples of color in the United States or around the world. That, in these respects, he was merely a "man of his times" made the consequences no less detrimental for the cause of real democratization in the United States or in Latin America and America's overseas colonies. Indeed, Wilson's narrow, if not hypocritical, interpretation of democracy and self-determination detracted seriously from America's postwar message to Europe and to peoples subjected to European colonialism.

Taken together, Woodrow Wilson's policies seamlessly melded America's historical sense of global mission and democratic exceptionalism with interventionist polices abroad and repression of racial minorities and political dissidents at home. That was *normalcy*, for America, even before it was taken on as a slogan by Wilson's successor, Warren G. Harding. In the name of democracy and freedom, Wilson reaffirmed racial segregation, attacked organized labor, and approved military and FBI surveillance of the peace movement, the suffragists, and the organizations struggling for the advancement and civil rights of people of color. His foreign policies presumed an American crusade to "make the world safe for democracy" — as American elites perversely understood the term.[22] Wilson's "liberal internationalism" also required periodic U.S. military intervention in the Western Hemisphere and elsewhere, a precedent for the righteous military and ideological crusades of future administrations from John F. Kennedy, Richard Nixon, Jimmy Carter, and Ronald Reagan to George W. Bush.

The League of Nations and Postwar Politics

As World War I wound down and Woodrow Wilson looked toward establishing his visionary framework for world peace, he finally decided to support female suffrage. On September 30, 1918, perhaps hoping for the suffragettes' support for his Fourteen Points, he urged Congress to approve an amendment to the Constitution: "We have made partners of the women in this war. . . . Shall we admit them only to a partnership of suffering and sacrifice and toil and not to a partnership of privilege and right?"[23] Despite rejection by eight states (and no approval by three), the Nineteenth Amendment extending the vote to women was ratified on August 18, 1920.

Wilson's battle to obtain Senate consent for the United States to join the League of Nations coincided with the upcoming presidential election. The

Republican candidate, Warren G. Harding, made keeping the United States out of the League a leading campaign issue. Joining the League of Nations seemed to require a commitment by the United States to come to the assistance of states seeking to ensure peace and sanction aggressors.[24] Such a commitment would have represented a dramatic departure from historical U.S. unilateralism.

Senator Henry Cabot Lodge, author of the Lodge Corollary to the Monroe Doctrine in 1912 and chairman of the Senate Foreign Relations Committee, opposed American entrance into the League of Nations, at least as it was conceived in the treaty submitted by Wilson to the Senate. He summed up his opposition to the core requirement of the League in barely coded racist and traditional unilateralist rhetoric: "Are you willing to put your soldiers and your sailors at the disposition of other nations?" Lodge's question was rhetorical, he thought. There could be no answer but no. Yet Lodge did not mention that thousands of African Americans in segregated units had been put under French command during the war, including units sent from Puerto Rico.[25] Lodge told his fellow citizens: "We are a great moral asset of Christian civilization. . . . How did we get there? By our own efforts. Nobody led us, nobody guided us, nobody controlled us. . . . I would keep America as she has been — not isolated. . . . I wish her to be master of her own fate." Senator James Reed (D.-Mo.) was less elliptical on the racial impediments to American participation in the League, reminding his senatorial colleagues that should they be tempted by Wilson's and the pacifists' exhortations, the League would consist of fifteen white nations and seventeen nations "of black, brown, yellow and red races."[26]

In 1919–20, no amount of supposed American idealism could make the country's racist premises, institutions, and practices compatible with recognizing the sovereign equality of "black, brown, yellow and red" nations. In any case, as former president Taft (who supported the League with reservations) explained, Latin Americans and others like them could not be relied upon to protect American interests or even their own: "An ignorant people without the slightest experience in the restraints necessary in successful self-government and subject to the wildest imaginings under the insidious demagoguery of venal leaders may well not know what is best for them."[27]

All of the Latin American countries entered the League except Mexico and Ecuador, though some, such as Costa Rica and Brazil, later withdrew. Nine were original members by virtue of signing the Treaty of Versailles and six by acceding to the Covenant as a separate document within two months of it coming into force.[28] Senator Reed counted none of the Latin Americans as "white" nations. Danger existed that whites would be outnumbered — and perhaps outvoted. Even the unanimity provisions eventually adopted for collective action could not overcome this genetic defect of the League of Nations. Americans remained determined to "command their own fortunes." Expressing its reservations to the League Covenant, the Senate resolved emphatically: "The United States will not submit to arbitration or inquiry by the assembly or by the council of the league of nations . . . any questions which in the judgment of the United States depend upon or relate to its long-established policy, commonly known as the Monroe doctrine; said doctrine is to be interpreted by the United States alone and is hereby declared to be wholly outside the jurisdiction of said league of nations."[29] The Olney Corollary remained in place. For the United States after World War I, the Monroe Doctrine still meant that "its fiat [was] law upon the subjects to which it confines its interposition."

Warren G. Harding won the presidency in 1920, campaigning against Wilson's Fourteen Points, the Versailles Treaty, and the League of Nations and even against the American occupations in Haiti and Santo Domingo. In the first presidential election in which women voted in every state, Harding defeated Democratic candidate James Cox in a landslide. In his inaugural address, Harding told the country: "I must utter my belief in the divine inspiration of the founding fathers. Surely there must have been God's intent in the making of this new-world Republic." Harding reaffirmed the trope of America's special Providence, its civilizing mission, its shining example for all the world to follow, and its core commitment to unilateralism: "America, our America, the America built on the foundation laid by the inspired fathers, can be a party to no permanent military alliance. It can enter into no political commitments, nor assume any economic obligations which will subject our decisions to any other than our own authority."[30] Harding reminded Americans of their virtue, righteousness, and exceptionalism, calling now for a return to *normalcy*. America, he claimed, had never made offensive warfare, never used force to acquire territory, never deployed military force until all diplomatic efforts had been exhausted. This synthesis of American popular culture and national identity is what Harding referred to when he told the country in his inaugural address: "Our supreme task is the resumption of our onward, normal way."

Harding either did not know American history or believed that Americans wanted to hear only the sacred version: "When the Governments of the earth shall have established a freedom like our own and shall have sanctioned the pursuit of peace as we have practiced it, I believe the last sorrow and the final sacrifice of international warfare will have been written."[31] In his December 6, 1921, State of the Union address, the first such address carried on radio, Harding told the country again that he favored a return to normalcy. In 1920, the

United States signed a peace treaty with Austria-Hungary (Treaty of Trianon) and, in 1921, a separate agreement with Germany (Treaty of Berlin). For the next twelve years, Republican administrations recommitted the country to what was called "independent internationalism," seeking through treaties on disarmament, naval limitations, trade, and agreed-upon spheres of influence with Japan, Great Britain, and France to keep the country out of another war while promoting prosperity at home.[32]

The United States sought a world order in which the industrial powers, particularly the victors in World War I, would police the colonial territories and divide up the natural resources (and peoples) of Asia, the Pacific, and Africa, yet still compete for markets and investment opportunities within peaceful limits. America desired what historian Robert Freeman Smith called an "Open Door World," allowing, in Harding's catchy phrase, "the peaceful commercial conquest of the world."[33] It did not isolate itself from international politics. Rather, it sought to manage the postwar world in its own way on its own terms.[34] That meant, in particular, reaffirmation of the Monroe Doctrine and hegemony in the Western Hemisphere as the foundation of grand strategy. The "new isolationists" of the 1920s oversaw "greater American participation in both economic and political affairs of Europe as well as wider relations of the world," even as they reaffirmed the unilateralist and autonomist tradition that stretched from George Washington to Theodore Roosevelt.[35]

Unfortunately, the effort to achieve peace through loans, investments, trade, and disarmament treaties failed. In one way or another, all the signatories violated the spirit and letter of the 1922 Naval Disarmament Treaty and other agreements, whether through building numerous nonprohibited vessels, such as submarines, through outsourcing weapons contracts and testing to other countries (for example, the Germans looked to South America), or through defying verification while seeking expanded influence in Asia, Africa, and the Middle East. Trade policy presented dilemmas for the victors as well as the defeated. In the United States, the Republican Party found it difficult to reconcile its traditional constituencies with the realities of a changing country — more urban, more industrial, more African American migrants escaping Jim Crow into northern cities, more southern European and Russian immigrants added to the "melting pot."

The commitment to protective tariffs was emblematic. Some Republican constituencies and northern urban groups sought to lower consumer prices and expand exports by lowering tariffs. Major manufacturing and agricultural interests demanded protection. As had been the case since the first debates after American independence, tariff policy reflected a jumble of competing, sometimes incompatible domestic interests, thus making difficult its use as an effective and coherent instrument of foreign policy. The Ford-McCumber Tariff (1922) and the highly protectionist Smoot-Hawley Tariff (1930), which raised rates and likely deepened the incipient depression after the 1929 stock market crash, demonstrated the conflictive relationship between domestic politics and the requirements of the "open door" for the Republican administrations from 1921 to 1933.[36] From Harding's first State of the Union message, it was clear that the Republicans would continue to favor a protectionist policy while making concessions to domestic political requirements (and the electoral constituencies of their various legislators) as best they could in forging the coalitions necessary to pass legislation through Congress. Only Latin America, where before the 1930s over 50 percent of government revenues commonly originated in customs duties, tended to have higher tariffs than the United States.[37]

The push for a world of treaties to "contractualize" international relations, whether with regard to trade, armaments, boundary disputes, or other matters, and to arbitrate international disputes culminated with the utopian Kellogg-Briand Pact of 1928, ostensibly outlawing war. By the end of 1928, some forty countries had signed on to the Pact — even the Soviet Union, to whose government the United States had not extended diplomatic recognition.[38] In the U.S. Senate, the only vote against the Pact came from John J. Blaine (R.-Wis.), author of the Twenty-first Amendment ending Prohibition. Blaine objected to continued British dominion over 400 million colonial subjects, including the Irish.

The United States refused to join the League of Nations, despite its global commercial and financial interests, military and naval deployments, contracts for military equipment, and security concerns even grander than before 1917. It would not be bound by the votes or influence of inferior nations, possibly allied with great power competitors. Moreover, the United States set about to reduce the flow of immigrants into the country to reassert its right to independent and sovereign decisions regarding its national security and over the sort of nation it wished to be.

The Immigration Debate

In 1921 (the "Emergency" Immigration Law) and 1924 (the Johnson-Reed Act), America adopted legislation to limit entry by Southern and Eastern Europeans and virtually to exclude Asians.[39] The Japanese government sent a formal protest to the secretary of state, dated May 31, 1924.[40] Shortly thereafter, Japan imposed 100 percent tariffs on goods imported in quantity from the United States and took its protests to the League of Nations.

Japanese protests were to no avail. Senator David A. Reed (R.-Pa.) proclaimed:

> There has come about a general realization of the fact that the races of men who have been coming to us in recent years are wholly dissimilar to the native-born Americans; that they are untrained in self-government — a faculty that it has taken the Northwestern Europeans many centuries to acquire. America was beginning also to smart under the irritation of her "foreign colonies" — those groups of aliens, either in city slums or in country districts, who speak a foreign language and live a foreign life, and who want neither to learn our common speech nor to share our common life. From all this has grown the conviction that it was best for America that our incoming immigrants should hereafter be of the same races as those of us who are already here.[41]

Senator "Cotton Ed" Ellison DuRant Smith (D.-S.C.) connected the anti-immigrant legislation to the Red Scare and labor strife and also to the current academic and political fad: "scientific" racism.[42] (Cotton Ed was a founder in 1905 of the Southern Cotton Association; he served in the Senate from 1909 until his death in 1944):

> We have been called the melting pot of the world. We had an experience just a few years ago, during the great World War, when it looked as though we had allowed influences to enter our borders that were about to melt the pot in place of us being the melting pot. . . . It is the breed of the dog in which I am interested. I would like for the Members of the Senate to read that book just recently published by Madison Grant, "The Passing of a Great Race." Thank God we have in America perhaps the largest percentage of any country in the world of the pure, unadulterated Anglo-Saxon stock; certainly the greatest of any nation in the Nordic breed. It is for the preservation of that splendid stock that has characterized us that I would make this not an asylum for the oppressed of all countries, but a country to assimilate and perfect that splendid type of manhood that has made America the foremost Nation in her progress and in her power.[43]

Paradoxically, the 1924 legislation excluded Asian immigrants but set no quota on immigrants from nations of the Western Hemisphere. (The quotas, based on the 1890 census — that is, on population before the wave of late nineteenth-century and post–World War I immigration — were to approximate 2 percent of the total of a "nation's" contribution to the U.S. population — for example, Northwestern European stock would receive 75 percent of the total quota.) Congressman Albert Johnson (R.-Wash.), a sponsor of the legislation, made explicit that "with this new immigration act the United States is undertaking to regulate and control the great problem of the commingling of races. Our hope is in a homogeneous Nation. At one time we welcomed all, and all helped to build the Nation. But now asylum ends. The melting pot is to have a rest. This Nation must be as completely united as any nation in Europe or in Asia. Self-preservation demands it."[44] Not only did self-defense sometimes require preemptive war. In accord with the spirit of the 1790 Naturalization Act, Congress returned to the idea of racially restrictive immigration legislation in the name of "self-preservation."

If so, why was there a permissive loophole for peoples of the Western Hemisphere?

The answer, like many anomalies in American foreign policy, could be found in Washington's complex and confusing bureaucratic politics and in special interest groups successfully defending their terrain in congressional horse trading. To that must be added the provisions of the Treaty of Guadalupe Hidalgo (1848) ending the War against Mexico.[45]

First, within the Department of State a small group of influential policymakers wished to avoid offending the Latin Americans in an era promoting Pan Americanism and dollar diplomacy. Senator Reed favored this "tradition of Pan Americanism." He told his colleagues: "We have for many years followed the policy of encouraging the spirit of fraternity between this country and our neighbors in North and South America. . . . To establish free trade in human beings, so to speak, with them, is believed to be desirable by those persons who had the Pan American Union most at heart."[46] He added that, in any case, with the exception of Mexico and Canada, no more than 8,000 persons entered the United States from other hemispheric nations annually, most as tourists, and most left, so there was no need to restrict immigration from within the hemisphere. Moreover, Reed explained that it was a physical impossibility to guard effectively the thousands of miles of Mexican and Canadian borders with the United States to prevent smuggling of immigrants.

Second, "in deference to the need for labor in Southwestern agriculture and American diplomatic and trade interests with Canada and Mexico," the legislators agreed not to fix a quota for the Western Hemisphere states. There seemed no politically plausible manner of fixing quotas for Mexico and not Canada. Third, the Treaty of Guadalupe Hidalgo provided for citizenship for Mexicans in the conquered territory, unless they explicitly renounced American citizenship.[47] This presented a "genetic" problem. The baseline for naturalization was the 1790 Naturalization Law, which provided "that any alien, *being a free white person*, who shall have resided within the limits and under the jurisdiction of the United States for the term of two years, may be admitted to become a citizen thereof, on application to any common law court of record, in any one of the States wherein he shall have resided for the term of one year at least."[48] The meaning of "white" for purposes of naturalization was litigated extensively into the 1920s and 1930s, when courts ruled in contradictory fashion but eventually concluded that Japanese were not "white" and, like other Asians, not eligible for citizenship.[49] Since Mexicans had been granted citizenship by the Treaty of Guadalupe Hidalgo, for purposes of the law they were, ipso facto, eligible, and therefore "white," or at least white enough for citizenship. They could be excluded from citizenship for other reasons, such as "likely to be a public charge" or "not of good moral character," but not for failure to meet the requirement of being a "free white person."

Racism inspired the 1924 immigration law, but, for the moment, politics and the "Pan-American spirit" seemed to provide *Latin* Americans a window of opportunity. Despite some amendments proposing quotas on Western Hemisphere immigrants, the legislation eventually passed with no quotas applied to nations of the hemisphere.[50]

President Harding had vigorously supported the restrictionist immigration legislation. He also asked Congress to legislate regarding registration of all aliens in the country: "The Nation has the right to know who are citizens in the making or who live among us and share our advantages while seeking to undermine our cherished institutions." Harding would not bring this idea to fruition. Plagued by corruption scandals and tales of multiple mistresses, he died in San Francisco, supposedly of a heart attack, in August 1923.

Harding's successor, Vice President Calvin Coolidge, proved to be one of America's most conservative, laconic, and predictable presidents. He wanted lower taxes, probusiness policies, and world peace. He wanted America for Americans, immigration restriction (which he urged on Congress in 1923 and signed off on in 1924), and less government meddling in people's daily lives. (In the 1980s, Ronald Reagan would have Coolidge's portrait hung prominently in the White House.) In foreign affairs, Coolidge spelled out emphatically the meaning of "the American principle," especially the commitment to unilateralism: "Our country has one cardinal principle to maintain in its foreign policy. It is an American principle. It must be an American policy. We attend to our own affairs, conserve our own strength, and protect the interests of our own citizens; but we recognize thoroughly our obligation to help others, reserving to the decision of our own Judgment the time, the place, and the method. . . . The League [of Nation] exists as a foreign agency. We hope it will be helpful. But the United States sees no reason to limit its own freedom and independence of action by joining it."[51]

Unilateralism redux. Shortly after Coolidge signed legislation restricting "undesirable" immigration, the Senate, in 1926, also refused to ratify U.S. participation in the Permanent Court of International Justice. But after World War I, the place of the United States in the world, its economic weight, and its influence in the international system gave unilateralism a new and more ominous meaning for the rest of the planet. The Republican administrations of the 1920s would seek to organize and manage an international order conducive to American economic and political interests, based in part on reaffirmation of the Monroe Doctrine and more complete U.S. hegemony in the Western Hemisphere. This would mean countering the influence of the Mexican revolution and nationalism in Latin America while combating socialism, Marxism, and Soviet-inspired communism within the hemisphere and across the Atlantic. America's equivocal idealism and belief in a civilizing mission, mixed imperfectly with a desire for economic prosperity based on expanding markets, foreign investment, and control of global financial networks, would foster Dr. Jekyll–Mr. Hyde foreign policies into the 1930s.

Americans often failed to understand the impact of what Europeans and Latin Americans perceived as their hypocrisy and self-serving idealism. As would occur in the early twenty-first century, Americans in the 1920s wanted to believe in their own exceptionalism and generosity; other peoples, particularly in Latin America, misunderstood U.S. intentions and were seemingly ungrateful for America's export of its versions of democracy and capitalism. Capturing the American spirit of the times, Congressman Fiorello H. La Guardia (Progressive Republican-N.Y.) had told the House of Representatives in 1919 that he would go to Mexico with beans in one hand and hand grenades in the other, and "God help them in case they do not accept our well-intended and sincere friendship."[52]

So began the return to "normalcy" for America's neighbors in the Western Hemisphere after World War I. For Latin America, normalcy in the United States meant imperious pretensions of hegemony. Until the onset of the economic depression of the 1930s, America seemed reluctant to temper the impact of its imperial benevolence toward Latin American beneficiaries of its "well-intended and sincere friendship." Meanwhile, normalcy at home meant reaffirmation of racism and Jim Crow, repression of labor unions and political dissidents, expansion of corporate capitalism, marital bliss for big business and probusiness governments, and deepening corruption of American politics and government.

Chapter Nine

Independent Internationalism

America seeks no earthly empire built on blood and force. No ambition, no temptation, lures her to thought of foreign dominions. The legions which she sends forth are armed, not with the sword, but with the cross. The higher state to which she seeks the allegiance of all mankind is not of human, but of divine origin. — CALVIN COOLIDGE, Inaugural Address, March 4, 1925

Republican presidents Warren Harding (1921–23) and Calvin Coolidge (1923–29) presided over a dramatic increase in American political influence and weight in the world economy. Massive augmentations of foreign investment, trade, lending, and octopus-like extension of financial networks made the United States the world's leading economic power. Americans increasingly controlled natural resources and communication, transportation, and energy networks around the world. This pattern was especially notable in Latin America.

In 1914, no U.S. bank operated in South America, and no American steamship line served the region. By 1921, over fifty U.S. banks had established branches in addition to expanded operations in the Caribbean and Central America.[1] Latin American economic policy was part of the global effort by the State Department and other American agencies to champion the "imperative demands of American business" and to coordinate "the work of all departments bearing upon the same great object of American prosperity."[2] Of 10 billion dollars invested abroad by U.S. firms and individuals, 40 percent (4 billion dollars) corresponded to Latin America. Accompanying these trends came fierce competition to place loans, bribe government officials, and employ U.S. experts, such as Edwin W. Kemmerer (the "money doctor") to supervise Latin American governments' fiscal and monetary policies.[3]

A less noticeable penetration of Latin America — one that would become much more important after World War II — came with U.S. government subsidies for a nascent Pan American Federation of Labor, using the American Federation of Labor (AFL) and Samuel Gompers as instruments. At first intended to influence Mexican labor organizations and the policies of the government of Venustiano Carranza, the Pan American Federation of Labor was, according to Santiago Iglesias Pantín (a Puerto Rican labor leader and pro-statehood senator), "the instrumentality through which the influence of radical labor unions in Latin America, inspired by the example of the Bolshevik Revolution of 1917 in Russia would be checked."[4] This initiative was the AFL corollary to the Monroe Doctrine, seeking to limit the reach of "extra-hemispheric" labor ideologies into the Western Hemisphere.

Though often with competing, even conflicting, agendas, the various agencies of the U.S. government sought to influence congressional decision making regarding Latin America and meddled extensively in constituting, toppling, and "orienting" the region's governments.[5] The multiple actors in U.S. foreign affairs — official, business, religious, philanthropic, and others, and the parallel activities of the Pan American Union — made difficult deciphering a coherent Latin American policy. Even more difficult to anticipate were the particulars: which bank consortium should be supported for which loan; which corporation for the cable concession; which shipping line for the mail service; and so on.

President Harding and his secretary of state, Charles Evan Hughes, had decided it was time to give a different face to the Caribbean and Central American protectorates. Hughes repeatedly referred to the Monroe Doctrine in his speeches but also sought to mollify Latin American critics by assuring them that it did not signify American designs of conquest or establishment of new protectorates. With rhetorical nuance, Hughes also further expanded the implications of the Monroe Doctrine, claiming that it opposed (1) any non-American action encroaching upon the political independence of American states under any guise and (2) the acquisition in any manner of the control of additional territory in the Western Hemisphere by any non-American power. Such language reaffirmed the unilateralist character of the Monroe Doctrine as an instrument to defend, first, U.S. interests (in the name of protecting Latin America against "encroachment" on political independence, whatever that meant), while seemingly reiterating the Lodge Corollary of 1912. European governments and political commentators responded with incredulity and satire to American protestations of idealism and noninterventionism.

According to Hughes, the United States enjoyed the *"recognized right to object to acts done by other powers which might threaten its own safety."*[6] This included the right of preemptive self-defense, based on a unilateral judgment that "acts" by other powers in the Western Hemisphere might threaten the United States. Hughes denied that the United States sought "overlordship" or that it sought "to make our power the test of right in this hemisphere." Nevertheless, the United States reaffirmed the exclusive right to determine "the occasions upon which the principles of the Monroe Doctrine shall be invoked or the measures that shall be taken in giving it effect." American sovereignty, self-defense, and vital interests required "unhampered discretion."

The United States sought peace and prosperity through treaties (like the 1923 Central American Treaty of Peace and Amity, which provided for nonrecognition of governments that came to power through coups), conferences (like the one sponsored by the United States to settle a variety of disputes among the Central American states in 1922–23), and arbitration of disputes — unless American security and vital interests, as defined by the United States, came into play. The country then demanded "unhampered discretion." That is what "independent internationalism" was about: leaving America in command of its own destiny. Despite this double standard for Latin American countries and the United States, by 1933, when the string of Republican administrations ended, the United States had established itself as a proxy inter-American court by arbitrating numerous boundary disputes involving almost three-quarters of the Latin American nations.

Haiti, Race Politics, and the Monroe Doctrine

By the early 1920s, with no immediate European challenge in the hemisphere, the military interventions, occupation regimes, and protectorates enforced by the Wilson administration had become an embarrassment. In his campaign for the presidency, Warren Harding not only denounced the League of Nations but also the "rape of Hayti and Santo Domingo." But, as in the past, policies toward the Caribbean and Central America in the 1920s, indeed toward Latin America more generally, could not be divorced from race politics in the United States.

American political elites presumed that keeping people of color "in line" required coercion and periodic repression. So ingrained was racism in domestic politics that the Republican platform for 1920 barely brought itself to denounce lynching and would not address the Jim Crow regime, peonage in the South, or disenfranchisement. President Harding did call lynching "a stain on the fair name of America" and met several times with African American leaders during the election campaign. His Democratic opponent, James Cox, with Franklin Delano Roosevelt as vice presidential candidate, called Republicans the "Afro-American Party" (and Roosevelt accused the Republicans of "appealing to race hatreds").[7] Such language, after the Red Scare and widespread racial violence, mainly violence against people of color, could not have heartened African American voters in the North.[8] Neither did pamphlets released by Democrats in Ohio, Cox's home state, with such pleasant titles as "A Timely Warning to the White Men and Women of Ohio" and "The Threat of Negro Domination."

After consultation with NAACP leaders recently back from Haiti, Harding decided to attack the Democrats for their handling of the Haitian and Dominican occupations. Perhaps ironically, W. E. B. Du Bois used language borrowed from Thomas Jefferson, declaring that Negroes were free from "entangling alliances" since neither of the candidates was "a friend of the Negro or democracy."[9] Du Bois proved prescient. Once elected, and after his 1921 message to Congress, Harding failed to take up the evils that screamed out for federal government attention. For Harding, "Racial amalgamation there cannot be. . . . Partnership of the races there must be."[10]

Partnership of the races? Only four months previous the African American community in Tulsa, Oklahoma, had been subjected to a pogrom worthy of czarist Russia. Harding expressed his "regret and horror at the recent Tulsa tragedy" but did nothing to provide federal assistance or reparations for the human tragedy that had been inflicted by the massacre (estimates ranged up to 300 killed; 35 city blocks were destroyed by fire and some 10,000 were left homeless). Harding did support antilynching legislation, which was passed by the House of Representative in October 1922 (231–119), but the bill was defeated in the Senate by a Democrat filibuster. From the African American community and the northern "radicals" came pleas for justice and a warning for the future: "What is America going to do after such a horrible carnage? . . . There is a lesson in the Tulsa affair for every American who fatuously believes that Negroes will always be the meek and submissive creatures that circumstances have forced them to be during the past three hundred years. . . . Perhaps America is waiting for a nationwide Tulsa to wake her. Who knows?"[11]

Shortly after Harding took office, the Senate Foreign Relations Committee created a special subcommittee, the Select Committee on Haiti and Santo Domingo, to investigate the atrocities allegedly committed by the American military occupation forces in Haiti.[12] The Select Committee, chaired by Senator Joseph Medill McCormick (R.-Ill.), expressed its "chagrin at the improper or criminal conduct of some few members of the Marine Corps and at the same time feels it to be its duty to condemn the process by which biased or interested individuals and committees and propagandists have seized on isolated instances . . . to bring into general disrepute the whole American naval force in Haiti. The committee wishes to express its admiration for the manner in which our men accomplished their dangerous and delicate task."[13]

Editorials in anti-imperialist media were not so forgiving. Ernest H. Gruening wrote in the *Nation:*

> Senator McCormick, who long before the Commission was created recorded himself publicly in favor of our retention for twenty years of the Civil Occupation of Haiti, but now accepts the military view completely, told me in conversation that his interpretation of the Monroe Doctrine gave us "militant rights down to the Orinoco Basin." ' This, I take it, means that we can according to our needs more or less gobble up everything in and around the Caribbean. . . . Mr. McCormick's successor may substitute the Amazon for the Orinoco, and Senator Someone-else may feel that our sphere of militancy should not stop short of the Straits of Magellan. But the fruits of this policy are already visible in our actual, partial, potential, and rapidly increasing domination of the weaker states of the Caribbean.[14]

Among African American activists, the Haitian occupation and mistreatment of the civilian population had become a cause célèbre.[15] W. E. B. Du Bois proclaimed: "If ever a Senator deserved defeat for betrayal of the Negro race, Medill McCormick is that man."[16] Yet the committee findings could hardly be surprising when Woodrow Wilson's secretary of state, Robert Lansing, had opined that "the experience of Liberia and Haiti shows that the African races are devoid of any capacity for political organization and lack genius for government. Unquestionably there is in them an inherent tendency to revert to savagery and to cast aside the shackles of civilization which are irksome to their physical nature. . . . It is that which makes the negro problem practically unsolvable."[17]

President Harding's death in August 1923 did nothing to modify domestic racial relations, foreign policy in general, or relations with Latin America. When Calvin Coolidge took office, Secretary of Commerce Herbert Hoover and Secretary of State Charles Evan Hughes stayed in place. Taxes came down, tariff protectionism was reaffirmed, and, as Harding had promised, there would be still "less government in business and more business in government."[18]

The Fifth Pan American Conference, 1923

Three months before Harding's death, the Fifth Pan American Conference met in Santiago, Chile (March 25–May 3, 1923). Refusal by the United States to join the League of Nations, which many of the Latin Americans saw as a chance to promote equality among states, and the ongoing U.S. occupations in the Caribbean and Central America proved problematic. Worse still, the United States, before rejecting membership in the League, had insisted on inserting article 21 into the League Covenant: "Nothing in this Covenant shall be deemed to affect the validity of international engagements such as treaties of arbitration or regional understandings like the Monroe Doctrine, for securing the peace."[19] It seemed, despite U.S. absence from the League, that Latin American members had acknowledged the legitimacy of the Monroe Doctrine, whatever its current interpretation by the government in Washington, D.C.

Held in the 100th anniversary year of Monroe's 1823 message to Congress, the Santiago conference provided an ideal moment for Latin Americans to attack its application in the hemisphere. Paradoxically, in an effort to curtail American unilateralism, the Uruguayans brought forth a resolution to make the Monroe Doctrine a collective security principle implemented by a regional "American League of Nations." Costa Rica proposed a Pan American Court of Justice. The United States opposed both of these ideas but did eventually support the proposal by Paraguay's two-time former president Manuel Gondra for a "Treaty to Avoid or Prevent Conflicts between the American States" (ratified by twenty of the twenty-one members and entered into force October 8, 1924). This treaty provided for a "cooling-off period" of six months in disputes among the members and for commissions to help arrive at settlements by agreement between the disputants. The Gondra Treaty was a symbolic achievement of a conference that deadlocked on other issues, especially the American refusal to clarify the meaning of the Monroe Doctrine or commit itself to nonintervention.

In Santiago, the U.S. delegates had instructions to avoid discussion of the League of Nations. They sought, as usual, to focus on commercial issues and arbitration agreements. Mexico, whose government had not been recognized by the United States, sent no delegate; neither did Bolivia or Peru, with the Tacna-Arica issue still unresolved from the War of the Pacific against Chile. According to American missionary, diplomat, and historian Samuel Inman, who lunched or dined with Chile's president, Arturo Alessandri, frequently during the conference, Alessandri told him that the most influential person at the Conference was the Mexican ambassador, "because the other delegates . . . go from the meetings to the Mexican Ambassador's home and there discuss what positions they should take the next day [regarding reform of the Pan American Union and the dilution of U.S. hegemony]."[20] Inman recollected: "The tragedy of the Santiago conference was that it came at the time when the United States, under President Harding, had hit one of its lowest moral levels. . . . Most of the delegates were 'lame ducks' — senators whose terms were soon to expire, with a trip to Santiago awarded as a kind of consolation prize. They knew nothing whatever of the Pan American movement."[21] He also recalled that his circuitous return voyage through Paris and Geneva "taught me that there [in Europe] . . . were the real centers of Latin American thought and of discussion concerning the international relations of Hispanic America — whose diplomats at times referred to the Pan American Union as the 'colonial division of the Department of State.' "[22]

Determined to Be Independent and Free

In foreign policy, first with Charles Evan Hughes and then with his new secretary of state, Frank B. Kellogg, Coolidge pushed forward the "civilizing and humanizing method adopted by means of conference, discussion, deliberation, and determination" to further American objectives: peace and business. In his 1924 address to Congress, Coolidge observed: "Ultimately nations, like individuals, cannot depend upon each other but must depend upon themselves. Each one must work out its own salvation. . . . While we desire always to cooperate and to help, we are equally determined to be *independent and free*."[23]

Coolidge followed the American principle: unilateralism in all matters of security and vital interests. In the same message, Coolidge found time also for a passing mention of Latin America: "While we are desirous of promoting peace in every quarter of the globe, we have a special interest in the peace of this hemisphere. It is our constant desire that all causes of dispute in this area may be tranquilly and satisfactorily adjusted." Four years later, in his last message to Congress, on December 4, 1928, Coolidge expressed his self-satisfied pleasure at American prosperity, the lowering of taxes, and the country's peace and progress in foreign relations. As a metric, he noted that during the last year alone "we have signed 11 new arbitration treaties, and 22 more are under negotiation." Relations had improved with Mexico, and the United States had arbitrated the Tacna-Arica dispute between Peru and Chile. Even in Nicaragua, Coolidge (wrongly) saw great progress and no cause to expect that the insurgency, what he called "a few bandits," would persist, as it did, for another five years.

Coolidge and Stimson sent more marines to Nicaragua in 1927 to suppress liberal guerrilla leader Augusto César Sandino's supposed Bolshevik orientations. They also sought to contain the ideological and political influence of Mexican revolutionary nationalism. As Coolidge's special envoy to Nicaragua in 1927, Stimson proclaimed that the Nicaraguans "were not fitted for the responsibilities that go with independence and still less fitted for popular self-government."[24] Notwithstanding the supposed racial and cultural inferiority of the Latin Americans, Stimson shared with most American policymakers the premise that hegemony in the Western Hemisphere was the cornerstone of American grand strategy: "That locality [Latin America] has been the one spot external to our shores which nature has decreed to be most vital to our national safety, not to mention our prosperity."[25] For that reason, the United States desired "order and stability" in Latin America. President Coolidge explained, for example, that American military interventions in Haiti and Nicaragua aimed "to assist the peoples and governments of those two countries in establishing stability, in maintaining orderly and peaceful institutions in harmony with civilized society."[26] More bluntly, the previous year, Undersecretary of State Robert Olds had written in a confidential memorandum: "We do control the destinies of Central America and we do so for the reason that the national interest absolutely dictates such a course. There is no room for any outside influence other than ours in this region. We could not tolerate such a thing without incurring grave risks. . . . Central America has always understood that governments which we recognize and support stay in power while those we do not recognize and support fall."[27]

Once again the institutional and personal overlay of colonial administration and the prejudices of foreign policy elites perverted American relations with Latin America. But these prejudices and American hubris were bipartisan.[28] Throughout the 1920s, policymakers believed that American prestige and influence, globally, depended on its ability to sustain effective overlordship and ideological contraception — whether of bolshevism, fascism, or revolutionary nationalism in its Latin American backyard. Precisely because Latin America itself did not threaten U.S. security, and its governments were generally weak, exclusion of extra-hemispheric influences and protection of American citizens and property remained a central premise of American regional policy.

Looking far beyond Latin America, Coolidge added in his 1928 address that American troops in China sought to ensure "peaceful conditions under which the rights of our nationals and their property may receive that protection to which they are entitled under the terms of international law."[29] He believed that sending more troops to China and recognizing the Nationalist government had improved the situation in Asia and that trade had increased. As historian William Appleman Williams wrote in 1954, the foreign relations of the United States in the 1920s "were marked by express and extended involvement with — and intervention in the affairs of — other nations of the world. . . .

The isolationists of the twenties . . . were in fact engaged in extending American power."[30] From the Western Hemisphere America exported its efforts to establish "order and stability," to protect American lives and property, and to exert its political and military influence globally.

Since extending American power required a partnership between business and government to create a peaceful and stable world, Coolidge applauded the Kellogg-Briand Pact that renounced *aggressive* war (August 27, 1928). He affirmed that the Pact "promises more for the peace of the world than any other agreement ever negotiated among the nations." Yet commitment to "the peace of the world" did not affect American adhesion to the No Transfer Principle or the Monroe Doctrine. As Secretary of State Kellogg declared to the Senate Committee on Foreign Relations on December 7, 1928, "The Monroe Doctrine is simply a doctrine of self-defense." A doctrine of self-defense cannot be renounced by sovereign states; it is an integral aspect of international law and the international system. In any case, the Senate committee reporting on the Kellogg-Briand Pact made clear that "under the right of self-defense allowed by the treaty must necessarily be included the right to maintain the Monroe Doctrine, which is part of our system of national defense."[31]

In renouncing "aggressive war," the United States did not abrogate its right of self-defense or even preemptive war. That would not be possible because, as Coolidge explained: "Our investments and trade relations are such . . . that it is almost impossible to conceive of any conflict anywhere on earth which would not affect us injuriously."[32] Coolidge assured Congress that the Pact "does not supersede our inalienable sovereign right and duty of national defense or undertake to commit us before the event to any mode of action which the Congress might decide to be wise."[33]

The Clark Memorandum

In January 1928 (several months before the signing of the Kellogg-Briand Pact), President Coolidge addressed the Sixth International Conference of American States in Havana, Cuba. He was the only sitting American president to do so. He told the delegates that

> an attitude of peace and good will prevails among our nations. A
> determination to adjust differences among ourselves, not by a resort
> to force, but by the application of the principles of justice and equity,
> is one of our strongest characteristics. The sovereignty of small nations
> is respected. It is for the purpose of giving stronger guaranties to the
> principles, of increasing the amount and extending the breadth of

"The Fox Preaches a Sermon on the Sovereignty of Small Nations." Cartoon published in *De Groene Amsterdammer*, Amsterdam, reprinted in the *American Review of Reviews*, April 1928. The "fox," American president Calvin Coolidge, has the "chicken," Nicaragua, in his basket, all the while preaching on the equality of nations to the other "chickens" of Latin America. Coolidge spoke at the Pan American Conference in 1928.

> these blessings, that this conference has been assembled. . . . A Divine
> Providence has made us a neighborhood of republics. It is impossible
> to suppose that it was for the purpose of making us hostile to each
> other, but from time to time to reveal to us the methods by which we
> might secure the advantages and blessings of enduring friendships.

He added: "It is among the republics of this hemisphere that the principle of human rights has had its broadest application; where political freedom and equality and economic opportunity have made their greatest advance. Our most sacred trust has been, and is, the establishment and expansion of the spirit of democracy."[34]

Despite Coolidge's platitudes, the chief of the U.S. delegation to the conference, Charles Evan Hughes, reasserted the American right of "temporary interposition" (not intervention!) as a matter of sovereignty and self-defense. Latin Americans vociferously denounced U.S. unwillingness to renounce preventive interventions and particularly opposed any explicit resurrection of the Roosevelt Corollary. Secretary of State Kellogg assigned Undersecretary of State J. Reuben Clark Jr. to devise a response to the Latin Americans' anger. Clark produced an extensively documented history of the Doctrine — the

"Equal Voices." Cartoon published in *Isvestia*, reprinted in *American Review of Reviews*, April 1928. Criticism from Russia of President Coolidge's statement that all nations at the Pan American Conference spoke with equal authority. The small voice is Nicaragua's.

"Memorandum on the Monroe Doctrine." Clark concluded, in diplomatic language, that the Roosevelt Corollary was a bastard offspring, not justified by the terms of the original Doctrine, but that U.S. intervention for purposes of self-defense and self-preservation derived from international law itself.[35]

According to Clark, Roosevelt had misinterpreted the Monroe Doctrine, but the policies he pursued in the hemisphere were justified by the principle of "self-defense." That being the case, the United States could not renounce potential unilateral action required to defend its sovereignty as permitted by the law of nations. Thus Clark had reaffirmed the legitimacy of applying the Roosevelt Corollary by renouncing it because it had neglected the most basic principle of all: the inalienable right of "self-defense" as interpreted by American policymakers.[36]

Where states were unable to guarantee protection to American citizens and property, when instability threatened U.S. or regional security, then "temporary interposition" might be required. As in the early nineteenth century, whether against pirates or governments that failed to meet their international obligations, the United States, like the European colonial regimes, reserved the right to bring the weight and reign of "civilization" to bear on the malefactors.

Toward the "Good Neighbor," Toward the New Deal

Herbert Hoover became the Republican candidate to succeed Calvin Coolidge in 1928. Hoover had extensive overseas experience since his days during the Boxer rebellion in China in 1900 and relief work during World War I. He served both Harding and Coolidge as secretary of commerce. The Republican platform proclaimed that the "United States has an especial interest in the progress of all the Latin American countries. . . . In the case of Nicaragua, we are engaged in co-operation with the government of that country upon the task of assisting to restore and maintain peace, order and stability, and in no way to infringe upon sovereign rights." Nicaraguan nationalists, such as Augusto César Sandino, whose guerrilla bands engaged U.S. marines in a brutal counterinsurgency campaign replete with tactical aircraft firing on the "bandits," thought otherwise. Sandino became a symbol throughout Latin America of resistance against American interventionism.

In his acceptance speech at the Republican convention, Hoover proclaimed: "We in America today are nearer to the final triumph over poverty than ever before in the history of this land. . . . We shall soon with the help of God be in sight of the day when poverty will be banished from this land." One of the Republicans' memorable campaign slogans was "a chicken in every pot and a car in every garage." Prosperity seemed to favor the Republicans, who campaigned on a platform of continuing the good times, continuing Prohibition, and maintaining high tariffs.

The Democrats nominated their first Catholic presidential candidate, Alfred Smith. Smith campaigned hard to overcome anti-Catholic bigotry and against Prohibition (he favored repeal of the Eighteenth Amendment) and Republican corruption and for tariff reform to safeguard the public "against monopoly created by special tariff favors." The Democrats proclaimed that the Philippines should be granted their immediate independence, "which they so honorably covet," and favored eventual statehood for Puerto Rico.[37]

On Latin America, the Democrats called for "non-interference with the elections or other internal political affairs of any foreign nation. This principle of non-interference extends to Mexico, Nicaragua, and all other Latin American nations. Interference in the purely internal affairs of Latin-American countries must cease." The Democrats also called for an end to executive initiatives that committed the country to protect other governments against revolution or foreign attack without congressional approval. (The Democrats conveniently ignored Woodrow Wilson's eight years of interventionism in the Western Hemisphere.)

The Democrats' mild criticism of Republican Latin American policy — what were "purely internal affairs" when protection of American citizens, their property, and U.S. security were at stake? — played little role in the electoral outcome.[38] Democrats won in only seven states, not even holding the "solid south." Hoover won 444 electoral votes against Smith's 87 and had more than 6 million more popular votes than his Democrat adversary.

Before taking office, Hoover took an unprecedented ten-week tour of Latin America. He promised Latin Americans that the United States would be a good (noninterventionist) neighbor. In his first message to Congress, on March 4, 1929, broadcast on a worldwide radio network, he commented: "Fortunately the New World is largely free from the inheritances of fear and distrust which have so troubled the Old World. We should keep it so." He also reiterated the "American principle": "Our people have determined that we should make no political engagements such as membership in the League of Nations, which may commit us in advance as a nation to become involved in the settlements of controversies between other countries. They adhere to the belief that the independence of America from such obligations increases its ability and availability for service in all fields of human progress."

In 1929, American policymakers still hoped that economic diplomacy, disarmament, and peace treaties could be the foundation of a new era. They failed to address the unraveling of the post-Versailles international system. The United States had refused to cancel war debts and the loans made to finance German reparation payments, further complicating any downward adjustments of the burden placed on the vanquished. Worse still, the Smoot-Hawley tariff raised duties and further eroded German ability to make reparation payments, thus adversely affecting Western European repayment of loans owed to U.S. banking consortiums.

In fairness to Hoover, despite his reservations on the tariff legislation, he followed the course of Republican policy since Harding, who had declared in his December 6, 1921, State of the Union message: "Much has been said about the protective policy for ourselves making it impossible for our debtors to discharge their obligations to us. This is a contention not now pressing for decision." A difference in 1930, of course, especially with the advantage of hindsight, was that Hoover could not claim that "this is not a contention now pressing for decision."

In Latin America, Hoover sought to extricate the country from the remaining military occupations and the obligations incurred under the protectorate regimes. He told the nation in his first message to Congress on December 3, 1929: "We still have marines on foreign soil — in Nicaragua, Haiti, and China. In the large sense we do not wish to be represented abroad in such manner." Hoover proved more or less true to his word; he orchestrated withdrawal of marines from Nicaragua (January 1933), and he refused to intervene either to emplace or overthrow dictators, for example, in the case of Gerardo Machado in Cuba.[39] Hoover's initiatives toward Latin America represented a genuine change in tactics, a distancing from military intervention and occupation as a principal instrument for achieving U.S. objectives. This change responded both to U.S. public opinion, grown tired of the unsuccessful counterinsurgency efforts, and to the onset of economic depression that made marines in Nicaragua or elsewhere in Latin America an unwelcome burden. It also responded, however grudgingly, to persistent diplomatic endeavors by Latin Americans to push the United States toward more respectful treatment of its sovereign sister republics in the Western Hemisphere.

Hoover and his team believed on taking office that prosperity would bring world peace. Seven months later, on October 29, 1929, Wall Street crashed, and the Great Depression began. First in Asia, with Japanese invasions of China, then in Europe, with the rise of fascism in Italy and nazism in Germany, the dream of prosperity and world peace turned into a nightmare. In January 1932, Japan declared the establishment of the Republic of Manchukuo (1932–45), a puppet government for Japanese control of Manchuria. The U.S. secretary of state responded with the Stimson Doctrine, protesting the Japanese occupation (but doing little else). Hoover refused to counter the Japanese military moves in Asia with the U.S. Navy; likewise, he failed to build U.S. naval forces even to the levels permitted by the treaties in force with Japan, Great Britain, and other powers.[40] Even in Latin America, war between Bolivia and Paraguay (June 1932–1935), both nonmembers of the League of Nations, broke the magical spell of regional peace, as did a brief conflict in late 1932 between Colombia and Peru over the territory around Leticia, Colombia's only outlet to the Amazon River. This last conflict was settled by League of Nations mediation and the first-time use of "international peacekeepers" (albeit Colombians) wearing League of Nations armbands as a face-saving device for Peru.[41]

The monumental contraction of the world economy, exacerbated by U.S. and European protectionism, devastated Latin America. Prices for raw materials dropped precipitously. Loans came due and could not be paid. Labor conflict, urban street protests, student demonstrations, and generalized discontent focused on American bankers and customs house administrators. Economic catastrophe undermined political stability. Between 1930 and 1935, fifteen Latin American countries experienced military coups. Many of the officers who took power favored European fascism or milder corporatist dictatorships to the sort of liberal democracy that Woodrow Wilson and his Republican successors had promised to spread around the globe.

A tide of economic nationalism followed in much of Latin America, accompanied by anti-Marxism, anticommunism, and antiliberalism. Internal dissent, provoked by massive unemployment and widespread misery, engendered repression, some of it locally administered but some of it also facilitated by America's new "noninterventionist" interpretation of independent internationalism. American military advisers assisted General Jorge Ubico's construction of a military dictatorship in Guatemala (1931–44), and U.S. military attachés in Central America witnessed (but did not orchestrate) the rise in El Salvador of General Maximiliano Hernández Martínez, perpetrator of the 1932 massacre of thousands of peasants in the name of anticommunism. Initially, the United States refused to recognize the Hernández Martínez government, in accord with its formal ties to the Central American treaty regime it had helped to create, but by 1935 (now under Franklin Delano Roosevelt's "Good Neighbor Policy"), the United States extended recognition to the Hernández Martínez dictatorship.[42]

In retrospect, from the mid-1920s until 1934, the United States gradually found an alternative to the protectorates and military occupations in Central America and the Caribbean. The marines left Cuba (1922), the Dominican Republic (1924), Nicaragua (1925 — but returned 1927–33), and Haiti (1934). After Herbert Hoover assumed the presidency in 1929, the United States sent no new military expeditions to restore or maintain order in the Caribbean. Although eschewing military intervention, the United States used nonrecognition or delayed recognition of governments as a principal policy instrument — as Wilson had done in Mexico. Nonrecognition complicated international trade and finance for the targeted nations.[43] It also made obtaining U.S. recognition a critical dimension of domestic political competition for political parties and would-be presidents in the Western Hemisphere. In Cuba, the Dominican Republic, and Central America, politicians and would-be dictators vied for U.S. blessings, even as nationalists denounced American intervention.

Against the Soviet Union and Japan (1931–32), nonrecognition of "illegitimate" governments proved a useless policy. Against Latin American governments, it was somewhat more effective. As it turned out (in the 1930s), some U.S. objectives could be achieved, especially "stability" and a commitment by Latin American governments to meet "international obligations," by installing "elected" dictatorships, buttressed by the constabularies created during the American occupation regimes. Such governments could be substituted for direct U.S. administration. So eventually Rafael Trujillo came to power in the Dominican Republic, as did the Somoza dynasty in Nicaragua, among other American-supported tyrants.[44]

New Deal?

In 1932, the position of the United States in the international system faced threats from internal economic collapse and political strife, from a surge of socialist and communist sentiments within the working classes, and from the rising tide of militarism and fascism in Japan and Europe. The international appeal of the Soviet alternative also menaced U.S. security. Franklin Delano Roosevelt's New Deal would have to address domestic immiseration and the threat of class warfare by restructuring the American federal government, "incorporating" labor through the National Labor Relations Act (1935), and establishing a social security system (1935). Government regulatory and planning agencies multiplied; the old capitalist order would never be quite the same.

Roosevelt adapted social democratic policies and institutions from Europe, understanding that status quo laissez-faire policies and discourse had run their course but also seeking not to overturn basic capitalist institutions or to undermine the racialist foundations of American society.[45] Thus African American sharecroppers suffered the consequences of the Agricultural Adjustment Act (1933) subsidies to landowners for taking land out of production.[46] More than a million Mexicans and Mexican Americans, as well as Filipinos, were repatriated to ease unemployment amid a campaign to rid the country of alien "cheap labor."[47]

Both fascism and international communism as ideological alternatives to liberal democracy invaded the Western Hemisphere. Agents of these ideological and political views organized political and social movements within most Latin American nations. On multiple fronts, the Western Hemisphere seemed vulnerable, if not already deeply penetrated by enemies that had to be taken seriously. Some of the threat scenarios that had agitated Theodore Roosevelt and Alfred T. Mahan resurfaced. Would a rearmed Germany resurrect the Kaiser's dream of bases in the Caribbean, a German colony in southern Brazil, or even strategic alliances with Argentina or Chile? Would international communism's appeal spread through Latin America? Would Japan go after the Philippines, Pacific islands, and Hawaii? How could Latin America, virtually sanitized of extra-hemispheric influence between 1914 and 1930, be preserved as the bastion of American power and influence? How would Latin America fit into this rapidly changing international system?

For Franklin Delano Roosevelt (1933–45), the overwhelming victor in the 1932 presidential election against a devastated Herbert Hoover, Latin America seemed the least of his problems. Yet he moved quickly to shore up the U.S. position in the hemisphere. In his inaugural address on March 4, 1933, borrowing from Herbert Hoover, he told the country: "In the field of world policy I would dedicate this nation to the policy of the good neighbor — the neighbor who resolutely respects himself, and because he does so, respects the rights of others." He repeated the message on April 12, 1933, at the Pan American Union: "The essential qualities of a true Pan Americanism must be the same as those which constitute a good neighbor, namely, mutual understanding." Yet Roosevelt characterized the Monroe Doctrine, the quintessential moment in American unilateralism, as a "Pan American doctrine of continental self-defense" and then returned to Henry Clay's focus on opening Latin American markets to the United States: "It is of vital importance to every Nation of this Continent that the American Governments, individually, take, without further delay, such action as may be possible to abolish all unnecessary and artificial barriers and restrictions which now hamper the healthy flow of trade between the peoples of the American Republics"[48] (fast forward to Ronald Reagan, George H. W. Bush, or Bill Clinton — the Good Neighbor now wants "free trade" "as may be possible").

At the Seventh Pan American Conference (December 3–28, 1933), at Montevideo, Uruguay, Roosevelt and his secretary of state, Cordell Hull, would have a chance to give more concrete meaning to the Good Neighbor Policy in Latin America. Hull announced that the United States "is as much opposed as any other government to interference with the freedom, the sovereignty, or the other internal affairs or processes of the government of other nations." He also declared that the U.S. government would not serve as the military arm of international bankers to collect debts owed by sovereign governments, a repudiation of gunboat and dollar diplomacy that was welcome to Latin Americans. President Roosevelt followed up on Hull's speech on December 28, declaring that "the definite policy of the United States from now on is one opposed to armed intervention." Latin Americans generally responded favorably to Roosevelt's rhetoric; he is still remembered in the region for his supposed adherence to the "nonintervention principle" as a foundation of inter-American relations.

Yet the question remained whether this change in rhetoric and tactics constituted a change in attitudes toward Latin Americans or a change in the underlying American grand strategy, which required as its cornerstone hegemony in the Western Hemisphere. Economic conditions in the United States made any new markets for American manufactures or investment opportunities in Latin America extremely welcome.[49] Likewise, American public opinion had turned against dollar diplomacy and military interventionism in the Caribbean and Central America. Latin American insurgents and Latin American diplomats had resisted U.S. militarism and unilateralism since 1898; the Good Neighbor Policy represented a modest acknowledgment that their efforts had not been entirely in vain. Thus, Roosevelt's reluctant acceptance of the nonintervention pledge (it was limited to a ban on *military* intervention, indeed the meaning of "intervention" for Roosevelt was limited to *military* incursions) responded to domestic and international contingencies that called for a change in tactics. As had all the post–World War I presidents, Roosevelt continued to rely on "nonrecognition" as a tool to discipline or alter Latin American governments.[50]

In the Convention on the Rights and Duties of States, adopted at Montevideo in 1933, the United States formally recognized the equality of states and agreed to equal votes and representation within the Pan American Union.[51] The memorable article 8 of this document stated plainly: "No state has the right to intervene in the internal or external affairs of another." According to Samuel Inman, who helped Hull develop the policy and the document language, "The afternoon of December 19, 1933, was the greatest hour in the history of the Inter-American movement since July 18, 1826, when the first treaty on Union, League, and Confederation was signed at Panama. It was also one of the greatest moments in the life of this writer, who had struggled for a decade to bring about such a change."[52]

Recognizing the catastrophic effects of global economic nationalism and U.S. protectionism, Roosevelt's Good Neighbor Policy resurrected James

Blaine's efforts to negotiate reciprocal trade agreements and, more important, moved away from the American stance that tariffs were strictly matters of domestic politics. President McKinley had called tariffs a matter of domestic politics; Hughes, in Havana (1928), had said that "tariffs are a national problem; their discussion would wreck the Pan American Union." The Good Neighbor Policy abandoned this position, confronting reality: trade policy affects both domestic interests and foreign relations, particularly bilateral relations in the case of reciprocal trade agreements.

The 1934 Reciprocal Trade Agreements Act authorized the president to reduce tariffs by 50 percent when trading partners did the same for U.S. products.[53] From 1934 to 1941, U.S. trade with Latin America tripled. Between 1934 and 1940, the United States signed eleven reciprocal trade agreements with Latin American nations, not without some opposition from Latin American nationalists looking for commercial opportunities in Germany, which received in 1938 around 10 percent of Latin America's exports and accounted for 17 percent of its imports.[54]

The year following the Montevideo Conference, the United States withdrew marines from Haiti and abrogated the Platt amendment in the Cuban constitution. Roosevelt refused to intervene militarily in a Cuban political crisis, though he did send warships to Havana to "encourage" a political solution acceptable to the United States. Emblematically, the United States refused to recognize a reformist government (September 1933–January 1934) headed by Ramón Grau San Martín, then recognized the transitory government of Colonel Carlos Mendieta. President Roosevelt explained to Cuban leaders that the United States "could not promise recognition to any individual or group in advance of the fulfillment of the conditions we have consistently set forth."[55] Roosevelt, like Woodrow Wilson, would use recognition policy in efforts to impose American preferences in the Western Hemisphere.

Nonintervention meant no troops on the ground, but not an end to *political* intervention (or to warships in Havana harbor as a reminder of American interest in Cuba's affairs as a Good Neighbor). Roosevelt and Hull also returned to Jeffersonian policy on recognition of governments in control of their territory, as judged by the United States, instead of Woodrow Wilson's moralistic insistence on "legitimacy" and "democracy." All these departures from the policies of Republican "protective imperialism" and also from Wilson's moral crusades met approval in Latin America. For the Roosevelt administration, they represented modalities for meeting domestic political exigencies and restructuring the architecture of hemispheric defense. Latin American policy, as always, seemed tangential, but on closer retrospection formed an essential part of a U.S. global agenda.

For Latin Americans, the Good Neighbor Policy marked an important break by the American president with over three decades of gunboat diplomacy in the Caribbean basin. No U.S. military intervention in a Latin American country would occur again until Lyndon Johnson sent an invasion force to the Dominican Republic in 1965. The Good Neighbor Policy also marked a discursive departure from the demeaning characterizations of Latin Americans by generations of American policymakers — though, in practice, respect for Latin Americans remained hard to find within the U.S. government.

By 1936, the war clouds over Europe and Japanese military operations in China further motivated the Roosevelt administration to attend to its Western Hemisphere home base. As in the time of Madison and Monroe, international developments drove hemispheric policy. A special conference for the maintenance of peace at Buenos Aires (December 3–26, 1936) adopted an agreement for consultation of the members if peace in the hemisphere were threatened by external forces or war among or between American states (as in the Chaco War). A protocol introduced by Mexico to reaffirm the nonintervention agreements arrived at in Montevideo obtained unanimous approval.

Two years later, on convening the Eighth Pan American Conference at Lima (December 9–27, 1938), according to Samuel Inman, "the threat to the American continent was in fact more critical than that of the Holy Alliance a century before."[56] Writing in the early 1960s, and comparing the threat of 1936 to that of 1823, might be taken as a big historical stretch. Or it might be taken as an indirect comment on the Cold War and the Cuban Revolution's implications for the United States and Latin America by a confirmed missionary Pan Americanist. In either case, at the moment, the "Western Hemisphere Idea" had been reaffirmed unanimously at Montevideo and Lima. For the next decade, it served as part of the discursive arsenal for American global strategy, particularly after the United States entered World War II and sought Latin American collaboration in rounding up, detaining, and sometimes deporting Germans, Japanese, and Italians from Central and South America to the United States, as potential threats to security and the war effort.[57]

Yet some of the Latin American nations still feared German, Italian, or Spanish intervention less than that of the United States. In parts of the hemisphere, sympathies for fascism and authoritarian government were strong. The United States ultimately extracted the Declaration of Lima from the 1938 Conference at Lima: "In case the peace, security or territorial integrity of any American Republic is thus threatened by acts of any nature that may impair them, they proclaim their common concern and their determination to make effective their solidarity, co-ordinating their respective sovereign wills by means of the procedure of consultation." But this Declaration of Lima would not convince Argentina and Chile to loosen ties with Italy and Germany until well into World War II.

Roosevelt's Good Neighbor Policy at least made the Latin Americans amenable to such a declaration of solidarity and to an abstract commitment to democracy as a hemispheric vision. Rising tensions in Europe made the Roosevelt administration more amenable to flexibility and patience in its Latin American policies, always with an eye to regional security as a foundation for the U.S. global position. Thus potentially serious disputes over oil concessions in Bolivia (1937–42) and Mexico (1938–40) found the Roosevelt administration carefully protecting access to resources and peaceful relations in the hemisphere, partly at the expense of U.S. and multinational corporations.[58] The claims of *particular* corporations could be sacrificed to the necessities of U.S. security and *global* business interests.

In July 1940, with German troops in Holland and France, Western Hemisphere foreign ministers met in Havana, where the United States obtained a monumental and ironic victory: multilateral acceptance of the premises of the 1811 No Transfer Principle in what came to be called the "Act of Havana." Cordell Hull told the foreign ministers:

> Specifically, there is before us the problem of the status of European possessions in this hemisphere. These geographic regions have not heretofore constituted a menace to the peace of the Americas. . . . Any effort, therefore, to modify the existing status of these areas — whether by cession, by transfer, or by any impairment whatsoever in the control here-to-fore exercised — would be of profound and immediate concern to all the American republics. It is accordingly essential that we consider a joint approach to this common problem.[59]

The foreign ministers agreed unanimously to the following resolution:

> The Second Meeting of the Ministers of Foreign Affairs of the American Republics
>   Declares:
>
>   That any attempt on the part of a non-American state against the integrity or inviolability of the territory, the sovereignty or the political independence of an American state shall be considered as an act of aggression against the states which sign this declaration.
>   In case acts of aggression are committed or should there be reason to believe that an act of aggression is being prepared by a non-American nation against the integrity or inviolability of the territory, the sovereignty or the political independence of an American nation, the

nations signatory to the present declaration will consult among themselves in order to agree upon the measure it may be advisable to take.

All the signatory nations, or two or more of them, according to circumstances, shall proceed to negotiate the necessary complementary agreements so as to organize cooperation for defense and the assistance that they shall lend each other in the event of aggressions such as those referred to in this declaration.

In principle, the new-and-improved No Transfer Principle could be invoked by "two or more" of the signatory Pan American states in the event of aggression or if there be "reason to believe that an act of aggression is being prepared." For the United States, this provided cover for preemptive or reactive military measures against extra-hemispheric powers by agreement with a single Latin American nation.

In January 1939, President Roosevelt had warned the Senate Military Affairs Committee in secret session: "The next perfectly obvious step, which Brother Hitler suggested in the speech yesterday, would be Central and South America. . . . We cannot afford to sit here and say it is a pipe dream. . . . It is the gradual encirclement of the United States by the removal of its first line of defense."[60] The same year as the Act of Havana, the German government granted a contract to Messerschmitt to create "the America Bomber," capable of reaching from the Azores to New York City.

Concerned with German influence and economic interests in the Western Hemisphere, the U.S. Council of National Defense created the Office for Coordination of Commercial and Cultural Relations between the American Republics in August 1940. This agency became the multifaceted Office of Inter-American Affairs (OIAA), which sought to coordinate U.S. economic and cultural policies in the region. Headed by Nelson Rockefeller, the OIAA penetrated Latin American governments and societies as an integral part of the war effort against the Axis, helping also to compile the "Black List" ("Proclaimed List of Certain Blocked Nationals"), which would be a precedent for American counterintelligence and counterinsurgency targeting of "subversives" after World War II. Many of these individuals lost their homes and businesses; some were incarcerated; others were repatriated; still others were deported — for detention in the United States. Among its other economic and cultural warfare operations, the OIAA "initiated blacklisting procedures on its own against movie theaters exhibiting Axis-produced films and newsreels," while working with American radio, film, and media networks "to bring the production of commercial feature films and newsreels into line with the requirements of the Good Neighbor policies and hemisphere defense."[61]

Addressing the nation in his 1941 message to Congress (the "Four Freedoms Speech," January 6, 1941), Roosevelt warned that

> it is not probable that any enemy would be stupid enough to attack us by landing troops in the United States from across thousands of miles of ocean, until it had acquired strategic bases from which to operate. But we learn much from the lessons of the past years in Europe — particularly the lesson of Norway, whose essential seaports were captured by treachery and surprise built up over a series of years. The first phase of the invasion of this Hemisphere would not be the landing of regular troops. The necessary strategic points would be occupied by secret agents and their dupes — and great numbers of them are already here, and in Latin America. As long as the aggressor nations maintain the offensive, they, not we, will choose the time and the place and the method of their attack. That is why the future of all the American Republics is today in serious danger.[62]

Quickly thereafter, the United States moved to obtain the cooperation of the Latin American nations, but even after the Japanese attack on Pearl Harbor, December 7, 1941, several of the South American countries maintained their neutrality, profiting from the war and seeking to avoid its costs. In Panama, the United States toppled the uncooperative government of Arnulfo Arias, and American military attachés and advisers moved into most of the Latin American nations. Beginning around May 1940, the United States replaced Europeans as the main supplier of the Latin American military forces, as the United States sought bases from which to defend the hemisphere against potential German invasion.[63]

Although Latin Americans went along with declarations of solidarity, they did not agree to a unified collective security policy in the hemisphere. They did consent, in 1942, to create the Inter-American Defense Board, in which military officers from the member countries would plan and prepare for extracontinental attacks in the hemisphere (an antecedent to the 1947 Rio Treaty for hemispheric collective security).[64] By then, the U.S. Congress had repealed most provisions of the Neutrality Acts adopted between 1935 and 1939 and entered into a de facto alliance with Britain.[65] According to historian George Herring, Roosevelt "stretched the powers of his office to unprecedented extents. . . . He used dubious if not illegal means to spy on his political foes. He created the basis for what would be called the imperial presidency and for the Cold War national security state."[66] Although Herring perhaps overstates the extent to which Roosevelt exceeded the duplicity and stretch of presidential authority by various of his predecessors, especially Theodore Roosevelt and

Woodrow Wilson, there could be no doubt that World War II challenged the security of the United States to a degree not seen since the Civil War.

As the war proceeded, Mexico, Brazil, Cuba, and the Central Americans provided varying degrees of assistance. Brazil sent troops to fight in Europe, participating in the Allied invasion of Italy in 1944. It also provided crucial air bases and port facilities to the war effort after declaring war on Germany and Italy in August 1942. American leaders, civilian and military, appreciated access to Latin American resources, air bases, ports, and communications facilities. Yet, for the most part, they also retained their disdain for Latin American peoples and their capabilities. As political scientist Lars Schoultz put it, "The Good Neighbor policy did not reach into the minds of U.S. leaders and public to change the way in which they thought about Latin Americans."[67]

Defending Democracy, Defending Racism

Like Woodrow Wilson, Franklin Delano Roosevelt favored democracy in the abstract. He tolerated, if not promoted, racial segregation at home. Having congratulated himself for "writing the Haitian constitution" while assistant secretary of the navy, he banned African American reporters from his presidential news conferences. He refused to support antilynching legislation, for fear of alienating southern congressional committee chairmen. He did issue Executive Order 8802 in 1941 barring discrimination in defense industries and creating the Fair Employment practices committee — but only after A. Philip Randolph proposed a massive protest march on Washington, D.C.[68] Roosevelt characterized Randolph, the leader of the Brotherhood of Sleeping Car Porters, as an "uppity nigger."[69]

Under Roosevelt, the armed forces remained segregated, as did the blood banks, upon which lives depended.[70] African Americans benefited from many of the New Deal programs focused on employment, education, and public works, but the War Department, under former colonial administrator Henry Stimson, refused to desegregate the armed forces or push for an end to Jim Crow laws more generally. According to military historian Morris J. Mac-Gregor Jr., Stimson "professed to believe in civil rights for every citizen, but he opposed social integration. He never tried to reconcile these seemingly inconsistent views; in fact, he probably did not consider them inconsistent. Stimson blamed what he termed Eleanor Roosevelt's 'intrusive and impulsive folly' for some of the criticism visited upon the Army's racial policy, just as he inveighed against the 'foolish leaders of the colored race' who were seeking 'at bottom social equality,' which, he concluded was out of the question 'because of the impossibility of race mixture by marriage.'"[71]

On the day after the Japanese attack at Pearl Harbor, the army adjutant general explained to a group of African American newspaper publishers:

> The Army is made up of individual citizens of the United States who have pronounced views with respect to the Negro just as they have individual ideas with respect to other matters in their daily walk of life. Military orders, fiat, or dicta, will not change their viewpoints. The Army then cannot be made the means of engendering conflict among the mass of people because of a stand with respect to Negroes which is not compatible with the position attained by the Negro in civil life. . . . The Army is not a sociological laboratory; to be effective it must be organized and trained according to the principles which will insure success. Experiments to meet the wishes and demands of the champions of every race and creed for the solution of their problems are a danger to efficiency, discipline and morale and would result in ultimate defeat.[72]

The African American press and social movements adopted the "Double-V" as their symbol of struggle: victory abroad and victory at home, an end to segregation! In a very-low-profile decision in 1944, the U.S. Supreme Court upheld segregation in the army but refused to rule on the substantive issues of a case in which Wynford W. Lynn had agreed to serve in any unit that was not segregated by race. He was charged with draft resistance; the court told him that in order to challenge the law he had to allow himself to be inducted. To challenge segregation in the army, Lynn agreed to induction and then filed suit against his superior officer. The New York Federal District Court refused to hear the case; the Circuit Court of Appeals upheld the decision. On appeal to the Supreme Court, the justices refused to hear the case because Lynn was serving overseas, out of the Court's jurisdiction, and the military officer against whom he had brought suit had retired from the military.[73]

So ended the legal challenge to Jim Crow in the military during World War II.[74] The army viewed the case pragmatically. Selective Service director General Lewis B. Hershey commented: "What we are doing is simply transferring discrimination from everyday life into the army. Men who make up the army staff have the same ideas [about African Americans] as they had before they went into the army." Perhaps. But the African American leadership had different ideas about how these racist ideas and practices should change. The NAACP monthly publication, the *Crisis*, declared itself "sorry for brutality, blood, and death among the peoples of Europe, just as we were sorry for China and Ethiopia. But the hysterical cries of the preachers of democracy for Europe leave us cold. We want democracy in Alabama, Arkansas, in

Mississippi and Michigan, in the District of Columbia — in the *Senate of the United States*."[75]

In short, for American relations with Latin America as well as for racial discrimination at home there existed an insistence on "normalcy" — not only by Harding, Coolidge, and Hoover, but now by the U.S. Army and the Selective Service System under Roosevelt's New Deal. Racism at home and abroad permeated U.S. foreign policy, though it never formed an official component of any administration's foreign policy platform. Racism did not determine foreign policy principles but it did color their interpretation and implementation. Legal and de facto racism remained an integral, largely unchallenged, "naturalized" part of American domestic politics; it therefore permeated foreign affairs in 1945 as it had in 1848 when Manifest Destiny "Providentially" severed half of Mexico in order to be annexed to the United States, and as it had since the Indian Removal Act in 1830 had made ethnic cleansing of "savage" Indians national policy.

Inexorably, racism also undermined American security at home and abroad and made American "democracy" a less attractive north star for Latin America and the colonized peoples of Asia and Africa. Racism tarnished the appeal of the American dream and made the United States a less credible partner in what came to be called the Third World after World War II. It also made the United States an unlikely champion of global and hemispheric democracy as it sought to design a new international order in the wake of World War II's massive devastation and human tragedy.

Chapter Ten

Not-So-Cold War, I

We should cease to talk about vague and . . . unreal objectives such as human rights, the raising of the living standards, and democratization. . . . We are going to have to deal in straight power concepts. The less we are then hampered by idealistic slogans, the better.
— GEORGE KENNAN, director of Policy Planning, U.S. State Department 1948

Conventional periodization calls the years from shortly after World War II until 1990 the "Cold War." For much of the world, including most of Latin America, this description is a terrible misnomer. The two global superpowers — the United States and the Soviet Union — never directly warred against each other.[1] Yet their surrogate wars around the world left millions of casualties in the names of "Democracy" and "Communism." U.S.-Soviet contestation transformed decolonization movements, civil wars, and even reformist politics into surrogate battles between the two superpowers.

Major hot wars in China (1946–50), Korea (1950–53), and Southeast Asia (1954–75) left several hundred thousand U.S. and allied military casualties. In the Chinese civil war, estimates for dead and wounded range from 2 to 4 million.[2] In Korea from 1950 to 1953, military and civilian casualties, including Chinese and Koreans, are estimated at around 4 million. The end result was a fortified border at the 38th parallel, about where it had been when the war started, thus "containment" had occurred. In the Vietnam War, unlike the Korean conflict, the United States failed to prevent unification, leading to the creation of the Socialist Republic of Vietnam. American dead and wounded numbered close to 300,000; total casualties, civilian and military, in Vietnam, Laos, and Cambodia likely numbered more than 6 million.[3]

The battle between the Soviets and the Americans sometimes resembled a religious war. The discourse of American policymakers conflated American national interests and the defense of "Western Civilization" fighting against

"Godless Communism." Future secretary of state John Foster Dulles wrote in 1949: "Terrorism, which breaks men's spirit, is, to Communists, a normal way to make their creed prevail, and to them it seems legitimate because they do not think of human beings as being brothers through the Fatherhood of God."[4] For its part, the Soviet Union fused Soviet grand strategy and Russian nationalism with "liberation movements" in the battle against "capitalist wage slavery." No matter that Third World and European peoples had their own agendas and internal conflicts. American and Soviet leaders subsumed such struggles under their own interpretations and sought to use them for their own ends in the global superpower contest.

Whether the Cold War started with a January 1944 memo from Soviet deputy minister Ivan Maisky to Josef Stalin, in August 1945 with the atomic blasts at Hiroshima and Nagasaki, or in the late 1940s when Stalin refused to remove Russian troops from Eastern Europe, the Cold War framework structured international politics for the next half century.[5] It also mangled the dreams and destinies of peoples around the world.[6]

The Soviets' global interests and ideological orientation positioned them to support nationalist and anticolonial movements, even as they imposed surrogate dictatorships on their client states in Eastern Europe. Military interventions established and sustained puppet governments and restored "order" when nationalist or democratizing movements challenged Soviet hegemony, such as occurred with the Hungarian revolt of 1956. Most exemplary of this Soviet policy was Soviet leader Leonid Brezhnev's justification (the Brezhnev Doctrine) for the invasion of Czechoslovakia in 1968. The Soviet Union sought to cover the 1968 repression in Czechoslovakia with the moral legitimacy of "international socialism" and the vestments of a regional security alliance, the Warsaw Pact:

> When a socialist country seems to adopt a "non-affiliated" stand, it retains its national independence, in effect, precisely because of the might of the socialist community, and above all the Soviet Union as a central force, which also includes the might of its armed forces. The weakening of any of the links in the world system of socialism directly affects all the socialist countries, which cannot look indifferently upon this. . . . Discharging their internationalist duty toward the fraternal peoples of Czechoslovakia and defending their own socialist gains, the U.S.S.R. and the other socialist states had to act decisively and they did act against the antisocialist forces in Czechoslovakia.[7]

The Brezhnev Doctrine thus denied the right of self-determination to peoples already blessed by "socialist gains." It proclaimed a Soviet protectorate and right of intervention where self-determination came into conflict with a nation's "own vital interests" — as determined by the Soviet Union. Like the American No Transfer Principle and the Monroe Doctrine, the Brezhnev Doctrine was based on an elastic interpretation of the sovereign right of "self-defense." Coincidentally, Brezhnev even replicated language routinely used in the nineteenth century by American policymakers: The socialist countries "could not look on indifferently" when "forces that are hostile to socialism try to turn the development of some socialist country towards capitalism." Explication and justification of the doctrine in *Pravda*, even before the invasion of Czechoslovakia, echoed the contorted rhetorical efforts by American policymakers between 1898 and 1933 to reconcile the sovereignty of Latin American nations with recurrent U.S. interventionism: "Needless to say, communists in the fraternal countries could not have stood idly by in the name of abstract sovereignty while [Czechoslovakia] was under the threat of anti-socialist degeneration."[8] Perhaps Brezhnev had an old copy of Theodore Roosevelt's Corollary to the Monroe Doctrine: "Chronic wrongdoing, or an impotence which results in a general loosening of the ties of civilized [socialist] society," required "intervention by some civilized [socialist] nation."

In the American case, inability or indisposition of policymakers to distinguish between nationalist, anticolonialist, and pro-Soviet movements and governments often put the United States on the side of right-wing dictatorships and military regimes in the name of containment or rollback of "communism" (most notably in Iran in 1953, Guatemala in 1954, Brazil in 1964, Indonesia in 1965–66, and Chile in 1973). The United States often reacted to economic nationalism as if it were the same as "communism" or "socialism" and thus ipso facto a threat to American interests.[9] Such policies gave "democracy" and the "free world" a bizarre significance in much of the world, as the United States supported coups against elected governments and as ferocious dictatorships became America's allies.

The two superpowers exported the battle for global and regional hegemony around the world. As Richard Bissell, former CIA director of plans, put it: "My responsibilities as deputy director for plans encompassed crises all over the globe," from the Congo to Guyana, from Vietnam and Cambodia to Cuba, and (illegally) to operations in the United States.[10] In the words of Michael Lind, senior fellow at the New America Foundation, who places most of the onus for the Cold War on Soviet efforts to dominate Europe and Asia, "the Cold War was the third world war. But it was a world war in slow motion, fought over four decades rather than a few years."[11]

The Cold War story has been told many times, from the point of view of peoples in the remotest village to that of the leaders deposed by American or

Soviet interventions — or, alternately, sustained in power with their support. The full story with all its local twists and regional intricacies will not be known for a very long time, if ever. Likewise, the role played by "peripheral" states in global and regional conflicts will be further revealed as declassification of documents in American, Soviet, and European archives and newly published memoirs and oral histories gradually deepen and sharpen our knowledge regarding the "slow motion" four-decade war.[12] The suffering caused, the "errors" made by Americans and Soviets in the name of democracy and communism, became a living legacy around the globe in the post-1990 period.[13] In Europe, memories of Soviet military occupation and political domination color post-1990s politics and national political culture. For many Third World peoples, including millions of Latin Americans, the Cold War made the United States an enemy of their freedom and right of self-determination. Such legacies of the Cold War have ongoing consequences for the United States in the twenty-first century.

A complicating factor for the United States in this story was the parallel anticolonial struggles in Asia and Africa and the ongoing struggle against racism in everyday life in America. In the 1950s, when the United States claimed to champion democracy around the world, American racism was not subtle. Jim Crow laws (de jure segregation of African Americans in schools, buses, parks, and public accommodations, along with disenfranchisement) remained on the books in much of the country. Breaches of these laws met repression, both official and "private."

To the surprise of many, given his upbringing in southern politics, President Harry Truman sent Congress a special message on civil rights in February 1948. Truman urged Congress to pass an antilynching law, to outlaw the poll taxes that disenfranchised African American voters, and to create a permanent Fair Employment Practices Commission and a Commission on Civil Rights. He also urged home rule for the District of Columbia. Congress rejected Truman's initiatives. The president then desegregated the armed forces by executive order. Truman, perhaps understanding the disconnect between America's democratic mission in the Cold War and the reality of racial segregation, perhaps seeking African American votes in the 1948 presidential election, became the first American president to actively promote an end to the Jim Crow regime.[14]

Truman's sometimes-forgotten attack on institutionalized racism prefigured the more successful civil rights movement of the 1960s. His support for racial equality and fundamental democratization of American politics led to a split in the Democratic Party and formation of the States' Rights Democratic Party (Dixiecrats) in the 1948 presidential election. Dismantling the Jim Crow regime in America would require decades more of struggle. As late as 1967, sixteen American states still outlawed "race-mixing."[15]

Such flagrant *legal* discrimination against people of color could not be ignored by two-thirds of the world's peoples, whom the United States claimed to defend from communist tyranny. How could such circumstances be explained to the international community (and their representatives in Washington, D.C., who experienced racism directly) in a country that preached democracy and respect for human rights?[16] In an era of decolonization and the arrival at the United Nations of newly independent African and Asian countries, the history of "states' rights" and the nature of American federalism offered not even a lame leg to stand on. For the Soviet Union, the persistence of racism and racial violence in the United States was a valuable propaganda tool in the not-so-Cold War. Racism gave American democracy a bad name in much of the world, including Latin America.

Even as the U.S. president launched an initial postwar attack on de jure racism, jingoistic American ideological hypocrisy competed for influence against jingoistic Soviet ideological hypocrisy — with the planet sometimes a chessboard and sometimes a battlefield in the Cold War.[17] Among the casualties of the smaller wars and covert operations of the Cold War would be hundreds of thousands of Latin Americans caught in the vice between the two superpowers preaching their own for-export-only utopias.

Security Architecture

Implementing U.S. Cold War grand strategy required restructuring global international relations and reorganizing regional security architecture. The creation of the United Nations and its charter that provided vetoes in the Security Council for the victorious World War II powers went far enough toward overcoming U.S. concerns of losing "command of its own fortune" to obtain congressional approval — unlike the failure to do so with the League of Nations in 1919. Regional collective security regimes such as the Rio Treaty (1947) and the North Atlantic Treaty Organization (NATO, 1949) provided the building blocks for the new global security architecture.[18] The NATO treaty marked the definitive end of the Founding Fathers' policy of staying out of European alliances. It also repudiated the Monroe Doctrine's pledge to stay neutral in European quarrels and pledged the United States to defend its allies from Soviet aggression.[19]

Within the Republican Party, Ohio senator Robert Taft led opposition to this departure from the traditional policies of the United States, arguing that a "policy of the free hand" rather than alliance politics would best protect

American postwar interests. Critics labeled Taft and his allies "isolationists," but that characterization neglected Taft's assessment of the international situation and his belief that America's radical break with its historical unilateralism would make the nation less secure, rather than more secure, and would lead to resentment against the United States around the world. In the emergent Cold War security architecture and alliances, as well as in Truman's foreign policies, Taft foresaw the dangers of a "garrison state" and erosion of American civil liberties, especially if moralizing internationalism required massive defense expenditures to impose an American vision of "democracy" around the world.[20] Taft also resisted further enhancement of executive authority — the move toward a still more imperial presidency: "Think of the tremendous power which this proposal gives to the President to involve us in any war throughout the world, including civil wars where we may favor one faction against the other. . . . I am opposed to the whole idea of giving the President power to arm the world against Russia or anyone else, or even to arm Western Europe, except where there is a real threat of aggression."[21] But Taft also called for a worldwide propaganda campaign in a war against communism that he said had to be won "in the minds of men." In *A Foreign Policy for Americans* (1951), Taft explicitly grounded his objections to America's early Cold War policies in the country's historical grand strategy:

> Our traditional policy of neutrality and non-interference with other nations was based on the principle that this policy was the best way to avoid disputes with other nations and to maintain the liberty of this country without war. From the days of George Washington that has been the policy of the United States. It has never been isolationism; but it has always avoided alliances and interference in foreign quarrels as a preventive against possible war, and it has always opposed any commitment by the United States, in advance, to take any military action outside of our territory. It would leave us free to interfere or not interfere according to whether we consider the case of sufficiently vital interest to the liberty of this country. It was the policy of the free hand.[22]

In Europe, the United States promoted the Marshall Plan to stimulate reconstruction and economic recovery. U.S. policy conditioned aid in each European beneficiary state upon meeting American political and financial terms. In some cases, the United States also used the conditionality of the Marshall Plan assistance to punish recalcitrant or "difficult" Latin American governments, for example, the authoritarian-populist regime of Juan Perón in Argentina (1946–55). Under the Marshall Plan, Europeans could use dollars

TABLE 10.1. Selected U.S. Interventions, 1946–1958

1946	*Iran.* Troops deployed in northern province
1946–49	*China.* Major U.S. army presence of about 100,000 troops, fighting, training, and advising local combatants
1947–49	*Greece.* U.S. forces wage a three-year counterinsurgency campaign
1948	*Italy.* Heavy CIA involvement in national elections
1948–54	*Philippines.* Commando operations, "secret" CIA war
1950–53	*Korea.* Major forces engaged in war on Korean peninsula
1950–55	*Formosa (Taiwan).* In June 1950, at the beginning of the Korean War, President Truman ordered the U.S. Seventh Fleet to prevent Chinese attacks upon Chiang Kai-shek on Taiwan
1953	*Iran.* CIA overthrows government of Prime Minister Mohammed Mossadegh
1954	*Vietnam.* Financial, matériel, and air support for colonial French military operations, which leads eventually to direct U.S. military involvement
1954	*Guatemala.* CIA overthrows the government of President Jacobo Arbenz
1954–55	*China.* Naval units evacuate U.S. civilians from the Tachen Islands
1956	*Egypt.* A marine battalion evacuates U.S. civilians from Alexandria during the Suez Crisis
1957	*Colombia.* Special operations and counter-insurgency
1958	*Indonesia.* Failed covert operations
1958	*Lebanon.* U.S. marines and army units totaling 14,000 land
1958	*Panama.* Clashes between U.S. forces and local citizens in Canal Zone
1959	*Tibet.* Covert operations against People's Republic of China

Source: *Global Policy Forum,* "US Military and Clandestine Operations in Foreign Countries."

for overseas food purchases; in 1948, the American government prohibited purchase of Argentine goods with Marshall Plan financing. Instead, the United States would subsidize U.S. farmers and finance grain sales in Europe, thereby making for a convenient connection between domestic political constituencies, reconstruction of Western Europe, and anticommunism, with a slap at Perón's efforts to find a "third way" for Argentines (and other Latin Americans) between communism and capitalism.[23]

In the Western Hemisphere, the United States failed to provide economic assistance similar to the Marshall Plan, engendering resentment throughout the region for the lack of appreciation by America for its neighbors' support during World War II. In contrast, the United States sponsored the first regional collective security regime and the first regional organization under the UN Charter in the Western Hemisphere: the Rio Pact and the Organization of American States (OAS). These new treaty regimes balanced the competing "globalist" and "regionalist" views in American policy circles (always with the Monroe Doctrine in mind and with the No Transfer Principle out of immediate recall but part of the subliminal premises for regional policy).

The U.S. government intended the Rio Pact and the OAS to serve as the military and legal architecture for postwar retrofitting of the Western Hemisphere bastion. Policy dictated that the bastion be free from extra-hemispheric threats, including governments sympathetic to socialist ideals or, more concretely, amenable to Soviet influence. Latin Americans initially viewed the new multilateral institutions with hope. For the most part, they were to be disappointed.

From the major World War II theaters, unlike the post–World War I experience, American troops would not all go home. More than half a century later, there would still be American military bases in Germany and Japan — along with over 100 other countries.[24] Between 1945 and 1990, within the Cold War framework, the United States created a far-flung, only partly visible, military empire. At home, this global military strategy would entail the maturation and political embedding of a gigantic military-industrial complex with roots in almost every congressional district.

Cold War Institutions and Alliances

The basic story of American post–World War II security and economic policy toward Europe and Japan is well known. At Bretton Woods, New Hampshire, in the summer of 1944, the Allies put in place arrangements for an International Bank of Reconstruction and Development (IBRD, to assist financing reconstruction of postwar Europe), the General Agreement on Trade and Tariffs (GATT, to promote more open markets and expand trade), and the International Monetary Fund (IMF, as a clearinghouse for international payments and short-term loans). The IRBD and the IMF came into formal existence in December 1945; the IBRD made its first loan, for reconstruction in France, on May 9, 1947. Taken together, these institutions made the United States the dominant nation in international commerce and finance. The system was based on the dollar as a world currency, and the United States retained vetoes over most global economic decisions emanating from the newly created multilateral institutions.

On March 12, 1947, President Harry Truman spoke to a joint session of Congress and proclaimed what came to be called the Truman Doctrine.[25] Reacting to insurgencies, nationalist movements, and the threat of communism in Greece and Turkey, Truman asked Congress for 400 million dollars to "assist free peoples to work out their own destinies in their own way." He claimed that the United States must be "willing to help free peoples to maintain their institutions and their national integrity against aggressive movements that seek to impose upon them totalitarian regimes. . . . Totalitarian regimes imposed upon free peoples, by direct or indirect aggression, undermine the foundations of international peace *and hence the security of the United States*."[26] American self-defense doctrine now extended well beyond the Western Hemisphere (and the Pacific); but the basic concept of self-defense as a right inherent in sovereignty, involving defense of foreign territory from "enemies" and *potential* threats, embraced the No Transfer Principle, the Monroe Doctrine, the pronouncements of Olney (1895) and Theodore Roosevelt (1904), and the Clark Memorandum (1928). Adherence to the Montevideo Convention (1933) on nonintervention did not preclude preemptive intervention in "self-defense" anywhere on the planet.

Truman told Congress that the very existence of the Greek state "is today threatened by the terrorist activities of several thousand armed men, led by Communists." Communists *were* terrorists. Truman did not mention that a major resistance group against the Nazi occupation had been the National Popular Liberation Army, largely but not entirely controlled by the Greek Communist Party — which remained a legal political party in Greece until its proscription in 1948 (the party would remain outlawed until 1974). For Turkey, Truman asked Congress for assistance to "maintain its national integrity," which "is essential to the preservation of order in the Middle East."

On July 26, 1947, the president signed the National Security Act, creating the National Security Council (NSC) and the Central Intelligence Agency (CIA).[27] In theory, the NSC would centralize security and defense policy within the executive branch, thereby overcoming the bureaucratic clientelism and turf wars of the Defense and State Departments. The very ambiguity of the CIA's charter (authority to correlate, evaluate, and disseminate intelligence and to perform "such other functions and duties related to intelligence affecting the national security") would provide legal cover for covert operations for the next seven decades.[28]

As the 1948 presidential election approached, Republicans were optimistic they might regain the White House for the first time since 1933. Truman, having succeeded Franklin Roosevelt upon his death in 1945, seemed without sufficient popular base of his own, and his party was divided. Truman's support for African American civil rights had eroded his appeal in the South. On foreign policy, however, both Republicans and Democrats adopted platforms that committed the United States to what was called a "new internationalism." The Democrats expressed the conviction "that the destiny of the United States is to provide leadership in the world toward a realization of the Four Freedoms."[29] They boasted that Roosevelt had established the Good Neighbor Policy and applauded "the Western Hemisphere defense pact [The Rio Treaty], *which implemented the Monroe Doctrine* and united the Western Hemisphere in behalf of peace."[30] The Republican platform seemed to agree with the Democrats, at least on the Western Hemisphere: "We particularly commend the value of regional arrangements as prescribed by the Charter [of the United Nations]; and we cite the Western Hemispheric Defense Pact as a useful model. We shall nourish these Pan-American agreements in the new spirit of cooperation *which implements the Monroe Doctrine*."[31]

Despite American election rhetoric that melded the Monroe Doctrine to the Truman Doctrine, the Rio Pact, and the OAS, few Latin Americans understood the OAS or UN charters as implementation of the Monroe Doctrine. Nor did they associate the Doctrine with a "spirit of cooperation." To the contrary, they aspired to a new era of nonintervention, respect for the sovereign equality of states as stipulated in the 1933 Montevideo Convention, and recognition of universal human rights.[32] The Cold War would undermine these aspirations.

Truman's 1948 election victory shocked much of the nation. The immediate foreign policy challenges shocked it more. For the United States, the Cold War marked the end of traditional distrust of standing armies and overseas (non-naval) deployments. The United States stationed armed forces in Europe and Japan, first as instruments of occupation then as a more permanent policy of global military presence. As mentioned, the Rio Pact and NATO departed fundamentally from U.S. disinclination toward permanent, peacetime, collective security alliances. This was no small change in policies that had been proclaimed by George Washington, Thomas Jefferson, and their successors and reiterated (with the exception of the 1846 treaty with Colombia) by American presidents and policymakers up to the outbreak of World War II.

Following proclamation of the Truman Doctrine, almost two more years of guerrilla warfare ensued in Greece. The communist insurgent armies operated across the Albanian and Yugoslav frontiers until Yugoslavia's Josip Tito closed that border in mid-1949. The United States and England provided arms, supplies, aircraft, fire support, and military advisers to the Greek National Army. Civil war in Greece ended officially in October 1949 with an announcement of cessation of hostilities by the main communist radio station. In January 1951, the Greek General Staff weekly newspaper, *Stratiotika*, published a summary of losses suffered during this first Cold War confrontation between American and Soviet surrogates. It gave Greek Army deaths at 12,777, with 37,732 wounded and 4,527 missing. It said a further 4,124 civilians and 165 priests had been executed by the communists. Property and infrastructure damage had been extensive. Estimates of the number of "communists" killed vary greatly, but 38,000 is considered a reliable figure, with 40,000 captured or surrendering.[33] Other sources put deaths at closer to 85,000 with over 600,000 refugees, many leaving Greece for Macedonia, Yugoslavia, Bulgaria, or Albania. Tactical air support provided to the Greek National Army greatly assisted in the victory over massed insurgent forces, which abandoned guerrilla tactics to engage in conventional warfare. The Free World thus won the Cold War's first not-so-Cold War conflict. Many hundreds more would follow.

From the Truman Doctrine to Korea

With announcement of the Truman Doctrine, the United States had made virtually the entire planet subject to a greatly expanded ideological and military No Transfer Doctrine, in which "free peoples" would be defended against "communists" who sought to impose totalitarianism, whether by direct or indirect aggression. The United States "could not see with indifference," to use the language of the early nineteenth century, the imposition of "communism" on "free peoples." As it would turn out, "free peoples," were not altogether free to choose socialist, communist, or even nationalist governments if they were perceived as threats to U.S. interests and national security. The No Transfer Principle, applied first to Spanish Florida, then to Cuba and the rest of the Caribbean, would now be recycled as "containment" of Soviet influence. For good measure, that part of the Monroe Doctrine that proscribed "European doctrines and systems" from the "New World" could also be resurrected and refined for the Cold War. Marxism and communism certainly qualified as European doctrines or systems and were thus subject, according to the Monroe Doctrine, to exclusion from the Western Hemisphere.[34]

To shore up Western Europe against the communist threat and to resurrect the international economy, the Marshall Plan transferred billions of dollars of economic assistance to Europe for reconstruction. Secretary of State George Marshall announced that such aid "will come to an abrupt end in any country that votes communism into power."[35] American tolerance for self-determination had its limits. The United States established the Economic Cooperation Administration to oversee Marshall Plan assistance to Europe. In exchange for aid, the United States heavily influenced trade, fiscal, and resource policies in the European beneficiary states.

Parallel to the economic assistance program, NATO would serve, in the words of historian and West Point graduate Andrew Bacevich, "not only as a bulwark against Soviet aggression but as an instrument to promote Europe's political and economic transformation while cementing the advantageous position that America had secured in Europe as a result of victory in World War II."[36] Perhaps more important, the United States promised to treat an attack on any NATO member as an attack on itself. Of course, upon signing the NATO treaty, the United States enjoyed a (very temporary) monopoly on the atomic bomb, and its use would be a unilateral decision in the event the NATO allies needed America to ward off Soviet aggression.

U.S. government agencies embedded clandestine operations within the policies to reconstruct the European economies. American intelligence agents infiltrated European labor movements, political parties, mass media, and government institutions, insisting on purges of left-leaning politicians and communists in postwar government coalitions. The United States also created "stay-behind" clandestine paramilitary forces to be activated in case of "need." For a time, the Americans treated European allies almost as if they were Caribbean or Central American puppet regimes. Under the direction of Frank Wisner, the Office of Policy Coordination clandestinely went to war against the Soviet Union and its allies, or potential allies, with an array of psychological, economic, and political measures, as well as "preventive direct action."[37]

Between late March 1948 and May 12, 1949, the Soviet Union enforced a land blockade of West Berlin. The United States and its allies responded with an airlift to supply their sectors of the occupied city. In January 1949, Mao Zedong's communist forces took Beijing; they declared establishment of the People's Republic of China in October. Six months later (April 14, 1950), Truman's NSC adopted a classified memorandum, NSC-68 (declassified only in 1975), a blueprint for military defense and grand strategy for the next three decades. This document insisted that U.S. objectives could only be met by "the virtual abandonment by the United States of trying to distinguish between national and global security." A year after NSC-68 was drafted, Truman asked for more than 60 billion dollars for the armed services, a five-fold increase from the previous year.[38]

Two months later, on June 25, 1950, North Korea invaded South Korea, seeking to unify the peninsula in a national state controlled by the communist government supported by the Soviet Union and China. The North Korean invasion seemed to justify the sweeping assumptions regarding Soviet designs on Asia and Europe. Truman sent American forces to Korea to counter the invasion without a congressional declaration of war, under cover of a vague UN Security Council resolution (June 25, 1950) demanding "an immediate cessation of hostilities and a withdrawal of North Korean forces to the 38th parallel." The United Nations called for "every assistance" to support the resolution. Senator Robert A. Taft (R.-Ohio) objected that, "in the case of Korea, where a war was already under way, we had no right to send troops to a nation, with whom we had no treaty, to defend it against attack by another nation, no matter how unprincipled that aggression might be, unless the whole matter was submitted to Congress and a declaration of war or some other direct authority obtained."[39] Taft and other conservatives saw in Truman's decision a precedent in executive war-making discretion. Indeed, Truman departed from constitutional practice, which had relied on congressional resolutions, legislation, and appropriations for major deployments of armed forces since the 1798 Quasi-War against France and the 1801–5 operations against the Barbary powers.

American policy garnered further UN cover on June 27 (with the Soviets still absent, having walked out in protest of the UN refusal to seat Communist China), when the Security Council asked members to provide military assistance to South Korea. This would not be the last UN commitment of military force to carry out Security Council resolutions, but it would be the last time the Soviet Union made the mistake of failing to exercise its veto in the Security Council on matters that concerned its interests or its allies.

For the Chinese communist government, American deployments to Korea and U.S. naval forces interposed between Taiwan and the mainland, combined with refusal to recognize the communist government, presaged an effort to overturn the revolution and reimpose Chiang Kai-shek. This perception, along with secret Soviet promises of support, brought massive Chinese involvement (and clandestine Soviet deployments) to the Korean conflict.[40] The four years of war that followed facilitated construction of a Cold War consensus in the United States that international communism, centered in the Soviet Union, could only be contained through permanent military preparedness and enormous defense budgets. The Founders' warnings against the dangers of standing armies went by the wayside. The not-so-Cold War against communist tyranny would justify almost a half century of American hyper-militarization of its foreign policy — and also of its domestic economy.

Taken together, the Soviet capture of Czechoslovakia in 1948, the "loss" of China, the Soviet blockade of Berlin, the Soviet acquisition of the atomic bomb, and then the Korean War transformed American domestic politics and the country's perspective on the international system. What did not change, however, was American reluctance to accept international norms or collective security agreements without explicit reservations. The U.S. government insisted on its discretion to act unilaterally, where and when necessary — even if cover of the United Nations or OAS resolutions might be used to legitimate American initiatives. Both Truman and his secretary of state, Dean Acheson, were convinced that the United States had to take the lead in containing the threat of communism, whether or not other nations or international organizations immediately came on board. If, in principle, the United States would be willing to assist "free peoples" anywhere against tyranny, it would, in practice, choose where, when, and with what means to do so. The Truman administration did not embark on a global crusade against communism nor did it commit itself to fighting communism everywhere without considering American economic and military limitations.[41]

Domestic Politics and National Security

The Cold War also had immediate effects on U.S. domestic politics. Oceans no longer protected America as they had in the past. Overwhelming technological and military superiority could not be assured. Realization that much of the United States could be obliterated if the Soviets chose to pay the price of retaliation significantly altered American politics and foreign policy. Fear of the Soviet Union's growing power and perceived belligerence inspired a wave of national security legislation and attacks on "communists" and "fellow-travelers," led by Senator Joseph McCarthy (R.-Wis.). McCarthy and his allies claimed that the State Department had been infiltrated with communists, that communists were active in the arts, the universities, and the labor movement — they were everywhere.[42]

As the 1952 presidential elections approached, the Republican Party selected a World War II hero for its presidential candidate: Dwight David Eisenhower. Eisenhower promised to bring an end to the Korean War. President Truman, whose popularity ratings with a war-weary public had plummeted, decided not to seek reelection. Instead, the Democrats nominated Illinois governor Adlai Stevenson II. The Republicans attacked the Democrats for permitting the great advances of international communism. Their platform proclaimed that the Truman administration had "squandered the unprecedented power and prestige which were ours at the close of World War II. . . . More than 500 million non-Russian people of fifteen different countries have been absorbed into the power sphere of Communist Russia, which proceeds confidently with its plan for world conquest."[43] Beyond the Cold War frame, Eisenhower believed that "foreign policy is, or should be, based primarily upon one consideration. That consideration is the need for the U.S. to obtain certain raw materials to sustain its economy and, when possible, to preserve profitable foreign markets for our surpluses. Out of this need grows the necessity for making certain that those areas of the world in which essential raw materials are produced are not only accessible to us, but their populations and governments are willing to trade with us on a friendly basis."[44]

After a landslide electoral victory, Eisenhower agreed to an armistice in Korea in July 1953. He resisted hard-line pressure in the United States to use atomic weapons against China; rather he accepted a demilitarized zone at the 38th parallel, in effect a "victory" against aggression but no military defeat of the communists. In the meantime, Eisenhower, his evangelical secretary of state John Foster Dulles, Dulles's brother and CIA director Allen Dulles, and their close inner circle further transformed the making of American foreign policy into a highly secretive and often rogue operation. To contain or roll back communism, the CIA established parallel military capabilities, front businesses and financial enterprises, radio and media networks, and intelligence and sabotage operations around the world.[45] Government officials circulated disinformation in the United States and overseas. They lied to Congress and to each other. American ambassadors often knew little of CIA operations in the countries to which they were posted; the Department of State frequently neither made policy nor implemented it, except to the extent that the Dulles brothers shared information in private meetings. According to Tim Weiner's history of the CIA, "[John] Foster [Dulles] firmly believed that the United States should do everything in its power to alter or abolish any regime not openly allied with America. Allen [Dulles] wholeheartedly agreed. With Eisenhower's blessings, they set out to remake the map of the world."[46]

In 1954, Eisenhower created the Planning Coordination Group (Special

Group) within the NSC framework, with secret directive NSC-5412/2. This directive provided broad, vague, and menacing "authority" (seemingly beyond the president's constitutional authority, if subjected to congressional or judicial test—which it was not). The NSC determined that the United States should make covert war on the Soviet Union, its allies, its potential allies, and even its sympathizers—all without explicit congressional approval or oversight. It made the decision that covert operations should, among other activities:

> Create and exploit troublesome problems for International Communism, impair relations between the USSR and Communist China and between them and their satellites, complicate control within the USSR, Communist China and their satellites, and retard the growth of the military and economic potential of the Soviet bloc.
> Discredit the prestige and ideology of International Communism and reduce the strength of its parties and other elements.
> Counter any threat of a party or individuals directly or indirectly responsive to Communist control to achieve dominant power in a free world country.
> Reduce International Communist control over any areas of the world.[47]

This vision of foreign policy and covert operations—a death struggle between two incompatible ways of life—left no room for concerns such as international law, sovereignty, or the UN Charter. Nor could policymakers take seriously America's repeatedly proclaimed commitment to democracy and self-determination. Such discourse was largely marketing slogans for managing American public opinion and ideological propaganda for competing with Soviet communism.

As the new "national security state" developed within the United States, its agents expanded their operations and experimented with the virtually limitless range of global interventions possible in the planetary war against international communism. The U.S. Congress progressively lost its remaining effective oversight capabilities and, for the most part, even its disposition to constrain the executive branch's initiatives. From time to time, investigations, hearings, and even reports on foreign policy failures would gain public attention. By the late 1950s, however, the Cold War mentality that gripped the country suppressed most congressional opposition to the secret government that, in practice, was supplanting the Republic in making and implementing foreign policy. Self-reinforcing zealotry and immunity from oversight or sanction for egregious failures allowed small groups of policymakers and operatives to press forward with clandestine and illegal foreign policies. Congress and the judiciary failed to sufficiently reassert their political and constitutional roles that might have spared the country, and its targets, many of the Cold War's most embarrassing and shameful foreign policy debacles.

Hundreds of clandestine operations in Europe and Asia left thousands dead in poorly planned intelligence schemes and covert attacks on "communism." In this clandestine war, the CIA tested mind-altering drugs and a variety of torture techniques in secret prisons on political prisoners in Europe, Japan, and Panama and in the United States, creating precedents for the American overseas gulag that was in place in the first decade of the twenty-first century.[48] Simultaneously, the world of never-ending, and always more daunting, threats manufactured by the Cold Warriors and the Cold War itself, nourished the military-industrial complex, which Eisenhower would warn the country about, much too late and without acknowledging his own part in its growth, as he left office in 1961: "In the councils of government, we must guard against the acquisition of unwarranted influence, whether sought or unsought, by the military-industrial complex. The potential for the disastrous rise of misplaced power exists and will persist. We must never let the weight of this combination endanger our liberties or democratic processes."[49]

From 1953 to 1961, the CIA, National Security Agency (NSA), and related overseas activities wasted billions of dollars in unsuccessful intelligence and covert warfare operations. Beyond the waste of money and resources, these operations undermined American moral and political credibility. Weiner's history of the CIA counts 170 new major covert actions in 48 countries during the Eisenhower years.[50] This count is surely underestimated, though to what extent we may only know years from now, as still more declassified documents, memoirs, and "confessions" become available.

Events in, and policy toward, Latin America would play their part in the larger story, just as they had since 1789. Likewise, on the home front, the interplay of domestic politics, including tariff and immigration policy, racial and labor conflicts, and internal security legislation, would influence and be influenced by policies toward Latin America. The No Transfer Principle and the Monroe Doctrine now faced their most serious challenge since the 1860s.

Not-So-Cold War in the Western Hemisphere

The Latin American front in the Cold War had its own idiosyncratic regional institutions (the Rio Treaty of 1947, the OAS founded in 1948, the Inter-American Development Bank founded in 1959, among others) that paralleled the global economic and security institutions initiated at Bretton Woods in

TABLE 10.2. Not-So-Cold War in the Western Hemisphere, 1945–1954

1945	Act of Chapultepec. Calls for collective measures in case of attack on signatory state by extracontinental power
1947	Inter-American Treaty of Reciprocal Assistance (Rio Treaty)
1948	OAS Created in Bogotá, Colombia, at the Ninth International Conference of American States
1948	*Bogotazo*. Initiates La Violencia
1948	Communist Party outlawed in Chile, Costa Rica
1948	Military coups in Peru, Venezuela
1949	El Salvador coup
1950	Haiti coup
1951	Bolivia coup
1952	Mutual Defense Assistance Agreements begin in Latin America with Ecuador, Cuba, Colombia, Peru, Chile
1952	Batista coup in Cuba
1952	Beginning of Bolivian Revolution led by Víctor Paz Estenssoro
1952	NSC-141. Application of NSC-68 to Latin America
1952	Eisenhower administration announces rollback policy
1953	Rojas Pinilla coup in Colombia
1954	Caracas Declaration
1954	Overthrow of Jacobo Arbenz government in Guatemala

1944.[51] It also had its own battles, with local actors and agendas from Mexico to Argentina caught in the web of the larger global confrontation. During this period — from George Kennan's warning on the Soviet threat and his 1950 report on Latin America[52] to the Committee of Santa Fe report (1980), which influenced President Ronald Reagan's policies toward Latin America — U.S. policymakers saw Latin America as a crucial battleground in the Cold War.

The American focus on containing or rolling back "communist" threats to U.S. regional hegemony stimulated a wave of anticommunist legislation and persecution of political and labor leaders. Between 1946 and 1948 Communist Parties were outlawed in much of Latin America, including Brazil,

Chile, Colombia, Costa Rica, Ecuador, Peru, and Venezuela. The campaign continued into the 1950s. With American support and intelligence collaboration, secret police forces penetrated "leftist" and Marxist parties and labor movements. American leaders and Latin American governments constructed the institutional and discursive instruments for a half-century crusade against communist subversion in the hemisphere as the regional element in America's Cold War grand strategy.[53]

From 1945 to 1948, dictatorships in Central America and the Caribbean had given way to elected, reformist governments. A democratic opening seemed to be under way. But socialist and communist participation in reform movements and even government coalitions worried policymakers in Washington. U.S. Army intelligence observed: "Where dictatorships have been abolished, the resulting governments have been weak and unstable." The FBI's J. Edgar Hoover claimed that communism was "making considerable headway in Latin America by playing on the theme of U.S. imperialism."[54] In January 1946, the American Federation of Labor appointed Serafino Romualdi as its official representative in Latin America. He would work for the eventual establishment of an anticommunist labor federation to rival the Confederación de Trabajadores de América Latina. Romualdi received support from the State Department and, as it turned out, worked for the CIA.[55] As in Europe, the United States would seek to infiltrate, orient, and influence organized labor and political parties in the Western Hemisphere.

At Rio de Janeiro in 1947, the United States coordinated agreement on a regional collective security treaty, the Inter-American Treaty of Reciprocal Assistance (the Rio Pact). The treaty provided for first response to threats and crises by regional actors rather than the United Nations, thus preempting but not disallowing recourse to article 51 of the UN Charter. The Rio Pact became a cornerstone in regional security architecture. The treaty seemingly committed the United States to do what it had refused to do in 1822–23 and what it had only done in a more limited way in 1846 with Colombia: oblige itself to provide military defense for Latin American republics in the event of external aggression. And to protection against external threats was added protection against internal subversion by communists.

Within the Cold War framework, the U.S. government interpreted the Rio Treaty as reaffirmation of its inherent sovereign right of self-defense. The treaty thus supplemented the No Transfer Principle and the Monroe Doctrine as additional legal cover for U.S. intervention when "international communism" threatened the sovereignty of any of the Latin American nations. Thus, article 3 provided that "an armed attack by any State against an American State shall be considered as an attack against all the American States and, consequently, each one of the said Contracting Parties undertakes to assist in meeting the attack in the exercise of the inherent right of individual or collective self-defense recognized by Article 51 of the Charter of the United Nations." The treaty further provided that "each one of the Contracting Parties may determine the immediate measures which it may individually take in fulfillment of the obligation contained in the preceding paragraph." Still to be decided was the relative weight to be given to the decisions of the United Nations regarding threats in the Western Hemisphere ("measures of self-defense provided for under this Article may be taken until the Security Council of the United Nations has taken the measures necessary to maintain international peace and security"). In practice, the United States would successfully impose the priority of OAS "peacekeeping" over UN action until the 1980s.[56]

For Latin Americans, the OAS Charter reaffirmed the principles of the Montevideo Conference (1933) on equality of states, within the UN framework and the OAS itself: "States are juridically equal, enjoy equal rights and equal capacity to exercise these rights, and have equal duties. The rights of each State depend not upon its power to ensure the exercise thereof, but upon the mere fact of its existence as a person under international law." Article 15 upheld the nonintervention pledge of the Good Neighbor Policy: "No State or group of States has the right to intervene, directly or indirectly, for any reason whatever, in the internal or external affairs of any other State."

American policymakers and Latin American nationalists read the OAS Charter differently. Latin Americans sought respect for self-determination, equality of states, and sovereignty. In the Cold War context, the United States intended to emphasize the "external threat" of international communism and the "inherent right of self-defense" *for the United States* against such a threat. For the United States, the Rio Pact and the OAS Charter were regional props in the international regime it sought to erect as part of its post–World War II grand strategy.

With these pieces of the regional architecture in place, George Kennan traveled to Latin America in early 1950. He found that Latin America was "cursed by geography, history, and race." Still, its "loss" to communism would be catastrophic for the United States. What to do? Kennan declared that the U.S. government should

> not be too dogmatic about the methods by which local communists can be dealt with. . . . Where the concepts and traditions of popular government are too weak to absorb successfully the intensity of the communist attack, then we must concede that harsh governmental measures of repression may be the only answer; that these measures

may have to proceed from regimes whose origins and methods would not stand the test of American concepts of democratic procedures, and that such regimes and such methods may be preferable alternatives, and indeed the only alternatives, to further communist success.[57]

Like Franklin Roosevelt's Good Neighbor Policy, American Cold War policy for Latin America would subordinate democracy to security (and support for dictatorships) when the choice had to be made.

By U.S. definition, local communists or, sometimes, even leftists, were agents of an extra-hemispheric power. George Kennan offered prospective insight into American policy in Latin America for the next half century. His advice anticipated John F. Kennedy's support for "modernizing" military governments as in El Salvador in 1961, Lyndon Johnson's support for a Brazilian military coup in 1964 and invasion of the Dominican Republic in 1965, the Nixon-Kissinger assault on Chile's elected socialist government (1970–73), and the arguments of the Reagan administration in the 1980s regarding "authoritarian" versus "totalitarian" regimes as it carried out clandestine war against the Sandinista government in Nicaragua. Of course, Kennan could not have predicted in his 1950 memorandum the victory of Fidel Castro in Cuba, Soviet efforts to install offensive intermediate range missiles with nuclear warheads on the island, or the Cuban leader's support for guerrilla wars across the region. Nor could he have anticipated fully the wave of state terrorism that afflicted Latin America's people during the not-so-Cold War as a result of what he called "harsh governmental measures of repression."

An oft-forgotten admonition in the Kennan-inspired NSC-68 augured poorly, long term, for America's support of repression in the name of anti-communism:[58] "The integrity of our system will not be jeopardized by any measures, covert or overt, violent or non-violent, which serve the purposes of frustrating the Kremlin's design ... *provided only they are appropriately calculated to that end and are not so excessive or misdirected as to make us enemies of the people instead of the evil men who have enslaved them.*"[59] American policy over the next decades would make the United States "enemies of the people" more often than Kennan could have dreamed in his worst nightmares.

As early as 1948, there was already danger of making enemies of the people of Latin America. A secret memorandum of the Policy Planning Staff reported:

Several conditions which play into the hands of the Communists
exist in many of the American Republics. There is poverty that is so
widespread that it means a bare subsistence level for large masses of
people. There are ignorance and a high degree of illiteracy. There are

strong reactionary forces which, through extreme selfishness and lack of any sense of social responsibility, impose a minority will through military or other dictatorial governments and so alienate large segments of their populations which otherwise probably would be anti-Communist.[60]

In the same memorandum, the staff cautioned against too vigorous support for dictatorships that might alienate noncommunist groups in the hemisphere but recommended that "after consultation with the Federal Bureau of Investigation, the Central Intelligence Agency and other interested departments and agencies, the Department of State should work out a plan for police cooperation in the Americas to combat Communist activities, including the possible training in the United States of police officials from the other American Republics. . . . The Department of State should take whatever action may be possible to refuse passports to known Communists who are citizens of the United States, and who wish to go to any of the other American Republics."

The OAS and U.S. Policy

At the end of March 1948, the Ninth International Conference of American States met in Bogotá, Colombia. Here the OAS would be created. Two years earlier a split in the Colombian Liberal Party allowed a Conservative, Mariano Ospina Pérez, to win the presidency for the first time since 1930. The Conservatives, led by Laureano Gómez, had begun a campaign of persecution against the Liberals. Gómez was a vocal and vitriolic enemy of liberal democracy. He had openly supported Hitler and admired Spain's General Francisco Franco. Ospina named Gómez to chair the committee preparing the Ninth International Conference. In the words of the most-well-known historian of the Pan American conferences, Samuel Inman, "a few days before the Conference he [Laureano Gómez] was appointed Minister of Foreign Affairs. Thus the best known fascist in [Latin] America was lined up, by a kind of political *coup*, as his government's nominee for President of the Conference."[61] The American delegation (over ninety persons, few of whom had experience in Latin America or spoke Spanish) seemed oblivious to these events leading up to the conference.

On April 9, 1948, an assassin killed Colombia's leading Liberal Party politician, Jorge Eliécer Gaitán. Gaitán headed the nationalist, populist wing of the Liberal Party; his presidential candidacy in 1946 had divided the Liberals, giving victory to the Conservatives. Gaitán represented at least a symbolic departure from politics as usual and hope for the masses of Colombia and for social change. An angry crowd lynched the assassin and displayed his mutilated body in public view at the Colombian president's residence.[62]

Days of violence followed, amounting virtually to an urban insurrection in which the site of the Pan American Conference, the Capitolio, suffered attacks. The *Bogotazo*, as the events came to be called, left a death toll estimated at anywhere from 1,200 to several thousand.[63] It also precipitated five years of widespread, bloody violence in Colombia, known afterward simply as *La Violencia* (the Violence). *La Violencia* would take the lives of hundreds of thousands of Colombians.

On November 9, 1948, President Ospina Pérez imposed a state of siege and closed the Colombian congress. When the Liberals refused to participate in the 1949 presidential elections, Laureano Gómez became president for the 1950–54 term. There followed censorship, repression of labor, purges of the public administration, and then constitutional "reforms" pushing the country toward a corporate state modeled on General Franco's Spain. Thus, the country hosting the creation of the oas and the American proclamations of the need for solidarity and democracy moved quickly to authoritarianism after the conference. (In 1951, the Gómez regime became the only government in Latin America to send military units to Korea. All the rest failed to see an attack on South Korea as a "trigger" for applying the provisions of the Rio Treaty or the oas Charter on collective defense.) Following a period of widespread political violence and atrocities, the army, led by Gustavo Rojas Pinilla, ousted Gómez, on June 13, 1953. Rojas Pinilla established a dictatorship, supported by a broad spectrum of Colombians hoping for the end to the civil war.

U.S. secretary of state George Marshall had gone to Bogotá in 1948 to inform the Latin Americans that European recovery had priority over their requests for economic assistance. He also carried the message that Latin Americans should look to foreign private capital to meet their development needs. At the same time, he expected the Latin Americans to join the anticommunist crusade. He blamed the violence in Bogotá on communist agitators, though Gaitán's assassination seemed more connected either to ongoing Conservative-Liberal tensions or even to a personal vendetta. Subsequent secret reports by the U.S. Department of State explored various theories regarding Gaitán's assassination and the extent of communist involvement in the *Bogotazo*.[64]

Within this climate of virtual dissolution of Colombian government authority, the Bogotá Conference had adopted a resolution for "The Preservation and Defense of Democracy in America." The resolution declared that "by its anti-democratic nature and its interventionist tendency, the political activity of international communism or any totalitarian doctrine is incompatible with the concept of American freedom, which rests upon two undeniable postulates, the dignity of man as an individual and the sovereignty of the nation." The declaration set the stage for inter-American intelligence operations to "proceed with a full exchange of information concerning any of the aforementioned activities that are carried on within their respective jurisdictions."[65]

In October, a top secret directive on information-sharing among the American republics regarding "subversive communist activities" was circulated among U.S. diplomatic representatives in the Western Hemisphere.[66] As an antecedent for what became massive anticommunist counterintelligence (and then counterinsurgency and antiterrorist) operations, this document deserves resurrection from the archives:

Sirs:

At the Bogotá Conference in April of this year there was approved unanimously an anti-Communist resolution providing among other things that the American Republics will exchange information among themselves to assist in checking subversive Communist activities. This proposed exchange of information may properly be considered a commitment on the part of the United States as well as the other American Republics, and it is appropriate therefore that the United States should implement this resolution in cooperation with the Governments of the other American Republics.

You are instructed therefore, to discuss this matter with the Foreign Minister and any other appropriate authorities of the country to which you are accredited and to arrange for the establishment of a suitable liaison and procedure by which information of the type mentioned in the Bogotá Resolution may be exchanged. Liaison with some countries may be directly with the Foreign Office, while in other instances more suitable regular arrangements for the interchange may be established with another ministry or with the police. In all cases the liaison, particularly the designation of specific officials of both the Embassy and the other government, should be arranged personally by the Chief of Mission directly with the appropriate high official or officials of the other government.

For the information of the mission, the Department recognizes that arrangements for exchange of information under the Bogotá

Anti-Communist Resolution may be modified as experience is gained. The nature, quantity and quality of the information which will be exchanged will vary with each country and may well develop only after a period of trial.

The recommendations and comments of the missions are requested on this matter, as well as a report specifically on (a) the arrangements that have been negotiated with the Foreign Office, and (b) the arrangements effected within the mission and the name of the officer designated for liaison duty.

Very truly yours,

For the Acting Secretary of State
W. Park Armstrong, Jr.
Special Assistant for Research and Intelligence

From 1948 on, the United States established as secret policy the creation of information exchange networks with "appropriate authorities," civilian, police, or others, in order to monitor and "check" subversive activities in the hemisphere. With time, full-on police and military training programs, including courses and practicums in psychological operations and "interrogation" techniques, would be offered to thousands of Latin Americans in the Panama Canal Zone and also in their home countries.

In the months after the Bogotá Conference, military coups ousted elected governments in Peru (October) and Venezuela (November). The United States recognized the government of General Manuel Odría in Peru a month after the coup. The leaders of the military coup in Venezuela assured the U.S. ambassador of their opposition to national and international communism and a desire to intensify Venezuela's relationship with the U.S. military missions and to respect free enterprise and foreign capital. In a memorandum for Acting Secretary of State Robert A. Lovett, George Kennan recommended that "recognition should be accorded after an interval neither so short as to be undignified nor so long as to make a prestige issue of the recognition question."[67]

In December, a military coup toppled the government of El Salvador; U.S. recognition followed in late January 1949. Ten days later, a coup took place in Paraguay. The United States delayed recognition, contributing to another coup in late February. U.S. recognition for the new government came in April. In December 1949, Arnulfo Arias, supported by the National Police, took over the presidency of Panama, followed by a military coup in Haiti (May 1950), a coup in Bolivia (June 1951), and a military coup in Cuba (March 10, 1952) led by Fulgencio Batista. On March 21, 1952, the Cuban foreign minister assured the American ambassador, Willard L. Beaulac, that Cuba would fulfill its international obligations without reservations of any kind and "would take steps to curtail communist activities, and would do everything practicable within the law to attract and to guarantee foreign private capital."[68] The United States formally recognized the Batista government six days later.[69]

The harvest of the resolution for "The Preservation and Defense of Democracy in America" was only beginning. Dictatorships and repression of the political left and communist parties spread throughout the hemisphere.[70] The United States created or expanded military missions from the Caribbean and Central America to the Southern Cone. Beginning with Ecuador, the U.S. government negotiated bilateral Mutual Defense Assistance Agreements (MDAAS) with Cuba, Colombia, Peru, and Chile (1952); with Brazil, the Dominican Republic, and Uruguay (1953); and with Nicaragua and Honduras (1954). After a covert operation ousted the government of Jacobo Arbenz in Guatemala, MDAAS came into place for Guatemala and Haiti (1955); Bolivia (1958); El Salvador, Panama, and Costa Rica (1962); and Argentina (1964). Congressional debates resulted in seesaw loosening and tightening of restrictions on military assistance from 1952 to 1959. Critics complained that the programs supported dictators, and supporters insisted that they were necessary to defend the hemisphere against international communism.[71]

Latin American military officers recognized and were frustrated by the gap between U.S. rhetoric and policy. The threat to the Western Hemisphere of Soviet-inspired communism in the 1950s seemed of little credibility, although perhaps useful as a pretext for repressing internal opposition and the small communist and socialist movements that challenged the status quo. In 1952, the Truman administration had elaborated its containment policy for Latin America in NSC-141, essentially a regional footnote to NSC-68: "In Latin America we seek first and foremost an orderly political and economic development which will make the Latin American nations resistant to the internal growth of communism and to Soviet political warfare. . . . Secondly, *we seek hemisphere solidarity in support of our world policy* and for cooperation of the Latin American nations in safeguarding the hemisphere through individual and collective defense measures against external aggression and internal subversion."[72]

As in the United States itself, internal subversion in Latin America had to be countered. This would require intensifying the work of the secret police, military intelligence, and the inter-American networks of anticommunist agents in the press, political parties, labor movements, and religious organizations. A nascent counterinsurgency system would link the United States and Latin America in an anticommunist, antisubversive crusade involving hundreds of covert operations and overt "public safety" programs.

In 1954, the government of Jacobo Arbenz in Guatemala found itself on the top of the list for immediate attention in the crusade against international communism. Arbenz and Guatemala would be the first high-profile victims as "rollback" came to Latin America.

Cold War and Intervention in Guatemala

In the 1952 electoral campaign, Republican leaders charged that the Democrats had sought to achieve their goal of "national socialism" for the last twenty years and had fomented "class strife," "shielded traitors to the Nation in high places," and "created enemies abroad where we should have friends." They charged the Democrats with abandoning Latvia, Lithuania, Estonia, Poland, and Czechoslovakia to communist aggression and with surrendering China to the communists, thereby substituting "on our Pacific flank a murderous enemy for an ally and friend." All this had started at Yalta and Potsdam and had led to the Korean War and "to a policy of containment that does not contain, and to swinging erratically from timid appeasement to reckless bluster."

The Republicans promised to purge the traitors and incompetents from the State Department and all federal offices, "wherever they may be." They also repudiated "all commitments contained in secret understandings such as those of Yalta, which aid Communist enslavement . . . looking forward to the genuine independence of those captive peoples." The Republicans understood communism as "a world conspiracy against freedom and religion."[73]

By the time Eisenhower negotiated the armistice in Korea, the communists in Vietnam were less than a year from defeating the French at Dien Bien Phu (May 7, 1954). French withdrawal from Indochina followed. North Vietnamese leader Ho Chi Minh had been betrayed at Potsdam, where the Russians, the Americans, and the British had decided on the postwar division of Vietnam — the North controlled by China (that is, by Chiang Kai-shek) and the South by the British — instead of allowing for independence as promised at the time the Vietnamese had fought as allies against the Japanese. Ho Chi Minh had declared the formation of the Democratic Republic of Vietnam (September 1945); Chinese forces arrived days later north of the 16th parallel. To the south, the French eventually convinced the British to cede them control.

For eight years, the Viet Minh guerrilla forces fought the French. French casualties are estimated at over 90,000 dead, wounded, and captured. Gradually the United States took over the position of the French in supporting a noncommunist regime in South Vietnam, refusing to abide by the accords made at Geneva in 1954 for national elections. Put simply, the United States understood that in free and fair elections, Ho Chi Minh, ally in the war against Japan and nationalist hero, would be elected the leader of a united Vietnam. American leaders also knew that Ho Chi Minh was a communist. In the Cold War context, his leadership over a unified Vietnam was not acceptable.

One month after the French defeat at Dien Bien Phu, the CIA executed Operation PBSUCCESS in Guatemala. American covert operations to contain or "rollback" communism had come to Central America.[74] Guatemala became a target for the frustration of early Cold War setbacks in Europe and Asia and of frenzied domestic anticommunism in the United States. Arbenz's nationalist rhetoric, collaboration with the local Communist Party in an agrarian reform program affecting the holdings of the United Fruit Company, and labor reforms all pushed too hard on the U.S. anticommunist button. U.S. policymakers were also concerned about the possible "demonstration effect" of agrarian reform and nationalization for U.S. interests elsewhere in the hemisphere. Moreover, some Guatemalan elites and military officers looked favorably on any rationale that would suppress social reform, organization of peasant unions, and disruption of the old order.

To prepare cover for the covert operation, Secretary of State John Foster Dulles cajoled, threatened, squeezed, and coerced the governments of the region to take a strong anticommunist stand at the Tenth Inter-American Conference at Caracas (March 1–28, 1954). Governed by dictator Marcos Pérez Jiménez, whose secret police notoriously persecuted and tortured regime opponents, Venezuela seemed a less-than-ideal location for sermons on democracy in the hemisphere. The congresses of Chile, Uruguay, and Bolivia objected to holding the conference in Caracas; officials from Ecuador, Panama, Mexico, and even Colombia expressed reservations. In the end, only Costa Rica refused to send a delegation.[75]

Over the objections of Guatemala and without the votes of Mexico and Argentina, the conference adopted a resolution that melded and updated the No Transfer Principle and the Monroe Doctrine to the Cold War by applying selectively the terms of the Rio Treaty, the OAS Charter, and the Bogotá Declaration. The Caracas Declaration provided plausible collective security rationale for combating "international communism" everywhere or anywhere in the hemisphere, despite a sop to sovereignty and nonintervention in the last section of the document.

The Tenth Inter-American Conference

DECLARES:

... That the domination or control of the political institutions of any American State by the international communist movement extending to this Hemisphere the political system of an extra continental power, would constitute a threat to the sovereignty and political independence of the American States, endangering the peace of America. ...

RECOMMENDS:

That without prejudice to such other measures as they may consider desirable, special attention be given by each of the American governments to the following steps for the purpose of counteracting the subversive activities of the international communist movement within their respective jurisdictions:

1. Measures to require disclosure of the identity, activities, and sources of funds, of those who are spreading propaganda of the international communist movement or who travel in the interests of that movement, and of those who act as its agents or in its behalf; and

2. The exchange of information among governments to assist in fulfilling the purpose of the resolutions adopted by the Inter-American Conferences and Meetings of Ministers of Foreign Affairs regarding international communism.[76]

In some sense, this resolution merely reaffirmed the commitment to regional counterintelligence and anticommunism spelled out at Bogotá in 1948. Given the immediate political context, however, it provided symbolic support for U.S. claims that Guatemala's government represented a grave threat, the camel's nose of communism slipping into the hemispheric tent. By this interpretation, even Latin American governments that failed to repress communists might be so much a threat to the hemisphere as to require invocation of the updated Monroe Doctrine and the right of collective or unilateral self-defense against "communist penetration of the hemisphere."

In June 1954, the CIA executed Operation PBSUCCESS, using exiled colonel Carlos Castillo Armas as the figurehead of a "liberating army." A haphazard covert operation ousted Guatemala's elected president, imposed Castillo Armas as dictator (until his assassination in 1957), and commenced three decades of repressive military governments in Guatemala. The overthrow of Arbenz (characterized as the "rollback" of communism) made clear to Latin Americans that the United States intended to use whatever means necessary to rid itself of perceived threats to its own security, defined not only as communists, but also as populists, nationalists, and reformers who might "destabilize" the region's political systems or open the door to subversive influences.[77]

Castillo Armas flew to Guatemala City, attended a party at the U.S. Embassy on July 4, 1954, and was "elected" president by the military junta four days later.[78] Arbenz's ouster generated regional and international protests. Crowds burned American flags from Santiago, Chile, to Rangoon, Burma. In Latin America, this intervention left an enduring legacy of anti-Americanism. The Castillo Armas government detained, interrogated, and tortured hundreds of "communists," and thousands of Guatemalans fled into exile. Reversal of the agrarian reforms and repression of the labor movement, frequently at the initiative of local landowners and militia, anticipated the genocidal campaigns against Indian peoples in the counterinsurgency wars that would bloody Guatemala in the 1980s.

The American "victory" in Guatemala, so applauded by Eisenhower, Dulles, and Bissell in their memoirs, became a gangrenous wound in U.S.–Latin American relations and a torturous memory for Guatemala's peasants, workers, and Indian peoples. It also became an over-glorified benchmark for future CIA adventures, serving to mythologize in the annals of covert lore what had been a shoddy operation, only successful by luck in ousting Arbenz. Under Dwight D. Eisenhower, the CIA would carry out many more such operations, on a grander scale and with very poor results, for example in Burma and Indonesia. Nevertheless, PBSUCCESS became the model for a failed invasion of Cuba at the Bay of Pigs in 1961, involving some of the same operatives who had carried out the Guatemalan operation. Like the Soviet invasion of Hungary two years later, the 1954 Guatemalan intervention gave the lie to superpower respect for self-determination of peoples and adherence to the UN Charter.

From 1954 to the early 1960s, the United States directly financed training for Guatemalan secret police and military officials, oversaw intelligence collection, and participated quietly in covert anticommunist operations. It did the same in the Caribbean, Central America, and parts of South America. Military dictators in Cuba, Nicaragua, El Salvador, the Dominican Republic, Peru, Colombia, and Venezuela received vigorous American support. In 1954, President Eisenhower conferred the Legion of Merit decoration on Peru's Manuel Odría and Venezuela's Marcos Pérez Jiménez. The symbolism could not be lost on Latin Americans, particularly the tortured inmates in Pérez Jiménez's dungeons and the prison cells of Cuba's Fulgencio Batista's secret police — and others like them throughout the hemisphere. For these Latin Americans, there was no *Cold* War. And for millions more, the everyday significance of the crusade of "Democracy" against "Communism" had come to mean continuing poverty, lack of opportunity, and repression for those who dared to challenge the old order that kept them down.

In 1959, an unforeseen revolution in Cuba would not only challenge the old order on the island but the basic premises of American hemispheric security doctrine and grand strategy since 1811. Rather than a "natural appendage" of the United States, Cuba would become a chink in the armor of the Western Hemisphere bastion as the not-so-Cold War waged by the superpowers afflicted peoples to the furthest reaches of the planet.

Chapter Eleven

Not-So-Cold War, II

We are engaged in a mortal struggle to determine the shape of the future world. Latin
America is a key area in the struggle. . . . We must ensure that it is neither turned against us
nor taken over by those who threaten our vital national interests. — GENERAL VERNON
WALTERS, U.S. military attaché in Paris, November 3, 1970

Fidel Castro took power in Cuba after two years of insurgency against Fulgencio Batista's dictatorship. The United States had pushed Batista in 1956 to create a more effective anticommunist intelligence apparatus (the BRAC [Buró
de Represión de las Actividades Comunistas]).[1] When CIA inspector General
Lyman Kirkpatrick returned to Havana in 1957, he found "evidence that BRAC
might be too enthusiastic in some of its interrogations." By March 1958, the
U.S. government cut off military assistance (but not CIA intelligence liaison)
to the Batista regime.

On January 1, 1959, Batista fled the island. Six days later, Washington recognized the new government. Secretary of State John Foster Dulles sent a memo
to President Eisenhower stating: "The Provisional Government appears free
from Communist taint and there are indications that it intends to pursue
friendly relations with the United States." But by mid-1959, U.S. policymakers had decided otherwise. In November, Undersecretary of State Christian
Herter told Eisenhower: "All actions of the United States Government should
be designed to encourage within Cuba and elsewhere in Latin America opposition to the extremist, anti-American course of the Castro regime."[2]

J. C. King, head of the CIA's Western Division, wrote a memorandum on
December 11, 1959, for Richard Bissell, CIA director of plans, and CIA director
Allen Dulles. The memo stated that Castro had established a far-left dictator-
ship. King concluded that "violent action" was the only means of breaking
Castro's grip on power. He recommended that "thorough consideration be
given to the elimination of Fidel Castro," apparently the first time that the idea

of assassinating Castro was committed to paper.[3] According to Kirkpatrick, "By 1960 Cuba was in all respects a Communist country."[4] President Eisenhower directed U.S. oil companies not to refine oil coming to Cuba from the Soviet Union, embargoed Cuban sugar imports, and cut off all military and economic aid. By year's end, the United States had imposed an embargo on exports to Cuba, excepting only food and medicine.[5] American efforts to isolate and punish the Cuban regime would endure through the first decade of the twenty-first century — long after the Cold War ended.

The Kennedy administration (1961–63) picked up where Eisenhower's team left off. Kennedy authorized, then took full responsibility for, an invasion by CIA-supported Cuban exiles at the Bay of Pigs in April 1961. The invasion failed miserably.[6] But the Bay of Pigs fiasco did not stop clandestine operations against Cuba. Between April 1961 and October 1962, Soviet and U.S. miscalculations made Cuba the focus of one of the Cold War's most dramatic and nearly cataclysmic confrontations.

The Soviet Union sent military assistance, trainers, and troops to Cuba. It also installed intermediate range missile launchers and provided nuclear warheads for the missiles — though the U.S. government apparently did not know that the warheads had already reached Cuba in October 1962.[7] For two weeks, the people of the world held their collective breath as the United States and the Soviets (largely ignoring Castro and the Cubans, let alone NATO and Warsaw Pact allies) fortuitously negotiated a settlement to the crisis, and the Soviets removed their missiles. They retained bases in Cuba, and thereafter, into the 1980s, installed and enhanced facilities for submarines, military aircraft, and intelligence operations on the island. They also seemed to have exacted a promise from the Kennedy administration to remove Jupiter missiles (of little remaining value, though they pointed at the Soviet heartland) from Turkey and not to invade Cuba. Unreported at the time was Soviet deployment of nuclear torpedo-armed submarines to the region and to stations off Pearl Harbor, with orders to defend Soviet transport ships and to attack Pearl Harbor "if the crisis over Cuba escalated into U.S.-Soviet war."[8]

Acclaimed as a great victory by President Kennedy, the bottom line of the Cuban missile crisis was that the Soviet Union had successfully challenged the Monroe Doctrine and U.S. Cold War regional strategy. This was a landmark in inter-American relations and American policy toward Latin America. The Soviets established a military presence on an island that, since 1811, had been a primary preoccupation of American policymakers. Cuba became an ally for the Soviets, a base for supporting insurgency and revolution in the rest of the hemisphere and a permanent thorn in the side of American governments. Its leader also became a rogue revolutionary, sometimes defying Soviet preferences with his romantic, global anti-imperialism, which extended Cuban influence and prestige far beyond the Western Hemisphere.

In response to the Cuban Revolution, the United States reconfigured regional and global strategic doctrine and revamped its military assistance programs and counterinsurgency operations in Latin America. Kennedy also approved increased clandestine operations in the Congo (Zaire), where Fidel Castro and Che Guevara had decided to extend their support for a nationalist movement, and to Southeast Asia (Thailand, Laos, and Vietnam). The U.S. military assistance group in Vietnam grew, officially, from fewer than 700 to over 12,000 from the time Kennedy took office until mid-1962.[9]

Meanwhile, the U.S. government directed clandestine operations against Cuba, including various unsuccessful plots to assassinate Fidel Castro.[10] Through programs of "economic denial" and a mélange of sabotage, disinformation campaigns, and "dirty tricks" against the island, the Kennedy administration sought to eliminate the Castro government. Chief cheerleader for this so-called Operation Mongoose was Attorney General Robert Kennedy, the president's brother.[11] For their part, the Cubans undertook covert military and diplomatic missions throughout Latin America, assisting and encouraging insurgent groups to "make revolution" instead of just talking about it. Cuban-inspired and supported guerilla movements would become a widespread phenomenon in Latin America during the 1960s.

Consistent with the history of U.S. grand strategy, the Western Hemisphere formed the bastion from which global policies emanated like the web of a spider. After 1961, however, the spiderweb had a close-at-home enemy base in Cuba. The United States would move in 1961 to counter international communism in the hemisphere by instituting an "Alliance for Progress" — a package of U.S.-supported socioeconomic reforms and infrastructure projects intended as a prophylactic to revolution. A play on the Spanish verb *parar* (to stop) prompted some Latin Americans to translate the policy in a different way: the "alliance stops progress" (*la alianza para al progreso*).

Just as the Marshall Plan had allotted special funds for covert operations across Europe, the Alliance for Progress provided cover and resources for such operations in Latin America. U.S. operatives recruited intelligence assets, suborned civilian politicians and military personnel, infiltrated local mass media, and subverted domestic politics in targeted nations. Beyond a persistent campaign of sabotage and subversion against Cuba itself, the American government supported military coups, dictatorships, and transnational assassination networks.[12] U.S. agents infiltrated universities, political parties, labor unions, and religious organizations. They bribed government officials and paid mercenaries to carry out illegal activities, from disinformation campaigns to murder. American policy mocked its own public calls for democracy and defiled its claims to favor human rights and civil liberties in a struggle against tyranny. Such policies spawned millions of resentful enemies for the United States — as George Kennan had presaged.

The Cuban Revolution also profoundly affected American domestic politics. Cuban exiles flowed into the United States, and especially to Florida, gradually transforming that state into a center of political intrigue and a base for covert operations against Cuba and other Latin American nations. By influencing the outcome of presidential elections with Florida's votes in the electoral college, the anti-Castro Cubans eventually (from the early 1980s, if not as early as 1968) "captured" American policy toward Latin America and parts of Africa. They also dominated aspects of local politics in Florida cities, especially Miami — what many people came to call the northernmost city in Latin America. In addition to an expanding presence in Florida state politics, anti-Castro Cubans would serve as ambassadors, State Department personnel in key posts, CIA assets, and operatives. The Cuban exiles' special brand of anticommunism sometimes overdetermined U.S. policies in the rest of Latin America.[13]

Policy toward Cuba formed an important part of the global Cold War drama. For the first time, an independent country in the Western Hemisphere had allied with America's most feared and fearsome adversary. The Cuban government celebrated its anti-Americanism, its amity with the Soviet Union, its own support for revolutionary movements in other Latin American countries, and its solidarity with anticolonial struggles in Asia and Africa. Fidel Castro tweaked the Eagle's beak in marathon speeches, with support for leftist political and guerrilla warfare in Latin America and in small, covert operations that did not make the evening news. Cuba had become an important element in the grand strategies of the United States and the Soviet Union (much more so than it had been for Britain, Spain, France, and the United States throughout the nineteenth century).

Not-So-Cold War America

Policy toward Cuba reflected more general tendencies in not-so-Cold War America. As always, electoral considerations, presidential personalities, and perceptions of public opinion played an important role in shaping policy. Whether it was President Kennedy's visceral anticommunism, Lyndon Johnson's big Texas ego, Richard Nixon's insecurity and alcoholic tantrums, or Jimmy Carter's moralism, presidents and their close advisers made decisions from 1962 into the 1980s not easily understood simply in terms of "rational choices." Despite underlying continuities in policy premises and grand strategy, particular decisions and methods of implementation (invasion, covert operations, military assistance, economic aid) could be determined by presidential personality and the immediate political context. Such idiosyncratic features of American foreign policy became ever more important as secret government gave increasing power to small cliques of policymakers ever less accountable to Congress.[14] Legislative checks and balances were sacrificed to concerns for "national security" as poorly advised executive initiatives stretched further and further the supposed inherent constitutional powers of the American presidency.

In the name of national security, political practice virtually eliminated the remaining *effective* accountability of the executive branch. Often neither Congress, even members of key committees, nor officials in the Department of State knew what the National Security Council (NSC), the CIA, or the president's closest advisers had determined *real* foreign policy to be. Frequently, American officials overseas and in Washington worked at cross-purposes for lack of interdepartmental coordination and because advisers close to the president, officials within the CIA and the National Security Agency (NSA), or key congressional committee chairs and cloaked bureaucrats conceived and ordered implementation of clandestine operations in private meetings.[15] What had begun 150 years earlier with Thomas Jefferson's secret orders to the Lewis and Clark expedition and James Madison's covert operations in the Spanish Floridas became a permanent, internally conflicted, and often jerry-built conglomeration of global and domestic military and intelligence operations in the name of freedom and anticommunism. American foreign policy became a crusade, framed by a frankly religious abomination of the satanic communistic enemy. As in the past, America's leaders, with the collaboration of the mass media, disseminated fear of the enemy as a tool of domestic governance — this time fear of communism rather than the French, British, Spanish, German, or Japanese demons of the past. The Cold War and Cold War discourse took on a life of their own, permeating daily life and premising domestic and foreign policy decisions.

Foreign adversaries had always existed, some with malevolent intentions. During the Cold War, there existed serious, even cataclysmic threats to American security. No doubt existed that the Soviets had terrifying military capabilities and incontrovertible global pretensions, nor was there doubt that Soviet-style regimes were tyrannical and cynical. Yet, as James Madison had prophesied, secret governance in response to foreign threats (and intensification of domestic political corruption) menaced the Republic from within.[16] American foreign policies weakened democracy in the United States. They violated the American Constitution and the law, and they undermined the moral credibility of the country around the globe.[17] The Cold War thus deepened the gradual and cumulative erosion of constitutional government and corruption of republican institutions that had been under way since the failure of Reconstruction after the Civil War.

The Cold Warriors in both the major political parties saw it otherwise. To defend the Free World, fire must be fought with fire, terror with counterterror. Presidents required broad discretion in deploying U.S. armed forces. Proclamation of the Truman Doctrine and congressional financing of the Greek counterinsurgency war were first steps. President Eisenhower and his secretary of state, John Foster Dulles, then set the tone for the next four decades of congressional resolutions, which effectively authorized the president to *make* war without a *declaration of war*. In 1955, Eisenhower obtained from Congress a joint resolution that gave him great latitude to take military action off the coast of mainland China in order to protect Formosa (Taiwan) and the Pescadores Islands from mainland Chinese military action. The resolution authorized the president "to employ the Armed Forces of the United States *as he deems necessary* for the specific purpose of securing and protecting Formosa and the Pescadores against armed attack." In 1956, Eisenhower used the same tactic to gain congressional support for a resolution that authorized deployment, *as judged necessary*, of U.S. military forces in the "general area" of the Middle East to counter "overt armed aggression" on the part of "any nation controlled by international Communism."[18]

The communist enemy also was at work in the Western Hemisphere. When Vice President Richard Nixon faced angry mobs in Lima and came menacingly close to being stoned in Caracas during his May 1958 trip to Latin America, he emphasized that communists had inspired the riots.[19] Nixon argued that the United States "must join the battle in Latin America on the field of propaganda. Otherwise the Communists would ultimately win out."[20] The fact that Venezuela's ex-dictator, Marcos Pérez Jiménez, and his notorious chief of secret police had taken refuge in the United States might have influenced Nixon's "welcome" in Caracas did not seem to occur to the American government. In Pérez Jiménez's prisons, jailors committed unspeakable atrocities against regime opponents. American support for such a government made ironic, if not pathetic, the clichéd speeches by American presidents heralding democracy. Yet Nixon believed, or said he believed, that propaganda could overcome Latin American distaste for American condescension, hypocrisy, and support for tyrants like Pérez Jiménez.[21]

When the torch passed from Eisenhower to the charismatic Kennedys and their youthful public idealism, there was a momentary hope for review of

Cold War policies. It lasted at the most only several months. Notwithstanding divisions within his policy team and his own sympathy for reform and economic opportunity, John F. Kennedy (1961–63) eventually came down on the same side of the hard-line Cold War divide as Eisenhower and Dulles. What mattered most was defending the hemisphere against international communism. Lyndon Johnson (1963–69) made the same choice after Kennedy's assassination in November 1963, as did Richard Nixon (1969–74) and Gerald Ford (1974–77).

For Latin America, this underlying continuity in U.S. policy would mean that limiting Soviet and Cuban influence and halting revolutionary advances took priority over hopes for democratization and social reform. Covert operations in Latin America corrupted and deformed other U.S. foreign policy initiatives. Intelligence operatives worked under cover in the Agency for International Development, the Office for Public Safety (created in 1957 to train foreign police forces), the International Association of Police Chiefs, police training programs in universities within the United States, news organizations, private businesses, labor organizations, and, of course, U.S. embassies. CIA proprietary firms, for example, International Police Services, Inc. (created in 1952), assisted the Agency for International Development in avoiding congressional oversight of programs directly related to foreign intelligence and political operations.[22]

Almost any U.S. government agency, many private organizations, and individual academic researchers *might* be doing CIA business — making Latin American policymakers and citizens suspicious of Americans in residence. Even Peace Corps volunteers often found themselves accused of working for the CIA, though few of them had contact with or knowledge of the CIA's work.[23] Latin Americans believed, correctly, that the United States did and would intervene in their internal affairs, to defend the "free world" as deemed necessary by American policymakers. Unseemly as it might seem, the "free world" included the rising number of Latin American military governments, which U.S. governments helped to install and sustain, and even General Francisco Franco's Spanish dictatorship.

"No More Cubas"

The not-so-Cold War in Latin America was never unilateral nor was it imaginary. Cubans fanned the embers of revolution where they could, supporting nationalist and internationalist movements opposed to international capitalism or simply to governments supported by U.S. policy.[24] Cuban and Soviet-supported Latin American insurgencies presented threats to weak and unpopular governments. They also attacked popularly elected governments promoting social reform, like that of Rómulo Bentacourt in Venezuela. Latin American reformers and revolutionaries had their own agendas and sought to carry them out, often in opposition to U.S. plans for the Western Hemisphere. For American policymakers and presidents, local conditions and national idiosyncrasies in Latin America mattered little except as they were perceived to affect the Cold War.

Soviet leader Nikita Khrushchev had declared in January 1961 that the Soviet Union would support "wars of liberation" around the world. Shortly thereafter, President Kennedy told the U.S. Congress that "the free world's security can be endangered . . . by being slowly nibbled away at the periphery, by forces of subversion, infiltration, intimidation[,] . . . guerrilla warfare or a series of limited wars."[25] With this in mind, U.S. policy was pragmatic and eclectic. American policymakers routinely conditioned "aid" to Latin American governments on supporting the American hemispheric agenda and voting as the United States desired at meetings of the Organization of American States (OAS) and the United Nations. The CIA covertly funded political parties, religious organizations, peasant cooperatives, trade unions, and mass media enterprises as if what happened in those countries were an extension of U.S. national politics and a natural part of U.S. defense and security policymaking. The U.S. government could oust dictators, even sponsor their assassination, when they no longer served American purposes (as with Rafael Trujillo in the Dominican Republic in 1961) or facilitate installation of "modernizing" military governments (as with Colonel Julio Adalberto Rivera in El Salvador in the same year). To combat communism, the United States could support military dictatorships, masked by the legal fiction of periodic elections (as in Guatemala and El Salvador from the early 1960s into the 1980s), or outright "salvationist" military juntas that promised to rescue their countries from the terrors of international Marxism, with little or no pretense of democratic legitimation (as in Brazil, 1964–85; Chile, 1973–90; Uruguay, 1973–84; and Argentina, 1976–83).[26] It could support elected civilian governments that fought insurgencies using constitutional regimes of exception, including martial law, as occurred in Colombia from 1958 to 1974 and in Venezuela in the 1960s. U.S. agencies could even operate covertly in British Guiana, still a colony but close to independence, to prevent a "communist" from coming to power.[27] When other measures failed to accomplish U.S. objectives, it could create and direct clandestine paramilitary forces, as would occur with the proxy "freedom fighter" army deployed against Nicaragua's Sandinista government from the early 1980s, or, as a last resort, intervene directly with U.S. armed forces, as occurred in the Dominican Republic in 1965.

Despite the "loss" of Cuba, indeed because of its incorporation into the Soviet orbit, the amalgamated No Transfer Principle and Monroe Doctrine became the "No More Cubas" policy. As part of Cold War grand strategy, the Kennedy administration prevailed on most members of the OAS in 1962 to exclude Cuba from that organization. Those governments that failed to break off diplomatic relations with Cuba (except Mexico, which collaborated in different fashion with U.S. intelligence agencies and the FBI) faced hostility if not U.S.-supported coups, as occurred in Argentina in 1962. By way of illustration, Secretary of State Dean Rusk told U.S. legislators in an executive session that "what led to the overthrow of the [Arturo] Frondizi government was the direct consequence of the attitude of Frondizi toward Castro."[28]

Even in the early 1960s, however, President Kennedy found his policies toward Latin America constrained by domestic political considerations — the old trade and tariff conundrums, with subsidies for American agriculture and protection for American producers, investors, and financiers arrayed against Latin America's post–World War II nationalism and its focus on government-driven development to overcome dependency on U.S. and European industrial imports and technology.[29] For Latin Americans, improved access to American and European markets for their products would often have been the most efficient form of "foreign aid," but this alternative negatively affected various American political constituencies. U.S. governments preferred to provide "food aid" (Public Law 480) rather than to create Latin American competition for American producers; they preferred loans and credits rather than the sort of grants that had rebuilt Europe under the Marshall Plan.[30] U.S. policymakers recommended that Latin America seek billions of dollars in foreign investment to generate development and insisted that Latin American governments provide "stability" and favorable business conditions to allure foreign investors to the region. These ineluctable facts of American politics, with slight adjustments and new slogans, persisted across Democratic and Republican administrations from 1959 into the 1990s.

The Cold War, thus, did not eliminate or overcome core elements of "politics as usual" in the United States, again to the disadvantage of Latin America. Indeed, in some ways, the continuity from the economic policies toward the region from the 1920s through the Eisenhower and Kennedy administrations, and even to the first decade of the twenty-first century, are striking: the United States pushed fiscal restraint, reducing government regulation, attracting private investment to stimulate economic growth, and opening markets. American governments publicly favored political democracy (elected governments) and capitalism, broadly understood, as a cure-all for Latin America's ills. It also prescribed the paradoxical formula of "less government" combined with more "state capacity" to provide "stability." In translation, that often meant starving the civil administration while buttressing the Latin American militaries, police, and intelligence agencies.

When push came to shove, "democracy" would be sacrificed to stability and national security concerns. So much was this the case that John F. Kennedy eventually departed publicly from the nonintervention principle that had characterized inter-American political culture (if not practice) since the 1933 Montevideo Conference and Franklin Roosevelt's Good Neighbor Policy. Only days before his assassination, President Kennedy declared that it was necessary "to come to the aid of any government requesting aid to prevent a takeover aligned to the policies of foreign communism." He made an expansive commitment to impede "more Cubas": "Every resource at our command [must be used] to prevent the establishment of another Cuba in this hemisphere."[31]

Kennedy's words were prophetic. Whether they be considered an update to the Truman Doctrine, iteration of the Caracas Declaration, reaffirmation of the 1954 intervention in Guatemala, or a warning to all Latin American governments and peoples against the temptation of "communism," they foretold almost three more decades of American "anything goes" to fight communism in the Western Hemisphere. As historian Stephen Rabe concluded: "President Kennedy brought high ideals and noble purposes to his Latin American policy. Ironically, however, his unwavering determination to wage Cold War in 'the most dangerous area in the world' led him and his administration ultimately to compromise and even mutilate those grand goals for the Western Hemisphere."[32]

From 1961 to 1963, the Kennedy administration greatly expanded the army's Special Forces and installed a Special Action Force in the Canal Zone at Fort Gulick, designated for special warfare missions in Latin America. The U.S. Southern Command shifted its emphasis to counterinsurgency. Between 1961 and 1964, the School of the Americas in the Canal Zone (called the U.S. Army Caribbean School until 1963) trained over 16,000 Latin American personnel in counterinsurgency and civic action programs. Police training against communist subversion also dramatically increased — from 1962, the Inter-American Police Academy at Fort Davis in the Canal Zone focused on internal threats while special programs focused on counterinsurgency and counterterrorism. U.S. military journals highlighted the new hemispheric approach with colorfully titled articles such as "MATA (Military Assistance Training Adviser) Army Conditioning Course Puts Cold Warriors on the Spot" and "Counterinsurgency: Global Termite Control."[33]

TABLE 11.1. Latin American Military Coups, 1961–1964

El Salvador	January 24, 1961
Ecuador	November 8, 1961
Argentina	March 29, 1962
Peru	July 18, 1962
Guatemala	March 31, 1963
Ecuador	July 11, 1963
Dominican Republic	September 25, 1963
Honduras	October 8, 1963
Brazil	March 31, 1964
Bolivia	November 4, 1964

Note: The 1961 coup in El Salvador was against a reformist military junta;
all the others ousted civilian governments.

That Kennedy frequently called Latin America "the most dangerous area in the world" put him in good company. From John Adams to Woodrow Wilson, U.S. grand strategy had presumed the need for a safe bastion in the Western Hemisphere. Kennedy's successors would use every resource imaginable (and some unimaginable, except to the "cowboys" engaged in Special Operations) to keep communism out of the rest of Latin America. The early harvest reaped from American militarization of its Latin American policy was ten military coups from Central America to the Southern Cone from 1961 to 1964 in the name of "Democracy" and "No More Cubas."

After Camelot: The Mann Doctrine

Vice President Lyndon Baines Johnson took office upon John F. Kennedy's assassination in late November 1963. At first, Johnson claimed to follow in Kennedy's footsteps (and those of Franklin Delano Roosevelt) in Latin American affairs: "Thirty-one years ago this month Franklin Roosevelt proclaimed the policy of the good neighbor. Three years ago this month John Kennedy called for an Alliance for Progress among the American Republics. Today my country rededicates itself to these principles and renews its commitment to the partnership of the hemisphere to carry them forward."[34] Even more so than Kennedy, Johnson emphasized the crucial role of private capital for development and the need to make conditions for such capital alluring: "Public funds are not enough. We must work together to insure the maximum use of private capital, domestic and foreign; without it, growth will certainly fall far behind." For Johnson as for Kennedy, however, the bottom line was anti-communism and "No More Cubas." He told America: "We must protect the Alliance against the efforts of communism to tear down all that we are building. . . . I now, today, assure you that *the full power of the United States is ready to assist any country whose freedom is threatened by forces dictated from beyond the shores of this continent.*"[35]

Even before this speech, the United States had gained support in 1963 for a Central American Defense Council (CONDECA) as a subsidiary organ of the Organization of Central American States (ODECA).[36] CONDECA determined "after careful analysis . . . [that] the most immediate threat to the area seemed to be that of insurgency fostered by Communist guerrilla forces from without."[37] Within this multilateral cover for its strategic agenda, the United States developed "intelligence-sharing arrangements," periodic meetings of regional military officers, and expanded regional surveillance and counterinsurgency networks, which would foster death squads and right-wing militias for the next two decades in the battle against international communism.

As the 1964 presidential elections approached, the Democratic Party platform claimed that the Alliance for Progress had "immeasurably strengthened the collective will of the nations of the Western Hemisphere to resist the massive efforts of Communist subversion that conquered Cuba in 1959 and then headed for the mainland." It also reminded the American electorate that the Agency for International Development (AID), created by the Kennedy administration in 1961, increased the percent of aid-financed commodities purchased in the United States from 41 percent in 1960 to 85 percent in 1964. To wit, the Cold War foreign aid program was more and more a program with a domestic constituency, even if not widely popular. The Democrats also boasted of the "carefully planned and prepared" response to the Cuban Missile Crisis of 1962, a monumental misrepresentation of the chaotic brush with nuclear catastrophe, which was made apparent by later-declassified documents.

Republicans accused the Democrats of aiding and abetting communism around the world with their inept policies, of allowing a communist takeover in Laos, increased aggression in Vietnam, and the building of a wall in East Berlin, and of having "forever blackened our nation's honor at the Bay of Pigs, bungling the invasion plan and leaving brave men on Cuban beaches to be shot down."[38] The Republicans asserted that "the supreme challenge is . . . an atheistic imperialism — Communism." They proclaimed: "We will take the Cold War offensive on all fronts . . . and mount a psychological warfare attack on behalf of freedom and against Communist doctrine and imperialism."[39]

The particulars of the Latin American plank in the Republican platform of 1964 included action to restore a "free and independent government in Cuba," recognizing a Cuban government in exile, and "assisting Cuban freedom fighters in carrying out guerrilla warfare against the Communist regime" (language that would be resuscitated by Ronald Reagan in the 1980s to support "freedom fighters" against the Sandinista government in Nicaragua). The platform added that "Republicans will make clear to all Communists now supporting or planning to support guerrilla and subversive activities, that henceforth *there will be no privileged sanctuaries* to protect those who disrupt the peace of the world."[40] Like the pirates of the 1820s, the communists would be attacked wherever found. They were enemies of humanity.

Although the Republicans lost the election and President Lyndon Johnson became increasingly more preoccupied with the rapidly escalating war in Southeast Asia, U.S. foreign policy moved in the direction favored by the Republicans. In 1964, Johnson ordered air strikes against North Vietnam and then followed the precedent set by Eisenhower (and John Adams, James Buchanan, and Benjamin Harrison) by requesting congressional support for expanding the undeclared war in Southeast Asia. The Tonkin Gulf resolution declared that "the United States is . . . prepared, *as the President determines*, to take all necessary steps, including the use of armed force to assist any member or protocol state of the Southeast Asia Collective Defense Treaty requesting assistance in defense of its freedom."[41] A treaty regime (like the seminal Bidlack-Mallarino Treaty with Colombia in 1846) would provide "legitimacy" for presidential war making, buttressed with congressional approbation and appropriations — but without a formal declaration of war.[42] The resolution further provided that this authority would remain in effect *until the president determined* that "the peace and security of the [Southeast Asia] area is reasonably assured by international conditions created by the United Nations or otherwise, except that it may be terminated earlier by concurrent resolution of Congress." For the moment, Congress left itself language insinuating a shred of remaining authority to rein in presidential war making.

After 1964, U.S. policy in Latin America became even more aggressive. Military invasion of the Dominican Republic in 1965 to prevent "more Cubas" was followed by support for a military coup in Argentina in 1966. Reflecting on the Dominican operation, in which the official justification of the United States for the insertion of some 20,000 troops was to "protect American lives and property," former assistant secretary of state Thomas Mann returned to America's unilateralist tradition and the "self-defense" version of the Monroe Doctrine put forth in the Clark Memorandum of 1928 (see chapter 9):

Monroe was talking about self-defense. Self-defense is as different from intervention as a steak is from a potato. They have no relationship to each other at all. The purpose of self-defense is not to dictate to a country how to manage its affairs; it's to enable a country to survive against a real or threatened attack. Now, there are many things wrong with the law of self-defense, but it should never be confused with intervention. . . . Once I became convinced, and it didn't take me very long (in fact, everybody was convinced) that if the rebels won, the Communist military component in the rebel movement had the military strength to take over and would take over — that you would have another Cuba — then all my problems disappeared, because I didn't think we were dealing with the problem of intervention; we were dealing with a problem of self-defense. . . . I was impressed during the Dominican crisis with interpretations by legal advisors in the State Department of OAS charter provisions, which cast doubt, in their opinion, on whether the U.S. had the right of unilateral self-defense. That just scared the pants off of me.[43]

What came to be called the Mann Doctrine was generally consistent with the Olney and Roosevelt Corollaries to the Monroe Doctrine, dusted off for the Cold War. President Johnson made no bones about U.S. policy: the United States "could not and would not permit the establishment of another Communist government in the Western Hemisphere."[44] Barely a pretense of favoring democracy (more accurately, civilian elected governments) over military governments would remain, so long as the governments in power provided stability, eschewed radical social reform, and toed the anticommunist line. As in the 1930s and 1940s, the Good Neighbor might support dictatorship when it suited its interests.[45] But the constitutional rationale for sending in the troops rested on the president's authority to protect American citizens abroad, a return to J. Reuben Clark Jr.'s less-well-remembered Memorandum on the Right to Protect Citizens in Foreign Countries by Landing Forces (1912) from the days of dollar diplomacy. Under this interpretation there was no need for consultation with Congress.

Mann, however, went well beyond Clark's 1912 memorandum. According to Mann's interpretation, the United States reserved a unilateral right of self-defense to intervene in any Latin American country to prevent or overturn a "communist" government. This right was inherent in U.S. sovereignty itself, notwithstanding the 1933 Montevideo Convention and the Good Neighbor Policy. No "intervention" occurred where the purpose was "self-defense." This right of self-defense, whether rooted in the Monroe Doctrine or not, combined with the inherent constitutional authority of the president as commander in chief, trumped all other treaty obligations, as well as the OAS and the UN Charter. And it would be the American president who would decide when "self-defense" required armed intervention in Latin America or elsewhere.

The Cold War and the "No More Cubas" policy had made reality of the nightmares of Senator Tom Corwin in 1847 ("the right of the President, without the control of Congress, to march your embodied hosts to Monterey, to Yucatán, to Mexico, to Panama, to China") and Senator Robert La Follette in 1917 ("to give the President the power to determine the purposes for which this Nation will engage in war, and the conditions on which it will make peace . . . can not long be tolerated if even the forms of free government are to remain"). As Senator Jacob Javits (R.-N.Y.) would put it in 1973: "Out of the crisis of World War II and the ensuing Cold War, . . . lawyers for the President had spun a spurious doctrine of 'inherent' commander-in-chief powers broad enough to cover virtually every 'national security' contingency."[46] Between the NSA's global surveillance of friend and foe and the secret NSC's National Security Intelligence Directives (NSCIDS), which expanded the CIA's and other agencies' operations, the presidency operated a parallel clandestine government.

As had occurred with John Adams and the Alien and Sedition Acts, Woodrow Wilson and the Palmer Raids after World War I, and McCarthyism in the 1950s, concern for internal security under Lyndon Johnson and Richard Nixon (1969–74) drove the FBI and the CIA to conflate domestic political opposition, the civil rights movement, and antiwar organizations with the external enemy. The FBI and the CIA surveilled and infiltrated civil rights and peace networks in the United States. Frustrated by the rising antiwar movement and more than seventy urban riots, President Lyndon Johnson ordered the CIA in late 1967 to monitor the possible relationship between peace, civil rights, and Black Power movements and Moscow. They found none.[47] This illegal operation, ongoing until 1974, included the NSA and the FBI in collaboration with local police departments. It produced extensive files on thousands of American citizens in the fashion of European and Latin American police states.

Domestic Politics and the Foreign Policy Agenda

Escalation in Vietnam, expanded covert operations in Asia and the Pacific, and anticommunist interventions and counterinsurgency operations in Latin America paralleled social mobilization on the home front, which greatly complicated war-making and security policy. The U.S. antiwar movement overlapped the sometimes violent struggle to end legal segregation in the United

States. Civil rights tactics included "sit-ins," "freedom rides," silent vigils, marches, and picketing — often met by Ku Klux Klan and official repression. Police violence against civil rights activists was reported and televised around the world. The offspring of the Reconstruction era Redeemer Democrats sought to terrorize African Americans and their allies once again into submission to the Jim Crow regime.

Neither Kennedy nor Johnson wished to emulate Andrew Johnson after Lincoln's assassination or Hayes's shameful bargain of 1877. The Kennedy administration sent federal marshals and then army troops to enforce desegregation. Kennedy proposed civil rights legislation in 1963. After Kennedy's assassination, Lyndon Johnson strongly urged that such legislation be passed as a tribute to the slain president — though perhaps a tribute to Harry Truman would have been more appropriate. Like Truman, Johnson was a Southern Democrat, and he would preside over the frontal attack on Jim Crow. A century after the Civil War ended, the American federal government would renew a serious, if not always full-bore, assault on segregation and racism. More blood would be shed and more time would pass, but, painfully, America was moving toward a fit between the ideals of the Declaration of Independence and its everyday politics — a time when the unalienable rights of "Life, Liberty, and the pursuit of Happiness" would be protected by the federal government for all Americans. If that dream could be realized *in* America, then hope might exist for a real change in the country's traditional unilateralist and ethnocentric foreign policies.

The turmoil of social change and resistance throughout the American South resulted in a spate of legislation and a growing agenda for the federal courts. As the civil rights movement pushed for the definitive end to legal segregation in the United States, President Johnson declared a War on Poverty. Johnson signed the Economic Opportunity Act in August 1964, under which he created a panoply of new social programs managed by the Office of Economic Opportunity: Volunteers in Service to America (VISTA), Job Corps, Head Start (later transferred to the Department of Health Education and Welfare), Legal Services, and the Community Action Program. Soon thereafter came Medicaid, Medicare (Social Security Act of 1965), and the Food Stamp program. Lyndon Johnson called his overall project for the country the Great Society. He pushed federal housing programs, created a Department of Housing and Urban Development (1965), and proposed environmental legislation and the first immigration reform of consequence since 1924. He also asked Congress to support new regulations regarding consumer safety and honesty in lending.

Viewed by most Republicans as an ill-advised, even dangerous, updating and expansion of the New Deal, the War on Poverty programs suffered attacks as examples of Democrat propensities to "tax-and-spend" and of "big government" and "welfarism." In part, the resistance to "welfare" programs (and to legal assistance for the poor) was barely disguised resistance to racial equality. Despite the efforts of the descendants of the Redeemer Democrats, this phase of the Cold War had provoked social and political movements that would progressively, if incompletely, overturn discrimination against African Americans, other minorities, and women. The dialectics of the Cold War inspired renewed appeals for realization of the American Dream — just as had occurred with the opposition to the Mexican War, the Spanish American War, and World War I. A diverse coalition of idealists called for a more universal and inclusionary version of American exceptionalism. It was time to take seriously the idea that "all men [and women] are created equal." But such a radical idea could not but meet significant resistance.

In practice, Vietnam and the Cold War overshadowed President Johnson's domestic initiatives, and the Great Society's domestic policies also polarized the American electorate. In March 1968, Johnson surprised the country by announcing that he would not run for a second term, much as Hayes had done in 1880 and Truman in 1952. He chose to focus, unsuccessfully as it turned out, on ending the Vietnam War. Simultaneously, conflict with Cuba again boiled to the surface as Castro cut off the water supply to the American base at Guantánamo and declared Cuba's intent to shoot down U-2 spy planes on missions over the island. President Johnson threatened Cuba with "severe action" if planes were downed and ordered construction of a water treatment plant to make the base self-sustaining.

The Cuban slap at a president already facing serious foreign policy failure further hardened American positions, providing ideal circumstances for the Republicans to remember the Monroe Doctrine. The Democrats had failed to secure the Western Hemisphere from the threat of international communism. To this the Soviets added the invasion of Czechoslovakia in August 1968, justified by the Brezhnev Doctrine. Cold War foreign policy, including relations with Cuba, would play an important part in the Republicans' 1968 election victory.

From Nixon to Carter

Republican Richard Nixon won the presidency in 1968 over the Democrat, Vice President Hubert Humphrey (in the popular vote, 43.4 to 42.7 percent, and 301–191 in the electoral college). The campaign, in a highly polarized country, was punctuated by widespread racial violence and war protests and the assassinations of civil rights leader Martin Luther King Jr. and President

Kennedy's brother and attorney general, Robert Kennedy. George Wallace's American Independent Party (with his vice presidential candidate, former air force chief of staff General Curtis LeMay) captured the electoral votes of five states of the former Confederacy. One hundred years later, the Civil War had not entirely ended. Wallace vehemently opposed the Great Society desegregation push — he had become famous for his slogan "Segregation now! Segregation tomorrow! Segregation forever!" LeMay was known for his advocacy of preemptive use of nuclear weapons and for his cavalier but serious remarks on Vietnam: "My solution to the problem would be to tell the North Vietnamese Communists frankly that they've got to draw in their horns and stop their aggression or we're going to bomb them into the stone age." The Wallace-LeMay ticket would win some 13 percent of the popular vote, pledging to "stand up for America." Public opinion pollsters reported that almost 50 percent of Americans believed that communists had something to do with the racial violence of the 1966–68 years. Like the racialization of radical politics in 1919 by Woodrow Wilson and the Military Intelligence Division after World War I, some of the Cold Warriors sought to conflate the civil rights movement and the women's liberation movement with the nation's Cold War enemy.[48] Communists favored racial equality. Communists favored women's rights. It was time to stem the liberal-pinko-communist tide.

Richard Nixon promised to restore law and order. He insinuated that he had a secret plan to end the Vietnam War. Yet not only did he lack a plan to end the war, secret or otherwise, but he had no plan to end the procession of military dictatorships supported by the United States in Latin America and around the world. In 1967, Nixon had characterized Latin America as a "tinder box for revolution." As president, he and his national security advisor, Henry Kissinger, would have no tolerance for further revolution or even radical reforms in the Western Hemisphere.[49]

In 1969, Nixon appointed Nelson Rockefeller to direct a study of U.S.–Latin American relations. Rockefeller's commission made four trips to Latin America, facing increasingly hostile crowds and anti-American demonstrations. The commission reported that "the seeds of nihilism and anarchy are spreading throughout the hemisphere" and found a wave of nationalism, Marxism, and anti-U.S. sentiment across the region.[50] It also worried that Castroite and communist subversion still threatened Latin America.[51] With this in mind, the commission recommended increased U.S. military assistance and training programs. It called for closer ties with the "new type of military man" who is "becoming a major force for constructive social change in the American republics."[52]

Thus, Nixon and his advisers reinforced the Mann Doctrine. Military regimes in Brazil, Bolivia, Argentina, and Central America received encouragement. The United States took a still harder line on reformist and populist movements that questioned American policies or favored more autonomous foreign policies for their countries. Explicitly socialist, pro-Castro, or excessively nationalist governments were targeted for American covert operations. There followed U.S.-supported coups and repressive military regimes in Honduras (1972), Chile (1973), and Uruguay (1973) — all with the encouragement of Nixon and Henry Kissinger. For them, Latin America mattered greatly for its implications in the Cold War. Nowhere was this more true than in Kissinger's worry that the legally elected socialist-communist coalition government in Chile in 1970 might provide a "negative example" for the rest of Latin America, Italy, or even France. As Kissinger put it in June 1970, "I don't see why we need to stand by and watch a country go communist because of the irresponsibility of its own people." Nixon and Kissinger ordered a no-holds-barred assault on Chile's newly elected government.[53] President Salvador Allende had to go.

Nixon and Kissinger's direct role in plotting CIA and paramilitary intervention in Chile is thoroughly documented in congressional hearings and official documents later declassified.[54] The same is true for support for military dictatorships in Honduras, Guatemala, Panama, Bolivia, and Uruguay. In this respect, the Nixon administration's Latin American policies followed, with its own crude and bizarre style, the path trod by Kennedy and Johnson. Although Kissinger repeatedly dismissed the importance of Latin America in world history, he dedicated himself ferociously to combating Marxism and even nationalism in the region.

Even as the Nixon administration escalated war in Southeast Asia with "secret" bombings of Cambodia and Laos, it encouraged harsh repression of leftist political movements in Latin America. Nixon and Kissinger covertly supported transnational terrorism by Latin American armed forces and secret police to extirpate "communism" from the Western Hemisphere. Kissinger's supposedly brilliant realpolitik promoted vicious dictatorships in the Southern Cone and elsewhere.[55] Kissinger deliberately and consciously dismissed the importance of human rights as an element in American foreign policy by privately conveying his support for Chile's General Augusto Pinochet and later (in the Gerald Ford administration) the Argentine military junta. His infatuation with hard power, especially military power and coercion, made his realpolitik a long-term losing strategy for American credibility, interests, and moral suasion. Among the many lamentable decisions made by Nixon and Kissinger, support for the Southern Cone military regimes' "Operation Condor" implicated the United States in a network of international state-sponsored terrorism that murdered America's "enemies." Operation Condor anticipated some of the techniques and "intelligence partnerships" again encouraged in Latin America in the Global War on Terror after September 11, 2001.[56]

The modern history of intelligence coordination efforts within the hemisphere went back to the proscribed lists of Germans, Japanese, and Italians during World War II. Postwar anticommunist intelligence operations had begun in Colombia, Chile, Brazil, and elsewhere in the mid-1940s and expanded greatly after 1959. In 1968, General Robert W. Porter (US SouthCom commander, 1965–69) stated that "in order to facilitate the coordinated employment of internal security forces within and among Latin American countries, we are . . . assisting in the organization of integrated command and control centers; the establishment of common operating procedures; and the conduct of joint and combined training exercises."[57] State terrorism by American-supported Latin American governments (and governments elsewhere) became a legacy of the "No More Cubas" era — and an indelible stain on the Nixon presidency. The Nixon Doctrine — military assistance for governments fighting subversion and "communism" while attempting to limit direct U.S. military involvement — would be applied in the Western Hemisphere and globally for years to come.[58] As Nixon put it: "Our idea is to create a situation in which those lands to which we have obligations or *in which we have interests*, if they are ready to fight a fire, should be able to count on us to furnish the hose and water."[59]

While the Nixon Doctrine provided a rhetorical rationale for withdrawal from Vietnam, it failed to turn around the Southeast Asian disaster. The political scandal that followed revelations regarding the use of the CIA, the NSA, and the FBI for surveillance and other illegal operations against Nixon's political opponents, symbolized by the break-in at the Watergate building in 1972, brought on the president's resignation on August 9, 1974, under threat of impeachment. Only one month earlier, the Supreme Court, overruling the Philadelphia Appeals Court in a 5–4 decision, had denied standing to a citizen challenging the constitutionality of the secret and disguised budget appropriations for the CIA and its covert operations.[60]

After Nixon's shame and resignation, his successor, Gerald Ford, persisted on the same foreign policy path, even retaining Kissinger as his primary foreign policy adviser and adding Donald Rumsfeld as his chief of staff to replace Kissinger's sometimes rival General Alexander Haig. President Ford issued a presidential pardon for Nixon, continuing the tradition of impunity for violations by a former president of the rule of law, established by Congress in 1844 when it revoked the fine assessed against Andrew Jackson for his contempt of judicial authority in 1815.

Nixon (with Kissinger) had conceived of foreign policy partly as an American crusade to protect Western "civilization," therefore justifying extreme, even extra-constitutional, measures. As biographer Robert Dallek described Nixon's decision to attack Cambodia: "It was as if he was willing himself, the country, and the world into seeing him as a great president rescuing civilization from the barbarians."[61] Like Andrew Jackson's ethnic cleansing against Native Americans (in contravention of rulings by the Supreme Court), what was done in the name of God, Civilization, and America should not be punished, notwithstanding violations of the U.S. Constitution, criminal codes, and — by the late 1950s — international law. There could be no higher law than the American mission, as defined by its president and his close advisers.

Fallout from the Watergate scandal and the defeat in Vietnam brought to Congress a more liberal contingent (the 93rd Congress, 1973–75). Kissinger and the national security establishment suffered a brief attack on presidential powers (the War Powers Act, 1973),[62] efforts at oversight of CIA covert operations (Hughes-Ryan amendment, 1974), an expanded Freedom of Information Act (1975), and new guidelines banning domestic covert operations.[63] Gerald Ford signed Executive Order 11905, prohibiting *peacetime* assassinations of foreign leaders. Congress also reduced or cut off military aid to governments identified as gross violators of human rights (Indonesia, Turkey, South Korea, Uruguay, and Chile) and shut down the Office of Public Safety, an AID front for CIA and military collaboration in overseas intelligence, training of secret police, and repression of "subversives" and "terrorists."

The Nixon scandal provided short-term opportunities to modify U.S. foreign policy and expose some of the domestic corruption and illegal operations that underlay its unconstrained interventionism. President Ford appointed a commission headed by Nelson Rockefeller to determine whether the CIA had engaged in illegal activities in the United States. The inquiry later expanded to include the CIA's foreign intelligence charter and to make suggestions for operational guidelines. Intended more as damage control than as a serious investigation and reform effort, the commission nevertheless confirmed the existence of a CIA domestic mail–opening operation; found that in the late 1960s and early 1970s the CIA had kept files on some 300,000 U.S. citizens and organizations relating to domestic dissident activities; and found that President Nixon had tried to use CIA records for partisan political ends.[64]

Parallel to the Rockefeller Commission, an investigation took place in the Senate headed by Senator Frank Church (D.-Idaho). The Committee to Study

Government Operations with Respect to Intelligence Activities (the Church Committee) produced a six-volume report released in April 1976. Highly critical of the intelligence community, which, as later revelations demonstrated, withheld key documents and information during the investigation, the Church Report recommended reforms for the intelligence agencies, most of which President Ford ignored. Ford responded more positively to the Rockefeller Commission.[65] Meanwhile, in the House of Representatives, the Select Committee on Intelligence to Investigate Allegations of Illegal or Improper Activities of Federal Intelligence, headed by Otis Pike (D.-N.Y.), operated from February 1975. The House of Representatives voted down the Pike Committee's report in January 1976, but portions nevertheless appeared in the *Village Voice*.[66]

Still another commission, headed by veteran diplomat Robert Murphy, examined the intelligence community and broader issues. The Commission on the Organization of the Government for the Conduct of Foreign Policy recommended that covert action should be employed only where it was clearly essential to vital U.S. purposes and only after a careful process of high-level review. President Ford appointed its chairman, Robert Murphy, to be the first chairman of the newly formed Intelligence Oversight Board.

Despite the congressional investigations, subpoenas of Kissinger, CIA officers, and other high officials, accusations of illegal activities, creation of new congressional oversight committees, and the fallout of defeat in Southeast Asia, the Ford administration authorized covert operations in Portugal, Madagascar, and Angola. In Angola, Cuban troops, supported by the Soviet Union, defeated the groups favored by the CIA. When questioned on the operations, the CIA (and President Ford) claimed that covert activities lay within the "inherent powers" of the president and were consistent with the CIA charter.[67] Shortly thereafter, future president George H. W. Bush replaced William Colby as CIA director. Bush skillfully resisted external pressures for reform of the CIA or more sincere cooperation with Congress.

Secret government continued, as did covert operations and collaboration with dictatorships. George H. W. Bush, like Ford, Kissinger, Secretary of Defense James Schlesinger, and the rest of the foreign policy elite, engaged in damage control. Other Nixon aides went to jail. Kissinger escaped sanction, largely retaining his prestige as a wise, realist policymaker.

Gerald Ford was a placeholder, promoting "reconciliation" after the bitter Nixon years. Presiding over the final agony of the war in Vietnam and the rest of Southeast Asia, he offered an unrepentant Kissinger and Schlesinger as his initial foreign policy duo. They sought to stonewall Congress and public opinion as best they could, reaffirming the need for covert operations and the legitimacy of the "inherent powers" of the president and, by extension, his advisers. Schlesinger lamented the lack of an American equivalent to the British Official Secrets Act. Regarding American support for military regimes and dictatorships, Schlesinger told Congress in 1974 that "this pattern of working relationships [with military regimes] reflects a coincidence of national security policy or foreign policy objectives between ourselves and those countries, but does not imply legitimization of the regimes."[68]

Ford brought Donald Rumsfeld to the White House staff and then appointed him as secretary of defense to replace Schlesinger. He named Dick Cheney as White House chief of staff and sent General Alexander Haig to Europe as NATO commander. He appointed George H. W. Bush to direct the CIA. A cohort of personalities who would be key policymakers in the post–Cold War years sought to reestablish decorum, while sustaining secret government and impunity for arguably illegal operations of the executive branch.

Ford's hard-line Cold Warriors sought to seal the leaks in the ship of state. They detested congressional oversight but learned also to doubt the effectiveness and loyalty of the CIA. They scarcely recalled the warnings of the CIA's first director, Rear Admiral Roscoe Hillenkoetter (1947–50), that sending "clandestine operatives into a foreign country against which the United States is not at war and instruct[ing] these agents to carry out 'black' operations . . . not only runs counter to the principles upon which our country was founded but also those for which we recently fought a war."[69]

Despite the routinization of secret government and the decline of the rule of law in the United States after 1947, the Nixon operations proved too blatant and too "political." President Ford and his team could not survive the Nixon legacy, losing the presidential election of 1976 to Georgia governor James Earl Carter. Unpredictably, the hard-core cadre of Nixon-Ford Cold War policymakers committed to secret government, covert operations, and an imperial authority for presidents in foreign policy would return to power in the 1980s — and beyond.

Latin America and the Carter Presidency

Jimmy Carter made Kissinger — his style, his policies, his deceit and vanity — campaign issues in the 1976 election. In one of the presidential debates, Carter declared: "As far as foreign policy goes, Mr. Kissinger has been the president of this country. Mr. Ford has shown an absence of leadership and an absence of a grasp of what this country is." On another occasion, Carter remarked on

Kissinger's secret and "amoral" style, adding that "our foreign policy should be as open and honest as the American people themselves."[70] Carter's attacks on the Nixon-Ford-Kissinger policy cabal struck a chord in the era after Vietnam and Watergate and the wave of congressional investigations on covert operations by the executive branch. To a lesser extent, human rights lobbies succeeded in making an unlikely campaign theme into an effective issue for the Democratic candidate.

President Carter was an anomaly in modern American politics. In some ways, however, he also captured the spirit of America's messianic belief in its civilizing mission. He took his oath of office on a Bible given to him by his mother, reading from it: "He hath showed thee, O man, what is good; and what doth the Lord require of thee, but to do justly, and to love mercy, and to walk humbly with thy God" (Micah 6:8). He told the country that "the bold and brilliant dream which excited the founders of this Nation still awaits its consummation." That dream, the *spread* of liberty and human freedom, was part of the moral obligations that, "when assumed, seem invariably to be in our own best interests."

Great distance existed between Carter's moral vision for American foreign policy and the realpolitik of the previous administrations. He said that he meant for government to be both "competent and compassionate." Perhaps most impressive, he insisted that "our commitment to human rights must be absolute, our laws fair, . . . the powerful must not persecute the weak, and human dignity must be enhanced." In his moral distancing from Nixon, Ford, and Kissinger, Carter retrieved the puritanical discourse of American exceptionalism, some of the Wilsonian missionary zeal to export democracy, and a belief that American national interests, broadly understood, would be served if America lived its ideals at home and practiced them abroad. This was no small charge, given the accreted corruption of American democracy and the perceived malevolence by millions around the globe of American foreign policy.

Carter proclaimed: "We are a strong nation, and we will maintain strength so sufficient that it need not be proven in combat — a quiet strength based not merely on the size of an arsenal, but on the nobility of ideas." Then, the just-inaugurated president set goals for foreign policy during his coming four years in office:

> I join in the hope that when my time as your President has ended, people might say this about our Nation: . . . That we had remembered the words of Micah and renewed our search for humility, mercy, and justice; . . . that we had enabled our people to be proud of their own Government once again. . . .

I would hope that the nations of the world might say that we had built a lasting peace, built not on weapons of war but on international policies which reflect our own most precious values. . . .

These are not just my goals . . . but the affirmation of our Nation's continuing moral strength and our belief in an undiminished, ever-expanding American dream.[71]

In Carter's first State of the Union Message, he gave more attention to the price of 5-10-15 fertilizer than to Latin America — except for Panama and the renegotiation of the canal treaties that had marred U.S.-Panama relations since the inception. Notwithstanding their absence in the message to Congress, for many Latin Americans Carter's emphasis on restoration of a moral foreign policy and its commitment to human rights around the world had great significance: "We stand for human rights because we believe that government has as a purpose to promote the well-being of its citizens. This is true in our domestic policy; it's also true in our foreign policy. The world must know that in support of human rights, the United States will stand firm."[72] A month later, Carter issued a Presidential Directive ordering that "it shall be a major objective of U.S. foreign policy to promote the observance of human rights throughout the world."[73]

Carter continued to hammer away at the human rights theme throughout his presidency. Such "intervention" into the internal affairs of other nations bothered adversaries, allies, and the so-called realist critics in both political parties.[74] But Carter's secretary of state, Cyrus Vance, cautioned that administration zeal for human rights would be implemented on a country-by-country basis: "In each case we must balance a political concern for human rights against economic or security goals."[75] Carter's human rights policy would not be quite so absolute as originally proclaimed.

Although Carter, Vance, and the State Department from 1977 to 1981 rejected the spirit of the Mann Doctrine and the Nixon-Kissinger policies, they found that combining a crusade for human rights with anticommunism in the Western Hemisphere proved problematical. For decades, American governments had overtly and covertly supported repressive regimes so long as they more or less toed the American line. Carter's national security advisor, Zbigniew Brzezinski, publicly acknowledged that for most Latin Americans the Monroe Doctrine signified the historical record of American interventionism and disdain rather than defense of human rights and protection of the hemisphere from outside influences.

To shape policy toward Latin America, Carter relied heavily on the recommendations of the private Commission on U.S.–Latin American Relations, at

New York's Center for Inter-American Relations. Chaired by former ambassador to the OAS Sol M. Linowitz, the commission produced two reports (1974, 1976) with extensive proposals for policy toward the region.[76] Linowitz himself became part of the negotiating team for the Panama Canal treaties. Various members of the commission joined the Carter administration. According to Robert Pastor, national security advisor for Latin America (1977–81), twenty-seven of the twenty-eight commission recommendations in 1976 became part of Carter's policy toward Latin America.[77]

President Carter faced a Latin America replete with military regimes and authoritarian civilian governments. Many of the governments had been installed with American acquiescence, encouragement, or covert intervention. Carter's human rights initiatives annoyed these regimes, to put it mildly. But Carter's most serious hemispheric challenges played out in the close-in bastion of earlier times: Panama, the Caribbean, Central America, and Mexico. The commission headed by Linowitz had identified creating a new relationship with Panama and the Canal Zone as the "most urgent" issue in U.S.-Latin American relations.

American quasi-sovereignty over the Canal Zone and periodic interventions in Panama were emblematic of American gunboat diplomacy. Carter sought to renegotiate the Panama Canal treaties, a long-standing source of irritation in Panama and the rest of Latin America. Overcoming opposition in both parties, and especially from the Ronald Reagan wing of the Republican Party, Carter convinced the Senate (barely) to approve two new canal treaties, in March and April of 1978. Unfortunately for Carter, many Americans opposed these treaties, which relinquished American sovereignty over a path through Panama and seemingly abandoned a pillar of hemispheric hegemony. "Giving away the canal" would be one of the issues that would lead to Carter's defeat in the 1980 presidential elections.

Toward Cuba, the Carter administration looked for gradual normalization of relations, or at least decompression. It intended to end covert operations against the Castro government. In September 1977, Cuba and the United States opened "interest sections" in their respective former embassy buildings in Havana and Washington, D.C. After some initial progress, Cuban foreign policy in Africa, charges of increased Soviet military presence on the island, and hard-line Cold War constituencies and legislators in the United States derailed the Carter initiative toward Cuba.[78]

Even Carter's national security advisor added his voice to the reticent: "Cuba is an active surrogate for foreign policy which is not shaped by itself, and is paid for by economic and military support on a scale that underlines Cuba's status as a dependent client of the Soviet Union."[79] As had been the case since 1811, the United States could not be indifferent to extra-hemispheric control of Cuba — but now it had occurred, and Carter would pay the price for his administration's apparent naïveté regarding Soviet intentions and Cuban unwillingness to sacrifice revolutionary principles and support for insurgencies in the hemisphere (and nationalist struggles in Africa) to improving relations with the United States.

Nowhere was that clearer than in Nicaragua. After more than forty years of dictatorship, the Somoza family dynasty faced a mortal threat. On-and-off-again insurgent movements had challenged the regime's national guard since the late 1950s. Now, in 1976–77, the opposition to Anastasio Somoza Debayle received encouragement from American liberals and the Carter administration. For their own disparate reasons, the governments of Cuba, Venezuela, and Panama provided the guerrillas (and their political front, the *Frente Sandinista de Liberación Nacional*) with military and logistical support. The Carter administration's human rights policies (combined with efforts to invent a legitimate opposition to forestall a Sandinista government) meant declines in American economic and military assistance to Somoza just as he faced mounting political and military pressure from his adversaries. Ousted in 1979, Somoza denounced President Carter from exile: "When it comes to Cuba and Fidel Castro, Mr. Carter and his State Department have consistently used blindfolds and earplugs. I told the proper U.S. authorities on many occasions that Cuba was our common enemy. . . . I wanted the United States to understand that in Cuba we both faced a mortal enemy and that Cuba wanted, and if unopposed would ultimately get, far more than Nicaragua."[80]

After Somoza's fall, the Carter administration unsuccessfully sought to arrange for a moderate coalition government to replace the dynasty. But the Sandinista military victory and the popular insurrection that accompanied it made such a stopgap measure implausible. Somoza, who would soon be assassinated in Paraguay (September 17, 1980) after being asked to leave the United States, proclaimed: "It wasn't unhappiness and poverty that forced me to leave, but an international Communist plot, blessed by the greatest killer, Carter."[81]

Republicans accused Carter of giving away the Panama Canal, of losing Nicaragua to communism, and of appeasing the Cubans, who further strengthened their alliance with the Soviets, exported revolution to Central America and the Caribbean, and sent military forces to assist American adversaries in Africa. For the Republican candidate in the 1980 election, Ronald Reagan, Carter's Latin American policies had betrayed the Founding Fathers and besmirched the Monroe Doctrine. Reagan recalled a phrase attributed to Lenin:

"Once we have Latin America, we won't have to take the United States, the last bastion of capitalism, because it will fall into our outstretched hands like overripe fruit."[82]

The bastion was under siege; it had been breached in Cuba and now in Nicaragua. Not only that — a fundamentalist anti-American revolution in Iran toppled America's ally, the Shah, in one of the world's most strategic regions. Jimmy Carter, the champion of human rights and global peacemaker, now enunciated the Carter Doctrine: "Let our position be absolutely clear: An attempt by any outside force to gain control of the Persian Gulf region will be regarded as an assault on the vital interests of the United States of America, and such an assault will be repelled by any means necessary, including military force."[83] "Outside force?" Not even Theodore Roosevelt would have imagined that the Persian Gulf was part of the United States' immediate security perimeter, oil or no oil. The No Transfer Principle and frequent corollaries to the Monroe Doctrine now applied to the Persian Gulf, as they had to Samoa in 1870 and Hawaii a bit later. But the Carter Doctrine also emulated the language of Calvin Coolidge in 1928. The United States had vital interests to defend everywhere in the world. To defend such interests, military force or even preemptive war might be required. For the United States, there was no higher law than its vital interests — and on that principle there existed bipartisan agreement.

After undercutting the Shah, as it had discarded Somoza, the United States would "regard any attempt by an outside power [such as the Soviet Union — or Iran?] to gain control of the Persian Gulf region as an assault on its vital interests" and would create a Rapid Deployment Force (RDF) dedicated to defense of the Persian Gulf — although as early as 1977 President Carter had ordered the Department of Defense to organize a mobile strike force for use in non-NATO contingencies. Despite Carter's reputation as a defender of human rights, he shared the view that America's global civilizing mission sometimes required unilateral use of military force. Planning for the RDF included plans for *preemptive* strikes where the *possibility* of Soviet intervention or threats to U.S. vital interests existed.[84]

Distracted by a hostage crisis in Iran (American diplomats were held hostage after the revolution for 444 days, from November 4, 1979, to January 20, 1981), and then, worse still, a Soviet invasion of Afghanistan, President Carter did not mention the Western Hemisphere in his 1980 State of the Union address. This omission occurred despite the recent Sandinista victory in Nicaragua and the obvious connections between the Cuban Revolution, the Soviet Union, and the new government in Managua. Instead, Carter pointed to three principal challenges: "the steady growth and increased projection of Soviet military power beyond its own borders; the overwhelming dependence of the Western democracies on oil supplies from the Middle East; and the press of social and religious and economic and political change in the many nations of the developing world, exemplified by the revolution in Iran." He claimed that "the Soviet invasion of Afghanistan could pose the most serious threat to the peace since the Second World War."

The not-so-Cold War had reerupted with a vengeance. Carter's efforts to bring peace to the world through further strategic arms limitations (SALT II) agreements conflicted with his criticism of Soviet human rights violations. So too did his effort to play China against the Soviet Union. In 1979, the Soviets invaded Afghanistan, an Islamic revolution toppled the Shah, and the Sandinistas took Managua. Carter's dream of peace, "built not on weapons of war but on international policies which reflect our own most precious values," evaporated. Combined with the administration's ineptitude in congressional relations, surging interest rates, inflation, and a growing energy crisis, Carter's foreign policy failures doomed him to be a one-term president.

Ronald Reagan, on a white charger, was coming to the rescue. He would fight to cleanse the Western Hemisphere bastion of enemies and, from there, launch a crusade against international communism. Waving the banner of a resurrected Monroe Doctrine and America's Providential mission, Reagan would restore the glory and the power of an America that sought to command its own destiny — and the world's.

Chapter Twelve

American Crusade

We cannot escape our destiny, nor should we try to do so. The leadership of the
free world was thrust upon us two centuries ago in that little hall of Philadelphia.
— RONALD REAGAN, 1974

Ronald Reagan campaigned aggressively against policies of the Carter administration. His acceptance speech at the Republican convention in Detroit was
a brilliant piece of rhetoric and touched virtually every thematic element in
the cantata of American patriotic discourse. He began with the pilgrims and
the New World myth: "Three hundred and sixty years ago, in 1620, a group
of families dared to cross a mighty ocean to build a future for themselves in a
new world."[1] He moved to the heroes of the War of Independence and then,
as Jefferson had after the 1800 election, called for unity "to overcome the injuries that have been done to America these past three and a half years [by the
Carter administration]": "More than anything else, I want my candidacy to
unify our country; to renew the American spirit and sense of purpose." Like
Jefferson, Reagan declaimed against "big government," modernizing this motif as an assault on the New Deal and Great Society social programs that had
become "givens" in American politics. Then he attacked the dismal economic
policies of the incumbent administration as "a new and altogether indigest-
ible economic stew, one part inflation, one part high unemployment, one part
recession, one part runaway taxes, one part deficit spending and seasoned by
an energy crisis. It's an economic stew that has turned the national stomach."

Reagan promised to cut back the federal government, reduce taxes, and
put Americans back to work. He reminded Americans that they lived in the
greatest country in the world, though under Carter it had suffered setbacks,
and proclaimed that "for those who have abandoned hope, we'll restore hope
and we'll welcome them into a great national crusade to make America great
again." The crusade at home would be accompanied by a crusade abroad:

"The United States has an obligation to its citizens and to the people of the world never to let those who would destroy freedom dictate the future course of human life on this planet. I would regard my election as proof that we have renewed our resolve to preserve world peace and freedom." Remembering Thomas Paine, Reagan affirmed: "We have it in our power to begin the world over again." He also echoed Franklin Delano Roosevelt as the country faced economic depression in the 1930s: "I believe that this generation of Americans today has a rendezvous with destiny." He queried (rhetorically, emulating Harding and Coolidge): "Can we doubt that only a Divine Providence placed this land, this island of freedom, here as a refuge for all those people in the world who yearn to breathe freely?" Then he concluded: "I'll confess that I've been a little afraid to suggest what I'm going to suggest — I'm more afraid not to — that we begin our crusade joined together in a moment of silent prayer. God bless America."[2]

Regarding the Western Hemisphere, Reagan claimed to cherish the Monroe Doctrine, or at least his version of it. During his presidency, he would iterate and reiterate the fundamental importance of Monroe's message: "Our commitment to a Western Hemisphere safe from aggression did not occur by spontaneous generation on the day that we took office. It began with the Monroe Doctrine in 1823 and continues our historic bipartisan American policy. Franklin Roosevelt said we 'are determined to do everything possible to maintain peace on this hemisphere.' President Truman was very blunt: 'International communism seeks to crush and undermine and destroy the independence of the Americans. We cannot let that happen here.' And John F. Kennedy made clear that 'Communist domination in this hemisphere can never be negotiated.'"[3]

Reagan denounced giving away "our" canal and the "shameful abandonment of Nicaragua to the Sandinistas."[4] Once in office, he reversed most of Carter's Latin American policies and added the Reagan Doctrine to the American foreign policy proclamations since 1947. Reagan's policy team emphasized more than ever America's supposed commitment to democracy and human liberty. Paradoxically, in Reagan's crusade for freedom, respect for human rights would no longer be a major condition for receiving U.S. military and economic assistance.

Reagan believed that détente veiled Soviet deceit and deception. He turned away from the arms control negotiations favored by Nixon, Ford, and Carter and announced a Strategic Defense Initiative for antimissile defense, which critics dubbed "Star Wars." In the spirit of the Committee on the Present Danger, Reagan called for a military buildup and a broad ideological assault on communism.[5] U.S. military spending increased dramatically, fueling a

TABLE 12.1. Foreign Policies and Doctrines, 1947–1989

Truman Doctrine, 1947 (Greece and Turkey). I believe that it must be the policy of the United States to support free peoples who are resisting attempted subjugation by armed minorities or by outside pressures. I believe that we must assist free peoples to work out their own destinies in their own way. . . . The world is not static, and the status quo is not sacred. But we cannot allow changes in the status quo in violation of the Charter of the United Nations by such methods as coercion, or by such subterfuges as political infiltration.

Eisenhower Doctrine, 1957 (Middle East). The action which I propose would have the following features. It would, first of all, authorize the United States to cooperate with and assist any nation or group of nations in the general area of the Middle East in the development of economic strength dedicated to the maintenance of national independence.

It would, in the second place, authorize the Executive to undertake in the same region programs of military assistance and cooperation with any nation or group of nations which desires such aid.

It would, in the third place, authorize such assistance and cooperation to include the employment of the armed forces of the United States to secure and protect the territorial integrity and political independence of such nations, requesting such aid, against overt armed aggression from any nation controlled by International Communism.

Kennedy Doctrine, 1963 (Latin America). [It is necessary] to come to the aid of any government requesting aid to prevent a takeover aligned to the policies of foreign communism. . . . Every resource at our command [must be used] to prevent the establishment of another Cuba in this hemisphere.

Johnson Doctrine, 1964 (Latin America). We must protect the Alliance against the efforts of communism to tear down all that we are building. . . . I now, today, assure you that the full power of the United States is ready to assist any country whose freedom is threatened by forces dictated from beyond the shores of this continent.

Nixon Doctrine, 1969 (Persian Gulf, Middle East, Vietnam). First, the United States will keep all of its treaty commitments.

Second, we shall provide a shield if a nuclear power threatens the freedom of a nation allied with us or of a nation whose survival we consider vital to our security.

Third, in cases involving other types of aggression, we shall furnish military and economic assistance when requested in accordance with our treaty commitments. But we shall look to the nation directly threatened to assume the primary responsibility of providing the manpower for its defense.

Carter Doctrine, 1980 (Persian Gulf, Afghanistan). Let our position be absolutely clear: An attempt by any outside force to gain control of the Persian Gulf region will be regarded as an assault on the vital interests of the United States of America, and such an assault will be repelled by any means necessary, including military force.

Reagan Doctrine, 1985 (Afghanistan, Nicaragua, global). We must stand by all our democratic allies. And we must not break faith with those who are risking their lives — on every continent, from Afghanistan to Nicaragua — to defy Soviet-supported aggression and secure rights which have been ours from birth. Support for freedom fighters is self-defense.

"war machine economy."[6] Massive defense budgets would also create indirect pressures for reduced spending for social programs in the name of fiscal responsibility — an ideal situation for Reagan's domestic political coalition of the Religious Right and highly ideological anti–New Deal Republicans bent on reconfiguring American politics.[7]

The Reagan policy shifts illustrated again the extent to which small groups of advisers and the powers concentrated in the presidency could alter the tone and favored instruments of American foreign relations. It also demonstrated how much strong personalities in key positions, infighting among cabinet officers and the national security advisor, and institutional turf battles shape foreign policy. Differences among cabinet officers from 1981 to 1989, beginning with the tussle between hard-liner secretary of state (and retired general) Alexander Haig and the secretary of defense, Caspar Weinberger, influenced key policy choices in the 1980s. Haig saw the troubles in the Western Hemisphere as an "externally managed and orchestrated interventionism" by the Soviets and their Cuban surrogates. He wanted to "deal with it at its source," that is to blockade or invade Cuba.[8] Haig also accused the Soviet-Cuban adversary of "training, funding, and equipping" international terrorists.[9] Weinberger was more cautious, as was Ambassador to the United Nations Jeanne Kirkpatrick. All of them, however, repeatedly emphasized the strategic and symbolic importance of the Western Hemisphere.[10]

By the beginning of his second term (1985), Reagan would put into use the idea of "a confederation of terrorist states" (Libya, Iran, North Korea, Nicaragua, and Cuba). He insisted that the United States must act "unilaterally if necessary, to insure that terrorists have no sanctuary — anywhere."[11] "Terrorists" meant enemies using asymmetric tactics against the United States and its allies. In contrast, "freedom fighters" meant U.S.-supported insurgents using the same tactics against governments the United States opposed. As Lewis Carroll so brilliantly told us in *Through the Looking Glass*:

> "When I use a word," Humpty Dumpty said, in a rather scornful tone, "it means just what I choose it to mean — neither more nor less."
>
> "The question is," said Alice, "whether you can make words mean so many different things."
>
> "The question is," said Humpty Dumpty, "which is to be master — that's all."[12]

Reagan's foreign policy team wished for America to be master — and not, like George Washington, only of its own fortune. Reagan linked events in Central America and the Caribbean to America's superpower status and its credibility as an ally. He asked, rhetorically: "If Central America were to fall, what would the consequences be for our position in Asia, Europe, and for alliances such as NATO? If the United States cannot respond to a threat near our own borders, why should Europeans or Asians believe that we are seriously concerned about threats to them?"[13]

For inspiration on Latin American policy, the Reagan team relied initially on the advice of conservative think tanks such as the Heritage Foundation and the Committee of Santa Fe's apocalyptic "A New Inter-American Policy for the Eighties" (July 1980). The Santa Fe document warned against the threat to national survival posed by Soviet incursions and surrogates in the hemisphere: "Detente is dead. Survival demands a new foreign policy. America must seize the initiative or perish. . . . Latin America and Southern Asia are the scenes of strife of the third phase of World War III. . . . America is everywhere in retreat. . . . Even the Caribbean . . . is becoming a Marxist Leninist Lake. Never before has the Republic been in such jeopardy from its exposed southern flank. . . . The hour of decision can no longer be postponed."[14] Reagan's crusade, in the tradition of presidents since 1810, invoked self-defense to justify covert operations, interventionism, and American-orchestrated regime change. Now American and Free World *survival* was at stake.

To redress the errors of Carter's State Department, Reagan opted for both covert and open support for authoritarian civilian governments and military regimes. Simultaneously, the Reagan team purged the State Department of personnel viewed as too "liberal" — especially in the ranks of Latin American specialists.[15] In shaping its policies toward Latin America, the Reagan administration resuscitated Alfred Thayer Mahan's insistence on the strategic importance of the Caribbean and Central America. It was time, once again, to clean up the neighborhood, in the bellicose spirit of Theodore Roosevelt, but also of Woodrow Wilson's "idealistic" interventionism. Unlike the 1895–1919 assault on "chronic wrongdoing" that threatened regional stability by inviting naval intervention by European competitors to collect debts, sanitizing the neighborhood in the 1980s was part of the global crusade against the Soviet evil empire.[16]

Reagan's Latin American policy also followed the mold of earlier presidents, with its focus on opening markets and "fair trade." Like many of his predecessors, Reagan saw foreign markets as a partial solution for the need for jobs at home. But globalization and off-shore production for the American market by multinational corporations presented new challenges. Selective protectionism for American sectors unable to compete with Japanese, Korean, European, or Brazilian exports took domestic political constituents into account. McKinley and Herbert Hoover, and also Franklin Delano Roosevelt, would have understood Reagan's balancing act on tariffs and nontariff protectionism versus trade liberalization. Reagan promised that "we will vigorously pursue our policy of promoting free and open markets in this country and around the world. . . . But let no one mistake our resolve to oppose any and all unfair trading practices. It is wrong for the American worker and American businessman to continue to bear the burden imposed by those who abuse the world trading system."

Access to American markets was particularly important for Latin American producers of commodities for which the United States provided subsidized prices within a quota regime. For example, for sugar producers in Latin America, the U.S. quota was critical. A U.S. decision to reduce the Nicaraguan quota by 90 percent in 1983 (with the bulk reassigned to Honduras) reeked of imperial bullying. Nicaragua protested at the Organization of American States (OAS) Special Committee for Consultation and Negotiation, and U.S. spokespersons accused Nicaragua of providing arms and training to El Salvadoran insurgents. A dozen Latin American countries called the U.S. actions violations of the OAS Charter and the General Agreement on Tariffs and Trade (GATT). Appeals to international law and Good Neighbor noninterventionism did not move the Reagan administration.

The particulars of Nicaraguan policy were driven by Cold War concerns, but Reagan's linkage of trade policy to domestic politics followed the tradition established in the 1790s. American partisan and interest-group politics "required" such linkage. As in the distant and recent past, "foreign" policies, such as trade, tariffs, and immigration, depended in part on domestic political considerations, even in the highly ideological Reagan administration. Trade liberalization as ideology did not automatically bring enhanced access to U.S. markets for most Latin American countries. Moreover, trade and financial sanctions, even embargos, might befall Latin American governments, such as Grenada and Nicaragua, that defied U.S. dictates. For the Caribbean basin nations, President Reagan offered an initiative that favored their products in U.S. markets. For the rest of Latin America, no such favorable treatment resulted.

Ideological free traders lamented the pragmatic aspects of Reagan's policies. One critic produced a long list of Reagan administration tariffs and "forced voluntary export quotas" for European, Asian, Canadian, and Latin American producers, in characterizing Reagan as a "protectionist."[17] But Reagan's rhetorical commitment to "free and fair" trade was vintage American politics. What was novel was the gradual melding of a new governing Republican coalition of neoconservative foreign policy hard-liners, the rising American Religious Right, and the neoliberal technocrats with an ideologi-

cal commitment to reversing the New Deal/Great Society paradigm. This coalition was determined to rally American public opinion to the crusade for
exporting "market democracy" abroad and for overturning New Deal/Great
Society liberalism at home.[18] For this coalition, trade liberalization might be a
way to break the power of organized labor in the United States in the name of
benefiting consumers (that is, "all of us").

There was another innovation. Through the National Security Council
(NSC) and the CIA, the Reagan team organized itself in 1983 to manipulate
American public opinion on its Latin American policy, because it understood
how opposition to the Vietnam War had undermined Lyndon Johnson and
Richard Nixon. Directed by Otto Reich, a vehemently anti-Castro Cuban
exile, the Office of Public Diplomacy for Latin America and the Caribbean
(formally within the State Department) secretly and illegally disseminated
"white propaganda" — that is, lies and "disinformation" — in American media
with fictitious bylines. Reich's office harassed television, radio, and newspaper editors who did not support the administration's Caribbean and Central
American policies.[19] In this initiative, the Reagan administration carried out
the equivalent of military psychological operations against America itself, especially but not only regarding policies toward Latin America.[20]

As the Reagan administration launched its global crusade against the evil
empire, Latin America faced its gravest economic challenge since the 1930s.
Afflicted by surging oil prices in 1979–81, rising interest rates, and price declines for most exports, Latin America experienced a debt crisis that brought
misery throughout much of the region. Mexico defaulted on its foreign debt
in 1982. Between 1982 and 1989 Latin America sent over $200 billion to its
creditors in Western Europe, the United States and Asia — more by far than
the Marshall Plan aid provided after World War II by the United States to
Europe.[21] According to a report from the Inter-American Dialogue in 1990,
"Since the debt crisis struck in 1982, the region has been mired in depression, its deepest and most prolonged ever. . . . More people than ever are
trapped in poverty."[22] By 1989, the 1980s were being called Latin America's "lost
decade."

To some extent, the Reagan administration's policies provoked the debt
crisis and its political consequences in Latin America. The U.S. government,
in alliance with private bankers and the International Monetary Fund, imposed
strict repayment terms on Latin American borrowers at a time of crashed
commodity prices and rising interest rates. Secretary of the Treasury Paul
Volcker (appointed by Carter and reappointed in 1983 by Reagan) exported
"monetarism." Fiscal policy "conditionality" imposed by the multilateral

lenders on Latin American governments incubated increasing social and political conflict in the region. Ironically, the debt crisis would undermine military regimes supported by the Reagan administration throughout the hemisphere, accelerating a transition back to civilian government in much of the Southern Cone: Bolivia (1982), Argentina (1983), Uruguay (1984), Brazil (1985), and Chile (1990). In Central America, however, insurgency and civil war intensified.

Rollback in the Caribbean and Central America

American support for counterinsurgency operations and military regimes had "saved" South America from communism in the 1960s and 1970s. The Reagan administration reaffirmed support for authoritarian governments and military regimes that oppressed their own people if that served American interests — as in Chile, Argentina (until the Falklands War fiasco of 1982), and Brazil. Reagan's advisers now meant to "take back" the Caribbean and Central America by attacking Soviet allies and surrogates. They vociferously rejected the 1968 Brezhnev Doctrine. The United States would support freedom fighters who rose up against Soviet-inspired communist tyranny.[23]

Long before the official unveiling of what came to be called the Reagan Doctrine, in 1985, its tenets had been put into practice. The number of U.S. covert actions overseas globally jumped from a dozen small ones in 1980 to about forty major operations in 1986, including operations against Nicaragua authorized in 1981.[24] Supporting freedom fighters against the Soviets in Afghanistan was partly payback for Soviet support for Ho Chi Minh in the Vietnam War. But the Reagan team's rhetoric also expertly connected its policies to the dreams of the Founding Fathers. American support for freedom fighters was morally essential; it was part of America's historical mission and of the global quest for liberty begun in 1776: "In the 19th century Americans smuggled guns and powder to Simon Bolivar, the Great Liberator; we supported the Polish patriots and others seeking freedom. We well remembered how other nations, like France, had come to our aid during our own revolution."[25] Secretary of State George P. Shultz also repeatedly tied America's moral and legal obligations to combat tyranny and promote democracy directly to the conflicts being waged in Central America and Asia: "The UN and OAS Charters reaffirm the inherent right of individual and collective self-defense against aggression — aggression of the kind committed by the Soviets in Afghanistan, by Nicaragua in Central America, and by Vietnam in Cambodia. Material assistance to those opposing such aggression can be a lawful form of collective self-defense."

Grenada

President Reagan ordered an invasion of the tiny island of Grenada in 1983, ostensibly to rescue American medical students in the midst of an internal political conflict on the island.[26] Protection of citizens was a traditional, and legitimate, rationale for limited incursions into foreign territory. But American intervention in Grenada in 1983 went beyond protection of medical students. Since 1979, Grenada's government, dominated by the New Jewel Movement, had implemented a radical reform agenda, moving ever closer to the Castro regime in Cuba and the Sandinista government in Nicaragua. The Carter administration had adopted policies discouraging tourism to the island, limiting economic assistance, and allowing regime opponents to operate in the United States almost as in the times of the filibuster expeditions to Cuba and Central America in the nineteenth century. The Reagan administration upped the ante, blocking World Bank and Caribbean Development Bank loans and refusing to include the country in the Caribbean Basin Initiative.

A naval exercise off Puerto Rico simulated an invasion of Grenada in August 1981 (much like the threat to Germany insinuated by Admiral Dewey's fleet in the 1902 Venezuelan episode). Grenada exemplified Cuban and Soviet gains in the Western Hemisphere on Carter's watch. Usually left unmentioned, the Grenada regime also tweaked the sensitive nerves of racism as an issue in U.S. domestic politics. Grenadians, mostly descendants of the British colonial slave system, speak English. The New Jewel government was a radical Afro-Caribbean socialist regime with great appeal to the Black Power movement in the United States. The symbolism of a successful black anti-imperialist government in the Caribbean gave special political significance to the Grenadian revolution.

Regime change required only the pretext. A violent intra-regime coup in 1983 set the stage for the American invasion. On October 25, 1983, American forces landed in Grenada in Operation Urgent Fury, fought against Cuban construction workers, military personnel, and allied Grenadians. (Only two days earlier, a suicide bomber had destroyed marine barracks in Beirut, Lebanon, killing 240 marines. Reagan diverted the task force headed to Lebanon for the Grenada operation.) Accounts published by the U.S. Navy Historical Center estimate that "three or four dozen Cuban Army regulars were in Grenada. . . . They were not organized into a regular military unit, but were primarily advisers and instructors to the Grenadian military."[27] Misinformation, disinformation, and a strongly felt desire in the United States for a victory in the resurgent Cold War crusade provided President Reagan with bipartisan support for the invasion. The administration's claim that an airport under construction would become a base for Cuban and Soviet forces also proved effective in mobilizing public opinion.[28] (After the invasion, the U.S. government finished the airport for tourism.)

Secretary of State Shultz explained that the Grenada invasion had not only purged the hemisphere of a dangerous Soviet-Cuban surrogate regime, but it had also served global notice of American determination to roll back Soviet influence in the Western Hemisphere. In Congress, as from the time of the Hamilton-Jefferson debates, minority voices questioned the president's authority to deploy armed forces without legislative approval.[29] The Congressional Black Caucus denounced the Grenada invasion, and seven Democratic congressmen, led by Ted Weiss (D.-N.Y.), urged impeachment of President Reagan. (Weiss, a naturalized U.S. citizen, was ten years old when his family fled the Nazi invasion of his native Hungary in 1938.) In contrast to the Weiss initiative, the *New York Times* reported: "Speaker Thomas P. O'Neill Jr., who initially criticized President Reagan for 'gunboat diplomacy' in the invasion of Grenada, said today that a House fact-finding mission had convinced him the action was 'justified' to rescue endangered Americans. His switch marked what some Democrats acknowledged was 'a strategic retreat' politically. It came amid strong public support for the United States–led invasion."[30] Opinion polls showed considerable support (over 60 percent favorable) for Reagan's decision to take down the Grenada government. Salutary demonstration effects also followed. The day after the invasion, Suriname's dictator, previously a wild card in northern South America's Cold War, closed down the Cuban embassy in his capital and expelled its diplomats.[31]

The UN Security Council deplored the invasion by a vote of 11–1 (the one dissenting vote being the United States). On November 3, 1983, over 100 members of the UN General Assembly adopted a resolution "deeply deploring" the U.S. armed intervention in Grenada. The next day, the *New York Times* reported: "President Reagan said today that he had conducted a rescue mission, not an invasion of Grenada, and that no comparison was possible with the warfare being waged in Afghanistan by the Soviet Union. The President . . . smiled as he dismissed the United Nations General Assembly vote Wednesday that deplored armed intervention in Grenada. 'It didn't upset my breakfast at all,' he said."

For good measure, as it had since 1846, the U.S. government sought to cover the unilateralist intervention in Grenada with the fig leaf of a treaty regime — this time, the Organization of Eastern Caribbean States.[32] The United States was not a member of this treaty regime but claimed that it had been requested to intervene in Grenada by its members. Barbados and Jamaica also provided token troops for the intervention. The Grenada operation gave

Reagan a quick, high visibility and a low-cost victory in the crusade to purge the Western Hemisphere of international communism. Speculation abounded on a follow-up operation in Nicaragua or even Cuba.

President Reagan had explained the importance of fighting against communist gains in Central America and the Caribbean at the annual meeting of the National Association of Manufacturers in 1983, in terms that would have been immediately understood by Thomas Jefferson, James Madison, and James Monroe: "The Caribbean Sea and Central America constitute this nation's fourth border. If we must defend ourselves against large, hostile military presence on our border, our freedom to act elsewhere to help others and to protect strategically vital sea lanes and resources has been drastically diminished. They [the Soviets] know this; they've written about this."[33] Presumably, the Soviets had read Alfred Thayer Mahan and understood that America's premier late nineteenth-century global strategist had considered the Caribbean basin the linchpin of U.S. grand strategy. Without its strategic underbelly secured and the region cleared of threats, the country's global posture would be adversely affected.[34]

El Salvador

El Salvador became a battleground in the not-so-Cold War from the late 1970s. Leftist political movements and guerrillas inspired by the Cuban Revolution challenged the old order. After the Sandinista victory in Nicaragua in 1979, the Salvadoran rebels counted on logistical support from Managua and Havana. Their political arm, the Farabundo Martí Liberation Movement (the FMLN, created in 1980), established headquarters in Nicaragua. Cuba, Nicaragua, and, indirectly, the Soviet Union would fight a surrogate war in El Salvador, supporting the FMLN against the United States and its local allies.

As elsewhere in Latin America, the U.S. government claimed to favor democracy in El Salvador. To promote democracy, U.S. policymakers and military advisers designed and financed an increasingly repressive counterinsurgency war to defeat the Salvadoran guerrillas.[35] In the same 1983 National Association of Manufacturers speech in which he defended the Grenada invasion, Reagan reaffirmed the Nixon Doctrine for El Salvador. He borrowed directly from the language regarding Vietnam toward the end of that war: "Only Salvadorans can fight this war, just as only Salvadorans can decide El Salvador's future. . . . Without playing a combat role themselves and without accompanying Salvadoran units into combat, American specialists can help the Salvadoran Army improve its operations."

To buttress its policy in El Salvador (and Nicaragua), President Reagan brought Henry Kissinger back to official Washington to chair a bipartisan commission on Central American policy. Kissinger repeatedly insisted on the importance of Central America and the Caribbean in U.S. security policy:

> The ability of the United States to sustain a tolerable balance of power on the global scene at a manageable cost depends on the inherent security of its land borders. This advantage is of crucial importance. It offsets an otherwise serious liability: our distance from Europe, the Middle East, and East Asia. . . . To the extent that a further Marxist-Leninist advance in Central America leading to . . . further projection of Soviet and Cuban power in the region required us to defend against security threats near our borders, we would face a difficult choice between unpalatable alternatives. We would either have to assume a permanently increased defense burden, or see our capacity to defend distant trouble spots reduced, and as a result have to reduce important commitments elsewhere in the world. From the standpoint of the Soviet Union, it would be a major strategic coup to impose on the United States the burden of defending our southern approaches, thereby stripping us of the compensating advantage that offsets the burden of our transoceanic lines of communication.[36]

According to Kissinger, the wars in Central America, the thrusts of the Soviets into the Caribbean, and U.S. support for counterinsurgency and military regimes in Latin America were part of World War III on slow cook — waged within the perimeter of the Western Hemisphere bastion. He did not consider for a moment the local or historical nature of the political and military circumstances in Central America or the rest of region — nor take seriously anything but the supposed realpolitik upon which he prided himself. Kissinger's ignorance on Latin America undermined U.S. policy. His intellectual inspiration, and (unrecognized) alter ego, Prince Clemens Wenzel von Metternich, would no doubt have been disappointed in Kissinger's unrealistic "realism" regarding the long-term political consequences for the United States of his Latin American operations.[37]

Notwithstanding vocal opposition from the antiwar movement and from some groups in Congress, the 1984 Salvadoran presidential election elicited bipartisan support in the United States for military assistance and some economic aid to the Salvadoran regime from 1984 to 1987. It did not hurt that President Reagan had won an overwhelming reelection victory in 1984 against Democrat Walter Mondale, carrying forty-nine states, all except the District of Columbia and his opponent's home state of Minnesota. Economic recovery, tax cuts, declines in inflation, and Reagan's personal popularity overwhelmed the Democratic candidate. Reagan's rhetorical appropriation of key pieces of the Jeffersonian tradition (especially promoting an "empire of liberty," keeping "kings and monarchs [and communists] out of our hemisphere," and attacking federal government overreach) effectively linked his policies to touchstones of American political culture and foreign relations.[38] Discouraged Democrats in the House of Representatives barely raised their voice against the El Salvador war for the next three years.[39]

By 1987, the Salvadoran military, with U.S. assistance, had fought the guerrillas to a stalemate. No military victory was in sight, but neither was the revolutionary regime change for which the Salvadoran insurgents had been fighting.[40] For five more years, the war would continue — until, after the Cold War ended, a peace accord was signed at the Castle of Chapultepec in Mexico on January 16, 1992.[41] Salvadorans paid a high price for the not-so-Cold War overlay on their internal conflicts.

To the end of his presidency, Reagan and his advisers would continue to lie to the public, to Congress, and to themselves about U.S. operations in El Salvador. Massive human rights violations against the civilian population (most, but not all, by the American-trained Salvadoran army and security services) and increasing flows of refugees to neighboring countries and the United States persisted into the early 1990s. As political scientist William LeoGrande puts it, the Reagan administration learned from its El Salvador policies that it could get away with pretty much whatever it wanted, "if the White House was willing to do whatever was necessary to keep the policy going until a congressional majority could be assembled behind it — even if that meant circumventing legal restrictions imposed by Congress in the meantime."[42]

This lesson would not be lost on future presidents.

Nicaragua and the Reagan Doctrine

The Nicaraguan Revolution was the first successful revolutionary insurgency in Latin America since 1959. For the Reagan administration, it represented everything that was wrong with Carter's Latin American policies. The Nicaraguan government, declaring that its revolution had "no frontiers," inadvertently confirmed the credibility of President Reagan's warnings that it represented another Soviet-Cuban surrogate in the Western Hemisphere.

To roll back Soviet-Cuban influence in Nicaragua, the Reagan administration devised a barely clandestine war against the Sandinista government by "freedom fighters" (in Spanish, *contrarevolucionarios* — or Contras, for short) based in Honduras. Financed and supplied largely by the United States, the Contras did not limit their attacks to military and police forces. They assassinated civilian government officials and destroyed economic infrastructure. Many from the original group had been national guardsmen under the Somoza regime. Using terrorist tactics to intimidate their opponents came "naturally." Nevertheless, they had support within Nicaragua from regime opponents, especially as the Sandinista government became more corrupt and less tolerant and American pressure on the regime ground down the economy.

Speaking to a forum of Latin American legislators on Nicaragua in 1985, President Reagan rolled out the self-defense interpretation of the Monroe Doctrine. He claimed that support for the Contras was consistent with the OAS and UN charters: "The Sandinistas have been attacking their neighbors through armed subversion since August of 1979. Countering this by supporting Nicaraguan freedom fighters is essentially acting in self-defense and is certainly consistent with the United Nations and OAS Charter provisions for individual and collective security."[43] Given the long history of U.S. elastic interpretation of "self-defense," it was not surprising that President Reagan could claim that supporting attacks on Nicaragua by the Contras was consistent with the OAS and UN charters. In his February 1985 State of the Union Address, Reagan proclaimed: "We must not break faith with those who are risking their lives — on every continent from Afghanistan to Nicaragua — to defy Soviet aggression and secure rights which have been ours from birth. Support for freedom fighters is self-defense." The Reagan Doctrine reasserted that self-defense, for the United States, had no geographical or tactical limits, including resort to paramilitary operations — that is, attacks by surrogate militias on the infrastructure and civilian officials of sovereign nations.[44]

Viewed in retrospect, the Soviet threat to the survival of the United States and its people, *if war should ensue between the two powers*, was catastrophically more consequential than anything the United States had faced before World War I. In the past, assertion by the United States of its supposed right of self-defense implied only defense of "armed neutrality," or national honor, or protection of citizens and their property, or of "its" hemisphere against outside intrusion, or, with the Carter Doctrine, of oil in the Persian Gulf. It was not likely that the Soviets would risk their nation for Nicaragua, or even for Cuba. But Reagan's crusade and support for freedom fighters in Afghanistan killed Russian soldiers and threatened, as it turned out, the very existence of the Soviet Union and the Warsaw Pact. According to the Defense Department, the operation that "drove the Soviet army out of Afghanistan" was the "largest covert action program" in the history of the CIA.[45] In its own self-defense, did the Soviet Union also have a right to make preemptive war?

According to Charles Krauthammer, writing in *Time* magazine's April Fool's Day issue in 1985: "The Brezhnev Doctrine proclaimed in 1968 that the Soviet sphere only expands. The Reagan Doctrine is meant as its antithesis. It declares that the U.S. will work at the periphery to reverse that expansion. How? Like the Nixon Doctrine, it turns to proxies. Unlike the Nixon Doctrine, it supports not the status quo but revolution." Anticipating an important post–Cold War dilemma of U.S. policy, Krauthammer then posed a key question: "How awful must a government be before it forfeits the moral protection of sovereignty and before justice permits its violent removal?" Without answering directly his own question, he concluded with a more or less congratulatory assessment of the Reagan Doctrine: "The Reagan Doctrine is more radical than it pretends to be. It pretends that support for democratic rebels is 'self-defense' and sanctioned by international law. That case is weak. The real case rests instead on other premises: that to be constrained from supporting freedom by an excessive concern for sovereignty (and a unilateral concern, at that) is neither especially moral nor prudent."[46]

In accord with the premise that support for freedom fighters was self-defense, the CIA carried out military attacks and bombing missions against Nicaraguan infrastructure, ports, and oil facilities. It mined Nicaraguan harbors. When Nicaragua protested at the United Nations in 1984, asking for a Security Council resolution condemning American aggression, the United States vetoed the resolution. When Nicaragua took the case to the International Court of Justice at the Hague, the United States claimed the court lacked jurisdiction and that the matter should be handled within the framework of the Rio Treaty and the OAS. The court rejected the American arguments. In 1985, the United States withdrew its general adherence to the compulsory jurisdiction of the International Court of Justice regime. The next year, the court decided in Nicaragua's favor and ordered the United States to pay reparations. The U.S. government ignored the decision.

Meanwhile, partisan opposition to the Contra war increased in Congress, led by Edward Boland (D.-Mass.) and Clement Zablocki (D.-Wis.). In 1982, Congress had adopted language (the first Boland amendment) in a continuing resolution that prohibited the CIA or Department of Defense from supporting "any group or individual, not part of a country's armed forces, for the purpose of overthrowing the Government of Nicaragua or provoking a military exchange between Nicaragua and Honduras."[47] The language did not prohibit assistance that intended to interdict arms shipments or logistical support by the Sandinistas for the guerrillas in El Salvador. Likewise, it did not explicitly restrict operations against Nicaragua by the NSC. Supporting the Contras did not violate the first iteration of the Boland amendment so long as the *intent* was not to overthrow the Sandinista government or to provoke a military confrontation between Honduras and Nicaragua.

When evidence revealed in 1984 that the CIA had mined Nicaraguan harbors, Congress added to the Boland amendment: "It is the sense of Congress that no funds heretofore or hereafter appropriated in any Act of Congress shall be obligated or expended for the purpose of planning, executing, or supporting the mining of the ports or territorial waters of Nicaragua."[48] Then, in October 1984, Congress attempted to prohibit further aid to the Contras. The legislation stipulated that "during fiscal year 1985, no funds available to the Central Intelligence Agency, the Department of Defense or any other agency or entity of the United States involved in intelligence activities may be obligated or expended for the purpose or which would have the effect of supporting, directly or indirectly, military or paramilitary operations in Nicaragua by any nation, group, organization, movement or individual."[49]

The Reagan administration found ways (some legal, some illegal) to circumvent the Boland amendment.[50] The administration solicited private funds to support the Contras; it also obtained resources from foreign governments in exchange for "solutions" to other bilateral issues.[51] Within the CIA, Deputy Director Robert Gates (later, secretary of defense in the George W. Bush and Barack Obama administrations) sent a memorandum to Director William Casey arguing that the United States could not stand a second Cuba in the Western Hemisphere and that "the only way to prevent such a dire outcome was to bring down the Sandinista regime, recognize a government in exile, and direct American air strikes against the Sandinistas."[52] In 1985, the United States imposed an embargo against Nicaragua. President Reagan justified this action by declaring that "the policies and actions of the Government of Nicaragua constitute an unusual and extraordinary threat to the national security and foreign policy of the United States."

The U.S. government was waging "low-intensity" war on Nicaragua, though no declaration of war would be forthcoming from Congress. In the 1986 fiscal year, Congress approved $27 million in aid for the Contras but stipulated that none of it could be spent on weapons. Congress authorized the administration to solicit Contra aid from other nations, but only if that aid was not used to buy weapons. In November, Congress also authorized the CIA to share intelligence with the Contras — in practice, a U.S. surrogate army (although also with its own counterrevolutionary agenda) deployed against a sovereign nation.

Iran-Contra Affair

Public support for U.S. efforts to overthrow the Sandinista government fluctuated. Congress restricted aid to the Contras but did not prohibit the use of unappropriated funds for carrying out administration policy. National Security Advisor Robert McFarlane and his successor, Admiral John Poindexter, authorized a covert operation run by a member of their staff, marine lieutenant colonel Oliver North, in which funds from the sale of arms to Iran were diverted to the Contras. In October 1986, the Nicaraguans downed a plane carrying military supplies to the Contras. They took prisoner an American crew member, who confessed his connections to the CIA, the Contras, and the operation run by Lieutenant Colonel North. Making matters worse, the next month, *Al-Shiraa*, a Lebanese newspaper, reported the unauthorized sale of arms to Iran and the linkage of these sales to negotiations for the freedom of American hostages captive since the Iran embassy takeover of 1979. President Reagan had promised never to negotiate with terrorists — the Iranians.

In January 1987, a joint House-Senate Select Committee on Secret Military Assistance to Iran and the Nicaraguan opposition heard testimony on what was now called the Iran-Contra Affair.[53] It determined the illegality of various aspects of the operations but not a "smoking gun" that directly connected President Reagan to what had transpired. National Security Advisor John M. Poindexter testified to Congress: "My objective all along was to withhold from the Congress exactly what the NSC staff was doing in carrying out the president's policy."[54] Along the way, key documents were lost or shredded. Reagan avoided impeachment, but the report of the congressional committees investigating the affair determined that "fundamental processes of government were disregarded and the rule of law was subverted."[55]

Like many of his predecessors, the Teflon President pushed executive war powers and interpretations of national security beyond the constitutional and legal envelope. He operated clandestinely, intervened in the affairs of other sovereign states, and recognized no higher law than his own version of American self-defense.[56] He also found himself engaged in a typical battle with opponents in Congress over executive initiatives in foreign policy and covert operations.[57] During the rest of his administration, Reagan continued the war against the Sandinista government, increased support for El Salvador's military against the insurgency in that country, and insisted by radio, television, public addresses, and in messages to Congress on the moral rightness of the American crusade in Central America and the Caribbean. He also insisted that the Nicaraguan government represented "an unusual and extraordinary threat to the national security and foreign policy of the United States." On May 1, 1987, he told Congress: "I shall continue to exercise the powers at my disposal to apply economic sanctions against Nicaragua as long as these measures are appropriate and will continue to report periodically to the Congress on expenses and significant developments." James K. Polk, Benjamin Harrison, and Theodore Roosevelt would have appreciated Reagan's expansive use of his authority as commander in chief in the name of the Monroe Doctrine and self-defense.

PARALLEL TO THE U.S. policies in Central America, and sometimes at cross-purposes, Latin American governments sought to bring peace to the isthmus. Eventually these efforts would produce a Peace Accord (Esquipulas II, August 7, 1987), involving negotiations supported by the Contadora Group (named for Contadora Island off Panama where foreign ministers from Panama, Colombia, Venezuela, and Mexico first met in 1983). The leadership of Costa Rican president Oscar Arias, members of the inter-American system, and then the United Nations contributed to the peace accord. The essential foundation for the accord was agreement on the end of outside support for Central American insurgencies, accompanied by elections and internal democratization.

The Reagan administration opposed the Contadora efforts. Initially, it also rejected the Esquipulas II Peace Agreement, believing that it further legitimated the Sandinista government and gave prestige to the multilateral Contadora efforts, to the detriment of U.S. policies focused on regime change in Nicaragua. For Nicaragua, the Esquipulas II accord was a desperate effort to end the surrogate war, the economic sanctions, and the suffering of its people. Looking backward from ten years later, some revolutionary Sandinistas saw Nicaragua as "the donkey striving to reach a carrot at the end of a stick tied to its own harness, with the difference that the cart the Nicaraguan donkey was hauling was full of cadavers, destruction, and suffering."[58]

For the Reagan administration, and for many Americans, only the Contras and U.S. firmness against communism had made the 1987 agreements possible. President Reagan told the country in November 1987: "It's the Nicaraguan freedom fighters who brought the Sandinistas to the negotiating table. It is the freedom fighters — and only the freedom fighters — who can keep them there."[59] Even if Reagan were right, by late 1988 Congress had limited Contra aid to "humanitarian assistance." But still Reagan insisted: "Our policy in Nicaragua remains the same: America must stand with those who fight for freedom in Nicaragua, as it has stood with the valiant freedom fighters in Afghanistan and Angola. . . . Their struggle is our struggle, and together we can achieve democracy in Nicaragua."[60] For the Reagan team, of course,

Nicaragua was part of the bigger story: the ongoing global crusade against the Soviet Union and international communism.

In retrospect, admirers of President Reagan would point to what they claimed were his successes: toppling a pro-Cuban regime in Grenada, saving El Salvador from the Marxist guerrillas, and undermining the Sandinista regime in Nicaragua. Reagan's policies meant that there were "no more Nicaraguas" in Central America. Most important, Reagan had supported the freedom fighters in Afghanistan and, indirectly, helped bring an end to the Soviet Empire. In this version, the Free World had emerged triumphant, even as the United States had reclaimed and purged (except for Cuba) communist influence in the Western Hemisphere.

Critics of the Reagan administration pointed to the government's flouting of the law and the Constitution, its use of emergency powers to deliver military assistance to brutal military governments in Argentina, Chile, and especially El Salvador, and its contempt for congressional opposition and international law.[61] Unknowable at the time, many of the political tactics of the Reagan team (and many of the key policymakers — Cheney, Abrams, Negroponte, Poindexter, Gates, among others) would reappear in Washington in the first decade of the twenty-first century to renew and extend the global crusade for democracy and freedom in the administration of George W. Bush (2001–9). Some even would be holdovers in the first phase of the administration of Barack Obama (2009–).

When it came time for Reagan to leave office, the Teflon was slightly scratched, but he ably campaigned for his successor, Vice President George H. W. Bush. He also contributed greatly to the Republicans' national election efforts, as this typical stump speech in San Diego illustrates: "[The liberals] opposed the liberation of Grenada. They opposed the blow we struck against terrorist Libya. They oppose our policy of helping freedom fighters advance the cause of liberty around the world. George Bush and I did all these things, and I tell you proudly right now: We'd both do every single one of them over again."[62]

Reagan was right. George H. W. Bush would do similar things again — in Panama, in Nicaragua, in El Salvador, in Iraq — all in "self-defense," wherever necessary for America to "command its own fortune" and fulfill its crusade for freedom.

The First Bush Presidency: George H. W.

Capitalizing on Reagan's popularity and a pathetic campaign by Democratic candidate Michael Dukakis, George H. W. Bush won the presidency, with

53.4 percent of the popular vote versus 45.6 percent for Dukakis. Bush garnered 420 votes in the electoral college; Dukakis received only 111. The Republicans successfully painted Dukakis as a northeastern liberal, out of touch with the real America, soft on crime, and unknowledgeable about national security issues. Bush promised the Republican convention that "the most important work of my life is to complete the mission we started in 1980." The crusade would continue, at home and abroad.

When he took the oath of office in January 1989, George H. W. Bush was the only chief executive to have served as director of the CIA. He was a Cold Warrior to the core. Bush inherited the major covert operations of the last Reagan years — Angola, Afghanistan, Nicaragua, Cambodia, and the ongoing war in El Salvador. He had approved, monitored, and sometimes directed such operations. He believed in and practiced interventionist foreign policies, recognizing no limits to American covert initiatives deemed necessary to defend the country's vital interests.

Controversy exists over the extent of Bush's role in the Iran-Contra Affair. Toward the end of his presidency (December 24, 1992), twelve days before former secretary of defense Caspar W. Weinberger was to go to trial, Bush pardoned him. He gave the same gift to former national security advisor Robert C. McFarlane, former assistant secretary of state Elliott Abrams, former CIA Central American Task Force chief Alan D. Fiers Jr., former CIA deputy director for operations Clair E. George, and former CIA counterterrorism chief Duane R. Clarridge. In the Weinberger case, there existed the likelihood that the president would be called as a witness. The imperial presidency depended on impunity for its key agents. President Ford had pardoned Nixon; George H. W. Bush pardoned executors of American clandestine policies during the Reagan administration.[63]

Bush proclaimed that Weinberger was a "true American patriot," and that for all those pardoned the "common denominator of their motivation — whether their actions were right or wrong — was patriotism." Bush's language sounded ominously similar to that used by members of the Argentine military junta, the Chilean generals, and other Latin American dictators and accomplices who had violated human rights since the 1970s. All of them were patriots. They killed their enemies, violated international law, tortured the subversives, and ignored basic human decency in the name of patriotism — *for la patria.*[64] Why should American leaders have more discretion to violate human rights and international law than Latin American dictators?

According to Webster G. Tarpley and Anton Chaitkin's *George Bush: The Unauthorized Biography*, when the designated congressional committees filed their joint report on the Iran-Contra Affair, "Wyoming Representative Richard

Cheney, the senior Republican member of the House Select Committee to Investigate Covert Arms Transactions with Iran, helped steer the joint committees to an impotent result." George H. W. Bush was totally exonerated. After being elected president, he appointed Cheney secretary of defense when the Senate refused to confirm John Tower — who had chaired the Reagan-appointed Tower Commission, which whitewashed the Iran-Contra Affair.[65] Cheney's minority report on the Iran-Contra episode recalled, correctly, that "during the country's first century, Presidents used literally hundreds of secret agents at their own discretion." It then asserted, more arguably, that "the presidents were simply using their inherent executive powers under Article II of the Constitution. . . . The use of Executive power for these kinds of covert activities raised no constitutional questions." In an interview discussing the Iran-Contra Report, Cheney offered views that he would put into practice during his later tenure as vice president (2001–9): "I think you have to preserve the prerogative of the President in extraordinary circumstances not to notify the Congress at all [of covert actions] . . . [and] to exercise discretion to wait for days or weeks, or even months. I think that's within his constitutional prerogative. . . . I think we have to guard against passing laws now that will restrict some future president in a future crisis that we can only guess at present."[66]

As Cheney began his tenure as secretary of defense in April 1989, surprising events brought an end to the Cold War and the beginnings of regime change in most of Eastern Europe. Soviet troops had completed withdrawal from Afghanistan in February. In September, Poland installed its first noncommunist government since the 1940s; the Berlin Wall was opened in early November; and by the end of March 1990, both Lithuania and Estonia had declared their independence.

In Latin America, the events of 1989–90 did not immediately change American policy. Secretary of Defense Cheney reaffirmed that the drug war initiated by President Nixon and extended by President Reagan remained "a high priority national security mission of the Department of Defense." In Central America, the guerrilla war in El Salvador heated up.[67] President Bush labeled Nicaragua and Cuba "Brezhnevite clients" at a summit meeting with Mikhail Gorbachev at Malta in early December 1989 and refused to believe Gorbachev's claim that military assistance to Nicaragua's and El Salvador's guerrillas had ended, despite Gorbachev's joking reference to his newly announced "Sinatra Doctrine" (October 1989), which would allow neighboring Warsaw Pact nations to "go their own way."[68]

Bush did recognize, however, the need for some debt relief for the Latin American nations. On June 27, 1990, the president announced a new policy called "Enterprise for the Americas Initiative" to establish a free trade zone from Anchorage to Tierra del Fuego, expand foreign investment, and provide official debt relief, administered in part by the Inter-American Development Bank. The initiative featured privatization of government enterprises as a tool for downsizing government and encouraging foreign investment. Bush told the assembled diplomats and the rest of the crowd at the White House that the United States proposed the Enterprise for the Americas with the full understanding that in some cases bilateral agreements might be preferable to regional treaties, at least for the present — a view that could have been expressed by James Blaine in 1889 or Franklin Roosevelt in 1933. Domestic politics and the idiosyncrasies of local economies would also have to be taken into account. Nonetheless, and with all the caveats, Bush explained:

> The three pillars of our new initiative are trade, investment, and debt. To expand trade, I propose that we begin the process of creating a hemisphere-wide free trade zone; to increase investment, that we adopt measures to create a new flow of capital into the region; and to further ease the burden of debt, a new approach to debt in the region with important benefits for our environment. . . . Framework agreements will enable us to move forward on a step-by-step basis to eliminate counterproductive barriers to trade and towards our ultimate goal of free trade. And that's a prescription for greater growth and a higher standard of living in Latin America and, right here at home, new markets for American products and more jobs for American workers. . . . We're ready to play a constructive role at this critical time to make ours the first fully free hemisphere in all of history.[69]

By 1992, all Latin American governments except Cuba, Haiti, and Suriname had signed "framework agreements" with the United States. A North American Free Trade Agreement (NAFTA) was programmed as the highest priority objective, to serve as the foundation for the hemispheric project.[70] However, opposition in Latin America to Bush's proposals emerged quickly. An International NGO Forum meeting in Rio de Janeiro proposed an alternative "Treaty of the People of the Americas," based on sustainable development and social justice: "We reject the Enterprise of the Americas initiative, the payment of the debt and structural adjustment and we commit ourselves to promote an initiative of the People of the Americas."

For the next fifteen years, the push for bilateral and regional free trade agreements, privatization, structural adjustment, and the rest of the so-called neoliberal package would be the core of U.S. economic policy toward Latin America — an old dream, with many associated old nightmares, transformed into "neo" language with modern political complications. The skeletal critique of Bush's policies made in the Treaty of the People of the Americas would serve as a beginning for resistance to American hemispheric policies by NGOs, leftist parties, nationalists, antiglobalization social movements, and various Latin American governments. A resurgence of nationalism and populism and varied efforts to craft alternatives to the neoliberal package coming out of Washington would confront American post–Cold War triumphalism.

In the interim, the Sandinistas' electoral loss in February 1990 ended any need for the United States to support the Contras and also halted most arms shipments to El Salvador. By 1991, the Soviet Union had greatly reduced aid to Cuba, essentially cutting the Cubans loose to fend for themselves. With the dissolution of the Soviet Union in December 1991, no lifeline remained for Cuba or the Central American revolutionaries. As the Central American wars ended, the Bush administration intelligently accepted a United Nations' Observer Force to monitor demobilization by the adversaries. This departure from U.S. unilateralism greatly served American and Central American interests. The United States even agreed to work with the Russians in negotiating a peace settlement in El Salvador. Then, in late 1992, the Russians and the Cubans announced that the Soviet infantry brigade posted to the island since 1962 would be withdrawn.[71]

Despite this end to the Cold War in the Western Hemisphere, Fidel Castro had not signed on to the new program. Likewise, the ever-stronger Cuban-American lobby in the United States called for tightening the screws on the Cuban regime. The result — the Cuban Democracy Act of 1992 — strengthened the embargo that had been in place for more than thirty years. It also increased potential sanctions against countries trading with Cuba and made "regime change" (elections, free press — essentially an end to the Castro government) a condition for improved relations. The former Spanish colony of most concern to the American Founding Fathers still plagued the makers of U.S. foreign policy and would play a special role in American domestic politics for the next two decades. As in the early nineteenth century, with or without a Cold War, Cuba had a special place in American foreign policy.[72]

Panama — Operation Just Cause

Other than Cuba and Mexico, the Panamanian isthmus had been the focus of the greatest historical concern for the United States in Latin America. The 1846 Bidlack-Mallarino Treaty, the Isthmian Canal Convention between the United States and Panama (1903, and as modified in 1936 and 1955), and the first Panamanian constitution had provided rights of U.S. intervention to protect the canal and maintain law and order until 1977. Article IV(2) of the 1977 treaty negotiated during the Carter administration retained authority for the United States to use military force to protect the canal.

Then, a month after the opening of the Berlin Wall, the United States inexplicably invaded Panama to oust a dictator. Manuel Noriega had a sordid history. He was corrupt. He ran drugs. He laundered money for assorted criminals, and he played both sides of the Cuban-American conflict.[73] He had worked for the CIA, the Drug Enforcement Agency, and the Defense Intelligence Agency. And, like so many Latin American military officers, he had been trained in U.S. military schools.[74] He was an American Frankenstein in Panama, a creature of the not-so-Cold War.

In 1987, the Reagan administration decided that Noriega had to go, but other matters took priority. The Department of Justice indicted Noriega in 1988 on drug trafficking charges. A failed coup in 1988 by dissidents of the Panamanian Defense Forces (PDF) left Noriega in power, and the U.S. government cut off military and economic assistance programs. In early 1989, U.S. Southern Command forces began aggressively exercising treaty rights of free passage through Panama by such actions as ignoring road blocks, conducting short-notice military exercises, and keeping maximum pressure on the PDF, "while at the same time complying with the Panama Canal Treaties in order to maintain the legal high ground."[75]

Noriega lost bitterly contested elections in May 1989, but he nullified them. An abortive coup attempt by PDF dissidents in October 1989 brought severe repression. US SouthCom had been in contact with the coup plotters. Secretary of Defense Cheney had agreed to asylum for family members if necessary but apparently never fully committed to the coup makers. The coup leader, Major Moisés Giroldi, surrendered to PDF officers loyal to Noriega, and they tortured and murdered him. A botched American covert operation had cost Giroldi his life.

President Bush declared that "the will of the people should not be thwarted by this man and his Doberman thugs." From October 1989, under the direction of Cheney and the chairman of the Joint Chiefs of Staff, General Colin Powell, the U.S. military revised operational plans to take down the Noriega government.[76] The Panamanian legislature declared Noriega president on December 15, 1989, and announced that the United States and Panama were in a state of war. The U.S. Congress did not bother to declare war against Panama, but tensions increased rapidly. Following the shooting death of an off-duty marine lieutenant and wounding of three other officers and an attack on a navy lieutenant and threats of assault on his wife while in "police custody" in mid-December 1989, President George Bush ordered U.S. forces to invade

Panama in Operation Just Cause.[77] According to Bush, the operation had the following objectives: protect American lives and key sites and facilities; capture and deliver Noriega to competent authority; neutralize the PDF; neutralize PDF command and control; support establishment of a U.S.-recognized government in Panama; and restructure the PDF.[78] Congress played no formal role in this decision.

The United States deployed its high technology air force and committed more than 25,000 troops (most already in Panama, but thousands more deployed from other bases) — its largest invasion since World War II other than Vietnam — to capture Noriega and bring "democracy" to Panama. President Bush also announced that the invasion on December 20, 1989, was in accord with article 51 of the UN Charter (self-defense, that is, protecting American lives in Panama).[79] Despite U.S. appeals to international law and the OAS Charter, on December 22, 1989, the OAS voted 20–1 (the dissenting vote coming from the United States) to condemn the U.S. operation in Panama and called for the withdrawal of American troops. A week later, the UN General Assembly condemned the invasion by a vote of 75–20. In the Security Council, the United States, England, and France vetoed a resolution condemning the invasion.

American forces quickly overwhelmed the Panamanian PDF. Without law and order, widespread looting and violent crime followed. The U.S. military units were ill-prepared to assume an occupation role, to restore order, or to quickly repair the vast damage done to the civilian economy by the invasion. For many observers, the reason that George H. W. Bush deployed so much U.S. military force in Panama in 1989 still remains a mystery, although there has been no dearth of second-guessing. Some critics claim that Bush was just "pissed off" after the events of December 16, 1989 — if so, the invasion should have been called "Operation Just Because!" The official joint chiefs' history of the invasion records Bush saying, "Okay, let's do it. The hell with it." But the anti-Noriega policy had been in place since 1987, if not before.

On the eve of the invasion, American agents were discussing the next government with the "winners" of the May 1989 election overturned by Noriega. (The CIA had spent millions of dollars to finance the campaign of Guillermo Endara; Noriega denounced U.S. intervention in the electoral process.) Cheney had favored increasing military pressure on Noriega. On July 22, 1989, Bush issued National Security Directive 17, providing for measures to implement Cheney's recommendations. Apparently, the commander of US South-Com, General Fred Woerner, opposed the invasion, and he was replaced at the end of July.[80] In August, General Colin Powell took over as chairman of the Joint Chiefs of Staff. Undersecretary of Defense for Policy Paul Wolfowitz would also participate in the final decision to invade Panama.[81] Less than fifteen years later, Powell, Wolfowitz, and Cheney would make an even more disastrous mess in Iraq than they had made in Panama in 1989. In Iraq, they would have no American-Muslim equivalent to U.S. brigadier general Marc Cisneros, who had been able, through his personal relationships with Panamanian officers, to avert massive civilian casualties and destruction of infrastructure.

President Bush told the nation: "The goals of the United States have been to safeguard the lives of Americans, to defend democracy in Panama, to combat drug trafficking and to protect the integrity of the Panama Canal Treaty." Secretary of State James A. Baker III claimed that article 51 of the UN Charter and article 21 of the OAS Charter recognized the right of self-defense; moreover, article IV of the Panama Canal Treaty justified the invasion. For good measure, the politicians who had been denied power in the May 1989 elections, and whom the United States had now installed to replace Noriega, "welcomed the U.S."[82] Noriega took refuge with the Papal Nuncio and then surrendered to U.S. authorities on January 3, 1990. Tried in federal court in Florida, he was sentenced to forty years in prison for drug trafficking, money laundering, and related crimes.

The Panama invasion and subsequent looting inflicted widespread civilian casualties and property damage. Legal claims for the damages continued in U.S. courts into the 1990s, as did condemnations by the Inter-American Commission on Human Rights. Five years after the invasion, the president of Panama would declare the anniversary of the intervention a day of national mourning.

With Operation Just Cause, President Bush officially joined the company of American presidents who had ordered unilateral military interventions in Latin America, for one reason or another, but always with a claim of righteousness. Civilized government had broken down, America was offended, its interests were at risk, its honor and credibility were challenged. As in the times of Theodore Roosevelt, "misbehavior" by Latin Americans required punishment and, perhaps, rehabilitation, at the hands of the American hegemon. No higher law existed than American sovereignty and interests, but, just in case, both the UN Charter and the OAS were said to allow for such "self-defense." Anticipating Latin American and global condemnation of the invasion, the U.S. House of Representatives passed a resolution declaring that the Panama operation was "a response to a unique set of circumstances and does not undermine the commitment of the United States to the principle of nonintervention in the internal affairs of other countries."[83]

The most astonishing justification for the Panama invasion was Secretary of

Defense Cheney's reinterpretation of the Reconstruction era *Posse Comitatus* Act. On December 20, 1989, Cheney approved modification of Department of Defense Directive 5525.5 to state: "With regard to military actions outside the territorial jurisdiction of the United States, however, the Secretary of Defense will consider for approval, on a case by case basis, requests for exceptions to the policy of restrictions against direct assistance by military personnel to execute the laws. Such requests for exceptions to policy outside the territorial jurisdiction of the United States should be made only when there are compelling and extraordinary circumstances to justify them." Cheney then issued a memo making Operation Just Cause such an exception.

According to Cheney's memo, because Noriega was under federal indictment for alleged drug trafficking, American military forces could be used to assist law enforcement officers to apprehend him — in Panama.[84] Reconstruction in the United States ended in 1877. Americans believed (perhaps naively) that the *Posse Comitatus* legislation meant that the military would not be involved in domestic law enforcement. Cheney reinterpreted this legislation, by memo, into a rationale for invading Panama to arrest Manuel Noriega. He would do more bizarre things later, but for now this would qualify as unusual, had anyone noticed.

Cheney's rewriting of the *Posse Comitatus* Act set the stage for SouthCom's increasing focus on its war on drugs mission after 1990.[85] Operation Just Cause and the follow-up, Operation Promote Liberty (establishment of a democratic government, a new national police force, and reconstruction in Panama), were also the first of many U.S. "Military Operations Other Than War" (MOOTW) that would follow in the first post–Cold War decade.[86]

ON JUNE 12, 1987, President Ronald Reagan went to Berlin. In a moving speech, he proclaimed that "freedom and security go together" and that "the advance of human liberty can only strengthen the cause of world peace." He then called out theatrically to Mikhail Gorbachev: "General Secretary Gorbachev, if you seek peace, if you seek prosperity for the Soviet Union and Eastern Europe, if you seek liberalization: Come here to this gate! Mr. Gorbachev, open this gate! Mr. Gorbachev, tear down this wall!"[87]

Less than three weeks before the Panama invasion, President Bush had met Soviet leader Mikhail Gorbachev at Malta to discuss rapidly moving events in Eastern Europe and other topics of mutual interest. Gorbachev assured Bush that "we pursue no goals in Central America. We do not want to gain bridgeheads, strong-points, you should be certain of this." More specifically, Gorbachev told Bush that no arms were going from the Soviet Union to Nicaragua or El Salvador. According to *Time* magazine: "The toughest part of the

Summit meeting between U.S. president George H. W. Bush and Soviet president Mikhail Gorbachev on the *Maxim Gorkiy* on December 2, 1989. The person to the left of Gorbachev is Aleksandr Yakovlev, considered the ideological father of glasnost. (National Archive image, courtesy of Michael Pocock and www.maritimequest.com)

President's message concerned Central America. If the Nicaraguan Sandinistas have told you they are not supplying weapons to El Salvador's rebels, they are misleading you. He warned the Soviet leader not to miscalculate how seriously Washington regarded the escalating violence in Latin America."[88] Bush and Gorbachev also discussed a broad range of political and economic issues, including the end of Soviet domination of the Warsaw Pact nations and the "transition" in Afghanistan. Perhaps most astonishing, Gorbachev essentially declared that the Cold War had ended: "The world leaves one epoch of Cold War and enters another epoch."[89] Hardly anyone present, including President Bush, believed what he heard or immediately grasped the full significance of the momentous announcement made by Gorbachev.[90]

Apparently the American crusade had been victorious. Despite the opening of the Berlin Wall, on November 9, 1989, however, and the hints dropped at the Malta Summit (December 2–3, 1989), when George H. W. Bush launched Operation Just Cause on December 20, America (and President Bush) was not convinced that the Cold War had ended. According to Soviet expert Vladislav M. Zubok: "Robert Gates, Richard Cheney, and Brent Scowcroft, among others, dismissed 'new thinking' as atmospherics at best and a deception campaign at worst, especially since Gorbachev posed as a neo-Leninist who gave no inkling of abandoning the goals of communism. . . . Only after his first six months in power did Bush decide to move 'beyond containment,' toward engaging the Soviet Union in the process of peaceful unification of Europe."[91]

Yet not even the growing awareness in the next two years that the Soviet challenge had evaporated would end America's global messianism. The end of the Cold War encouraged America to pursue its global mission, to install a planetary "empire of liberty," and to export "market democracy" around the globe.

Chapter Thirteen

Not the End of History

A total dismantling of socialism as a world phenomenon has been taking place. This may be
inevitable and good. For this is a reunification of mankind on the basis of common sense.
And a common fellow from Stavropol [Gorbachev] set this process in motion.

— ANATOLY CHERNAEV,[1] October 5, 1989

With the end of the Cold War, a resurgent messianism (mis)informed American foreign policy. In the words of historian and international expert on insurgency and terrorism Walter Laqueur, "When the Cold War came to an end in 1989 with the dismantling of the Berlin Wall, when the countries of Eastern Europe regained independence, and when finally the Soviet Union disintegrated, there was widespread feeling throughout the world that at long last universal peace had descended on Earth."[2] American philosopher and political economist Francis Fukuyama captured the essence of this euphoric pretension that the Soviet implosion meant that liberal democracy and capitalism would spread their blessings around the world. Fukuyama claimed: "The triumph of the West, of the Western *idea*, is evident first of all in the total exhaustion of viable systematic alternatives to Western liberalism. . . . What we may be witnessing is . . . the end of history as such: that is, the end point of mankind's ideological evolution and the universalization of Western liberal democracy as the final form of human government."[3]

Rather than the "end of history," universal peace, and the global victory of liberal democracy predicted by Fukuyama, the end of the Cold War bequeathed the United States "a jungle full of poisonous snakes."[4] The end of bipolarity as the frame for world politics made more visible the underlying conditions suppressed by the Cold War, such as ethnic strife, cultural and religious conflict, secessionist movements, civil wars, and pervasive poverty in much of the world. The dangers posed by rogue states, failing states, and failed states became painfully evident as UN membership increased from 159 in 1990 to 185 in 1994. And, although some ex-Soviet republics transformed themselves into nations that favored Western-style party politics, in much of the world, governments and peoples rejected liberal, secular, "market democracy." They also resisted American pretensions of global primacy.

A first hint of what would follow came with Iraq's invasion of Kuwait in August 1990, two months after East Germany began dismantling the Berlin Wall. Iraqi leader Saddam Hussein sought control of Kuwait's oil, but also harked back to Great Britain's creation of Kuwait in 1961 (the same year construction began on the Berlin Wall). Hussein claimed that Kuwaiti oil wells were sucking oil across the Iraqi frontier and that, in any case, Kuwait was part of Iraq.

Contributing to the crisis was a diplomatic "misunderstanding" between Iraq and the United States. Saddam Hussein had been told by the U.S. ambassador, shortly before the invasion, that "we have no opinion on the Arab-Arab conflicts, like your border disagreement with Kuwait. . . . We hope you can solve this problem using any suitable methods via Klibi [Chadli Klibi, secretary general of the Arab League] or via President Mubarak [of Egypt]. All that we hope is that these issues are solved quickly."[5] At a meeting in Aspen, Colorado on August 2, 1990, Margaret Thatcher reminded President Bush that, with Kuwait, Hussein would have 65 percent of the world's oil reserves: "He could blackmail us all." She added: "We have to move to stop the aggression . . . stop it quickly. If we let it succeed, . . . no small country can ever feel safe again [and] the law of the jungle would take over from the rule of law."[6] Fearful of Hussein's next move, Saudi Arabia's king authorized the United States to base troops in his country — a dangerous move for the nation that hosts Islam's most holy sites. Meanwhile, Hussein announced that the Iraqi and Kuwaiti people were "now one." In late September, he warned the United States that military intervention in Iraq and Kuwait would be followed by a repeat of its experience in Vietnam.

On November 29, 1990, the UN Security Council authorized the use of "all necessary means" if Hussein did not order withdrawal from Kuwait by January 15, 1991. President Bush asked Congress for authorization to join the United Nations in enforcing the Security Council resolution and protecting Saudi Arabia (and its oil) against Hussein. Despite the brutality of the invasion of Kuwait, the Senate only narrowly approved U.S. participation in Operation Desert Shield. (The Senate voted 52–47; the House 250–183). On January 17, 1991, Desert Shield morphed into Operation Desert Storm. American and allied ground forces invaded Iraq in late February and defeated the Iraqi army in five days. At war's end, Bush and his advisers invoked a UN Security Council resolution that applied sanctions against Iraq but allowed Hussein to remain in power. Hussein took advantage of this decision to repress the internal

Kurd and Shi'a opposition. (In 2001, Saddam Hussein would describe the first Gulf War as a "confrontation between good and evil that continues today," the "aggression" by the "followers of Satan.")[7] Apparently, he had still not heard about the end of history.

The quick victory temporarily distracted public opinion in the United States from other flash points in the Middle East, Africa, and the Balkans. Even so, President Bush, who no longer could rely on the Reagan legacy alone, lost his reelection bid in 1992 to Bill Clinton. Clinton focused his campaign on domestic economic woes. His acceptance speech at the Democratic convention barely touched on foreign policy or security issues except to say that his proposal for a "New Covenant" with America included: "An America with the world's strongest defense, ready and willing to use force when necessary; An America at the forefront of the global effort to preserve and protect our common environment—and promoting global growth; An America that will not coddle tyrants, from Baghdad to Beijing; An America that champions the cause of freedom and democracy from Eastern Europe to Southern Africa—and in our own hemisphere, in Haiti and Cuba."[8] Clinton donned the mantle of the American crusade for freedom and promotion of "market democracy." He celebrated the Cold War victory, while lamenting America's economic decline under Bush's mentorship: "The Cold War is over. . . . Freedom, democracy, individual rights, free enterprise—they have triumphed all around the world. And yet, just as we have won the Cold War abroad, we are losing the battles for economic opportunity and social justice here at home."[9]

Like many of his predecessors, both Republican and Democrat, Clinton sought to ameliorate domestic economic problems, at least in part, by "opening markets." Reaching back to the Great Society and the New Deal, he also proposed "reinvestment" by the federal government in domestic infrastructure, health care, and education and even in combating crime. He proclaimed: "Now that we have changed the world, it's time to change America."[10] (The same mantra of "change" would again dominate the presidential election in 2008, after George H. W. Bush's son occupied the White House for eight years, ending his term in 2009 with a much less successful war in Iraq and implosion of the domestic economy.)

Despite Clinton's mindless claim that freedom, democracy, individual rights, and free enterprise had "triumphed all over the world," he inherited the post–Cold War global jungle, full of snakes and other dangers. Somalia, where Bush had bequeathed Clinton a failing UN humanitarian mission, hosted more than a few of them: warlords, pirates, Islamist militia, terrorists, and more. From 1993 to 1995, Mogadishu became a symbol of American failure in humanitarian and peacekeeping interventions in the post–Cold War world. Somali militiamen shot down American helicopters, killed Americans and other UN peacekeepers, and dragged the mutilated remains through the streets. All this was televised around the world. Shortly after, American troops withdrew. Most Americans wondered why they had been there in the first place.[11] Somalia would become a tragic example of American ineptitude and hubris in exporting democracy or even stable government. Ethnic, religious, tribal, and warlord violence persisted. Piracy against international shipping in the Gulf of Aden would become endemic and, by 2008, was frequently headline news.[12]

After Somalia, Clinton usually preferred cruise missiles and airpower to putting American troops on the ground in combat against Third World peoples. But he did not abandon selective unilateralism (although failure to intervene during the Rwandan genocide of 1994 dramatically illustrated that the "critical interests" of the United States usually did not include human rights in sub-Saharan Africa). Clinton repeatedly deployed U.S. armed forces abroad without prior congressional authorization: Haiti (1994); Bosnia (1994–95); Iraq (1998); Sudan (1998); Afghanistan (1998); and, most notably, in the seventy-nine-day air war against Serbia/Kosovo (March 24 to June 10, 1999) under cover of the NATO Treaty.[13] Russia, China, India, and other nations opposed the NATO action, which bypassed the United Nations and, arguably, international law, threatening the sovereignty and internal security of other nations facing potential secessionist movements.

John C. Yoo, a law professor at Boalt Hall in Berkeley, who would later justify torture by other names and defend presidential war-making authority in the George W. Bush administration, lamented that "when it comes to using the American military, no president in recent times has had a quicker trigger finger [than Clinton]." Yoo drew attention to a significant change in the *rationale* for American military deployments abroad: "During the Reagan and Bush administrations, the United States often intervened unilaterally, quickly, and generally in pursuit of purely American interests. American invasions in Grenada and Panama, for example, occurred without any significant multilateral participation, were executed within the 60-day War Powers Resolution period, and did not receive Security Council approval." Yoo was not opposed to American military interventions or unilateralism; he was uncomfortable with treaty regime justification for presidential commitment of American armed forces:

> Under this new paradigm, the approval of the U.N. or other international organizations has become the foundation upon which justifications for intervention are built. In sending troops to Haiti and Bosnia,

for example, President Clinton expressly relied upon the need to carry out U.N. Security Council resolutions as support, rather than domestic legal mandates. . . .

The Clinton administration . . . may believe that the President's authority to interpret and execute treaty commitments may buttress his constitutional authority to send American troops abroad. At the level of domestic law, however, the Clinton administration's refusal to seek affirmative congressional authorization . . . may have been consistent with historical practice, but it is still open to constitutional question.

Despite Yoo's criticism, Clinton simply followed in the tradition of American unilateralism with treaty regime cover, dating from the Bidlack-Mallarino Treaty of 1846. Since the 1947 Rio Treaty, the NATO Treaty, and entry into the Korean conflict, U.S. unilateralism, with or without congressional approval, had been packaged in multilateral discourse. Still, Yoo spelled out clearly that whatever additional legitimacy international regimes might provide for American deployment of armed forces abroad, "Kosovo verifies that international law amounts to nothing more than a constitutional placebo. . . . As demonstrated by the Clinton administration's bombing of Serbian targets without U.N. sanction, international law places no constraints upon the President's exercise of his Commander-in-Chief or executive war powers."[14]

Yoo believed that the American president could do whatever was necessary to assure American self-defense, as defined by the President. International law might be a useful cover but did not constrain presidential initiative. Yoo worried, like other neoconservatives, that multilateralism might become a *real* rationale (and therefore, a potential constraint), rather than a (sometimes) convenient justification for American unilateralist foreign policy.[15] Yoo believed that no higher law, of whatever sort, limited the American president's "inherent" constitutional authority to preserve, protect, and defend the Constitution of the United States.

Yet, in the post–Cold War era, it was increasingly difficult to make American unilateralism compatible with the sovereignty of almost 200 other countries.[16] What of the interests and security of other nation-states that conflicted with American interests or American interpretation of treaty regimes? American insistence on nonproliferation, for example, meant that sovereign states should voluntarily abstain or be prevented from acquiring nuclear, biological, and chemical weapons. On what basis did the United States, NATO, Russia, China, and other nuclear powers expect to retain their oligopoly over weapons which they, themselves, relied on for deterrence? Why was nuclear deterrence unimaginable as a policy for India, Pakistan, North Korea, or Iran, particularly against U.S. or Western interventions, if it had been a premise of U.S. and Soviet defense policies since the early 1950s and Israeli security policy since the 1970s?[17] With what alternative instruments would other nation-states deter the United States, NATO, or regional competitors?

Beyond U.S. policies that reaffirmed the anomaly of unequal sovereign nations, the Clinton administration's insistence on its "pivotal and inescapable" role in the international system also encountered the legacies of resentment rooted in thousands of U.S. covert operations of the Cold War era. By American calculation, resistance to global hegemony from diverse quarters represented threats to American security. President Clinton asserted the equivalency of the new threats to the old threats of fascism and communism: "Just as surely as fascism and communism once did, so, too, are our freedom, democracy, security and prosperity now threatened by regional aggressors and the spread of weapons of mass destruction; ethnic, religious, and national rivalries; and the forces of terrorism, drug trafficking and international organized crime."[18] Clinton claimed also that the spread of capitalism was part of the security agenda: "Our national security strategy is therefore based on enlarging the community of market democracies. . . . The more that democracy and political and economic liberalization take hold in the world, particularly in countries of strategic importance to us, the safer our nation is likely to be and the more our people are likely to prosper."[19] (Could Calvin Coolidge or Ronald Reagan have said it better?)

Exporting market democracy was a hard sell when such a package reeked of America's sense of cultural superiority and disdain for other ways of life. The "American package" included downscaling or privatization of public enterprise. In much of the world, this meant loss or erosion of public services such as health care, pensions, and education and the elimination of subsidies for food, water, and transportation. Privatization of government enterprises from Chile and Nicaragua to Russia and the former Soviet republics entailed, in practice, transfers of public assets at fire-sale prices to favored clients of outgoing regimes, whether communist, socialist, or military regimes in Latin America. The free-trade policies disadvantaged peasants in Latin America and around the world, while American and European agricultural subsidies drove small farmers off the land. When the victims of such globalization sought to find jobs in the United States, they confronted the limits to economic liberalization. Market democracy meant "opening" for capital and trade, not for labor and people. All these consequences of the American post–Cold War formula for "progress" cultivated renewed nationalism, populism, sectarianism, and antiliberal discourse belying further the "end of history" thesis.

Clinton's national security team shared fundamental premises with its two Republican predecessors: America had a civilizing mission as the vanguard of global freedom; this mission depended upon American military superiority over all regional or global competitors; and America's mission and military superiority required a regional strategy. Such a strategy had to take into account the "full spectrum" of potential threats — thus the need for "full spectrum threat dominance."[20] Despite the end of the Cold War, America required massive defense budgets to counter actual, potential, and imaginable threats. It also required bases and "lily pads" to the corners of the earth for projection of American military power and to protect energy supplies, pipeline routes, and other strategic resources.

Clinton's policies meant that the military Unified Commands took an ever-larger role in making and implementing foreign policy. As Boston University professor and retired U.S. Army officer Andrew Bacevich noted, a decade after the Cold War ended, it was the four-star commanders "who managed the far reaches of America's global imperium."[21] In the Balkans, Americans sought to enforce a "no fly zone" over Bosnia in 1993, then committed air power in 1995 in covert alliance with Croatians to defeat the Serbs in Bosnia. In Central and South Asia, the Clinton team deployed American forces to several former Soviet republics governed by dictatorial regimes. Plans to effect regime change against the Taliban in Afghanistan were also under discussion. American interests, and therefore potential threats to those interests, extended to the corners of the earth.

There would be no long-term peace dividend. Defense spending during the Clinton presidency averaged $278 billion, almost exactly the Cold War average (in 2002 dollars).[22] Clinton's national security advisor added two dangerously ambiguous concepts to security doctrine: enlargement and engagement. The United States would involve itself, as part of its mission to expand the "community of free nations," in wars big and small around the planet as well as in Military Operations Other Than War (MOOTW).[23] MOOTW encompassed everything from humanitarian intervention and peacekeeping missions to responses to natural disasters.[24] It also included "show of force" operations, support for insurgencies, support for counterinsurgency, combating terrorism, and participating in the global war on drugs. The executive summary of the Joint Doctrine Manual on MOOTW explained: "The use of military force in peacetime helps keep the day-to-day tensions between nations below the threshold of armed conflict or war and maintains U.S. influence in foreign lands."[25]

The use of military force in peacetime as an essential element of American foreign policy meant maintaining a vast global military presence, in effect a military empire. MOOTW doctrine presaged still further militarization of American foreign policy. In parts of Latin America, MOOTW brought re-militarization of internal administration and police functions, confounding the supposed commitment to democratization and civilian control over the military announced as SouthCom objectives in the early 1990s. The Clinton team accepted the premises of the 1993 *Regional Defense Strategy* document released by Secretary of Defense Dick Cheney, which emphasized the need for "the democratic nations of the region to defend themselves against the threat posed by insurgency and terrorism."[26] Thus, the "communist terrorists" against whom Eisenhower, the Dulles brothers, and John F. Kennedy protected America had been replaced by "international terrorists" as the country's main enemies, well before September 11, 2001. As American policy targeted inter-national terrorism, U.S. and Latin American military institutions reactivated and expanded collaborative intelligence networks established beginning in 1948 and enhanced in the "dirty wars" of the 1970s and 1980s.

Notably, the Clinton administration also resorted to new forums, so-called Summits of the Americas and Defense Ministerial meetings, to promote its hemispheric agenda, rather than relying primarily on the existing multilateral institutions, such as the Organization of American States (OAS) and the 1947 Rio Treaty regime.[27] In the name of "cooperative security," the United States would formulate and attempt to impose a "regional security agenda."[28] Such an agenda rarely coincided neatly with the security concerns of Latin Ameri-can governments and military institutions.

When Clinton accepted his party's nomination for the presidency again in 1996, his only mention of Latin America (other than the 1994 Operation Re-store Freedom "humanitarian intervention" in Haiti) referred to free trade.[29] Much of Clinton's speech could have been delivered by Ronald Reagan or George H. W. Bush, whether on security or economic matters.[30] Following this bipartisan vision, the 1997 *Quadrennial Defense Review* concluded that the United States "must remain engaged as a global leader and harness the unmatched capabilities of its armed forces to do three things: shape the inter-national security environment in favorable ways, respond to the full spectrum of crises when it is in our interests to do so, and prepare now to meet the challenges of an uncertain future by transforming U.S. combat capabilities and support structures to be able to shape and respond effectively well into the 21st century."[31]

As part of this effort to "shape and respond effectively," the Department of Defense in 1996–97 added considerable territory to SouthCom's jurisdiction and moved command headquarters to Miami, with implementation of the withdrawal from Panama specified in the 1977 treaty. According to South-

Com's description of these changes, "The new [Area of Responsibility] encompasses 32 nations (19 in Central and South America and 13 in the Caribbean), of which 31 are democracies, and 14 U.S. and European territories covering more than 15.6 million square miles." Overall, the revised strategy document announced an era of increased defense expenditures, force reconfiguration, and further overseas deployments. Indeed, the proposed global reach of the United States for engagement, enlargement, and shaping of the environment, "from Northern Asia to the Straits of Magellan and around the Cape back to the Mediterranean Sea," seemed astounding.[32] Even so, conservative critics of the Clinton administration's policies argued that the United States was squandering the opportunity to more fully "reshape the world" and that still much more defense spending was required.

In June 1997, the leaders of the Project for the New American Century (PNAC) — a conservative nongovernmental organization — declared: "We seem to have forgotten the essential elements of the Reagan Administration's success: a military that is strong and ready to meet both present and future challenges; a foreign policy that boldly and purposefully promotes American principles abroad; and national leadership that accepts the United States' global responsibilities."[33] Although the PNAC viewed the Clinton administration's security and defense postures as inadequate, the U.S. government's foreign polices could hardly be characterized as retrenchment. As an illustration, the *Special Operations Forces Posture Statement 2000* reported that in 1999 Special Operations Forces conducted "engagement operations" in over 100 countries and were deployed to 152 countries and territories — that is, to approximately 80 percent of the world's nations.[34]

To administer its global responsibilities, the Department of Defense divided the world into regional and functional "unified commands." Each regional command (in 2000) had its "area of responsibility" (AOR) and "area of interest" (AOI) around the planet. No other nation on earth even imagined such an imperial military architecture at the end of the twentieth century. After the September 11, 2001, attacks on the United States, the Unified Command Plan gradually was altered: U.S. Northern Command was established on October 1, 2002, "to provide command and control of Department of Defense . . . homeland defense efforts and to coordinate defense support of civil authorities." (A new U.S. Africa Command was announced in 2007 to "consolidate U.S. government efforts in Africa and the ability to work with partner nations," in response to "the increasing importance of Africa strategically, diplomatically and economically.")[35] Gradually, the regional commanders came to control larger budgets and to exercise more power and influence than all of the civilian agencies involved in U.S. foreign relations, including the Department

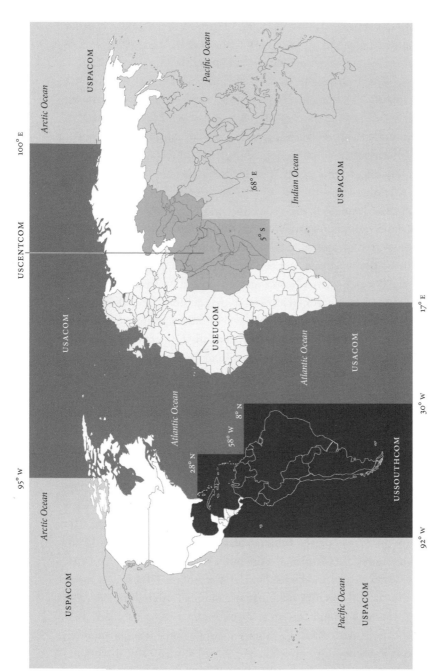

Map 13.1. Unified Command Plan Map, 1999. Based on a map in CRS Report for Congress, "Military Changes to the Unified Command Plan: Background and Issues for Congress," June 21, 1999. In October 2002 President George W. Bush created U.S. NorthCom to "defend America's homeland" and in 2007 created U.S. AfriCom "to promote a stable and secure African environment in support of U.S. foreign policy." See http://www.northcom.mil/; http://www.africom.mil/.

of State.[36] They also came to view themselves as responsible for "their" parts of the globe well beyond any narrow military tasking. For example, Admiral Dennis C. Blair, commander in chief (CINC) of the U.S. Pacific Command (Blair would become director of National Intelligence in the Barack Obama administration in 2009), commented in November 2000: "The U.S. role is critical. The United States *is the only Asian power* that does not have territory in Asia. . . . Our forward-based and forward-deployed military posture is really the key to the United States being able to make good things happen and keep bad things from happening in the theater."[37]

In short, the flexible architecture of America's global military reach was the foundation for the "hegemony strategy," whereby the United States sought to "extend unilateral protection over as many states as possible" in order to maximize U.S. security and protect American interests.[38] Such a strategy mimicked, on a grand scale, the "protectorate regime" strategy introduced in the Bidlack-Mallarino Treaty with Colombia in 1846. Protective imperialism in the Western Hemisphere had been transformed into a planetary grand strategy, accompanied by a national security doctrine and force structure to implement it.[39]

For American democracy, this development had consequences. Clinton viewed U.S. *global leadership* and *hegemony* as essential for American national security and international order. For Clinton's policy team, "national security" blurred into "global security." Thus, as political analyst Michael Lind put it, "the ambitious project of establishing solitary U.S. hegemony over the rest of the world, even in the absence of the threat of a rival superpower, created a new rationale for the imperial presidency."[40]

In 1998, the Senate passed unanimously the Iraq Liberation Act, making regime change in Iraq official policy.[41] The law declared that "it should be the policy of the United States to seek to remove the Saddam Hussein regime from power in Iraq and to replace it with a democratic government." The law, approved overwhelmingly (360–38 in the House and without amendment by unanimous consent in the Senate), authorized funds to support the opposition to Saddam Hussein, called for an international tribunal to indict, prosecute, and imprison Hussein and other Iraqi officials, and provided for humanitarian assistance after regime change to "support Iraq's transition to democracy." Regime change could now be announced by Congress as *official* policy not only for Cuba, but also for nations of the Middle East, as if the United States had an international mandate to police decency and export democracy, or at least the American version. And, by 1998, the post–Cold War crusade for democracy had achieved impressive bipartisan support. Senator Trent Lott

(R.-Miss.) reminded his colleagues that during the Reagan years "we supported freedom fighters in Asia, Africa, and Latin America willing to fight and die for a democratic future."[42]

Not surprisingly, however, the post–Cold War crusade was about more than exporting freedom and democracy. On Clinton's watch, the Department of Defense and the Joint Chiefs of Staff had anticipated an "oil war" in the Persian Gulf (an updating of President Jimmy Carter's creation of the Rapid Deployment Force for precisely this mission). By 2000, American aircraft were attacking Iraqi targets routinely to enforce American and British interpretations of UN sanctions and the "no fly zone" established over that nation's sovereign territory after the first Gulf War in 1991. The U.S. government claimed that UN Security Council Resolution 688 (April 5, 1991) justified enforcement of the no fly zones; the UN secretary general called the U.S. and British operations illegal. No mention of such operations or anything similar appeared in Resolution 688 itself.[43] Iraq announced it would no longer respect the no fly zones in December 1998. From that time, British and U.S. air forces took fire from Iraqi antiaircraft installations. American and British operations continued until the end of the Clinton administration. They would escalate in preparation for the invasion of Iraq in March 2003, two years after George W. Bush succeeded Clinton at the White House.[44]

Enlargement and Engagement in the Western Hemisphere

As always, for America to "make the difference" and to achieve its global objectives, it had first to reconfirm the security of the Western Hemisphere bastion. In the early 1990s, it was not clear how post–Cold War policies would be applied to Latin America. U.S. policymakers celebrated the decline of insurgencies in the region but also lamented the ongoing and increasing violence associated with the drug cartels, especially in Colombia.[45] By 1994–95, an emerging U.S. hemispheric security policy sought to incorporate the drug war into a more comprehensively defined range of threat scenarios.[46] After the December 1994 Summit of the Americas and the July 1995 Defense Ministerial at Williamsburg, Virginia, the U.S. Department of Defense released its assessment, in "United States Security Strategy for the Americas: a New Concept of 'Cooperative Security.'" The Department of Defense document concluded that threats to the United States were more diverse and that the line between domestic and foreign policies had blurred. Threats in the hemisphere to U.S. security in the 1990s included narco-trafficking, terrorism, illegal immigration, and environmental degradation. Pointedly, *migration of people* joined the list of threats along with terrorism and drug trafficking.

In the mid-1995 Defense Ministerial of the Americas, "the first ever gathering of the hemisphere's civilian and military leaders," the U.S. secretary of defense announced that "the bedrock foundation of our approach to the Americas is a shared commitment to democracy, the rule of law, conflict resolution, defense transparency, and mutual cooperation." In his testimony to the House National Security Committee in March 1995, the commander of SouthCom, General Barry R. McCaffrey, stressed what had become the party line: increased economic integration, the prevalence of "market principles," democratization, and cooperative security arrangements were the wave of the future in the region.[47] Such rhetoric had also been the wave of the past. Underlying the Western Hemisphere policies, as usual, were a focus on "better trade partners" and "stability." For the United States' Latin American neighbors, of course, old problems remained: border disputes, political violence, insurgencies, poverty, and economic insecurity that menaced regime stability.

And there was Cuba. Fidel Castro had survived the end of the Cold War and had not signed on to the end of history story. With elections upcoming, President Clinton wished, this time, to carry the electoral votes from Florida that had escaped him in his first campaign for the presidency.[48] That meant catering to the anti-Castro lobby that could make the difference. President Clinton had enforced the Cuban Democracy Act of 1992 and the annual condemnations of human rights violations in Cuba during his first term.[49] When he convoked the first Summit of the Americas in Miami in December 1994, he excluded Cuba. Fidel Castro complained, in response, that the United States sought to control the hemisphere, isolate Cuba, and retain Latin America as an American enclave.[50] No end to history here, either — just the same old story that dated from 1959.

At the Ibero-American Summit, held in Bogotá, Colombia, in June 1994, heads of state from Latin America, Spain, and Portugal called for free trade throughout the Americas and an end to all trade barriers, including the U.S. embargo of Cuba. This forum would continue to serve as an alternative to the American-sponsored Summits of the Americas through the end of Clinton's term and beyond — presaging a growing movement in Latin America that challenged post–Cold War U.S. hemispheric policies.[51] At the Bogotá meeting, Cuba denounced assassination attempts against Fidel Castro and continuous acts of terrorism against the island launched from the United States, as well as the exclusion of Cuba from the Summit of the Americas: "The presumed bosses of the hemisphere have prohibited Cuba from participating in this [Miami] meeting. . . . What cowardice."[52]

Despite discussions on strengthening democracy, poverty alleviation, and sustainable development, the headlines coming out of the first Summit of the

Americas focused on the promise of an expanded (from the North American Free Trade Agreement [NAFTA]) free trade area for the region by 2005.[53] A Jamaican newspaper editorialized: "The Americans look at the hemisphere and see a market of 800 million consumers. That is why they declare in no uncertain terms that this summit is really about economic growth. Dare we say the same?" From Spain's *El País* (December 16, 1994) came more critical coverage: "To hold a hemispheric summit in the number two Cuban city in the world [Miami] and not speak of Cuba is senseless. The Summit of the Americas has ended as if Cuba did not exist. This quarantine does not appear to be the best formula for a democratic system to evolve within Cuba."[54]

Clinton cared less about democracy in Cuba than being reelected. In 1996, he endorsed the Helms-Burton law (Cuban Liberty and Democratic Solidarity Act), "an act to seek international sanctions against the Castro government in Cuba, to plan for support of a transition government leading to a democratically elected government in Cuba, and for other purposes."[55] As it would in Iraq in 1998, the U.S. government promoted regime change in Cuba in 1996: "The Cuban people deserve to be assisted in a decisive manner to end the tyranny that has oppressed them for 36 years." Both Houses of Congress overwhelmingly approved the legislation (74–24 in the Senate; 294–130 in the House of Representatives).

The Helms-Burton legislation had been introduced in 1995 by Representative Dan Burton (R.-Ind.) and Senator Jesse Helms (R.-N.C.) but was tabled when Helms could not overcome a Democratic filibuster in the Senate. President Clinton had opposed the legislation for a variety of reasons, including its impact on American trade partners and allies. With elections approaching, however, the president and the Democrats could not resist the political tide. Clinton signed slightly revised Helms-Burton legislation on March 12, 1996.

Helms-Burton challenged the sovereign interests of America's European allies, former Soviet republics, and other Western Hemisphere nations. Mexico and Canada strongly protested the legislation.[56] Canada passed a law prohibiting compliance by Canadian corporations with any "extraterritorial measure of the United States" and with any "communications" received from persons in a position to direct or influence the policies of such corporations. The United Kingdom passed legislation providing criminal sanctions *for complying with* Helms-Burton. Most of the international community rejected the law's extraterritorial pretensions.

A month before Clinton signed the Helms-Burton legislation, Cuban fighter jets had shot down two small aircraft operated by the *Hermanos al Rescate* (Brothers to the Rescue). Four Cuban-Americans died as they ostensibly sought to assist would-be migrants to the United States on rafts and boats of all sorts (the *balseros*). The Brothers to the Rescue were not simply good-hearted humanitarians bent on rescuing Cubans fleeing Castro's dictatorship. Created in 1991, the group actively engaged in operations against the Cuban government, claiming that it sought to overthrow Fidel Castro through active nonviolent means.[57]

The Cuban government had repeatedly warned the Brothers to the Rescue about violations of Cuban airspace; it also accused the group of carrying out terrorist activities in Cuba. In more than one case, a Brothers' plane dropped anti-Castro leaflets over Havana. Some of its member worked with, and for, American intelligence agencies. Nevertheless, the Cubans had shot down unarmed civilian aircraft and killed American citizens. (They had also penetrated the Brothers group with a spy — who returned to Cuba just before the planes were shot down.) A UN Security Council resolution condemned the Cuban action, which was in violation of International Civil Aviation Organization (an agency of the United Nations) regulations.[58] The European Union did the same. A spokesperson for the Cuban Foreign Ministry rejected these resolutions, noting that the United States would not tolerate repeated violations of its airspace and that "these people knew what they were doing. They were warned. They wanted to take certain actions that were clearly intended to destabilize the Cuban government and the US authorities knew about their intentions."

In an election year, this incident could not be downplayed.[59] Republicans accused Clinton of weakness in responding to the Cuban pilots' deaths. Even some Democrats publicly questioned the usefulness of merely strengthening an embargo that had not worked for thirty-seven years. Representative José Serrano (D.-N.Y.) commented: "I think what he's going to do now is try to tell the Florida community that he's going to get tough against Castro by putting this legislation forth. This legislation does nothing. . . . The world community is going to laugh at us because I don't think that the Canadians and the British and the Japanese are going to go along." Congresswoman Ileana Ros-Lehtinen (R.-Fla.) declared: "Castro shot them down. And now we're going to sit down and negotiate with Castro? That's like negotiating with the Japanese government after Pearl Harbor!"[60] Ros-Lehtinen exaggerated slightly. Cuba had shot down two small planes piloted by anti-Castro exiles. A crime, perhaps, but not an attack on America. Still, as in the past, presidential elections sometimes gave special meaning to such events and significantly impacted foreign policy decisions.

President Clinton won reelection on November 5, 1996, carrying Florida this time, unlike in 1992. But the Helms-Burton law created continuing friction with allies from Israel to Germany. Until the end of the Clinton presidency, it engaged American negotiators in fractious meetings with representatives of the European community and provoked bilateral problems with Canada, Mexico, Spain, Argentina, and Brazil, among other nations. The law seriously challenged the fundamental principles of sovereignty in international law: equality of states; nonintervention; and the coextensiveness of territory and jurisdiction. It also seemed to violate the UN and OAS charters, NAFTA, and the General Agreement on Trade (GATT).[61] But for the United States, there was no higher law than its own.

In his second inaugural address, Clinton went back to the beginning, to the Founders' dreams, to the country's Providential destiny. He seemed to echo presidents Wilson, Harding, and Coolidge — and Reagan: "Guided by the ancient vision of a promised land, let us set our sights upon a land of new promise. . . . America stands alone as the world's indispensable nation." As to the future: "We will stand mighty for peace and freedom, and maintain a strong defense against terror and destruction. . . . And the world's greatest democracy will lead a whole world of democracies."[62]

With an expanding economy, drastically reduced fiscal deficits, and a program of targeted tax cuts, Clinton received frequent applause from the Republican-dominated Congress when he delivered his State of the Union message in 1998. He returned repeatedly to America's global mission and the need to "seek opportunity not just at home, but in all the markets of the world," aiming to "shape this global economy, not shrink from it." He continued: "I will also renew my request for the fast track negotiating authority necessary to open more new markets, create more new jobs, which every President has had for two decades." Clinton also addressed expansion of NATO, the "peacekeeping" mission in Bosnia, the UN weapons inspectors in Iraq, and the "new hazards of chemical and biological weapons and the outlaw states, terrorists, and organized criminals seeking to acquire them."[63]

About Latin America, Clinton made one passing reference to security strategy toward South America. Yet, on the ground, the United States was not idle in the Western Hemisphere.

SouthCom and the Regional Security Strategy

At the end of the 1990s, despite the discourse on human rights and democracy, the operative U.S. security agenda for the Western Hemisphere, measured in dollars and other resources committed, had become predominantly the drug war. Fighting international terrorism, guaranteeing "stability," promoting trade liberalization, and expanding opportunities for private enterprise filled out the package. By Clinton's second term, however, almost the entire policy agenda for Latin America had been "securitized." Security policy encompassed everything from democratization and trade liberalization to undocumented immigration and urban gangs. The Department of Defense had become the "lead agency" for the detection and monitoring of illicit drug smuggling into the United States. In principle, this lead agency function included "coordination with the State Department," but the most important missions involved support for bilateral and multilateral cross-border operations, particularly in the Andean region (between Colombia and Ecuador, Colombia and Venezuela, and Peru and Brazil).[64] Unlike the Reagan administration's focus on Central America, from the early 1990s U.S. policy put Colombia and the Andean region in the spotlight.

Terrorism and narco-guerrillas had replaced the Marxist threat of the past. Like the communist menace during the Cold War, the narco-terrorists challenged democracy and internal security in the hemisphere. At the end of 1998, Secretary of Defense William S. Cohen anticipated the tensions between fighting against terrorists and maintaining constitutional democracy in the United States and the hemisphere. Cohen told the attendees at the Defense Ministerial III in Cartagena:[65]

> The best deterrent that we have against acts of terrorism is to find out who is conspiring, who has the material, where are they getting it, who are they talking to, what are their plans. In order to do that, in order to interdict the terrorists before they set off their weapon, you have to have that kind of intelligence-gathering capability, but it runs smack into Constitutional protections of privacy. And it's a tension which will continue to exist in every free society — the reconciliation of the need for liberty and the need for law and order. . . .
>
> What we need most of all is to have an understanding that we must share intelligence about terrorist activities. If you pick up information about groups that are planning attacks within your own countries who are cross-border, then that is information that should be shared. The same is true for all of us in the hemisphere. We have an obligation to do that and I believe that it will in fact provide the kind of deterrence that we are all looking for.[66]

Cohen's remarks preceded the September 11, 2001, attacks on the United States by almost three years. Terrorism and regional counterterrorist operations already were at the top of the U.S. agenda. For Latin American military officers, however, the idea of "shared intelligence" had very concrete referents.[67] With American knowledge and complicity, Latin American military intelligence operations in the 1970s had attacked and assassinated "subversives" and "terrorists" in Europe, the United States, and throughout the Western Hemisphere. Latin American military officers and security forces understood the *real* balance between "democracy" and "security" in the U.S. agenda for the hemisphere. As in the Cold War, elected civilian governments might serve U.S. interests, but only if they meant stability and cooperation with the broader U.S. regional agenda. What had "worked" in Guatemala, Nicaragua, El Salvador, Haiti, and the Southern Cone during the Cold War might now be exported elsewhere, along with all the old tricks of regime change and supervised elections that dated from the interventions of the early twentieth century. The Marine Corps' 1940 *Small Wars Manual* remained, implicitly, the blueprint for exporting democracy: creation of surrogate armies or national police forces to maintain order and guarantee the "rule of law," followed by elections as legitimation of "democratic" governments.[68]

In 1999, the only threats to U.S. security in the Western Hemisphere worthy of mention in official policy documents were drug trafficking and its spin-offs, along with undocumented immigration to the United States. According to Professor Gabriel Marcella, teaching at the U.S. Army War College, SouthCom "became the unified command par excellence for counternarcotics. At one time, nearly 90 percent of its operations involved counternarcotics support."[69] The United States was engaged, whether covertly or through military assistance programs, in low-intensity war and counter-drug operations in the Andean region — and had been for some time.[70] American military forces engaged in a variety of training missions throughout Latin America, often justified as part of the drug war. Sometimes the training went over the line established by Congress. In addition, numerous private contractors performed military and quasi-military missions, thereby evading congressional limits on U.S. military deployments (and also despite numerical caps on the contractors) and making efforts to audit these operations more difficult.[71]

Clinton announced in 1999 that "Plan Colombia" would provide greatly increased military, counter-drug, and economic assistance to Colombia and its Andean neighbors. Of the initial funding, 80 percent went to military and police assistance aimed at attacking the Colombian guerrilla armies and drug lords in addition to drug crop eradication. However, Clinton's commitment of aircraft and helicopters to Colombia in mid-2000 alarmed neighboring nations. At a meeting in Brazil, Venezuelan president Hugo Chávez remarked, "That's how Vietnam started."[72] The day before, Brazil's foreign minister, Luiz Felipe Lampreia, declared that his country was "greatly preoccupied" with the potential military consequences of Plan Colombia, predicting that the war would be even worse by the beginning of 2001.[73]

Clinton signed a presidential determination waiving human rights conditionality (the law's requirement that Colombian armed forces and police improve their human rights record to receive assistance) in the aid package for Colombia in August 2000.[74] By September 2000, Peru, Ecuador, Venezuela, and Brazil had deployed special units to their frontiers, anticipating the spillover from the fumigation operations and drug sweeps. Immigrants fleeing Plan Colombia created new security and humanitarian challenges for Ecuador and, to a lesser extent, for Colombia's other neighbors.[75]

Even as the war in Colombia intensified and spilled over to its neighbors and even as the ongoing drug wars transformed politics in Mexico, the Caribbean, and Central America, American civilian and military policymakers repeated ad nauseam the nostrum of democracy and "free markets." Throughout the 1990s, economic insecurity for millions of Latin Americans increased, as did personal insecurity with the rise in violent crime, including contracted murders and kidnapping for hire and profit. The pressures exerted on Latin American governments by the economic policies promoted by the United States, the International Monetary Fund, and the World Bank, the unrelenting war on drugs, and the lack of nuance and local knowledge by U.S. policymakers contributed significantly to these outcomes.

In response to these trends, anti-U.S. and antiglobalization social and political movements surged throughout the region. In Mexico, the Zapatistas rose in arms in 1994, proclaiming that NAFTA and free trade was a "death certificate for the Indian peoples of Mexico." In Venezuela, Hugo Chávez came to office in 1998 with a colorful antiglobalization and antineoliberal flourish. In 1999, massive protests overturned privatization of the water supply in Cochabama, Bolivia, and peasants mobilized to oppose President Hugo Banzer's collaboration with the American drug war.[76] The antiglobalization movement would grow worldwide into the twenty-first century, with sometimes-violent protests against international financial institutions, the World Trade Organization, and the G-8 Summit Meetings around the world, beginning in Seattle in 1999. The drug war and the American neoliberal economic package generated disorder and discontent not only in the Western Hemisphere but around the globe.

Once again, the Western Hemisphere would be a laboratory for policy later exported elsewhere. In 1999, the Pentagon transferred its Office for Inter-American Affairs from the Bureau for International Security to a bureau called Special Operations and Low-Intensity Conflict. Under the reorganization, Latin America was the only geographic area assigned to an office focused on issues like terrorism, drug enforcement, and other activities of Special Forces dedicated to MOOTW. Though unknown at the time, the war on terrorism in Latin America drew on the counterinsurgency experience of the Cold War. Civilian and military officials blooded in Latin America's not-so-Cold War would soon be directing key components of America's war on drugs and its global war on terror.

The 2000 Election

As the 2000 presidential election approached, the Republican Party reminded voters of a paradise lost by the Democrats since the end of the Cold War. In 1990, "around the globe, the word, the ideals and the power of the United States commanded respect." The Clinton administration had "squandered the opportunity granted to the United States by the courage and sacrifice of previous generations: The administration has run America's defenses down over the decade through inadequate resources, promiscuous commitments, and the absence of a forward-looking military strategy." The Republicans also echoed Harding, Coolidge, and Reagan: "International organizations can serve the cause of peace, but they can never serve as a substitute for, or exercise a veto over, principled American leadership. The United Nations was not designed to summon or lead armies in the field and, as a matter of U.S. sovereignty, American troops must never serve under United Nations command. Nor will they be subject to the jurisdiction of an International Criminal Court."

Republicans favored a "distinctly American internationalism" (Harding and Coolidge had called this idea "independent internationalism"). On Latin America, the Republican platform regurgitated the formulaic bipartisan liturgy, beginning with "democracy and free markets." Republicans also promised more active support for the anti-Castro dissidents and proclaimed that "under no circumstances should Republicans support any subsidy of Castro's Cuba or any other terrorist state."[77] The platform also listed Clinton's other failures in the Western Hemisphere: the problems of Mexico had been ignored, as the indispensable neighbor to the south struggled with too little American help to deal with its formidable challenges; the tide of democracy in Latin America had begun to ebb, with a sharp rise in corruption and narcotrafficking; a military intervention in Haiti displayed administration indecision and incoherence and, after billions of dollars had been spent, accomplished nothing of lasting value.

Although many domestic policy differences existed between the Republicans and the platform adopted by the Democrats, on foreign policy the parties agreed that the U.S. military must be kept strong and that the United States should promote increased trade and democracy. The Democrats called for "Prosperity, Progress, and Peace," even as violent antiglobalization protests marred the convention in Los Angeles, California, which nominated Clinton's vice president, Al Gore, as the party's presidential candidate. The platform called for "open trade" but also for trade agreements to protect labor and the environment. As to national security, the Democrats declared that "we must be able to meet any military challenge from a position of dominance" and reaffirmed the policy of "forward engagement," although, unlike the Republicans, the Democrats emphasized the importance of multilateralism, alliances, international organizations, and the United Nations. On Latin America, the platform mentioned the need to continue to combat narco-traffickers, especially in Colombia, and to "increase cooperation and trade." There was also the obligatory mention of bringing democracy to Cuba.[78] The Democrats emphasized what they characterized as the successes of the Clinton administration (Haiti, Bosnia, strengthening alliances in Asia, and NATO enlargement). Latin America, mentioned in passing, was described as "a focal point of our efforts to enhance economic development, stability, and prosperity." Candidate Gore repeatedly told Americans that he believed that America had a responsibility to lead in the world, and that the United States needed a security agenda for a global age based on "forward engagement."[79]

Andrew Bacevich captured exquisitely the foreign policy convergence of the Republican and Democratic parties in 2000: "They found the same intimate connection between U.S. foreign policy and America's domestic well-being. They shared an identical belief in the importance of U.S. military supremacy. They embraced the same myths about the past."[80] Of course, this was not new—Democrats and Republicans had agreed on the linkage between foreign markets, protectorate regimes in the Western Hemisphere, American naval power, and "domestic tranquility" since before the American Civil War.

In November 2000, Republican George W. Bush narrowly lost the battle for popular votes in the presidential election (47.9 percent to 48.4 percent). But Bush won the presidency in the electoral college after a contentious legal battle over the outcome in Florida. A controversial 5–4 Supreme Court decision gave Bush the keys to the White House, confirming a 271–266 electoral college margin for the Bush candidacy.[81]

Although they shared the same premises and some of the same blind spots, Gore and George W. Bush would not bring to the White House the same sort of advisers. Bush went back to hard-line Reaganites, members of the Committee on the Present Danger, the PNAC hawks, and personalities such as Otto Reich, John Negroponte, John Poindexter, and others who had orchestrated Reagan's Central American and Caribbean policies. His vice president, former secretary of defense Dick Cheney, had directed the Panama invasion in

1989 and had signed the Regional Defense Security document in 1993. Bush brought former secretary of defense and corporate magnate Donald Rumsfeld back to Washington as secretary of defense and appointed as secretary of state Colin Powell. Powell had overseen the invasion of Panama, as chairman of the Joint Chiefs of Staff. The Bush administration would again demonstrate how the concentrated powers of the presidency, the personalities and personal agendas of a small group of policymakers, and the debilitation of congressional oversight in the foreign policy process could shape American commitments and use of military force. With the PNAC, Committee on the Present Danger, Heritage Foundation ideologues, and corporate oil interests prominent in the National Security Council, Defense Department, and Department of State, the practical meaning of American "leadership" and full spectrum threat dominance would soon resonate around the globe.

Regarding Latin America, Bush's advisers criticized Clinton's neglect of the region and highlighted the failures: "Over the past decade, political unrest, transnational crime, drug trafficking and wars, and economic mismanagement reversed the encouraging democratic and economic reforms begun in the 1980s. The Clinton Administration neglected the commitments America made to support these reforms, and the opportunity for President Bush to recoup lost progress and set a new course is shrinking."[82] Bush's Latin American team lamented the growing diversification of Latin American military suppliers (including China) and also the gradual loss of U.S. economic weight, as investors and firms from the European Union, Japan, South Korea, Australia, Russia, and China took advantage of privatization schemes and market opportunities in the Western Hemisphere. In a sense, globalization and resistance in parts of Latin America to American policies eroded U.S. economic predominance and political influence (especially in the Southern Cone). Victory in the Cold War thus brought paradoxical consequences for the United States in Latin America. Instead of the "end of history," would there be an end to U.S. hegemony?

Quadrennial Defense Review 2001

By the time the second *Quadrennial Defense Review* (QDR) appeared in 2001, with a letter of transmittal signed by Secretary of Defense Donald Rumsfeld, U.S. national security concerns had understandably focused even more intensely on international terrorism than during the Clinton years. Shortly after the September 11, 2001, al Qaeda attacks on the World Trade Center and the Pentagon, defense policy analysts had also shifted subtly from assessing threats to *countering capabilities of potential adversaries.*[83] The 2001 QDR identified six operational goals for U.S. forces, including: "Deny enemies sanctuary by providing persistent surveillance, tracking, and rapid engagement" and "enhance the capability and survivability of space systems."[84] U.S. national defense and security included "the mission of space control . . . to ensure the freedom of action in space for the United States and its allies and, when directed, to deny such freedom of action to its adversaries."[85]

If this new mission made sense from a military perspective, its political and strategic implications, particularly for the sovereignty of almost 200 other nation-states, could not be disregarded. U.S. security doctrine and military missions seemed to preclude sovereignty for countries with interests incompatible with those of the United States, both on the earth's surface and now in space. With the number of potential state and nonstate adversaries, and the range of their known (and unknown) capabilities, greatly increasing, there seemed no rational limit to defense expenditures or to the sacrifices of civil liberties that Americans would have to make to achieve "full spectrum protection." Would the United States, if it deemed it vital to its self-defense, deny satellite communications and reconnaissance to other nations? Would article 51 of the UN Charter, as interpreted by American leaders, or the traditional doctrines of imminent threat and self-defense, justify American attacks on any country that it deemed a *potential* threat to its vital interests? Might American electoral politics "require" preemptive attacks? If so, did not America's forward presence and its strategic doctrine represent a potential threat to most every country in the world? What if Russia, China, Iran, or Brazil adopted and took seriously an analogue of U.S. national security doctrine, including American interpretations of anticipatory self-defense?

U.S. Navy captain Sam J. Tangredi (a senior military fellow, Institute for National Strategic Studies, National Defense University) remembered that the 2001 QDR had much in common with the approach to national security and global reach of Alfred Thayer Mahan's vision in the 1890s: "In the Quadrennial Defense Review Report of 2001, the Bush administration indicated its desire to move to a capabilities-based approach to defense, which it defines as a model focused 'more on how an adversary might fight than who the adversary might be and where a war might occur.' . . . Such would be a method of which Captain Mahan, with his desire to analyze the underlying principles of current history, would have undoubtedly approved."[86] In the final chapter of his edited volume *Globalization and Maritime Power*, Tangredi (along with more than thirty other authors) seemed to be a good disciple of Mahan.[87] Tangredi concluded: "*Homeland security blends with forward security, which blends with global security.* Global navies are the prime means of projecting sustained yet unobtrusive power across the great commons and into regions of potential crisis."[88] Predictably, a return to Mahan's strategic thinking reaffirmed the importance of the Caribbean basin to American security.

Dr. Colin S. Gray, a dual U.S./UK citizen and author of *The Sheriff: America's Defense of the New World Order*, went further.[89] Deliberately using the metaphor of a sheriff in the American Wild West, Gray, like Clinton and Bush, argued that the United States has a "global role as principal guardian of world order" and that, "despite heavy criticism from home and especially abroad, there is a need for the United States to be willing and able, very occasionally, to take preventive action in order to forestall future dangers."[90]

Whether it be the global navy — with its cruise missiles — satellite surveillance, space weapons, or deployment of ground forces, American civilian and military elites and leaders of both parties agreed that the United States had a unique historical mission in the era of globalization — as it had, in different ways, in every era since the inception. They also agreed, like Theodore Roosevelt's generation and much before, that America had to command its own destiny, to decide for itself when, where, and with what instruments to protect its vital interests and exercise its global benevolence. As in the past, a starting point for American grand strategy in the twenty-first century would be efforts to establish and sustain hegemony in the Western Hemisphere. And further militarization of U.S. foreign policy, as occurred during the Cold War in the Western Hemisphere, would be exported around the world. Military Operations Other Than War might encompass everything from disaster relief and humanitarian intervention to deterrence, special operations, and civic action. All such operations would help to "consolidate the Cold War victory."[91]

Chapter Fourteen

The New Normalcy?

The way I think about it, it's a new normalcy. . . . [The war] may never end [, at] least, not in our lifetime. — VICE PRESIDENT RICHARD CHENEY, 2001

Nine days after the September 11, 2001, attacks on the United States, President George W. Bush declared a Global War on Terror. As in America's war on the pirates of the Caribbean in the 1820s, there would be no sanctuaries in the Global War on Terror. Those who harbored the terrorists would also face America's wrath: "We will pursue nations that provide aid or safe haven to terrorism. Every nation in every region now has a decision to make: Either you are with us or you are with the terrorists. . . . From this day forward, any nation that continues to harbor or support terrorism will be regarded by the United States as a hostile regime." Bush added: "Our war on terror begins with al Qaeda, but it does not end there. It will not end until every terrorist group of global reach has been found, stopped and defeated."[1]

Responding to the attacks on the United States, the NATO Council invoked article 5 of the treaty regime for the first time — the attack on the United States represented an attack on all members of NATO. The alliance created in 1949 to contain the Soviet Union would now go on the offensive against militant Islamists in Afghanistan.[2] On October 7, 2001, Bush announced that the United States and its allies had begun strikes on al Qaeda camps and the military installations of the Taliban regime in Afghanistan.[3] America and its allies quickly ousted the country's Taliban government but failed to capture or kill al Qaeda leader Osama bin Laden.

A year later, the White House released the 2002 "National Security Strategy of the United States of America." The document began by acclaiming the Cold War victory and, seemingly, accepting Professor Francis Fukuyama's "end of history" thesis: "The great struggles of the twentieth century between liberty and totalitarianism ended with a decisive victory for the forces of freedom — and *a single sustainable model for national success*: freedom, democracy, and free enterprise. . . . We will defend the peace by fighting terrorists and tyrants."[4] As in the time of Woodrow Wilson's democratic crusade almost a century earlier, as America fought international terrorism it would also "use this moment of opportunity to . . . bring the hope of democracy, development, free markets, and free trade to every corner of the world."

Missed in this litany was the fact that al Qaeda had not attacked the United States to oppose democracy in America, free markets, or free trade. Nor were the Taliban in Afghanistan or millions of Muslims around the world, nor millions of other people of diverse faiths and ethnicities particularly attracted by the cultural and religious gifts offered by the most recent American civilizing mission. More broadly, much of the world and many of its sovereign governments, including China, Russia, and most of South Asia, did not share American enthusiasm for liberalism or "market democracy," whether in its conservative or liberal versions.[5] As historian and cofounder of the Project for a New American Century Robert Kagan put it: "To non-liberals, the international liberal order is not progress. It is oppression."[6]

In this most recent war on America's enemies, the United States was updating the concept of "imminent threat," which was first introduced with the No Transfer Resolution in 1811 and continued with Henry Clay's discourse on the need for anticipatory self-defense in the American annexation of West Florida in 1810. A basic premise of American strategy in the Western Hemisphere from 1810 to the 1930s had gradually become a first principle for global strategy. In the spring of 2002, Simon Serfaty, director of the Europe Program at the U.S.-based Center for Strategic and International Studies, concluded that "as deterrence of the groups willing (let alone able) to inflict such violence ceases to be credible, *preemption becomes the only reliable solution.*" Paraphrasing remarks by Vice President Cheney in late October 2001, Serfaty added that the "new normalcy" had "restored the legitimacy of force as the central pillar of a new international order that accommodates vital concerns of national security."[7] But to continue the war on terror until, literally, "every terrorist group of global reach has been found, stopped and defeated" was a recipe for perpetual war. Was that what Cheney meant by the "new normalcy"?[8]

In June 2002, President George W. Bush told the country that "we must take the battle to the enemy, disrupt his plans, and confront the worst threats before they emerge. . . . Our security will require all Americans . . . to be ready for preemptive action when necessary to defend our liberty and to defend our lives." Bush requested that Congress authorize deployment of U.S. armed forces against Iraq (the next target, after Afghanistan, in the war on terrorism). He followed precedents from the time of John Adams in 1798 in the Quasi-War against France to President Lyndon Johnson with the Tonkin Gulf Resolution in 1964 by asking for authorization to wage war without a declaration of war.[9] Theoretically, he risked a negative response from Congress, as had occurred with the various requests by James Buchanan to deploy forces to Central America and Mexico in the 1850s. But the September 11 attacks had transformed American politics, making congressional rejection of Bush's preemptive war unlikely.

After intense debate, Congress agreed (in the Senate, 77–23, and in the House of Representatives, 296–133) on a joint resolution giving the president broad, vague, and seemingly unlimited (by time or place of deployment) authority: "The President is authorized to use the Armed Forces of the United States as he determines to be necessary and appropriate in order to — (1) defend the national security of the United States against the continuing threat posed by Iraq; and (2) enforce all relevant United Nations Security Council resolutions regarding Iraq."[10]

Senator Robert Byrd (D.-W.Va.) unsuccessfully opposed S.J. 46, sponsored by Senator Joseph Lieberman (D.-Conn.) and John Warner (R.-Va.).[11] He sought to amend the resolution by imposing a one-year time limit on the authority granted to the president. Byrd's plea for restraint echoed those of legislators in the past — Whig senator Tom Corwin during the Mexican War, Speaker of the House Thomas Brackett Reed before the war with Spain in 1898, and Senator Robert La Follette in World War I — imploring his colleagues to put limits on presidential war making and to resist preemptive war. Byrd's remarks went to the heart of the moral, political, and constitutional issues of the last fifty years of American foreign policy:

> Mr. President, 38 years ago I, Robert C. Byrd, voted on the Tonkin Gulf Resolution — the resolution that authorized the President to use military force to "repel armed attacks" and "to prevent further Communist aggression" in Southeast Asia.
>
> It was this resolution that provided the basis for American involvement in the war in Vietnam.
>
> It was the resolution that led to the longest war in American history.
>
> . . . It was a war that destroyed the Presidency of Lyndon Johnson and wrecked the administration of Richard Nixon.
>
> After all that carnage, we began to learn that, in voting for the Tonkin Gulf Resolution, we were basing our votes on bad information. We learned that the claims the administration made on the need for

the Tonkin Gulf Resolution were simply not true, and history is repeating itself.

. . . So many people, so many nations in the Arab world already hate and fear us. Why do we want them to hate and fear us even more?

People are correct to point out that September 11 changed everything. We need to be more careful. We need to build up our intelligence efforts and our homeland security. But do we go around pounding everybody, anybody, who might pose a threat to our security? If we clobber Iraq today, do we clobber Iran tomorrow?

When do we attack China? When do we attack North Korea? When do we attack Syria?

. . . September 11 should have made us more aware of the pain that comes from being attacked. We, more than ever, are aware of the damage, the deaths, and the suffering that comes from violent attacks.

. . . This is what we are about to do to other countries. We are about to inflict this horrible suffering upon other people.

Of course, we do not talk about this. We talk about taking out Saddam Hussein. We are talking about taking out Iraq, about "regime change."

I do not want history to remember my country as being on the side of evil.

. . . Before I vote for this resolution for war, a war in which thousands, perhaps tens of thousands or hundreds of thousands of people may die, I want to make sure that I and this Nation are on God's side. I want more time. I want more evidence.

I want to know that I am right, that our Nation is right, and not just powerful.

On March 19, 2003, President Bush sent the following letter to the Speaker of the House and the President of the Senate:

Dear Mr. Speaker: (Dear Mr. President:)

Consistent with section 3(b) of the Authorization for Use of Military Force Against Iraq Resolution of 2002 (Public Law 107-243), and based on information available to me, including that in the enclosed document, I determine that:

(1) reliance by the United States on further diplomatic and other peaceful means alone will neither (A) adequately protect the national security of the United States against the continuing threat posed by Iraq nor (B) likely lead to enforcement of all relevant United Nations Security Council resolutions regarding Iraq; and

(2) acting pursuant to the Constitution and Public Law 107-243 is consistent with the United States and other countries continuing to take the necessary actions against international terrorists and terrorist organizations, including those nations, organizations, or persons who planned, authorized, committed, or aided the terrorist attacks that occurred on September 11, 2001.

Sincerely,
George W. Bush

The next day, the invasion of Iraq began. Congress had provided the president with sweeping authority — and a raft of blank checks. It next appropriated the funds to cover them, and continued to do so until the end of Bush's presidency. President Bush and his advisers, despite the warnings received from some of the country's most knowledgeable military officers, began a gigantic spending spree on a preemptive war.[12] No one could say that Bush lacked congressional authorization (unlike several of the instances when President Clinton had deployed American combat forces overseas) nor could it be said that American public opinion initially opposed the war in Iraq (according to a USA Today/Gallup poll in March 2003, around 75 percent of Americans approved of the invasion). President Bush was able to successfully link the invasion of Iraq to the Global War on Terror.[13]

The Iraq war gradually pushed up oil prices, devalued the American dollar, ground up American military equipment, eroded the strength of the U.S. Army, and undermined the George W. Bush presidency. It inflicted great misery on the Iraqi people and spread the pain, and refugees, to Iraq's neighbors. It threatened to provoke war with Iran and undermined American efforts to rebuild and stabilize Afghanistan. American casualties, dead and wounded, multiplied into the thousands. And the way America made war in Iraq corroded its remaining political and moral credibility in most of the world.

President Bush had justified the invasion of Iraq as both self-defense and as implementation of UN resolutions (particularly UN Resolution 687 from 1991) requiring Iraqi cooperation with UN weapons inspection teams. In this respect, Bush acted in accord with the war-making practices of American presidents that had evolved since 1798 and been greatly amplified since 1947, after formulation of the Truman Doctrine. Like President Clinton, he sought cover of legitimacy in collective security "entanglements" and alliances, as well as in the traditional sovereign right of self-defense.

Yet Iraq had not attacked the United States, or any of its NATO allies, and no evidence surfaced subsequently to suggest that Saddam Hussein intended to do so. After the invasion, no weapons of mass destruction were found.

Whether this outcome reflected bad intelligence or deliberate misrepresentation by the president, the vice president, the secretary of defense, and others regarding Iraqi weapons programs remains unclear, although as more revelations were made by the intelligence community, former presidential advisers, and foreign sources, the case for "ignorance" weakened.

In any case, UN Resolution 687 had no reference to enforcement by force of arms, either by the United Nations or by any of its member states. The United States and the United Kingdom claimed that since Iraq was in "material breach" of the cease-fire agreement arranged after the first Gulf War (1990), that they had suspended the cease-fire and renewed hostilities. Going back thirteen years to a 1990 UN resolution to find legal cover for the Iraq invasion in 2003 was a long stretch. The UN Security Council did not authorize military action against Iraq in 2003 nor would it update the 1990 resolution. The Anglo-American allies made their own determination and dressed their decision in the garb of dated UN resolutions.

The Bush administration had sought, clumsily and unsuccessfully, to influence the votes of key countries in the UN Security Council by threatening bilateral relationships with the United States. Chile, for example, was reminded that the U.S. Senate had under consideration a free-trade agreement, which might be rejected if the Chileans voted against the U.S.-sponsored resolution authorizing UN action against Iraq. The Chileans refused to be coerced, believing that Iraq had agreed to cooperate with the UN inspection teams, seeking a peaceful solution to the ongoing conflict in February and March 2003.[14] A temporary chill in U.S.-Chilean bilateral relations ensued. Likewise, President Bush sought unsuccessfully to pressure Mexican president Vicente Fox to support the United States in the Security Council. To punish Mexico's recalcitrance, Bush put bilateral trade and immigration negotiations on the back burner.[15] In the end, although Bush preferred the legal cover of an *updated* UN Security Council resolution, authorization by the U.S. Congress was sufficient for him to unleash the invasion.

When the invasion began, President Bush explained that it was meant "to disarm Iraq of weapons of mass destruction, to end Saddam Hussein's support for terrorism, and to free the Iraqi people."[16] Like many of his predecessors had, George W. Bush assured the country that America acted righteously to defend its own security and the peace of the world, even using the unfortunate term "crusade" to characterize this military mission to a Muslim country.[17] And like presidents since James K. Polk, Bush and his administration misinformed Congress and the American people as they sought to conflate the war on terrorism, the events of September 11, 2001, and the Iraq invasion.[18] Although the Bush team perhaps took media spin and outright lies to the American people to new levels, it nevertheless emulated the tactics of the administrations of Woodrow Wilson, Lyndon Johnson, Richard Nixon, and Ronald Reagan, with his Office of Public Diplomacy. Manufacturing fear of enemies, misrepresenting the military capabilities and intentions of potential adversaries, and manipulating public opinion with the equivalent of military psychological operations had become a routine instrument of governance by American presidents, no matter the occupant of the White House. Formulation and implementation of American foreign policy had come to depend on such deception of Americans and of Congress itself, beginning even before President Polk's negotiations of the Canadian boundary in the 1840s and the war against Mexico.[19]

Also, like many of his predecessors, Bush proclaimed that the United States acted not only to defend its own security but *to defend the world* against terrorism and tyranny: "Our nation entered this conflict reluctantly, yet with a clear and firm purpose. The people of the United States and our friends and allies will not live at the mercy of an outlaw regime that threatens the peace with weapons of mass murder. . . . This will not be a campaign of half-measures. It is a fight for the security of our nation and the peace of the world, and we will accept no outcome but victory."[20]

The United States and its allies routed the Iraqi military, deposed the government, and took Saddam Hussein prisoner. An Iraqi government emplaced by the American military occupation executed Hussein on December 30, 2006, after a theatrical "trial." Saddam Hussein had been guilty of many crimes against his own people and others, yet the trial he suffered shamed American commitments to the rule of law. After the rapid military victory over Iraq's armed forces, the messianism, ethnocentrism, and hypocrisy of American foreign policy historically was condensed in the extended debacle occasioned by the American occupation regime, with its gradually shrinking "coalition of the willing." In practice, the United States (approximately 250,000 troops) and Britain (approximately 45,000 troops) carried out the invasion, with small contingents from Australia (2,000 troops) and Poland (194 troops). Between 2003 and 2009, other governments committed forces to the Iraq war but then gradually withdrew them, including Honduras, Nicaragua, El Salvador, and the Dominican Republic.[21] The cost of deploying the Latin American troops was underwritten by the United States, provoking sarcastic commentary regarding the "coalition of the billing."[22] Among the Latin American nations, only El Salvador still maintained troops in Iraq in 2008; the last Salvadoran troops, involved in humanitarian and reconstruction missions, returned home in February 2009.[23]

In the years following the 2003 invasion, Senator Byrd's fears were realized.

America was mired in an Iraqi civil war and was engaged in counterinsurgency against countless and varied enemies. American use of secret prisons, "extraordinary rendition" (kidnapping, disappearing, and shipping prisoners to third countries to outsource torture), and American torture of prisoners at detention facilities like Abu Ghraib and Guantánamo belied American claims to support human rights around the world.[24] Attorney General Alberto Gonzales, with the approval of President Bush and Vice President Cheney, among others, claimed that the prisoners were "unlawful combatants" not covered by the Geneva Conventions. Gonzales sought to reinterpret the meaning of torture and to circumvent compliance with American and international law against it.[25] And, as in the past, a minority of Americans, some from within the military services, voiced their patriotic condemnation of the country's abandonment of its fundamental principles and commitment to human rights.

The U.S. Supreme Court seemed to reject the effort to make torture (called "enhanced interrogation" or "alternative procedures") both legal and official policy in 2006.[26] Nevertheless, Bush, Cheney, and Rumsfeld all insisted that some enhanced interrogation techniques (such as "water-boarding," that is, simulated drowning — a technique similar to the *tormenta de toca* used by the Spanish Inquisition) did not constitute torture. Such a claim flagrantly contrasted with American prosecution of Japanese military personnel after World War II for the same crimes, blatantly contradicted the Convention against Torture (1987) ratified by the United States in 1994, and violated American military law, field manuals, and practices.[27]

Within a year of the Anglo-American invasion, the struggle of Iraq's diverse peoples against the occupation had become a rallying cry across the Middle East, Eurasia, and South Asia for resistance against America's "civilizing mission." Iraq became a seed bed for Islamic militancy against the American crusade. In Afghanistan, the Taliban experienced a resurgence.

There had been no end to history.

BETWEEN 2003 AND 2009 America lost much of its remaining credibility around the world and in the Western Hemisphere — even with its allies. Its honor was tarnished and its economy was in crisis. Its "package" of democracy, free trade, and free enterprise was not in great demand. Privatization and the deregulation of capital and financial markets, which the United States had recommended to promote freedom and growth, had contributed to the massive debt crisis in Latin America in the 1980s and to another debt crisis in East Asia in the late 1990s (sometimes referred to as the IMF [International Monetary Fund] crisis). The implosion of the U.S. economy and massive efforts at government bailouts of the private financial sector came in the last year of George W. Bush's presidency, and the crisis continued into 2009. More "free enterprise" and less concern for human rights as the United States fought its war on terror had not improved conditions in the United States or in most of the world.

Most Latin Americans opposed the U.S. war in Iraq and questioned the sincerity of America's war on terror. American rhetoric was called to mind from the dirty wars and counterinsurgency campaigns of the Cold War.

With the end of the Cold War, the Clinton administration had made Latin America a laboratory for its globalization recipes — engagement, enlargement, and the Free Trade of the Americas initiative — just as Jefferson, Madison, Monroe, Polk, and Harrison had used the Western Hemisphere as a laboratory for American foreign policy doctrines and practices in the nineteenth century. Even before September 11, 2001, the war on drugs in the Western Hemisphere had become the war on narco-*terrorists*. The Clinton team resurrected dormant intelligence networks and training programs and created new ones similar to those that had nurtured Operation Condor and state terrorism in the 1970s and 1980s. In the post-Cold War era, they would be deployed against transnational terrorism and drug lords instead of international communism. As in the times of James Madison, James Monroe, James Buchanan, Benjamin Harrison, and Theodore Roosevelt, public order, stability, protection of foreign nationals, and investments in Latin America required the U.S. government to exercise a quasi-police power in the hemisphere. And, as had been the case since the mid-nineteenth century, some Latin American elites collaborated in implementing U.S. policies because they seemed to serve their own interests. But, despite billions of dollars in expenditures, the war on drugs and narco-terrorists failed. The blowback in terms of organized crime and surging violence wracked Latin America from the Southern Cone to Mexico, and it boomeranged back to the United States.[28]

Within Latin America, a resurgent wave of anti-neoliberal social and political movements gradually brought populist, nationalist governments to power in Venezuela, Argentina, Bolivia, Ecuador, and Nicaragua. More moderate, but still reformist, social democratic governments presided in Chile, Brazil, Uruguay, and even Honduras. Democratization in Latin America necessarily meant that elected governments, to be successful, had to distance themselves from unpopular American foreign policies. Indeed, for real democratization to take hold in Latin America required dilution if not the end of American regional hegemony. George W. Bush's policies and arrogant foreign policy style provided the ideal target for anti-Americanism. He became the most detested American president in Latin America since Theodore Roosevelt.

Yet, despite the failed drug war, increased criminal violence, and the challenges of globalization, the end of the Cold War had also brought unanticipated economic and political opportunities for Latin America. Liberation from surrogate superpower wars in the region and intensified technological and economic globalization gradually diluted U.S. influence. Just as Bolívar sought in the 1820s to buffer American dominance by establishing counterbalancing relations with Great Britain and other European powers, and just as European powers contested American efforts to establish economic and military predominance in the hemisphere before World War I, the post-Cold War era offered opportunities for Latin America to elude and challenge American hegemony. Alternatives for markets, investment capital, manufactured goods, and even military equipment and training existed in the European community, Russia, Canada, Australia, New Zealand, China, Japan, and South Korea, among the most prominent. European Union investors took advantage of privatization policies to acquire telecommunications, public utilities, and banking assets from Mexico to Brazil and Chile. Trade with China of 200 million dollars in 1975 had grown to 50 billion dollars by 2005; Chile and China signed a bilateral free trade agreement in November 2005, China's first such agreement in Latin America. South America looked increasingly to Europe and Asia; many of the countries in the Western Hemisphere bastion consolidated between the 1880s and World War II no longer remained so dependent or so vulnerable to American policies, investors, or even military assistance.

Some Americans worried about declining U.S. influence in the hemisphere. In 2006, Congressman Dan Burton (R.-Ind.), coauthor of the Helms-Burton legislation), observed that the Chinese presence in Latin America "is not conducive to the United States in pursuing her own goals." In the same year, Juan Gabriel Tokatlian, an Argentine policy analyst with years of experience in Colombia, asked dramatically: "Will the United States overcome its addiction to failed policies for its own sake and for the sake of its neighbors in the Western Hemisphere?"[29] Political scientist Jonathan Graubart and political economist Dipak Gupta asked rhetorically whether self-serving unilateralism and lack of regard for morality were "the inevitable outcomes of the U.S. foreign policy processes"?[30] Tokatlian's questions, and the answer provided by Gupta and Graubart, pointed toward the obvious conclusion: The way that American policy was formulated and its connection to domestic politics had created and sustained foreign policies in conflict with the country's proclaimed values and supposed exceptionalism since the 1790s. The policies of the George W. Bush administration were the most recent chapter is this story.

In response to American post-Cold War policies formulated by the George

H. W. Bush and Clinton administrations, there reemerged in the Western Hemisphere a "culture of resentment," a "rage against the prevailing system brought on by social exclusion and persistent poverty."[31] Past American wrongs and disgust for the present regional agenda fueled resistance to American policy. American policymakers and associated academics connected what they called radical populism and a "transnational culture of resentment" with "anti-globalization mobs," Islamic militants, revolutionaries, and terrorists of the past. According to Gabriel Marcella at the U.S. Army Strategic Studies Institute, all these created a crisis of legitimacy, authority, democracy, and governability in the Western Hemisphere.[32]

Writing in 2006, Peter Hakim, president of the Inter-American Dialogue think tank, observed: "Anti-Americanism has surged in every country in Latin America. People in the region, rich and poor, resent the Bush administration's aggressive unilateralism and condemn Washington's disregard for international institutions and norms."[33] A Zogby poll of Latin America's elites found that 86 percent disapproved of Washington's management of conflicts around the world.[34] Yet Hakim, like Marcella and many analysts of U.S. policy, was trapped in the present. The so-called culture of resentment was only the most recent expression of Latin American resistance to American disdain for the region's peoples, its cultures, and its countries' sovereignty. Venezuela's "radical populist" president Hugo Chávez sounded, in many ways, like an up-dated Juan Domingo Perón of Argentina, who insisted just after World War II on a "third way" for Latin America, "neither capitalist nor communist." Chávez exploited the legacy of ill will toward American governments and policies (theatrically suggesting that George W. Bush was the Devil at the United Nations in 2007), just as Nicaraguan poet Rubén Darío (*To Roosevelt*, 1904) had told President Theodore Roosevelt, "And, although you count on everything, you lack one thing: God!"

Yes, Darío told America that its mission lacked God; it was self-interested and unprincipled — profane. Darió's powerful message resounded backward and forward for American relations with Latin America:

You are the United States,
future invader of our native America
with its Indian blood, an America
that still prays to Christ and still speaks Spanish.
You think that life is a fire,
that progress is an irruption,
that the future is wherever
your bullet strikes.

What American policymakers and academics connected to the Pentagon called a "culture of resentment" stemmed from two centuries of American hubris and hypocrisy in its policies toward Latin America, many of them later exported worldwide. American policymakers have been addicted to failure, unable to empty the historical bilges of ethnocentrism and sentiments of cultural and political superiority. American governments have been unwilling to abide by international law or to respect the sovereignty of the country's supposedly equal Latin American neighbors.[35]

From the early nineteenth century, American governments had exported failed policies — even, most recently, the war on drugs and counterinsurgency and antiterrorism policies — from the Western Hemisphere around the globe. The George W. Bush administration renewed this unenviable legacy as part of its Global War on Terror. In September 2007, the official home page of the U.S. Southern Command explained that it continued "to support the War on Terrorism within our [Area of Responsibility] and provides a forward defense against known threats transiting through or emanating from it. We seek to deter aggression and coercion while retaining the capability to act promptly *in self-defense* and remain cognizant that the deterrence and defeat of certain threats, particularly Weapons of Mass Destruction . . . may require preemptive action. USSOUTHCOM will remain vigilant against threats at all times."

For Spanish America, preemptive U.S. intervention in self-defense — whatever the immediate threat used to justify the intervention — was very old news, dating from American annexation of West Florida and continuing with Texas, the Mexican War, the Spanish American War and the era of gunboat diplomacy. In the first decade of the twenty-first century, SouthCom would now monitor and seek to prevent internal or transnational threats to the stability of "democratic government" *as defined by the United States*. Washington and SouthCom echoed the Caracas Declaration of 1954, which preceded the U.S. intervention and regime change in Guatemala and the extension of the Cold War battle against communism, bringing military regimes and state terrorism to much of Latin America. That should not be a big surprise. In many ways, the war on terror had roots in the Cold War counterinsurgency operations in the Western Hemisphere and U.S. covert operations in Afghanistan in the 1980s.

During 2008, a renewed quest within Latin America for autonomy and regional multilateralism, excluding the United States, took form in the Union of South American States (UNASUR) and a new regional security agreement called the South American Defense Council. Brazil and Venezuela, for their own reasons, spearheaded this initiative, with Venezuela's Hugo Chávez re-

membering Simón Bolívar's call for a Hispanic American nation or confederation of larger states to balance American power in the hemisphere. Colombia
announced its reticence to join the new organization, partly because the conservative Álvaro Uribe government depended on Washington's support and
partly as a response to the recent conflicts over Revolutionary Armed Forces
of Colombia (FARC) guerrilla bases or sanctuaries in Venezuelan and Ecua-
dorean territory and Colombian intrusions (with U.S. intelligence and logistical support) into northern Ecuador to kill Raúl Reyes, a high-level guerrilla
FARC commander, and other combatants.

Less than two months earlier, the U.S. Navy had announced reestablishment of its Fourth Fleet (created in 1943 to patrol against German submarines
and blockade runners and then disestablished in 1950) "for U.S. Navy ships,
aircraft and submarines operating in the U.S. Southern Command . . . area of
focus, which encompasses the Caribbean, and Central and South America
and the surrounding waters."[36] The chief of Naval Operations, Admiral Gary
Roughead, who had served as the Department of the Navy's chief of legislative
affairs, declared that "re-establishing the Fourth Fleet recognizes the immense
importance of maritime security in the southern part of the Western Hemisphere, and signals our support and interest in the civil and military maritime
services in Central and South America." The reestablished fleet would "conduct varying missions including a range of contingency operations, counter
narco-terrorism, and theater security cooperation activities" and would be
commanded by Rear Admiral Joseph D. Kernan, at the time serving as commander of the Naval Special Warfare Command.

Of course, this Fourth Fleet was part of a much bigger vision. As Admiral Roughead told a Fredericksburg, Virginia, Chamber of Commerce dinner
crowd in March 2009: "A gray ship flying the American flag in every corner
of the world is a statement about who we are, what we are interested in, and
how we assure and deter in the far reaches of the earth."[37] Admiral Roughead
likely did not consider what memories such words would conjure up for Latin
Americans. He did not mention Alfred Thayer Mahan or Theodore Roosevelt's
Great White Fleet — perhaps because the navy ships "flying the American flag
in every corner of the world" were now painted battleship gray.

The Venezuelan government reacted quickly to the announcement: "They
don't scare us in the least. . . . Along with Brazil we're studying the creation of a
South American Defense Council [which would defend South America from
foreign intervention]. If a North Atlantic Treaty Organization exists, . . . why
can't a [South Atlantic Treaty Organization] . . . exist?" Bolivian president Evo
Morales called the U.S. naval force "the Fourth Fleet of intervention." Fidel
Castro suggested in early May 2008 that the move constituted a return to U.S.

gunboat diplomacy as well as a message to Venezuela and the rest of the region that had been electing left-wing governments opposed to U.S. hegemony in the Americas.[38]

At the least, the revived Fourth Fleet constituted a symbolic message to the "radical populists" and renewed support for Colombia in its war against the narco-terrorists and the FARC and threats from Venezuela and Ecuador if Colombia were to again violate the territory of its neighbors. The Venezuelan government responded with an invitation for Russian strategic bombers to visit the country in September 2008 and planned joint naval exercises with the Russians for later in the year. Russia, Iran, and Venezuela explored creation of a "natural gas OPEC" (Organization of Petroleum Exporting Countries), and Chávez called for creation of a strategic alliance with Russia "to protect Venezuela against an American invasion." In February 2009, the Bolivian government announced that Russia had agreed to provide military helicopters for antidrug operations and entered into contracts for development of natural gas fields. Russian interests already controlled major gambling businesses in Bolivia.

Meanwhile, China accelerated its investments in Latin American natural resources and expanded its trade throughout the region. More important, speculation existed that "for Latin America, China provides a compelling illustration that an underdeveloped country can achieve rapid economic growth and prosperity without liberalizing its political system. . . . The Chinese success story, coupled with Chinese economic and diplomatic overtures to Latin America, provide a compelling argument to those in the region who wish to resist the U.S. agenda for democratic institutionalization, free trade and economic reform."[39]

The old American dream of a separate sphere in the Western Hemisphere over which the United States could exercise primacy could not be sustained. Of course, the counterpart was that the United States had China surrounded by its bases and fleets in Asia and had populated Russia's perimeter with American bases and the expansion of NATO into former Warsaw Pact nations. Russia, China, and India were still digesting the Clinton administration's dismantling of Yugoslavia, and they witnessed repeated military interventions by the United States around the globe. Thus, Russian and Chinese diplomatic initiatives and military cooperation in Latin America could also be taken as a sort of tit for tat, as well as reminders that American engagement in "their" parts of the world might have consequences for the United States close to home.

At the end of 2008, before Barack Obama, America's first African American president, assumed office, the U.S. Western Hemisphere and global vision — "the new normalcy" — constituted a doctrinal formulation for perpetual war against terrorism and *other actual or potential threats* in the name of peace and security. American policy and official rhetoric seemed an unintentional parody of George Orwell's *1984*. In the name of democracy, American policy often subverted it. In the name of human rights and antiterrorism, American policy operated secret detention centers and practiced torture. In the name of freedom and self-determination, America engaged in global interventionism, creating and sustaining an empire of military bases and "lily pads" to the furthest reaches of the planet, with announced intentions of controlling outer space.[40] Without a trace of irony, a prominent sign visible from Interstate Highway 5 outside the U.S. Marine Corp's amphibious training base in Oceanside, California, proclaimed: "No Beach Beyond Reach."

Like America's Cold War policies toward Latin America, from 2001 to 2009 clandestine wars and intelligence operations in North Africa, the Persian Gulf, South Asia, and parts of the former Soviet Union were brewing poisonous spirits for America in the first decade of the twenty-first century. Congressional appropriations were diverted from their sanctioned purposes to intelligence and covert operational missions. The CIA and Special Forces operated well outside their legal mandates — and beyond the pale of international law. Lawyers in the Justice Department, at the orders of the president, the vice president, and other high-ranking officials, crafted legal opinions to justify barbarous treatment of prisoners and preposterous interpretations of the American Constitution itself. If the United States were not so powerful, who could doubt that Bush, Cheney, Rumsfeld, Alberto Gonzales, and other Americans would have faced the same sort of international sanctions, even trials for war crimes, as former Argentine, Chilean, Rwandan, and Serbian dictators? And who could say for sure that in future years their travels to Europe or elsewhere would not be interrupted with detention and trial — as occurred with General Augusto Pinochet in 1998 on an extradition request from Spain to Great Britain?

The world perceived that the former American president, vice president, secretary of defense, and attorney general had condoned cruel and unusual punishment, plainly put, *torture*, while claiming to defend democracy and human rights. But exaggerated presidential claims of "inherent constitutional powers" and "executive privilege," coupled to the Global War on Terror and congressional authorization of billions and more billions of dollars to continue the atrocities, no longer shocked the American public or the world community. Even most Americans who opposed the war in Iraq shared the belief that no higher law should govern American policy than its own interpretation of the requirements of national security — not its own laws, not international human rights law, no law at all beyond America's desire to command its own fortune. (In this respect, at least, American views were no more exceptional than those of British, Russian, Indian, Korean, French, and Chinese patriots defending their nations' sovereign rights.)

Yet, despite these widely shared tenets of American political culture, America's "fortune" was (and is) not entirely in its own hands. The 9/11 Commission report told Americans in 2004: "Terrorism against American interests 'over there' should be regarded just as we regard terrorism against America 'over here.' In this same sense, the American homeland is the planet."[41] By this reasoning, homeland security was planetary security. Just as American policymakers in 1811, 1823, 1846, and after announced that European initiatives that affected the Western Hemisphere, its backyard and bastion, might justify an American response in self-defense, now the entire planet had become the American homeland. Self-defense for America — reactive, anticipatory, or even preventive — extended to every remote spot on the globe.[42] Just as the No Transfer Policy and the expanded Monroe Doctrine had been exported to Asia and the Pacific by the late nineteenth century, now, in the twenty-first century, American security and national interests required forward deterrence, forward deployment, a global network of military bases, and control of outer space. America's military doctrine of "full spectrum threat dominance" imagined and created threats where none previously existed, precisely because it required security against *potential capabilities of potential adversaries*. Existing threats were ominous enough; defending against potential threats of potential enemies left little room for limited government, civil liberties, or tolerance of domestic opposition. Such policies also left virtually no place on the planet for other nations and peoples to exercise their sovereignty.

By 2008, the Bush administration had been discredited at home and abroad. The U.S. economy was in shambles, the war in Iraq had dragged on interminably, and there was a Taliban resurgence in Afghanistan. Most Americans believed that the Bush administration had eroded the country's image abroad. Only 11 percent of respondents in a Pew Research Center survey conducted in December 2008 said that Bush would be remembered as an outstanding or above-average president; his approval ratings had dropped to historic lows for an American president.[43] Both the Democratic and the Republican candidates in the presidential election campaigned on a slogan of "change" — and against Bush's record as president. Both agreed, however, that more troops had to be sent to Afghanistan, that the war on drugs and the war on terrorism were national priorities, that America must resist further intrusion by European and Asian nations into "our hemisphere," and that America was still the beacon of hope for the rest of the world.

Neither Republican John McCain nor Democrat Barack Obama questioned seriously how the American political system, its institutions, and the underlying political culture might be responsible for the current difficulties of the nation or the international system. They did not wonder out loud (how could they in an election campaign?) whether America's determination to be restrained by no higher law must be shed if America were to be once again seen as a beacon of freedom. They sought the presidency in a time of political and cultural polarization accompanied by international crisis — like Adams, Clay, Calhoun, Jackson, and Crawford in the 1824 electoral struggle that gave America, and the world, the Monroe Doctrine. As in 1822–24, American politics still required that the candidates out-patriot each other, reinforcing the myths and practices of an imperfect, aggressive democracy.

In November 2008, America elected its first African American president, Democrat Barack Obama. Obama promised change; his election was, in itself, symbolic of change — the hard-won, but still partial, victories of the civil rights movement dating back to the nineteenth century. America had changed — there could be no doubt of that. But it had also stayed the same. It believed in its own exceptionalism and that it should be the "leader" of the world.

Epilogue

When Barack Obama took office in January 2009, the United States confronted its worst economic crisis since the 1930s. Polarizing policy debates on social and economic issues resembled the early years of the New Deal under Franklin D. Roosevelt. Underlying the policy debates were "culture wars" anchored in religious, moral, and philosophical divisions within the country, along with racist undercurrents from groups ill-disposed to accept an African American president. Bitter opponents of Obama called him a "socialist" (an epithet in the United States) — and much worse. And the war on terror continued.

Despite the enthusiasm generated in some quarters by a president publicly committed to "change," the new national security advisor, retired marine general James L. Jones, quickly affirmed the administration's commitment to a "pro-active military" and to full spectrum dominance ("the ability of U.S. forces, operating alone or with allies, to defeat any adversary and control any situation across the range of military operations").[1] Obama retained former CIA director and Cold Warrior Robert Gates as his secretary of defense. In a wide-ranging speech at Kansas State University in November 2007, Gates had applauded the words of historian Donald Kagan in *On The Origins of War and the Preservation of Peace* (1995): "What seems to work best in world affairs . . . is the possession by those states who wish to preserve the peace of the preponderant power and of the will to accept the burdens and responsibilities required to achieve that purpose."[2] In short, Gates (and Obama) sought American global primacy and regional hegemony as outlined in the Defense Department's *Defense Strategy for the 1990s: The Regional Strategy* (January 1993).

Whatever changes in foreign policy might be ordered by President Obama, from greater respect for international human rights law to less rigid diplomacy with allies and adversaries, he seemed to share with his principal foreign policy advisers a belief in (or, at least, the usual rhetoric regarding) America's right and obligation to act unilaterally in the name of freedom, liberty, vital interests, and national security. Obama also implicitly accepted the premises of the "new normalcy" proclaimed by former vice president Cheney after September 11, 2001. His first budget message (February 26, 2009) reflected the fundamental continuity of American security policy, framed by a global war on the "enemies of freedom."[3] Although Obama mentioned the importance of alliances, partners, and cooperative security, the language in the budget message retained the focus on domination, by the United States, of the full spectrum of threats *around the world*, and also the sense of urgency of the last eight years under Bush's doctrine of preemptive war.[4]

To wage the global war on terrorists, Obama initially relied on experienced hands in the interagency labyrinth in which foreign policy was formulated and implemented. "Experienced" meant Cold War–hardened. By way of illustration, Assistant Secretary of Defense Michael G. Vickers had cut his teeth on counterinsurgency in the Western Hemisphere laboratory, and then he had gone on to Afghanistan and the Global War on Terror. He was a principal strategist for the Afghan war against the Soviets. He had operational and combat experience in Central America and the Caribbean.[5] According to one unofficial biography, "It was in Central America in particular that Mr. Vickers gained practical experience in insurgency and counterinsurgency operations," and Vickers received a citation for combat in Grenada. The *Washington Post* reported that "some Pentagon officials once jokingly referred to his efforts [at the Defense Department] as the 'take-over-the-world plan.'"[6] President Obama reconfirmed Vickers in his position at the Department of Defense. No doubt he was a capable and knowledgeable Cold Warrior, but would he, and would many more of his colleagues with shared experiences and worldviews, bring change to American grand strategy, covert operations, and special forces warfare around the world?

A first insight into how Obama might approach U.S.–Latin American relations was provided at the Fifth Summit of the Americas (April 17–19, 2009) in Port of Spain, the capital of Trinidad and Tobago. In March, Obama announced the appointment of career diplomat Jeffrey Davidow as White House adviser for the summit meeting. Among his many assignments during his more than thirty years of service, including as assistant secretary for Inter-American Affairs in the Clinton administration and as U.S. ambassador to Venezuela and Mexico, Davidow was a political officer in Chile from 1971 to 1974, during the period of the Nixon-Kissinger covert operations against Chile's president, Salvador Allende. By 2009, as a retired career ambassador, he was regarded as a highly qualified liberal internationalist (or, as some critics characterize this approach to foreign affairs, liberal interventionist). He took a leave from his position as president of the Institute of the Americas in San Diego, California, to serve in the Obama administration.

In presummit interviews, Davidow seemed to reaffirm, with updates, the familiar U.S. agenda for Latin America, especially free trade and democracy (meaning elected governments) and the usual concern with narco-traffickers, public security, and reducing poverty in the region.[7] However, Davidow also mentioned the need for gradual redefinition of relations with Cuba. During the summit, Davidow noted the strained relations of the United States with Venezuelan president Hugo Chávez but put the onus on Chávez to "take some steps" to improve bilateral relations.[8]

Davidow was keenly aware of Latin America's historical resentments toward the United States. But he exercised caution regarding concrete measures to improve hemispheric relations, especially any changes that might provoke immediate political opposition from the complex domestic coalitions that shaped U.S.-Latin American policies. Davidow's approach would characterize Obama's initiatives toward Latin America during his first year in office: a rhetoric of change constrained by the politics, policies, and personalities of the past.

During the 2008 presidential campaign, Obama recognized the burden of this legacy of American policy toward Latin America. He revived the spirit of Franklin D. Roosevelt's Good Neighbor Policy, emphasizing respect for sovereignty and pluralism in the hemisphere. He declared that it was "time to turn the page on the arrogance in Washington" and that he would promote "aggressive, principled and sustained diplomacy in the Americas from day one." In the first moments of his administration, Obama announced that the United States would close the Guantánamo prison in Cuba and that Americans would not torture captured enemy prisoners, an implicit criticism of his predecessor and also an indication that the United States might return to an emphasis on human rights last seen during the Carter administration.

Yet Obama also announced that CIA and other officials who had "acted under orders" would not be prosecuted for torturing prisoners of the American war on terror — a questionable decision by the president of a country that had signed the UN Convention against Torture. Although it was an "understandable" political move in the first months of his presidency, this decision might reaffirm the tradition of impunity that had begun with General Andrew Jackson in 1844. Bruce Fein, a Justice Department official in the Reagan administration, commented: "Obama has set a precedent of whitewashing White House lawlessness in the name of national security that will lie around like a loaded weapon ready for resurrection by any commander in chief eager to appear 'tough on terrorism' and to exploit popular fear."[9] Of course, Obama had not set the precedent; impunity for high officials committing crimes in the name of patriotism had a long history in America. It remained to be seen, however, whether Obama's Justice Department might find a way to overcome this legacy, just as Chilean, Argentine, and other Latin American governments had sought to overcome the tradition of impunity in the region by bringing to justice some of the military and civilian leaders responsible for human rights violations from the 1970s into the 1990s. How could the United States effectively promote human rights in the hemisphere while systematically violating such rights in its global war on terrorist organizations and then justifying impunity for such crimes on grounds of national security? Wasn't that exactly how the Argentine, Brazilian, Chilean, and other Latin American dictatorships sought to justify the atrocities they committed against their opponents (whom they called terrorists) from the 1960s into the 1990s?

Obama acknowledged that "mistakes" had been made in past U.S. policy toward Latin America. Addressing the hemisphere's political leaders, Obama reached out rhetorically, and literally, with handshakes for critics of American policy. His opening remarks at the summit brought applause, as he noted historical defects in American policy toward the region:

> I know that promises of partnership have gone unfulfilled in the past, and that trust has to be earned over time. While the United States has done much to promote peace and prosperity in the hemisphere, we have at times been disengaged, and at times we sought to dictate our terms. But I pledge to you that we seek an equal partnership. [Applause.] There is no senior partner and junior partner in our relations; there is simply engagement based on mutual respect and common interests and shared values. So I'm here to launch a new chapter of engagement that will be sustained throughout my administration. [Applause.]

Obama won over his fellow presidents and delegates with humor: "To move forward, we cannot let ourselves be prisoners of past disagreements. I am very grateful that President Ortega — [Applause] — I'm grateful that President Ortega did not blame me for things that happened when I was three months old. [Laughter.]" He also demonstrated once again his oratorical skill: "I didn't come here to debate the past — I came here to deal with the future. [Applause.] I believe, as some of our previous speakers have stated, that we must learn from history, but we can't be trapped by it." Obama promised future engagement based on equality and mutual respect.[10]

Like Franklin D. Roosevelt, in a time of economic strife and international conflict Obama had dressed the United States in its best Good Neighbor vestments. The interventionism of the past was supposedly over (as Franklin Roosevelt had promised in 1933); the treatment as unequal and inferior nations and peoples was history, to be learned from but not repeated. But whether Obama could overcome entrenched domestic interests that dominated hemispheric policies, such as the failed drug war, the country's perverse immigration policies, and the insulting annual "human rights certification" process, remained doubtful.

More important, Obama, like Roosevelt and his successors, was steeped in the tradition of American exceptionalism and the belief in the nation's historical mission. Such beliefs made unlikely an "equal partnership" with Latin American nations. From the first moments of his administration, Obama donned the mantle of the American crusader for freedom and took on the renamed global war on terrorist organizations as his own. In this crusade for freedom, the war against terrorists, and the war on drugs, the Western Hemisphere was a crucial element in U.S. grand strategy.

U.S. regional and global military strategy depended on a network of air bases for strategic airlift, aerial refueling, disaster relief, and "air mobility contingencies," a term elastic enough to cover U.S. operations around the world, including the war on drugs and the war against terrorist organizations. In Latin America and the Caribbean, the United States operated air bases in Puerto Rico and at Comalpa (El Salvador), Soto Cano (Honduras), Reina Beatrix (Aruba), Hato (Curaçao), and Manta (Ecuador). Theoretically, the base at Manta was limited to use in the drug war, but the war on drugs routinely overlapped counterinsurgency missions and even surveillance of illegal migration. In 2008, Ecuador's government gave official notice that the lease on the Manta facility would not be renewed. The last U.S. troops left in September 2009.

After a meeting between Obama and Colombia's president Álvaro Uribe, on June 30, 2009, the Pentagon announced that Colombia would make five facilities available during ten years (that is, beyond Obama's presidency, even if reelected for a second term) for U.S. air missions in the drug war and the war against terrorists. Colombia would also allow the U.S. Navy access to installations at Cartagena and Málaga Bay. Although these would not technically be U.S. bases, in its budget request of some 46 million dollars for "upgrades" at Colombia's Palanquero air base, the White House asked for funds to finance "contingency operations," a term as elastic as the commitment to "full spectrum dominance."

In geostrategic terms, beyond replacing the base at Manta, the agreement on Palanquero was an update of Alfred Thayer Mahan's call in the 1890s for coaling stations in the hemisphere to support America's "New Navy" and its emerging global grand strategy. According to the U.S. Air Mobility Command, current U.S. grand strategy required "cooperative security locations" for regional airlift and global contingency operations. Replacing the base at Manta with Palanquero and other Colombian facilities meshed with U.S. global strategic doctrine for the twenty-first century.[11] (The Pentagon also sought new facilities in French Guiana, which would allow airlift capability into Africa.)[12] As part of the new Colombian agreement, the Obama administration requested increased funding for military assistance, including counterinsurgency equipment and training for the Colombian armed forces, despite frequent allegations of human rights violations by Colombian security forces.[13]

These initiatives were consistent with candidate Obama's campaign literature, which promised increased support for the war on drugs and the fight against the Revolutionary Armed Forces of Colombia (FARC) guerrillas, further promising that "in an Obama administration, we will support Colombia's right to strike terrorists who seek safe-haven across its borders, to defend itself against FARC, and we will address any support for the FARC that comes from members of neighboring governments because this behavior must be exposed to international condemnation and regional isolation."[14] Thus, Obama's campaign document lent support to Colombia's attack on FARC camps in Ecuadorian territory — a measure condemned by governments throughout the hemisphere. As Americans had done since the 1820s, including Bill Clinton and George W. Bush most recently, Obama proposed a policy of "no sanctuary" for terrorists. As an added benefit for U.S. Southern Command (SouthCom), the agreement with Colombia would put new American intelligence and special forces operations close to the Ecuadorian and Venezuelan borders.

Some Colombians protested that the new base agreement with the United States would violate the country's constitution, article 173, prohibiting foreign troops on Colombian soil except in transit — and then only after approval by the Colombian senate. This objection seemed tardy, since U.S. forces and private military contractors already operated out of almost a dozen Colombian installations as part of Plan Colombia, initiated in the Clinton administration. Elsewhere in South America, with the exception of Peru, reaction to the expansion of the U.S. military footprint on the continent was generally negative. Venezuela's Hugo Chávez labeled the agreement part of a plan to invade Venezuela; in early September he announced the purchase of 100 Russian tanks. Simultaneously, Chávez also reaffirmed preferential access of Russian energy firms to Venezuelan oil, followed by an announcement of a multibillion-dollar contract and joint venture with China for exploration and production in the Orinoco oil field.

With the news regarding the U.S. base agreement with Colombia, President Rafael Correa announced that Ecuador was shopping for Israeli drones to monitor the border with Colombia and revealed new contracts with Brazil to provide Ecuador with military aircraft. Bolivian president Evo Morales revealed that he would buy a presidential plane from Russia, that the Russians would construct an installation to service Russian-built aircraft in Bolivia, and that he would seek fighter aircraft from Brazil or China—since the United States had vetoed acquisition of planes from Czechoslovakia made with U.S. components.[15] Meanwhile, Brazilian president Lula da Silva declared: "I don't see why we need an American military presence on our continent."[16] (Lula had been the first Latin American president to meet with Obama after his inauguration, in March 2009.) Even Chilean president Michelle Bachelet found the plan for new bases "disquieting."

In early September 2009, the presidents of twelve South American nations held a special summit meeting of the Union of South American States (UNASUR) in Bariloche, Argentina, to discuss the implications of the new U.S. bases and to consider regional policy on bilateral base agreements. No agreement could be reached on a proposal by Bolivian president Evo Morales to "declare foreign bases unacceptable in South America."[17] Nevertheless, Obama's bilateral agreement with Colombia would further militarize U.S. policy in the region without prior consultation with concerned Latin American nations. American unilateralism had been reaffirmed, seemingly in contradiction to Obama's pledge of "engagement among equal partners." This lack of consultation particularly offended Brazilian policymakers, who shared permeable borders and security threats with Colombia, Venezuela, Peru, and Bolivia.

If the United States intended to enhance its political and economic influence in the Western Hemisphere, to deter a South American arms race, or even to give the appearance of a "good neighbor," Obama's initial policies were not working. For some Latin Americans, rather than change, Obama's first moves in the hemisphere seemed more of the same.

Yet it was still early in the Obama administration. Overall policy toward Latin America and bilateral relations in the hemisphere were in flux. On June 28, 2009, Latin America witnessed a perplexing U.S. government response to an apparent coup d'état in Honduras. The coup ousted President Manuel Zelaya in favor of a clique of conservative politicians and military officers headed by Roberto Micheletti (president of the Honduran congress).[18] Coup supporters proclaimed that they had defended the constitution and democracy against usurpation by an incumbent president — a common claim of coup makers in Latin America throughout the nineteenth and twentieth centuries. They also rejected the term "coup," claiming that the constitution allowed the supreme court to order the president's removal from office.

What had provoked Zelaya's ouster? Zelaya, a wealthy Liberal Party politician, had made himself over into a populist reformer. He had declared in August 2008 that Honduras would join the Bolivarian Alliance of the Americas (ALBA, *Alianza Bolivariana para los Pueblos de Nuestra América*), the Venezuelan-sponsored regional alternative to U.S. "development" institutions and free trade policies.[19] According to Venezuelan president Hugo Chávez, ALBA was a reincarnation of Simón Bolívar's dream of Spanish American regional integration (to protect itself from American domination), updated with his own vision of "socialism for the 21st century."[20] In late May 2009, Zelaya had announced that the Soto Cano base, the headquarters for U.S. Joint Task Force Bravo, would be converted into an international civilian airport, using funds provided by Venezuela.[21] Honduras also received oil subsidies from the Venezuelan-financed PetroCaribe, created, according to the Venezuelan government, to overcome the corrupt and exploitative networks of multinational corporate oil interests. Thus, Zelaya had challenged the Honduran political elite, multinational corporations, and the long-standing U.S. influence and military presence in Honduras.

The U.S. government denied any involvement in Zelaya's ouster.[22] The day after the coup, Obama declared: "It would be a terrible precedent if we start moving backwards into the era in which we are seeing military coups as a means of political transition, rather than democratic elections."[23] Notwithstanding Obama's pronouncement, many Latin American and U.S. observers saw the hand of the U.S. government in the coup. They immediately noted that, like tens of thousands of Latin American military personnel, the coup leaders, General Romeo Vásquez Velásquez (head of the armed forces, who was dismissed by Zelaya shortly before the coup but restored to command by the Honduran supreme court) and air force general Luis Javier Prince Suazo (commander at the Soto Cano base), had attended courses at the U.S. School of the Americas (now the Western Hemisphere Institute for Security Cooperation, WHINSEC).[24] A week before Zelaya's ouster, Assistant Secretary of State for Western Hemisphere Affairs Thomas Shannon and Deputy Assistant Secretary of State Craig Kelley met in Honduras with the civilian and military groups that later participated in Zelaya's ouster — ostensibly to avert the coup. In addition, John Negroponte, former ambassador to Honduras (during the Contra war against Nicaragua) and George W. Bush's director of Intelligence, was working as an adviser to Secretary of State Hillary Clinton. Clinton initially refrained from characterizing Zelaya's ouster as a military coup d'état, because under U.S. law such a label would trigger trade sanctions against Honduras.[25]

The Honduran coup presented Obama with a familiar challenge: whether to support a U.S.-friendly government that had overthrown a Latin American reformer or to affirm support for a democratically elected government and insist on compliance with the Inter-American Democratic Charter proclaimed in Lima on September 11, 2001.[26]

In late July, at a news briefing, Assistant Secretary of State Philip J. Crowley reinforced the idea that the tepid U.S. policy toward the Honduras coup makers formed part of a broader hemispheric thrust against the spread of Chávez-style populism: "We certainly think that if we were choosing a model government and a model leader for countries of the region to follow, that the current leadership in Venezuela would not be a particular model. If that is the lesson that President Zelaya has learned from this episode, that would be a good lesson."[27]

Despite this apparent expression of satisfaction with the results of the coup (if not with the coup itself), in late August the Obama administration curtailed some 30 million dollars of aid to Honduras, revoked the visas of Honduras's interim president and also of fourteen supreme court judges, and threatened to cancel 200 million dollars in pending foreign aid. A week later, Congressman Howard Berman, chair of the House Committee on Foreign Affairs, called for the State Department to make a formal determination that a coup had occurred in Honduras, followed by a cutoff of most foreign aid. Nevertheless, Honduran officers continued their courses at WHINSEC, and the base at Soto Cano operated routinely. Toward the end of September, Joint Task Force Bravo heralded its participation in PAMAX 2009, an annual SouthCom joint and multinational training exercise tailored to the defense of the Panama Canal, involving civil and military forces from around the world.[28]

Obama's dilemma in making policy toward the Honduran coup was emblematic of the gap between his calls for "change" and the special interests, entrenched bureaucratic agendas, and Pentagon security doctrine in the Western Hemisphere. Obama faced opposition to a more aggressive policy against the interim Honduran government within the State Department, Defense Department, and in Congress from the old anti-Castro and Cold Warrior coalition. Congressman Connie Mack (R.-Fl.) declared: "The Honduran people seek freedom, security and prosperity for their country. They deserve our support, not punishing sanctions and severe reductions in aid."[29] Mack, the ranking member of the House Western Hemisphere Subcommittee, had previously called Honduras "the epicenter of the struggle for freedom and democracy in Latin America" and had called Chávez a "thugocrat" who should be treated "in the way U.S. policy used to deal with communist nations." In early September 2009, Mack called upon Obama to "stand firm against Chávez and other enemies of freedom. We can start by adding Venezuela to the list of state sponsors of terrorism. I call on the President to do just that."[30] Mack did not offer any insight on how such a decision would affect U.S. imports of Venezuelan oil — through June 2009 Venezuela was the fourth-leading exporter of oil to the United States.[31]

To register their opposition to Obama's policy toward Honduras, Republicans held hostage the confirmation of his nominee for assistant secretary of state for Western Hemisphere Affairs, Arturo Valenzuela, a well-known academic and expert on Latin America who had served in the first Clinton administration as deputy assistant secretary for Inter-American Affairs. Senator Jim DeMint (R.-S.C.) complained that "President Obama rushed to side with [Venezuelan President Hugo] Chávez and [Cuban leader Raúl] Castro before getting the facts. . . . Now it's clear that the people of Honduras were defending the rule of law, yet this administration still supports Zelaya's efforts to become a dictator and return to power."[32] Right-wing bloggers and lobbyists maligned Valenzuela with clearly false accusations about his writings and policy views in efforts to deter Obama from more forceful support for Zelaya's return to the presidency.[33] The attacks on Valenzuela and on Obama's Honduras policy melded with domestic debates on health care, social issues, deregulation, and the more general "tea party protests" against "big government," "socialism," "bailouts," and a range of other issues, including welfare reform and protection of property rights.[34] As with the battles between the Federalists and the Jeffersonians in the beginnings of the Republic, there could be no easy separation of foreign policy and domestic politics for Obama in 2009.

In the months after the coup, the Obama administration waffled on its Honduran policy, hoping for a solution from mediation by former Costa Rican president Oscar Arias, who had won a Nobel Prize for his efforts to end the Central American civil wars and insurgencies of the 1980s. Arias proposed the return of Zelaya to the presidency until the elections scheduled for November and immunity for the coup makers for their actions. Such an outcome would allow a symbolic return to "democracy" and provide legitimacy for a newly elected Honduran government toward the end of 2009.

The Obama administration could hope that a new Honduran government might break with Chávez and ALBA and reaffirm the country's historic collaboration with U.S. policy in Central America and beyond. But, short term, the coup makers complicated U.S. tactics by rejecting Zelaya's return and threatening him with prosecution for violating the constitution and for a raft of other supposed crimes, should he dare to enter Honduras.

On September 15, Zelaya celebrated Central American independence from Spain (in 1821) with Nicaraguan president Daniel Ortega at the historic Hacienda San Jacinto, where Nicaraguan forces defeated American filibusterer William Walker in 1856. Zelaya proclaimed: "On this historic site . . . we continue struggling for *la Patria*, because our adversaries and enemies continue to be the same [as in 1856, meaning Americans intervening in Central American affairs]."[35] Six days later, Zelaya sneaked back into Honduras and took refuge in the Brazilian embassy. From this refuge, he called for dialogue with the coup makers. After military and security forces surrounded the embassy, cut off power, and arrested hundreds of Zelaya supporters, the U.S. State Department issued a statement calling for calm and urging the contending forces to accept Organization of American States (OAS) mediation: "We stress the need for dialogue; the United States supports the proposed mission by the Organization of American States to promote this dialogue. We encourage the parties to sign and implement immediately the San Jose Accord [proposed by Oscar Arias], which remains the best approach to resolve this crisis."[36] Quickly, U.S. diplomats moved to restore electricity to the Brazilian embassy, and Brazil's president proposed a meeting with Obama to work together on a solution to the Honduran political crisis.

Perhaps Obama could turn the crisis to the good, particularly if it could lead to high visibility cooperation with Brazil and the OAS. But U.S. domestic politics could not be overlooked. On September 24, Congressman Aaron Schock (R.-Ill.), citing a Congressional Research Service report, insisted that Zelaya's ouster had been legal and that no coup had occurred (although flying the Honduran president out of the country did violate the Honduran constitution's prohibition on banishment or expatriation).[37] The congressman called on Obama to renew U.S. aid to Honduras and end the visa sanctions imposed against the interim government.

As September ended no immediate resolution of the Honduran crisis was in sight. The interim government faced regional and domestic pressures to negotiate with Zelaya but insisted he could not return to the presidency — nor could his plebiscite on constitutional reform be reconsidered. Zelaya called for a "peaceful insurrection" to restore him to the presidency and considered the possibility of a parallel government, financed by ALBA, PetroCaribe, and other foreign supporters. Such a proposal created diplomatic problems for Brazil, the OAS, and the United States. Allowing Zelaya to remain as a short-term "guest" was acceptable to Brazil, but the embassy could not be used as a base for an insurrectionary movement against the interim government. All parties looked toward the late November elections as the obvious longer-term break from the impasse, although the period between the elections and the inauguration of a new president, scheduled for January 27, 2010, left room for more political surprises.

In November, Hondurans elected Porfirio "Pepe" Lobo of the National Party as their next president. The day before Lobo's inauguration, the Honduran congress proclaimed an amnesty for all involved in the June coup and the supreme court dismissed charges against the military commanders who had ousted Zelaya. Lobo then arranged Zelaya's safe conduct from the Brazilian embassy, en route to the Dominican Republic.

The Obama administration had negotiated with Senator DeMint over recognition of the election outcome, without Zelaya's reinstatement, in return for Senate confirmation of Valenzuela as assistant secretary of state and Shannon's confirmation as ambassador to Brazil. At least that was the post on Senator DeMint's website on November 5, 2009: "I trust Secretary Clinton and Mr. Shannon to keep their word. I will . . . continue closely monitoring our administration's future actions with respect to Honduras and Latin America."

Obama's response to Zelaya's ouster reflected discord in the U.S. policy establishment and Congress over regional policy, and erosion of U.S. control over hemispheric events. It also highlighted the gap between Obama's rhetoric and the degree and kind of "change" he would promote in the hemisphere. The events in Honduras revealed the influence on Obama's Latin American policy of old guard politicians and Cold Warriors, U.S. business interests, the Cuban lobby, Clinton-era advisers, and the Pentagon's global strategic vision. Although the United States and several Latin American governments recognized the electoral outcome, most members of the OAS faulted the United States for failing to uphold the 2001 Inter-American Democratic Charter.

OBAMA'S FIRST DECISIONS on U.S.-Cuban relations also demonstrated the tension between "change" and the ossified policies toward Latin America — especially toward Cuba — still favored by many executive-branch policymakers, legislators, and lobbyists. Notwithstanding the president's declared intention to "seek a new beginning" with Cuba, shortly after the April summit meeting in Trinidad and Tobago Secretary of State Hillary Clinton told Congress that the Castro government was a "regime that is ending," and the State Department reaffirmed Cuba's membership on the list of "state sponsors of terrorism." Cuban foreign minister Bruno Rodríguez responded by calling the U.S. government an "international criminal." He added: "In matters of terrorism, the government of the United States has had a long record of state-sponsored acts of terrorism, not only against Cuba."[38] On September 11, 2009, the Obama administration extended the trade embargo on Cuba for one year.

In a memorandum addressed to Secretary of State Clinton and Treasury Secretary Timothy Geithner, Obama wrote: "I hereby determine that the continuation for one year of the exercise of those authorities with respect to Cuba is in the national interest of the United States."[39]

Why was the embargo on Cuba still in the national interest of the United States? What threat did Cuba represent to U.S. national security in 2009? Why did the Obama administration insist on Cuba's continued inclusion on the membership list of "state sponsors of terrorism," along with only three other countries — Iran, Sudan, and Syria?[40] How did these decisions reflect a new policy of "engagement and mutual respect?" Or did Obama's memorandum really mean that reaching agreements on too many other pending political issues might depend on Republican and moderate Democratic votes, thus making change in policy toward Cuba impracticable in the administration's first year? Was this decision simply an implicit acknowledgment that U.S. policies toward Cuba and Latin America were still formulated, largely, by people identified with the ideas, special interests, policies, and practices of the past? And was it also acknowledgment that Obama believed that he could not afford to confront directly the Cuban lobby and its conservative allies — at least not until Congress acted on crucial domestic legislation such as health care, financial reform, and perhaps energy policy?

In still another illustration of Obama's inability to quickly break free from his predecessor's policies in the Western Hemisphere, he decided in late June 2009 to maintain Bolivia's suspension from the trade benefits of the Andean Trade Promotion and Drug Eradication Act (ATPDEA). The Bush administration had implemented this suspension because, allegedly, Bolivia was not complying with its obligations to control the drug trade. In January 2009, Bolivia's president had ordered Drug Enforcement Agency agents out of the country, for "engaging in espionage" and for "illegal political activities, abuse, and arrogance." The Washington Office on Latin America, a liberal think tank in Washington, D.C., reported: "Evidently, the Obama administration was internally divided about reinstating Bolivia as an ATPDEA beneficiary, and faced strong opposition from some lawmakers, including Senator Charles Grassley, the Iowa Republican whose membership on the powerful Finance Committee positions him to play a pivotal role on some of the Administration's top legislative priorities this year. The forward-looking aspirations from the April Summit succumbed to bureaucratic inertia in Washington — Obama's eventual ATPDEA decision remained tethered to the past."[41] Whether or not Grassley had been the key, the decision to continue the exclusion of Bolivia from the ATPDEA hardly demonstrated a new policy of "equal partnerships," with "no senior or junior partners."[42]

Such decisions in the first year of the Obama administration raised serious questions about U.S. policy toward Latin America. How could Obama make good his pledge of a "new partnership?" How could he transform the conflicting interests that shape U.S. trade, immigration, antidrug, security, and "democracy promotion" policies into a more benign agenda toward its southern neighbors? How could he break the connections among the lobbyists, donors, political parties, and corporate interests that dominated the country's politics (and continued to be represented within his administration at the highest levels)? How could he end the addiction to the failed war on drugs—in the United States and abroad? How could Obama give a different meaning to the American mission and commitment to democracy in the Western Hemisphere? How could he undo two centuries of disdain for Latin Americans in American government and public opinion?

OBAMA'S TETHER TO the past was not limited to policy toward the Western Hemisphere. In his first address to Congress, he reaffirmed America's role as global leader: "There is no force in the world more powerful than the example of America. . . . As we stand at this crossroads of history, the eyes of all people in all nations are once again upon us—watching to see what we do with this moment; waiting for us to lead."[43] Obama did, however, offer some hint of change in foreign policy style and tactics. At the G-20 Summit in early April 2009 he remarked: "I do not buy into the notion that America can't lead in the world. I just think, in a world that is as complex as it is, that it is very important for us to be able to forge partnerships as opposed to simply dictating solutions."[44]

In spite of the need for partnerships and Obama's opposition to the invasion of Iraq in 2003, he proclaimed repeatedly that the war against al Qaeda and other terrorists had to be intensified. Shortly after taking office, he ordered more troops to Afghanistan and authorized increased missile attacks by drones against targets in Pakistan. Albeit with a new name ("war on terrorist organizations"), Obama inherited and expanded America's global war against al Qaeda and other groups designated as terrorists by the U.S. government. On March 27, 2009, Obama declared: "The core goal of the U.S. must be to disrupt, dismantle, and defeat al Qaeda and its safe havens in Pakistan, and to prevent their return to Pakistan or Afghanistan."[45]

In modern times, no power has ever fully conquered Afghanistan nor effectively controlled its territory. Indeed, no Afghan government has done so. There is no reason to believe that the United States could succeed in such an endeavor at which the Mongols, Persians, British, and Russians have failed. Beyond Afghanistan, al Qaeda might have operatives in more than fifty countries. As he ran the risk of making the war in Afghanistan "Obama's war" (like Madison made the War of 1812 "Mr. Madison's war" and Lyndon Johnson made the war in Vietnam "Johnson's war"), Obama did not indicate what limit there would be to American determination to pursue the enemy until, in the words of his predecessor, "every terrorist group of global reach has been found, stopped and defeated." On the other hand, Obama did express some skepticism regarding expanding the objectives of the war in Afghanistan. On CBS's *Face the Nation*, on September 20, 2009, Obama told the television audience: "We're not going to put the cart before the horse and just think by sending more troops we're automatically going to make Americans safe."[46]

Although Obama had doubts on the war in Afghanistan, he would not be constrained in the war against terrorist organizations by Pakistan's (or any other nation's) sovereignty. And, although he ruled out torture and proclaimed American support for human rights, many of the Obama administration's early decisions on matters of national security, state secrets, and civil liberties led the *Wall Street Journal* to editorialize that "it seems that the Bush administration's antiterror architecture is gaining new legitimacy."[47]

Obama had inherited not only Bush's "antiterror architecture," but also the legacy of two centuries of America's belief in its own exceptionalism and global mission. This legacy had led to disaster and defeat in Vietnam and, more recently, to civil war, tragedy, and the creation of a seedbed for terrorism and regional anti-Americanism in Iraq. Expanding the war in Afghanistan promised more of the same — with no likelihood of victory — even if the nature of such a "victory" could be defined. There was no prospect that U.S. economic and military assistance could transform Afghanistan into a western liberal democracy, or that, in the immediate future, a government in Kabul could gain effective control over the national territory.

Toward the end of 2009, Obama faced pressure from some of his generals, the old Cold Warriors, and the Pentagon–Drug Enforcement Agency addicts of the war on drugs to send thousands more troops, at great expense in money and blood, to fight a war that would, inevitably, make more enemies for America. If he failed to answer the call, he might be accused of "losing Afghanistan" (as Truman had "lost" China and Carter had "lost" Iran and Nicaragua). If he upped the ante, as his generals requested, he risked the fate of Lyndon Johnson, a one-term president, and America risked another gruesome failed mission in South Asia.

George W. Bush had left Obama a crashed economy and some hard foreign policy choices. Among the most visible were what to do in Iraq, Afghanistan, and Pakistan; how to engage Iran and North Korea on their nuclear programs; how to redefine and restructure the NATO alliance; how to respond to China's growing power, to changing politics in Japan, and to Russian resentment of U.S. policy in Central Europe; and, in the Western Hemisphere, how to manage the erosion of U.S. influence and the appeals of what the Pentagon had called "radical populism." Underlying each of these challenges was a common geostrategic dilemma: If Obama did not shed the Pentagon's post–Cold War security doctrines, including the quest for full spectrum dominance and preemptive war, and if he did not reject Cheney's "new normalcy" for the United States itself, there would be no fundamental change for American politics, for inter-American relations, or for the international community — only perpetual war, with its nefarious domestic consequences.

American ascendancy to superpower status and, after the Cold War, to pretensions of global primacy made America's tradition of messianism and unilateralism ever more dangerous for the rest of the planet and for America itself. At the same time, in practice, it made American primacy, and perhaps American democracy, ever less sustainable. Could Obama pursue the wars in Afghanistan and Pakistan and send thousands more American troops to Afghanistan, former Soviet republics, Africa, and Asia without following in the deceptive practices of his predecessors? Could he establish new American "cooperative security locations" in Latin America (and around the world) without rekindling bitter memories from the past and resurgent anti-Americanism? Could he accept the implications of the unending quest for full spectrum dominance without further bloating the budget for the military and intelligence establishments and further corroding America's republican institutions and democracy?

Even America, with all its vast wealth and military power, cannot withstand forever endless war, corruption, malfeasance, stupidity, and arrogance. It must share the Earth with other nations and peoples on a more equitable basis or lose itself and its dream. James Madison, though he did not always follow his own advice, had it right in his oft-quoted reflections on war, fear, and the Republic: "It is a universal truth that the loss of liberty at home is to be charged to the provisions against danger, real or pretended, from abroad. [For no] nation could preserve its freedom in the midst of continual warfare." But perhaps America's second president, John Adams, understood even better the risks of a president and a country that recognizes no higher law than its own decisions: "An empire is a despotism, and an emperor is a despot, bound by no law or limitation but his own will; it is a stretch of tyranny beyond absolute monarchy. For, although the will of an absolute monarch is law, yet his edicts must be registered by parliaments. Even this formality is not necessary in an empire."

America's liberal-corporate warfare state is not the sort of empire imagined by John Adams. But George Washington, John Adams, and other founders of the Republic well understood that foreign threats, economic ambitions, political corruption, and a perverse interplay of foreign policy and domestic politics constituted a threat to survival of republican institutions. The George W. Bush administration reconfirmed the insightfulness of the founders in their fears for survival of limited government and republican institutions in times of crisis. Bush and his advisers pushed the outer limits (and beyond) of what Arthur M. Schlesinger Jr.'s classic work called the "imperial presidency."

The American crisis, however, is not simply about presidential authority. It is about America itself and its place on a shrinking planet. Only fundamental reform of the corrupt American political system and a parallel jettisoning of American political myths may spare the United States, Latin America, and the rest of the planet further catastrophes resulting from an America that recognizes no higher law than its own definition of national security and its quest for global primacy. Without more transparency, greater accountability, and less hubris in American government, the prognosis seems gloomy. To move America in that direction requires inspired and courageous political leadership, buttressed by a multiplicity of grassroots social movements intent on a long-term battle to reform the country's political institutions — for the vast majority of Americans are in no mood for revolution or even constitutional reform.

Popular and elite belief in American exceptionalism, in the country's civilizing mission, and in its providential destiny has reinforced, sustained, and reproduced the unilateralism and jingoism of its elected leaders. As British diplomats in the United States observed of the Monroe Doctrine at mid-nineteenth century, American politics seem to require of its politicians jingoism and imperial hubris to be elected at all. It is a rare politician in the United States who does not remind Americans that "we are the greatest nation in the world." Still rarer is the politician who questions this mantra or asks how Americans know that it is true, or what it is that makes America the "greatest nation," beyond its aircraft carriers, global military deployments, and command of outer space. The idea of America — freedom, liberty, tolerance, opportunity, and the championing of human rights around the world — remains an inspiration for many of the world's peoples. Yet American foreign policy has demeaned and besmirched the idea and dream of America.

In this quandary, not only reform of political institutions is required to rescue the country from its self-defeating foreign policies, but also transformation of American political culture itself. Political and institutional reform requires extraordinary political leadership, even in ordinary times. Making a global war against terrorist organizations, confronted by proliferation of nuclear weapons and enhanced military capabilities of regional powers around the world and facing a deep economic crisis, it will be no easy task for America's president and his administration to transform the country's self-perpetuating system of corrupt domestic politics and messianic militarism. Obama's election was a minor miracle. Asking him and his administration to do more than change the direction of American politics and foreign policy and to give that change some momentum might be asking too much.

Obama came to national prominence with his keynote address to the Democratic Convention in 2004: "The Audacity of Hope." The idea of Hope had elected Obama: "The hope of slaves sitting around a fire singing freedom songs; the hope of immigrants setting out for distant shores; the hope of a young naval lieutenant bravely patrolling the Mekong Delta; the hope of a mill worker's son who dares to defy the odds; the hope of a skinny kid with a funny name who believes that America has a place for him, too. Hope in the face of difficulty. Hope in the face of uncertainty. The audacity of hope." When Obama turned the keynote address into a book, the subtitle became *Reclaiming the American Dream*. If Obama wishes to reclaim the American Dream, for Americans, for Latin Americans, and for the rest of the world, he will eventually have to break cleanly from the Cold Warriors that surround him and from national security doctrines that propelled the United States toward endless war. Such a break would signify a monumental new beginning for America, for the Western Hemisphere, and for the international community. It is not likely to occur, but there remains the audacity of hope.

Neither the Roman empire nor the British empire survived imperial overreach. Rome succumbed, corrupted from within and overrun by "barbarians." After World War II, Great Britain carried on, gradually letting go of the imperial urge and the impossible task of managing and policing the planet. It remains to be seen whether the United States will circumscribe the meaning given to its enlarged sense of manifest destiny in time and in a fashion that allows for self-determination of peoples in Latin America and elsewhere — and for the United States to salvage and repair its own republican institutions. In the midst of economic crisis and political polarization, this is the challenge facing President Barack Obama and all Americans in 2010.

Notes

Abbreviations

NATO   North Atlantic Treaty Organization
NSC   National Security Council
NSC-PD   Presidential Directive/National Security Council
PPS   Policy and Planning Staff
Stat.   *Public Statutes at Large of the United States of America, 1789–March 3, 1845.*
          Vol. 2, edited by Richard Peters. Boston: Little, Brown, 1861.

Introduction

1 As I was finishing this book, newly elected president Barack Obama moved toward renaming the war. Instead of a "war on terror," it would be a war against terrorist organizations.

2 Clinton, "A National Security Strategy of Engagement and Enlargement," February 1996. Emphasis added.

3 The essentials of the Bush Doctrine were put forth in George W. Bush, "The National Security Strategy of the United States of America," on September 17, 2002. Its basic components are unilateralism, *when necessary* (alliances if possible and convenient); preemptive strikes (or preventive strikes) against existing or potential threats; and regime change, where necessary to "extend the benefits of freedom across the globe."

4 Article 51 of the UN Charter reads: "Nothing in the present Charter shall impair the inherent right of individual or collective self-defence if an armed attack occurs against a Member of the United Nations, until the Security Council has taken measures necessary to maintain international peace and security. Measures taken by Members in the exercise of this right of self-defence shall be immediately reported to the Security Council and shall not in any way affect the authority and responsibility of the Security Council under the present Charter to take at any time such action as it deems necessary in order to maintain or restore international peace and security." However, the legality of preemptive war is controversial. Preemptive war doctrine builds upon the seventeenth-century formulation of the Dutch scholar Hugo Grotius ("The Law of War and Peace," 1625), who argued that "self-defense" may be permitted "not only after an attack has already been suffered, but also in advance, where the deed may

be anticipated." Later, in *The Law of Nations* (1758), Swiss jurist Emmerich de Vattel affirmed: "A nation has the right to resist the injury another seeks to inflict upon it, and to use force and every other just means of resistance against the aggressor." Under this broader, and perhaps more controversial, interpretation of self-defense, Article 51 of the UN Charter would not override the customary right of anticipatory self-defense or even preemptive attack. Interestingly enough, the works of Grotius and Vattel were favorite readings of Thomas Jefferson, who relied very heavily upon them for crafting the Declaration of Independence.

5 Gray, "Implications of Preemptive and Preventive War Doctrine."

6 The West Florida Republic lasted three months; today its territory forms part of Louisiana, Mississippi, and Alabama. The Texas Republic existed from 1836 to 1845. The California "Bear Flag" Republic lasted less than a month (1846). The Republic of Hawaii, created with the intervention of the American minister to Hawaii and the U.S. Navy, lasted from 1894 to 1898, before annexation by joint resolution of the U.S. Congress.

7 The most widely used textbook on U.S.–Latin American relations (Peter Smith, *Talons of the Eagle*, 7–8) focuses especially on the character and transformation of the international system that "guided the management of inter-American relations," with special attention to "the ultimate content of policy, rather than with struggles over its formation." This book also enters this terrain, but much more attention is given here to domestic politics and to the shaping, directly and indirectly, of foreign policy and relations with Latin America by partisan, sectional, racial, and even personal conflicts within the United States.

8 I use the term "grand strategy" in this book in the broad sense of the effort to define a state's strategic interests and to focus and coordinate diplomatic, economic, cultural, and military assets of its government and peoples to achieve its self-defined national objectives. Such objectives always include security (survival), but the definition of interests and other objectives may change over time, requiring reformulation of grand strategy in relation to changing international, regional, and domestic contingencies. Other authors limit "grand strategy" to "the means by which a state plans to use force or the threat of force to achieve political ends" (see Desch, *When the Third World Matters*, 1). There is no single correct definition for "grand strategy." I simply alert the reader at the outset to the usage I have adopted in this volume.

9 For a very different opinion, see Schweikart and Allen, *A Patriot's History*.

10 Thus McDougal (*Promised Land*, 11) refers to a "bible of [American] foreign affairs," replete with conflicting and overlapping precepts that make American policy analogous to the Sergio Leone spaghetti western *The Good, the Bad, and the Ugly*: As America gained weight in international affairs, "predictably, the Good the United States did magnified enormously, but so too did the Bad and the Ugly."

11 This premise implies that histories of the foreign policies of other nations would also include reference to national myths, political culture, territorial ambitions, domestic politics, perceptions of threats by adversaries, geopolitics, security doctrine, and so on. Those histories, whether of Great Britain, Spain, or France in the nineteenth century or of Germany, Russia, Japan, or China in the twentieth century, among many more, are for others to write. In this spirit, I share the observations of historian

William Appleman Williams ("Confessions," 339): "I do not approve of imperial actions by Russia *or* by Israel, and I do not approve of repression in Brazil *or* in France, but most of all I like them least by and in my own America."

12 Postcolonial and postmodern studies have added to the various "schools" of international relations theorists concerns with diverse cultural elements of influence and power, from sport, film, mass media, public health, and military psychological operations to U.S. and European business and religious penetration of colonized or "neo-colonially dominated" regions.

13 See Cherry, *God's New Israel.*

14 Formulation of basic foreign policy principles and doctrines began with George Washington's admonitions regarding the danger of foreign meddling and partisanship in American politics and the desirability of armed neutrality as a basic principle of foreign policy and continued with Thomas Jefferson's admonitions against "entangling alliances," the No Transfer Resolution of 1811, and the Monroe Doctrine of 1823. This book brings such principles, doctrines, and corollaries into the twenty-first century, with the so-called Bush Doctrine of 2002.

15 The idea of American exceptionalism has been interpreted in many different ways. One version is that the United States has a special, God-given role to play in human history. Associated with this version is the idea that the Western Hemisphere could be a "separate sphere" from Europe and avoid its evils. Within the Western Hemisphere, the unique constitutional and republican institutions of the United States would be an example for the world. From this basic formulation, American exceptionalism may include many different ways in which the United States is supposedly unique among nations — from lack of a strong Marxist labor movement to a foreign policy based on ideals and benevolence rather than on the power politics of other great powers. The idea of exceptionalism may also be applied in practice in many different ways. For a synopsis of different versions of American exceptionalism, see McCrisken, "Exceptionalism"; for a recent challenge to the idea of American exceptionalism, see Hodgson, *Myth of American Exceptionalism.*

16 McDougal, *Promised Land*, 18.

17 On the way in which attitudes toward Spanish America influenced formation of American national identity, see Jaksić, *Hispanic World.* For examples of influential textbooks that emphasized the racial and cultural inferiority of Latin Americans, see Hutton Webster, *History of Latin America*; and Sweet, *History of Latin America.*

18 Thus, before the advent of the Global War on Terror, Professor Robert J. Lieber, former chair of the Government Department at Georgetown University, wrote of the post–Cold War decade (in "Foreign Policy and American Primacy," 3) that "American primacy has been sustained and even enhanced, and it is likely to continue. The dimensions of this primacy include, *inter alia*, military strength, the capacity to project power at great distance, technology, economic dynamism, and culture (broadly defined to include lifestyle and entertainment)."

19 George W. Bush, "Address to a Joint Session of Congress and the American People," September 20, 2001.

20 "President Bush Discusses Global War on Terror," April 10, 2006, Paul H. Nitze School of Advanced International Studies, Johns Hopkins University, Washington, D.C., 21.

21 Negotiated on America's behalf by Benjamin Franklin, John Jay, and John Adams, the treaty recognized "the 13 colonies to be free, sovereign and independent States, and that his Majesty relinquishes all claims to the Government, propriety, and territorial rights of the same, and every part thereof."

Chapter 1

1 For convenience, and anticipating the correct objections of our neighbors in the hemisphere, I have often used the terms "American" and "America" to refer to the United States of America. This is common usage in the United States. In a broader sense, all citizens of the Western Hemisphere are "Americans," whether Central Americans, South Americans, North Americans (also Canadians and Mexicans), Caribbean Americans, or Native Americans.

2 For example, McDougal (*Promised Land*, 40) asserts that "our vaunted tradition of 'isolationism' is no tradition at all, but a dirty word that interventionists, especially since Pearl Harbor, hurl at anyone who questions their policies." Hunt (*Ascendancy*, 21) puts it simply: "Isolationism, a term that has come to be associated with this approach [nonentanglement] does not accurately apply." See also Zakaria, *From Wealth to Power*; and William Appleman Williams, "Rise of an American World Power Complex," 59.

3 George Washington, "A Farewell Address to the People of the United States," September 17, 1796, An open letter published in American newspapers on September 19, 1796. A recent restatement of this view of American foreign policy in its first century is Lind, *American Way of Strategy*.

4 Everett, *America*, 1–2. Everett was minister to Spain from 1825 to 1829 and later became editor of America's most important literary magazine, the *North American Review*.

5 Dexter Perkins, *American Approach*, 1.

6 Rieselbach, *Roots of Isolationism*, 3.

7 Jones, *Crucible of Power*, 3; Lind, *American Way of Strategy*, 58.

8 Loch Johnson, *Seven Sins*, 186.

9 "Providential" refers to "the foreseeing and caring guidance of God" in America's destiny.

10 On Spanish military and financial aid to the American independence movement, see Chávez, *Spain and the Independence of the United States*; on France and independence, see "Attitude of France to the United States," in *Revolutionary Diplomatic Correspondence*, vol. 1.

11 Hutson, "Early American Diplomacy," 60–61.

12 Weinberg, "Historical Meaning."

13 George Washington, Fifth Annual Message to Congress, Philadelphia, December 3, 1793.

14 George Washington, Seventh Annual Message to Congress, December 8, 1795.

15 The Neutrality Act of June 4, 1794, banned Americans from serving in the armed forces of foreign powers, from arming ships for war, or from providing for any military expedition against a nation with which the United States was not at war. This legislation was renewed in 1797 for two years and then became a permanent policy with the Neutrality Act of April 20, 1818. U.S. Congress, Act of April 20, 1818, ch. 88, 15th Cong., 1st sess., 3 *Stat.* 447.

16 Washington, Farewell Address.

17 George Washington, Eighth Annual Message to Congress, December 7, 1796.

18 Insights into American commercial and diplomatic activity in China and South Asia from the 1780s to the 1830s can be found in Gedalecia, "Letters from the Middle Kingdom."

19 Jefferson, *A Summary View*, 3.

20 At the outbreak of the Civil War, tariff revenues accounted for more than 90 percent of federal government income. U.S. Bureau of the Census, *Historical Statistics*.

21 North, *Economic Growth of the United States*.

22 Coatsworth, "American Trade," 243.

23 Ross M. Robertson, *History of the American Economy*, 229–30.

24 In 1801, the United States refused to pay further tribute to the Barbary powers to avoid seizures of American merchant ships. With the slogan "millions for defense, but not one cent for tribute," the United States sent naval squadrons into the Mediterranean. In 1805, Marines stormed the Barbary harbor fortress stronghold of Derna (Tripoli), commemorated in the Marine Corps Hymn invocation "To the Shores of Tripoli." Strictly speaking, this was a war against established governments — not against free-lance "pirates."

25 For the economic impact of these wars, see O'Rourke, "Worldwide Economic Impact."

26 Horsman, *Expansion and American Indian Policy*; Prucha, *Sword of the Republic*.

27 Herring, *From Colony to Superpower*, 100–101. Ongoing episodes of piracy, conflicts over treatment of vessels in times of war and peace, commercial disputes, and the terms of immigration and local business activities resulted in conflicts, wars, and treaties with the North African governments of the Barbary states (Morocco, 1786; Algeria, 1795; Tripoli, 1796, 1797; Tunis, 1797; Tripoli, 1805; Algeria, 1815, 1816; and Tunis, 1824). In the so-called Tripolitan War (1801–5) Thomas Jefferson sent naval units against Tripoli, which bombarded the city — on his own authority, while authorizing the U.S. consul at Tunis to conspire with the brother of the pasha of Tripoli in an unsuccessful plot for regime change. See Field, *America and the Mediterranean World*; and Allison, *Crescent Obscured*.

28 Washington, Farewell Address.

29 Lind (*American Way of Strategy*, 76–78) characterizes this part of the strategy as "averting a Balkanized North America."

30 For example, collaboration with the British in policing the international slave trade led to several important laws before 1820 and small naval deployments to restrict slavers. "An Act to Prohibit the Importation of Slaves into Any Port or Place within the Jurisdiction of the United States," March 2, 1807, 2 *Stat.* 429; Slave Trade Act, April 20, 1818, 3 *Stat.* 450 (outlawed the slave trade); "Act in Addition to the Acts Prohibiting the Slave Trade," 3 *Stat.* 532 (1819) (authorized the president to send a naval squadron into African waters to apprehend slave traders and appropriated $100,000 to resettle recaptured slaves in Africa).

31 On the history of public lands, see Clawson, *Federal Lands Revisited*.

32 As the federal government increased its size and functions, from road building and canals to other public works and services, along with navy and army recruitment and procurement, patronage and corruption permeated American politics. See Grossman, *Political Corruption*.

33 Tariff policy debates repeatedly occupied Congress, with outcomes sometimes determined by upcoming presidential and congressional elections. For example, rejection in 1845 of a commercial treaty with Prussia, which would have lowered duties on tobacco, lard, rice, and raw cotton in exchange for reducing American duties on German wine and other goods, was the result of party politics before the 1845 election. See Holt, *Treaties Defeated by the Senate*, 77–82.

34 George Washington had asked for a "competent fund"; in 1790, the Congress created a "Contingent Fund of Foreign Intercourse," which became known as the "secret service fund." *Annals*, 1st Cong., 2nd sess., 2292; 1 *Stat.* 128.

35 Sayle, "Historical Underpinnings."

36 The 1790 legislation provided funds for two years and was renewed in 1793 and 1794. *Annals*, Act of February 9, 1793, 2nd Cong., 2nd sess., 1412. Emphasis added.

37 "An Act Making Further Provision for the Expenses Attending the Intercourse of the United States with Foreign Nations," March 4, 1794, *Stat.*, 3rd Cong., 1st sess., 345. Sayle ("Historical Underpinnings," 9) adds that the manner of "accounting by certificate" for the covert operations authorized for George Washington was essentially "the same procedure delegated to the Director of Central Intelligence by the Central Intelligence Act of 1949."

38 The Northwest Ordinance of 1787 provided rules for incorporating the Northwest Territory into the Union. The ordinance prohibited slavery in any state created out of the territory, which included the present states of Minnesota, Michigan, Wisconsin, Ohio, Indiana, and Illinois. Ohio was the first state formed from the Northwest Territory; its 1803 constitution prohibited slavery in accord with the 1787 ordinance but failed, by one vote, to extend the suffrage to African Americans.

39 Hamilton to McHenry, June 27, 1799, Hamilton, *Works of Hamilton*, 7:97.

40 Ibid., 6:282, 284.

41 Jefferson to Edward Rutledge, July 4, 1790, in Jefferson, *Writings of Jefferson*, 8:61.

42 At the end of the French and Indian Wars in 1763, France lost all its continental possessions in North America. Louisiana, west of the Mississippi, was ceded to Spain. In the 1795 Pinckney Treaty, Spain conceded to the United States the right of navigation on the Mississippi River and the right of deposit of U.S. goods at the port of New Orleans for export. The treaty was to remain in effect for three years, with the possibility of renewal. In October 1800, Napoleon Bonaparte concluded the Treaty of San Ildefonso with Spain, returning Louisiana to France in exchange for a Spanish kingdom in Italy. This made possible the Louisiana Purchase from France by the United States in 1803. Spain retained East and West Florida, Texas, what became the New Mexico Territory, and California.

43 Neutrality Proclamation, April 22, 1793.

44 White, *Critical Years*, chaps. 1–4.

45 The Jay Treaty, also known as the Treaty of London, resolved issues outstanding from the War of Independence, including British vacation of forts in the Northwest and concession to the United States of rights to trade with India and British West Indies colonies. Although it avoided war with Britain, it sharply divided the American political elite. Approval in the Senate barely obtained the necessary two-thirds (20–10). *Annals*, 4th Cong., 4th sess., 861–62. Opponents in the House of Representatives at-

tempted to block appropriations to carry out the treaty, losing this battle (51–48). *Annals*, House of Representatives, 4th Cong., 1st sess., 1282–91.

46 President John Adams, Special Message to the Senate and the House, May 16, 1797.

47 "An Act to Suspend the Commercial Intercourse between the United States and France, and the Dependencies Thereof," 1 *Stat.* 565; "An Act to Authorize the Defense of the Merchant Vessels of the United States against French Depredations," 1 *Stat.* 572.

48 U.S. Department of the Navy, Navy Historical Center, "Reestablishment of the Navy."

49 DeConde, *Quasi-War*; U.S. Department of the Navy, Navy Historical Center, "Reestablishment of the Navy."

50 DeConde, *Quasi-War*, 68–69.

51 In the election of 1796, Adams defeated Thomas Jefferson in the electoral college by a margin of 71–68. The second-place finisher was awarded the vice presidency. Thus Federalist Adams had as his vice president Thomas Jefferson, his most prominent political opponent.

52 U.S. policymakers and modern-day enthusiasts for exporting U.S.-style democracy around the world frequently forget how early in American history that political corruption became an endemic and systematic feature of American politics. See Grossman, *Political Corruption*.

53 DeConde, *Quasi-War*, 90.

54 For alternative views on Adams, Jefferson, the Alien and Sedition Acts, and the Fries rebellion, see Diggins, *John Adams*; and McCullough, *John Adams*.

55 *Bas v. Tingy* (1800). Justice Bushrod Washington distinguished between a "solemn war" and an "imperfect war." He, and other justices, reasoned that war could exist, de facto and de jure, without a congressional declaration. Sofaer, *War, Foreign Affairs*, 145–46, 164.

56 From this controversy in the country's first undeclared war against a European power there developed ongoing constitutional disputes over the extent to which Congress could delegate contingent authority to the president. See Fisher, *Constitutional Conflicts*, 84–99.

57 The last of these provisions, adopted July 14, 1798, was called "An Act for the Punishment of Certain Crimes against the United States."

58 What became the Democratic-Republican Party emerged in the early 1790s, led by Jefferson and Madison. It was variously referred to as Jeffersonians, Republicans, and Democratic-Republicans.

59 A "land and dwellings" tax (a direct levy on real estate and slaves) to support the war and enforcement of the Alien and Sedition Acts induced rebellion in Pennsylvania, the so-called John Fries Rebellion or House Tax Rebellion of 1797–98. The leaders were sentenced to execution, but Adams issued an amnesty in May 1800. See Newman, *Fries's Rebellion*.

60 In the Convention of Môrtefontaine (September 30, 1800), the French refused to pay reparations for the ships and goods lost during the war; they agreed to void the treaty of 1778 and agreed to a new alliance that would allow the United States to remain neutral in the European wars. Napoleon kept secret his pending agreement with Spain for retrocession of Louisiana.

61 On the 1800 election, see Larson, *Magnificent Catastrophe*; and DeConde, *Quasi-War*, 259–93.

62 Thomas Jefferson, First Inaugural Address, March 4, 1801.

63 Jefferson, *Writings of Jefferson*, 10:318.

64 Theriault ("Party Politics," 316) reports that twenty-five of thirty Federalists in the House opposed the appropriation bill to implement the purchase (on a vote of 90–25).

65 *Annals*, Senate, 7th Cong., 2nd sess., 96. See the debates at pp. 84–97, 171–257.

66 Ibid., 189–90.

67 Thomas Jefferson to James Monroe, January 1803, Library of Congress, Thomas Jefferson Exhibition, Manuscript Division, 196.

68 Cited in Scroggs, *Story of Louisiana*, 161.

69 The territory of West Florida had been transferred among Spain, France, and England since the late seventeenth century after various colonial wars. At the end of the Seven Years War (French and Indian War, 1756–63), the British received Spanish Florida and parts of French Louisiana. From these possessions, the British created East Florida (most of the present state of Florida) and West Florida (bounded by the Mississippi River and Lake Pontchartrain in the west, by the 31st parallel on the north and the Apalachicola River on the east). After the American Revolution, the British agreed to a boundary between the United States and West Florida at 31° north latitude between the Mississippi and Apalachicola Rivers — a strip extending east from the Mississippi River and along the Gulf Coast to the Perdido River (the westernmost border of today's state of Florida). Spain continued to govern the territory and resisted the boundaries defined in 1783 until 1795 (Treaty of San Lorenzo).

70 See Onuf and Onuf, *Federal Union*.

71 *Senate Journal*, December 5, 1810, 1789–1873.

72 Stagg, "James Madison and George Mathews," 26.

73 For documentation on these debates, see David Hunter Miller, *Secret Statutes*.

74 Congress had anticipated the Florida landgrab on February 24, 1804, by authorizing President Thomas Jefferson, "whenever he shall deem it expedient," to establish a separate customs district at Mobile, *within the disputed territory*. Act of February 24, 1804, 2 *Stat.* 252, 254. In correspondence with Madison and others, Jefferson repeatedly made clear his desire to annex the Floridas. In 1807, he wrote to Madison: "Our southern defensive force can take the Floridas, volunteers for a Mexican army will flock to our standard, and rich pabulum will be offered to our privateers in the plunder of their commerce & coasts. Probably Cuba would add itself to our confederation." Cited in Sofaer, *War, Foreign Affairs*, 469 n. 33.

75 Emphasis added. Clay here was referring to smuggling, settlement of escaped slaves, piracy, and other "transnational crime" based in the Spanish Floridas. Settlers and policymakers were also offended by Spain's use of free colored and mulatto (*pardo*) militia to uphold law and order and engage American (white) troops in the region.

76 U.S. Congress, *Abridgement of the Debates of Congress*, January 1811, 264. Emphasis added.

77 "Resolved by the Senate and House of Representatives of the United States of America in Congress assembled, That the act, passed during the present session of Congress, entitled 'An act to enable the President of the United States, under certain contingen-

cies, to take possession of the country lying east of the river Perdido, and south of the State of Georgia, and the Mississippi Territory, and for other purposes,' and the declaration accompanying the same, be not printed or published, unless directed by the President of the United States, any law or usage to the contrary notwithstanding." *Annals*, 11th Cong., 3rd sess., 378.

78 See Wriston, *Executive Agents*; and Sofaer, *War, Foreign Affairs*.

79 Stagg, "James Madison and George Mathews."

80 *Annals*, House of Representatives, 11th Cong., 2nd sess., 1308.

81 Confidential message from President James Madison to the Senate and House of Representatives, January 3, 1811, *Annals*, 11th Cong., 3rd sess., 369–70.

82 Logan (*No Transfer*) traces the "no transfer idea" back to the Washington administration (the Nootka crisis, 1790, involving contending Spanish, British, and, to a lesser extent, Russian claims over the northwestern coast of North America) and concerns regarding transfer by Spain of any of its colonial territory to Great Britain.

83 In the 1980s, a modified version would be applied by the administration of Jimmy Carter to the Persian Gulf. See Record, *Rapid Deployment Force*.

84 *Stat.* 3, 15th Cong., 1st sess., April 20, 1818, 439–40, "An Act to Provide for the Publication of the Laws of the United States, and for Other Purposes." The administration journal, the *National Intelligencer*, had published the legislation on October 17, 1812, at 3, column 1, after it was first revealed in an opposition newspaper in Connecticut.

85 See the history of the executive proceedings, in *Annals*, 11th Cong., 3rd sess., 369–80, 1117–48.

86 The Perdido River, part of the modern boundary between the states of Alabama and Florida, formed the boundary (1682–1763) between Spanish Florida and French Louisiana. Defeated in the Seven Years War, the French ceded territory west of the Perdido River to England, which also received Spanish Florida. Spain retained territory west of the Mississippi. In the Treaty of Paris (1783), England returned all of Florida to Spain, giving it control of the Gulf of Mexico. When Spain ceded Louisiana to France (Treaty of San Ildefonso, 1800), it retained territory east of the Mississippi, as Spanish Florida. However, after the Louisiana Purchase by the United States, Spain claimed that only the portion of Louisiana west of the Mississippi had been returned to France. This created a territorial dispute between Spain and the United States over the Gulf Coast between the Mississippi and Perdido Rivers.

87 Knott, *Secret and Sanctioned*, 87–107.

88 Mr. Monroe to Mr. Foster, November 2, 1811, *Annals*, House of Representatives, 12th Cong., 1st sess., 439–40.

89 Stagg, *Mr. Madison's War*; Stagg, "James Madison and George Mathews"; Cusick, *Other War of 1812*.

90 From the Secretary of State to General George Mathews and Colonel John M'Kee, Department of State, January 26, 1811, *House Journal*, July 1, 1812.

91 Knott, *Secret and Sanctioned*, 107.

92 Secretary of State to Mathews, April 4, 1812, *House Journal*, Wednesday, July 1, 1812.

93 Stagg, "James Madison and George Mathews," 23.

94 In the same year, Congress also passed a first "foreign aid" bill for the relief of earthquake victims in Venezuela (May 8, 1812). Debates on this bill raised the question of

using American tax dollars to assist foreign peoples in times of disaster as a component of foreign policy.

95 War Message, June 1, 1812, *Annals*, 12th Cong., 1st sess., 1714–19.

96 The expanding scholarship on Jefferson's contribution to American political development and foreign policy is superbly reviewed in Jenkinson, "Ordeal of Thomas Jefferson."

97 Crackel, *Mr. Jefferson's Army*, 173.

98 "Report and Resolutions of the Hartford Convention," January 5, 1815, in MacDonald, *Documentary Source Book*, 293–302.

99 See Latimer, *1812*; and Stewart, *United States Army and the Forging of a Nation*, chap. 6.

100 *Annals*, House of Representatives, 12th Cong., 1st sess., December 1811, 428.

101 American merchants and sea captains had shared copies of the American Declaration of Independence and the federal Constitution with Latin Americans since the early nineteenth century. Some hoped that liberation from Spain would bring increased opportunities for trade; others saw themselves as political missionaries promoting "liberty." See Richard J. Cleveland, *Voyages of a Merchant Navigator*.

102 *Annals*, House of Representatives, 12th Cong., 1st sess., 425–27.

103 See Rippy, *Rivalry of the United States and Great Britain*.

104 The Great Seal of the United States, with its resplendent bald eagle on the face and the "Eye of Providence" accompanied by the script *Annuit Coeptis* (He [God] has favored our undertakings) on the reverse side, was approved on June 20, 1782.

105 See Gleijeses, "Limits of Sympathy"; and Waddell, "British Neutrality."

106 Sofaer, *War, Foreign Affairs*, 340.

107 See Remini, *Legacy of Andrew Jackson*; and Remini, *Andrew Jackson and His Indian Wars*.

108 Bassett, *Correspondence of Jackson*, 2:374–75.

109 After the Battle of New Orleans (January 8, 1815), Jackson declared martial law and declared himself de facto military governor. A judge (whom Jackson detained, then banished) issued writs of habeas corpus in favor of prisoners taken by Jackson. At the end of hostilities, the judge fined Jackson $1,000 for his abuse of authority and contempt. He paid the fine, submitting to civilian authority, but justified his actions as necessary for the American cause.

110 On the Seminole War, see *Annals*, 15th Cong., 1st sess., 515–30, 583–1138.

111 *Annals*, House of Representatives, 15th Cong., 2nd sess., 600–606.

112 Letter from General Andrew Jackson to his Excellency Don José Callava, Governor of West Florida at Pensacola, April 30, 1821, *Annals*, 17th Cong., 1st sess., Appendix, 1835–36.

113 Decades later (February 16, 1844), in the heat of presidential elections, Congress rescinded the fine and passed into oblivion Jackson's patriotic excesses. Congress ordered that, with interest, he be paid $2,700 — a little more than a year before he died in June 1845. *Stat.*, 28th Cong., 1st sess., 651. See *Congressional Globe*, Senate, 28th Cong., 1st sess., 194–96, for Senator William Woodbridge's (Whig-Mich.) objections to rescinding the fine for a general who "forgot he was not a Roman dictator." He called on his colleagues not to "blot out this whole page from your country's history" (ibid., February 1844, 196).

114 Castlereagh to Bagot, November 10, 1817, cited in Charles K. Webster, *Foreign Policy of Castlereagh*, 448–49.

115 The boundary was to be the Sabine River, north from the Gulf of Mexico to the 32nd parallel north, then due north to the Red River, west along the Red River to the 100th meridian, due north to the Arkansas, west to its headwaters, north to the 42nd parallel north, and finally west along the parallel to the Pacific Ocean.

Chapter 2

1 Kaplan and Pease, *Cultures*; Pratt, *Imperial Eyes*.

2 Jaksić, *Hispanic World*, 3–6.

3 Richardson, *Compilation of the Messages and Papers*, 2:116.

4 Conference committee report on the Missouri Compromise, March 1, 1820, Joint Committee of Conference on the Missouri Bill, March 1–March 6, 1820, Record Group 1281, National Archives.

5 *Annals*, Senate, 16th Cong., 1st sess., 374–88.

6 In 1820–21, the Missouri constitution prohibited free blacks from entering the state and forbade manumission without specific authorization of the state legislature. Henry Clay orchestrated a compromise — that no provision of the Missouri constitution should be construed as denying any citizen the privileges and immunities of citizens of the United States. This has been called the "second Missouri compromise."

7 The "City on the Hill" is a reference to Puritan leader John Winthrop's passage in "A Model of Christian Charity" (1630): "For we must consider that we shall be as a city upon a hill. The eyes of all people are upon us." Winthrop had in mind the Sermon on the Mount: "You are the light of the world. A city set on a hill cannot be hid. . . . Let your light so shine before men, that they may see your good works and give glory to your Father who is in heaven" (Matthew 5:14–16).

8 Article 4, section 2, of the Constitution provided that "no Person held to Service or Labour in one State, under the Laws thereof, escaping into another, shall, in Consequence of any Law or Regulation therein, be discharged from such Service or Labour, but shall be delivered up on Claim of the Party to whom such Service or Labour may be due." Thus the states' rights advocates relied on the federal Constitution to impede manumission by virtue of escaping to states where slavery had been outlawed. This clause was removed when the Thirteenth Amendment abolished slavery in December 1865. George Washington signed the first fugitive slave law in 1793 (February 12, 1793, ch. 7, 1 *Stat.* 302).

9 James E. Lewis Jr., *American Union*, 35–40, chap. 6. In principle, Spain had abolished slavery at home and in all its colonies except Cuba, Puerto Rico, and Santo Domingo (Dominican Republic) in 1811.

10 Holt, *Treaties Defeated by the Senate*, 43.

11 On the personalities and intrigues of the 1824 election and competing views over its role in formulation of the Monroe Doctrine, see Turner, *Rise of the New West*, chap. 11; Ernest R. May, *Making of the Monroe Doctrine*, 254–60; and Ammon, "Monroe Doctrine."

12 Schoultz, *Beneath the United States*, 11.

13 Henry Clay to Francis Preston Blair, January 29, 1825, Clay, *Papers of Henry Clay*, 4:46–48. Blair was a journalist who became an avid supporter of Andrew Jackson in the 1830s.

14 Cited in Holt, *Treaties Defeated by the Senate*, 45. Emphasis added.

15 In 1804, the Twelfth Amendment to the Constitution altered the manner of presidential and vice presidential selection; the 1800 election had demonstrated the defects of the original process, especially that the president and vice president might be from different parties and work at cross-purposes, as occurred with John Adams and Thomas Jefferson. In 1824, Jackson would lose the presidency despite receiving a plurality of the popular vote and also a plurality in the electoral college. The fourth-highest vote getter, Henry Clay, Speaker of the House and longtime political enemy of Jackson, threw his support to Adams. Adams then named Clay as his secretary of state. Jackson called this a "corrupt bargain." He would return to defeat John Quincy Adams in the 1828 election.

16 The Senate approved an amended treaty (29–13) to suppress the slave trade in May 1824 but struck the clause providing for patrols off America's coast, leaving only Africa and the West Indies. This change made the treaty unacceptable to the British, as its opponents among slave state senators and, more important, supporters of Crawford's presidential candidacy intended. All thirteen senators voting against the treaty supported Crawford; the seven additional senators whose votes assured British rejection of the treaty opposed Adams's presidential bid. Holt, *Treaties Defeated by the Senate*, 47–51.

17 For a contemporary (1828) analysis of the American position in the international system and the Western Hemisphere in the 1820s, see Everett, *America*, chap. 2.

18 President Monroe informed Congress that the United States had appointed diplomatic representatives to Colombia, Buenos Aires, Chile, and Mexico in his message of December 1823. *Annals*, Senate, 18th Cong., 1st sess., 15–17.

19 Monroe consulted with former presidents Madison and Jefferson on the Canning proposal. Both agreed that Monroe should accept the British offer. But Adams and Clay (both of them presidential candidates) disagreed, convincing Monroe that the message should be unilateral.

20 Hugh Nelson served as a congressman from Virginia from 1811 to 1823, when he was appointed minister plenipotentiary to Spain.

21 "Adams to Hugh Nelson," Washington, D.C., April 28, 1823, in Worthington Chauncey Ford, *Writings of Adams*, 7:381.

22 Ibid., 7:369–73.

23 Larson, *Magnificent Catastrophe*, 192–202.

24 Slaves accounted for approximately 20 percent of the population of the newly independent United States. The Constitution (article 1, section 2) stated that, apart from free persons, "all other persons," meaning slaves, are each to be counted as three-fifths of a white person for the purpose of apportioning congressional representatives on the basis of population. Since most slaves lived in the South, this implied "over-representation" for white southerners. Article 1, section 9, stated that the importation of "such Persons as any of the States now existing shall think proper to admit," meaning slaves, would be permitted until 1808. The Constitution did not explicitly mention "slaves."

25 Partially as a result of this foiled insurrection, South Carolina authorities passed the Negro Seaman Act (1822), which authorized the detention of any black seaman in the port of Charleston. This legislation complicated U.S.-British relations when black seamen on British vessels were detained while their ships were at port. Secretary of State John Quincy Adams denounced the law as unconstitutional, but South Carolina's governor continued to enforce the legislation.

26 This is the largest number of executions ever ordered by a civilian court in the United States. For varying interpretations of the Vesey conspiracy and trial, see David Robertson, *Denmark Vesey*; Starobin, *Denmark Vesey*; and Michael Johnson, "Denmark Vesey."

27 See Barcia, "Revolts"; and Barcia, *Seeds of Insurrection*.

28 Thus Alexander H. Everett, American minister to Spain and later editor of the *North American Review*, wrote in 1827 (*America, A General Survey*, 182) that "it is one thing to love liberty, and another to love desolation, slaughter, and universal uproar, which would be the consequence of the simultaneous and general emancipation of the blacks."

29 The final House vote to admit Missouri as a slave state passed, 90–87. Many of the congressmen spoke of the possible destruction of the Union if a compromise was not reached. The final vote on prohibiting slavery north of the 36°30′ latitude line was not close (134–42), but it took place only after rejection of a bill from the Senate that prohibited slavery in all the Louisiana Territory, including Missouri. *Annals*, House of Representatives, 16th Cong., 1st sess., 1585–88. In the Senate, the prohibition of slavery in *all* the Louisiana Territory had been approved by a vote of 24–20. *Annals*, Senate, 16th Cong., 1st sess., 427–28.

30 Adding to the mix, in 1811 the Spanish liberals proclaimed abolition of slavery in all colonies except Cuba, Puerto Rico, and Santo Domingo (Dominican Republic). Gran Colombia (Colombia, Venezuela, and Ecuador), recognized by the United States in 1822, had promulgated a plan for gradual abolition of slavery in 1821. Chile abolished slavery in 1811 and again in 1823.

31 Adams to Rush, November 29, 1823, cited in Logan, *No Transfer*, 169.

32 John Jay's father was one of the largest slave owners in New York, but John Jay became an advocate of manumission. See John Jay to Egbert Benson, Jay, *Papers of John Jay*, September 18, 1780, Jay #1713. In 1799, as governor of New York (1795–1801), Jay signed into law "An Act for the Gradual Abolition of Slavery." Hamilton came to oppose slavery. Indeed, he had racial attitudes closer to the spirit of the Declaration of Independence's affirmation of equality than had its author, Thomas Jefferson, who believed in the natural inferiority of black people. See Horton, "Alexander Hamilton."

33 James Monroe, Annual Message to Congress, December 2, 1823.

34 James Monroe, Inaugural Address, March 4, 1817.

35 James Monroe, Special Message, March 30, 1824.

36 Monroe had some difficulty convincing the Senate to approve a treaty with Great Britain making the slave trade "piratical." See James Monroe, Special Message, May 21, 1824.

37 Rivas, *Relaciones Internacionales*; Rivas, *Historia Diplomática*; Taussig, *Tariff History*.

38 *Annals*, Senate, 18th Cong., 1st sess., 22.

39 *Annals*, House of Representatives, 18th Cong., 1st sess., 805–6.

40 Ibid., 1085–86.

41 Ibid., 1083–1100.

42 Ibid. (Congressman Rollin Carolas Mallary, R.-Vt.), 879–80.

43 Poinsett served as secretary of war from March 7, 1837, to March 5, 1841, and presided over the continuing "removal" of Indians west of the Mississippi.

44 *Annals*, House of Representatives, 18th Cong., 1st sess., 1104–9.

45 Adams to Luriottis, August 23, 1823, ibid., 1109–10.

46 *Annals*, House of Representatives, 18th Cong., 1st sess., 1110–11.

47 Ibid., 1112–76, 1181–1212.

48 James Monroe, Message to Congress, December 2, 1823.

49 *Annals*, House of Representatives, 12th Cong., 1st sess., December 1811, 427–28.

50 Thus a widely used textbook (Spanier and Hook, *American Foreign Policy*, 293) refers to the "traditional moralism that had so often in the past fueled America's sense of mission" and noted that "American idealists [in the 1990s] equated the country's national values — democracy, religious tolerance, human rights — with universal values."

51 This was made clear in the Polignac memorandum, in which Canning was informed by France's ambassador in London that the French did not intend to spearhead a reconquest of the Spanish colonies. See Temperley, "Documents Illustrating the Reception"; and Temperley, "French Designs."

52 John F. T. Crampton to Lord Clarendon, February 7, 1853, in Barnes and Barnes, *Private and Confidential*, 66.

53 On the interplay between foreign policy and private interests, including businessmen, missionaries, and filibusters, see O'Brien, *Making the Americas*.

54 See Cox, *War, Foreign Affairs*, 42.

55 This episode certainly involved blatant corruption, but American diplomats in this period were typically political appointees, and most mixed private interests with their diplomatic chores.

56 Parks, *Colombia*, 188.

57 *Senate Journal*, 24th Cong., 2nd sess., January 10, 1837.

58 *Stat.* 9, 881.

59 The vote on the treaty (29–7) reflected the electoral victory of the Democrats and the ascent of slave interests. All the dissenting votes were by northern Whig senators, some of whom had also opposed annexation of Texas and expansion of slavery within the Union. *Senate Executive Journal*, 30th Cong., 1st sess., June 3, 1848, 424; U.S. Congress, *Biographical Directory of the United States Congress*.

60 Clayton to Letcher, September 18, 1849, S. Exec. Doc. 97 (32.1): 11–13.

61 Parks, *Colombia*, 249.

62 Among the notable opponents of the war were John Quincy Adams and Abraham Lincoln.

63 *Congressional Globe*, Senate, 29th Cong., 2nd sess., 548–51. The Wilmot Proviso provided "that, as an express and fundamental condition to the acquisition of any territory from the Republic of Mexico by the United States, by virtue of any treaty which may be negotiated between them, and to the use by the Executive of the moneys herein appropriated, neither slavery nor involuntary servitude shall ever exist in any part of said territory, except for crime, whereof the party shall first be duly convicted."

64 Ealy, *Yanqui Politics*, 17–27.

65 Campbell, *From Revolution*, chap. 6.

66 O'Brien, *Making the Americas*, 43.

67 Corwin, *President*, 201.

68 For detailed case material on the period to 1857, see Cox, *War, Foreign Affairs*, chaps. 1–2; and Prucha, *American Indian Treaties*.

69 The idea of manifest destiny encompassed a number of religious, racial, and political themes, which were not entirely compatible with one another and which changed over time and were appropriated by different political movements for their particular use. See Horsman, *Race and Manifest Destiny*; Merk, *Manifest Destiny and Mission*; and William Earl Weeks, *Building the Continental Empire*.

70 Cited in Bemis, *John Quincy Adams*, 182.

71 Pletcher, *Diplomacy of Annexation*.

72 *Naturalization Law of March 26, 1790*, 1st Cong., 2nd sess., 103.

73 In response to hundreds of thousands of petitions gathered by the American Anti-Slavery Society, the House of Representatives adopted a resolution on March 26, 1836 (117–68), that automatically tabled all petitions relating to slavery, the so-called gag rule. The House reaffirmed the rule in January 1837 (129–69). This procedure remained in place until 1844. On the history of the gag rule, see Jenkins and Stewart, "Gag Rule."

74 On the complex impact of racism on U.S. territorial ambitions, see Love, *Race over Empire*.

75 In some ways, the *Potomac*'s career represented the history of the U.S. Navy from the 1830s to the 1850s. See Navy Historical Center, *Dictionary of American Naval Fighting Ships*, <http://www.history.navy.mil/danfs/index.html>. Accessed February 22, 2009.

76 Downes to Levi Woodbury, Secretary of the Navy, February 17, 1832, in Bauer, *New American State Papers: Naval Affairs*, 22nd Cong., 1st sess., 156.

77 See General Instructions to Commodore John Downes, in ibid., 150. Downes had general instructions on neutrality, the slave trade, piracy, and protection of American commerce off the coast of South America and for collecting intelligence on Dutch and British activities in the region.

78 Annual Report of the Secretary of the Navy, Showing the Condition of the Navy in 1832, December 3, 1832, in Bauer, *New American State Papers: Naval Affairs*, 22nd Cong., 2nd sess., 158.

79 Herring, *From Colony to Superpower*, 171.

80 Collier, "Instances of the Use of Force"; Long, *Gold Braids*.

81 Mr. J. R. Ingersoll, *Congressional Globe*, House of Representatives, 28th Cong., 1st sess., 79.

82 *Congressional Globe*, House of Representatives, 28th Cong., 1st sess., 80.

83 *Congressional Globe*, Senate, 28th Cong., 1st sess., 383.

84 Excerpted from "The Great Nation of Futurity," *United States Democratic Review* 6, no. 23 (1845): 426–30.

85 The British eventually accepted the 49th parallel as the boundary, except for the southern tip of Vancouver Island.

86 By the Treaty of Wanghia (Wangxia) (1844), U.S. merchants in China obtained most favored status and access to five Chinese ports. The Treaty of Tientsin (Tianjin) (1858)

afforded U.S. missionaries the right to preach Christianity in China. In 1854, Admiral Matthew Perry "opened" Japan at ship's cannon point and proposed that the United States claim sovereignty over Formosa (Taiwan).

87 See U.S. Navy, Historical Section, Fourteenth Naval District, Rare Books Room, *Administrative History of the Fourteenth Naval District and the Hawaiian Sea Frontier*, vol. 1, *Hawaii, 1945*.

88 John F. T. Crampton to Lord Clarendon, November 20 and February 7, 1853, in Barnes and Barnes, *Private and Confidential*, 66, 87.

89 Mexican War hero Zachary Taylor had been elected president in 1848, but he died in office. The Whigs dropped Taylor's vice president and the incumbent president, Millard Fillmore, as their candidate, replacing him with General Winfield Scott, opposing the Democrats' General Franklin Pierce. Every American president before the Civil War except for the two Adamses and Martin Van Buren served in uniform, though not all served in combat.

90 "An Act to Organize the Territories of Nebraska and Kansas," May 30, 1854, in Bevans, *Statutes: Treaties and Other International Agreements*, 10:277. See Potter, *Impending Crisis*.

91 The Compromise of 1850 had allowed California into the Union as a free state; compensated Texas for the loss of New Mexico; organized the New Mexico Territory (Arizona, New Mexico, and part of Nevada) without prohibiting slavery; and implemented a harsh fugitive slave law (Fugitive Slave Act of 1850, 9 *Stat.* 462). Federal marshals had a duty to capture runaway slaves and were rewarded with a fee; persons assisting runaways were subject to fines and jail; and alleged runaways were not entitled to a trial, making free blacks also vulnerable to enslavement.

92 After Collier, "Instances of the Use of Force."

Chapter 3

1 I mean by "did not happen Providentially" that I do not believe that "the foreseeing and caring guidance of God" explains American territorial expansion or its place in the international system.

2 The Neutrality Act of 1794 forbade "anyone other than the U.S. [government] from raising an army within the territory of the United States to attack a state with which the United States is at peace." Reenacted and modified several times, it was "finalized" in the Neutrality Act of 1818, partly in response to Spanish complaints regarding insurgents' use of American ports.

3 John Quincy Adams, Address to the House of Representatives, July 4, 1821.

4 Boot, *Savage Wars*, 339.

5 James Monroe, First Inaugural Address, March 4, 1817.

6 Jackson did add to the public domain. His Indian Removal policies added millions of acres of land for white settlement and encouraged the expansion of slavery.

7 In theory, the Texas Republic encompassed all of the present state of Texas and parts of today's New Mexico, Oklahoma, Kansas, Colorado, and Wyoming.

8 Andrew Jackson, Special Message to Congress, February 6, 1837.

9 Andrew Jackson, Special Message to Congress, March 3, 1837.

10 Tyler was the first president to occupy the office as a result of succession after the death of an incumbent, in this case the demise of William Henry Harrison in 1841.

11 Holt, *Treaties Defeated by the Senate*, 67–77.

12 In his classic work on U.S.–Latin American relations, Samuel Flagg Bemis (*Latin American Policy*, 87) wrote that "to block annexation, Anglo-French mediation had brought Texas to sign a protocol of preliminaries of peace by which Mexico would consent to acknowledge the independence of Texas and Texas would agree never to annex herself or be subject to any country whatever. . . . Mexico proposed that the mediating states guarantee Texan independence forever. Great Britain was willing to do this, but France refused to go that far."

13 See Adams, *British Interests*.

14 Cited in Dexter Perkins, *Monroe Doctrine: 1826–1867*, 71.

15 Ibid., 71–72.

16 James K. Polk, A Special Message Calling for a Declaration of War against Mexico, Washington, D.C., May 11, 1846.

17 Silverstone, "Federal Democratic Peace."

18 James K. Polk, Message to Congress, December 2, 1845.

19 *Congressional Globe*, Senate, 30th Cong., 1st sess., 590–642, 738.

20 Appendix to the *Congressional Globe*, 30th Cong., 1st sess., 591.

21 *Congressional Globe*, Senate, 30th Cong., 1st sess., 591–92.

22 Ibid., 595.

23 Ibid., 596–97.

24 Ibid., 598.

25 Westcott, in alliance with military officers who had figured prominently in the Seminole War, sponsored legislation to drain the Florida everglades in order to use the land for rice and sugar cultivation. General Thomas S. Jessup, quartermaster general of the army in 1848, wrote to Westcott that cultivation of limes, oranges, and olives in the drained everglades "by a numerous white population, which would be interposed between the sugar plantations cultivated by slaves and the free blacks of the West Indies [would be] from a military point of view highly important, and add greatly to the strength of the South." S. Doc. 242, 30th Cong., 1st sess., 42, 607.

26 Ibid., 42, 599. Emphasis added.

27 "Nat Turner's Insurrection," *Atlantic Monthly*, August 1861, 173–87.

28 Polk sent no troops to Yucatán, but a filibuster expedition led by a lieutenant recently released from the army after the Mexican War did reach Yucatán in December 1848. The group suffered some casualties and returned to New Orleans by March 1849. In addition, Commodore Matthew Perry, commander of the Home Squadron, delivered supplies and armaments to the white *Yucatecos*. See Joseph, "United States, Feuding Elites"; and O'Brien, *Making the Americas*, 38–39.

29 James K. Polk, State of the Union Address, December 7, 1847.

30 See Morison, Merk, and Freidel, *Dissent*.

31 In 1848, the House of Representatives (85–81) attached a censure of Polk for "unnecessarily and unconstitutionally" starting a war to a resolution commending Zachary Taylor and others for the victories in Mexico. *Congressional Globe*, 30th Cong., 1st sess., 1848, 95. Abraham Lincoln supported this resolution: "Allow the President to invade a neighboring nation whenever he shall deem it necessary to repel invasion, and you allow him to do so whenever he may choose to say he deems it necessary for such purpose, and you allow him to make war at pleasure."

32 *Congressional Globe*, Senate, 29th Cong., 2nd sess.

33 In the colonial period, the western boundary of Spanish "Tejas" had been the Nueces River. After Mexican independence, from 1821 to 1845, Spanish and Mexican maps and documents reaffirmed the Nueces River as the boundary. Some Anglos in Texas and their backers in the United States claimed that the western boundary was the Rio Grande. Approximately 150 miles separated the Nueces from the Rio Grande in southern Texas, but the differing claims affected thousands of square miles of territory to the northwest, including half of New Mexico.

34 H. Exec. Doc. 351, 25th Cong., 2nd sess., serial 332, 313–14.

35 See Garber, *Gadsden Treaty*.

36 Einstein, "Lewis Cass," 326.

37 For the interplay among manifest destiny, domestic racial politics, slavery, white working-class identity, and popular culture, see Streeby, *American Sensations*; and Saxton, *Rise and Fall of the White Republic*.

38 Bourne, *Britain and the Balance of Power*; Jones and Rakestraw, *Prologue*.

39 Upper Canada had legislated gradual abolition of slavery in 1793. In 1833, Parliament ended slavery in all of the British Empire. Act against Slavery, July 9, 1793; Slavery Abolition Act, 1833 (British Imperial Act, August 28, 1833, which excepted territories in the possession of the East India Company, the Island of Ceylon, and the Island of Saint Helena).

40 U.S. Congress, *Abridgement of the Debates of Congress*, June 1844, 142. Emphasis added.

41 *Congressional Globe*, Senate, 29th Cong., 1st sess., 867–69. In the debates over the treaty, President Polk asserted "executive privilege," refusing to deliver certain "confidential documents" to the Senate for publication regarding Minister McLane's negotiations with the British — an important precedent in executive-congressional relations on foreign policy. See *Senate Executive Journal*, July 21, 1846.

42 *Senate Journal*, June 18, 1846. Controversy over the precise boundaries in the Juan de Fuca Strait persisted. In 1859, the United States sent troops to occupy the San Juan Islands, claimed by both England and the United States under the terms of the 1846 treaty ("Treaty with Great Britain, in Regard to Limits Westward of the Rocky Mountains"). In 1872, the United States agreed to arbitration of the dispute, and its claims were upheld ("Protocol of Agreement between Her Majesty and the United States of America, Defining the Boundary Line through the Canal de Haro, in Accordance with the Award of the Emperor of Germany," October 21, 1872).

43 The Fugitive Slave Act, September 18, 1850, 9 *Stat.* 462–65. In 1856, the Supreme Court ruled in the *Dred Scott* decision not only that slaves brought to free states remained the property of their owners and that Negroes, free or slave, could never be citizens and had no standing in court, but that the 1820 compromise was unconstitutional, violating the Fifth Amendment by depriving persons of their property without due process of law. Recently elected James Buchanan had lobbied for this decision with two of the justices before taking the oath of office — an unprecedented effort by a presidential candidate to influence a pending court decision.

44 The term "Slave Power" was used in the period in the North to refer to the slaveocracy that dominated southern politics and society before the Civil War. In practice, both

constitutional arguments and sectional politics limited the scope of federal policy before the Civil War.

45 Millard Fillmore, Third Annual Message to Congress, December 6, 1852.

46 Scientific racism purported to demonstrate the inferiority of some races and the superiority of others, especially "Caucasians." Such "science" permeated popular culture and was taken for granted among policymakers. Perhaps the most well known of the scientific racists was Louis Agassiz (*Contributions*), a Harvard professor and America's leading naturalist. He argued that the human races came from separate creations, and he remained an opponent of Darwin's theories for his entire life. See also Fitzhugh, *Sociology for the South*; and Fitzhugh, *Cannibals All.*

47 Cited in Horsman, *Race and Manifest Destiny*, 282.

48 Franklin Pierce, Inaugural Address, March 4, 1853.

49 Palmerston's Speech to Parliament, June 25, 1850, defending his use of the fleet to uphold the claims of a Jew from Gibraltar (and British subject) whose house had been invaded and damaged by a Greek mob in 1847.

50 Franklin Pierce, Inaugural Address, March 4, 1853.

51 Pletcher, *Diplomacy of Trade*, 150. Quote is from Ostend Manifesto (October 18, 1854), *House Executive Documents*, 33rd Cong., 2nd sess., 10:127–36.

52 See the correspondence from 1850 to 1854 between the British minister, John F. T. Crampton, and the foreign ministers in London, in Barnes and Barnes, *Private and Confidential*, 38–117.

53 Ostend Manifesto (October 18, 1854), *House Executive Documents*, 33rd Cong., 2nd sess., 10:127–36.

54 *Congressional Globe*, 35th Cong., 2nd sess., Appendix, 90, "Report on the Acquisition of Cuba."

55 James Buchanan, Message to Congress, December 19, 1859.

56 On the Confederate states' diplomacy, see Owsley, *King Cotton Diplomacy*.

57 Thus Sir John Alexander Macdonald, one of the founders of the Canadian Confederation, proclaimed in 1865: "If we are not blind to our present position we must see the hazardous situation in which all the great interests of Canada stand in respect to the United States" (Speech delivered in Parliament, February 1865).

58 Pinkett, "Efforts to Annex Santo Domingo."

59 Herring, *From Colony to Superpower*, 212.

60 Pletcher, *Diplomacy of Annexation*, 153.

61 *Nation*, November 20, 1873, 438.

62 "Treaty Concerning the Cession of the Russian Possessions in North America by His Majesty the Emperor of All the Russias to the United States of America," March 30, 1867.

63 Foner, *Forever Free*; Foner, *Reconstruction*.

64 The most significant of the European conflicts was the Franco-Prussian War (1870), which brought down France's Second Empire and served as a prelude for World War I.

65 Iriye, *From Nationalism*, 71.

66 An interesting exception is Walter Hixon, *The Myth*, 19–20.

67 Indian Removal Act, May 28, 1830.

68 Andrew Jackson, Fifth Annual Message to Congress, December 3, 1833.

69 For Andrew Jackson's obsession with Indian Removal and the history of treaties and despoiling of Indian peoples, see Remini, *Andrew Jackson and His Indian Wars*.

70 *Worcester v. State of Georgia* (1832).

71 *Allegheny Democrat*, March 16, 1835, cited in Ehle, *Trail of Tears*, 275–78.

72 *Journal of Cherokee Studies* 3, no. 3 (1978): 145, cited in Ehle, *Trail of Tears*, 324–25.

73 "Reading 3" in the National Park Service's "Lesson Plan for Teachers on the Trail of Tears" ("Every Cherokee man, woman or child must be in motion," <http://www.nps .gov/trte/forteachers/index.htm>. Accessed May 30, 2008.

74 There was, of course, Indian resistance to the removal policy. A notable case was the Seminole people in Florida. In May 1842, President John Tyler declared that "further pursuit of these miserable beings by a large military force, seems to be as injudicious as it is unavailing." Cited in Prucha, *Sword of the Republic*, 300, 304–6.

75 Theodore Roosevelt, "Expansion and Peace," *Independent* 51 (December 21, 1899): 3403–4, cited in Walter Williams, "United States Indian Policy."

76 U.S. Army, *American Military History*, 318. Emphasis added.

77 After Collier, "Instances of the Use of Force."

Chapter 4

1 North, *Growth and Welfare*, 75–77.

2 Eric Williams, *Capitalism and Slavery*.

3 Land sales from 1820 to 1860 contributed an average of 10.8 percent of federal government income; in some peak years, for example 1836 (48 percent), the total was much higher. See Paul W. Gates, *History of Public Land Law Development*; Rohrbough, *Land Office Business*; and Clawson, *Federal Lands Revisited*.

4 Slaves (approximately 3.2 million) accounted for 13.2 percent of America's population (23 million) in 1850, down from a high of 17.6 percent in 1800.

5 U.S. Bureau of the Census, 1860, *Population*, 598–99.

6 North, *Growth and Welfare*, 79–80.

7 Ross M. Robertson, *History of the American Economy*, 109–11.

8 Horton and Horton, *Slavery*.

9 The word "slave" did not appear in the Constitution. Instead, article 1 referred to "all other persons" in regard to the three-fifths rule and "such persons" in regard to "importation" of more slaves until 1808 (article 1, section 9). During this period, the federal government could tax, per capita, the importation of slaves (not exceeding ten dollars a person). Article 4, section 2, provided: "No Person held to Service or Labour in one State, under the Laws thereof, escaping into another, shall, in Consequence of any Law or Regulation therein, be discharged from such Service or Labour, but shall be delivered up on Claim of the Party to whom such Service or Labour may be due."

10 Robert E. May, *Southern Dream*.

11 In 1800, for example, customs duties provided about 84 percent of federal revenue; customs duties accounted for over 90 percent of federal receipts in most years prior to the Civil War. U.S. Bureau of the Census, *Historical Statistics*.

12 "An Ordinance to Nullify Certain Acts of the Congress of the United States, Purporting to Be Laws Laying Duties and Imposts on the Importation of Foreign Commodities," November 24, 1832.

13 Proclamation to Congress Regarding Nullification, December 10, 1832.

14 The United States outlawed the slave trade beginning in 1808: "An Act to Prohibit the Importation of Slaves into Any Port or Place within the Jurisdiction of the United States, from and after the First Day of January, in the Year of Our Lord One Thousand Eight Hundred and Eight," March 2, 1807.

15 The idea of an "American System" is associated with Henry Clay and gradually evolved after the War of 1812. It consisted of protective tariffs to encourage American manufactures, a program of federal government public works, such as canals and roads, a national bank, and a quest for foreign markets (especially in Latin America) for American agriculture.

16 "Privateers" refer to privately owned vessels, armed and equipped for the purpose of carrying on a maritime war by the authority of one of the belligerent parties. However, pirates became privateers when European states contracted them, or, in the case of the Spanish American independence movements, when they attacked Spanish or neutral shipping.

17 *Annals, Register of Debates*, Senate, 18th Cong., 2nd sess., 158–61.

18 Ibid., 198.

19 Ibid., 160.

20 Ibid., 276–77.

21 Barbour later served as John Quincy Adams's secretary of war (1825–28), presiding over negotiations for removal of Cherokee Indians from Georgia, and then was appointed minister to England (1828–29). In 1839, he presided over the first Whig national convention, which nominated William Henry Harrison as its presidential candidate.

22 *Annals, Register of Debates*, Senate, 18th Cong., 2nd sess., 275–85, 304–14, 377–407, 461–63; ibid., House of Representatives, 714–39.

23 Ibid., Senate, 277–78.

24 For details on the antipiracy campaign and its complexities, see Long, *Gold Braids*, 58–67.

25 John Quincy Adams, Fourth Annual Message to Congress, December 2, 1828.

26 On the naval operations and legislative debates, see Sofaer, *War, Foreign Affairs*, 365–79.

27 John Quincy Adams, First Annual Message to Congress, December 6, 1825.

28 Note to John Quincy Adams from Salazar, 1824, and note from Adams to Salazar, August 6, 1824, cited in Dexter Perkins, "John Quincy Adams," 81.

29 Dexter Perkins, *Monroe Doctrine: 1823–1826*, 84.

30 Cited in Burton, "Henry Clay," 141; *Annals, Register of Debates*, Senate, 19th Cong., 1st sess., 152, 153–346; ibid., bill passed, 671.

31 Cited in Burton, "Henry Clay," 144.

32 Hayne is most remembered for the Hayne-Webster debate of 1830 in which he defended the "nullification manifesto," arguing that states could nullify federal legislation.

33 *Annals, Register of Debates*, Senate, 19th Cong., 1st sess., 153–56.

34 Ibid., 671.

35 Logan, *No Transfer*, 101.

36 Madison to Armstrong, February 22, 1808, in *American State Papers: Foreign Relations*, 3:252.

37 Memo by Jefferson, cabinet meeting, October 22, 1808, cited in Logan, *No Transfer*, 106.

38 Madison to Pinkney, October 30, 1810, cited in Latané, *American Foreign Policy*, 285.

39 Cited in ibid., 228.

40 Cited in Bartlett, *Record of American Diplomacy*, 232–33.

41 James E. Lewis Jr., *American Union*, 194. See the recollection of Adams's and Clay's efforts by Senator George Smith Houston (D.-Ala.) in debates on the proposed occupation of Yucatán in 1848, in *Congressional Globe*, Senate, 30th Cong., 1st sess., 603.

42 John Quincy Adams to Hugh Nelson, April 28, 1823, U.S. Department of State, *Diplomatic Instructions*, 9:183–243, with extract in Bartlett, *Record of American Diplomacy*, 231–32. Emphasis added.

43 H. Exec. Doc. 121, 32nd Cong., 1st sess., cited in Latané, *American Foreign Policy*, 290.

44 Secretary of State John Middleton Clayton (1849–50) had already instructed the American representative in Madrid to inform the Spanish that "transfer of the island to another foreign power would be the immediate signal for war." Mary Wilhelmine Williams, "John Middleton Clayton," 14.

45 Reeves, *American Diplomacy*; James Buchanan to Romulus M. Saunders, June 17, 1848 (offer to purchase Cuba), in Bartlett, *Record of American Diplomacy*, 234–37.

46 Robert E. May, *Southern Dream*.

47 Quitman was charged with violations of the Neutrality Act of 1818; he resigned the governorship to defend himself against the charges. After three "hung juries," the charges were dropped. He was subsequently elected to Congress in 1855 (D.-Miss.), supporting annexation of Cuba and filibusters in Central America until his death in 1858.

48 President Zachary Taylor blocked Narciso López's first expedition in accord with the U.S. Neutrality Act of 1818. On his third try, in 1851, López was captured and executed by Spanish authorities.

49 Cited in Bailey, *Diplomatic History*, 288.

50 Crittenden to Comte de Sartiges, October 22, 1851, in Latané, *American Foreign Policy*, 296.

51 "Cuba and the United States, the Tripartite Treaty," *New York Times*, January 6, 1853 (article includes texts of messages regarding Cuba between Webster and British and French diplomats).

52 Ostend Manifesto (October 18, 1854), *House Executive Documents*, 33rd Cong., 2nd sess., 10:127–36.

53 Moore, "Pierre Soule," 209.

54 Cited in Henry Nash Smith, *Virgin Land*, 154.

55 Robert E. May, *Southern Dream*.

56 *Dred Scott v. Sanford* (1857). The decision found the 1820 Missouri Compromise unconstitutional, thus permitting slavery in all of the country's territories.

57 William M. Blackford, U.S. Chargé d'Affaires at Bogotá, to Daniel Webster, Secretary of State of the United States, extract in Manning, *Diplomatic Correspondence: Inter-American Affairs*, 5:591–92.

58 Ibid., 5:621.

59 Bidlack to Buchanan, November 27, 1846, in ibid., 5:627–28. Emphasis in the original.

60 Buchanan to Livingston, May 13, 1848, in Buchanan, *Works of Buchanan*, 8:64–69.

61 Article 1, section 8, para. 18. This paragraph in the U.S. Constitution reads that Congress has the authority "to make all Laws which shall be necessary and proper for carrying into Execution the foregoing Powers, and all other Powers vested by this Constitution in the Government of the United States, or in any Department or Officer thereof." In debates over ratification of the Constitution, many of the anti-Federalists objected to the "undefined, unbounded and immense power which is comprised in [this] clause." See Frohnen, *The Anti-Federalists*; and Laurence M. Vance, "The Anti-Federalists Were Right Again," <http://www.lewrockwell.com/vance/vance107.html>. Accessed April 2, 2009.

62 Report by Manuel María Mallarino, minister of foreign affairs, translation in Manning, *Diplomatic Correspondence: Inter-American Affairs*, 5:630–33.

63 Bidlack to Buchanan, December 14, 1846, in ibid., 5:634–37.

64 Ibid. Emphasis in the original.

65 The nay votes in the Senate came from six Whigs and an Independent Democrat who later became a Free Soiler. They were antislavery legislators who had also opposed the Mexican War, seeing in it an effort to expand the empire of slavery with increased presidential foreign policy initiatives in Central America.

66 Clayton to Foote, July 19, 1849, cited in Parks, *Colombia*, 215. Thomas M. Foote replaced Bidlack in Bogotá after Bidlack's death on February 6, 1849.

67 Safford and Palacios, *Colombia*, 218.

68 "Randolph Runnels," <http://www.trainweb.org/panama/runnels.html>. Accessed March 11, 2009.

69 The Panama Railroad, "History of the Panama Railroad," <http://www.trainweb.org/panama/history1.html>. Accessed March 10, 2009.

70 Report of Amos B. Corwine, United States Commissioner, Respecting the Occurrences at Panama on April 15, 1856, Department of State, Record Group 59, Microfilm Series 159, National Archives.

71 Corwine to Jefferson Davis, December 31, 1857, cited in Parks, *Colombia*, 287.

72 "Important from New Granada," *New York Times*, June 26, 1858, 1; "The Attitude of New Granada," July 29, 1858, *New York Times*, 4; Malloy, *Treaties, Conventions, International Acts*, 1:319–21.

73 Malloy, *Treaties, Conventions, International Acts*, 1:246.

74 March 8, 1889, cited in Parks, *Colombia*, 363.

75 Parks (*Colombia*, 219) documents American troop deployments to Panama from 1856 to 1902.

76 Senator Albert G. Brown (*Speeches, Messages*, 593–94) told his Mississippi constituents that William Walker, an American filibusterer, "was doing us a good service, and he ought to have been let alone . . . because slavery must go South, if it goes at all. If Walker had been allowed to succeed, he would have planted such a state, and the Southern States would have populated it."

77 According to Secretary of State Abel Parker Upshur (cited in Randolph Adams, "Abel Parker Upshur," 113–14), "England was trying to get Texas at such a disadvantage that a commercial treaty could be dictated from London creating a terrific social problem

with a free state adjoining the South — and the ensuing border strife, Negro insurrections, and English manufactures smuggled into the country."

78 On early schemes for an isthmian canal, see Stephens, *Incidents of Travel*.

79 Jones, *Course of American Diplomacy*, 168–69.

80 "Las Dos Americas," *El Correo de Ultramar*, February 15, 1857. ("La raza de la América latina, Al frente tiene la sajona raza, Enemiga mortal que ya amenaza, Su libertad destruir y su pendón.")

81 Estrade, "El invento de 'América Latina'"; Quijada, "Sobre el origen."

82 Long, *Gold Braids*, 141.

83 Lyons to Palmerston, July 1859, in Barnes and Barnes, *Private and Confidential*, 216–17.

84 Cited in Einstein, "Lewis Cass," 356. See also Robert E. May, "James Buchanan, the Neutrality Laws."

85 See Mary Wilhelmine Williams, *Anglo-American Isthmian Diplomacy*, 41–66.

86 Einstein, "Lewis Cass," 350.

87 Cass to Dimitry, no. 15, May 3, 1860, *Instructions, Central American States*, 16:125, in Bemis, *American Secretaries of State*, 6:360–61.

88 *Congressional Globe*, House of Representatives, 35th Cong., 2nd sess., February 7, 1859, 87–100.

89 "Convention between the United States of America and Her Britannic Majesty," April 19, 1850.

90 Cited in Latané, *American Foreign Policy*, 316.

91 Cited in ibid., 322.

92 Cited in Schlesinger, *Imperial Presidency*, 57.

93 James Buchanan, State of the Union Message to Congress, December 19, 1859. Emphasis added.

94 Cited in Horsman, *Race and Manifest Destiny*, 217.

95 Lyons to Russell, October 11, 1859, cited in Barnes and Barnes, *Private and Confidential*, 217–18.

96 Callahan, *American Foreign Policy*, 148.

97 Ibid., 267–75.

98 These failed treaties were a precedent for both the Hay-Bunau Varilla Treaty with Panama in 1903 and the Platt amendment making Cuba a virtual protectorate from 1902 until 1934.

99 See Henry Wilson, *History of the Rise and Fall of the Slave Power*.

100 James Buchanan, Annual Message to Congress, December 19, 1859.

101 Einstein, "Lewis Cass," 361.

102 For the incredible stupidity of American naval officers, Buchanan, and American diplomacy in this incident, see Long, *Gold Braids*, 161–68.

103 *Congressional Globe*, Senate, 35th Cong., 1st sess. (1858), 1963.

104 *Congressional Globe*, 35th Cong., 1st sess., 1961, 1963 (May 5, 1858); James Bowlin to Cass, December 20, 1858, in Manning, *Diplomatic Correspondence: Canadian Relations*, Document 4582, 10:184.

105 James Buchanan, State of the Union Message to Congress, December 19, 1859; *Congressional Globe*, 36th Cong., 1st sess., Appendix, 1–7.

106 James Buchanan, Message to Congress, April 5, 1860. Emphasis added.

107 Policies toward South America could be detailed to make some of the same points. See Leonard, *United States–Latin American Relations*; Shurbutt, *United States–Latin American Relations*; and Joseph Smith, *Illusions*.

108 Secretary of State William Seward would share Buchanan's views on Mexico: "For a few years past, the condition of Mexico has been so unsettled as to raise the question on both sides of the Atlantic whether the time has not come when some foreign power ought, in the general interest of society, to intervene to establish a protectorate or some other form of government in that country and guaranty its continuance there." Cited in Percy F. Martin, *Maximilian in Mexico*, 66.

Chapter 5

1 I use the term "Reconstruction" to refer to the period from 1865 to 1877 and to the policy debates over how best to reincorporate the former Confederate states into the Union. Where I use the term "reconstruction," I refer to postwar rebuilding of southern infrastructure and the economy.

2 Andrew Johnson, First Annual Message to Congress, December 5, 1865.

3 Johnson's veto of the Civil Rights Act, *Senate Journal*, March 27, 1866.

4 Trefousse, *Andrew Johnson*, 198.

5 It was not accidental that Johnson specified white *men* instead of *persons*. Despite the activism of some women in the abolition movement, the Fourteenth and Fifteenth Amendments did not apply to women. See Gurko, *Ladies of Seneca Falls*; and Melder, *Beginnings of Sisterhood*.

6 Owsley, *King Cotton Diplomacy*, 547–58.

7 Museum of Modern Art, "Manet and the Execution of Maximilian," <http://www.moma.org/exhibitions/2006/Manet/timeline.htm>. Accessed September 3, 2008.

8 "Hampton Roads Conference, A. H. Stephens Private Secretary Writes about It," *New York Times*, July 22, 1895 (Stephens was vice president of the Confederacy).

9 Seward to Motley, April 16, 1866, 39th Cong., 1st sess., H. Doc. 93, 46–47.

10 Andrew Johnson, Second Annual Message to Congress, December 3, 1866.

11 As commander of the Division of the Missouri, Sheridan carried out wars of extermination against the Cheyenne, Arapaho, Kiowa, and Comanche, forcing survivors onto reservations. By one account, Sheridan, who ended his career as commander of the U.S. Army (1884–88), proclaimed: "If a village is attacked and women and children killed, the responsibility is not with the soldiers but with the people whose crimes necessitated the attack."

12 On the financiers, arms merchants, and other groups involved in financing the Mexican war effort and the wave of post–Civil War investment in Mexico, see John Mason Hart, *Empire and Revolution*.

13 The Lincoln government had promoted Canadian, Irish, German, and other European immigration during the Civil War, recruiting them as laborers with bounties of $500 and then enlisting them in the ranks of the Union Army. See Owsley, *King Cotton Diplomacy*, 496–99.

14 Andrew Johnson, Second Annual Message to Congress, December 3, 1866.

15 Senior, *Last Invasion*; Jenkins, *Fenians*.

16 Ged Martin, *Britain and the Origins of Canadian Confederation*.

17 Evidence exists that bribes to congressmen by the Russians made the purchase of Alaska possible. See Goulder, "Purchase of Alaska," 424. Herring (*From Colony to Superpower*, 257) explains that Midway was acquired "under an 1850s 'Guano Law' that permitted acquisition of uninhabited Pacific islands."

18 Cited in Holt, *Treaties Defeated by the Senate*, 109; *Congressional Globe*, June 30, 1868, 3630ff.

19 "Treaty Concerning the Cession of the Russian Possessions in North America by His Majesty the Emperor of All the Russias to the United States of America," March 30, 1867; ratified by the United States, May 28, 1867; exchanged, June 20, 1867; proclaimed by the United States, June 20, 1867.

20 Andrew Johnson, Third Annual Message to Congress, December 3, 1867.

21 Ibid.

22 Veto of the Freedmen's Bureau Bill, *Senate Journal*, February 19, 1866; first reading of the Articles of Impeachment, *Journal of the House of Representatives*, February 29, 1868; voting on the Articles of Impeachment, *Journal of the House of Representatives*, March 2, 1868.

23 Andrew Johnson, Fourth Annual Message to Congress, December 9, 1868.

24 O'Brien, *Making the Americas*, 58.

25 Democratic Party Platform, July 4, 1868, New York.

26 Republican Party Platform, May 21, 1868, Chicago.

27 Grant's message to Congress on annexation of Santo Domingo, May 31, 1870, *Senate Executive Journal*, Tuesday, May 31, 1870, 41st Cong., 2nd sess.

28 Memorandum to Congress, S. Exec. Doc., July 14, 1870, 41st Cong., 2nd sess.

29 Fuller, "Hamilton Fish," 125–214.

30 Grant issued instructions to the representatives of the United States in Bolivia, Ecuador, and Colombia and to the consular officers for whom no appropriation had been made, "to close their respective legations and consulates and cease from the performance of their duties."

31 Ulysses S. Grant, First Inaugural Address, March 4, 1869.

32 "Treaty of Reciprocity between the United States of America and the Hawaiian Kingdom"; ratifications exchanged in Washington, D.C., June 3, 1875; entered into force, September 9, 1876.

33 Ulysses S. Grant, Eighth Annual Message, December 5, 1876.

34 Foner, *Reconstruction*, 575–76.

35 De Santis, "Rutherford B. Hayes"; Foner, *Reconstruction*, chap. 12.

36 The Fifteenth Amendment to the Constitution, section 1, read: "The right of citizens of the United States to vote shall not be denied or abridged by the United States or by any State on account of race, color, or previous condition of servitude." Section 2 read: "The Congress shall have power to enforce this article by appropriate legislation."

37 Laurie and Cole, *Role of Federal Military Forces*, chap. 2.

38 Ibid., 54–55.

39 "New imperialism" refers to the period from the end of the Franco-Prussian War (1871) to 1914. In the Act of Berlin (1885), the Great Powers carved up Africa into "spheres of influence." Participants included Great Britain, Austria-Hungary, France, Germany, Russia, the United States, Portugal, Denmark, Spain, Italy, the Netherlands, Sweden, Belgium, and Turkey.

40 On the failures of Reconstruction, see Fitzgerald, *Splendid Failure*; and Foner, *Reconstruction*.

41 Rutherford B. Hayes, Annual Message to Congress, December 3, 1877.

42 Rutherford B. Hayes, Annual Message to Congress, December 6, 1880. Emphasis added.

43 For the painful details, see Millington, *American Diplomacy*.

44 A railroad and banking attorney, Frelinghuysen served from 1871 to 1877 in the Senate, chairing the Committee on Foreign Affairs during the *Alabama* claims negotiations. He also served on the electoral commission that awarded the presidency to Hayes in 1877.

45 *New York Herald*, December 16, 17, 20, 1881, January 10, 1882, cited in Healy, *James G. Blaine*, 98–99.

46 The German Imperial Navy dated from 1872, just after Prussian victory in the Franco-Prussian War (1870–71). From 1880 to 1914, German industrial development was the fastest in the world. By 1914, Germany would have the world's second-largest navy.

47 Cited in Crapol, *James G. Blaine*, 166–67.

48 Chester A. Arthur, Annual Message to Congress, December 6, 1881.

49 Michael Palmer, "The Navy."

50 See Loveman, *For la Patria*, chap. 3.

51 Doenecke, *Presidencies of Garfield and Arthur*.

52 Grover Cleveland, First Inaugural Address, March 4, 1885.

53 Grover Cleveland, Special Message to Congress, March 13, 1885.

54 Grover Cleveland, First Annual Message to Congress, December 8, 1885.

55 Grover Cleveland, Proclamations, March 13, April 17, July 23, 1885.

56 See Zakaria, *From Wealth to Power*.

57 On the role of tariffs in U.S. economic policy, see Irwin, "Historical Aspects of U.S. Trade Policy."

58 Grover Cleveland, Proclamation, September 9, 1885.

59 LaFeber, *Inevitable Revolutions*, 78–79.

60 On corporate influence and tariff politics, see Josephson, *Politicos*, chap. 16.

61 See Laurie and Cole, *Role of Federal Military Forces*, chaps. 2–7.

62 *Congressional Record*, 53rd Cong., 2nd sess., May 9, 1894, 4512.

63 Josephson, *Politicos*, 570.

64 Stromberg, "Political Economy of Liberal Corporatism"; Kolko, *Triumph of Conservatism*; Kolko, *Railroads and Regulation*.

65 Scheips, "United States Commercial Pressures."

66 Martí, *Argentina y la Primera Conferencia*, 120.

67 Mahan, "United States Looking Outward," 819.

68 Josephson, *Politicos*.

69 Message from the President of the United States, H. Exec. Doc. 35, December 21, 1842, 27th Cong., 3rd sess.

70 On U.S. regime change in Hawaii and annexation, see Kinzer, *Overthrow*, 9–30.

71 Emphasis added.

72 Hawaiian treaty, 44th Cong., 1st sess., 1876, House of Representatives, 116, pt. 1.

73 Bowers, "William M. Evarts," 238.

74 Shufeldt to Thompson, no. 64, November 24, 1879, Cruise of the *Ticonderoga*, vol. 2, Record Group 45, National Archives, cited in Hagan, *American Gunboat Diplomacy*, 99–100.

75 See "The War," special telegram to the Liverpool *Daily Post*, July 11, July 12–13, 1882.

76 Committee on Naval Affairs, House of Representatives, 47th Cong., 1st sess., no. 653: VII, cited in Davis, *Navy Second to None*, 33.

77 Davis, *Navy Second to None*, 32.

78 *Congressional Record*, 48th Cong., 1st sess., July 5, 1884, 6082.

79 *Congressional Record*, 50th Cong., 1st sess., August 16, 1888, 19, 7633.

80 Treaty of Friendship and Commerce, January 17, 1878. See Message from the President, H. Exec. Doc. 44, February 24, 1877.

81 Treaty of Reciprocity between the Kingdom of Hawaii and the United States of America, 1875, renewed in 1884; Hagan, *This People's Navy*, 201.

82 9 *Stat*. 169, Act of March 3, 1847.

83 For the debates on this issue, see *Congressional Record*, 46th Cong., sess. 1–3, 10, 128, 133, 1392, 1699, 1775, 1777, 4508, 4610.

84 Cox, *War, Foreign Affairs*, 273.

85 For details, see Goldberg, *"Baltimore" Affair*.

86 According to the Nebraska State Historical Society official website, Egan was the president of the Irish National League in Lincoln, the center for Irish home-rule activity in the United States. Unlike most Irishmen, "he joined the Republicans because he regarded American 'free-trade theories as certain to produce the same calamities as British free-trade has brought to Ireland.'"

87 J. F. Van Ingen to Blaine, January 14, 1891, State Department Consular Dispatches from Talcahuano, Record Group 122, National Archives.

88 *U.S. v. the Itata* (1893).

89 For the American war plan against Chile, including blockades of major ports and landing marines at Caldera, offers of Argentine assistance to the Americans, and reports on war hype in the press, see Goldberg, *"Baltimore" Affair*, 118–23.

90 Cited in Hagan, *This People's Navy*, 199.

91 Thus, on October 26, 1893, the *New York Times* ("Gross Military Anomaly: Improved Southern Harbors with No Proper Protection") reported that Congress had neglected the defense of the country's ports and harbors and that "when the Chilean war scare was at its height, Fort Jefferson [America's largest coastal fortification, off Florida on Garden Key] was looked on as the place most likely to be attacked by the first Chilean fleet sent to the United States, because it holds a position that has been called the military key to the Gulf of Mexico." The article called for new fortifications for various ports and harbors, including Pensacola.

92 Congressman Nelson Dingley (R.-Minn., 1881–99) cited in Goldberg, *"Baltimore" Affair*, 110. Dingley would be most remembered for the highly protectionist Dingley Act tariff of 1897.

93 The contract for the first ships of the New Navy went to John Roach's Morgan Iron Works (Roach was a prominent Republican). On the beginnings of a U.S. military-industrial complex, see Hackemer, *U.S. Navy*.

94 Topik, *Trade and Gunboats*, 146.

95 Republican Party Platform, July 7, 1892.

96 Democratic Party Platform, June 21, 1892.

Chapter 6

1 Mahan's *Influence of Sea Power on History* (1890) was the most influential text on naval policy and grand strategy in the United States for decades.

2 On Mahan's ideas, see Musicant, *Empire by Default*.

3 Mahan, "United States Looking Outward."

4 Democratic Party Platform, June 21, 1892, Chicago.

5 A collection of Mahan's articles was published as *The Interest of America in Sea Power, Present and Future* (Boston: Little Brown, 1898).

6 Healy, *James G. Blaine*, 180–204.

7 Hammett, *Hilary Abner Herbert*, 199.

8 McKinney to Gresham, January 12, April 2, 1894, U.S. Department of State, *Colombia*.

9 Protected cruisers, with armor on their decks to protect boilers and steam engines, appeared in the 1880s. The first was the Chilean *Esmeralda*, built in England. The first such ships in the American New Navy were the *Atlanta* and the *Boston* (1884) and the *Chicago* (1885).

10 LaFeber, *Inevitable Revolutions*, 121–22; Mitchell, *Danger of Dreams*, 108–18, 126–27.

11 Grover Cleveland, State of the Union Address, December 4, 1893.

12 Herrick, *American Naval Revolution*, 170.

13 On November 1, 1893, the *New York Times* headline read "Six More Ships for Brazil: Ten Vessels Now Secured to Fight Mellos Fleet." The article reported that "all ten craft were purchased through Messrs. Flint & Co."

14 Topik, *Trade and Gunboats*, 151.

15 Ibid.

16 This is sometimes written as "Mosquito Coast," and the territory is other times referred to as "Mosquitia," from the San Juan River into Honduras.

17 Annual Report, 1893, H. Exec. Doc. 1, pt. 3, 53rd Cong., 2nd sess., 340–41. Herbert served as a Democratic congressman from Alabama from 1877 to 1893, chairing the Committee on Naval Affairs in the 49th to the 52nd Congresses. He had championed the navy modernization program.

18 Annual Report, 1896, H. Doc. 3, 7, 54th Cong., 2nd sess.

19 Joseph Smith, "Brazil: On the Periphery," 217.

20 Hagan, *American Gunboat Diplomacy*, 203–4.

21 See Inter-American Commission on Human Rights, "Report on the Situation."

22 U.S. Navy Historical Center, *Dictionary of American Fighting Ships*, <http://www.history.navy.mil/danfs/m4/marblehead-ii.htm>. Accessed October 30, 2008.

23 Cited in Berman, *Under the Big Stick*, 136.

24 Leonard, "Central America," 87.

25 Sprout and Sprout, *Rise of American Naval Power*, 213–20.

26 Grenville and Young, *Politics, Strategy*, 133.

27 "Corinto in Danger," *Washington Post*, April 25, 1895, 1; "Corinto's Delivery Confirmed; The Alert Reports All Well and Quiet at San Juan del Sur," *New York Times*, May 7, 1895.

28 "Gunboats to Nicaragua," *New York Times*, April 30, 1895. Emphasis added.

29 Cleveland, *Venezuelan Boundary Controversy*.

30 Cited in Schuyler, "Richard Olney," 282.

31 Josephson, *Politicos*, 586–87.

32 In 1900, Olney called for annexation of Cuba: "The spectacle now exhibited of a President and his Cabinet sitting in Washington with an appointee and sort of imitation President sitting with his Cabinet in the Antilles must have an end, the sooner the better, and will end when Congress ceases to ignore its functions and makes Cuba in point of law what she already is in point of fact, namely, United States territory." Olney, "Growth of Our Foreign Policy."

33 Metaphorical, because in the first decade of the twentieth century the most modern dreadnought battleships had only ten- to thirteen-inch guns — nothing close to the "20-inch guns" of the Olney message. The *Maine*, sunk in Havana harbor in 1898, carried ten-inch guns. See *New York Times*, "Guns for the New Navy," October 8, 1893.

34 Cited in Dexter Perkins, *Monroe Doctrine: 1867–1907*, 190.

35 Josephson (*Politicos*, 620–24) suggests that perhaps Olney and Cleveland created a "war scare" to divert attention from a Senate investigation of the government response to the Pullman Strike and another committee investigation of a loan from an international (or "British") syndicate to stem the pending financial crisis.

36 Lord Salisbury to Olney, cited in Dexter Perkins, *Monroe Doctrine: 1867–1907*, 177–78.

37 Cited in Schuyler, "Richard Olney," 309.

38 Lodge, "England, Venezuela," 657–58.

39 Cited in Brands, *Reckless Decade*, 302.

40 Grenville and Young, *Politics, Strategy*, 176.

41 Quoted in *Literary Digest* 16, no. 1 (January 1898): 261; and cited in Dexter Perkins, *Monroe Doctrine: 1867–1907*, 282.

42 Grover Cleveland, Fourth Annual Message (second term), December 7, 1896.

43 Porter and Johnson, *National Party Platforms*, 88.

44 Ibid., 94.

45 Ibid., 99–100.

46 On the Bryan campaign, see Josephson, *Politicos*, chap. 19.

47 Porter and Johnson, *National Party Platforms*, 108.

48 Ibid., 108–9.

49 Pérez, *Cuba: Between Reform and Revolution*, 115–21.

50 Pérez, *Cuba and the United States*; LaFeber, *New Empire*.

51 Rothbard, *Wall Street, Banks, and American Foreign Policy*. Rothbard's work is controversial and looks at parts of modern American history as deriving from conflicts between the Morgan and Rockefeller interests. He explains why large corporations favor state capitalism and cartelization rather than *real* capitalism, arguing that taxation, regulation, and perpetual war are the result.

52 Olney to Cleveland, September 1895, cited in Schuyler, "Richard Olney," 282.

53 Cited in ibid., 287.

54 Teller was elected as a "Silver Republican" in 1897 but switched to the Democratic Party for the rest of his career in the Senate.

55 William McKinley, War Message, U.S. Department of State, *Papers Relating to Foreign Affairs*, 1898, 750–60. Emphasis added.

56 U.S. Navy Historical Center, "Battle of Manila Bay, 1 May 1898," <http://www.history.navy.mil/faqs/faq84-1.htm>. Accessed September 8, 2008.

57 Treaty of Paris, December 10, 1898, ending the Spanish American War.

58 Senator Orville Platt (R.-Conn.) attached the amendment, essentially authored by Secretary of War Elihu Root, to an army appropriations bill in 1901. As a condition imposed by the United States to end the military occupation, the Cuban constitutional convention accepted the terms of the amendment as an appendix to the new nation's constitution. The "Treaty of Relations" between the United States and Cuba in 1903 then incorporated the terms of the amendment.

59 "The Platt Amendment," in Bevans, *Treaties and Other International Agreements*, 8:1116–17.

60 For a brief account of German plans (1899–1903) for taking Puerto Rico and invading the U.S. eastern seaboard, see Grenville and Young, *Politics, Strategy*, 305–7.

61 Kane (*Civil Strife*, 41–43) notes that the naval planners found existing British bases tolerable, particularly in Jamaica, given the existing relationship between the United States and Great Britain.

62 Theodore Roosevelt, "Letter to Mahan: Obstacles to Immediate Expansion, 1897," <http://www.mtholyoke.edu/acad/intrel/trmahan.htm>.

63 See Hill, *Roosevelt and the Caribbean*.

64 Between 1885 and 1894, over 25,000 Japanese migrated to Hawaii, most as contract laborers in the plantations. See Wilson and Hosokawa, *East to America*, 141.

65 Bailey, *Diplomatic History*, 482–83.

66 Grover Cleveland, Message to the Senate and House of Representatives, December 18, 1893.

67 Queen Liliuokalani went to Washington, D.C., to protest the proposed treaty of annexation. The official protest began: "I, Liliuokalani of Hawaii, by the will of God named heir apparent on the tenth day of April, A.D. 1877, and by the grace of God Queen of the Hawaiian Islands on the seventeenth day of January, A.D. 1893, do hereby protest against the ratification of a certain treaty, which, so I am informed, has been signed at Washington by Messrs. Hatch, Thurston, and Kinney, purporting to cede those Islands to the territory and dominion of the United States. I declare such a treaty to be an act of wrong toward the native and part-native people of Hawaii" (Official Protest to the Treaty of Annexation, June 17, 1897).

68 55th Cong., 2nd sess., July 7, 1898.

69 Protest Resolution to Secretary of State W. R. Day, August 6, 1898, <www.hawaiiankingdom.org/protest_1898.shtml>. Accessed September 8, 2009.

70 U.S. Department of State, "Annexation of Hawaii 1898," <http://www.state.gov/r/pa/ho/time/gp/17661.htm>. Accessed September 4, 2008.

71 Congressional debate on the Hawaii Organic Act, 56th Cong., 1st sess., December 4, 1899–June 7, 1900; University of Hawaii Libraries, Special Collections at <http://libweb/hawaii.edu/digcoll/annexation/organic/oa001.html>. Accessed September 8, 2009.

72 U.S. Congress, *House Journal*, April 6, 1900, 3851–64.

73 Ibid., 3855.

74 In 1900, President McKinley sent 5,000 American troops from the Philippines to China to "protect American lives and property" during the Boxer rebellion. Schlesinger (*Imperial Presidency*, 88–89) calls this deployment "a spectacular case of military

intervention for political purposes. . . . The Chinese government even declared war against the United States. Although the United States declined to declare war in response, the Courts later ruled that a state of war had existed. But at no point was Congress consulted." *Hamilton v. McLaughry* (1905).

75 Herwig, *Germany's Vision*; Herwig, *Politics of Frustration*.

76 Pillsbury, "The Destiny of Duty," 170n77.

77 Soldiers' letters, reprinted in Foner and Winchester, *Anti-Imperialist Reader*, 316–23.

78 See John Bassett Moore, "The Interoceanic Canal and the Hay-Pauncefote Treaty," *New York Times*, March 4, 1900, 23.

79 For example, in 1901 British and German pressure under the guns of warships had convinced Guatemalan dictator (1898–1920) Manuel Estrada Cabrera to repay debts to those nations, without U.S. objection. See Kneer, *Great Britain and the Caribbean*.

80 Louis Labadie Driggs, "Uncle Sam's Naval Base in the Caribbean Sea," *New York Times*, October 5, 1902.

81 See Beale, *Theodore Roosevelt*, 399–432, for a detailed account of this episode.

82 Livermore, "Theodore Roosevelt, the American Navy."

83 For German diplomatic correspondence on this incident, see Dugdale, *Growing Antagonism*. Collin (*Theodore Roosevelt's Caribbean*, chap. 4) offers an extended discussion of the incident.

84 Jonas (*United States and Germany*, 72) suggests that the German Foreign Office "had reached the decision to accept arbitration of its own accord, moved not by ultimata but by genuine concern for maintaining good relations with the United States."

85 See Morris, *Rise of Roosevelt*; and Morris, "A Matter of Extreme Urgency."

86 *New York Herald*, January 31, 1903, cited in Jonas, *United States and Germany*, 73.

87 Theodore Roosevelt, Fourth Annual Message, December 6, 1904.

88 Ibid.

89 Albert B. Hart, *Monroe Doctrine*, 232.

90 Ibid., 233. Emphasis added.

91 Theodore Roosevelt, Fifth Annual Message, December 5, 1905.

92 Ibid.

93 "This conjunction of an immense military establishment and a large arms industry is new in the American experience. The total influence — economic, political, even spiritual — is felt in every city, every State house, every office of the Federal government. We recognize the imperative need for this development. Yet we must not fail to comprehend its grave implications." "Farewell Radio and Television Address to the American People" [commonly known as the "Military-Industrial Complex Speech"], January 17, 1961, online at American Presidency Project.

Chapter 7

1 Cited in Pérez, *Cuba: Between Reform and Revolution*, 141.

2 *Cherokee Nation v. Georgia* (1831). See Walter L. Williams, "United States Indian Policy."

3 *United States v. Kagama* (1885), 379–82; *Elk v. Wilkins* (1884), 99–103; cited in Walter L. Williams, "United States Indian Policy."

4 Walter L. Williams, "United States Indian Policy."

5 Collin, *Theodore Roosevelt's Caribbean*, 431–32.

6 Elihu Root, private letter, cited in Kane, *Civil Strife*, 66–67.

7 Pérez, *Cuba: Between Reform and Revolution*, 137.

8 Cited in ibid., 332.

9 Cited in McCulloch, *Path between the Seas*, 383–84.

10 Report of the Special Committee on the Termination of the National Emergency, November 19, 1973, 93rd Cong., 1st sess., S. Rep. 93-549, Emergency Powers Statutes, Provisions of Federal Law Now in Effect Delegating to the Executive Extraordinary Authority in Time of National Emergency.

11 Cited in Ninkovich, "Theodore Roosevelt," 233.

12 TR to John Davis Long, 23 June and 30 September, 1897, cited in ibid., 237.

13 Roosevelt established the receivership within the Bureau of Insular Affairs (War Department), the same agency that administered the Philippines, pursuant to an executive arrangement between the United States and the Dominican Republic in February 1905.

14 Vargas Vila, *Ante los Bárbaros*. First published in the magazine *Nemesis*, the book went through multiple editions. Vargas Vila was expelled from the United States.

15 Translated by Bonnie Frederick, in Brians et al., *Reading about the World*.

16 On Hispanism, see Pike, *Hispanismo*.

17 Kane, *Civil Strife*, 74–76.

18 Ibid., 75. Reference is to the plan by Alfred Graf van Schlieffen, adopted before 1906 by the German General Staff, for attacks against France on the Western Front while also fighting a war on the Eastern (Russian) Front.

19 Department of the Navy, Navy Historical Center, "The Cruise of the Great White Fleet," <http://www.history.navy.mil/library/online/gwf_cruise.htm>. Accessed May 18, 2008.

20 Austin Bay, "TR's Big Stick: The Great White Fleet's Voyage," December 12, 2007, at <www.realclearpolitics.com/articles/2007/12/trs_big_stick_the_great_white.html>. Accessed September 8, 2009.

21 Department of the Navy, Navy Historical Center, "The Great White Fleet," <http://www.history.navy.mil/faqs/faq42-1.htm>. Accessed September 2, 2008.

22 William H. Taft, Annual Message to Congress, December 3, 1912. Taft, as governor general in the Philippines, had remarked, "We are doing God's work here." See Karnow, *In Our Image*, 228.

23 On business expansion to Latin America, see O'Brien, *Making the Americas*, chap. 3.

24 On Clark's influence, including later opposition to the League of Nations and, still later, to the United Nations, see Fox, *J. Reuben Clark*.

25 Address to the Third National Peace Conference, Baltimore, May 4, 1911, in Fred M. Wilson Papers (Ursinus College), cited in Iriye, *From Nationalism*, 214–15.

26 Wilson to Baldwin, January 19, 1910, Fred M. Wilson Papers (Ursinus College), cited in Iriye, *From Nationalism*, 215.

27 Bryce to Foreign Office, June 15, 1910, FO 371 (U.S.), 1910, vol. 1023; Knox to the American Society for Judicial Settlement of International Disputes, November 8, 1911; both cited in Callcott, *Western Hemisphere*, 111.

28 Address of Assistant Secretary of State Adolph Berle Jr., "The Policy of the United States in Latin America," Academy of Political Science, New York City, May 3, 1939, U.S. Department of State, Press Releases, XX, 501, Publication 1328: 378.

29 Albert B. Hart, *Monroe Doctrine*, 234.

30 The patriarch of historians of U.S.–Latin American policy, Samuel Flagg Bemis (some called him Samuel "wave the flag" Bemis), called the post-1898 period the "new epoch of protective imperialism" (*Latin American Policy*, 140).

31 Emphasis added.

32 *Congressional Record*, 62nd Cong., 2nd sess., 10045.

33 García Calderón, *Latin America*, 298–99.

34 Ibid., 312.

35 Cited in Blum, *Reforging the White Republic*, 240.

36 Crichfield, *American Supremacy*, 1:386.

37 Taft was an exception. He identified with Unitarianism and got along well with Bishop Gregorio Aglipay, a Roman Catholic priest who had formed the new Philippine Independent Church. For this deviation, evangelical Protestants criticized him in the 1908 election.

38 Bemis, *Latin American Policy*, 169.

39 Woodrow Wilson, Circular Note to European Powers, November 24, 1913, explaining his policies, cited in Healy, *Drive to Hegemony*, 177.

40 Bemis, *Latin American Policy*, 185.

41 Petrie, "American Neutrality."

42 John Mason Hart, *Revolutionary Mexico*; O'Brien, *Revolutionary Mission*.

43 Colby N. Chester, "Present Status of the Monroe Doctrine," cited in Callcott, *Western Hemisphere*, 128.

44 Shortly after the Cuban Revolution of 1959, with U.S. support, a successor institution (*Corte Centroamericana de Justicia*, or *CCJ*) was created in December 1962.

45 Woodrow Wilson, Speech to Congress, April 2, 1917.

46 Albert B. Hart, *Monroe Doctrine*, 374.

47 See Calder, *Impact of Intervention*.

48 Seligmann, "Conquest of Haiti," 35.

49 For trade and commercial data, see Tulchin, *Aftermath of War*, chap. 3.

50 Ibid., 67.

51 See Lloyd Gardner, "American Foreign Policy."

52 Grimmett, "Instances of Use of United States Armed Forces Abroad," 8–14.

Chapter 8

1 Declaration Concerning the Laws of Naval War, in Parry, *Consolidated Treaty Series*, 208:338 (1909). This declaration attempted to specify the rights of neutral shipping in war, the rules governing blockades, the types of commodities that might be considered "contraband of war," and the conditions under which neutral shipping might be seized or destroyed.

2 "U.S. 'Strict Accountability' Warning to Germany," February 10, 1915, U.S. Department of State, *Foreign Relations of the United States*, 1915 Supplement, 95–97.

3 Robert Lansing's cover-up on the *Lusitania* affair contributed to the resignation of Secretary of State William Jennings Bryan. Lansing then became secretary of state.

4 Zimmermann to Heinrich von Eckhardt, German minister to Mexico, cited in Tuchman, *Zimmermann Telegram*, 146.

5 Woodrow Wilson, Speech to Congress, April 2, 1917.

6   See Ohl, "The Navy, the War Industries Board," 17–22.

7   Wolper, "Wilsonian Public Diplomacy."

8   For Colonel House's effort to elaborate on the Fourteen Points for dissemination in the American media, see U.S. Department of State, *Foreign Affairs of the United States*, 1918, Supplement 1, *The World War*, 1:405–13.

9   March 4, 1919, cited in Lloyd Gardner, "American Foreign Policy," 223.

10 Commonly cited estimates put total combatant dead at approximately 9 million and wounded at 21 million. Including civilians, dead and wounded are estimated at 40 million.

11 "The Allies Conditional Acceptance of the Fourteen Points," November 5, 1918, U.S. Department of State, *Foreign Relations of the United States*, 1918 Supplement, 1:468–69.

12 For a radical assessment of the process, see Spector, "Record of the Democracies."

13 Later applications of the nonrecognition policy would include governments in China, Japan, Italy, and the post-1940 Soviet Union in Eastern Europe under the Stimson Doctrine — first applied to the Japanese-created "Manchuko" regime upon invading China in 1931–32.

14 For a remarkable account of this tragic misadventure, see Graves, *America's Siberian Adventure*. Graves's book features a foreword by the secretary of war, who delivered a secret memorandum to him from Woodrow Wilson regarding the mission.

15 In 1918, ex-president Taft declared: "Then there is Russia, controlled by the Bolsheviki. I do not know what we are going to do about Russia. I know what we ought to have done. We ought to have sent two hundred thousand men in there originally, and with additional forces from our Allies we could have stamped out Bolshevism" (address delivered at dinner of editors and publishers, in New York City, December 6, 1918, in Marburg and Flack, *Taft Papers on League of Nations*, 158).

16 Murray, *Red Scare*; Feuerlicht, *America's Reign of Terror*; Higham, *Strangers in the Land*.

17 On racial violence after World War I, see Laurie and Cole, *Role of Federal Military Forces*, chap. 12; and Brophy, *Reconstructing the Dreamland*.

18 Dray, *At the Hands of Persons Unknown*.

19 According to Laurie and Cole (*Role of Federal Military Forces*, 233), the Military Intelligence Division "cooperated with the Office of Naval Intelligence; the U.S. Secret Service; the Bureau of Investigation (later FBI); the War Trade Intelligence Board; the Department of Labor; the Plant Protection Service; state and local law enforcement agencies; and volunteer groups, especially the American Protective League (APL). By mid-June 1917 the APL had six hundred branches and a membership of 100,000, soon to peak at well over 250,000. Its membership assisted MID in its surveillance of radicals, aliens, and labor groups and was commended by the Army chief of staff in 1919."

20 See Talbert, *Negative Intelligence*; and Jensen, *Army Surveillance*.

21 Senator Robert La Follette, "Free Speech and the Right of Congress to Declare the Objects of the War," Senate Chamber, October 6, 1917, *Congressional Record*, 65th Cong., 1st sess., 786–87.

22 See Hunt, *Ideology*; Calhoun, *Power and Principle*; and Clements, *Presidency of Woodrow Wilson*.

23 Justice, "Women, Wilson, and Emergency War Measures."

24 Article 10 of the Covenant of the League of Nations reads: "The Members of the League undertake to respect and preserve as against external aggression the territorial integrity and existing political independence of all Members of the League. In case of any such aggression or in case of any threat or danger of such aggression the Council shall advise upon the means by which this obligation shall be fulfilled."

25 In 1917, the Jones-Shafroth Act granted Puerto Ricans a "special" citizenship status, making them eligible for conscription. Organic Act of Puerto Rico ("Jones Act," 39 *Stat.* 461, March 2, 1917).

26 Ambrosius, *Woodrow Wilson*, 139.

27 Marburg and Flack, *Taft Papers on League of Nations*, 137.

28 Kelchner, *Latin American Relations*, 1–2, 10.

29 Cited in Gaddis Smith, *Last Years*, 31. Emphasis added.

30 Warren G. Harding, Inaugural Address, March 4, 1921.

31 Ibid.

32 Thomas G. Paterson et al. (*American Foreign Relations*) use the term "independent internationalism" to include a "non-military" foreign policy, dating from the Washington Naval Conference (November 12, 1921–February 6, 1922).

33 Robert Freeman Smith, "American Foreign Relations," 232–62.

34 William Appleman Williams, "The Legend"; William Appleman Williams, "A Note."

35 Powaski, *Toward an Entangling Alliance*, 27–29.

36 Senator Reed Smoot, (R.-Utah) the first native-born Utah senator, served simultaneously as an Apostle of the Mormon Church. His election created considerable controversy in the Senate, and hearings on his seating lasted from 1904 until 1907. Smoot was reelected until 1933, serving as the chairman of the Foreign Finance Committee.

37 Coatsworth and Williamson, "Roots of Latin American Protectionism"; Clemens and Williamson, "Closed Jaguar."

38 *Stat.*, vol. 46, pt. 2, 2343.

39 "An Act to Limit the Migration of Aliens into the United States," May 26, 1924. This act was approved in the Senate with only six dissenting votes. It extended screening authority to consular officials abroad, who would issue, or deny, visas, thereby placing the actual restriction at overseas posts rather than in American ports and, incidentally, creating opportunities for the exercise of discretion — and for corruption.

40 Trevor, *An Analysis*. Harding expressed his regret regarding the Japanese exclusion in his signing message, May 26, 1924, noting that he would have liked to sever it from the legislation.

41 *Literary Digest*, May 10, 1924, 12–13.

42 This connection was consistent with the eugenics movement's and scientific racism movement's beliefs that bolshevism was a dangerous theory because it advocated universal equality rather than white supremacy. See Stoddard, *Rising Tide of Color*; and Grant, *Passing of the Great Race*.

43 Ellison DuRant Smith, April 9, 1924, *Congressional Record*, 68th Cong., 1st sess., vol. 65, 5961–62.

44 *Congressional Record*, June 24, 1924, 68th Cong., 1st sess., 11744. In the case of European colonies in the Caribbean and in South America, immigrants would be

charged to the quota of the colonial power (for example, from Jamaica, the immigrant would be charged to Great Britain's quota). In practice, the 1924 legislation remained in place, with minor changes, until 1965, when "national origins" quotas were eliminated.

45 See Ngai, *Impossible Subjects*, 23, 50.

46 *Congressional Record*, Senate, April 3, 1924, 68th Cong., 1st sess., 5474.

47 Article 8 of the 1848 treaty provided that any Mexicans who remained in the United States had to declare their preference to retain Mexican citizenship within one year, or "[they] shall be considered to have elected to become citizens of the United States."

48 Emphasis added.

49 In its decision in the case of *U.S. v. Bhagat Singh Thind* (1923), the Supreme Court decided that Asian Indians were ineligible for citizenship because U.S. law allowed only free whites to become naturalized citizens. The Court concluded that Indians were "Caucasians" and that anthropologists considered them to be of the same race as white Americans, but "the average man knows perfectly well that there are unmistakable and profound differences."

50 See, for example, the proposals by Senator William J. Harris (D.-Ga.), April 7, 1924, 5739, and Senator Morris Sheppard (D.-Tex.), April 14, 1924, 6314, 68th Cong., 1st sess., 65, pt. 6. Harris had served as director of the Census Bureau (1913–15). A "Wilson Democrat," he continued to campaign for exclusion of Mexicans and Latin Americans (but not Canadians) throughout the 1920s.

51 Calvin Coolidge, First Message to Congress, December 6, 1923.

52 *Congressional Record*, 66th Cong., 1st sess., 1919, vol. 58, pt. 3, 2421, cited in Robert Freeman Smith, "American Foreign Relations," 239.

Chapter 9

1 Inman, *Inter-American Conferences*.

2 Secretary of State Charles Evan Hughes, "Some Aspects of the Work of the Department of State," 67th Cong., 2nd sess. (1922), S. Doc. 206, 10.

3 Kemmerer supervised fiscal and economic reforms in Colombia, Chile, Ecuador, Bolivia, Peru, Mexico, and Guatemala, in addition to missions in Europe, China, Turkey, and South Africa. See Drake, *Money Doctor*.

4 Iglesias, "Pan-American Federation of Labor," 390–92.

5 Tulchin, *Aftermath of War*, 79–82; Robert Freeman Smith, "Latin America, the United States, and the European Powers."

6 Charles E. Hughes, Address to the American Bar Association, August 30, 1923, "Observations on the Monroe Doctrine," *American Journal of International Law* 17, no. 4 (October 1923): 611–28. Emphasis added.

7 Sherman, *Diplomatic and Commercial Relations*, 153.

8 The term "race riot" was the term used most often at the time. In some cases, "massacre" might have been more appropriate.

9 Sherman, *Diplomatic and Commercial Relations*, 154.

10 Warren Harding, Speech in Birmingham, Alabama, October 26, 1921.

11 Walter White, *Nation*, June 15, 1921; "The Eruption of Tulsa," *Nation*, June 29, 1921, <http://www.thenation.com/doc/20010820/1921tulsa>. Accessed April 9, 2008.

12 Senate, 67th Cong., 2nd sess., S. Rep. 794. For a colorful and provocative summary of these events, see Schoultz, *Beneath the United States*, 256–60.

13 U.S. Department of the Navy, Navy Historical Center, "Inquiry into Occupation and Administration of Haiti."

14 Editorials by Ernest H. Gruening against the Haitian and Dominican Republic occupations were "Haiti and Santo Domingo Today — I," *Nation* 114 (February 8, 1922); and "Haiti under American Occupation," *Century* 103 (April 1922).

15 For the Wilson administration's retrospective justification of the Haiti intervention, see Letter from Hon. Robert Lansing, Former Secretary of State, to the Chairman of the Select Committee on Haiti and the Dominican Republic, Washington, D.C., May 4, 1922, in Gantenbein, *The Evolution of Our Latin American Policy*, 36. In addition to the financial chaos and political disorder in Haiti, Lansing emphasized the German "menace to the position of the United States in the Caribbean Sea, to the security of the Panama Canal and, consequently, to the peace of this hemisphere."

16 Cited in Sherman, "Harding Administration and the Negro," 164.

17 Cited in Prince, *Haiti: Family Business*, 62–63.

18 The Fordney-McCumber Tariff (1922) raised tariffs to around 38 percent ad valorem, with the usual package of negotiated privileges for certain industries and agricultural interests.

19 Covenant of the League of Nations, article 21.

20 Inman, *Inter-American Conferences*, 101.

21 Ibid., 102.

22 Ibid., 104.

23 Emphasis added.

24 Appointed governor general of the Philippines (1927–29), Stimson opposed Philippine independence for the same reasons — racial incapacity for civilized government.

25 U.S. Department of State, *United States and Other American Republics*, 5.

26 Calvin Coolidge, Speech at the Gettysburg Battlefield, Decoration Day, May 30, 1928.

27 Confidential Memorandum by Undersecretary of State Robert Olds, January 2, 1927, Document 817.00/4456, Record Group 59, National Archives.

28 See Dean, *Imperial Brotherhood*.

29 Calvin Coolidge, Speech at the Gettysburg Battlefield, Decoration Day, May 30, 1928.

30 William Appleman Williams, "The Legend," 76.

31 Cited in Gaddis Smith, *Last Years*, 33.

32 Calvin Coolidge, Speech at the Gettysburg Battlefield, Decoration Day, May 30, 1928.

33 Calvin Coolidge, Sixth Annual Message to Congress, December 4, 1928.

34 Calvin Coolidge, Address before the Pan American Conference, Havana, Cuba, January 16, 1928.

35 Clark, "Memorandum on the Monroe Doctrine."

36 Robert Freeman Smith, "Latin America, the United States, and the European Powers," 115.

37 Porter and Johnson, *National Party Platforms*, 278.

38 For the 1928 electoral campaign, see ibid., 270–324.

39 Cohen, *Empire without Tears*, 118–23.

40 Gaddis Smith (*Last Years*, 35) notes that as early as 1905 Theodore Roosevelt suggested that Japan adopt its own version of the Monroe Doctrine; in 1934 Japan declared that it

had "special responsibilities in East Asia." See Blakeslee, "Japanese Monroe Doctrine," 671–81.

41 For a brief account of this dispute, see Woolsey, "Leticia Dispute," 94–99.

42 Thomas P. Anderson, *Matanza*, 151.

43 See Ellis, *Republican Foreign Policy*, chaps. 7–8.

44 "Withdrawal of Military Forces from Haiti; Agreement between the United States of America and Haiti, modifying the agreement of August 7, 1933," signed July 24, 1934, Executive Agreement Series No. 68 (Washington D.C.: Government Printing Office, 1934).

45 There is ongoing debate over the significance of the New Deal for American domestic politics and foreign relations. For diametrically opposing views, see Bernstein, "The New Deal," 281–82; and Schweikart and Allen, *A Patriot's History*.

46 Agricultural Adjustment Act, Public Law 73-10, enacted May 12, 1933.

47 Ngai, *Impossible Subjects*.

48 Franklin Delano Roosevelt, Address before the Special Session of the Governing Board of the Pan American Union in Celebration of Pan American Day, Washington, D.C., April 12, 1933.

49 Fraser and Gerstle, *Rise and Fall*.

50 Green, *Containment of Latin America*.

51 Montevideo Convention on the Rights and Duties of States, Signed at Montevideo, December 26, 1933; Article 8 reaffirmed by Protocol, December 23, 1936.

52 Inman, *Inter-American Conferences*, 156–57. Inman's book was published posthumously — he did not live to see the U.S. invasion of the Dominican Republic in 1965.

53 Chap. 474, 48 *Stat.* 943, codified at *U.S. Code* 19 (June 12, 1934), §1351.

54 Bulmer-Thomas, *Economic History of Latin America*, 201–23; Gellman, *Good Neighbor Diplomacy*, 48.

55 U.S. Department of State, Bureau of Public Affairs Historical Office, "U.S. Policy toward Latin America."

56 Inman, *Inter-American Conferences*, 180.

57 Friedman, *Nazis and Good Neighbors*.

58 Gilderhus (*Second Century*, 84–91) describes these events in Bolivia and Mexico.

59 Hull, *Memoirs*, 1:823.

60 Cited in Lind, *American Way of Strategy*, 104.

61 According to Cramer and Prutsch ("Nelson A. Rockefeller's Office," 786–89, 795), the Office of Inter-American Affairs used five subsidiary corporations, including Prencin-radio, to serve as a screen for covert operations that the U.S. government did not wish to be associated with in public.

62 In April 1941, the United States put Iceland (part of the Western Hemisphere) under its protection and in July occupied Greenland. Roosevelt's advisers persuaded him that West Africa could not be included within the reach of the Monroe Doctrine. Gaddis Smith, *Last Years*, 39.

63 Sicker, *Geopolitics of Security*, 100–101.

64 See Child, *Unequal Alliance*.

65 On the 1930s neutrality acts, see Powaski, *Toward an Entangling Alliance*, 66–91.

66 Herring, *From Colony to Superpower*, 536–37, 588.

67 Schoultz, *Beneath the United States*, 314–15.

68 Executive Order 8802, June 25, 1941, "Prohibition of Discrimination in the Defense Industry."

69 "Getting to Know the Racial Views of Our Past Presidents," 44–46.

70 Dalfiume, "Military Segregation"; Charles Johnson, "The Army, the Negro"; McGuire, "Desegregation of the Armed Forces."

71 MacGregor, *Integration of the Armed Forces*; Stimson and Bundy, *On Active Service*, 461–64. The quotations are from Stimson, *Diaries of Stimson*, January 24, 1942.

72 Colonel Eugene R. Householder, Speech before Conference of Negro Editors and Publishers, Washington, D.C., December 8, 1941, cited in Gibson, *Knocking Down Barriers*, 5–6.

73 *U.S. ex rel Lynn v. Downer* (1944). A minority opinion in the case is included as Appendix A in Ken Lawrence, "Thirty Years of Selective Service Racism" (1971), <http://www.sojournertruth.net/waybdf.pdf>. Accessed September 10, 2008.

74 Breckinridge, "Winfred Lynn Case," 370; MacDonald, "Novel Case of Winfred Lynn."

75 "Editorial," *Crisis* 47: 209.

Chapter 10

1 They did not officially war against each other if one does not count clandestine combat between American and Soviet forces, as occurred in Korea and elsewhere.

2 Westad, *Decisive Encounters*.

3 Vietnam's Ministry of Labor, War Invalids, and Social Affairs released figures on April 3, 1995, reporting that the war caused 1.1 million fighter — Viet Cong guerrillas and North Vietnamese soldiers — and nearly 2 million civilian deaths in the North and the South between 1954 and 1975. Other estimates are much higher, even without counting casualties in Laos and Cambodia.

4 Cited in Van Dusen, *Spiritual Legacy*, 5–12.

5 On the Maisky memo (a memo outlining a scenario for dominating Europe — uncovered after the Cold War ended), see Pechatnov, "Big Three after World War II." For contradictory views on the beginning of the Cold War, see Lens, *Forging of the American Empire*, 347, 349; and Lind, *American Way of Strategy*, 122.

6 In the years since 1990, newly opened archives, memoirs, and revisionist research have begun to provide a more multidimensional history of the not-so-Cold War for much of the planet. An important contribution for Latin America is Joseph and Spenser, *In from the Cold*.

7 Speech by Leonid Brezhnev, November 13, 1968, at the Fifth Congress of the Polish United Workers' Party.

8 S. Koralev, "Sovereignty and the International Obligations of Socialist Countries," *Pravda*, September 26, 1988; Ouimet, *Rise and Fall*.

9 Thus, at an inter-American conference in Mexico in 1945, the U.S. delegation supported a draft resolution calling for the end of economic nationalism "in all its forms," urging Latin Americans to open their markets to American exports and investment. See Green, *Containment of Latin America*.

10 Bissell, *Reflections*, 142.

11 Lind, *American Way of Strategy*, 111.

12 On the Soviet perspective, see Zubok and Pleshakov, *Inside the Kremlin's Cold War*; and Mastny, *Cold War*.

13 On American covert operations, see Prados, *Safe for Democracy*; and Weiner, *Legacy of Ashes*.

14 Michael R. Gardner, *Harry Truman*.

15 The Supreme Court ruled such provisions unconstitutional in *Loving v. Commonwealth of Virginia* (1967), a case on appeal from Virginia, in which the judge told the "mixed" couple: "Almighty God created the races, white, black, yellow, Malay and red, and he placed them on separate continents. And but for the interference with his arrangement there would be no cause for such marriages. The fact that he separated the races shows that he did not intend for the races to mix."

16 Borstelmann, *Cold War and the Color Line*.

17 I use the term "jingoism" here in its standard dictionary meaning: "extreme patriotism in the form of aggressive foreign policy" or "bellicose chauvinism."

18 See North Atlantic Treaty Organization, "NATO, the First Five Years."

19 Brands (*Devil We Knew*, 24–27) notes that the NATO treaty also demonstrated U.S. lack of confidence in the United Nations and collective security.

20 See Doenecke, *Not to the Swift*; and Taft, *A Foreign Policy for Americans*.

21 Robert A. Taft, "Washington Report," August 3, 1949, cited in Moser, "Principles," <http://www.ashbrook.org/publicat/dialogue/moser.html#10>. Accessed April 2, 2009.

22 Taft, *A Foreign Policy for Americans*, 12–13.

23 Rock, *Argentina*, 289–96.

24 In no year from 1953 to 1973 did fewer than twenty countries host 1,000 or more U.S. troops. On average, from 1950 to 2000, 535,000 troops (23 percent of all military personnel) were deployed on foreign soil. See Kane, "Global U.S. Troop Deployment."

25 Truman established the foundations of American global anticommunism and containment for the next half century informed by George F. Kennan's "long telegram" from the Soviet Union (February 22, 1946, to Washington, D.C.).

26 Emphasis added.

27 Three weeks before Truman signed the National Security Act, the Russian delegation had walked out of a meeting in Paris at which participants discussed distribution of Marshall Plan aid and then prohibited receipt of such aid by their Eastern European "allies."

28 According to Weiner (*Legacy of Ashes*, 24–25), eighty-one such operations occurred during Truman's second term.

29 Porter and Johnson, *National Party Platforms*, 430.

30 Ibid., 432. Emphasis added.

31 Ibid., 453. Emphasis added.

32 In Bogotá in 1948, the American nations adopted the "American Declaration of the Rights and Duties of Man," the first such declaration on human rights adopted after World War II.

33 Cooper, "Greek Civil War, 1944–1949." Herring (*From Colony to Superpower*, 617) estimates 100,000 killed, 5,000 executed, and 800,000 refugees.

34 At the time, James Reston commented in the *New York Times*: "Like the Monroe Doctrine [the Truman Doctrine] warned that the United States would resist efforts to impose a political system or foreign domination on areas vital to our security" (Gaddis Smith, *Last Years*, 56).

35 Cited in Lens, *Forging of the American Empire*, 357. Marshall's threats were reiterated

by Truman and others. See James E. Miller, "Taking Off the Gloves"; and Powers, *Not without Honor.*

36 Bacevich, *American Empire*, 4.

37 Prados, *Safe for Democracy*, chap. 3.

38 Historian Ernest R. May (*American Cold War Strategy*, vii, 1–19) provides valuable insight into the bureaucratic, intellectual, and political process that created NSC-68; see also Chace, *Acheson*, 274–79.

39 Taft, *A Foreign Policy for Americans*, 33.

40 Mark O'Neill writes that "the intervention of the U.S. 7th Fleet saved the remnants of the Chinese nationalist forces opposed to Mao and led by Chiang Kai-shek. This assistance from the United States virtually guaranteed Mao's entry into the Korean War." O'Neill, "Soviet Involvement," 21.

41 Spaulding, *First Cold Warrior*; Gaddis, *Strategies of Containment.*

42 In 1948, using the authority of the Smith Act (1940), the Truman administration ordered the arrest of leaders of the U.S. Communist Party. The Supreme Court upheld convictions against those arrested, essentially declaring the Communist Party a criminal conspiracy.

43 Porter and Johnson, *National Party Platforms*, 496.

44 Cited in Cook, *Declassified Eisenhower*, 122–23.

45 Soley and Nichols, *Clandestine Radio Broadcasting.*

46 Weiner, *Legacy of Ashes*, 77.

47 Cited in Prados, *Safe for Democracy*, 150–51.

48 Weiner, *Legacy of Ashes*, 66–68.

49 Office of the Public Register, *Public Papers of the Presidents*, Dwight D. Eisenhower, 1960, 1035–40.

50 Weiner, *Legacy of Ashes*, 76.

51 The World Bank's official history of the institutional redesign of the postwar global system, "World Bank Group Historical Chronology," updated November 2008, <http://siteresources.worldbank.org/extarchives/resources/wb_historical_chronology_1944_2005.pdf>.

52 George F. Kennan to the Secretary of State, March 29, 1950, U.S. Department of State, *Foreign Relations of the United States, 1950*, 2:598–624, cited in Gaddis Smith, *Last Years*, 238.

53 Klare and Kornbluh, *Low Intensity Warfare*; Loveman, *For la Patria*, 155–226.

54 Gaddis Smith, *Last Years*, 63–64.

55 For his career as "labor ambassador to Latin America," see Romualdi, *Presidents and Peons.*

56 "Inter-American Treaty of Reciprocal Assistance" (Rio Treaty), 1947.

57 George F. Kennan to the Secretary of State, March 29, 1950, U.S. Department of State, *Foreign Relations of the United States, 1950*, 2:598–624.

58 NSC-68, "United States Objectives."

59 U.S. Department of State, *Foreign Relations of the United States, 1950*, 1:244. Emphasis added.

60 PPS-26, "Problem to Establish U.S. Policy."

61 Inman, *Inter-American Conferences*, 236.

62 Ibid., 248.

63 Dix, *Colombia*, 105.

64 U.S. Department of State, "Communist Involvement in the Colombian Riots."

65 "Final Act of Bogotá," Resolution 32.

66 "The Acting Secretary of State to Diplomatic Representatives in the American Republics," top secret, October 15, 1948, U.S. Department of State, *Foreign Relations of the United States, 1948*, vol. 9.

67 U.S. Department of State, Bureau of Public Affairs Historical Office, "U.S. Policy toward Latin America: Recognition and Non-Recognition," 42.

68 Batista had found ways to work with the Communists in the 1930s and 1940s, but he was also willing to board the Cold War bus to gain Washington's support — as he did until 1958.

69 U.S. Department of State, Bureau of Public Affairs Historical Office, "U.S. Policy toward Latin America: Recognition and Non-Recognition," 52–53.

70 An important exception was the 1952 revolution in Bolivia, in which the United States was able to co-opt the "reluctant revolutionaries." See Klein, *Bolivia*, chap. 8; and Blasier, *Hovering Giant*.

71 Loveman, *For la Patria*, 149–56.

72 NSC-141, "Reexamination of U.S. Programs." Emphasis added.

73 Porter and Johnson, *National Party Platforms*, 497–500.

74 On the intervention in Guatemala, see Gleijeses, *Shattered Hope*; Schlesinger and Kinzer, *Bitter Fruit*; and Schneider, *Communism*.

75 Inman, *Inter-American Conferences*, 258–59.

76 Sklar and Hagen, "Declaration of Solidarity for the Preservation of the Political Integrity."

77 "Operation PBSUCCESS: The United States and Guatemala, 1952–1954," CIA History Staff document by Nicholas Cullather, 1994. Excerpts of this declassified document are available on the online site of the National Security Archive.

78 McClintock, *State Terror*, 29.

Chapter 11

1 Lyman Kirkpatrick, *Real CIA*, chap. 7.

2 Department of State Memorandum, "Current Basic United States Policy toward Cuba" [Herter to Eisenhower], November 5, 1959, cited in National Security Archive, "Bay of Pigs Forty Years After: Chronology."

3 Cited in National Security Archive, "Bay of Pigs Forty Years After: Chronology."

4 Lyman Kirkpatrick, *Real CIA*.

5 U.S. Department of State, *Foreign Relations of the United States, 1961–1963*, vol. 10, *Cuba, 1961–62*; Michael Warner, "The CIA's Internal Probe of the Bay of Pigs Affair"; Kornbluh, *Bay of Pigs Declassified*.

6 Schoultz (*Infernal Little Cuban Republic*, 142–69) provides a detailed account of the planning for the Bay of Pigs invasion, including the possibility that CIA officials expected the invasion to fail but also expected President Kennedy to send in American forces to save the day and overthrow Castro. See also Kornbluh, *Bay of Pigs Declassified*; and Jones, *Bay of Pigs*.

7 Chang and Kornbluh, *Cuban Missile Crisis.*

8 Burr and Blanton, "Submarines of October."

9 Prados, *Safe for Democracy*, 338–39.

10 U.S. Department of State, *Foreign Relations of the United States, 1961–1963*, vol. 10, Documents 270 and 278. According to the U.S. State Department Office of the Historian, "The Special Group and the 303 Committee approved 163 covert actions during the Kennedy administration and 142 during the Johnson administration through February 1967."

11 Schoultz, *Infernal Little Cuban Republic*, 175–83, 187–91.

12 Loveman, *For la Patria*, chaps. 6–7.

13 For details on Cuban exile influence in the Nixon government's clandestine activities and the Watergate scandal, see Cooperative Research History Commons, "Profile: Nixon Administration," <http://www.cooperativeresearch.org/>. Accessed June 14, 2008.

14 Of course, these policymakers make decisions from among "a repertoire of possibilities that are a product of their experience" and of how they understand the "principles and traditions of the nation." See Dean, *Imperial Brotherhood*, 1–10.

15 Cuba was often the topic of bureaucratic and personal conflicts among presidential advisers over foreign policy. See Stansfield Turner's foreword to Newsom, *Soviet Brigade in Cuba.*

16 Writing to Thomas Jefferson in 1798 during the Quasi-War, Madison penned the oft-quoted line: "No nation can preserve its freedom in the midst of continual warfare." In 1799, commenting on the French Revolution in *Aurora General Advertiser* (Philadelphia, February 23, 1799), Madison wrote that "the fetters imposed on liberty at home have ever been forged out of the weapons provided for defence against real, pretended, or imaginary dangers from abroad."

17 Presidential pardons for the "overzealous" patriots induced a growing sense of impunity for those who committed crimes in the name of national security. President Gerald Ford pardoned ex-president Nixon (1974). President George H. W. Bush pardoned ex–secretary of defense Caspar Weinberger and six other policymakers, including Robert McFarlane and Elliott Abrams, in the Iran-Gate affair (1992).

18 Emphasis added in congressional resolutions.

19 Zahniser and Weis, "A Diplomatic Pearl Harbor."

20 Schmitz, *Thank God*, 212.

21 "Embarrassing Exiles," *Time*, June 2, 1958. The United States eventually extradited Pérez Jiménez to Venezuela in 1963 for trial on charges of murder, corruption, and other crimes.

22 Agee, *Inside the Company*; Marks, *CIA's Corporate Shell Game*; Huggins, *Political Policing.*

23 I can testify to this from personal experience as a Peace Corps volunteer in Chile from 1965 to 1968, in a region so remote from global politics that even most Chileans did not know the name or location of the town (Trovolhue) where my wife and I lived for more than two years.

24 See Loveman and Davies, *Che Guevara.*

25 Cited in McClintock, *State Terror*, 13.

26 On the Argentinean case, see the declassified documents posted by the National Se-

curity Archive, "New Declassified Details on Repression and U.S. Support for Military Dictatorship."

27 Rabe, *Most Dangerous Area in the World*, 79–95.

28 Senate Committee on Foreign Relations, Executive Sessions, 1962, 14:691, 760, cited in ibid., 62.

29 See Prebisch, *Towards a Dynamic Development Policy*.

30 Title I of the Public Law 480 program ((Agricultural Trade Development and Assistance Act of 1954, as amended, Public Law 480, 83rd Congress) was administered by the U.S. Department of Agriculture (Foreign Agricultural Service and Title II by the Agency for International Development).

31 *Department of State Bulletin* 49 (December 9, 1963): 900–904.

32 Rabe, *Most Dangerous Area in the World*, 199.

33 In Spanish, "MATA" — you kill, it kills, he kills, she kills, kill! — was a less than subtle acronym. For more detail on these programs, see Loveman, *For la Patria*, chap. 6.

34 Lyndon Johnson, Remarks on the Third Anniversary of the Alliance for Progress, March 16, 1964.

35 Ibid. Emphasis added.

36 The Organization of Central American States (ODECA) was created in 1951 and suspended in 1973.

37 Laun C. Smith Jr., "Central American Defense Council."

38 Porter and Johnson, *National Party Platforms*, 653–54, 678–79.

39 Ibid., 689.

40 Ibid. Emphasis added.

41 American-trained and American-equipped special commando groups — many of whom died in these missions — were carrying out operations in North Vietnam several years before the dramatic and fraudulent Gulf of Tonkin incident in 1964 that precipitated large-scale U.S. military intervention. Congress passed the Tonkin Gulf Resolution (Southeast Asia Resolution, Public Law 88-408) in response to misinformation and lies provided by Johnson and Secretary of Defense Robert McNamara regarding supposed attacks on American naval units. Wayne Morse (D.-Ore.), one of two senators who opposed the resolution, declared: "I believe that within the next century, future generations will look with dismay and great disappointment upon a Congress which is now about to make such a historic mistake." *Congressional Record*, August 6–7, 1964, 88th Cong., 2nd sess., 18132–33, 18406–7, 18458–59, 18470–71.

42 House Joint Resolution 1145, August 7, 1964.

43 Truman Presidential Library and Museum, Oral History Interview with Thomas C. Mann, Undersecretary of State, Economic Affairs, 1965–66 (previously, Assistant Secretary of State for Inter-American Affairs), transcript of tape-recorded interview, June 12, 1974.

44 Sicker, *Geopolitics of Security*, 121–24.

45 On the Latin American reaction to the Dominican intervention from a U.S. military viewpoint, see Yates, *Powerpack*.

46 Cited in Marchetti and Marks, *CIA*, 324.

47 Weiner, *Legacy of Ashes*, 285–87.

48 Dan T. Carter, *Politics of Rage*, 306.

49 Address by Richard M. Nixon to the Bohemian Club, San Francisco, July 29, 1967.

50 Rockefeller, *Rockefeller Report on the Americas*.

51 Tad Szulc, "Rockefeller Fear of New 'Castros' Voiced in Report; Governor's Findings on Trip Term U.S. Ties to Latins Perilously Deteriorated," *New York Times*, November 9, 1969, 1.

52 Many U.S. academics jumped on the "military as modernizers" bandwagon, most notably political scientist Samuel Huntington (Huntington, *Political Order*) and, for Latin America, Stanford University historian John J. Johnson (*Military*).

53 National Security Archive, "Chile and the United States: Declassified Documents Relating to the Military Coup, 1970–1976."

54 See Kornbluh, *Pinochet File*; and Dallek, *Nixon and Kissinger*, 238.

55 National Security Archive, "Kissinger Transcripts: A Verbatim Record of U.S. Diplomacy"; National Security Archive, "The Kissinger State Department Telcons."

56 McSherry, *Predatory States*; Dinges, *Condor Years*.

57 Cited in Herman, *Real Terror Network*.

58 See Kimball, "Nixon Doctrine."

59 Richard Nixon, on-the-record interview with C. L. Sulzberger, March 8, 1971, *New York Times*, March 10, 1971, 14. Emphasis added.

60 *U.S. v. Richardson* (1974), 167–202.

61 Dallek, *Nixon and Kissinger*, 199.

62 Public Law 93-148 (Section 2a).

63 Partly in reaction to CIA operations in Angola, Congress passed the Hughes-Ryan amendment to the Foreign Assistance Act, which for the first time required that the president report covert CIA operations in a foreign country (other than for intelligence collection) to the relevant congressional committees.

64 Commission on the Roles and Capabilities of the United States Intelligence Community, "Evolution of the U.S. Intelligence Community." The Nixon team had also used the Internal Revenue Service to blackmail George Wallace to keep him out of the 1972 presidential race. See Dan T. Carter, *Politics of Rage*.

65 The Church Report documented the history of U.S. intervention in Chilean politics from 1963 to 1973 — from financing candidates and political parties to support for the military coup in 1973.

66 On February 19, 1975, the House voted to create a House Select Intelligence Committee (the Nedzi Committee). Five months later this committee was replaced by the Pike Committee, headed by Congressman Otis Pike (D.-N.Y.). Two days before the Pike Committee was scheduled to conclude its activities (January 29, 1976), the House voted to withhold public release of the committee's final report. For details, see Haines, "Pike Committee Investigations."

67 Prados, *Safe for Democracy*, 455–57.

68 Testimony of Secretary of Defense James Schlesinger, Hearings before the Committee on Foreign Relations, Senate, 93rd Cong., 2nd sess., S. Doc. 3394, to amend the Foreign Assistance Act of 1961 and for other purposes, June 7, 21, 26, July 24, 25, 1974, 241.

69 Cited in Winks, *Cloak and Gown*, 451.

70 Cited in Isaacson, *Kissinger*, 700–701.

71 Jimmy Carter, Inaugural Address, January 20, 1977.

72 Jimmy Carter, State of the Union Address, January 19, 1978.

73 NSC-PD 30, "Human Rights."

74 On Carter's human rights policy and Latin America, see Schoultz, *Human Rights*, chap. 3.

75 U.S. Congress, Senate, Committee on Appropriations, Subcommittee on Foreign Assistance and Related Programs, "Foreign Assistance and Related Programs Appropriations Fiscal Year 1978," 95th Cong., 1st sess., 1977, 161, 196.

76 Commission on U.S.–Latin American Relations, "Americas in a Changing World"; Commission on U.S.–Latin American Relations, "United States and Latin America."

77 Pastor, "Carter Administration and Latin America."

78 On the history of these initiatives, see Wayne S. Smith, *Closest of Enemies*. For a history of the "back-channel efforts by Kennedy, Kissinger, Carter and Clinton to improve and even attempt to normalize relations with the Castro regime," see Peter Kornbluh and William LeoGrande (forthcoming), *Talking with Fidel: The Untold History of Dialogue between the United States and Cuba*.

79 Newsom, *Soviet Brigade in Cuba*, Appendixes B and C.

80 Cited in Loveman and Davies, *Che Guevara*, 361.

81 Cited in Gaddis Smith, *Last Years*, 156.

82 Reagan, *An American Life*, 471–74.

83 Jimmy Carter, State of the Union Address, January 23, 1980.

84 Prados, *Safe for Democracy*, 472; Record, *Rapid Deployment Force*; NSC-PD 18, "U.S. National Strategy"; Klare, *Beyond the "Vietnam Syndrome."*

Chapter 12

1 Reagan often referred to John Winthrop's "City on the Hill" sermon, which was given on the *Arabella*. For example, see "We Will Be as a City on a Hill," Speech at the Conservative Political Action Conference, January 25, 1974.

2 Ronald Reagan, Nomination Acceptance Speech, Republican National Convention, Detroit, July 17, 1980.

3 Ronald Reagan, Address before a Joint Session of Congress Reporting on the State of the Union, January 27, 1987.

4 In 1976, Reagan had criticized then-president Ford and Secretary of State Kissinger: "Well, the Canal Zone is not a colonial possession. It is not a long-term lease. It is sovereign United States Territory every bit the same as Alaska and all the states that were carved from the Louisiana Purchase. We should end those negotiations and tell the General: We bought it, we paid for it, we built it, and we intend to keep it." Ronald Reagan, Speech to America, March 31, 1976.

5 According to its official website, the Committee on the Present Danger "was formed in 1950 as a bipartisan education and advocacy organization to build a national consensus behind President Truman's policy of 'containment' against Soviet expansionism. The [committee] then re-emerged in 1976 when its original leaders and others believed that America's will to win the Cold War was flagging and that the United States should pursue policies to bring that war to a successful conclusion. . . . Now, the [committee] has returned to confront the new 'present danger'—militant Islamism and the terrorism that it is spawning." <http://www.committeeonthepresentdanger.org/>.

6 Greg Schneider and Renae Merle, "Reagan's Defense Buildup Bridged Military Era's Huge Budgets, Brought Life Back to Industry," *Washington Post*, June 9, 2004.

Schneider and Merle report that defense spending hit a peak of $456.5 billion in 1987 (in projected 2005 dollars), compared with $325.1 billion in 1980 and $339.6 million in 1981.

7 Grandin (*Empire's Workshop*, 182) sees in this confluence of massive defense budgets, tax cuts, high interest rates, and cuts in social program spending "the institutionalizing of a perpetual system of global austerity that rendered political liberalism, both domestic and international, not viable."

8 Pastor, "Reagan Administration and Latin America"; Haig, *Caveat*.

9 *Philip Taubman*, "U.S. Tries to Back Up Haig on Terrorism," *New York Times*, May 3, 1981, 1.

10 An important exception to this devotion to the Monroe Doctrine was support for the British in a brief war against Argentina (1982) regarding sovereignty over the Malvinas (Falklands) Islands, occupied by Great Britain since 1833 but claimed by Argentina.

11 Bernard Weinraub, "President Accuses 5 'Outlaw States' of World Terrorism," *New York Times*, July 9, 1985, 1.

12 Lewis Carroll's *Through the Looking Glass, and What Alice Found There* (1871) was the sequel to *Alice's Adventures in Wonderland* (1865). It is often treated as "children's literature," but few children can make sense of Carroll's sardonic treatment of politics and international relations.

13 Reagan, "Central America: Defending Our Vital Interests."

14 Council for Inter-American Security, "A New Inter-American Policy for the Eighties," 1–2.

15 For examples, see Bird, "Reagan's Foreign Service."

16 Reagan used the term "evil empire" in his March 8, 1983, Speech to the National Association of Evangelicals in Orlando, Florida.

17 Richman, "Ronald Reagan: Protectionist."

18 Grandin (*Empire's Workshop*, 180–82) finds the underlying foundations of this new coalition in "a rapid transformation in the class and political relations that defined how [America] acted in the world" after the first "oil shock" (1973–74), as "economic internationalists joined with militarists and Christian capitalists to defeat world Bolshevism, avenge Vietnam, and push for open markets."

19 For declassified documents on this topic, see National Security Archive, "Public Diplomacy and Covert Propaganda, Declassified Record of Ambassador Otto Juan Reich," March 2, 2001.

20 Army Field Manual 33-5, "Psychological Operations — Techniques and Procedures," defined psychological operations (psyops) as the use of propaganda and other means to influence opinions, attitudes, emotions, and behavior of friendly, neutral, or hostile groups.

21 Reagan's battle against inflation through Federal Reserve hikes in interest rates, deregulation of the savings and loan industry, and the Tax Reform Act of 1986, which eliminated deductibility of losses on investment real estate, contributed to a massive financial failure, requiring a government bailout to the tune of more than 120 billion dollars — a crisis bequeathed by Reagan to the George H. W. Bush administration. Large-scale government intervention through the Resolution Trust Corporation gradually brought the crisis under control — in retrospect, a "small" version of the crisis that would occur in 2008–9.

22 Inter-American Dialogue, *The Americas in a New World.*

23 Shultz, *Turmoil and Triumph,* 471–75.

24 Bodenheimer and Gould, *Rollback.*

25 George P. Schultz, *Department of State Bulletin* (April 1985).

26 For official justification of the invasion, see Kenneth W. Dam, Statement on Grenada before the House Committee on Foreign Affairs, October 25, 1983, cited in Leich, "Protection of Nationals," 200–217.

27 U.S. Department of the Navy, Navy Historical Center, "Grenada, Operation Urgent Fury," October 23–November 21, 1983, <http://www.history.navy.mil/faqs/faq95-1.htm>. Accessed April 4, 2009.

28 Stuart Taylor Jr., "In Wake of Invasion Much Official Misinformation by U.S. Comes to Light," *New York Times,* November 6, 1983, A20.

29 U.S. Congress, House, Committee on Foreign Affairs, *Grenada War Powers.*

30 Hedrick Smith, "O'Neill Now Calls Grenada Invasion 'Justified' Action," *New York Times,* November 9, 1983, A1.

31 For an official accounting of Operation Urgent Fury, see *Grenada Documents: An Overview and Selection,* OCLC 11273740; *Situation in Grenada: Communication from the President of the United States Transmitting a Further Report on the Situation in Grenada* (Washington, D.C.: Government Printing Office, 1984), OCLC 10561282; Committee on Foreign Relations, *The Situation in Grenada,* 98th Cong., 1st sess., 1983, OCLC 10583467.

32 Treaty of Basseterre, Establishing the Organization of Eastern Caribbean States (Antigua, Dominica, Grenada, Montserrat, St. Kitts/Nevis, Santa Lucia, St. Thomas, and the Grenadines). See <http://www.oecs.org/about_origin.html>.

33 Ronald Reagan, Remarks on Central America and El Salvador at the Annual Meeting of the National Association of Manufacturers, March 10, 1983.

34 See Vaky, "Reagan's Central American Policy."

35 See LeoGrande, *Our Own Backyard;* and Manwaring and Prisk, *El Salvador at War.*

36 *Report of the President's National Bipartisan Commission on the Americas,* 109–10.

37 See Kissinger, *A World Restored.*

38 Thomas Jefferson wrote to James Monroe in 1823: "Although we have no right to intermeddle with the form of government of other nations, yet it is lawful to wish to see no emperors nor kings in our hemisphere," in Jefferson, *Writings of Jefferson,* 10:164.

39 LeoGrande, *Our Own Backyard,* 274–77.

40 For details and analysis of the war in El Salvador, see Bacevich et al., *American Military Policy.*

41 Negotiated between 1989 and 1992, under the auspices of the United Nations, with the special cooperation of Colombia, Mexico, Spain, and Venezuela (the "friends of the secretary-general"), the Salvadoran Peace Accords provided for a "Truth Commission" to investigate "serious acts of violence that occurred between 1980 and 1991, whose impact on society urgently demands that the public should know the truth." See UN Commission for Truth for El Salvador, *From Madness to Hope.* The Farabundo Martí Liberation Movement would transform itself into a legal political party, participate in elections beginning in 1994, and become one of the two most important political groups in the country (almost 40 percent of the electorate in the 2006 legislative assembly elections). The party elected a president for the first time in March 2009.

42 LeoGrande, *Our Own Backyard*, 281.

43 Remarks at the Western Hemisphere Legislative Leaders Forum, January 24, 1985, co-sponsored by the Western Hemisphere Affairs Subcommittee of the House Foreign Affairs Committee, Boston University, and the Center for Democracy.

44 For critical analysis of the policies, see LaFeber, *Inevitable Revolutions*, 275–328.

45 Department of Defense, "Special Operations/Low Intensity Conflict and Interdependent Capabilities," http://www.defenselink.mil/policy/sections/policy_offices/solic/index.html>. Accessed March 13, 2009.

46 *Time*, April 1, 1985, <http://www.time.com/time/magazine/article/0,9171,964873-5,00.html>. Accessed August 21, 2008.

47 Further Continuing Appropriations Act, Public Law 97-377, §793, 96 *Stat.*, 1830, 1865 (1982).

48 Deficit Reduction Act of 1984, Public Law 98-369, §2907, 98 *Stat.* 494, 1210.

49 Continuing Appropriations Act for Fiscal Year 1985, Public Law 98-473, §8066(a), 98 *Stat.*, 1837, 1935 (1984).

50 Louis Fisher ("How Tightly Can Congress Draw the Purse Strings," 758–66) notes that a memorandum (September 12, 1985) by Bretton G. Sciaroni, counsel to the President's Intelligence Oversight Board, maintained that the National Security Council was not covered by the Boland amendment.

51 Inouye and Hamilton, *Report of the Congressional Committees Investigating the Iran-Contra Affair* (the Iran-Contra Report).

52 Public Law 97-377 (1982), H. Amdt. 974 (Boland amendment, passed 411–0), prohibited CIA and Department of Defense use of funds for military purposes in Nicaragua. See Congressional Research Service, "Congressional Use of Funding Cutoffs since 1970," January 10, 2001.

53 On the Iran-Contra Affair, see LeoGrande, *Our Own Back Yard*, chaps. 18–20.

54 Inouye and Hamilton, *Report of the Congressional Committees Investigating the Iran-Contra Affair*, 140–42, cited in ibid., 477.

55 Inouye and Hamilton, *Report of the Congressional Committees Investigating the Iran-Contra Affair*, with Supplemental Minority and Additional Views, H. Rep. 100-433, S. Rep. 100-216, 100th Cong., 1st sess., 11. A minority report (sec. 2, pt. 2), written by political scientist Michael J. Malbin, assisted, among others, by David Addington (later Vice President Cheney's chief of staff), spelled out Reagan and Cheney's view of presidential authority to carry out foreign policy beyond congressional oversight.

56 The CIA justified the mining of Nicaraguan harbors as a legitimate means of self-defense. *Congressional Quarterly Weekly Report*, April 14, 1984, 835.

57 For a retrospective lament on congressional "poaching" on the executive foreign policy authority, see Rogers, "Constitution and Foreign Affairs."

58 Zamora, "Contadora and Esquipulas."

59 Remarks to Administration Supporters at a White House Briefing on Arms Control, Central America, and the Supreme Court, November 23, 1987.

60 Reagan, Statement on Aid to the Nicaraguan Democratic Resistance, October 14, 1988.

61 See, for example, Bodenheimer and Gould, *Rollback*.

62 Reagan, Remarks at a Republican Campaign Rally, San Diego, October 27, 1988.

63 Illustratively, Elliott Abrams, who pleaded guilty to withholding information from

Congress, was pardoned by George H. W. Bush and then under George W. Bush was appointed to the position of deputy national security advisor for global democracy strategy.

64 Loveman, *For la Patria*, chap. 8.

65 See Kitts, *Presidential Commissions*.

66 *Frontline*, November 18, 1987.

67 Richard Cheney, Memorandum for the Commanders of the Unified and Specified Combatant Commands, Subject: Elevation of the Mission Priority of Counternarcotics Operations, September 1989. See Claudio and Stewman, "Oplan Narco."

68 The phrase "Sinatra Doctrine" was apparently invented by Soviet foreign ministry spokesperson Gennadi Gerasimov on U.S. television, on the *Good Morning Show* (October 25, 1989). " 'Sinatra Doctrine' at Work in Warsaw Pact, Soviet Says," *Los Angeles Times*, October 25, 1989.

69 President George H. W. Bush, Remarks Announcing the Enterprise for the Americas Initiative, June 27, 1990.

70 Conditionality under the "Framework Agreements" was legislated in U.S. Code, Title 22, chap. 32, subchap. 3-A, §2430g, America's Framework Agreements.

71 Gaddis Smith, *Last Years*, 217.

72 See Schoultz, *Infernal Little Cuban Republic*, chap. 13.

73 For background on Noriega, see Scranton, *Noriega Years*.

74 Powell, *My American Journey*, 415.

75 Gray and Manwaring, "Panama: Operation Just Cause"; Gilboa, "Panama Invasion Revisited"; Flanagan, *Battle for Panama*.

76 Office of the Chairman of the Joint Chiefs of Staff, History Office, *Operation Just Cause: Panama*.

77 Ibid.

78 Joint Chiefs of Staff Plan 90-2, December 17, 1989.

79 Office of the Public Register, *Public Papers of the Presidents*, George H. W. Bush, 1989, 2:1734. See also Quigley, "Legality of the United States Invasion of Panama," 276.

80 On the disagreement between Woerner and officials in Washington, see Woodward, *Commanders*, 82–99; and Millet, "Panama and Haiti," 144–48.

81 The Panamanian government had denied the use of Panama as a base for attacks on Nicaragua and El Salvador and also refused to extend the presence of the School of the Americas for fifteen years. See Vera Calderón, "United States Invasion of Panama."

82 Ibid.

83 *Congressional Record*, 101st Cong., 1st sess. (1990), 1507.

84 Ibid., chap. 4, notes 24, 25; "Modification of DOD Directive 5525.5, 'DoD Cooperation with Civilian Law Enforcement Officials,' " December 20, 1989; Secretary of Defense Dick Cheney, "Approval Consistent with Revised DOD Directive 5525.5, 'DoD Cooperation with Civilian Law Enforcement Officials,' of Assistance to Law Enforcement Apprehension of Manuel Noriega of Panama," December 20, 1989; both in Secretariat Joint Staff/Historical Division.

85 The modern "drug war" began with Richard Nixon's creation of the Drug Enforcement Agency in 1973. President Reagan's National Security Decision Directive 221 declared the drug trade a threat to U.S. national security in 1986. In the administration of George H. W. Bush, Secretary of Defense Cheney issued a memorandum calling

the drug trade "a direct threat to the sovereignty and security of the country" (Department of Defense Guidance for Implementation of the President's National Drug Control Strategy, 1989).

86 Flanagan, *Battle for Panama*.

87 Ronald Reagan, Remarks at the Brandenburg Gate, West Berlin, June 12, 1987.

88 "Turning Visions into Reality," *Time*, December 11, 1989.

89 "The Malta Summit; Transcript of the Bush-Gorbachev News Conference in Malta," *New York Times*, December 4, 1989.

90 For an invaluable collection of Cold War documents and insight into the end of the Cold War, see the growing collection of documents and investigations at the Cold War International History Project virtual archive; on the economic and technological conditions that undermined the Soviet system, see Brooks and Wohlforth, "Power, Globalization."

91 Zubok, "New Evidence on the End of the Cold War," 12.

Chapter 13

1 Chernyaev was Gorbachev's chief foreign policy aide.

2 Walter Laqueur, "After the Cold War," <www.laqueur.net>. Accessed May 8, 2008.

3 Fukuyama, "End of History." Fukuyama provided a retrospective on his influential 1989 article and 1992 book, *End of History*, in the *Guardian*, April 3, 2007. He attempted to "clarify" his argument (and distance himself from the George W. Bush foreign policy debacle).

4 "U.S. Military Unprepared for New Role, General Zinni Says," Seminar, Pew Fellowships in International Journalism, February 21, 2001.

5 "Excerpts from Iraqi Document on Meeting with U.S. Envoy," *New York Times*, September 23, 1990, 19.

6 Thatcher, *Downing Street Years*, 817.

7 *Frontline*, " The Gulf War," <http://www.pbs.org/wgbh/pages/frontline/gulf/>. Accessed March 23, 2009.

8 William Clinton, Presidential Nomination Address, "Our New Covenant," New York City, July 16, 1992.

9 Ibid.

10 Ibid.

11 Stewart, "United States Army in Somalia."

12 Middleton, "Piracy in Somalia."

13 On December 15, 1995, Clinton ordered the deployment of 22,000 U.S. ground troops to Bosnia. He explained in a letter to Congress that the decision was taken pursuant to his "constitutional authority to conduct the foreign relations of the United States and as Commander in Chief and Chief Executive," the same sort of justification given by the Reagan administration and, later, by the George W. Bush administration. See Healy, "Arrogance of Power Reborn."

14 Yoo, "Kosovo, War Powers, and the Multilateral Future."

15 On the divisions among the schools of Washington "policy wonks" and the role of the "neocons" in the George W. Bush administration, see Hadar, " 'X' Dreams."

16 Although official Department of Defense documents stated that the United States had

few strategic interests in sub-Saharan Africa, the United States intervened often in the region. See Catoire, "A CINC for Sub-Saharan Africa."

17 See SarDesai and Thomas, *Nuclear India*.

18 Clinton, "A National Security Strategy of Engagement and Enlargement," February 1996.

19 Ibid.

20 U.S. Department of Defense, *Defense Strategy for the 1990s*.

21 Bacevich, *American Empire*, 180. Bacevich points to General Leonard Wood's role in Cuba and the Philippines as the prototype of the "senior commander as proconsul."

22 Chalmers Johnson, *Sorrows of Empire*, 56.

23 See Joint Chiefs of Staff, *Joint Doctrine*.

24 Defined broadly, humanitarian intervention entails resort to force to remedy a situation of large-scale violation of fundamental human rights committed by a state against its own nationals, by one state against the nationals of another state, or due to internal war. Humanitarian intervention is controversial for many reasons, including determining who rightfully decides on intervention, the threshold criteria for intervention, accountability of forces that intervene, and the reality that only weak states need fear such interventions (for example, China and Russia are unlikely to intervene in the United States to defend human rights, and vice versa).

25 Joint Chiefs of Staff, *Joint Doctrine*, viii.

26 U.S. Department of Defense, *Defense Strategy for the 1990s*, 22.

27 See Rosenberg, "OAS and the Summit of the Americas."

28 U.S. Department of Defense, Office of International Security Affairs, "United States Security Strategy for the Americas," 1995; U.S. Department of Defense, Inter-American Affairs, "United States Security Policy for the Americas," October 2000.

29 William Clinton, Acceptance Speech at Democratic Convention, August 29, 1996.

30 William Kristol and Robert Kagan described America's role in 1996 as "benevolent global hegemony," in "Toward a Neo-Reaganite Foreign Policy," cited in Lind, *American Way of Strategy*, 129.

31 U.S. Department of Defense, *Report of the Quadrennial Defense Review*, May 1997.

32 President Clinton had stated that this was not a "democratic crusade" but "a pragmatic commitment to see freedom take hold where that will help us most." Clinton, "A National Security Strategy of Engagement and Enlargement," February 1996.

33 Project for a New American Century, "Statement of Principles," June 3, 1997. In the 2000 presidential campaign, the Project for a New American Century produced a major policy prescription (see Project for a New American Century, *Rebuilding America's Defenses*). Prominent members then became key policymakers in the Defense Department.

34 U.S. Department of Defense, *Special Operations Forces Posture Statement 2000*, Foreword, 15.

35 Current legislation requires that the chair of the Joint Chiefs of Staff review the missions, responsibilities, and geographical boundaries of each combatant command in the U.S. military every two years and recommend to the president, through the secretary of defense, any changes that may be necessary. See Unified Command Plan website, <http://www.defenselink.mil/specials/unifiedcommand/>.

36 For the disconnect between various U.S. agencies' "division of the world" and dilemmas of "interagency" coordination, see Wilcox, "Strategic Transformation."

37 "The U.S. Pacific Command Today: A New Course for Peace and Prosperity in Asia," *Sea Power Magazine* (December 2000): 9–10. Emphasis added. Interview with Admiral Dennis C. Blair, Commander in Chief, U.S. Pacific Command.

38 Lind, *American Way of Strategy*, 173.

39 On the growing political autonomy of the CINCs, see Priest, *Mission*.

40 Lind, *American Way of Strategy*, 165.

41 Public Law 105-338, October 31, 1998.

42 Cited in Grandin, *Empire's Workshop*, 225.

43 UN Security Council Resolution 688, April 5, 1991.

44 See Michael Smith, "The War before the War."

45 Office of the Secretary of State, Office of the Coordinator for Counterterrorism, *Patterns of Global Terrorism, 1992*.

46 Memorandum for the Commanders of the Unified and Specified Combatant Commands, Subject: Elevation of the Mission Priority of Counternarcotics Operations, 1989. President Clinton also followed this policy. See Joint Chiefs of Staff, *Joint Counterdrug Operations*, February 17, 1998.

47 Prepared statement of General Barry R. McCaffrey, House National Security Committee, March 8, 1995.

48 On Cuban-American influence in U.S. politics, see Schoultz, *Infernal Little Cuban Republic*, 435–52.

49 Sponsored by Congressman Robert Torricelli (D.-N.J.), the Cuban Democracy Act prohibited foreign-based subsidiaries of U.S. firms from trading with Cuba, limited travel and family remittances to Cuba, and sought to promote regime change on the island, while threatening countries and firms trading with Cuba with U.S. sanctions.

50 *El Tiempo* (Bogotá), June 16, 1994.

51 The Ibero-American Summit organization met first in Guadalajara, Mexico, in 1991, during preparations for the celebration of the Quincentenary of the Discovery of the Americas. It included twenty-one countries (Portugal, Spain, and all the Hispano-Luso-American nations).

52 "Terrorism against Cuba," <http://www.granma.cu/miami5/ingles/043.htm>; "Castro Slams U.S. for Exclusion from Miami Summit," *Miami Herald*, June 15, 1994, 18A.

53 The first Summit of the Americas in Miami (1994) was followed by meetings in Santiago, Chile (1998), Quebec, Canada (2001), Mar del Plata, Argentina (2005), and Trinidad (2009). For summit documents, see <http://www.summit-americas.org/>.

54 "Exploiting the Summit," *Jamaica Gleaner*, December 13, 1994; *El País* (Madrid), December 16, 1994.

55 Public Law 104-114, 110 *Stat.* 785 (March 12, 1996), *U.S. Code* 22, §6021–91.

56 Richard W. Stevenson, "Canada, Backed by Mexico, Protests to U.S. on Cuba Sanctions," *New York Times*, March 14, 1996, Late Edition — Final, A7.

57 In 2007, the *Hermanos'* official website included a tribute to the heroes shot down by Cuban pilots in 1996 and a warning to Americans that Castro had declared in May 2001 that Cuba and Iran could bring America to its knees (with accompanying photos of Fidel alongside Libya's Muammar el-Qaddafi and other "terrorists.") See <http://www.hermanos.org/>.

58 UN press release SC/6247: "Security Council condemns use of weapons against civil aircraft; calls on Cuba to comply with international law," July 27, 1996.

59 For detailed discussion of the politics surrounding the Helms-Burton legislation and the Brothers to the Rescue incident, see Schoultz, *Infernal Little Cuban Republic*, 475–98.

60 PBS On-Line Backgrounders, "Congress Reacts," February 26, 1996.

61 President Clinton suspended certain provisions of the Helms-Burton Act for six months.

62 William Clinton, Second Inaugural Address, January 20, 1997.

63 William Clinton, State of the Union Message, January 27, 1998.

64 U.S. Department of Defense, Office of International Security Affairs, "United States Security Strategy for the Americas," 1995, 22–24.

65 After developing a post–Cold War regional security policy for Latin America, the Department of Defense sponsored meetings of the region's defense ministers in 1995 (in Washington, D.C.) and in 1996 (in Bariloche, Argentina). At the third meeting in 1998, the Department of Defense hoped to further encourage "collegial post–Cold War security relationships."

66 "Hemispheric Cooperation in Combating Terrorism," Defense Ministerial of the Americas III, Secretary of Defense William S. Cohen, Cartagena, Colombia, Tuesday, December 1, 1998.

67 McSherry, *Predatory States*; Dinges, *Condor Years*.

68 Bacevich (*American Empire*, 178–79) calls this a strategy of "gunboats and Gurkhas," harking back to the days of Theodore Roosevelt, Taft, and Wilson.

69 Marcella, "United States and Colombia," 51.

70 U.S. Southern Command, "Profile of the United States Southern Command," 28–29, <www.southcom.mil/appssc/index.php>.

71 Many of the civilian contractors were ex-military personnel, and some came from other Latin American countries. For an assessment of the role of contractors in the Colombian conflict before the Uribe administration, see "U.S. Contractors in Colombia," compiled by CIP Colombia program intern Sara Vins, in November 2001.

72 "Chávez lanza nuevas críticas a Plan Colombia 'Así empezó Vietnam,'" *El Colombiano* (Medellín), September 6, 2000.

73 "Plan Colombia, protagonista en Cumbre Suramericana," *El Tiempo* (Bogotá), August 31, 2000.

74 Presidential Determination No. 2000-28, Memorandum for the Secretary of State, Subject: Presidential Determination on Waiver of Certification under Section 3201, "Conditions on Assistance for Colombia," August 22, 2000, in Title III, chap. 2, of the Emergency Supplemental Act, as Enacted in Public Law 106-246.

75 "Colombianos huyen a Ecuador por fumigación de plantaciones," *El Mostrador* (Chile), September 13, 2000; "Destruyen 5 mil hectáreas de coca y 90 laboratorios en Colombia," *El Mostrador*, September 14, 2000; "5 mil hectáreas de coca fueron eliminadas," *El Comercio* (Quito), September 14, 2000.

76 On the antiglobalization protests in Latin America, see Hansen, "Globalization Backlash"; O'Brien, *Making the Americas*, chap. 10; and Seoane, *Resistencias Mundiales*.

77 Republican Platform, 2000, July 31, 2000.

78 Democratic National Platform, 2000, "Prosperity, Progress, and Peace."
79 Ibid., 35.
80 Bacevich, *American Empire*, 214–15.
81 *Bush v. Gore* (2000).
82 Stephen Johnson, "A New U.S. Policy for Latin America."
83 U.S. law (*U.S. Code*, Title 50, chap. 15, sec. 404a) required an annual national security strategy report to Congress. This report also provided opportunities for lobbying for changes in doctrine and threat scenarios, with budget and program implications for the various armed services and intelligence agencies as well as for numerous defense contractors.
84 U.S. Department of Defense, *Quadrennial Defense Review Report*, May 1997.
85 U.S. Department of Defense, *Quadrennial Defense Review*, September 30, 2001, 2.
86 Tangredi, *Globalization and Maritime Power*, chap. 1.
87 According to the Executive Lecture Forum website at Mississippi State University, <http://www.msstate.edu/chair/radvanyi/elf.html>, Tangredi served as special assistant and speechwriter to the secretary of the navy and as the head of the Strategy and Concepts Branch, Office of the Chief of Naval Operations.
88 Tangredi, *Globalization and Maritime Power*. Emphasis added.
89 According to his official website, Gray was founding president of the National Institute for Public Policy, Fairfax, Virginia, between 1982 and 1987 (during the Reagan administration), and he served on the President's General Advisory Committee on Arms Control and Disarmament.
90 Gray, "Implications of Preemptive and Preventive War Doctrine," 51.
91 U.S. Army retired general Fred F. Woerner Jr., cited in Joint Chiefs of Staff, *Joint Doctrine*, A-22.

Chapter 14
1 George W. Bush, Speech to a Joint Session of Congress, September 20, 2001.
2 In principle, the NATO intervention in Bosnia and Yugoslavia was under cover of UN Security Council Resolutions 713 and 757 and then 781 in 1992 — not for collective security to protect an alliance member state. The U.S. and NATO bombing campaign against Serbia remains controversial. Carried out under the slogan "Serbs out, peacekeepers in, refugees back," the air war against Serbia destroyed civilian infrastructure, industrial facilities, and communication networks, led to thousands of civilian casualties, and left a legacy of resentment against the United States in the former Yugoslavia against CIA support for the Albanian-supported KLA guerrilla forces. See Thomas, *Yugoslavia Unraveled*.
3 "Bush Announces Opening of Attacks," CNN.com., October 7, 2001.
4 Emphasis added.
5 On the varieties of liberalism, see Wolfe, *Future of Liberalism*.
6 Kagan, "End of History."
7 Serfaty, "The New Normalcy," 218. Emphasis added. In 2007, Serfaty, listed by the World Affairs Council as "one of the 500 most influential Americans in foreign policy," called the Iraq invasion "a war that the administration failed to explain when it was launched, and now fails to understand after it has failed." "Which Past War Is Iraq?," *Washington Post*, August 29, 2007.

8   Bob Woodward, "CIA Told to Do Whatever Necessary to Kill Bin Laden," *Washington Post*, October 21, 2001, A22.

9   Southeast Asia Resolution, Public Law 88-408, August 10, 1964.

10 "H.J. Res. 114 [107th]: Authorization for Use of Military Force against Iraq Resolution of 2002," Public Law 107-243.

11 S.J. 46, 2002, 107th Cong., 2nd sess., <http://rpc.senate.gov/_files/L56defenseje100302 .pdf>.

12 Bacevich, *New American Militarism*, 230–32. Some analysts would not accept the characterization of the war in Iraq as a preemptive war because American policymakers did not honestly view Iraq as an imminent threat to the United States or even to the Middle East region at the time of attack. Instead, the war on Iraq would be characterized as a "resource war" — an effort to control oil supplies as world demand increased (especially from China and India). On the basic notion of "resource war," see Klare, *Resource Wars*; and Klare, *Blood and Oil*.

13 The Gallup Poll question read: "In view of the developments since we first sent our troops to Iraq, do you think the United States made a mistake in sending troops to Iraq, or not?" The USA Today/Gallup Poll indicated that 75 percent of Americans felt that the U.S. government did not make a mistake in sending troops to Iraq in March 2003. However, according to the same poll retaken in April 2007, 58 percent of the participants stated that the initial attack *was* a mistake. In May 2007, the *New York Times* and CBS News released similar results of a poll in which 61 percent responded that it had been a mistake (*New York Times*, May 25, 2007).

14 Ernesto Ekaizer, "No conocía la brutalidad con la que Bush advirtió a Chile," *El País* (Madrid), September 26, 2007; Muñoz, *Diplomat's Chronicle*.

15 Tim Weiner, "Threats and Responses: The UN Debate; Holding Swing Vote, Mexico Tells Bush It Won't Support Iraq Resolution U.S. Favors," *New York Times*, October 28, 2002.

16 White House, March 22, 2003, "Operation Iraqi Freedom," <http://www.whitehouse .gov/news/releases/2003/03/20030322.html>. Accessed December 4, 2008.

17 Peter Ford, "Europe Cringes at Bush's 'Crusade' against Terrorists," *Christian Science Monitor*, September 19, 2001.

18 Gershkoff and Kushner ("Shaping Public Opinion") report that the White House officially established the Office of Global Communications by executive order on January 21, 2003. It had been operating since 2002. Its message: "As the President plainly states, freedom is God's gift to every single person. Freedom is also the one true model for national success." White House Office of Global Communications, <http://www .whitehouse.gov/ogc/aboutogc.html>. Accessed September 27, 2007.

19 In an 1846 message to Congress, James Polk defended the use of contingency funds for secret operations and, implicitly, for influencing American public opinion in times of "emergency" or "for the public safety or the public good." He refused to provide information to Congress regarding the activities of Daniel Webster in negotiations on the Webster-Ashburton Treaty with Great Britain in 1842. President James K. Polk, Message to the House of Representatives, April 20, 1846. This information was highlighted on the CIA website in 2008 — along with vignettes on other presidents' "contributions" to developing U.S. intelligence operations.

20 President Bush's Weekly Radio Address to the Nation, March 22, 2003.

21 GlobalSecurity.org maintained a running list on countries participating with armed forces in the "coalition of the willing" and withdrawals of such forces, from 2003 to 2008, at <http://www.globalsecurity.org/index.html>.

22 Laura McClure, "Coalition of the Billing — or Unwilling?," Salon.com., March 12, 2003. American policymakers deployed various sorts of incentives — and threats of adverse consequences — involving trade concessions, foreign aid, and even eventual NATO membership, to entice participation in the "coalition of the willing."

23 Reuters, "El Salvador to Cut Small Troop Presence in Iraq," August 7, 2008; Associated Press, "El Salvador Withdraws Last Soldiers from Iraq," February 7, 2009.

24 Testimony by Tom Malinowski, Human Rights Watch, Washington Advocacy director, U.S. Senate Committee on Foreign Relations, Hearing on the CIA Secret Detention, Rendition, and Interrogation Program, July 26, 2007.

25 Scott Shane, David Johnston, and James Risen, "Secret U.S. Endorsement of Severe Interrogations," New York Times, October 4, 2007.

26 Hamdan v. Rumsfeld (2006).

27 See United Nations, Committee on Torture, Summary of the Record of the 703rd Meeting, May 12, 2006.

28 See Loveman, Addicted to Failure; Crandall, Driven by Drugs; and Youngers and Rosin, Drugs and Democracy.

29 Tokatlian, "After Iraq: Next Colombia," 257.

30 Gupta and Graubart, "Is the U.S. a Rogue Nation?," 302.

31 Marcella, "American Grand Strategy," 5.

32 Ibid., 5–10.

33 In March 2009, the Inter-American Dialogue issued a report calling for pragmatism in American policies regarding what it identified as a ten-item agenda for the Western Hemisphere. The report (A Second Chance) offered no new vision or recommendations for major departures in U.S. policies, beyond better relations with Cuba and the usual focus on crime, drugs, economic conditions, immigration, and trade policies, along with support for democracy in the region.

34 Hakim, "Is Washington Losing Latin America?"

35 Loveman, Addicted to Failure, chap. 1.

36 U.S. Department of Defense news release, "Navy Reestablishes U.S. 4th Fleet," April 24, 2008.

37 Remarks as delivered by Chief of Naval Operations Admiral Gary Roughead, Fredericksburg (Va.) Regional Chamber of Commerce Dinner, March 4, 2009.

38 Cited in Nikolas Kozloff, "U.S. Fourth Fleet in Venezuelan Waters," <http://www.venezuelanalysis.com/analysis/3496>. Accessed May 27, 2008. Castro added in late May that the United States and the European Union are "two hungry wolves disguised as 'good grandmothers,' competing over the Latin American Red Riding Hood [Caperucita]." "Fidel Castro califica a EEUU y a Europa de 'lobos hambrientos,'" Agence France Presse, May 19, 2008.

39 Ellis, "Military-Strategic Dimensions."

40 According to its home page, <http://www.stratcom.mil/> in March 2009, USSTRATCOM "is a global integrator charged with the missions of full-spectrum global strike, space operations, computer network operations, Department of Defense information operations, strategic warning, integrated missile defense, global C4ISR (Command,

Control, Communications, Computers, Intelligence, Surveillance, and Reconnaissance), combating weapons of mass destruction, and specialized expertise to the joint warfighter."

41 National Commission on Terrorist Attacks against the United States, July 22, 2004, 362, <http://govinfo.library.unt.edu/911/report/911Report.pdf>. Accessed June 4, 2008.

42 The *New York Times* reported on November 8, 2008, that "the United States military since 2004 has used broad, secret authority to carry out nearly a dozen previously undisclosed attacks against Al Qaeda and other militants in Syria, Pakistan and elsewhere." Eric Schmitt and Marc Mazzetti, "Secret Order Lets U.S. Raid Al Qaeda in Many Countries."

43 "Bush and Public Opinion," Pew Research Center for the People and the Press, December 3–7, 2008. 1,126 respondents were interviewed on a landline telephone, and 363 were interviewed on a cell phone, including 138 who had no landline telephone. Both the landline and cell phone samples were provided by Survey Sampling International.

Epilogue

1 This concept was adopted as doctrine in the Joint Chiefs of Staff document *Joint Vision 2010*: "Full Spectrum Dominance will be the key characteristic we seek for our Armed Forces in the 21st century." See also Engdahl, *Full Spectrum Dominance*.

2 Landon Lecture, Kansas State University, Remarks as Delivered by Secretary of Defense Robert M. Gates, Manhattan, Kansas, November 26, 2007.

3 Office of the President, "A New Era of Responsibility: Renewing America's Promise," (Office of Management and Budget, Washington, D.C.: Government Printing Office, 2009), 87.

4 For a much more technical discussion of full spectrum dominance, see Lieutenant Colonel Paul W. Phister Jr. and Igor Plonisch, "C2 of Space: The Key to Full Spectrum Dominance," Air Force Research Laboratory Information Directorate, <http://www.dodccrp.org/events/1999_CCRTS/pdf_files/track_6/109phist.pdf>. Accessed September 13, 2009.

5 For Vickers's role in Afghanistan, see Crile, *Charlie Wilson's War*.

6 Ann Scott Tyson, "Sorry Charlie, This Is Michael Vickers's War," *Washington Post*, December 28, 2007, A19.

7 Speech, America's Society, "Amb. Jeffrey Davidow on Expectations for the Summit of the Americas," April 3, 2009; speech, Jeffrey Davidow, Council on Foreign Relations, "Perspectives on the Fifth Summit of the Americas," April 9, 2009.

8 Interview with Jeffrey Davidow, "Obama More Popular Than Chávez in Venezuela, Says US Top Aide," SouthAtlantic News Agency, MercoPress, April 18, 2009, <http://en.mercopress.com/2009/04/18/obama-more-popular-than-chavez-in-venezuela-says-us-top-aide>. Accessed September 2, 2009.

9 Bruce Fein, "How Obama Excused Torture," <http://airamerica.com/blog/2009/apr/17/bruce-fein-how-obama-excused-torture>. Accessed April 20, 2009.

10 Remarks of President Obama for the Opening of the Summit of the Americas, April 17, 2009, Port of Spain, Trinidad and Tobago.

11 See U.S. Air Mobility Command, "Air Mobility Command en Route Strategy," 2008, <http://www.wola.org/media/GlobalEnRouteStrategy.pdf>. Accessed September 7,

2009. This document suggested a much broader role for the base at Palanquero: "Until recently, security concerns in South America have focused on the counter-narcotics mission. That mission has not required the use of strategic airlift in its prosecution. Recently, USSOUTHCOM has become interested in establishing a location on the South American continent that could be used . . . as a location from which mobility operations could be executed."

12 Thus the Overseas Basing Commission (2005) explained: "In keeping with U.S. policy for the region to strengthen democratic institutions, promote a prosperous hemisphere, investing in people, and bolstering security, the U.S. Government has taken a multi-departmental approach to dealing with the region's security issues. The U.S. Coast Guard, Drug Enforcement Agency, Central Intelligence Agency, U.S. Customs Service, Federal Bureau of Investigation, the Department of Defense, and others are all deeply involved with strengthening the region's democratic institutions and bolstering security in the region." See Commission on Review of Overseas Military Facility Structure of the United States (Overseas Basing Commission), Report to the President, May 5, 2005, <http://www.fas.org/irp/agency/dod/obc.pdf>. Accessed July 7, 2009.

13 Ecuador's president, Rafael Correa, had facetiously offered to renew the lease on the Manta base, whose use was theoretically limited strictly to the drug war, if the United States would reciprocate with an Ecuadorian base in Miami: "If there's no problem having foreign soldiers on a country's soil, surely they'll let us have an Ecuadorian base in the United States."

14 "A New Partnership for the Americas," Obama campaign, <http://obama.3cdn.net/f579b3802a3d35c8d5_9aymvyqpo.pdf>. Accessed August 12, 2009.

15 "Bolivia Looks to China, Brazil, for Fighter Aircraft," September 1, 2009, DefenceTalk, Global Defence and Military Portal, <http://www.defencetalk.com/bolivia-looks-to-china-brazil-for-combat-aircraft-21497/>. Accessed September 14, 2009.

16 Richard Reynolds, "Latin Fears about U.S. Plans to Open Bases in Colombia," *Sydney Morning Herald*, August 8, 2009, <http://www.smh.com.au/world/latin-fears-about-us-plans-to-open-bases-in-colombia-20090807-edoj.html>. Accessed August 29, 2009.

17 Corey Flintoff, "Uproar in South America over U.S. Base Deal," August 26, 2009, National Public Radio, <http://www.npr.org/templates/story/story.php?storyId=112247252>. Accessed September 7, 2009.

18 In Washington, D.C., Lanny Davis, a lawyer (and former counsel to President Bill Clinton and campaign adviser to Hillary Clinton) and now a lobbyist for the Honduran coup leaders and the Honduran branch of the Business Council for Latin America, explained that "the [Honduran] Congress, 95 percent of the Congress, even if you quarrel with plus or minus ten votes, voted to remove Mr. Zelaya, including a majority of his own party, as did fifteen members of the Supreme Court, including a majority of the Supreme Court justices who were liberal democrats." Davis did not add that neither the Honduran congress, nor the supreme court, nor the army had any constitutional authority to arrest the president in his pajamas and fly him out of the country to Costa Rica, with a stop to refuel at the Soto Cano air base. Lanny Davis, Interview with Amy Goodman, August 7, 2009, Democracy Now, <http://www.democracynow.org/2009/8/7/honduras>. Accessed August 28, 2009.

19 In 2009, members of the ALBA group (Alianza Bolivariana para los Pueblos de Nuestra América) included Antigua and Barbuda, Bolivia, Cuba, Dominica, Ecuador, Honduras, Nicaragua, Saint Vincent and the Grenadines, and Venezuela.

20 Chávez apparently borrowed this term from German sociologist Heinz Dieterich Steffan (see *Hugo Chávez; El socialismo del siglo XXI),* although the term may originate with Russian author A. V. Buzgalin (*El socialismo del siglo XXI,* Guanabo, Cuba, January 2000; original in Russian, 1996).

21 Joint Task Force Bravo's website describes its mission in the typical language of South-Com since 1995, <http://www.jtfb.southcom.mil>. Part of the mission is "to provide strategic flexibility for U.S. Southern Command regional engagement." Accessed September 2, 2009.

22 "U.S. Military Denies Role in Honduras Coup Flight," *USA Today,* <http://www .usatoday.com/news/world/2009-08-16-honduras-military_N.htm>; "SouthCom: No U.S. Role in Honduras Coup Flight," *ArmyTimes,* August 17, 2009.

23 "Obama Says Coup in Honduras Illegal," Reuters, June 29, 2009, <http://www.reuters .com/article/Disaster/idUSTRE55S5J220090629>. Accessed July 14, 2009.

24 José de Cordoba, "Honduras Lurches toward Crisis over Election," *Wall Street Journal,* June 26, 2009; Linda Cooper and James Hodge, "Honduran Coup Leader a Two-Time SOA Graduate," *National Catholic Reporter,* June 29, 2009, <http://ncronline .org/news/global/honduran-coup-leader-two-time-soa-graduate?nocache=1>. Accessed August 28, 2009.

25 Negroponte, as assistant secretary of state in the Bush administration, had traveled to Honduras in June 2008 to discuss the Soto Cano air base and the possibility of a new base in the Mosquito Coast region. In late January 2009, Negroponte became vice chairman of McLarty Associates, a leading international strategic advisory firm in Washington, D.C. In July 2009, he also took a part-time position at Yale University, his alma mater, teaching grand strategy.

26 Inter-American Democratic Charter, Lima, Peru, September 11, 2001, <http://www .oas.org/charter/docs/resolution1_en_p4.htm>.

27 U.S. Department of State, Philip J. Crowley, Assistant Secretary of State, Daily Press Briefing, Washington, D.C., July 20, 2009, <http://www.state.gov/r/pa/prs/dpb/2009/ july/126250.htm>. Accessed August 21, 2009.

28 News release posted on Joint Task Force Bravo website on September 21, 2009, <http:// www.jtfb.southcom.mil/news/index.asp>.

29 Paul Richter, "US Cuts Aid to Honduras," *Los Angeles Times,* September 3, 2009; Mark Weisbrot, "IMF Gives $164 million to Coup Government in Honduras, Following Familiar Pattern," *Guardian Unlimited,* September 3, 2009, <http://www.cepr .net/index.php/op-eds-&-columns/op-eds-&-columns/imf-honduras-coup/>. Accessed September 12, 2009. Tracy Williams, "Visas Pulled to Push Zelaya's Return," *Los Angeles Times,* September 13, 2009, A20.

30 Posted on Congressman Mack's website, <http://conniemack.com/news>. Accessed September 2, 2009.

31 U.S. Energy Information Administration, "Crude Oil and Total Petroleum Imports Top 15 Countries," August 28, 2009, <http://www.eia.doe.gov/pub/oil_gas/petroleum/ data_publications/company_level_imports/current/import.html>. Accessed September 14, 2009.

32 Lesley Clark, "Obama's Support for Zelaya Prompts Senator to Block Two State Department Appointments," *Miami Herald*, July 22, 2009, <http://www.miamiherald.com/honduras/story/1151874.html>.

33 Hans Bader, "Obama Nominee: Corrupt Foreign Rulers Have a Right to Remain in Office Until They Receive 'Judicial Process,'" Openmarket.org (Competitive Enterprise Institute), July 8, 2009. The CEI, founded during the Reagan administration, calls itself "the largest free-market environmental policy program in Washington," <http://cei.org/about>. Openmarket.org proclaimed: "Obama has joined Cuban dictator Castro and Venezuelan dictator Chávez in demanding that Zelaya be reinstated. He nominated Valenzuela despite his reputation as a loud defender of dictator Chávez. Obama, too, claims Zelaya's removal was 'illegal,' even though it was carried out on orders of Honduras's supreme court, and ratified by Honduras's Congress, pursuant to Articles 239 and 272 of the Honduran Constitution."

34 An extreme version of this resistance to the Obama agenda was the so-called Tenther Movement, a group that wished to revert to constitutional interpretations dating to before 1803. The Tenthers claimed that "New Deal–era reformers led an unlawful coup against the 'True Constitution,' exploiting Depression-born desperation to expand the federal government's powers beyond recognition. Under the tenther constitution, Barack Obama's health-care reform is forbidden, as is Medicare, Medicaid, and Social Security. The federal minimum wage is a crime against state sovereignty; the federal ban on workplace discrimination and whites-only lunch counters is an unlawful encroachment on local businesses. According to the tenthers, the Constitution contains an itemized list of federal powers — such as the power to regulate interstate commerce or establish post offices or make war on foreign nations — and anything not contained in that list is beyond Congress' authority." Posted on Military.com, <http://forums.military.com/eve/forums/a/tpc/f/409192893/m/8080040232001>. Accessed September 14, 2009.

35 Giorgio Trucchi, "80 días de lucha y resistencia en todo el país," Rebelion.com, <http://www.rebelion.org/noticia.php?id=91786>. Accessed September 20, 2009.

36 "Statement on Situation in Honduras," U.S. Department of State, September 22, 2009.

37 Congressman Schock cited Library of Congress, Report for Congress, August 9, 2009, "Honduras: Constitutional Law Issues," Directorate of Legal Research, written by Norma C. Gutierrez, <http://schock.house.gov/uploadedfiles/Schock_CRS_Report_Honduras_final.pdf>. Accessed September 24, 2009. Other legal experts disagreed with the constitutional interpretations in this report. See Doug Cassel, "Honduras: Coup d'Etat in Constitutional Clothing? *American Society of International Law* 13, no. 9 (July 29, 2009), <http://www.asil.org/files/insight090729pdf.pdf>. Accessed September 2, 2009.

38 "Cuba Reacts to US Blacklisting, Calls Washington 'International Criminal,'" May 1, 2009, SouthAtlantic News Agency, MercoPress, <http://en.mercopress.com/2009/05/01/cuba-reacts-to-us-blacklisting-calls-washington-international-criminal>. Accessed September 4, 2009.

39 "Obama Extends Cuba Embargo 1 Year," *New York Times*, September 14, 2009, <http://www.nytimes.com/aponline/2009/09/14/us/politics/AP-US-Obama-Cuba.html?_r=1>. Accessed September 14, 2009.

40 In 1979, the United States established a list of countries providing either direct or indi-

rect support to terrorist groups. This list was legislated in the Export Administration Act under the secretary of state's authority. The annual list is published in the Code of Federal Regulations and in Country Reports on Terrorism. On September 16, 2009, the State Department website, <http://www.state.gov/s/ct/c14151.htm>, explained that countries determined by the secretary of state to have repeatedly provided support for acts of international terrorism are designated pursuant to three laws: section 6(j) of the Export Administration Act, section 40 of the Arms Export Control Act, and section 620A of the Foreign Assistance Act. Taken together, the four main categories of sanctions resulting from designation under these authorities include restrictions on U.S. foreign assistance; a ban on defense exports and sales; certain controls over exports of dual-use items; and miscellaneous financial and other restrictions. Designation under the above-referenced authorities also implicates other sanctions laws that penalize persons and countries engaging in certain trade with state sponsors.

41 Kathryn Ledebur (Andean Information Network) and John Walsh (Washington Office on Latin America), "Obama's Bolivia ATPDEA Decision: Blast from the Past or Wave of the Future?" August 11, 2009, <http://www.wola.org/media/ATPDEA%20Blast%20from%20the%20Past%20final.pdf>. Accessed September 10, 2009.

42 See Memorandum to reporters and editors, re: the President's determinations regarding Bolivia and Ecuador under the Andean Trade Promotion and Drug Eradication Act, July 1, 2009, <http://finance.senate.gov/press/Gpress/2009/prg070109.pdf>. Grassley also wrote to Secretary of State Clinton expressing concern about Thomas A. Shannon's nomination as ambassador to Brazil, because Shannon had supported removing the tariff on Brazilian ethanol — a measure not favored by his Iowa constituents. See "Grassley Seeks Clarification of U.S. Stance on Ethanol Tariff before Nominee for Ambassador to Brazil Moves Forward," Press Release, July 28, 2009, on Senator Grassley's home page, <http://finance.senate.gov/press/Gpress/2009/prg072809.pdf>. Accessed September 12, 2009.

43 Barack Obama, Address to Congress, February 24, 2009.

44 Christi Parsons, "Obama Makes a Point with 1 Word," Los Angeles Times, April 3, 2009, A1, 24.

45 "White Paper of the White House Interagency Policy Group's Report on U.S. Policy toward Afghanistan and Pakistan," March 27, 2009, <http://www.whitehouse.gov/assets/documents/Afghanistan-Pakistan_White_Paper.pdf>. Accessed September 2, 2009.

46 "Transcript: Obama on 'Face the Nation.'" Interview conducted at the White House, September 18, 2009, <http://www.cbsnews.com/stories/2009/09/20/ftn/main5324077.shtml>. Accessed September 21, 2009.

47 "Obama's War on Terror May Resemble Bush's in Some Areas," New York Times, February 22, 2009.

Bibliography

In writing this book, I have relied on the work of generations of historians, social scientists, journalists, political analysts, literary scholars, and travel accounts. I have also drawn on forty years of reading and research, including immersion in congressional debates, contemporary newspapers, memoirs, letters, and other traditional historical source materials. For purposes of publication, I have limited the references here to works cited in the text, to books and articles that have so influenced my interpretations and conclusions that it would be improper not to mention them, and to important reference and bibliographical sources. A more comprehensive bibliography of works consulted is available at the website dedicated to this book at <http://www-rohan.sdsu.edu/dept/polsciwb/brianl/book18.html>.

For selected government documents and publications, I have used citations that most easily connect a reader to the document as mentioned in the text or notes. For some government publications, for example, the U.S. State Department series *Foreign Relations of the United States* (*FRUS*), I have relied on digital versions, but most of the time I have also verified content with printed sources. For presidential messages to Congress, speeches, proclamations, and related materials, I have often relied on the Avalon Project at Yale University (<http://avalon.law.yale.edu/>), the American Presidency Project at the University of California, Santa Barbara (<http://www.presidency.ucsb.edu/>), and the Office of the Public Register, *Public Papers of the Presidents of the United States* (<http://www.gpoaccess.gov/pubpapers/>). For the period since the Truman administration, the U.S. State Department offers online access to much material, along with a useful "search" function, <http://www.state.gov/r/pa/ho/frus/>, and also a list of all volumes (since 1861), with a chronological indication of content for each volume. Likewise, the Library of Congress website "A Century of Lawmaking for a New Nation: U.S. Congressional Documents and Debates, 1774–1875," <http://memory.loc.gov/ammem/amlaw/lawhome.html>, provides access to many of the debates and documents mentioned in the text, including references to *U.S. Statutes at Large* (*Stat.*), congressional debates, and House and Senate journals. For diplomatic correspondence in the first half of the nineteenth century, the compilations of William R. Manning, listed below, are invaluable. I have also relied on the National Security Archive at George Washington University and its internet site, <http://www.gwu.edu/ñnsarchiv/>, for declassified materials and for its valuable electronic briefing books.

The selective bibliography is divided into four sections. The first, Official Publications

and Collections of Official Documents, includes government publications and nongovernmental collections of documents cited in the text or relied on for documentation. The
second section, Selected Official and Nongovernmental Documents, includes individual
documents, such as presidential directives, commission reports, State Department memo-
randa (for example, the Clark Memorandum of 1928, brief reports by the Congressional
Research Service, or short policy statements by the Department of Defense). The third section, Books, Monographs, and Theses, includes full citations for publications cited in the
notes or upon which I have significantly relied in my research but that are not directly cited
in the notes. This includes bibliographic works and historiography on American politics
and foreign relations. The last section, Articles, Book Chapters, and Papers, includes full
citations of miscellaneous policy papers, reports, briefings, and other materials cited in
the notes.

Official Publications and Collections of Official Documents

American Presidency Project (University of California, Santa Barbara, <http://www
.presidency.ucsb.edu/>). Over 80,000 documents related to the presidency, including
presidential messages and papers. State of the Union messages are at <http://www
.presidency.ucsb.edu/sou.php>.

American State Papers: Foreign Relations. 6 vols. Washington, D.C., 1832–59.

Annals of Congress. 42 vols. Washington, D.C.: Gales and Seaton, 1834–56, <http://
memory.loc.gov/ammem/amlaw/lwac.html>. (Includes *Register of Debates*, 1824–37;
Congressional Globe, 1833–73); and part of the *Congressional Record*, 1873– .

Avalon Project (Yale University, <http://avalon.law.yale.edu/>). A large collection of
digital documents and supporting materials on Law, History, Economics, Politics,
Diplomacy, and Government and including internal links to American Diplomacy;
Major Treaties; Inter-American System: Agreements, Conventions, and Other Documents; Cold War Diplomacy; Defense Treaties of the United States; and Selected Treaties between the United States and Native Americans.

Bartlett, Ruhl J., ed. *The Record of American Diplomacy.* 4th ed. New York: Knopf, 1964.

Bauer, K. Jack. *The New American State Papers: Naval Affairs.* 10 vols. Wilmington, Del.:
Scholarly Resources, 1981.

Bevans, C. I., ed. *Treaties and Other International Agreements of the United States of
America, 1776–1949.* 13 vols. Washington, D.C.: Government Printing Office, 1968–76.

Cold War International History Project. <http://www.wilsoncenter.org/index.
cfm?fuseaction=topics.home&topic_id=1409.> Extensive virtual archive.

Commager, Henry Steele, ed. *Documents of American History.* 7th ed. New York: Appleton-Century-Crofts, 1963.

Congressional Research Service. *Inter-American Relations: A Collection of Documents,
Legislation, Descriptions of Inter-American Organizations, and Other Material Pertain-
ing to Inter-American Affairs: Report Prepared for the Use of the Committee on Foreign
Relations, United States Senate and Committee on Foreign Affairs, U.S. House of Representatives.* Washington, D.C.: Government Printing Office, 1989.

Gambone, Michael D., ed. *Documents of American Diplomacy: from the American Revolution to the Present.* Westport, Conn.: Greenwood Press, 2002.

Gantenbein, James W., ed. *The Evolution of Our Latin American Policy: A Documentary
Record.* New York: Octagon Books, 1971.

Inaugural Addresses of the Presidents of the United States: George Washington to George W. Bush. Washington, D.C.: Government Printing Office, 1989; New York: Bartleby, 2001.

Long, David F., ed. *A Documentary History of U.S. Foreign Relations: Selections from and Additions to Ruhl J. Bartlett's* The Record of American Diplomacy. Washington, D.C.: University Press of America, 1980.

Lowrie, Walter, and Matthew St. Clair, eds. *American State Papers: Documents, Legislative and Executive, of the Congress of the United States.* Washington, D.C.: Gales and Seaton, 1832–61.

MacDonald, William. *Documentary Source Book of American History, 1606–1926.* 3rd ed. New York: Macmillan, 1929.

Malloy, William M. *Treaties, Conventions, International Acts, Protocols, and Agreements between the United States and Other Powers, 1776–1909.* Senate Doc. 357, 61st Cong., 2nd sess. 2 vols. Washington, D.C.: Government Printing Office, 1910.

Manning, William R., ed. *Diplomatic Correspondence of the United States: Canadian Relations, 1784–1860.* 4 vols. Washington, D.C.: Carnegie Endowment for International Peace, 1940–45.

————, ed. *Diplomatic Correspondence of the United States: Inter-American Affairs, 1831–1860.* 12 vols. Washington, D.C.: Carnegie Endowment for International Peace, 1932–39.

————, ed. *Diplomatic Correspondence of the United States Concerning the Independence of the Latin-American Nations.* 3 vols. New York: Oxford University Press, 1925–26.

————, ed. *Early Diplomatic Relations between the United States and Mexico.* Baltimore: Johns Hopkins University Press, 1916.

Miller, Hunter. ed. *Treaties and Other International Acts of the United States of America.* 8 vols. Washington, D.C.: Government Printing Office, 1931–48.

————, ed. *Documents 1–40: 1776–1818.* Vol. 2 of *Treaties and Other International Acts of the United States of America.* Washington, D.C.: Government Printing Office, 1931–48.

Office of the Public Register. *Public Papers of the Presidents of the United States.* Electronic resource. Washington, D.C.: Federal Register Division, National Archives and Records Service, General Services Administration.

Parry, Clive. ed. *Consolidated Treaty Series with Index, 1648–1919.* 231 vols. Dobbs Ferry, N.Y.: Oceana Publications, 1969-.

Project on Defense Alternatives. *The Defense Strategy Review Page.* (Formerly a *Quadrennial Defense Review* page.) Official Strategy, Posture, and Commission Documents (online defense-related documents), <http://www.comw.org/qdr/offdocs.html>. Accessed April 2, 2009.

Public Statutes at Large of the United States of America, 1789–March 3, 1845. Vol. 2, edited by Richard Peters. Boston: Little, Brown, 1861.

Richardson, James D., ed. *A Compilation of the Messages and Papers of the Presidents, 1789–1897.* 10 vols. Washington, D.C.: Published by authority of Congress, 1899.

United States of America. Vol. 15 of *British Parliamentary Papers.* Shannon: Irish University Press, 1971.

U.S. Army. *American Military History.* Washington, D.C.: U.S. Army Center of Military History, 1989.

U.S. Bureau of the Census. *Historical Statistics of the United States, Colonial Times to 1970.* Washington, D.C.: Government Printing Office, 1975.

U.S. Congress. *Abridgement of the Debates of Congress, from 1789 to 1856.* New York: D. Appleton, 1857–61. From *Annals of Congress: Register of Debates* (Gales and Seaton); and from John C. Rives, *Official Reported Debates,* <http://quod.lib.umich.edu/cgi/t/text/pageviewer-idx?c=moa&cc=moa&idno=ahj4053.0004.001&frm=frameset&view=image&seq=3>.

———. *Biographical Directory of the United States Congress, 1774–2005: The Continental Congress, September 5, 1774, to October 21, 1788, and the Congress of the United States, from the First through the One Hundred Eighth Congresses, March 4, 1789, to January 3, 2005.* Washington, D.C.: Government Printing Office, 2005.

U.S. Department of State. *Diplomatic Instructions of the Department of State, 1801–1906.* Series M77. College Park, Md.: National Archives.

———. *Diplomatic Instructions of the United States Department of State to Special Missions, 1823–1906.* Record Group 59, M77. Reels 152–55. College Park, Md.: National Archives; distributed by Scholarly Resources, 1965.

———. *Foreign Relations of the United States* (*FRUS*). (Much of this is also available as an electronic resource at <http://www.state.gov/r/pa/ho/frus/>.) Washington, D.C.: Department of State Edition.

———. *Foreign Relations of the United States, 1961–1963.* Vol. 10, *Cuba, 1961–62.* Washington, D.C.: Government Printing Office, 1997.

———. *Papers: Despatches from U.S. Ministers to Colombia, 1820–1906.* Series T33. College Park, Md.: National Archives.

———. *Proclamations and Decrees during the War with Spain.* Washington, D.C.: Government Printing Office, 1899.

———. *The Revolutionary Diplomatic Correspondence of the United States.* 6 vols. Edited under direction of Congress by Francis Wharton, with preliminary index and notes historical and legal; published in conformity with act of Congress of August 13, 1888. Washington, D.C.: Government Printing Office, 1889.

———. *The State Department Policy Planning Staff Papers.* Introduction by Anna Kasten Nelson; foreword by George F. Kennan. New York: Garland, 1983.

———. *The United States and Other American Republics.* Department of State series no. 4. Washington, D.C., 1931.

U.S. Department of State and U.S. Department of Defense. *Grenada Documents: An Overview and Selection.* Washington, D.C., 1984.

U.S. Marine Corps. *Small Wars Manual.* NAVMC 2890. Reprint of 1940 edition, with an introduction by Ronald Schaffer. Manhattan, Kans.: Military Affairs, Department of History, 1972.

———. *U.S. Marines and Irregular Warfare, 1898–2007: Anthology and Selected Bibliography.* Compiled by Stephen S. Evans. Quantico, Va.: Marine Corps University Press, 2008.

U.S. Navy. Historical Section, Fourteenth Naval District, Rare Books Room. *Administrative History of the Fourteenth Naval District and the Hawaiian Sea Frontier.* Vol. 1, *Hawaii, 1945.* Washington, D.C., 1945. Extracts at <http://www.history.navy.mil/docs/wwii/pearl/hawaii.htm>.

U.S. Senate. Committee on Foreign Relations. *A Decade of American Foreign Policy: Basic Documents, 1941–49.* Prepared at the request of the Senate Committee on Foreign Relations by the Staff of the Committee and the Department of State. Washington, D.C.: Government Printing Office, 1950.

————. Committee on Foreign Relations. *United States–Latin American Relations.* Prepared under the direction of the Subcommittee on American Republics Affairs, document no. 125, August 31, 1960. Washington, D.C., Government Printing Office, 1960.

Selected Official and Nongovernmental Documents

Ackerman, David M. "International Law and the Preemptive Use of Force against Iraq." Washington, D.C.: Congressional Research Service, updated April 11, 2003.

Bush, George H. W. "National Security Strategy of the United States." White House Document. August 1991.

Bush, George W. "National Security Presidential Directive/NSPD-32, Western Hemisphere Strategy." Washington, D.C.: The White House, 2004.

————. "The National Security Strategy of the United States of America." White House Document, Washington, D.C., September 17, 2002, at <http://merln.ndu.edu/whitepapers/USnss2002.pdf>.

Carter, James. "The National Security Council System." Presidential Directive/National Security Council (NSC-PD) 2. January 20, 1977.

Clark, J. Reuben, Jr. "Memorandum by the Solicitor for the Department of State, Right to Protect Citizens in Foreign Countries by Landing Forces." Washington, D.C., 1912.

————. "Memorandum on the Monroe Doctrine" (December 17, 1928). Washington, D.C.: Department of State Publication no. 37, 1930.

Clinton, William. "A National Security Strategy of Engagement and Enlargement." White House Document. Washington, D.C., February 1995, <http://www.au.af.mil/au/awc/awcgate/nss/nss-95.pdf>.

————. "A National Security Strategy of Engagement and Enlargement." White House Document. Washington, D.C., February 1996, <http://www.fas.org/spp/military/docops/national/1996stra.htm>.

————. "A National Security Strategy for a New Century." White House Document, May 1997, <http://clinton2.nara.gov/WH/EOP/NSC/Strategy>.

————. "A National Security Strategy for a New Century." White House Document. December 1999, <http://clinton2.nara.gov/WH/EOP/NSC/Strategy>.

Collier, Ellen C. "Instances of the Use of Force by United States' Forces Abroad, 1783–1993." Washington, D.C.: Congressional Research Service, October 7, 1993.

Commission on the Roles and Capabilities of the United States Intelligence Community. "The Evolution of the U.S. Intelligence Community—An Historical Overview." Appendix A of *Preparing for the Twenty-first Century: An Appraisal of U.S. Intelligence.* Washington, D.C.: Government Printing Office, March 1, 1996.

Congressional Research Service. "Congressional Use of Funding Cutoffs since 1970 Involving U.S. Military Forces and Overseas Deployments." January 10, 2001.

"Final Act of Bogotá," Resolution 32, "The Preservation and Defense of Democracy in America," Bogotá, 1948. *Foreign Relations of the United States*, 1948, vol. 9.

Grimmett, Richard F. "Instances of Use of United States Armed Forces Abroad, 1798–2007." Rl 32170. Washington, D.C.: Congressional Research Services, 2008.

————. "The War Powers Resolution: After Thirty-four Years." Washington, D.C.: Congressional Research Services, updated March 10, 2008.

Inouye, Daniel K., and Lee H. Hamilton. *Report of the Congressional Committees Investigating the Iran-Contra Affair*. Washington, D.C.: Government Printing Office, 1987.

Inter-American Commission on Human Rights. "Report on the Situation of Human Rights of a Segment of the Nicaraguan Population of Mikito Origin." OEA/Ser. L./V.II.62, Doc. 10 rev. 3 (1983).

Johnson, Lyndon. "The Direction, Coordination, and Supervision of Interdepartmental Activities Overseas." National Security Action Memorandum (NSAM) 341. March 2, 1966.

Joint Chiefs of Staff. *Joint Doctrine for Military Operations Other Than War*. June 16, 1995.

————. *Joint Counterdrug Operations*. Joint Pub 3-07.4. February 17, 1998.

————. *Joint Vision 2010. America's Military: Preparing for Tomorrow*. Washington, D.C., 1996, <http://www.dtic.mil/jv2010/jv2010.pdf>.

————. *Joint Vision 2020. America's Military: Preparing for Tomorrow*. Washington, D.C.: Government Printing Office, June 2000.

Mages, Lisa. "U.S. Armed Forces Abroad: Selected Congressional Roll Call Votes since 1982." Washington, D.C.: Congressional Research Service, updated January 27, 2006.

Miller, David Hunter (U.S. Department of State). *Secret Statutes of the United States: A Memorandum*. Washington, D.C.: Government Printing Office, 1918.

NGO Global Forum. The NGO Alternative Treaties, Rio de Janeiro, June 1–15, 1992, <http://habitat.igc.org/treaties>.

North Atlantic Treaty Organization. "NATO, the First Five Years" (updated March 15, 2001). Signed by Lord Ismay, November 1, 1914, Paris, <http://www.nato.int/archives/1st5years/index.htm>. Accessed March 20, 2009.

Nixon, Richard M. "Reorganization of the National Security Council System." National Security Decision Memorandum (NSDM) 2. Nixon Presidential Library, January 20, 1969.

NSC 10/5: "Scope and Pace of Covert Operations," October 23, 1951. In *The CIA under Harry Truman*, edited by Michael Warner, 437–39. Washington, D.C.: Central Intelligence Agency, 1994.

NSC 68: "United States Objectives and Programs for National Security." A Report to the President Pursuant to the President's Directive of January 31, 1950. Washington, D.C.: National Security Council, April 14, 1950.

NSC 141: "Reexamination of U.S. Programs for National Security," January 19, 1953. In U.S. Department of State, *Foreign Relations of the United States*, 1952–54, 2:209–31, 1984.

NSC-PD 18: "U.S. National Strategy," August 24, 1977, <http://www.jimmycarterlibrary.org/documents/pd18.pdf>. Accessed April 2, 2009.

NSC-PD 30: "Human Rights," February 17, 1978, <http://www.jimmycarterlibrary.org/documents/pd30.pdf>. Accessed February 22, 2009.

Office of Inter-American Affairs. *History of the Office of the Coordinator of Inter-American Affairs: Historical Reports on War Administration*. Washington, D.C.: Government Printing Office, 1947.

Office of the Chairman of the Joint Chiefs of Staff. Joint History Office (Ronald H. Cole). *Operation Just Cause: The Planning and Execution of Joint Operations in Panama, February 1988–January 1990*. Washington, D.C., 1995.

————. *Operation Urgent Fury: The Planning and Execution of Joint Operations in Grenada, 12 October–2 November 1983*. Washington, D.C., 1997.

Office of the President of the United States. Office of Management and Budget, Budget of the U.S. Government, Fiscal Year 2006. *Historical Tables*, <http://www.whitehouse.gov/omb/budget/fy2006/pdf/hist.pdf>. Accessed February 22, 2009.

Office of the Press Secretary. "White House Press Release: Classified National Security Information." *Executive Order #12958* (April 17, 1995), Sec. 4.4.

Office of the Secretary of State. Office of the Coordinator for Counterterrorism. *Patterns of Global Terrorism, 1992*. April 30, 1993.

PPS-26. "Problem to Establish U.S. Policy Regarding Anti-Communist Measures Which Could Be Planned and Carried Out within the Inter-American System." Secret. Washington, D.C., March 22, 1948.

President's Special Review Board. *The Tower Commission Report: The Full Text of the President's Special Review Board*. New York: Bantam, 1987.

Project for a New American Century (PNAC). Principal author, Thomas Donnelly. *Rebuilding America's Defenses: Strategy, Forces and Resources for a New Century*. Washington, D.C.: September 2000.

Reagan, Ronald. "Central America: Defending Our Vital Interests." Address before a Joint Session of Congress, April 27, 1983. *Department of State Bulletin* (June 1983): 4.

————. "Implementation of the Recommendations of the President's Special Review Board." National Security Decision Direction (NSDD) 266. March 31, 1987. Federation of American Scientists Intelligence Resource Program.

Report of the President's National Bipartisan Commission on the Americas. Foreword by Henry Kissinger. New York: Macmillan, 1984.

Rockefeller, Nelson. *The Rockefeller Report on the Americas: The Official Report of a United States Presidential Mission for the Western Hemisphere*. Introduction by Tad Szulc. Chicago: Quadrangle Books, 1969.

Roosevelt, Theodore. "Letter to Mahan: Obstacles to Immediate Expansion, 1897." <http://www.mtholyoke.edu/acad/intrel/trmahan.htm>.

Sklar, Barry, and Virginia M. Hagen, comp. "Declaration of Solidarity for the Preservation of the Political Integrity of the American States against International Communist Intervention." Ninth International Conference of American States, Caracas, Venezuela, March 28, 1954.

Truman, Harry. "United States Objectives and Programs for National Security." NSC 68/1, Annex 9, September 21, 1950. Digital National Security Archive, George Washington University, Melvin Gelman Library, Washington, D.C.

UN Commission for Truth for El Salvador. *From Madness to Hope: The Twelve-Year War in El Salvador*. New York: United Nations, March 15, 1993.

U.S. Congress. House. Committee on Foreign Affairs. *Grenada War Powers: Full Compliance Reporting and Implementation*. 98th Cong., 1st sess., 1983, OCLC 11649794.

————. Senate. Select Committee to Study Governmental Operations with Respect to Intelligence Activities. *Alleged Assassination Plots Involving Foreign Leaders*. 94th Cong., 1st sess., S. Rep. 465. Washington, D.C.: Government Printing Office, 1975.

U.S. Department of Defense. Inter-American Affairs. "United States Security Policy for the Americas." October 2000.

U.S. Department of Defense. Office of International Security Affairs. "United States Security Strategy for the Americas." September 1995.

U.S. Department of Defense. Office of the Secretary of Defense. *Defense Strategy for the 1990s: The Regional Strategy.* January 1993.

———. *Quadrennial Defense Review.* September 30, 2001.

———. *Quadrennial Defense Review Report.* February 6, 2006.

———. *Report of the Quadrennial Defense Review.* May 1997.

———. *Special Operations Forces Posture Statement 2000,* <http://www.dod.mil/pubs/sof/sof2000.pdf>. Accessed April 8, 2009.

U.S. Department of the Navy. Navy Historical Center. "Historical Overview of the Federalist Navy, 1787–1801." Naval History Bibliographies no. 4.

———. Navy Historical Center. "Inquiry into Occupation and Administration of Haiti and the Dominican Republic." 67th Cong., 2nd sess., S. Rep. 794. 1922.

———. Navy Historical Center. "The Reestablishment of the Navy, 1787–1801." Naval Historical Bibliographies no. 4.

U.S. Department of State. "Communist Involvement in the Colombian Riots of April 9, 1948." Office of Intelligence Research (OIR) Rep. 4696. October 14, 1948.

———. *Foreign Relations of the United States.* George F. Kennan to the Secretary of State, PPS/23. February 24, 1948, 1: 509–29.

———. *Foreign Relations of the United States, 1964–1968.* Vol. 32, *Dominican Republic, Cuba, Haiti, Guyana.* Edited by Daniel Lawler and Carolyn Yee. Washington, D.C.: Government Printing Office, 2005 (includes "Notes on Covert Action," 31–36).

———. *Foreign Relations of the United States, 1945–1950.* NSC 4-A, December 17, 1947, Emergence of the Intelligence Establishment. Document 257.

———. *Foreign Relations of the United States, 1945–1950.* NSC 10/2, June 18, 1948, Emergence of the Intelligence Establishment. Document 292.

U.S. Department of State. Bureau of Public Affairs Historical Office. "U.S. Policy toward Latin America: Recognition and Non-Recognition of Governments and Interruptions in Diplomatic Relations, 1933–1974." Washington, D.C., June 1975.

U.S. Senate. Select Committee on Intelligence. "CIA's Use of Journalists and Clergy in Intelligence Operations." 104th Cong., 2nd sess., July 17, 1996.

———. Select Committee on Intelligence. *Whether Disclosure of Funds for the Intelligence Activities of the United States Is in the Public Interest.* 94th Cong., 2nd sess., S. Rep. 95-274, June 16, 1977. Washington D.C.: Government Printing Office, 1977.

U.S. Southern Command. Command Strategy 2016 (CS-2016). "Partnership for the Americas." March 2007.

Books, Monographs, and Theses

Adams, Ephraim Douglas. *British Interests and Activities in Texas, 1838–1846.* Baltimore: Johns Hopkins University Press, 1910.

Adams, John. *Papers of John Adams.* 6 vols. Edited by Robert J. Taylor. Cambridge, Mass.: Belknap Press of Harvard University Press, 1977.

Adams, John Quincy. *Writings of John Quincy Adams.* 7 vols. Edited by Worthington Chauncey Ford. New York: Macmillan, 1913–17.

Agassiz, Louis. *Contributions to the Natural History of the United States of America.* 4 vols. Boston: Little, Brown, 1857–62.

Agee, Philip. *Inside the Company: CIA Diary*. London: Penguin, 1975.

Allison, Robert J. *The Crescent Obscured: The United States and the Muslim World, 1776–1815*. New York: Oxford University Press, 1995.

Alvarez, Alejandro. *The Monroe Doctrine: Its Importance in the International Life of the States of the New World*. New York: Oxford University Press, 1924.

Ambrosius, Lloyd E. *Woodrow Wilson and the American Diplomatic Tradition*. New York: Cambridge University Press, 1987.

"American Foreign Policy: Regional Perspectives." Ruger Workshop No. 4. Proceedings. A workshop sponsored by the William B. Ruger Chair of National Security Economics. Newport, R.I., May 13–15, 2009.

Anderson, Fred. *Crucible of War: The Seven Years' War and the Fate of Empire in British North America, 1754–1766*. New York: Vintage Books, 2000.

Anderson, Thomas P. *Matanza: El Salvador's Communist Revolt of 1932*. Lincoln: University of Nebraska Press, 1971.

Auster, Lawrence. *The Path to National Suicide: An Essay on Immigration and Multiculturalism*. Charlestown, W.Va.: Old Line Press, 1990.

Bacevich, Andrew J. *American Empire: The Realities and Consequences of U.S. Diplomacy*. Cambridge, Mass.: Harvard University Press, 2002.

———. *The Limits of Power: American Exceptionalism*. New York: Metropolitan Books, 2008.

———. *The New American Militarism: How Americans Are Seduced by War*. New York: Oxford University Press, 2005.

Bacevich, Andrew J., James D. Hallums, Richard H. White, and Thomas E. Young. *American Military Policy in Small Wars: The Case of El Salvador*. Washington, D.C.: Pergamon-Brassey, 1988.

Bailey, Thomas A. *A Diplomatic History of the American People*. 8th ed. New York: Appleton-Century-Crofts, 1969.

Barcia, Manuel. *Seeds of Insurrection: Domination and Resistance on Western Cuban Plantations, 1808–1848*. Baton Rouge: Louisiana State University Press, 2008.

Barnes, James J., and Patience P. Barnes. *Private and Confidential: Letters from British Ministers in Washington to the Foreign Secretaries in London, 1844–67*. London: Associated University Presses, 1993.

Bassett, John Spencer, ed. *Correspondence of Andrew Jackson*. 7 vols. Washington, D.C.: Carnegie Institution of Washington, 1926–35.

Beale, Howard. *Theodore Roosevelt and the Rise of America to World Power*. Baltimore: Johns Hopkins University Press, 1956.

Beede, Benjamin R. *Intervention and Counterinsurgency: An Annotated Bibliography of Small Wars of the United States*. New York: Garland, 1985.

Beisner, Robert L., ed. *American Foreign Relations since 1600: A Guide to the Literature*. 2nd ed. Santa Barbara, Calif.: ABC-CLIO, 2003.

Bemis, Samuel Flagg. *The Latin American Policy of the United States: An Historical Interpretation*. New York: Harcourt, Brace and World, 1943.

———. *John Quincy Adams and the Foundations of American Foreign Policy*. New York: Knopf, 1949.

———, ed. *The American Secretaries of State and Their Diplomacy*. 10 vols. New York: Knopf, 1927–29.

Berman, Karl. *Under the Big Stick: Nicaragua and the United States since 1848*. Boston: South End Press, 1986.

Bernstein, Barton J., ed. *Towards a New Past: Dissenting Essays in American History*. New York: Pantheon Books, 1968.

Bethell, Leslie, and Ian Roxborough, eds. *Latin America between the Second World War and the Cold War: Crisis and Containment, 1944–1948*. New York: Cambridge University Press, 1994.

Binder, Frederick Moore. *James Buchanan and the American Empire*. London: Associated University Presses, 1994.

Bissell, Richard M., Jr., with Jonathan E. Lewis and Francis T. Pudlo. *Reflections of a Cold Warrior: From Yalta to the Bay of Pigs*. New Haven: Yale University Press, 1996.

Blasier, Cole. *The Hovering Giant: U.S. Responses to Revolutionary Change in Latin America, 1910–1985*. Rev. ed. Pittsburgh: University of Pittsburgh Press, 1985.

Blight, James G., Bruce J. Allyn, and David A. Welch. *Cuba on the Brink: Fidel Castro, the Missile Crisis, and the Collapse of Communism*. New York: Pantheon, 1993.

Blight, James G., and Peter Kornbluh, eds. *Politics of Illusion: The Bay of Pigs Invasion Reexamined*. Boulder, Colo.: Lynne Rienner, 1997.

Blum, Edward J. *Reforging the White Republic: Race, Religion, and American Nationalism, 1865–1898*. Baton Rouge: Louisiana State University Press, 2005.

Blum, William. *Killing Hope: U.S. Military and CIA Intervention since World War II*. Updated ed. Monroe, Maine: Common Courage Press, 2004.

Bodenheimer, Thomas, and Robert Gould. *Rollback! Right-Wing Power in U.S. Foreign Policy*. Cambridge, Mass.: South End Press, 1989.

Boot, Max. *The Savage Wars of Peace: Small Wars and the Rise of American Power*. New York: Basic Books, 2002.

Borstelmann, Thomas. *The Cold War and the Color Line: American Race Relations in the Global Arena*. Cambridge, Mass.: Harvard University Press, 2001.

Bourne, Kenneth. *Britain and the Balance of Power in North America, 1815–1908*. Berkeley: University of California Press, 1967.

Brands, H. W. *The Devil We Knew: Americans and the Cold War*. New York: Oxford University Press, 1993.

———. *The Reckless Decade: America in the 1890s*. New York: St. Martins, 1995.

Brians, Paul, et al. *Reading about the World*. Vol. 2. 3rd ed. Harcourt, Brace Custom Publishing, 1999.

Brophy, Alfred L. *Reconstructing the Dreamland: The Tulsa Riot of 1921: Race, Reparations, and Reconciliation*. New York: Oxford University Press, 2002.

Brown, Albert G. *Speeches, Messages, and Other Writings*. Edited by M. W. McCluskey. Philadelphia: Jas. B. Smith, 1859.

Brown, Charles Henry. *Agents of Manifest Destiny: The Lives and Times of the Filibusters*. Chapel Hill: University of North Carolina Press, 1980.

Buchanan, James. *The Works of James Buchanan*. 10 vols. Collected and edited by John Bassett Moore. New York: Antiquarian Press, 1960.

Bulmer-Thomas, Victor. *The Economic History of Latin America since Independence*. New York: Cambridge University Press, 1994.

Buzgalin, A. V. *El Socialismo del siglo XXI*. Guanabo, Cuba, January 2000.

Calder, Bruce. *The Impact of Intervention: The Dominican Republic during the U.S. Occupation of 1916–1924*. Austin: University of Texas Press, 1984.

Calhoun, Frederick S. *Power and Principle: Armed Intervention in Wilsonian Foreign Policy*. Kent, Ohio: Kent State University Press, 1986.

Callahan, James M. *American Foreign Policy in Mexican Relations*. New York: Cooper Square, 1967.

Callcott, Wilfrid Hardy. *The Western Hemisphere: Its Influence on United States Policies to the End of World War II*. Austin: University of Texas Press, 1968.

Campbell, Charles S. *From Revolution to Rapprochement: The United States and Great Britain, 1783–1900*. New York: Wiley, 1974.

Carter, Dan T. *The Politics of Rage: George Wallace, the Origins of the New Conservatism, and the Transformation of American Politics*. 2nd ed. Baton Rouge: Louisiana State University Press, 2000.

Carter, John J. *Covert Action as a Tool of Presidential Foreign Policy: From the Bay of Pigs to Iran-Contra*. Lewiston, N.Y.: Edwin Mellen Press, 2006.

———. *Covert Operations and the Emergence of the Modern American Presidency, 1920–1960*. Lewiston, N.Y.: Edwin Mellen Press, 2002.

———. *Covert Operations as a Tool of Presidential Foreign Policy in American History from 1800 to 1920: Foreign Policy in the Shadows*. Lewiston, N.Y.: Edwin Mellen Press, 2000.

Center for the Study of the Presidency. *Forward Strategic Empowerment: Synergies between CINCs, the State Department, and Other Agencies*. New York: Center for the Study of the Presidency, August 2001.

———. *The Presidency and National Security Policy*. Edited by R. Gordon Hoxie. New York: Center for the Study of the Presidency, 1984.

Chace, James. *Acheson: The Secretary of State Who Created the American World*. New York: Simon and Schuster, 1998.

Chang, Laurence, and Peter Kornbluh, eds. *The Cuban Missile Crisis, 1962: A National Security Archive Documents Reader*. Rev. ed. New York: New Press, 1998.

Chávez, Thomas E. *Spain and the Independence of the United States: An Intrinsic Gift*. Albuquerque: University of New Mexico Press, 2002.

Cherry, Conrad, ed. *God's New Israel: Religious Interpretations of American Destiny*. Englewood Cliffs, N.J.: Prentice-Hall, 1971.

Child, John. *Unequal Alliance: The Inter-American Military System, 1938–1979*. Boulder, Colo.: Westview, 1980.

Chomsky, Noam. *Hegemony or Survival: America's Quest for Global Dominance*. New York: Metropolitan Books, 2003.

Clark, Wesley K. *Waging Modern War: Bosnia, Kosovo, and the Future of Combat*. New York: Public Affairs, 2001.

Clawson, Marion. *The Federal Lands Revisited*. Washington, D.C.: Resources for the Future, 1983.

Clay, Henry. *The Papers of Henry Clay*. 5 vols. Edited by James F. Hopkins. Lexington: University of Kentucky Press, 1972.

Clements, Kendrick A. *The Presidency of Woodrow Wilson*. Lawrence: University Press of Kansas, 1992.

Cleveland, Grover. *The Venezuelan Boundary Controversy*. Princeton, N.J.: Princeton University Press, 1913.

Cleveland, Richard J. *Voyages of a Merchant Navigator of the Days That Are Past: Compiled from the Journals and Letters of the Late Richard J. Cleveland*. New York: Harper, 1886.

Coakley, Robert W. *The Role of Federal Military Forces in Domestic Disorders, 1789–1878*. Washington, D.C.: U.S. Army Center of Military History, 1988.

Coatsworth, John H. *Central America and the United States: The Clients and the Colossus*. New York: Twayne, 1994.

Cohen, Warren I. *Empire without Tears: American Foreign Relations, 1921–1933*. Philadelphia: Temple University Press, 1987.

Collin, Richard. *Theodore Roosevelt's Caribbean: The Panama Canal, the Monroe Doctrine, and the Latin American Context*. Baton Rouge: Louisiana State University Press, 1990.

Combs, Jerald A. *American Diplomatic History: Two Centuries of Changing Interpretations*. Berkeley: University of California Press, 1983.

Commission on U.S.–Latin American Relations. *The Americas in a Changing World*. New York: Center for Inter-American Relations, 1974.

———. *The United States and Latin America, Next Steps*. New York: Center for Inter-American Relations, 1976.

Cook, Blanche Wiesen. *The Declassified Eisenhower: A Divided Legacy*. Garden City, N.Y.: Doubleday, 1984.

Cooling, Benjamin. *Gray Steel and Blue Water Navy: The Formative Years of America's Military-Industrial Complex, 1881–1917*. Hamden, Ct.: Archon Books, 1979.

Corwin, Edward S. *The President: Office and Powers, 1787–1984: History and Analysis of Practice and Opinion*. 5th rev. ed. New York: New York University Press, 1984.

Courtwright, David T. *Dark Paradise: Opiate Addiction in America before 1940*. Cambridge, Mass.: Harvard University Press, 1982.

Cox, Henry B. *War, Foreign Affairs, and Constitutional Power, 1829–1901*. New York: Ballinger, 1984.

Crandall, Russell. *Driven by Drugs: U.S. Policy toward Colombia*. 2nd ed. Boulder, Colo.: Lynne Rienner, 2008.

Crapol, Edward P. *James G. Blaine: Architect of Empire*. Wilmington, Del.: Scholarly Resources, 2000.

Crichfield, George W. *American Supremacy: The Rise and Progress of the Latin American Republics and Their Relations to the United States under the Monroe Doctrine*. 2 vols. New York: Brentano's, 1908.

Crile, George. *Charlie Wilson's War: The Extraordinary Story of How the Wildest Man in Congress and a Rogue CIA Agent Changed the History of Our Times*. New York: Atlantic Monthly Press, 2003.

Curti, Merle. *American Philanthropy Abroad: A History*. New Brunswick, N.J.: Rutgers University Press, 1963.

Cusick, James G. *The Other War of 1812: The Patriot War and the American Invasion of Spanish East Florida*. Gainesville: University Press of Florida, 2003.

Dalfiume, Richard M. *Desegregation of the United States Armed Forces: Fighting on Two Fronts, 1939–1953*. Columbia: University of Missouri Press, 1969.

Dallek, Robert. *The American Style of Foreign Policy: Cultural Politics and Foreign Affairs*. New York: Knopf, 1983.

———. *Nixon and Kissinger: Partners in Power*. New York: HarperCollins, 2007.

Dangerfield, George. *The Awakening of American Nationalism, 1815–1820*. New York: Harper and Row, 1965.

Daugherty, William J. *Executive Secrets: Covert Action and the Presidency*. Lexington: University of Kentucky Press, 2004.

Davis, George. *A Navy Second to None: The Development of Modern American Naval Policy*. New York: Harcourt, Brace, 1940.

Dean, Robert D. *Imperial Brotherhood: Gender and the Making of Cold War Foreign Policy*. Amherst: University of Massachusetts Press, 2001.

DeConde, Alexander. *A History of American Foreign Policy*. 2 vols. New York: Scribner's, 1978.

———. *The Quasi-War: The Politics and Diplomacy of the Undeclared War with France, 1797–1801*. New York: Scribner's, 1966.

———. *This Affair of Louisiana*. New York: Scribner's, 1976.

DeConde, Alexander, et al., ed. *Encyclopedia of American Foreign Policy*. 3 vols. 2nd ed. New York: Scribner's, 2002.

Desch, Michael C. *When the Third World Matters: Latin America and United States Grand Strategy*. Baltimore: Johns Hopkins University Press, 1993.

DeVoto, Bernard. *The Year of Decision: 1846*. Boston: Little Brown, 1943.

Dieterich Steffan, Heinz. *El socialismo del siglo XXI*. Also at <http://www.puk.de/download/elsocialismo.pdf>.

———. *Hugo Chávez y el socialismo del siglo XXI*. Caracas: Instituto Municipal de Publicaciones de la Alcaldía de Caracas, 2005.

Diggins, John Patrick. *John Adams*. New York: Times Books, 2003.

Dinges, John. *The Condor Years: How Pinochet and His Allies Brought Terrorism to Three Continents*. New York: New Press, 2004.

———. *Our Man in Panama: How General Noriega Used the United States — and Made Millions in Drugs and Arms*. New York: Random House, 1990.

Dix, Robert H. *Colombia: The Political Dimensions of Change*. New Haven: Yale University Press, 1967.

Doenecke, Justice D. *Not to the Swift: The Old Isolationists in the Cold War Era*. Lewisburg, Pa.: Bucknell University Press, 1979.

———. *The Presidencies of James A. Garfield and Chester A. Arthur*. Lawrence: Regents Press of Kansas, 1981.

Drake, Paul. *The Money Doctor in the Andes: The Kemmerer Missions, 1923–1933*. Durham, N.C.: Duke University Press, 1989.

Dray, Philip. *At the Hands of Persons Unknown: The Lynching of Black America*. New York: Random House, 2002.

Du Bois, W. E. B. *Black Reconstruction in America*. New York: Russell and Russell, 1962.

Dugdale, E. T. S., ed. and trans. *The Growing Antagonism, 1898–1910*. Vol. 3 of *German Diplomatic Documents, 1871–1914*. New York: Harper, 1930.

Dusinberre, William. *Slavemaster President: The Double Career of James Polk*. New York: Oxford University Press, 2003.

Ealy, Lawrence E. *Yanqui Politics and the Isthmian Canal*. University Park: Pennsylvania State University Press, 1971.

Eckes, Alfred E. *Opening America's Market: U.S. Foreign Trade Policy since 1776*. Chapel Hill: University of North Carolina Press, 1995.

Egerton, Douglas R. *Gabriel's Rebellion: The Virginia Slave Conspiracies of 1800 and 1802.* Chapel Hill: University of North Carolina Press, 1993.

Ehle, John. *Trail of Tears: The Rise and Fall of the Cherokee Nation.* New York: Doubleday, 1988.

Engdahl, F. William. *Full Spectrum Dominance: Totalitarian Democracy in the New World Order.* Baton Rouge: Third Millennium Press, 2009.

Ellis, L. Ethan. *Republican Foreign Policy, 1921–1933.* New Brunswick, N.J.: Rutgers University Press, 1968.

Everett, Alexander H. *America, or a General Survey of the Political Situation of the Several Powers of the Western Continent, with Conjectures on Their Future Prospects.* Philadelphia: H. C. Carey and I. Lea, 1827.

Farer, Tom J. *The Grand Strategy of the United States in Latin America.* New Brunswick, N.J.: Transaction Books, 1988.

Ferguson, Niall. *Colossus: The Price of America's Empire.* New York: Penguin, 2004.

Feuerlicht, Roberta Strauss. *America's Reign of Terror: World War, the Red Scare, and the Palmer Raids.* New York: Random House, 1971.

Field, James A., Jr. *America and the Mediterranean World, 1776–1882.* Princeton, N.J.: Princeton University Press, 1969.

Fisher, Louis. *Constitutional Conflicts between Congress and the President.* 5th ed. Lawrence: University Press of Kansas, 2007.

——— . *Presidential War Power.* Lawrence: University Press of Kansas, 1995.

Fiske, John. *American Political Ideas Viewed from the Standpoint of Universal History: Three Lectures Delivered at the Royal Institution of Great Britain in May, 1880.* New York: Harper, 1885.

Fitzgerald, Michael W. *Splendid Failure: Postwar Reconstruction in the American South.* Chicago: Ivan R. Dee, 2007.

Fitzhugh, George. *Cannibals All! or, Slaves without Masters.* Richmond Va.: A. Morris, 1857.

——— . *Sociology for the South, or, The Failure of Free Society.* Richmond, Va.: A. Morris, 1854.

Flanagan, Edward M., Jr. *Battle for Panama: Inside Operation Just Cause.* Washington, D.C.: Brassey's, 1993.

Foner, Eric. *Forever Free: The Story of Emancipation and Reconstruction.* New York: Knopf, 2005.

——— . *Reconstruction: America's Unfinished Revolution, 1863–1877.* New York: Harper and Row, 1988.

Foner, Philip S. *A History of Cuba in Its Relations with the United States.* 2 vols. New York: International Publishers, 1963.

Foner, Philip S., and Richard Winchester. *The Anti-Imperialist Reader: A Documentary History of Anti-Imperialism in the United States.* Vol. 1. New York: Holmes and Meier, 1984.

Forbes, Robert Pierce. *The Missouri Compromise and Its Aftermath: Slavery and the Meaning of America.* Chapel Hill: University of North Carolina Press, 2007.

Fox, Frank W. *J. Reuben Clark: The Public Years.* Provo, Utah: Brigham Young University Press, 1980.

Fraser, Steve, and Gary Gerstle, eds. *The Rise and Fall of the New Deal Order, 1930–1980*. Princeton, N.J.: Princeton University Press, 1989.

Friedman, Max Paul. *Nazis and Good Neighbors: The United States Campaign against the Germans of Latin America in World War II*. Cambridge: Cambridge University Press, 2003.

Frohnen, Bruce. *The Anti-Federalists: Selected Writings and Speeches*. Lanham, Md.: Regnery, 1999.

Fromkin, David. *A Peace to End All Peace: Creating the Modern Middle East, 1914–1922*. New York: Holt, 1989.

Fukuyama, Francis. *The End of History and the Last Man*. New York: Free Press, 1992.

Gaddis, John L. *The Cold War: A New History*. New York: Penguin, 2005.

———. *Strategies of Containment: A Critical Appraisal of Postwar American National Security Policy during the Cold War*. Rev. ed. New York: Oxford University Press, 2005.

Garber, Paul N. *The Gadsden Treaty*. Philadelphia: University of Pennsylvania Press, 1923.

García Calderón, Francisco. *Latin America: Its Rise and Progress*. Translated by Bernard Miall. London: T. Fisher Unwin, 1913.

Gardner, Lloyd C. *Imperial America: American Foreign Policy since 1898*. New York: Harcourt Brace Jovanovich, 1976.

Gardner, Michael R. *Harry Truman and Civil Rights: Moral Courage and Political Risks*. Carbondale: Southern Illinois University Press, 2002.

Gates, Paul W. *History of Public Land Law Development*. Washington, D.C.: Public Land Law Review Commission, 1968.

Gates, Robert M. *From the Shadows: The Ultimate Insider's Story of Five Presidents and How They Won the Cold War*. New York: Simon and Schuster, 1996.

Gerstle, Gary. *American Crucible: Race and Nation in the Twentieth Century*. Princeton, N.J.: Princeton University Press, 2001.

Gibson, Trumbull K., Jr., with Steve Huntley. *Knocking Down Barriers: My Fight for Black America*. Evanston, Ill.: Northwestern University Press, 2005.

Gilderhus, Mark T. *The Second Century: U.S. Latin American Relations since 1889*. Wilmington, Del.: Scholarly Resources, 2000.

Gleijeses, Piero. *Conflicting Missions: Havana, Washington, and Africa, 1959–1976*. Chapel Hill: University of North Carolina Press, 2002.

———. *The Cuban Drumbeat*. Chicago: University of Chicago Press, 2009.

———. *Shattered Hope: The Guatemalan Revolution and the United States, 1944–1945*. Princeton, N.J.: Princeton University Press, 1991.

Goldberg, Joyce S. *The "Baltimore" Affair*. Lincoln: University of Nebraska Press, 1986.

Golinger, Eva. *Bush versus Chávez: Washington's War on Venezuela*. New York: Monthly Review Press, 2008.

———. *The Chávez Code: Cracking U.S. Intervention in Venezuela*. Northampton, Mass.: Olive Branch Press, 2006.

Gould, Lewis L. *The Modern American Presidency*. Lawrence: University Press of Kansas, 2003.

———. *The Presidency of Theodore Roosevelt*. Lawrence: University Press of Kansas, 1991.

———. *The Spanish-American War and President McKinley*. Lawrence: University Press of Kansas, 1982.

Graebner, Norman A. *America as a World Power: A Realist Appraisal from Wilson to Reagan*. Wilmington, Del.: Scholarly Resources, 1984.

―――. *Foundations of American Foreign Policy: A Realist Appraisal from Franklin to McKinley*. Wilmington, Del.: Scholarly Resources, 1985.

Grandin, Greg. *Empire's Workshop: Latin America, the United States, and the Rise of the New Imperialism*. New York: Metropolitan Books, 2006.

Grant, Madison. *The Passing of the Great Race; or, The Racial Basis of European History*. 4th rev. ed. with a documentary supplement, with prefaces by Henry Fairfield Osborn. New York: Scribner's, 1921.

Graves, William S. *America's Siberian Adventure*. Reprint. New York: Peter Smith, 1941.

Gray, Colin S. *The Sheriff: America's Defense of the New World Order*. Lexington: University of Kentucky Press, 2004.

Green, David. *The Containment of Latin America: A History of the Myths and Realities of the Good Neighbor Policy*. Chicago: Quadrangle Books, 1971.

Grenville, John A. S., and George Berkeley Young. *Politics, Strategy, and American Diplomacy: Studies in Foreign Policy, 1873–1917*. New Haven: Yale University Press, 1966.

Griswold del Castillo, Richard. *The Treaty of Guadalupe Hidalgo: A Legacy of Conflict*. Norman: University of Oklahoma Press, 1990.

Grossman, Mark. *Political Corruption in America: An Encyclopedia of Scandals, Power, and Greed*. Santa Barbara, Calif.: ABC-CLIO, 2003.

Gurko, Miriam. *The Ladies of Seneca Falls: The Birth of the Women's Rights Movement*. New York: Macmillan, 1974.

Gurtov, Melvin. *SuperPower on Crusade: The Bush Doctrine in U.S. Foreign Policy*. Boulder, Colo.: Lynne Rienner, 2006.

Hackemer, Kurt. *The U.S. Navy and the Origins of the Military-Industrial Complex, 1847–1883*. Annapolis, Md.: Naval Institute Press, 2001.

Hagan, Kenneth J. *American Gunboat Diplomacy and the Old Navy, 1877–1889*. Westport, Ct.: Greenwood Press, 1973.

―――. *This People's Navy: The Making of American Sea Power*. New York: Free Press, 1991.

Haig, Alexander, Jr. *Caveat: Realism, Reagan, and Foreign Policy*. New York: Macmillan, 1984.

Hamilton, Alexander. *The Works of Alexander Hamilton*. 12 vols. Edited by Henry Cabot Lodge. New York: G. P. Putnam's, 1904.

Hammett, Hugh B. *Hilary Abner Herbert: A Southerner Returns to the Union*. Philadelphia: American Philosophical Society, 1976.

Hart, Albert B. *The Monroe Doctrine: An Interpretation*. Boston: Little, Brown, 1916.

Hart, John Mason. *Empire and Revolution: The Americans in Mexico since the Civil War*. Berkeley: University of California Press, 2002.

―――. *Revolutionary Mexico: The Coming and Process of the Mexican Revolution*. Berkeley: University of California Press, 1987.

Hartlyn, Jonathan, Lars Schoultz, and Augusto Varas, eds. *The United States and Latin America in the 1990s: Beyond the Cold War*. Chapel Hill: University of North Carolina Press, 1992.

Healy, David. *Drive to Hegemony: The United States in the Caribbean, 1889–1917*. Madison: University of Wisconsin Press, 1988.

―――. *James G. Blaine and Latin America*. Columbia: University of Missouri Press, 2001.

Herman, Edward S. *The Real Terror Network: Terrorism in Fact and Propaganda*. Montreal: Black Rose Books, 1985, 1982.

Herrick, Walter R., Jr. *The American Naval Revolution*. Baton Rouge: Louisiana State University Press, 1966.

Herring, George C. *From Colony to Superpower: U.S. Foreign Relations since 1776*. New York: Oxford University Press, 2008.

Herwig, Holger. *Germany's Vision of Empire in Venezuela, 1871–1914*. Princeton, N.J.: Princeton University Press, 1986.

————. *Politics of Frustration: The United States in German Naval Planning, 1889–1941*. Boston: Little, Brown, 1976.

Higham, John. *Strangers in the Land: Patterns of American Nativism, 1860–1925*. New York: Atheneum, 1974.

Hill, Howard C. *Roosevelt and the Caribbean*. Chicago: University of Chicago Press, 1927.

Hixson, Walter L. *The Myth of American Diplomacy: National Identity and U.S. Foreign Policy*. New Haven: Yale University Press, 2008.

————. *Parting the Curtain: Propaganda, Culture, and the Cold War, 1945–1961*. New York: St. Martin's, 1997.

Hodgson, Godfrey. *The Myth of American Exceptionalism*. New Haven: Yale University Press, 2009.

Hogan, Michael J. *A Cross of Iron: Harry S. Truman and the Origins of the National Security State, 1945–1954*. Cambridge: Cambridge University Press, 1998.

————. ed. *America in the World: The Historiography of American Foreign Relations since 1941*. New York: Cambridge University Press, 1995.

Hogan, Michael J., and Thomas G. Paterson. *Explaining the History of American Foreign Relations*. 2nd ed. New York: Cambridge University Press, 2004.

Holden, Robert J., and Eric Zolov, eds. *Latin America and the United States: A Documentary History*. New York: Oxford University Press, 2000.

Holt, W. Stull. *Treaties Defeated by the Senate*. Baltimore: Johns Hopkins University Press, 1933.

Horsman, Reginald. *The Causes of the War of 1812*. New York: A. S. Barnes, 1962.

————. *Expansion and American Indian Policy, 1783–1812*. East Lansing: Michigan State University Press, 1967.

————. *Race and Manifest Destiny: The Origins of American Racial Anglo-Saxonism*. Cambridge, Mass.: Harvard University Press, 1981.

Horton, James Oliver, and Lois E. Horton. *Slavery and the Making of America*. New York: Oxford University Press, 2005.

Huggins, Martha K. *Political Policing: The United States and Latin America*. Durham, N.C.: Duke University Press, 1998.

Hull, Cordell. *Memoirs*. 2 vols. New York: Macmillan, 1948.

Hunt, Michael H. *The American Ascendancy: How the United States Gained and Wielded Global Dominance*. Chapel Hill: University of North Carolina Press, 2007.

————. *Ideology and U.S. Foreign Policy*. New Haven: Yale University Press, 1987.

Huntington, Samuel. *Political Order in Changing Societies*. New Haven: Yale University Press, 1968.

Ignatieff, Michael, ed. *American Exceptionalism and Human Rights*. Princeton, N.J.: Princeton University Press, 2005.

Immerman, Richard H. *The CIA in Guatemala: The Foreign Policy of Intervention*. Austin: University of Texas Press, 1982.

Inman, Samuel Guy. *Inter-American Conferences, 1826–1954: History and Problems*. Washington, D.C.: University Press of Washington, D.C., and Community College Press, 1965.

Inter-American Dialogue. *The Americas in 1988: A Time for Choices, a Report of the Inter-American Dialogue*. Washington, D.C.: Aspen Institute, 1988.

———. *The Americas in a New World: The 1990 Report of the Inter-American Dialogue*. Washington, D.C.: Aspen Institute, 1990.

———. *A Second Chance: U.S. Policy in the Americas*. Washington, D.C., March 10, 2009.

Iriye, Akira. *From Nationalism to Internationalism: U.S. Foreign Policy to 1914*. London: Routledge and Kegan Paul, 1977.

Isaacson, Walter. *Kissinger: A Biography*. New York: Simon and Schuster, 1992.

Jaksić, Iván. *The Hispanic World and American Intellectual Life, 1820–1880*. New York: Palgrave-Macmillan, 2007.

Jay, John. *The Papers of John Jay*. Columbia University Libraries, <http://www.columbia.edu/cu/lweb/digital/jay/>.

Jefferson, Thomas. *Papers of Thomas Jefferson*. 10 vols. Edited by Julian P. Boyd. Princeton, N.J.: Princeton University Press, 1950.

———. *A Summary View of the Rights of British America*. Raleigh, N.C.: Alex Catalogue; Boulder, Colo.: NetLibrary.

———. *The Writings of Thomas Jefferson*. Edited by Andrew L. Lipscomb. 20 vols. Washington, D.C.: Thomas Jefferson Memorial Association, 1903–7.

———. *The Writings of Thomas Jefferson*. 10 vols. Collected and edited by Paul Leicester Ford. New York: G. P. Putnam's, 1892–99.

Jenkins, Brian A. *Fenians and Anglo-American Relations during Reconstruction*. Ithaca, N.Y.: Cornell University Press, 1969.

Jensen, Joan M. *Army Surveillance in America, 1775–1980*. New Haven: Yale University Press, 1991.

Jentleson, Bruce W., and Thomas Paterson, eds. *Encyclopedia of U.S. Foreign Relations*. 4 vols. New York: Oxford University Press, 1997.

Johnson, Chalmers. *Blowback: The Costs and Consequences of American Empire*. Rev. ed. New York: Henry Holt, 2001.

———. *Nemesis: The Last Days of the American Republic*. New York: Metropolitan Books, 2006.

———. *The Sorrows of Empire: Militarism, Secrecy, and the End of the Republic*. New York: Metropolitan Books, 2004.

Johnson, Donald Bruce, and Kirk H. Porter. *National Party Platforms, 1840–1972*. Urbana: University of Illinois Press, 1973.

Johnson, John J. *A Hemisphere Apart: The Foundations of United States Policy toward Latin America*. Baltimore: Johns Hopkins University Press, 1990.

———. *Latin America in Caricature*. Austin: University of Texas Press, 1980.

———. *The Military and Society in Latin America*. Palo Alto, Calif.: Stanford University Press, 1964.

Johnson, Loch K. *Seven Sins of American Foreign Policy*. New York: Pearson Longman, 2007.

Jonas, Manfred. *The United States and Germany: A Diplomatic History*. Ithaca, N.Y.: Cornell University Press, 1985.

Jones, Howard. *The Bay of Pigs*. New York: Oxford University Press, 2008.

———. *The Course of American Diplomacy: From the Revolution to the Present*. New York: Franklin Watts, 1985.

———. *Crucible of Power: A History of American Foreign Relations from 1897*. Wilmington, Del.: Scholarly Resources, 2001.

Jones, Howard, and Donald A. Rakestraw. *Prologue to Manifest Destiny: Anglo-American Relations in the 1840s*. Wilmington, Del.: Scholarly Resources, 1997.

Joseph, Gilbert M., Catherine C. Legrand, and Ricardo D. Salvatore, eds. *Close Encounters with Empire: Writing the Cultural History of U.S.–Latin American Relations*. Durham, N.C.: Duke University Press, 1998.

Joseph, Gilbert M., and Daniela Spenser, eds. *In from the Cold: Latin America's New Encounter with the Cold War*. Durham, N.C.: Duke University Press, 2008.

Josephson, Mathew. *The Politicos, 1865–1896*. New York: Harcourt, Brace, 1938.

Kagan, Richard L., ed. *Spain in America: The Origins of Hispanism in the United States*. Urbana: University of Illinois Press, 2002.

Kagan, Robert. *Dangerous Nation: America's Place in the World from Its Earliest Days to the Dawn of the 20th Century*. New York: Knopf, 2006.

———. *Of Paradise and Power: America and Europe in the New World Order*. New York: Knopf, 2003.

———. *The Return of History and the End of Dreams*. New York: Knopf, 2008.

Kane, William Everett. *Civil Strife in Latin America: A Legal History of U.S. Involvement*. Baltimore: Johns Hopkins University Press, 1972.

Kaplan, Amy, and Donald E. Pease, eds. *Cultures of United States Imperialism*. Durham, N.C.: Duke University Press, 1993.

Karnow, Stanley. *In Our Image: America's Empire in the Philippines*. New York: Random House, 1989.

Kelchner, Warren H. *Latin American Relations with the League of Nations*. Boston: World Peace Foundation, 1930.

Kennan, George F. *American Diplomacy, 1900–1950*. New York: Merton Books, 1951.

Kennedy, Paul. *The Rise and Fall of the Great Powers*. New York: Random House, 1987.

Kinzer, Stephen. *Overthrow: America's Century of Regime Change from Hawaii to Iraq*. New York: Times Books/Henry Holt, 2006.

Kinzer, Stephen C., and Stephen Schlesinger. *Bitter Fruit: The Untold Story of the American Coup in Guatemala*. Garden City, N.Y.: Doubleday, 1982.

Kirkpatrick, Jeanne. *Dictatorships and Double Standards: Rationalism and Reason in Politics*. New York: Simon and Schuster, 1982.

Kirkpatrick, Lyman. *The Real CIA*. New York: Macmillan, 1968.

Kissinger, Henry. *White House Years*. Boston: Little, Brown, 1979.

———. *A World Restored: Metternich, Castlereagh and the Problems of Peace, 1812–1822*. Boston: Houghton Mifflin, 1957.

Kitts, Kenneth. *Presidential Commissions and National Security: The Politics of Damage Control*. Boulder, Colo.: Lynne Rienner, 2006.

Klare, Michael T. *Beyond the "Vietnam Syndrome": U.S. Interventionism in the 1980s*. Washington, D.C.: Institute of Policy Studies, 1981, 1982.

————. *Blood and Oil: The Dangers and Consequences of America's Growing Petroleum Dependency*. New York: Metropolitan Books/Henry Holt, 2004.

————. *Resource Wars: The New Landscape of Global Conflict*. New York: Metropolitan Books, 2001.

Klare, Michael T., and Peter Kornbluh, eds. *Low Intensity Warfare: Counterinsurgency, Proinsurgency, and Antiterrorism in the Eighties*. New York: Pantheon Books, 1988.

Klein, Herbert S. *Bolivia: The Evolution of a Multi-ethnic Society*. 2nd ed. New York: Oxford University Press, 1992.

Kluger, Richard. *Seizing Destiny: How America Grew from Sea to Shining Sea*. New York: Alfred A. Knopf, 2007.

Kneer, Warren G. *Great Britain and the Caribbean, 1901–1913: A Study in Anglo-American Relations*. East Lansing: Michigan State University Press, 1975.

Knott, Stephen F. *Secret and Sanctioned: Covert Operations and the American Presidency*. New York: Oxford University Press, 1996.

Kolko, Gabriel. *The Age of War: The United States Confronts the World*. Boulder, Colo.: Lynne Rienner, 2006.

————. *Confronting the Third World: United States Foreign Policy, 1945–1980*. New York: Pantheon, 1988.

————. *Railroads and Regulation, 1877–1916*. Westport, Ct.: Greenwood Press, 1976, 1965.

————. *The Roots of American Foreign Policy: An Analysis of Power and Purpose*. Boston: Beacon Press, 1969.

————. *The Triumph of Conservatism: A Reinterpretation of American History, 1900–1916*. New York: Free Press of Glencoe, 1963.

Kornbluh, Peter. *The Pinochet File: A Declassified Dossier on Atrocity and Accountability*. New York: New Press, 2003.

————, ed. *Bay of Pigs Declassified: The Secret CIA Report*. A National Security Archive Documents Reader. New York: W. W. Norton, 1998.

Kramer, Paul A. *The Blood of Government: Race, Empire, the United States, and the Philippines*. Chapel Hill: University of North Carolina Press, 2006.

LaFeber, Walter. *The American Search for Opportunity, 1865–1913*. Vol. 2 of *The Cambridge History of American Foreign Relations*. New York: Cambridge University Press, 1993.

————. *Inevitable Revolutions: The United States in Central America*. 2nd rev. ed. New York: W. W. Norton, 1993.

————. *The New Empire: An Interpretation of American Expansion, 1860–1898*. Ithaca, N.Y.: Cornell University Press, 1967.

Larson, Edward J. *A Magnificent Catastrophe: The Tumultuous Election of 1800, America's First Presidential Campaign*. New York: Free Press, 2007.

Latané, J. H. *American Foreign Policy*. New York: Doubleday, Page, 1927.

————. *The United States and Latin America*. Garden City, N.Y.: Doubleday, Page, 1920.

Latham, Michael E. *Modernization as Ideology: American Social Science and "Nation Building" in the Kennedy Era*. Chapel Hill: University of North Carolina Press, 2000.

Latimer, Jon. *1812: War with America*. Cambridge, Mass.: Harvard University Press, 2007.

Laurie, Clayton D., and Ronald H. Cole. *The Role of Federal Military Forces in Domestic Disorders, 1789–1878*. Washington, D.C.: U.S. Army Center of Military History, 1977.

Laurie, Clayton D., and Ronald H. Cole. *The Role of Federal Military Forces in Domestic Disorders, 1877–1945*. Washington, D.C.: U.S. Army Center of Military History, 1977.

Lens, Sidney. *The Forging of the American Empire*. New York: Thomas Y. Crowell, 1971.

LeoGrande, William. *Our Own Backyard: The United States in Central America, 1977–1992*. Chapel Hill: University of North Carolina Press, 1998.

Leonard, Thomas M., ed. *United States–Latin American Relations, 1850–1903: Establishing a Relationship*. Tuscaloosa: University of Alabama Press, 1999.

Lewis, David Levering. *W. E. B. Du Bois: The Fight for Equality and the American Century, 1919–1963*. New York: Henry Holt, 2000.

Lewis, James E., Jr. *The American Union and the Problems of Neighborhood: The United States and the Collapse of the Spanish Empire, 1783–1829*. Chapel Hill: University of North Carolina Press, 1998.

Lieber, Robert J., ed. *Eagle Rules? Foreign Policy and American Primacy in the Twenty-first Century*. Upper Saddle River, N.J.: Prentice-Hall, 2002.

Lind, Michael. *The American Way of Strategy*. New York: Oxford University Press, 2006.

Link, Arthur S., ed. *Woodrow Wilson and a Revolutionary World, 1913–1921*. Chapel Hill: University of North Carolina Press, 1982.

Lippmann, Walter. *The Cold War*. New York: Harper, 1947.

Lipset, Seymour Martin. *American Exceptionalism: A Double-Edged Sword*. New York: W. W. Norton, 1996.

Logan, John A., Jr. *No Transfer: An American Security Principle*. New Haven: Yale University Press, 1961.

Long, David F. *Gold Braids and Foreign Relations: Diplomatic Activities of U.S. Naval Officers, 1798–1883*. Annapolis, Md.: Naval Institute Press, 1988.

Love, Eric T. *Race over Empire: Racism and U.S. Imperialism, 1865–1900*. Chapel Hill: University of North Carolina Press, 2004.

Loveman, Brian. *Chile: The Legacy of Hispanic Capitalism*. 3rd ed. New York: Oxford University Press, 2001.

——— . *For la Patria: Politics and the Armed Forces in Latin America*. Wilmington, Del.: Scholarly Resources, 1999.

——— , ed. *Addicted to Failure: U.S. Security Strategy in Latin America and the Andean Region*. Lanham, Md.: Rowman and Littlefield, 2006.

——— , ed. *Strategy for Empire: U.S. Regional Security Policy in the Post–Cold War Era*. Wilmington, Del.: Scholarly Resources, 2004.

Loveman, Brian, and Thomas M. Davies Jr. *The Politics of Antipolitics: The Military in Latin America*. 3rd rev. ed. Wilmington, Del.: Scholarly Resources, 1997.

Loveman, Brian, and Thomas M. Davies Jr., eds. *Che Guevara on Guerrilla Warfare*. 3rd rev. ed. Wilmington, Del.: Scholarly Resources, 1997.

Lowenthal, Abraham F. *Exporting Democracy: The United States and Latin America, Themes and Issues*. Baltimore: Johns Hopkins University Press, 1991.

MacGregor, Morris, Jr. *Integration of the Armed Forces, 1940–1965*. Washington, D.C.: U.S. Army Center of Military History, 1985.

Madsen, Deborah L. *American Exceptionalism*. Jackson: University Press of Mississippi, 1998.

Maddison, Angus. *Monitoring the World Economy, 1820–1992*. Paris: OECD Development Centre, 1995.

Madison, James. *The Writings of James Madison*. 9 vols. Edited by Gaillard Hunt. New York: G. P. Putnam's, 1908.

Mahajan, Rahul. *Full Spectrum Dominance: U.S. Power in Iraq and Beyond*. New York: Seven Stories Press, 2003.

Mahan, Alfred Thayer. *The Influence of Sea Power upon History, 1660–1783*. Boston: Little, Brown, 1890.

———. *The Interest of America in Sea Power, Present and Future*. Boston: Little, Brown, 1898.

Manwaring, Max G., and Court E. Prisk. *El Salvador at War: An Oral History*. Washington, D.C.: National Defense University, 1988.

Marburg, Theodore, and Horace E. Flack, eds. *Taft Papers on League of Nations*. New York: Macmillan, 1920.

Marchetti, Victor, and John D. Marks. *The CIA and the Cult of Intelligence*. New York: Knopf, 1974.

Marks, John. *The CIA's Corporate Shell Game*. Washington, D.C.: Center for National Security Studies, July 1976.

Martí, José. *Argentina y la Primera Conferencia Panamericana*. Edited by Dardo Cúneo. Buenos Aires: Ediciones Transición, n.d.

———. *Inside the Monster: Writings on the United States and American Imperialism*. Translated by Elinor Randall. New York: Monthly Review Press, 1975.

Martin, Ged. *Britain and the Origins of Canadian Confederation, 1837–67*. Vancouver: University of British Columbia Press, 1995.

Martin, Percy F. *Maximilian in Mexico: The Story of the French Intervention (1861–1867)*. New York: Charles Scribner's, 1914.

Mastny, Vojtech. *The Cold War and Soviet Insecurity: The Stalin Years*. New York: Oxford University Press, 1996.

May, Ernest R. *The Making of the Monroe Doctrine*. Cambridge, Mass.: Belknap Press of Harvard University Press, 1975.

———, ed. *American Cold War Strategy: Interpreting NSC 68*. Boston; New York: St. Martin's Press, 1993.

May, Ernest R., and Philip Zelikow, eds. *Dealing with Dictators: Dilemmas of U.S. Diplomacy and Intelligence Analysis, 1945–1990*. Cambridge, Mass.: MIT Press, 2007.

May, Robert E. *Manifest Destiny's Underworld: Filibustering in Antebellum America*. Chapel Hill: University of North Carolina Press, 2002.

———. *The Southern Dream of a Caribbean Empire, 1854–1861*. Baton Rouge: Louisiana State University Press, 1973.

McClintock, Michael. *Instruments of Statecraft: U.S. Guerrilla Warfare, Counter-insurgency, and Counter-terrorism, 1940–1990*. New York: Pantheon Books, 1992.

———. *State Terror and Popular Resistance in El Salvador*. Vol. 1 of *The American Connection*. London: Zed Books, 1985.

———. *State Terror and Popular Resistance in Guatemala*. Vol. 2 of *The American Connection*. London: Zed Books, 1985.

McCullough, David. *John Adams*. New York: Simon and Schuster, 2001.

———. *The Path between the Seas: The Creation of the Panama Canal, 1870–1914*. New York: Simon and Schuster, 1977.

McDougal, Walter A. *Promised Land, Crusader State: The American Encounter with the World since 1776*. Boston: Houghton Mifflin, 1997.

McLoughlin, William G. *After the Trail of Tears: The Cherokees' Struggle for Sovereignty, 1839–1880*. Chapel Hill: University of North Carolina Press, 1993.

McSherry, J. Patrice. *Predatory States: Operation Condor and Covert War in Latin America*. Lanham, Md.: Rowman and Littlefield, 2005.

Mead, Walter Russell. *God and Gold: Britain, America, and the Making of the Modern World*. New York: Knopf, 2007.

———. *Special Providence: American Foreign Policy and How It Changed the World*. New York: Knopf, 2001, 2003.

Mecham, J. Lloyd. *The United States and Inter-American Security, 1889–1960*. Austin: University of Texas Press, 1967.

Meinig, Donald W. *The Shaping of America: A Geographical Perspective on 500 Years of History*. 4 vols. New Haven: Yale University Press, 2004.

Melder, Keith. *Beginnings of Sisterhood: The American Woman's Rights Movement, 1800–1850*. New York: Schocken Books, 1977.

Merk, Frederick. *Manifest Destiny and Mission in American History: A Reinterpretation*. New York: Knopf, 1963.

Merk, Frederick, with Lois Bannister. *The Monroe Doctrine and American Expansionism, 1843–1849*. New York: Knopf, 1966.

Millington, Herbert. *American Diplomacy and the War of the Pacific*. New York: Columbia University Press, 1948.

Mitchell, Nancy. *The Danger of Dreams: German and American Imperialism in Latin America*. Chapel Hill: University of North Carolina Press, 1999.

Muñoz, Heraldo. *A Diplomat's Chronicle of the Iraq War and Its Lessons*. Golden, Colo.: Fulcrum, 2008.

Morison, Elting F. *The War of Ideas: The United States Navy, 1870–1890*. Colorado Springs, Colo.: U.S. Air Force Academy, 1969.

Morison, Samuel Eliot, Frederick Merk, and Frank Freidel. *Dissent in Three American Wars*. Cambridge, Mass.: Harvard University Press, 1970.

Morris, Edmund. *The Rise of Theodore Roosevelt*. Rev. ed. New York: Modern Library, 2001.

Munro, Dana G. *Intervention and Dollar Diplomacy in the Caribbean, 1900–1921*. Princeton, N.J.: Princeton University Press, 1964.

Murphy, Gretchen. *Hemispheric Imaginings: The Monroe Doctrine and Narratives of U.S. Empire*. Durham, N.C.: Duke University Press, 2005.

Murray, Robert K. *Red Scare: A Study in National Hysteria, 1919–1920*. Minneapolis: University of Minnesota Press, 1955.

Musicant, Ivan. *The Banana Wars: A History of United States Military Intervention in Latin America from the Spanish-American War to the Invasion of Panama*. New York: Macmillan, 1990.

———. *Empire by Default: The Spanish-American War and the Dawn of the American Century*. New York: Henry Holt, 1998.

Musto, David F. *The American Disease: Origins of Narcotics Control*. New Haven: Yale University Press, 1973.

National Security Archive. Digital Security Archive. *The Kissinger Transcripts: A Verbatim Record of U.S. Diplomacy, 1969–1977*.

Newman, Paul Douglas. *Fries's Rebellion: The Enduring Struggle for the American Revolution*. Philadelphia: University of Pennsylvania Press, 2004.

Newsom, David D. *The Soviet Brigade in Cuba*. Bloomington: Indiana University Press, 1987.

Ngai, Mae M. *Impossible Subjects: Illegal Aliens and the Making of Modern America*. Princeton, N.J.: Princeton University Press, 2004.

North, Douglass C. *The Economic Growth of the United States, 1790–1860*. Englewood Cliffs, N.J.: Prentice-Hall, 1961.

———. *Growth and Welfare in the American Past: A New Economic History*. Englewood Cliffs, N.J.: Prentice-Hall, 1966.

Nugent, Walter. *Habits of Empire: A History of American Expansion*. New York: Knopf, 2008.

Nye, Joseph S., Jr. *The Paradox of American Power: Why the World's Only Superpower Can't Go It Alone*. New York: Oxford University Press, 2002.

O'Brien, Thomas F. *The Century of U.S. Capitalism in Latin America*. Albuquerque: University of New Mexico Press, 1999.

———. *Making the Americas: The United States and Latin America from the Age of Revolutions to the Era of Globalization*. Albuquerque: University of New Mexico Press, 2007.

———. *The Revolutionary Mission: American Enterprise in Latin America, 1900–1945*. New York: Cambridge University Press, 1996.

Offutt, Milton. *Protection of Citizens Abroad by the Armed Forces of the United States*. Baltimore: Johns Hopkins University Press, 1928.

Offner, John L. *An Unwanted War: The Diplomacy of the United States and Spain over Cuba, 1895–1898*. Chapel Hill: University of North Carolina Press, 1992.

Onis, José de. *The United States as Seen by Latin American Writers*. New York: Hispanic Institute in the United States, 1952.

Onuf, Peter, and Nicholas Onuf. *Federal Union, Modern World: The Law of Nations in an Age of Revolution, 1776–1814*. Madison, Wisc.: Madison House Publishers, 1993.

Oren, Michael B. *Power, Faith, and Fantasy: America in the Middle East, 1776 to the Present*. New York: W. W. Norton, 2007.

Ouimet, Matthew. *The Rise and Fall of the Brezhnev Doctrine in Soviet Foreign Policy*. Chapel Hill: University of North Carolina Press, 2003.

Owsley, Albert B. *The Monroe Doctrine: An Interpretation*. Boston: Little, Brown, 1916.

Owsley, Frank Lawrence. *King Cotton Diplomacy: Foreign Relations of the Confederate States of America*. 2nd rev. ed. Chicago: University of Chicago Press, 1959.

Owsley, Frank L., Jr., and Gene A. Smith. *Filibusters and Expansionists: Jeffersonian Manifest Destiny, 1800–1821*. Tuscaloosa: University of Alabama Press, 1997.

Oye, Kenneth A., Robert J. Lieber, and Donald Rothchild, eds. *Eagle Resurgent? The Reagan Era in American Foreign Policy*. Boston: Little, Brown, 1987.

Pach, Chester J., Jr. *Arming the Free World: The Origins of the United States Military Assistance Program, 1945–1950*. Chapel Hill: University of North Carolina Press, 1991.

Palmer, David Scott. *U.S. Relations with Latin America during the Clinton Years: Opportunities Lost or Opportunities Squandered?* Gainesville: University of Florida Press, 2006.

Parks, E. Taylor. *Colombia and the United States, 1765–1934*. Durham, N.C.: Duke University Press, 1935.

Pastor, Robert A. *Whirlpool: U.S. Foreign Policy toward Latin America and the Caribbean.* Princeton, N.J.: Princeton University Press, 1992.

Paterson, Thomas G., J. Gary Clifford, Shane J. Maddock, Deborah Kisatsky, and Kenneth J. Hagan. *American Foreign Relations: A History since 1895.* 6th ed. Boston: Houghton Mifflin, 2005.

Pérez, Louis A., Jr. *Cuba: Between Reform and Revolution.* 3rd ed. New York: Oxford University Press, 2006.

———. *Cuba and the United States: Ties of Singular Intimacy.* 3rd ed. Athens: University of Georgia Press, 2003.

Perkins, Bradford. *The Creation of the Republican Empire, 1776–1865.* Cambridge History of American Foreign Relations. Cambridge: Cambridge University Press, 1993.

Perkins, Dexter. *The American Approach to Foreign Policy.* Rev. ed. Cambridge, Mass.: Harvard University Press, 1962.

———. *A History of the Monroe Doctrine.* Rev. ed. Boston: Little, Brown, 1963.

———. *The Monroe Doctrine, 1823–1826.* Cambridge, Mass.: Harvard University Press, 1927.

———. *The Monroe Doctrine, 1826–1867.* Baltimore: Johns Hopkins University Press, 1933.

———. *The Monroe Doctrine, 1867–1907.* Baltimore: Johns Hopkins University Press, 1937.

Phillips, David Atlee. *The Night Watch.* New York: Atheneum, 1977.

Pike, Frederick. *FDR's Good Neighbor Policy: Sixty Years of Generally Gentle Chaos.* Austin: University of Texas Press, 1995.

———. *Hispanismo, 1898–1936: Spanish Conservatives and Liberals and Their Relations with Spanish America.* South Bend, Ind.: University of Notre Dame Press, 1971.

———. *The United States and Latin America: Myths and Stereotypes of Civilization and Nature.* Austin: University of Texas Press, 1992.

Pletcher, David M. *The Diplomacy of Annexation: Texas, Oregon, and the Mexican War.* Columbia: University of Missouri Press, 1973.

———. *The Diplomacy of Trade and Investment: American Economic Expansion in the Hemisphere, 1865–1900.* Columbia: University of Missouri Press, 1998.

Plischke, Elmer. *U.S. State Department: A Reference History.* Westport, Conn.: Greenwood Press, 1999.

Polk, James K. *Correspondence of James K. Polk.* 6 vols. Edited by Herbert Weaver. Nashville, Tenn.: Vanderbilt University Press, 1969.

———. *The Diary of James K. Polk during His Presidency: 1845–1849.* 4 vols. Edited by Milo Milton Quaife. Chicago: A. C. McClurg, 1910.

Porter, Kirk H., and Donald B. Johnson, eds. *National Party Platforms, 1840–1960.* Urbana: University of Illinois Press, 1961.

Potter, David Morris. *The Impending Crisis, 1848–1861.* New York: Harper and Row, 1976.

Powaski, Ronald E. *Toward an Entangling Alliance: American Isolationism, Internationalism, and Europe, 1901–1950.* New York: Greenwood Press, 1991.

Powell, Colin, with Joseph E. Persico. *My American Journey.* New York: Random House, 1995.

Powers, Richard Gid. *Not without Honor: The History of American Anti-Communism.* New York: Free Press, 1995.

Prados, John. *Safe for Democracy: The Secret Wars of the CIA.* Chicago: Ivan R. Dee, 2006.

Pratt, Louise. *Imperial Eyes: Travel Writing and Transculturation*. New York: Routledge, 1992.

Prebisch, Raúl. *Towards a Dynamic Development Policy for Latin America*. New York: United Nations, 1963.

Prestowitz, Clyde. *Rogue Nation: American Unilateralism and the Failure of Good Intentions*. New York: Basic Books, 2003.

Priest, Dana. *The Mission: Waging War and Keeping Peace with America's Military*. New York: W. W. Norton, 2003.

Prince, Rod. *Haiti: Family Business*. London: Latin American Bureau, 1985.

Prucha, Francis Paul. *American Indian Treaties: The History of a Political Anomaly*. Berkeley: University of California Press, 1994.

———. *The Sword of the Republic: The United States Army on the Frontier, 1783–1846*. London: Collier-Macmillan, 1969.

Rabe, Stephen G. *Eisenhower and Latin America: The Foreign Policy of Anticommunism*. Chapel Hill: University of North Carolina Press, 1988.

———. *The Most Dangerous Area in the World: John F. Kennedy Confronts Communist Revolution in Latin America*. Chapel Hill: University of North Carolina Press, 1999.

———. *U.S. Intervention in British Guiana: A Cold War Story*. Chapel Hill: University of North Carolina Press, 2005.

Reagan, Ronald. *An American Life*. New York: Simon and Schuster, 1990.

Reckner, James R. *Teddy Roosevelt's Great White Fleet*. Annapolis, Md.: Naval Institute Press, 1988.

Record, Jeffrey. *The Rapid Deployment Force and U.S. Military Intervention in the Persian Gulf*. Cambridge, Mass.: Institute for Foreign Policy Analysis, February 1981.

Reeves, Jesse S. *American Diplomacy under Tyler and Polk*. Baltimore: Johns Hopkins University Press, 1990.

Reichley, A. James. *The Life of the Parties: A History of American Political Parties*. 2nd ed. Lanham, Md.: Rowman and Littlefield, 2000.

Remini, Robert V. *Andrew Jackson and His Indian Wars*. New York: Viking, 2001.

———. *The Legacy of Andrew Jackson: Essays on Democracy, Indian Removal, and Slavery*. Baton Rouge: Louisiana State University Press, 1988.

Renda, Mary A. *Taking Haiti: Military Occupation and the Culture of U.S. Imperialism, 1915–1940*. Chapel Hill: University of North Carolina Press, 2001.

Reuter, Frank T. *Trials and Triumphs: George Washington's Foreign Policy*. Fort Worth: Texas Christian University Press, 1989.

Rieselbach, Leroy N. *The Roots of Isolationism: Congressional Voting and Presidential Leadership in Foreign Policy*. Indianapolis: Bobbs-Merrill, 1966.

Rippy, J. Fred. *Latin America in World Politics*. 3rd ed. New York: Crofts, 1940.

———. *Rivalry of the United States and Great Britain over Latin America (1808–1830)*. Baltimore: Johns Hopkins University Press, 1929.

Rivas, Raimundo. *Historia Diplomática de Colombia, 1810–1934*. Bogotá: Imprenta Nacional, 1961.

———. *Relaciones Internacionales entre Colombia y los Estados Unidos*. Bogotá: Imprenta Nacional, 1915.

Robertson, David. *Denmark Vesey: The Buried History of America's Largest Slave Rebellion and the Man Who Led It*. New York: Knopf, 1999.

Robertson, Ross M. *History of the American Economy*. 2nd ed. New York: Harcourt, Brace and World, 1964.

Rock, David. *Argentina, 1516–1982: From Spanish Colonization to the Falklands War*. Berkeley: University of California Press, 1985.

Rodríguez González, Rodrigo. *El socialismo del siglo XXI*. Caracas: Centro de Economía Política Juan de Mariana, 2006.

Rohrbough, Malcolm. *The Land Office Business: The Settlement and Administration of American Public Lands, 1789–1837*. New York: Oxford University Press, 1968.

Romualdi, Serafino. *Presidents and Peons: Recollections of a Labor Ambassador in Latin America*. New York: Funk and Wagnalls, 1967.

Ronning, C. Neale. *Intervention in Latin America*. New York: Knopf, 1970.

Roosevelt, Theodore. *Presidential Addresses and State Papers of Theodore Roosevelt*. Edited by Albert Shaw. 4 vols. New York: P. F. Collier, 1905.

Rosenberg, Emily. *Spreading the American Dream: American Economic and Cultural Expansion, 1890–1945*. New York: Hill and Wang, 1982.

Rossignol, Marie-Jeanne. *The Nationalist Ferment: The Origins of U.S. Foreign Policy, 1792–1812*. Translated by Lillian A. Parrott. Columbus: Ohio State University Press, 2004.

Rothbard, Murray N. *Wall Street, Banks, and American Foreign Policy*. Burlingame, Calif.: Center for Libertarian Studies, 1995.

Safford, Frank, and Marco Palacios. *Colombia: Fragmented Land, Divided Society*. New York: Oxford University Press, 2002.

SarDesai, D. R., and Raju G. C. Thomas, eds. *Nuclear India in the Twenty-first Century*. New York: Palgrave-Macmillan, 2002.

Sater, William F. *Chile and the United States: Empires in Conflict*. Athens: University of Georgia Press, 1990.

Saunders, Frances Stonor. *The Cultural Cold War: The CIA and the World of Arts and Letters*. New York: New Press, 2000.

Savelle, Max. *The Origins of American Diplomacy: The International History of Anglo-America, 1492–1763*. New York: Macmillan, 1967.

Saxton, Alexander. *The Rise and Fall of the White Republic: Class Politics and Mass Culture in Nineteenth-Century America*. New York: Verso, 2003.

Schlesinger, Arthur M., Jr. *The Imperial Presidency*. Boston: Houghton Mifflin Company, 1973.

———. *A Thousand Days: John F. Kennedy in the White House*. Boston: Houghton Mifflin, 1965.

Schlesinger, Stephen, and Stephen Kinzer. *Bitter Fruit: The Untold Story of the American Coup in Guatemala*. 2nd ed. Garden City, N.Y.: Anchor Books, 1983.

Schmidt, Hans. *The United States Occupation of Haiti, 1914–1934*. New Brunswick, N.J.: Rutgers University Press, 1971.

Schmitz, David E. *Thank God They're on Our Side: The United States and Right-Wing Dictatorships, 1921–1965*. Chapel Hill: University of North Carolina Press, 1999.

Schneider, Ronald M. *Communism in Guatemala, 1944–1954*. New York: Praeger, 1958.

Schoultz, Lars. *Beneath the United States: A History of U.S. Policy toward Latin America*. Cambridge, Mass.: Harvard University Press, 1998.

————. *Human Rights and United States Policy toward Latin America*. Princeton, N.J.: Princeton University Press, 1981.

————. *National Security and United States Policy toward Latin America*. Princeton, N.J.: Princeton University Press, 1987.

————. *That Infernal Little Cuban Republic: The United States and the Cuban Revolution*. Chapel Hill: University of North Carolina Press, 2009.

Schweikart, Larry, and Michael Allen. *A Patriot's History of the United States: From Columbus' Great Discovery to the War on Terror*. New York: Sentinel, 2004.

Scranton, Margaret. *The Noriega Years*. Boulder, Colo.: Westview, 1991.

Scroggs, William O. *The Story of Louisiana*. 3rd ed. Indianapolis: Bobbs-Merrill, 1943.

Scruggs, William Lindsay. *British Aggressions in Venezuela, or the Monroe Doctrine on Trial*. 1894. Franklin Printing and Publishing, 1896.

Scudder, Evarts Seelye. *The Monroe Doctrine and World Peace*. Port Washington, N.Y.: Kennikat Press, 1939.

Senior, Hereward. *The Last Invasion of Canada: The Fenian Raids, 1866–1870*. Toronto: Dundurn Press, 1991.

Seoane, José. *Resistencias Mundiales: de Seattle a Porto Alegre*. Buenos Aires: Consejo Latinoamericano de Ciencias Sociales, 2001.

Shafer, Byron E., ed. *Is America Different? A New Look at American Exceptionalism*. New York: Oxford University Press, 1991.

Sherman, William R. *The Diplomatic and Commercial Relations of the United States and Chile, 1820–1914*. Boston: Russell, 1926.

Shultz, George P. *Turmoil and Triumph: My Years as Secretary of State*. New York: Scribner's, 1983.

Shurbutt, T. Ray, ed. *United States–Latin American Relations, 1800–1850: The Formative Generations*. Tuscaloosa: University of Alabama Press, 1991.

Sicker, Martin. *The Geopolitics of Security in the Americas: Hemispheric Denial from Monroe to Clinton*. Westport, Conn.: Praeger, 2002.

Simpson, Christopher, ed. *National Security Directives of the Reagan and Bush Administrations: The Declassified History of U.S. Political and Military Policy, 1981–1991*. Boulder, Colo.: Westview, 1995.

Skidmore, Thomas E., and Peter H. Smith. *Modern Latin America*. 6th ed. New York: Oxford University Press, 2005.

Small, Melvin. *Democracy and Diplomacy: The Impact of Domestic Politics on Foreign Policy, 1789–1994*. Baltimore: Johns Hopkins University Press, 1996.

Smith, Gaddis. *The Last Years of the Monroe Doctrine: 1945–1993*. New York: Hill and Wang, 1994.

Smith, Henry Nash. *Virgin Land: The American West as Symbol and Myth*. New York: Vintage Books, 1950.

Smith, Joseph. *Illusions of Conflict: Anglo-American Diplomacy toward Latin America, 1865–1896*. Pittsburgh: University of Pittsburgh Press, 1979.

Smith, Peter. *Talons of the Eagle: Dynamics of U.S.–Latin American Relations*. 3rd ed. New York: Oxford University Press, 2008.

Smith, Robert Freeman, ed. *Era of Caribbean Intervention, 1890–1930*. Vol. 1 of *The United States and the Latin American Sphere of Influence*. Malabar, Fla.: Robert E. Krieger, 1981.

Smith, Wayne S. *The Closest of Enemies: A Personal and Diplomatic Account of U.S.-Cuban Relations since 1957*. New York: W. W. Norton, 1987.

Sofaer, Abraham. *War, Foreign Affairs, and Constitutional Powers: The Origins*. Cambridge, Mass.: Ballinger, 1976.

Soley, Lawrence C., and John S. Nichols. *Clandestine Radio Broadcasting: A Study of Revolutionary and Counterrevolutionary Electronic Communication*. New York: Praeger, 1987.

Spanier, John, and Steven W. Hook. *American Foreign Policy since World War II*. 13th ed. Washington, D.C.: Congressional Quarterly, 1995 (16th ed., 2004).

Spaulding, Elizabeth Edwards. *The First Cold Warrior: Harry Truman, Containment, and the Remaking of Liberal Internationalism*. Lexington: University Press of Kentucky, 2006.

Spiro, Jonathan Peter. *Defending the Master Race: Conservation, Eugenics, and the Legacy of Madison Grant*. Lebanon, N.H.: University of Vermont Press, 2009.

Sprout, Harold, and Margaret Sprout. *The Rise of American Naval Power, 1776–1918*. Princeton, N.J.: Princeton University Press, 1940.

Stagg, J. C. A. *Mr. Madison's War: Politics, Diplomacy, and Warfare in the Early American Republic, 1783–1830*. Princeton, N.J.: Princeton University Press, 1983.

Starobin, Robert S., ed. *Denmark Vesey: The Slave Conspiracy of 1822*. Englewood Cliffs, N.J.: Prentice-Hall, 1970.

Stephens, John L. *Incidents of Travel in Central America, Chiapas, and Yucatán*. 2 vols. New York: Harper, 1841.

Stewart, Richard W., ed. *The United States Army and the Forging of a Nation, 1775–1917*. Vol. 1 of *American Military History*. Washington, D.C.: U.S. Army Center of Military History, 2005.

———. *The United States Army in a Global Era*. Vol. 2 of *American Military History*. Washington, D.C.: U.S. Army Center of Military History, 2005.

Stimson, Henry L. *The Diaries of Henry Lewis Stimson (1909–1945)*. Microfilm. 9 rolls. Wilmington, Del.: Scholarly Resources.

Stimson, Henry, and McGeorge Bundy. *On Active Service in Peace and War*. New York: Harper, 1947.

Stoddard, Lothrop. *The Rising Tide of Color against White World-Supremacy*. New York: Scribner's, 1920.

Streeby, Shelley. *American Sensations: Class, Empire, and the Production of Popular Culture*. Berkeley: University of California Press, 2002.

Strong, Josiah. *Our Country: Its Possible Future and Its Present Crisis*. New York: Baker and Taylor, 1886.

Suskind, Ron. *The One Per Cent Doctrine: Deep Inside America's Pursuit of Its Enemies since 9/11*. New York: Simon and Schuster, 2006.

Sweet, William Warren. *A History of Latin America*. New York: Abingdon, 1919.

Taft, Robert A. *A Foreign Policy for Americans*. Garden City, N.Y.: Doubleday, 1951.

Talbert, Roy, Jr. *Negative Intelligence: The Army and the American Left, 1917–1941*. Jackson: University of Mississippi Press, 1991.

Tangredi, Sam J., ed. *Globalization and Maritime Power*. Washington, D.C.: National Defense University, 2002.

Taubman, Philip. *Secret Empire: Eisenhower, the CIA, and the Hidden Story of America's Space Espionage*. New York: Simon and Schuster, 2003.

Taussig, Frank W. *The Tariff History of the United States*. 2nd ed. New York: G. P. Putnam's, 1892.

Taylor, Arnold H. *American Diplomacy and the Narcotics Traffic, 1900–1939*. Durham, N.C.: Duke University Press, 1969.

Temperley, Harold W. V. *The Foreign Policy of Canning, 1822–1827: England, Neo-Holy Alliance, and the New World*. London: G. Bell, 1925.

Thatcher, Margaret. *The Downing Street Years*. New York: HarperCollins, 1993.

Thomas, Raju G. C., ed. *Yugoslavia Unraveled: Sovereignty, Self-Determination, Intervention*. Lanham, Md.: Lexington Books, 2003.

Topik, Steven C. *Trade and Gunboats: The United States and Brazil in the Age of Empire*. Palo Alto, Calif.: Stanford University Press, 1996.

Trefousse, Hans Louis. *Andrew Johnson: A Biography*. New York: Norton, 1997.

Trevor, John Bond. *An Analysis of the American Immigration Act of 1924*. New York: Carnegie Endowment for International Peace, Division of Intercourse and Education, 1924.

Tuchman, Barbara W. *The Zimmermann Telegram*. New York: Macmillan, 1958, 1966.

Tucker, Robert W. *Woodrow Wilson and the Great War: Reconsidering America's Neutrality, 1914–1917*. Charlottesville: University of Virginia Press, 2007.

Tulchin, Joseph. *The Aftermath of War: World War I and U.S. Policy toward Latin America*. New York: New York University Press, 1971.

Turner, Frederick Jackson. *The Frontier in American History*. New York: Holt, 1920.

———. *Rise of the New West, 1819–1829*. New York: Harper, 1906.

Ugarte, Manuel. *The Destiny of a Continent*. Translated by Catherine A. Phillips. New York: Knopf, 1925.

Van Dusen, Henry P., ed. *The Spiritual Legacy of John Foster Dulles*. Philadelphia: Westminster, 1960.

Vargas Vila, José María. *Ante los Bárbaros. El Yanki; He Ahí el Enemigo*. Barcelona: Ramón Palacio Viso, 1930.

Vattel, Emmerich de. *The Law of Nations, or the Principles of Natural Law Applied to the Conduct and to the Affairs of Nations and of Sovereigns*. Translated from the French. 1758. Philadelphia: P. H. Nicklin and T. Johnson, 1829.

Walker, William O. *Drug Control in the Americas*. Rev. ed. Albuquerque: University of New Mexico Press, 1989.

Waltz, Kenneth. *Realism and International Politics*. New York: Routledge, 2008.

Waltzer, Michael. *Just and Unjust Wars: A Moral Argument with Historical Illustrations*. New York: Harper, 1977.

Warburg, Gerald F. *Conflict and Consensus: The Struggle between Congress and the President over Foreign Policymaking*. New York: Harper and Row, 1989.

Warner, Michael, ed. *The CIA under Harry Truman*. Washington, D.C.: Central Intelligence Agency, 1994.

Warshauer, Matthew. *Andrew Jackson and the Politics of Martial Law: Nationalism, Civil Liberties, and Partisanship*. Knoxville: University of Tennessee Press, 2006.

Webster, Charles K. *The Foreign Policy of Castlereagh, 1815–1822: Britain and the European Alliance*. London: G. Bell, 1925, 1934.

————, ed. *Britain and the Independence of Latin America, 1812–1830: Select Documents from the Foreign Office Archives*. New York: Octagon Books, 1970.

Webster, Hutton. *History of Latin America*. Boston: D.C. Heath, 1924.

Weeks, Gregory. *U.S. and Latin American Relations*. Longman, 2008.

Weeks, William Earl. *Building the Continental Empire: American Expansion from the Revolution to the Civil War*. Chicago: Ivan R. Dee, 1996.

Weiner, Tim. *Legacy of Ashes: The History of the CIA*. New York: Doubleday, 2007.

Westad, Odd Arne. *Decisive Encounters: The Chinese Civil War, 1946–1950*. Palo Alto, Calif.: Stanford University Press, 2003.

Whitaker, Arthur P. *The United States and the Independence of Latin America, 1800–1830*. New York: Russell and Russell, 1962.

————. *The Western Hemisphere Idea: Its Rise and Decline*. Ithaca, N.Y.: Cornell University Press, 1954.

White, Patrick C. T., ed. *The Critical Years: American Foreign Policy, 1793–1823*. New York: John Wiley, 1970.

Wilkerson, Marcus M. *Public Opinion and the Spanish-American War: A Study in War Propaganda*. 1932. New York: Russell and Russell, 1967.

Williams, Eric. *Capitalism and Slavery*. 1944. London: A. Deutsch, 1987.

Williams, Mary Wilhelmine. *Anglo-American Isthmian Diplomacy, 1815–1915*. Washington, D.C.: American Historical Association, 1916.

Williams, William Appleman. *Empire as a Way of Life: An Essay on the Causes and Character of America's Present Predicament along with a Few Thoughts about an Alternative*. New York: Oxford University Press, 1980.

————. *The Tragedy of American Diplomacy*. Cleveland: World Publishing, 1959, rev. ed., 1962, 1972.

————, ed. *From Colony to Empire: Essays in the History of American Foreign Relations*. New York: John Wiley, 1972.

Wilson, Charles Morrow. *The Monroe Doctrine: An American Frame of Mind*. Princeton, N.J.: Auerbach, 1971.

Wilson, Henry. *History of the Rise and Fall of the Slave Power in America*. 3 vols. Boston: J. R. Osgood, 1875–77.

Wilson, Robert A., and Bill Hosokawa. *East to America*. New York: William Morrow, 1980.

Wimmel, Kenneth. *Theodore Roosevelt and the Great White Fleet*. London: Brassey's, 1998.

Winks, Robin. *Cloak and Gown: Scholars in the Secret War, 1939–1961*. New Haven: Yale University Press, 1987.

Wittkopf, Eugene R., and James M. McCormick, eds. *The Domestic Sources of American Foreign Policy: Insights and Evidence*. 4th ed. Lanham, Md.: Rowman and Littlefield, 2004.

Wolfe, Alan. *The Future of Liberalism*. New York: Knopf, 2009.

Wood, Bryce. *The Dismantling of the Good Neighbor Policy*. Austin: University of Texas Press, 1985.

————. *The Making of the Good Neighbor Policy*. New York: Norton, 1961.

Woodward, Bob. *The Commanders*. New York: Simon and Schuster, 1991.

Wright, Thomas C. *Latin America in the Era of the Cuban Revolution*. Rev. ed. Westport, Ct.: Praeger, 2001.

Wriston, Henry M. *Executive Agents in American Foreign Relations*. Baltimore: Johns Hopkins University Press, 1929.

Wyden, Peter. *Bay of Pigs: The Untold Story*. New York: Simon and Schuster, 1979.

Yates, Lawrence A. *Powerpack: U.S. Intervention in the Dominican Republic, 1965–1966*. Fort Leavenworth, Kans.: U.S. Army Command and General Staff College, July 1988.

York, Neil Longley. *Turning the World Upside Down: The War of Independence and the Problem of Empire*. Westport, Conn.: Praeger, 2003.

Youngers, Coletta A., and Eileen Rosin, eds. *Drugs and Democracy in Latin America*. Boulder, Colo.: Lynne Rienner, 2005.

Zakaria, Fareed. *From Wealth to Power: The Unusual Origins of America's World Role*. Princeton, N.J.: Princeton University Press, 1999.

Zinn, Howard. *A People's History of the United States: 1492–Present*. 20th anniversary ed. New York: HarperCollins, 1999.

Zinni, Anthony, and Tony Koltz. *The Battle for Peace: A Frontline Vision of America's Power and Purpose*. New York: Palgrave-Macmillan, 2006.

Zorilla, Luis G. *Historia de las relaciones entre México y los Estados Unidos de América, 1800–1958*. 2 vols. Mexico City: Editorial Porrúa, 1965–66.

Zubok, Vladislav M., and Constantine Pleshakov. *Inside the Kremlin's Cold War: From Stalin to Khrushchev*. Cambridge, Mass.: Harvard University Press, 1996.

Articles, Book Chapters, and Papers

Adams, Randolph G. "Abel Parker Upshur, Secretary of State." In vol. 5 of *The American Secretaries of State and Their Diplomacy*, edited by Samuel F. Bemis, 67–124. New York: Knopf, 1927–29.

Ammon, Harry. "Monroe Doctrine: Domestic Politics or National Decision." *Diplomatic History* 5 (Winter 1981): 53–70.

Antoniou, Giorgos. "The Greek Civil War Historiography, 1945–2001: Toward a New Paradigm." *Columbia Journal of Historiography* 1 (2004), <http://www.politikinet .gr/who_is_who/Personal/maranjidis_nikos/The_Greek_Civil_War_Historiography .doc>. Accessed April 2, 2009.

Barcia, Manuel. "Revolts among Enslaved Africans in Nineteenth-Century Cuba: A New Look to an Old Problem." *Journal of Caribbean History* 39, no. 2 (2005): 173–200.

Berbusse, E. J. "The Origins of the McLane-Ocampo Treaty of 1859." *Américas* 14 (1958): 223–45.

Bernstein, Barton J. "The New Deal: The Conservative Achievements of Liberal Reform." In *Towards a New Past: Dissenting Essays in American History*, edited by Barton J. Bernstein, 263–88. New York: Pantheon Books, 1968.

Bird, Kai. "Reagan's Foreign Service." Alicia Patterson Foundation, *APF Reporter* 7, no. 3, <http://www.aliciapatterson.org/APF0703/APF0703.html>. Accessed August 22, 2007.

Blakeslee, George H. "The Japanese Monroe Doctrine." *Foreign Affairs* 11 (July 1993): 671–81.

Bogue, Allan G., and Mark Paul Marlaire. "'Of Mess and Men': The Boardinghouse and Congressional Voting, 1821–1842." *American Journal of Political Science* 19 (May 1975): 207–30.

Bowers, Claude. "William M. Evarts, Secretary of State, March 12, 1877, to March 3, 1881."
In vol. 7 of *The American Secretaries of State and Their Diplomacy*, edited by Samuel F.
Bemis, 217–59. New York: Knopf, 1927–29.

Breckinridge, S. P. "The Winfred Lynn Case Again: Segregation in the Armed Forces."
Social Service Review 18 (September 1944): 369–71.

Brooks, Stephen G., and William C. Wohlworth. "Power, Globalization, and the End of
the Cold War: Reevaluating a Landmark Case for Ideas." *International Security* 25, no. 3
(Winter 2000/2001): 5–53.

Burr, William, and Thomas S. Blanton, eds. "The Submarines of October: U.S. and Soviet
Naval Encounters during the Cuban Missile Crisis." National Security Archive Electronic Briefing Book no. 75, October 31, 2002.

Burton, Theodore. "Henry Clay, Secretary of State, March 7, 1825, to March 3, 1829." In
vol. 4 of *The American Secretaries of State and Their Diplomacy*, edited by Samuel F.
Bemis, 115–58. New York: Knopf, 1927–29.

Calder, Bruce. "Caudillos and Gavilleros versus the U.S. Marines: Guerrilla Insurgency
during the Dominican Intervention, 1916–1924." *Hispanic American Historical Review*
58, no. 4 (November 1978): 649–75.

Catoire, Richard G. "A CINC for Sub-Saharan Africa? Rethinking the Unified Command
Plan." In *Strategy for Empire: U.S. Regional Security Policy in the Post–Cold War Era*,
edited by Brian Loveman, 135–51. Wilmington, Del.: Scholarly Resources, 2004.

Claudio, Arnaldo, and Stephan K. Stewman. "Oplan Narco." *Military Review* (December
1992): 64–73.

Clemens, Michael A., and Jeffrey G. Williamson. "Closed Jaguar, Open Dragon: Comparing Tariffs in Latin America and Asia before World War II." National Bureau of
Economic Research, Working Paper 9401 (December 2002).

Coatsworth, John H. "American Trade with European Colonies in the Caribbean and
South America, 1790–1812." *William and Mary Quarterly* 3rd series, 24 (1969): 243–66.
———. "United States Interventions: What For?" *Revista: Harvard Review of Latin
America* (Spring/Summer 2005): 6–9.

Coatsworth, John H., and Jeffrey G. Williamson. "The Roots of Latin American Protectionism: Looking before the Great Depression." *NBER Working Paper 8999*, National
Bureau of Economic Research, Cambridge, Mass. (June 2002).

Cooper, Tom. "The Greek Civil War, 1944–1949." Air Combat Information Group,
October 26, 2003, <http://www.acig.org/artman/publish/article_294.shtml>. Accessed
January 2008.

Council for Inter-American Security ("The Committee of Santa Fe"). "A New Inter-
American Policy for the Eighties." Washington, D.C., May 1980. Coauthored by Lewis
Tambs, Roger W. Fontaine, David C. Jordan, Gordon Sumner, and L. Francis Bouchey.

Cramer, Gisela, and Ursula Prutsch. "Nelson A. Rockefeller's Office of Inter-American
Affairs (1940–1946) and Record Group 229." *Hispanic American Historical Review* 86,
no. 4 (2006): 785–806.

Crapol, Edward. "Coming to Terms with Empire: The Historiography of Late Nineteenth-
Century American Foreign Relations." In *Paths to Power: The Historiography of Ameri-
can Foreign Relations to 1941*, edited by Michael Hogan, 79–116. New York: Cambridge
University Press, 2000.

Dalfiume, Richard M. "Military Segregation and the 1940 Presidential Election." *Phylon* 30, no. 1 (1969): 42–55.

DeSantis, Vincent P. "Rutherford B. Hayes and the Removal of the Troops and the End of Reconstruction." In *Region, Race, and Reconstruction*, edited by Morgan Kousser and James McPherson, 417–50. New York: Oxford University Press, 1982.

Drake, Paul. "From Good Men to Good Neighbors: 1912–1932." In *Exporting Democracy: The United States and Latin America: Themes and Issues*, edited by Abraham F. Lowenthal, 3–40. Baltimore: Johns Hopkins University Press, 1991.

Einstein, Lewis. "Lewis Cass, Secretary of State, March 7 1857, to December 12, 1860." In vol. 6 of *The American Secretaries of State and Their Diplomacy*, edited by Samuel F. Bemis, 297–384. New York: Knopf, 1927–29.

Ellis, R. Evan. "The Military-Strategic Dimensions of Chinese Initiatives in Latin America." Center for Hemispheric Policy, University of Miami, February 16, 2007.

Estrade, Paul. "El invento de 'América Latina' en París por LatinoAmericanos (1856–1889)." In *París y el mundo ibérico e iberoamericano*, compiled by Jacques Maurice and Marie-Claire Zimmerman, 179–88. Paris: Université Paris X-Nanterre, 1998.

Field, James A., Jr. "American Imperialism: The Worst Chapter in Almost Any Book." *American Historical Review* 83 (June 1978): 644–83.

Fisher, Louis. "How Tightly Can Congress Draw the Purse Strings?" *American Journal of International Law* 83, no. 4 (October 1989): 758–66.

Fukuyama, Francis. "The End of History?" *National Interest* (Summer 1989): 3–18.

Fuller, Joseph V. "Hamilton Fish, Secretary of State, March 11, 1869, to March 11, 1877." In vol. 7 of *The American Secretaries of State and Their Diplomacy*, edited by Samuel F. Bemis, 125–214. New York: Knopf, 1927–29.

Gardner, Lloyd. "American Foreign Policy, 1900–1921: A Second Look at the Realist Critique of American Diplomacy." In *Towards a New Past: Dissenting Essays in American History*, edited by Barton J. Bernstein, 202–31. New York: Pantheon Books, 1968.

———. "A Progressive Foreign Policy, 1900–1921." In *From Colony to Empire: Essays in the History of American Foreign Relations*, edited by William Appleman Williams, 204–51. New York: John Wiley, 1972.

Gedalecia, David. "Letters from the Middle Kingdom: The Origins of America's China Policy." *Prologue Magazine* 34, no. 4 (Winter 2002): 261–73.

Gershkoff, Amy, and Shana Kushner. "Shaping Public Opinion: The 9/11-Iraq Connection in the Bush Administration's Rhetoric." *Perspectives on Politics* 3, no. 3 (September 2005): 525–37.

"Getting to Know the Racial Views of Our Past Presidents: What about FDR?" *Journal of Blacks in Higher Education* 38 (Winter 2002–3): 44–46.

Gignilliat, John. "Pigs, Politics, and Protection: The European Boycott of American Pork, 1879–1891." *Agricultural History* 35 (January 1961): 3–12.

Gilboa, Eytan. "The Panama Invasion Revisited: Lessons for the Use of Force in the Post Cold War Era." *Political Science Quarterly* 110, no. 4 (Winter 1995/96): 539–62.

Gleijeses, Piero. "1898: The Opposition to the Spanish-American War." *Journal of Latin American Studies* 35, no. 4 (November 2003): 681–719.

———. "The Limits of Sympathy: The United States and the Independence of Spanish America." *Journal of Latin American Studies* 24, no. 3 (October 1992): 481–505.

Goulder, Frank A. "The Purchase of Alaska." *American Historical Review* 25, no. 2 (January 1920): 411–25.

Gray, Colin S. "The Implications of Preemptive and Preventive War Doctrine: A Reconsideration." Washington, D.C.: Strategic Studies Institute (July 2007).

Gray, Anthony, and Maxwell Manwaring. "Panama: Operation Just Cause." In *Policing the New World Disorder: Peace Operations and Public Security*, edited by Robert B. Oakley, Michael J. Dziedzic, and Eliot M. Goldberg, chap. 2. Washington, D.C.: Institute for National Strategic Studies, National Defense University, 1996.

Grenville, John A. S. "Diplomacy and War Plans in the United States, 1890–1917." *Transactions of the Royal Historical Society* 11 (1961): 1–21.

Gupta, Dipak, and Jonathan Graubart. "Is the U.S. a Rogue Nation?" In *Strategy for Empire: U.S. Regional Security Policy in the Post–Cold War Era*, edited by Brian Loveman, 289–313. Lanham, Md.: Rowman and Littlefield/Scholarly Resources, 2004.

Haass, Richard N. "What to Do with American Primacy?" *Foreign Affairs* (September/October 1999): 37–49.

Hadar, Leon T. "The 'X' Dreams of Washington's Wonks." *Asian Times*, April 4, 2007, <http://www.cato.org/pub_display.php?pub_id=8174>. Accessed August 14, 2008.

Haines, Gerald K. "The Pike Committee Investigations and the CIA: Looking for a Rogue Elephant. CIA, Studies in Intelligence (Winter 1998–99), <https://www.cia.gov/library/center-for-the-study-of-intelligence/csi-publications/csi-studies/studies/winter98_99/art07.html>. Accessed March 10, 2008.

Hakim, Peter. "Is Washington Losing Latin America?" *Foreign Affairs* 85 (January/February 2006): 39–53.

———. "Another Chance for U.S. Policy in the Americas." In *American Foreign Policy: Regional Perspectives*, 63–73. Ruger Workshop No. 4. A workshop sponsored by the William B. Ruger Chair of National Security Economics. Newport, R.I., May 13–15, 2009.

Hansen, Brian. "Globalization Backlash: Does Free Trade Hurt People in the Third World?" *CQ Researcher* 11, no. 33 (September 28, 2001): 761–84.

Hayes, Michael T. "The Republican Road Not Taken: The Foreign Policy Vision of Robert A. Taft." *Independent Review* 8, no. 4 (Spring 2004): 509–25.

Healy, Gene. "Arrogance of Power Reborn: The Imperial Presidency and Foreign Policy in the Clinton Years." Cato Institute, *Policy Analysis* 389 (December 2000).

Herwig, Holger H., and David F. Trask. "Naval Operations Plans between Germany and the USA, 1898–1913." In *The War Plans of the Great Powers, 1880–1914*, edited by Paul M. Kennedy, 39–74. Boston: Allen and Unwin, 1985.

Horton, James Oliver. "Alexander Hamilton: Slavery and Race in a Revolutionary Generation." *New York Journal of American History* 3 (Spring 2004): 16–24.

Hughes, Charles Evans. Address to the American Bar Association, August 30, 1923, Minneapolis. In *American Journal of International Law* 17, no. 4 (October 1923): 611–28.

Hutson, James H. "Early American Diplomacy: A Reappraisal." In *The American Revolution and "A Candid World,"* edited by Lawrence S. Kaplan, 40–68. Kent, Ohio: Kent State University Press, 1977.

Iglesias, Santiago. "Pan-American Federation of Labor, Creation of A.F. of L." *International Molders Journal* 63 (July 1927): 390–92.

Ikenberry, John. "America's Imperial Ambition." *Foreign Affairs* 81, no. 5 (September–October 2002): 44–60.

Irwin, Douglas A. "Historical Aspects of U.S. Trade Policy." National Bureau of Economic Research, *NBER Reporter* online (Summer 2006), <http://www.nber.org/reporter/summer06/irwin.html>. Accessed April 16, 2007.

Jenkins, Jeffrey R., and Charles Stewart III. "The Gag Rule, Congressional Politics, and the Growth of Anti-Slavery Popular Politics" (2005), <http://web.mit.edu/cstewart/www/gag_rule_v12.pdf>. Accessed September 8, 2008.

Jenkinson, Clay S. "The Ordeal of Thomas Jefferson: Whirl Is King." *Oregon Historical Quarterly* (Fall 2004): 509–16.

Johnson, Charles. "The Army, the Negro, and the Civilian Conservation Corps: 1933–1942." *Military Affairs* 36, no. 3 (October 1972): 82–88.

Johnson, Michael P. "Denmark Vesey and His Co-conspirators." *William and Mary Quarterly* 58, no. 4 (October 2001): 915–76.

Johnson, Paul. "The Myth of American Isolationism — Reinterpreting the Past." *Foreign Affairs* 74, no. 3 (May/June 1995): 159–64.

Johnson, Stephen. "A New U.S. Policy for Latin America: Reopening the Window of Opportunity." *Heritage Foundation Backgrounder* 1409 (February 15, 2001).

Joseph, Gilbert M. "The United States, Feuding Elites, and Rural Revolt in Yucatán, 1836–1915." In *Rural Revolt in Mexico: U.S. Intervention and the Domain of Subaltern Politics*, edited by Daniel Nugent, 173–206. Durham, N.C.: Duke University Press, 1998.

Justice, Lisa. "Women, Wilson, and Emergency War Measures," <http://userwww.sfsu.edu/ñepf/2001/justice.html>. Accessed October 30, 2008.

Kagan, Robert. "The Benevolent Empire." *Foreign Policy* 111 (Summer 1998): 24–35.

———. "The End of History: Why the Twenty-first Century Will Look Like the Nineteenth." *New Republic*, April 23, 2008, 40–47.

Kammen, Michael. "The Problem of American Exceptionalism: A Reconsideration." *American Quarterly* 45 (March 1993): 1–43.

Kane, Tim. "Global U.S. Troop Deployment." Heritage Foundation, *Center for Data Analysis Report* 04-11.

Kaplan, Lawrence S. "The Monroe Doctrine and the Truman Doctrine: The Case of Greece." *Journal of the Early Republic* 13, no. 1 (Spring 1993): 1–21.

———. "Toward Isolationism: The Rise and Fall of the Franco-American Alliance, 1775–1801." In *The American Revolution and "A Candid World,"* edited by Lawrence S. Kaplan, 134–57. Kent, Ohio: Kent State University Press, 1977.

Kimball, Jeffrey. "The Nixon Doctrine: A Saga of Misunderstanding." *Presidential Studies Quarterly* 36 (March 2006): 59–74.

Kirkpatrick, Jeanne J. "Dictatorships and Double Standards." *Commentary* (November 1979): 34–45.

Krauthammer, Charles. "The Unipolar Moment." *Foreign Affairs* 70, no. 1 (1990–91): 23–33.

LaFeber, Walter. "United States Depression Diplomacy and the Brazilian Revolution, 1893–1894." *Hispanic American Historical Review* 40 (1960): 107–18.

Leich, Marian Nash. "Protection of Nationals: Rescue Operation by Armed Forces–Grenada." *American Journal of International Law* 78 (1984): 200–217.

LeoGrande, William. "From the Red Menace to Radical Populism: U.S. Insecurity in Latin America." *World Policy Journal* (Winter 2005/6): 25–35.

Leonard, Thomas M. "Central America: The Search for Economic Development." In *United States–Latin American Relations, 1850–1903: Establishing a Relationship*, edited by Thomas M. Leonard, 81–106. Tuscaloosa: University of Alabama Press, 1999.

Lieber, Robert J. "Foreign Policy and American Primacy." In *Eagle Rules? Foreign Policy and American Primacy in the Twenty-first Century*, edited by Robert J. Lieber, 1–15. Upper Saddle River, N.J.: Prentice-Hall, 2002.

Livermore, Seward W. "Theodore Roosevelt, the American Navy, and the Venezuelan Crisis of 1902–1903." *American Historical Review* 51, no. 3 (April 1946): 452–71.

Lockey, Joseph B. "James Gillespie Blaine, Secretary of State, March 7, 1881, to December 18, 1881 (First Term)." In vol. 7 of *The American Secretaries of State and Their Diplomacy*, edited by Samuel F. Bemis, 263–97. New York: Knopf, 1927–29.

Lodge, Henry Cabot. "England, Venezuela, and the Monroe Doctrine." *North American Review* 160 (June 1895): 657–58.

Lowe, David. "Idea to Reality: NED at 25." National Endowment for Democracy, <http://www.ned.org/about/nedhistory.html>. Accessed June 5, 2009.

Lowenthal, Abraham. "Two Hundred Years of American Foreign Policy: The United States and Latin America, Ending the Hegemonic Presumption." *Foreign Affairs* 55, no. 1 (October 1976): 199–213.

MacDonald, Dwight. "The Novel Case of Winfred Lynn." *Nation* 156 (February 20, 1943): 268–70.

Mahan, Alfred Thayer. "The United States Looking Outward." *Atlantic Monthly*, December 1890, 816–24.

Marcella, Gabriel. "American Grand Strategy for Latin America in the Age of Resentment." U.S. Army War College Strategic Studies Institute, Carlisle Barracks, Pa., September 2007.

———. "The United States and Colombia: The Journey from Ambiguity to Strategic Clarity." U.S. Army War College Strategic Studies Institute, Carlisle Barracks, Pa., May 2003.

May, Ernest R. "National Security in American History." In *Rethinking America's Security: Beyond Cold War to the New World Order*, edited by Graham Allison and Gregory T. Treverton, 94–114. New York: W. W. Norton, 1992.

May, Robert E. "James Buchanan, the Neutrality Laws, and American Invasions of Nicaragua." In *James Buchanan and the Political Crisis of the 1850s*, edited by Michael Birkner, 123–45. Selinsgrove, Pa.: Susquehanna University Press, 1996.

McCrisken, Trevor B. "Exceptionalism." In *Encyclopedia of American Foreign Policy*, 2nd ed., edited by Alexander DeConde et al., 2:63–70. New York: Charles Scribner's, 2002.

McGuire, Phillip. "Desegregation of the Armed Forces: Black Leadership, Protest, and World War II." *Journal of Negro History* 68, no. 2 (Spring 1983): 147–58.

Middleton, Roger. "Piracy in Somalia: Threatening Global Trade, Feeding Local Wars." Royal Institute of International Affairs Briefing Paper. London: Chatham House, October 2008.

Miller, James E. "Taking Off the Gloves: The United States and the Italian Elections of 1948." *Diplomatic History* 7 (Winter 1983): 35–55.

Millet, Richard L. "Panama and Haiti." In *U.S. and Russian Policymaking with Respect to the Use of Force*, edited by Jeremy R. Azrael and Amil A. Payin, 137–61. Santa Monica, Calif.: Rand, 1996.

Moore, J. Preston. "Pierre Soule: Southern Expansionist and Promoter." *Journal of Southern History* 21, no. 2 (May 1955): 203–23.

Morris, Edmund. "'A Matter of Extreme Urgency': Theodore Roosevelt, Wilhelm II, and the Venezuela Crisis of 1902 — United States–Germany Conflict over Alleged German Expansionistic Efforts in Latin America." *Naval War College Review* (Spring 2002): 73–85.

Moser, John. "Principles without Program: Senator Robert A. Taft and American Foreign Policy." *Ohio History* 108 (September 2001): 177–92.

NAACP. "Chicago and Its Eight Reasons: Walter White Considers the Causes of the 1919 Chicago Race Riot," <http://historymatters.gmu.edu/d/4978/>. Accessed May 22, 2007.

Ninkovich, Frank. "Theodore Roosevelt: Civilization as Ideology." *Diplomatic History* 10, no. 3 (Summer 1986): 221–45.

Ohl, John K. "The Navy, the War Industries Board, and the Industrial Mobilization for War, 1917–1918." *Military Affairs* 40, no. 1 (February 1976): 17–22.

Olney, Richard. "The Growth of Our Foreign Policy." *Atlantic Monthly* 85, no. 509 (March 1900): 298–301.

O'Neill, Mark. "Soviet Involvement in the Korean War: A New View from the Soviet-Era Archives." *OAH Magazine of History* 14, no. 3 (Spring 2000): 20–24.

O'Rourke, Kevin. "The Worldwide Economic Impact of the Revolutionary and Napoleonic Wars." National Bureau of Economic Research Working Paper No. 11344, May 2005, <http://www.nber.org/~confer/2005/daes05/orourke.pdf>. Accessed August 22, 2008.

Ostrom, Charles, and Brian Job. "The President and the Political Use of Force." *American Political Science Review* 80, no. 2 (March 1986): 541–66.

Palmer, Michael. "The Navy: The Continental Period, 1775–1890." Department of the Navy, Navy Historical Center, Washington, D.C., <http://www.history.navy.mil/history/history2.htm>. Accessed April 12, 2008.

Pastor, Robert A. "The Carter Administration and Latin America: A Test of Principle." Carter Center, July 1992.

———. "The Reagan Administration and Latin America: Eagle Insurgent." In *Eagle Resurgent? The Reagan Era in American Foreign Policy*, edited by Kenneth A. Oye, Robert J. Lieber, and Donald Rothchild, 359–92. Boston: Little, Brown, 1987.

Pechatnov, Vladimir O. "The Big Three after World War II: New Documents on Soviet Thinking about Post-war Relations with the United States and Great Britain." Woodrow Wilson Center Working Paper no. 13, Washington, D.C., May 1995.

Perkins, Dexter. "John Quincy Adams, Secretary of State, September 22, 1817, to March 4, 1825." In vol. 4 of *The American Secretaries of State and Their Diplomacy*, edited by Samuel F. Bemis, 3–111. New York: Knopf, 1927–29.

Petrie, John N. "American Neutrality in the 20th Century: The Impossible Dream." Washington, D.C.: National Defense University, McNair Paper 33, January 1995.

Pillsbury, A. J. "The Destiny of Duty." *Overland Monthly and Out West Magazine* 33, no. 194 (February 1899): 168–70.

Pinkett, Harold T. "Efforts to Annex Santo Domingo to the United States, 1866–1871." *Journal of Negro History* 26, no. 1 (January 1941): 12–45.

Posen, Barry R. "Command of the Commons: The Military Foundations of U.S. Hegemony." *International Security* 28, no. 1 (Summer 2003): 5–46.

Prieto-Calixto, Alberto. "Rúben Darío and Literary Anti-Americanism and Anti-Imperialism." In *Beyond the Ideal: Pan-Americanism in Inter-American Affairs*, edited by David Sheinin, 57–65. Westport, Ct.: Greenwood Press, 2000.

Quigley, John. "The Legality of the United States Invasion of Panama." *Yale Journal of International Law* 15 (1990): 281–97.

Quijada, Mónica. "Sobre el origen y difusión del nombre "America Latina' (O una variación heterodoxa en torno al tema de la construcción social de la verdad)." *Revista de Indias* 58 (214) (September–December 1998): 595–616.

Richman, Sheldon L. "Ronald Reagan: Protectionist." *Free Market* (Mises Institute Monthly) 6, no. 5 (May 1988), <http://www.mises.org/freemarket_detail.asp?control=489>. Accessed August 20, 2007.

Rogers, William. "The Constitution and Foreign Affairs: Two Hundred Years." *American Journal of International Law* 83, no. 4 (October 1989): 894–900.

Rosenberg, Robin L. "The OAS and the Summit of the Americas: Coexistence, or Integration of Forces for Multilateralism." *Latin American Politics and Society* 43, no. 1 (Spring 2001): 79–101.

Sayle, Edward F. "The Historical Underpinnings of the U.S. Intelligence Community." *International Journal of Intelligence and Counterintelligence* 1 (1986): 1–27.

Scheips, Paul J. "United States Commercial Pressures for a Nicaragua Canal in the 1890's." *Americas* 20, no. 4 (April 1964): 333–58.

Schuyler, Montgomery. "Richard Olney, Secretary of State, June 8, 1895, to March 4, 1897." In vol. 8 of *The American Secretaries of State and Their Diplomacy*, edited by Samuel F. Bemis, 273–325. New York: Knopf, 1927–29.

Schweikart, Larry. "Why It's Time for a Patriot's History of the United States." *History News Network*, <http://hnn.us/articles/9536.html>. Accessed July 2, 2008.

Scott, John Brown. "Elihu Root, Secretary of State, July 7, 1905, to January 27, 1909." In vol. 9 of *The American Secretaries of State and Their Diplomacy*, edited by Samuel F. Bemis, 193–282. New York: Knopf, 1927–29.

Seligmann, Herbert J. "The Conquest of Haiti." *Nation* 111 (July 10, 1920): 35–36.

Serfaty, Simon. "The New Normalcy." *Washington Quarterly* 25, no. 2 (Spring 2002): 209–19.

Sherman, Richard B. "The Harding Administration and the Negro: An Opportunity Lost." *Journal of Negro History* 49, no. 3 (July 1964): 151–68.

Silverstone, Scott A. "Federal Democratic Peace: Domestic Institutions, International Conflict, and American Foreign Policy, 1807–1860." Ph.D. diss., University of Pennsylvania, 1999.

Smith, Alistair. "International Crises and Domestic Politics." *American Political Science Review* 92, no. 2 (June 1998): 623–38.

Smith, Joseph. "Brazil: On the Periphery I." In *United States–Latin American Relations, 1850–1903*, edited by Thomas M. Leonard, 197–225. Tuscaloosa: University of Alabama Press, 1999.

Smith, Laun C., Jr. "Central American Defense Council: Some Problems and Achievements." *Air University Review* (March–April 1969): 19–38.

Smith, Michael. "The War before the War." *New Statesman* 134 (May 30, 2005): 20–21.

Smith, Robert Freeman. "American Foreign Relations, 1920–1942." In *Towards a New Past: Dissenting Essays in American History*, edited by Barton J. Bernstein, 232–62. New York: Pantheon Books, 1968.

———. "Latin America, the United States, and the European Powers, 1830–1930." In *The Cambridge History of Latin America, c. 1870 to 1930*, vol. 4, edited by Leslie Bethell, 83–119. Cambridge: Cambridge University Press, 1986.

Spector, Maurice. "The Record of the Democracies." *New International* 4, no. 4 (April 1938): 115–19.

Stagg, J. C. A. "James Madison and George Mathews: The East Florida Revolution of 1812 Reconsidered." *Diplomatic History* 30, no. 1 (January 2006): 23–55.

Stewart, Richard W. "The United States Army in Somalia, 1992–1994." U.S. Army Center of Military History, <http://www.history.army.mil/brochures/Somalia/Somalia.htm>. Accessed June 5, 2008.

Stromberg, Joseph. "The Political Economy of Liberal Corporatism." Center for Libertarian Studies, 1997, <http://tmh.floonet.net/articles/strombrg.html>. Accessed May 1, 2007.

Tambs, Lewis, et al. "A New Inter-American Policy for the Eighties." Committee of Santa Fe Report. Washington D.C.: Council for Inter-American Security, 1980.

Temperley, Harold. "Documents Illustrating the Reception and Interpretation of the Monroe Doctrine in Europe, 1823–4." *English Historical Review* 39, no. 156 (October 1924): 590–93.

———. "French Designs on Spanish America in 1820–5." *English Historical Review* 40, no. 157 (January 1925): 34–53.

Theriault, Sean M. "Party Politics during the Louisiana Purchase." *Social Science History* 30, no. 2 (Summer 2006): 293–323.

Tokatlian, Juan Gabriel. "After Iraq: Next Colombia? The United States and (In)Security in South America." In *Addicted to Failure: U.S. Security Policy in Latin America and the Andean Region*, edited by Brian Loveman, 265–88. Lanham, Md.: Rowman and Littlefield, 2006.

Tyrrell, Ian. "American Exceptionalism in an Age of International History." *American Historical Review* 96, no. 4 (October 1991): 1031–55.

Vaky, Viron. "Reagan's Central American Policy: An Isthmus Restored." In *Central America: Anatomy of Conflict*, edited by Robert Leiken, 233–57. New York: Pergamon Press, 1984.

Van Aken, Mark. "British Policy Considerations in Central America before 1850." *Hispanic American Historical Review* 42, no. 1 (February 1962): 54–59.

Vélez, Federico. "U.S. Policy toward Latin America: A View from the Arab World." *Revista: Harvard Review of Latin America* (Spring/Summer 2005): 10–12.

Vera Calderón, Rodolfo. "The United States Invasion of Panama: A Tri-dimensional Analysis." *EntreCaminos* (Spring 2003), <http://clas.georgetown.edu/entre2003/Panama.html#_ftn8>. Accessed June 15, 2008.

Waddell, D. A. G. "British Neutrality and Spanish-American Independence: The Problem of Foreign Enlistment." *Journal of Latin American Studies* 19, no. 1 (May 1987): 1–18.

Walcott, Earle Ashley. "The War between Spain and the United States." *Overland Monthly and Out West Magazine* 31, no. 186 (June 1898): 528–45.

Warner, Michael. "The CIA's Internal Probe of the Bay of Pigs Affair." *Studies in Intelligence* (Winter 1998/99): 93–101.

Way, Almon Leroy, Jr. "How America Goes to War: The President, American Law, & U.S. Military Intervention into Foreign Conflicts." *Progressive Conservative* 1, no. 1 (June 10–December 31, 1999).

Weinberg, Albert K. "The Historical Meaning of the American Doctrine of Isolation." *American Political Science Review* 34, no. 3 (June 1940): 539–47.

Wilcox, Greg. "Strategic Transformation: Aligning National Security Policy/Operations," <http://www.d-n-i.net/wilcox/wilcox_strat_trans.pdf>. Accessed July 15, 2006.

Williams, Mary Wilhelmine. "John Middleton Clayton, Secretary of State, March 7, 1849, to July 1, 1850." In *The American Secretaries of State and Their Diplomacy*, vol. 6, edited by Samuel F. Bemis, 3–74. New York: Knopf, 1927–29.

Williams, Walter L. "United States Indian Policy and the Debate over Philippine Annexation: Implications for the Origins of American Imperialism." *Journal of American History* 66, no. 4 (March 1980): 810–31.

Williams, William Appleman. "Confessions of an Intransigent Revisionist." *Socialist Review* 17 (September–October 1973): 89–98.

———. "Latin America: Laboratory of American Foreign Policy in the Nineteen-Twenties." *Journal Inter-American Economic Affairs* 11 (Autumn 1957): 3–31.

———. "The Legend of Isolationism in the 1920s." *Science and Society* 18 (Winter 1954): 1–20. Reprinted in *A William Appleman Williams Reader*, edited by Henry W. Berger, 75–88. Chicago: Ivan R. Dee, 1992.

———. "A Note on American Foreign Policy in Europe in the 1920s." *Science and Society* 22 (Winter 1958): 1–20.

———. "The Rise of an American World Power Complex." In *Consensus at the Crossroads*, edited by H. Bliss et al., 58–72. New York: Dodd, Mead, 1972.

Wolper, Gregg. "Wilsonian Public Diplomacy: The Committee on Public Information in Spain." *Diplomatic History* 17 (Winter 1993): 17–34.

Woolsey, L. H. "The Leticia Dispute between Colombia and Peru." *American Journal of International Law* 29, no. 1 (January 1935): 94–99.

"X" [George Kennan]. "The Sources of Soviet Conduct." *Foreign Affairs* 25, no. 4 (July 1947): 566–82.

Yoo, John C. "Kosovo, War Powers, and the Multilateral Future." *University of Pennsylvania Law Review* 148 (2000): 1673, 1686–1704.

———. "War and the Constitutional Text." *Boalt Working Papers in Public Law*, paper no. 27. University of California, Berkeley, 2002.

Zahniser, Marvin R., and W. Michael Weis. "A Diplomatic Pearl Harbor? Richard Nixon's Goodwill Visit to Latin America in 1958." *Diplomatic History* 13 (Spring 1989): 163–90.

Zakaria, Fareed. "The Myth of America's 'Free Security' (Reconsiderations)." *World Policy Journal* 14, no. 2 (Summer 1997): 35–54.

Zamora, Augusto. "Contadora and Esquipulas Ten Years Later." *Revista Envío* 196 (November 1997), <http://www.envio.org.ni/articulo/2048>. Accessed March 2, 2009.

Zubok, Vladislav M. "New Evidence on the End of the Cold War: New Evidence on the 'Soviet Factor' in the Peaceful Revolutions of 1989." *Cold War International History Project Bulletin* 12/13 (Fall/Winter 2001): 5–72.

Acknowledgments

My first debt of gratitude in writing this book is to generations of historians, social scientists, and archivists who have investigated and written about American politics and foreign policy. I have relied on hundreds of interpretative works, monographs, and specialized articles in writing this history. For me, history, though written by individual historians, is a collective enterprise, a multigenerational, transnational cultural endeavor that bequeaths to each generation the work of multitudes of predecessors. I wish to acknowledge this debt in general, and to numerous scholars whose work has influenced my own. To my mentors, James Scobie, Vincent Ostrom, and Alfred Diamant, I wish to express my particular gratitude for inspiring a lifetime of scholarship.

Research for this book was supported by the Ford Foundation (Andean Region and Southern Cone Office, Santiago, Chile). I am especially grateful for the encouragement of Augusto Varas as Ford Foundation Representative at the time financing for this project was granted. I am also grateful to Augusto Varas as a respected colleague for more than twenty years for his intellectual contributions to this book. Along the way generous colleagues have read portions of the manuscript in its various stages of development, and their suggestions have made this a better book than it would have been otherwise. I thank in particular David Carruthers, Thomas M. Davies Jr., Paul Drake, Jonathan Graubart, Robert Holden, Iván Jaksić, Naoko Kada, Ron King, Guang Lei, Elizabeth Lira, Mara Loveman, J. Patrice McSherry, Michael Mitchell, David Scott Palmer, Jody Pavilack, Thomas O'Brien, Filippo Sabetti, Lars Schoultz, Louis Terrell, Latha Varadarajan, Gregory Weeks, and Alexander Wilde. Greg Grandin was one of three anonymous reviewers of the manuscript for the University of North Carolina Press. Much later, at my request, the Press asked if I could be in touch with anonymous "Reader 1" because the comments and suggestions had been so valuable, and I wished to both thank the reviewer directly, and request that (s)he look at some of the revisions. Greg generously agreed to both requests. None of the colleagues mentioned above, except Iván Jaksić, is responsible for any remaining errors or omissions on my part. I also wish to thank the anonymous reviewers for the UNC Press, who provided suggestions for improving the draft manuscript that allowed me to avoid errors and make revisions that, I hope, have made the book more useful to readers than it would otherwise have been.

As always, Sharon Siem Loveman has contributed to my work by encouraging my research, engaging my ideas, and patiently reviewing the draft manuscript. I extend my heartfelt thanks to members of the staff at the University of North Carolina Press, especially to Elaine Maisner, who has shepherded the project from its inception, as well as to Tema Larter, Paul Betz, Ian Oakes, Courtney Baker, Ellen Bush, and Dino Battista for their creative and professional assistance along the way. The book has also benefited greatly from the expert copyediting of Dorothea Anderson.

Index

Burton, Dan, 358, 378

Bush, George H. W., 243, 306, 307, 333, 333, 334–41, 346–47, 352, 448 (n. 17); photo of, 342

Bush, George W., 1, 6, 7, 217, 330, 356, 365, 366–68; and anti-Americanism in Bolivia, 399; Bush Doctrine of, 377, 405 (n. 3); and Hugo Chávez, 379; and Iraq war, 372–76; and preemptive war, 388; public opinion of, 384; and torture, 376, 383; unilateralism of, 379; and war on terror, 369–71, 380, 401

Butler, Elizur, 85

Byrd, Robert, 371, 375

Calhoun, John C., 48, 385

California, 12, 28, 33, 36, 56, 59, 60, 72, 75, 107, 109, 110, 175, 197, 365, 406 (n. 6); and Compromise of 1850, 420 (n. 91); gold rush in, 108, 143

Cambodia, 253, 255, 303, 305, 322, 334, 444 (n. 3)

Canada, 13, 16, 26, 29, 31–33, 39, 65, 73, 74, 78, 79, 82, 86, 94, 124, 138, 160, 170, 223, 358, 360, 378, 422 (n. 39), 423 (n. 57)

Canning, George, 44, 416 (n. 19), 418 (n. 51)

Caracas Declaration (1954), 280, 294, 380

Caribbean: and American grand strategy, 17, 55, 58, 70, 74–78, 79, 80, 110–14, 136, 142, 144, 145, 152, 158, 163, 168–70, 175, 183, 188, 189, 195, 243, 263, 311, 318, 319, 326, 368, 391, 442 (n. 15); and annexation debates, 57; and Cold War, 322–25; European colonies in, 33, 41, 45, 46; and Charles E. Hughes, 228; military intervention in, 186, 198, 211, 232, 244, 246; and Napoleonic wars, 29; piracy, 94–97; and Quasi-War, 19, 21; and race politics, 229, 231; and T. Roosevelt, 186; slave rebellions in, 45, 93; and slavery, 101, 103; U.S. trade in, 13, 19, 94. *See also specific countries*

Caribbean Development Bank, 323

Caribbean Region Initiative, 320, 323

Carnegie, Andrew, 139, 162

Carranza, Venustiano, 228

Carroll, Lewis, 318

Cartagena, Colombia, 361, 391

Carter, Jimmy (James Earl), 217, 233, 307–13, 315, 321, 323, 327, 338, 356, 389, 398

Carter Doctrine, 317, 328

Casey, William, 330

Cass, Lewis, 54, 69, 70, 109, 112, 116, 184

Cass-Herrán Treaty, 109

Cass-Yrisarri Treaty, 112

Castillo Armas, Carlos, 281–82

Castro, Fidel, 273, 285–88, 293, 301, 303, 310, 311, 323, 337, 357, 359, 364, 381

Castro, Raúl, 396

Center for Strategic and International Studies (CSIS), 370

Central America: and American grand strategy, 71, 118, 129, 132, 170, 175, 187, 189; Anglo-American rivalry in, 54–55, 77, 114, 116, 144–45, 155–56; and James Buchanan, 110–14; and canal proposals, 52–55, 111–13, 135, 136, 149, 152, 168, 175–76; and drug war, 363; and expansion of slavery, 75, 92, 101, 103; and filibusters, 111; military intervention in, 99, 186; and Robert Olds, 234; and R. Reagan, 316, 319, 325–33; and T. Roosevelt, 179, 186; and U.S. banks, 227; and U.S. Trade, 137, 138, 140, 142–43. *See also specific countries*

Central American Court of Justice, 195, 197, 200

Central American Defense Council (CONDECA), 296

Central American Treaty of Peace and Amity (1923), 229

Central Intelligence Agency. *See* U.S. Central Intelligence Agency

Central Powers, 208–10, 212

Chaco War (1932–35), 246

Chaitkin, Anton, 334

Charleston, S.C., 45, 93, 417 (n. 25)

Chávez Frías, Hugo, 362, 363, 379, 380, 383, 389, 392, 394–96, 465 (n. 20)

Cheney, Richard (Dick), 307, 333, 335, 338–41, 342, 352, 365, 369, 370, 376, 383, 388, 402

Chernaev, Anatoly, 345

Treaty, 244; navy of, 154; and Nicaragua, 116, 155; No Transfer policy, 27, 99; and Oregon Territory, 59, 73, 74; and Panama invasion (1989), 229; and A. Pinochet, 383; policies of, in Western Hemisphere, 17, 26, 27, 105, 115, 135; and Quasi-War, 17; and relations with France, 17, 18; and slavery, 101, 111; and Spanish-American independence movements, 101; Texas, 67, 76; Treaty of Ghent, 33; and U.S. Civil War, 123; and Venezuela, 157–58, 160–61, 177; and *Virginius* case, 80; in War of 1812, 28, 30–31; Webster-Ashburton Treaty, 74; in West Indies, 94; and West Florida, 412 (n. 69); and World War I, 199, 209–10, 212

Enterprise (ship), 144

Enterprise for the Americas Initiative, 336, 455 (n. 69)

"Era of good feelings," 40

Espionage Act (1917), 215

Esquipulas II (1987 peace accords), 332

Estonia, 212, 279, 335

Ethiopia, 251

European Union, 359, 366, 378, 462 (n. 38)

Evans, Robley ("Fighting Bob"), 188

Evarts, William A., 131, 143, 144

Everett, Alexander H., 10, 417 (n. 28)

Exceptionalism, American. *See* American exceptionalism

Failed states, 345

Falkland Islands (Malvinas), 58; war in, 322

Farabundo Martí Liberation Movement (FMLN), 325, 453 (n. 41)

FARC, 381, 382, 392

Fascism, 234, 240, 241, 242, 243, 246, 350

Federal Bureau of Investigation (FBI), 217, 271, 274, 293, 299, 304, 464 (n. 12)

Federalist Papers, 46

Federalist Party, 12, 17, 18, 19, 20, 23, 29, 31, 35, 56, 396

Fein, Bruce, 389

Fenians (Irish nationalists), 124

Ferdinand VII (king of Spain), 40, 43, 94

Fiers, Albert D., Jr., 334

Fiji Islands, 58, 88, 117

Filibusters (expeditions), 51, 55, 60, 65, 67, 102, 103, 110–12, 128, 129, 191, 208, 230, 323, 397, 421 (n. 28), 426 (n. 47), 427 (n. 76)

Fillmore, Millard, 75, 420 (n. 89)

Fish, Hamilton, 80, 128–29, 143

Fiske, John, 121

Fletcher, Thomas C., 122

Flint, Charles, 141; and Flint's Fleet, 154

Flores, Juan José, 105

Florida, 125, 130, 131, 184, 263, 288, 340, 357, 359; and elections (2000), 365. *See also* East Florida; West Florida

Food for Peace (P.L. 480), 293

Ford, Gerald, 291, 303–7

Fordney-McCumber Tariff (1922), 221, 442 (n. 18)

Foreign aid, 292, 296, 395, 413 (n. 94)

Forsyth, John, 73

Fort Ross (California), 56

Forty-ninth parallel (as U.S.-Canadian border), 74, 419 (n. 85)

Foster, John A., 158

Four Freedoms Speech (January 6, 1941), 249

Fourteen Points (W. Wilson), 210, 211, 212, 217, 219, 439 (n. 8)

France, 261, 339; and American independence, 11, 13, 322; and Central America, 104; Cuba policy of, 99, 102; empire of, in Mexico, 119, 123; in Franco-Prussian War, 129; and Louisiana Purchase, 17, 21–23; and Marshall Plan, 261; and Napoleonic wars, 30; and Panama invasion (1989), 339; and Polignac memorandum, 418 (n. 51); and Quasi-War, 6, 14, 18–21, 265, 371, 410 (n. 42); and Spanish-American independence, 44, 98, 101; and Texas; 68; and U.S. Civil War, 122; war with England, 12; World War I, 212

Franco, Francisco, 275, 291

Franco-Prussian War (1870), 129, 423 (n. 64), 431 (n. 46)

Franklin, Benjamin, 408 (n. 21)

McGregor, Morris J., Jr., 250

McKinley, William, 138, 139, 141, 163, 165–66, 170–73, 194, 245

McKinley Tariff, 138

McLane, Robert, 73

McLane-Ocampo Treaty (1859), 116

McNamara, Robert, 449 (n. 41)

Mediterranean, 9, 409 (n. 24); piracy in, 12; 14, 97; and U.S. grand strategy, 49, 161, 175, 353; and World War I, 209

Mediterranean Squadron, 57, 58, 87

Memorandum on the *Right to Protect Citizens in Foreign Countries by Landing Forces* (1912), 298

Mendieta, Carlos, 245

Mervine, William, 109

Messina, Italy, 189

Metternich, Prince von (Clemens Wenzel), 326

Mexico, 29, 45, 47, 89, 90, 92, 107, 114, 203, 204; and Adams-Onís Treaty, 36; and American Civil War, 79, 119, 122–23; and Anglo-American rivalry, 67–70; and annexation debates, 57; and James Buchanan presidency, 115–17; and George W. Bush, 374; and Caracas Declaration (1954), 280; debt default (1982), 321; dispute with Guatemala, 133; and Gadsden Purchase, 60; independence, 94; Isthmian canal route, 52; A. Jackson, 67; Maximilian I, 79, 122–23; and Montevideo Conference (1933), 246; and Pan American Conference (1923), 231; and slavery, 78, 101; and Taft presidency, 189; and Texas, 53, 59, 67; U.S. support for independence of, 29, 33, 51; violent crime, 377; war with U.S., 6, 54, 70–73, 74; and Wilson presidency, 194–95, 199, 211; and World War I, 208–10; Zapatistas, 363

Micheletti, Roberto (Honduras), 393

Middle East, 212, 220, 261, 290, 313, 317, 326, 347, 355, 376, 461 (n. 120)

Midway Island, 124

Military coups and U.S. policy, 241, 255, 270, 273, 277, 278, 287, 293, 295, 297, 303, 323, 338, 393; and Central American Treaty of Peace and Amity (1923), 229; and Honduras, 393–97, 464 (n. 18). *See also specific countries*

Military-industrial complex, 137, 139, 180, 210, 260, 269, 436 (n. 93)

Military Operations Other Than War (MOOTW), 341, 351

Military Reconstruction Act (1867), 126

Missionaries, 143, 146, 155, 161, 168, 194, 202

Mississippi River, 23, 41, 62, 85, 131, 410 (n. 42), 412 (n. 69) , 413 (n. 86)

Mississippi Territory, 82, 84, 413 (n. 77); and Indian Removal Act, 83; and U.S. grand strategy, 16, 22

Missouri, 415 (n. 6)

Missouri Compromise (1820), 40–41, 45, 46, 54, 60, 75, 92, 94, 96, 100, 103, 118, 415 (n. 4), 417 (n. 29), 426 (n. 56)

Mogadishu, Somalia, 347

Môle St. Nicholas, Haiti, 152

Mondale, Walter, 326

Monroe, James, 22, 23, 35–37, 39; and piracy, 95–97; presidency, 40–51 passim, 66–67

Monroe Doctrine, 3, 27, 37, chapter 2 passim, 66, 68, 70–76, 80, 91, 94, 95, 97, 101, 105, 106, 108, 118, 132, 142–44, 152, 162, 178, 182, 187, 189, 191, 195, 198, 210, 213, 220, 225, 255, 263–64, 269, 271, 301, 309, 311, 312, 384, 385, 403; and American Federation of Labor, 228; and Caracas Declaration, 280; and Civil War, 123; and Clark Memorandum, 238; and Clayton-Bulwer Treaty, 113, 135; and Cold War, 280–81, 286, 293; and Cuba, 162; as doctrine of self-defense, 159, 235, 297–98, 328, 332, 339; and Hamilton Fish, 128; and Good Neighbor Policy, 262; and Ulysses S. Grant, 128–29; and Ernest H. Gruening, 231; and Haiti, 229; and Charles Evan Hughes, 228–29; and Frank B. Kellogg, 235; and Philander Knox, 189, 191; and Robert Lansing, 199; and League of

and T. Roosevelt, 182; and U.S. grand strategy, 174, 210, 243

Pickering, Timothy, 23

Pierce, Franklin K., 60, 61, 75–76, 102–3, 111, 112, 129

Pike, James Shepherd, 75

Pike, Otis, 306, 450 (n. 66)

Pike, Zebulon, 15

Pinckney Treaty, 410 (n. 42), 412 (n. 69)

Pinkney, William, 100

Pinochet Ugarte, Augusto, 303, 383

Piracy, 41, 43, 95–97, 348, 409 (n. 27); and antipiracy legislation, 45, 95

Plan Colombia, 362, 363, 392

Planning Coordination Group (Special Group, 1954), 267

Platt Amendment, 167–68, 175, 182, 183, 186, 195, 197, 245, 435 (n. 58)

Poindexter, John M., 331, 333, 365

Poinsett, Joel R., 49, 50, 418 (n. 43)

Poland, 49, 50, 211, 212, 279, 335, 375

Polignac memorandum, 418 (n. 51)

Political corruption, 3, 20, 30, 129, 130, 131, 134, 136, 137, 142, 152, 224, 225, 239, 289, 290, 305, 308, 364, 402, 409 (n. 32), 411 (n. 52)

Polk, James K., 1, 67; and Bidlack-Mallarino Treaty, 105, 107; censure by House of Representatives, 421 (n. 31); and Cuba, 101; and manifest destiny, 54; and Mexico, 54; and Monroe Doctrine, 54, 69, 71; and Oregon, 74; presidential powers, 422 (n. 41), 461 (n. 19); and slavery, 60; and Texas, 106; war with Mexico, 67–69, 71, 74; and Yucatán, 69, 421 (n. 28)

Porter, David D., 143

Porter, Robert W., 304

Porter, W. D., 109

Portugal, 98, 306, 357, 430 (n. 39), 458 (n. 51)

Posse Comitatus Act (1878), 341

Potomac (ship), 57–58, 419 (n. 75)

Powell, Colin, 338, 339, 340, 366

Pravda, 255

Preemptive war, 1, 2, 188, 371; as "self defense," 22, 23, 26, 99, 101, 103, 223, 235;

and Act of Havana (1940), 247; Bush Doctrine of (2002), 370, 388, 405 (n. 3); and Carter Doctrine, 312; in Iraq, 373; and Monroe Doctrine, 71, 192, 229; and SouthCom, 380; and Truman Doctrine, 261

Presidential war powers, 20, 194, 305, 331, 348, 349

Privateers/privateering, 15, 19, 33, 41, 95, 412 (n. 74), 425 (n. 16)

Project for the New American Century (PNAC), 353, 365, 366

Prosser, Gabriel, 45

"Protective imperialism," chapter 7 passim, 245, 355

Providence/Providential destiny, 11, 39, 57, 76, 360, 403

Prussia, 70, 129, 410 (n. 33); Franco-Prussian War, 129, 423 (n. 64)

Public lands policy, 15, 48, 126

Public Law 480 (Agricultural Trade Development Assistant Act, 1954), 293, 449 (n. 30)

Puerto Cabello, Venezuela, 176

Puerto Rico, 41, 45, 46, 59, 93, 94, 95, 98, 111, 122, 132, 138, 167, 174, 175, 177, 183, 213, 218, 239, 323, 391, 440 (n. 25)

Pullman Strike, 139, 159, 162, 434 (n. 35)

Quadrennial Defense Review (QDR), 352, 366, 367

Quallah Battoo, 57

Quasi-War with France (1798), 6, 17, 18–21, 29, 265, 371

Quitman, John, 102, 426 (n. 47)

Rabe, Stephen, 294

Race and racism, 11, 57, 70, 75, 81, 82, 194, 198–99, 212–13, 222, 224, 225, 229, 250, 252, 256, 257, 300; and foreign policy, 6, 57, 70, 194, 198, 199, 323

Raleigh (ship), 166

Randolph, A. Philip, 250

Rankin, Jeannette, 210

Rapid Deployment Force (Carter administration), 312, 356, 413 (n. 83)

Ordinance, 410 (n. 38); and slave trade, 15, 41, 43–47, 64, 74, 75, 93, 96, 101, 113, 416 (n. 16), 425 (n. 14); U.S. Constitution, 415 (n. 8); and Wilmot Proviso, 418 (n. 63)

Slidell, John, 78

Small Wars Manual (U.S. Marine Corps), 362

Smith, Alfred, 239

Smith, Ellison Durant ("Cotton Ed"), 222

Smoot-Hawley Tariff (1930), 221, 240

Social Security, 242, 300, 455 (n. 34)

Soft power, 25

Somalia, 347, 348

Somoza Debayle, Anastasio (Somoza dynasty), 242, 311, 328

Soto Cano (air base), 391, 394, 395, 465 (n. 25)

Soulé, Pierre, 102–3

South American Defense Council (CDS), 380

Southeast Asia Collective Defense Treaty, 297

South Korea, 265, 275, 305, 366, 378

Soviet Union, 200, 213, 221, 242, 253, 255, 257, 265, 266, 268, 288, 306, 310, 313, 324–26, 328, 329, 333, 341, 343, 369, 383; and Afghanistan, 324; and Angola, 306; and Berlin blockade, 264; and Berlin Wall, 345; Cold War, chapters 10–12 passim; and Cuba, 286, 312, 337; and Czechoslovakia, 254; dissolution of, 337, 345; and El Salvador, 325; and wars of national liberation, 292

Spain, 2, 86, 87, 93, 94, 97–98, 136, 274, 357, 360; and Adams-Onís Treaty, 36; and Cuba, 75–78, 80, 99–103, 128, 140, 162–65; and Dominican Republic, 119, 122; and East Florida, 27–30, 34–36; French invasions of, 43, 65; independence of Spanish American colonies from, 33, 40–41, 44; and Louisiana, 21–23; and Monroe Doctrine, 45; and Napoleonic wars, 10, 18; and No Transfer Policy, 27, 44; and Oregon, 73; and Pinckney Treaty, 410 (n. 42); and Pinochet case, 373; and piracy, 95–96; and U.S. grand strategy, 14,

17, 170, 174–75; and Venezuela, 157; and *Virginius* incident, 129; war with the United States (Spanish-American War) 6, 10, 33, 95, 164–68, 169, 170, 173, 176, 183, 201, 301, 371, 380; and West Florida, 23–26

Special Forces, 294, 363, 383, 388, 392

Special Operations Forces Posture Statement 2000, 353

Stagg, J. C. A., 26, 29

Stalin, Josef, 254

Standard Oil, 153

Stanton, Edwin, 125

"Star Wars" program, 316

Stephens, Alexander, 78, 429 (n. 8)

Stevenson, Adlai, II, 267

Stimson, Henry, 233, 234, 250, 442 (n. 24)

Stimson Doctrine, 240, 439 (n. 13)

Stoddert, Benjamin, 19

Strategic Arms Limitation Treaties, 313

Strategic Defense Initiative (SDI), 316

Strikes (labor), 131–32, 134, 139, 159, 162, 213, 434 (n. 35)

Strong, Josiah, 193

Submarine warfare, 197, 204, 208–10, 220, 286, 381

Sudan, 348, 399

Suez Canal, 143, 176, 259

Sugar, 76, 91, 137, 138, 140, 143, 145, 164, 174, 286, 320, 421 (n. 25)

Summits of the Americas, 356, 458 (n. 53); in Miami (1994), 356–58; in Trinidad-Tobago (2009), 388

Sumner, Charles, 124

Supreme Court. *See* U.S. Supreme Court

Suriname, 324, 336

Syria, 399

Tacna-Arica dispute (Chile and Peru), 232–33

Taft, Robert A., 257–58, 265

Taft, William Howard, 187, 189, 191, 192, 194, 218, 439 (n. 15)

Taiwan (Formosa), 168, 265, 290, 420 (n. 86)

Taliban, 351, 369, 370, 376, 384

of War (1917), 210; and Dominican Republic, 179, 182; and Hawaii treaty, 173–74; and Hay-Herrán Treaty, 184; Helms-Burton legislation, 358; and Honduras, 118; impeachment of A. Johnson, 125; Indian Removal law, 84; Iran-Contra Affair, 331; Iraq Liberation Act (1998), 355; and A. Jackson, 36; Joint Resolution on Iraq War, 371–72; Kellogg-Briand Pact, 221, 235; League of Nations debate, 217–20; and Louisiana Purchase, 23; lynching debates, 230; and McLane-Ocampo Treaty, 116; Missouri Compromise, 41, 96; and Monroe Doctrine, 158, 235; and Operation Desert Shield, 346; and Oregon territory, 59, 74; and Panama canal treaties (1978), 310; Panama Congress debate (1826), 98; piracy debates, 96; Reconstruction policy, 124; resolution on Central America (1835), 52; and Teller Amendment, 166; and Treaty of Guadalupe Hidalgo, 53; and Treaty of New Echota, 84; and treaty on slave trade, 43; and treaty with Denmark (1869), 124–25; and War of 1812, 30

U.S. Council of National Defense, 248

U.S. Defense Intelligence Agency (DIA), 338

U.S. Department of Defense, 312, 329, 330, 335, 341, 352, 353, 356, 361, 388

U.S. Department of Justice, 338

U.S. Department of State, 82, 103, 173, 174, 179, 189, 210, 223, 227, 233, 262, 266, 267, 271, 274, 275, 279, 288, 289, 298, 309, 311, 319, 321, 361, 366, 395, 397, 398

U.S. Division of Insular Affairs, 182; Bureau of Insular Affairs, 182, 437 (n. 13)

U.S. Drug Enforcement Agency (DEA), 338, 399, 401, 455 (n. 85), 464 (n. 12)

U.S. Marine Corps (Marines), 61, 63, 64, 87, 88, 89, 156, 188, 198, 200, 201–4, 233, 238, 240, 241, 245, 259, 323, 409 (n. 24)

U.S. National Security Agency (NSA), 269, 289

U.S. Navy, 12, 19, 20, 58, 67, 74, 76, 79, 95, 96, 102, 124, 130, 135, 136, 143, 144–49,

chapter 6 passim, 183, 188, 194, 208, 240, 250, 323, 368, 381, 391, 406 (n. 6), 419 (n. 75), 432 (n. 93)

U.S. Office for Public Safety, 291

U.S. Peace Corps, 291

U.S. Southern Command (SouthCom), 338, 339, 341, 352, 357, 360–64, 380, 392, 395, 464 (n. 11)

U.S. Supreme Court, 20, 82, 84, 103, 181, 197, 251, 304, 305, 365, 376, 422 (n. 43), 441 (n. 49), 445 (n. 15), 446 (n. 42)

U.S. v. Bhagat Singh Thind (1923), 441

U.S. v. Kagama (1885), 436

U.S. v. Richardson (1974), 450

USA Today, 373

Upper Canada, 82, 94, 422 (n. 39)

Uribe, Álvaro, 381, 391

Valenzuela, Arturo, 396

Van Buren, Martin, 58, 84, 420 (n. 89)

Vance, Cyrus, 309

Vancouver Island, 74

Van Deman, Ralph H., 213

Vanderbilt, Cornelius, 111

Vargas Vila, José María, 187, 437 (n. 14)

Venezuela, 29, 66, 95, 104, 271, 277, 280, 282, 290, 292, 311, 323, 332, 361, 362, 363, 377, 379, 380–82, 388, 392, 393–96, 413 (n. 94); boundary dispute with Great Britain (1895), 157–61; conflict with Germany and England (1902), 176–78; and Olney Corollary, 159–60

Vera Cruz, Mexico, 194, 195

Versailles, Treaty of, 199, 212, 218, 219

Vesey, Denmark, 45, 93, 417 (n. 26)

Vickers, Michael, 388

Vietnam War, 253, 255, 279–80, 296, 297, 299, 301, 302, 304, 306, 308, 321, 322, 325, 339, 346, 362, 371, 400, 401, 449 (n. 41)

Village Voice, 306

Virginia, 44, 46, 46, 71, 193, 356, 381; Loving v. Commonwealth of Virginia (1967), 445 (n. 15)

Virgin Islands (Danish West Indies), 79, 195

Crow, 250–53, 257, 260, 263–64, 267; and onset of Cold War, 299; and postwar grand strategy, 272, 321; and postwar nationalism in Latin America, 293, 379

Wounded Knee massacre, 85–86

XYZ Affair, 19

Yalta Conference (1945), 279

Yoo, John C., 348–49

York (later Toronto), Canada, 31, 94

Yorktown (ship), 188

Yucatán, Mexico, 69, 70, 299, 421 (n. 28); Caste War in, 69–71

Yugoslavia, 212, 263, 382, 460 (n. 2)

Zablocki, Clement, 329

Zakaria, Fareed, 408 (n. 2)

Zapatistas (Mexico, 1994), 363

Zelaya, José Santos, 155, 156, 158, 195

Zelaya, Manuel (Mel), 393–98

Zemurray, Sam "the banana man," 191

Zimmermann Telegram, 209

Zogby Poll, 379

Zubok, Vladislav M., 342, 444 (n. 12)